If It's
April 2000
and you are still using this Directory, it's time to order the NEW 8th Edition.

Cabell Publishing Company (409) 898-0575

ALL ORDERS MUST BE PREPAID OR ACCOMPANIED BY A UNIVERSITY PURCHASE ORDER NUMBER

☐ Accounting, Economics and Finance (ISBN#0-911753-10-9) . . . . . . 7th Edition $89.95
☐ Management and Marketing (ISBN#0-911753-11-7) . . . . 7th Edition $89.95
☐ All of the Above $179.90

Price includes shipping and handling for all U.S. Add $20 for shipping via surface mail or $100 for shipping Air Mail to countries Outside United States.

Name _____ Rank _____

Department _____

University/College _____

Address _____

City _____ State _____ Zip _____ Country _____

FAX No. _____ EMAIL Address (if available) _____

Send Your Order To:
CABELL PUBLISHING COMPANY - 4 A 7
P.O. BOX 5428 TOBE HAHN STATION
BEAUMONT, TEXAS 77726
(409) 898-0575

To: Department Chairman
Acquisitions Librarian
Please order Cabell's Directory of Publishing Opportunities as checked for Library.

★ Allow 6 to 8 weeks for delivery

_____
Name (Printed)

ALL ORDERS MUST BE PREPAID OR ACCOMPANIED BY A UNIVERSITY PURCHASE ORDER NUMBER

☐ Accounting, Economics and Finance (ISBN#0-911753-10-9) . . . . . . 7th Edition $89.95
☐ Management and Marketing (ISBN#0-911753-11-7) . . . . 7th Edition $89.95
☐ All of the Above $179.90

Price includes shipping and handling for all U.S. Add $20 for shipping via surface mail or $100 for shipping Air Mail to countries Outside United States.

Name _____ Rank _____

Department _____

University/College _____

Address _____

City _____ State _____ Zip _____ Country _____

FAX No. _____ EMAIL Address (if available) _____

Send Your Order To:
CABELL PUBLISHING COMPANY - 4 A 7
P.O. BOX 5428 TOBE HAHN STATION
BEAUMONT, TEXAS 77726
(409) 898-0575

To: Department Chairman
Acquisitions Librarian
Please order Cabell's Directory of Publishing Opportunities as checked for Library.

★ Allow 6 to 8 weeks for delivery

_____
Name (Printed)

Cabell's Directory of Publishing Opportunities In Accounting, Economics and Finance

VOLUME I   A THROUGH J of D

SEVENTH EDITION 1997-98

David W. E. Cabell, Editor
McNeese State University
Lake Charles, Louisiana

Deborah L. English, Associate Editor

To order additional copies
send check or university purchase order to:

CABELL PUBLISHING CO.
Box 5428, Tobe Hahn Station
Beaumont, Texas 77726-5428
(409) 898-0575
FAX (409) 866-9554

$89.95 U.S. for addresses in United States

Price includes shipping and handling for all U.S.
Add $20 for shipping via surface mail or
$100 for shipping Air Mail to countries Outside United States.

ISBN # 0-911753-10-9

Although every reasonable effort has been made to ensure the accuracy of the information contained in this DIRECTORY, the author cautions the reader that there may be mistakes in the information provided. Thus, the reader is responsible for his or her actions resulting from the use of this information.

TABLE OF CONTENTS

TABLE OF CONTENTS

TABLE OF CONTENTS

TABLE OF CONTENTS

TABLE OF CONTENTS

TABLE OF CONTENTS

TABLE OF CONTENTS

TABLE OF CONTENTS

TABLE OF CONTENTS

PREFACE

The objective of CABELL'S DIRECTORY OF PUBLISHING OPPORTUNITIES IN ACCOUNTING, ECONOMICS AND FINANCE is to help you publish your ideas.

The DIRECTORY contains the editor's name(s), address(es), phone and fax number(s) for over 400 journals.

To help you in selecting those journals likely to publish your manuscripts the INDEX classifies the journals into fifteen (15) different topic areas. In addition, the INDEX provides information on the journal's type of review process, number of external reviewers and acceptance rate.

To further assist you in organizing and preparing your manuscript, the DIRECTORY includes information on the style and format of each journal. If a journal has its own set of manuscript guidelines, the DIRECTORY has published a copy of these guidelines. Also, it indicates the use of a standard set of guidelines by a journal. For example, some journals use the CHICAGO MANUAL OF STYLE or the PUBLICATION MANUAL OF THE AMERICAN PSYCHOLOGICAL ASSOCIATION.

Furthermore, the DIRECTORY describes the type of review process used by the editor(s) of a journal, type of review, number of reviewers, acceptance rate, time required for review, availability of reviewers comments, fees charged to review or publish the manuscript, copies required and manuscript topics. Also, the DIRECTORY provides information on the journal's circulation, readership and subscription prices.

Although this DIRECTORY focuses on Journals in the specialized areas of Accounting, Economics and Finance; the CABELL'S DIRECTORY OF PUBLISHING OPPORTUNITIES IN MANAGEMENT AND MARKETING focuses on its respective areas of specialization. The divison of business journals into two directories, more appropriately meets the researcher's need for publishing in his area specialization. Also, the division of business journals into two separate directories allows for some economies of scale in printing which makes the DIRECTORY more affordable to the individual researcher.

The decision to place journals in their respective classification for the two directories relies on the manuscript topics that each journal editor emphasizes and the journal's guidelines for authors.

The CABELL'S DIRECTORY OF PUBLISHING OPPORTUNITIES IN
    ACCOUNTING, ECONOMICS AND FINANCE focuses on the following topics:

Accounting Information Systems	Insurance
Accounting Theory & Practice	International & Economic
Auditing	International Finance
Capital Budgeting	Portfolio & Security Analysis
Cost Accounting	Public Policy Economics
Econometrics	Real Estate
Economic History	Tax Accounting
Government & Non Profit Acounting	

The CABELL'S DIRECTORY OF PUBLISHING OPPORTUNITIES IN
MANAGEMENT AND MARKETING focuses on the following topics:

Advertising & Promotion Management
Business Education
Business Information Systems (MIS)
Business Law, Public Responsibility
   & Ethics
Communication
Direct Marketing
Global Business
Health Care Administration
Labor Relations & Human Resource Mgt.
   (HRM)
Marketing Research
Non Profit Organizations
Office Administration/Management

Operations Research/Statistics
Organizational Behovior & Theory
Organizational Development
Production/Operations
Public Administration
Purchasing/Materials Management
Sales/Selling
Services
Small Business Entrepreneurship
Strategic Management Policy
Transportation/Physical
   Distribution
Technology/Innovation

Also, the DIRECTORY includes a section titled "What is a Refereed Article?"
The section describing a refereed article tends to emphasize the value of a
blind review process and use of external reviewers. However, it cautions
those using this criteria to also consider the journal's reputation for
quality. Also it indicates that differences in acceptance rates may be the
result of different methods used to calculate these percentages and the
number of people associated with a particular area of specialization.

ACKNOWLEDGEMENTS

The preparation of this DIRECTORY was made possible through the tremendous efforts of my associate editor, Deborah L. English. In addition, the efforts of Chris Koger, Consultant, Austin, Texas, helped us to make the changes in the computer program and hardware that greatly improved the DIRECTORY.

HOW TO USE THE DIRECTORY

To help you locate a publication, the DIRECTORY contains a Table of Contents and Index listing over 400 journals. The index classifies the journals according to fifteen (15) different manuscript topics. It also includes information on the type of review, number of external reviewers and acceptance rate.

The DIRECTORY provides the following information for each publication: EDITOR'S NAME(S), ADDRESS(ES), PHONE AND FAX NUMBER(S), and E-MAIL ADDRESS.

LENGTH OF MANUSCRIPT refers to the length of the manuscript in terms of the number of double-spaced typescript pages.

NUMBER OF COPIES REQUIRED indicates the number of copies of the manuscript you should submit to the editor.

FORMAT refers to the type of word processing programs or computer language the journal requires for reviewing the manuscript. Some examples of these programs are Microsoft Word, Word Perfect, ASCII or Wordstar.

TYPE OF REVIEW is either blind, editorial, or optional. A blind review indicates the reviewer(s) does not know who wrote the manuscript. An editorial review indicates the reviewer knows who wrote the manuscript. The term "optional" indicates the author may choose either one of these types of review.

NUMBER OF INTERNAL REVIEWERS
NUMBER OF EXTERNAL REVIEWERS
These two items refer to the number of reviewers who review the manuscript prior to making a decision regarding the publication of the manuscript. Although the editor attempted to determine whether the reviewers were on the staff of the journal or were outside reviewers, many of the respondents had trouble distinguishing between internal and external reviewers. Thus it may be more accurate to add these two categories and determine the total number of reviewers.

ACCEPTANCE RATE refers to the number of manuscripts accepted for publication relative to the number of manuscripts submitted within the last year. The method of calculating acceptance rates varies among Journals.

TIME REQUIRED FOR REVIEW indicates the amount of time that passes between the submission of a manuscript and notification to the author regarding the results of the review process.

REVIEWER'S COMMENTS indicates whether the author can obtain a copy of the reviewers' comments. In some cases, the author needs to request the editor to send these comments.

FEES CHARGED TO REVIEW MANUSCRIPT. Knowing this item permits the author to send the required funds with the manuscript. Thus, the manuscript enters the review process without waiting for a letter and reply regarding the need for funds.

PERCENTAGE OF INVITED ARTICLES indicates the percentage of articles in which the editor requests people to write specifically for publication in the journal. The percentage is the number of invited articles relative to the total number of articles that appear in a journal within the past year.

FEES CHARGED TO PUBLISH THE MANUSCRIPT assists the author in deciding whether to place the manuscript into the review process.

MANUSCRIPT TOPICS indicates those subjects the journal emphasizes.

MANUSCRIPT GUIDELINES/COMMENTS provides information on the journal's objectives, style and format for references and footnotes that the editor expects the author to follow in preparing the manuscript for submission.

TYPE OF READER indicates the predominant type of reader the publication seeks to attract. These are divided into a group designated as practitioners and professionals, or another group referred to as researchers in accounting, economics and finance.

FREQUENCY OF ISSUE indicates the number of times a journal will be published in a year.

COPIES PER ISSUE indicates the number of copies the journal distributes per issue.

SUBSCRIPTION PRICE indicates the cost to order a year's subscription unless otherwise indicated.

SPONSORSHIP OF PUBLICATION indicates the journal's affiliation with a professional association, university, profit-oriented corporation, non profit organization or government agency.

HOW THE DIRECTORY HELPS YOU PUBLISH YOUR IDEAS

Although a person must communicate their ideas in writing, the DIRECTORY helps the author determine which journal will most likely accept the manuscript. In making this decision, its important to compare the characteristics of your manuscript and the needs of each journal. The following table provides a frame work for making this comparison.

INFORMATION PROVIDED BY THE DIRECTORY FOR EACH JOURNAL	MANUSCRIPT CHARACTERISTICS
Topic(s) of Articles Manuscript Guidelines	Theme
Acceptance Rate Percentage of Invited Articles	Significance of Theme
Type of Reader	Methodology and Style
Circulation Review Process	Prestige
Number of Reviewers Availability of Reviewers Comments Time Required for Review	Results of Review

This framework will help the author determine a small number of journals that will be interested in publishing the manuscript. Although the DIRECTORY can assist the author in determining these journals, a set of unwritten and written laws prevent you from simultaneously sending your manuscript to more than one journal. However, a rejection by any one publication does not prevent you from sending it to another journal.

Also, the copyright laws and editorial policy of the publication will cause the author to choose only one journal. Furthermore, some journals will require the author to sign a statement indicating the manuscript is not presently under review by another publication.

Although publication of the manuscript in the proceedings of a professional association does not prevent the author from sending it to a journal, there usually are some restrictions attached. Most professional associations require that the author acknowledge the presentation of the manuscript at the association meeting.

Since the author is limited to sending the manuscript to only one journal and the review process for each journal requires a long period of time, a "query" letter may help the author determine the journal most likely to publish the manuscript. The query letter contains the following information.

-- Topic, major idea or conclusion of the manuscript.

-- The subject sample, research setting conceptual framework, methodology type of organization or location.

-- The reasons why the author thinks the journal's readers would be
   interested in your proposed article.

-- Asks the editor to make comments or suggestions on the usefulness of this
   type of article to the journal.

Although the query letter is helpful in selecting a journal that will be
likely to publish the manuscript, the author could use the DIRECTORY and the
framework presented to develop a set of journals which would be likely to
publish the manuscript. With this number of possible journals, it makes the
sending of a query letter more feasible and tends to achieve the objective
of finding the journal most likely to publish the manuscript.

RELATING THE THEME OF THE MANUSCRIPT TO
THE TOPICS OF ARTICLES PUBLISHED BY EACH JOURNAL

To begin the process of choosing the journals to receive the "query" letter
and at some future time the manuscript, the author needs to examine the
similarity between the theme of the manuscript and the editor's needs.
The DIRECTORY describes these needs by the topics each publication considers
important and the manuscript guidelines. To find those journals that publish
manuscripts in any particular area, refer to the topic index.

In attempting to classify the theme, the author should limit his choice to a
single discipline. With the increasing specialization in the academic world,
it is unlikely that reviewers, editors or readers will understand an article
that requires a knowledge of two different disciplines. If these groups do
not understand a manuscript, the journal will reject it.

If a manuscript emphasizes an interdisciplinary approach, it is important to
decide who will be reading the article. The approach should be to explain
the theoretical concepts of one discipline to the specialists in another
discipline. The author should not attempt to resolve theoretical issues
present in his discipline and explain their implications for specialists in
another discipline.

Although the discipline classifications indicate the number of journals
interested in your manuscript topic, the manuscript guidelines help the
author determine the journals which will most likely have the greatest
interest in the manuscript. The manuscript guidelines provide a detailed
statement of the criteria for judging manuscripts, the editorial objectives,
the readership and the journal's content and approach. This information
makes it possible to determine more precisely the congruence between the
manuscript and the type of articles the journal publishes. THE DIRECTORY
CONTAINS THE MANUSCRIPT GUIDELINES FOR A LARGE NUMBER OF JOURNALS.

THE RELATIONSHIP BETWEEN THE JOURNAL'S
ACCEPTANCE RATE AND THE SIGNIFICANCE OF THE
THEME OF THE MANUSCRIPT

In addition to determining the similarity between the topic of the manuscript and the topic of articles published by the journal, an examination of the significance of the theme to the discipline is also an important criteria in selecting a journal. The journals with the lowest acceptance rate will tend to publish those manuscripts which make the most significant contributions to the advancement of the discipline. Since these journals receive a large number of manuscripts, the editors can distinguish those manuscripts likely to make a significant contribution to the reader's knowledge.

Although defining newness or the contribution of any one study to the understanding of a discipline is difficult, it is possible to gain some insights into this definition by asking the following questions:

1. Is the author stating the existence of a variable, trend or problem, not previously recognized by the literature?

2. Is the author testing the interactions of a different set of variables or events?

3. Is the author presenting a new technique to cope with a problem or test an idea previously presented in the literature?

4. Is the author using a subject sample with different characteristics than previously presented in the literature?

If the manuscript does not satisfy one of the first two categories, it is unlikely that a journal with a low acceptance rate will accept it for publication. Thus, the author should send the manuscript to those journals where the acceptance rate is higher.

Although the DIRECTORY provides the acceptance rates of manuscripts for many different journals, it is important to examine the data on percentage of invited articles for each journal. A high acceptance rate may result because the editor has asked leaders in the discipline to write articles on a particular subject. These invited articles are usually accepted. Since the author of an unsolicited manuscript competes with the leaders in the discipline, the manuscript will have to make a significant contribution to receive the editor's approval.

THE RELATIONSHIP OF THE MANUSCRIPT'S STYLE AND
METHODOLOGY TO THE JOURNAL'S READERSHIP

Another factor in selecting the journal to receive the manuscript is the journal's readership. The readers of each journal include either practitioners and professionals, researchers in accounting, economics and finance, or a combination of these groups.

Since the most important goal for an author is to publish the manuscript, the author should consider the prestige of the journal only after the manuscript has a relatively high probability of being published by more than one journal. This probability is determined by the responses the author received to his query letter and the similarity between the finished manuscript and the needs of the journal.

The method of determining the prestige of a journal varies depending on its readership and the goals of the author. If the readership is primarily administrators or practicing professionals and the goal of the author is to improve the author's image and that of the institution, the journal's circulation would probably be the best indicator of prestige.

In contrast, the author whose goal is to become known among the author's colleagues might consider the type of review process the journal uses as well as its circulation. With a few exceptions, the most prestigious journals with academic readership use a refereed review process.

THE POSSIBLE RESULTS OF THE REVIEW PROCESS AND THE
SELECTION OF A JOURNAL TO RECEIVE THE MANUSCRIPT

Although the author may feel that a journal with lower prestige would most likely publish the article, the author might be willing to take a chance on a journal with a greater amount of prestige. Since this will decrease the manuscript's chances of being accepted, the author should also consider the consequences of rejection. The consequences include the knowledge the author will gain from having his manuscript rejected.

To determine the amount of knowledge the author is likely to gain requires consideration of the number of reviewers the journal uses in the review process, the availability of the reviewer's comments and the time required for the review process. If the journal makes the reviewer's comments available to the author, this provides the author with a great learning opportunity. Also, the more people that review the manuscript, the greater will be the author's knowledge of how to improve the present manuscript. Hopefully, the author will transfer the knowledge gained from writing this manuscript to future manuscripts.

Should the review process take a small amount of time relative to a long period of time, it will provide the author with a greater opportunity to use this knowledge to revise the manuscript. To assist the author in determining those journals which provide a suitable learning opportunity, each journal in the DIRECTORY includes information on the number of reviewers, availability of reviewer's comments to the author and time required for review.

SENDING THE MANUSCRIPT

Before sending the manuscript to an editor, the author should write a cover letter, make sure the manuscript is correctly typed, the format conforms to the journal's guidelines and the necessary copies have been included. THE AUTHOR SHOULD ALWAYS KEEP A COPY OF THE MANUSCRIPT.

The cover letter that is sent with the manuscript makes it easy for the editor to select reviewers and monitor the manuscript while it is in the review process. This letter should include the title of the manuscript, the author name(s), address(es) and phone number(s). In addition, this letter should provide a brief description of the manuscript theme, its applicability and significance to the journal's readership. Finally it should request a copy of the reviewer's comments regardless of whether the manuscript is accepted or rejected.

RECEIPT OF THE REVIEWER'S COMMENTS

Although the author may have followed this procedure and taken every precaution to avoid rejection, the reviewers may still reject the article. When this occurs, the author's attitude should be to make those changes which would make the manuscript more understandable to the next editor, and/or reviewer. These changes may include providing additional information and/or presenting the topic in a more concise manner. Also, the author needs to determine whether some error occurred in selecting the journal to receive the manuscript. Regardless of the source of the errors, the author needs to make those changes which will improve the manuscript's chances of being accepted by the next journal that receives it.

Unless the journal specifically requests the author to revise the manuscript for publication, the author should not send the manuscript to the journal which first rejected it. In rejecting the manuscript, the reviewers implied that it could not be revised to meet their standards for publication. Thus, sending it back to them would not improve the likelihood that the manuscript will be accepted.

If your manuscript is accepted, go out and celebrate but write another one very quickly. When you find you're doing something right, keep doing it so you won't forget.

WHAT IS A REFEREED ARTICLE?

With some exceptions a refereed article is one that is blind reviewed and has two external reviewers. The blind review requirement and the use of external reviewers are consistent with the research criteria of objectivity and of knowledge.

The use of a blind review process means that the author of the manuscript is not known to the reviewer. With the large number of reviewers and journals, it is also likely that the name of the reviewers for a particular manuscript is not known to the author. Thus, creating a double blind review process. Since the author and reviewers are frequently unknown, the manuscript is judged on its merits rather than on the reputation of the author and/or the author's influence on the reviewers.

The use of two (2) reviewers permits specialists familiar with research similar to that presented in the paper to judge whether the paper makes a contribution to the advancement of knowledge. When two reviewers are used it provides a broader perspective for evaluating the research. This perspective is further widened by the discussion among the editor and reviewers in seeking to reconcile these perspectives.

In contrast to these criteria, some journals that have attained a reputation for quality do not use either a blind review process or external reviewers. The most notable is HARVARD BUSINESS REVIEW which uses an editorial review process. Its reputation for quality results from its readership whose continual subscription attests to its quality.

In addition to these criteria, some researchers include the journal's acceptance rate in their definition of a refereed journal. However, the method of calculating acceptance rates varies among journals. Some journals use as a base for computing this rate all manuscripts received. Other journals allow the editor to choose which papers are sent to reviewers and calculate the acceptance rate on those that are reviewed which is less than the total manuscripts received. Also, many editors do not maintain accurate records on this data and provide only a rough estimate.

Furthermore, the number of people associated with a particular area of specialization influences the acceptance rate. If only a few people can write papers in an area, it tends to increase the journal's acceptance rate.

Although the type of review process and use of external reviewers is one possible definition of a refereed article, it is not the only criteria. Furthermore, in judging the usefulness of a journal to the advancement of knowledge requires the reader to be familiar with many journals in their specialization and make their own evaluation.

ABACUS

ADDRESS FOR SUBMISSION :

G.W. DEAN, EDITOR
ABACUS
UNIVERSITY OF SYDNEY
DEPARTMENT OF ACCOUNTING
SYDNEY, 2006
N.S.W. AUSTRALIA
61-02-351-3107
61-02-351-6638 (Fax)
E-Mail : graeme@abacus.econ.su.oz.au

CIRCULATION DATA :

Reader : Academic

Frequency of Issue : 2 Times/Year

Copies Per Issue : 1001-2000

Subscription Price : 35.00 US$

Sponsorship : University

PUBLICATION GUIDELINES :

Manuscript Length : 16-20

Copies Required : Three

Computer Submission : Yes

Format : N/A

Fees to Review : 35.00 US$
  For a Subscriber 35.00 US$

REVIEW INFORMATION :

Type of Review : Blind Review

No. of External Reviewers : Two

No. of In House Reviewers : One

Acceptance Rate : 11-20%

Time To Review : 4-6 months

Reviewer's Comments : Yes

Fees to Publish : 0.00 US$

Invited Articles : 5% or less

MANUSCRIPT TOPICS : ACCOUNTING INFORMATION SYSTEMS;
  ACCOUNTING THEORY & PRACTICE; AUDITING; CAPITAL BUDGETING; COST ACCOUNTING;
  GOVERNMENT & NON-PROFIT ACCOUNTING; TAX ACCOUNTING; ACCOUNTING HISTORY

PUBLICATION GUIDELINES :

MANUSCRIPT GUIDELINES/COMMENTS :

1. ABACUS has as its objective the publication of explanatory constructive and critical articles on all aspects of accounting and on those phases of the theory and administration of organizations and of economic behavior generally which are related to accounting and finance.

Manuscripts should be sent to the Editor and will be considered for publication only if accompanied by a submission fee of $35.00 U.S. The submission fee is waived if the author or a co-author is a personal subscriber to the journal. The general layout and style should follow the most recent Style Guide which is printed in the Journal from time to time.

2. Submit three copies of manuscript.

3. Use opaque quarto paper (207 mm x 260 mm) or A4 (210 mm x 297 mm); double space text; leave adequate (30 mm) margins on both sides.

ABACUS

4. Place name of author in BLOCK capitals above the title of the article. Give author's present position at the foot of the first page.

5. Use footnotes sparingly. Place them at the end of the manuscript, double-spaced with an extra line between entries. Number footnotes consecutively throughout the text; use superior numbering without point, thus: "...money".3 Cite books and articles in the text thus:...(Jones,1962, p. 21).

For page reference numbers use p. 21, pp. 423-32, pp. 406-571, but pp.11-13, pp.115-19.

6. List books and articles cited in alphabetical order at the end of the manuscript. When listing books and articles use the following forms respectively:

    Jones, A., Depreciation of Assets, Publisher & Co.,1962.

    Morrissey, Leonard, 'Intangible Costs' in Morton Backer (ed.), Modern Accounting Theory, Prentice Hall,1966.

    Revsine, L. and J. Weygandt, 'Accounting for Inflation: The Controversy', Journal of Accountancy, October 1974.

    Smith, B., 'An Aspect of Depreciation', The Journal of Accounting, August 1965.

Do not use brackets; use short titles for publishers unless it is essential to tracing.

7. Underline what is to be printed in italics. Use BLOCK capitals only for what is to be printed in capitals. Use italics and BLOCK capitals sparingly. Use the smallest number of styles for section headings; preferably side headings, in italics.

8. For quotations within the text use only single quotation marks, and double marks for quotes within quotes. Where quotations exceed four lines insert quoted material three spaces, but do not use quotation marks.

9. Do not use a point in standard abbreviations such as CPA, SEC, but use points in U.K., U.S.A., and similar abbreviations. Date style e.g.,19 February 1966.

10. Use double dashes (--) to indicate dashes in the text, single dashes (-) for hyphens.

11. Use 'z' for such words as capitalize; 's' for the smaller number of words such as advise, analyse, comprise, enterprise (see OXFORD ENGLISH DICTIONARY).

12. Use the simplest possible form for mathematical symbols.

13. Keep tables to a minimum but do not try to convey too much information, at the cost of simplicity, in any one table.

ACADEMY OF ACCOUNTING AND FINANCIAL STUDIES JOURNAL

ADDRESS FOR SUBMISSION :

JAMES CARLAND, EDITOR
ACADEMY OF ACCOUNTING AND FINANCIAL
  STUDIES JOURNAL
P.O. BOX 2689
CULLOWHEE, NC 28723
704-293-9151
704-293-9407 (Fax)
E-Mail : CARLAND@WCU.EDU

CIRCULATION DATA :

Reader : Academic

Frequency of Issue : 3 Times/Year

Copies Per Issue : Less than 1000

Subscription Price : 50.00 US$

Sponsorship : Non Profit Corp.

PUBLICATION GUIDELINES :

Manuscript Length : 16-20

Copies Required : Four

Computer Submission : Yes

Format : WordPerfect 6.1

Fees to Review : 0.00 US$

REVIEW INFORMATION :

Type of Review : Blind Review

No. of External Reviewers : Two

No. of In House Reviewers : Two

Acceptance Rate : 11-20%

Time To Review : 4-6 months

Reviewer's Comments : Yes

Fees to Publish : 0.00 US$
  Academy Member   50.00 US$

Invited Articles : 5% or less

MANUSCRIPT TOPICS : ACCOUNTING INFORMATION SYSTEMS;
  ACCOUNTING THEORY & PRACTICE; AUDITING; CAPITAL BUDGETING; COST ACCOUNTING;
  GOVERNMENT & NON-PROFIT ACCOUNTING; PORTFOLIO & SECURITY ANALYSIS;
  TAX ACCOUNTING; ACCOUNTING & FINANCE EDUCATION

PUBLICATION GUIDELINES : American Psychological Association

MANUSCRIPT GUIDELINES/COMMENTS :

COMMENTS. All authors of published manuscripts must be members of The Academy.
Membership fee is $50.00.

ACADEMY OF FREE ENTERPRISE EDUCATION JOURNAL

ADDRESS FOR SUBMISSION :

JIM CARLAND, EDITOR
ACADEMY OF FREE ENTERPRISE EDUCATION
  JOURNAL
ALLIED ACADEMY GROUP
P.O. BOX 2689
CULLOWHEE, NC 28723
704-293-9151
704-293-9407 (Fax)
E-Mail : CARLAND@WCU.EDU

CIRCULATION DATA :

Reader : Academic

Frequency of Issue : 3 Times/Year

Copies Per Issue : Less than 1000

Subscription Price : 50.00 US$

Sponsorship : Profit Oriented Corp.

PUBLICATION GUIDELINES :

Manuscript Length : 26-30

Copies Required : Five

Computer Submission : No

Format : N/A

Fees to Review : 0.00 US$

REVIEW INFORMATION :

Type of Review : Blind Review

No. of External Reviewers : Three

No. of In House Reviewers : One

Acceptance Rate : 21-30%

Time To Review : 4-6 months

Reviewer's Comments : Yes

Fees to Publish : 0.00 US$

Invited Articles : 5% or less

MANUSCRIPT TOPICS : COST ACCOUNTING; ECONOMIC HISTORY;
   PUBLIC POLICY ECONOMICS; ECONOMIC EDUCATION;SMALL BUSINESS ENTREPRENEURSHIP

PUBLICATION GUIDELINES : American Psychological Association

MANUSCRIPT GUIDELINES/COMMENTS :

There are no guidelines for submissions; publication guidelines are provided
to authors of accepted manuscripts.

ACCOUNTANCY

ADDRESS FOR SUBMISSION :

BRIAN SINGLETON-GREEN, EDITOR
ACCOUNTANCY
INSTITUTE OF CHARTERED ACCOUNTANTS
40 BERNARD STREET
LONDON, WC1N 1LD
ENGLAND
44-071-833-3291
44-071-833-2085 (Fax)
E-Mail : postmaster@theabg.demon.co.uk

CIRCULATION DATA :

Reader : Business Persons

Frequency of Issue : Monthly

Copies Per Issue : Over 25,000

Subscription Price : 44.00 U.K.$
  Overseas : 63.00 U.K.$

Sponsorship : Professional Assoc.

PUBLICATION GUIDELINES :

Manuscript Length : 2000 Words

Copies Required : One

Computer Submission : No

Format : N/A

Fees to Review : 0.00 US$

REVIEW INFORMATION :

Type of Review : Editorial Review

No. of External Reviewers : Zero

No. of In House Reviewers : Two

Acceptance Rate : 11-20%

Time To Review : One month or less

Reviewer's Comments : No

Fees to Publish : 0.00 US$

Invited Articles : Over 50%

MANUSCRIPT TOPICS : ACCOUNTING INFORMATION SYSTEMS;
    ACCOUNTING THEORY & PRACTICE; AUDITING; CAPITAL BUDGETING; COST ACCOUNTING;
    ECONOMETRICS; TAX ACCOUNTING; BUSINESS EDUCATION;
    BUSINESS LAW & PUBLIC RESPONSIBILITY; ECONOMICS; FINANCE & INVESTMENTS;
    INTERNATIONAL BUSINESS; MANAGEMENT; SMALL BUSINESS ENTREPRENEURSHIP;
    STRATEGIC MANAGEMENT POLICY; GENERAL BUSINESS

PUBLICATION GUIDELINES :

MANUSCRIPT GUIDELINES/COMMENTS :

Most feature articles published in ACCOUNTANCY are commissioned, and
commissioning usually takes place some months before the planned publication
date. Those wishing to write feature articles should first submit a written
synopsis to the features editor, who may then commission the article.
Unsolicited manuscripts will be considered but are unlikely to be accepted.

Where topics are of immediate news interest, contact should be made by
telephone to the news editor.

ACCOUNTING AND BUSINESS RESEARCH

ADDRESS FOR SUBMISSION :

PROFESSOR K.V. PEASNELL, EDITOR
ACCOUNTING AND BUSINESS RESEARCH
UNIVERSITY OF LANCASTER
LANCASTER, LA1 4YX
UK
+44 0 1524 593977
+44 0 1524 594334 (Fax)
E-Mail : k.peasnell@lancaster.ac.uk

CIRCULATION DATA :

Reader : Academic

Frequency of Issue : Quarterly

Copies Per Issue : 1001-2000

Subscription Price : 39.00 Lb.$
  Institution : 9.00 Lb.$

Sponsorship : Professional Assoc.

PUBLICATION GUIDELINES :

Manuscript Length :

Copies Required : Three

Computer Submission : No

Format : N/A

Fees to Review : 45.00 US$

REVIEW INFORMATION :

Type of Review : Blind Review

No. of External Reviewers : Two

No. of In House Reviewers : Zero

Acceptance Rate : 11-20%

Time To Review : 2-3 months

Reviewer's Comments : Yes

Fees to Publish : 0.00 US$

Invited Articles : 5% or less

MANUSCRIPT TOPICS : ACCOUNTING INFORMATION SYSTEMS;
  ACCOUNTING THEORY & PRACTICE; AUDITING; CAPITAL BUDGETING; COST ACCOUNTING;
  GOVERNMENT & NON-PROFIT ACCOUNTING; TAX ACCOUNTING

PUBLICATION GUIDELINES :

MANUSCRIPT GUIDELINES/COMMENTS :

ACCOUNTING AUDITING & ACCOUNTABILITY JOURNAL

ADDRESS FOR SUBMISSION :

LEE D. PARKER, JOINT EDITOR
ACCOUNTING AUDITING & ACCOUNTABILITY
   JOURNAL
FLINDERS UNIVERSITY OF SOUTH AUSTRALIA
SCHOOL OF COMMERCE
BEDFORD PARK, SA 5042
AUSTRALIA
61 08 201 2643
61 08 201 2644 (Fax)

CIRCULATION DATA :

Reader : Academic

Frequency of Issue : 6 Times/Year

Copies Per Issue : Less than 1000

Subscription Price : 599.00 US$

Sponsorship : Profit Oriented Corp.

PUBLICATION GUIDELINES :

Manuscript Length : 30+

Copies Required : Four

Computer Submission : Yes

Format : Windows Word 6

Fees to Review : 0.00 US$

REVIEW INFORMATION :

Type of Review : Blind Review

No. of External Reviewers : Two

No. of In House Reviewers : One

Acceptance Rate : 21-30%

Time To Review : 1-2 months

Reviewer's Comments : Yes

Fees to Publish : 0.00 US$

Invited Articles : 5% or less

MANUSCRIPT TOPICS : ACCOUNTING INFORMATION SYSTEMS; AUDITING;
   COST ACCOUNTING; NON PROFIT ORGANIZATIONS;
   BUSINESS EDUCATION; PUBLIC ADMINISTRATION

PUBLICATION GUIDELINES :

MANUSCRIPT GUIDELINES/COMMENTS :

ABOUT THE JOURNAL
Articles submitted to ACCOUNTING, AUDITING & ACCOUNTABILITY should be original
contributions and should not be under consideration for any other publication
at the same time. Submissions should be sent to:

THE EDITOR
Professor Lee D. Parker, Joint Editor, Accounting, Auditing & Accountability
Journal, School of Commerce, The Flinders University of South Australia,
Bedford Park, SA 5042, Australia.

EDITORIAL OBJECTIVES
The journal ACCOUNTING, AUDITING & ACCOUNTABILITY is dedicated to the
advancement of accounting knowledge and provides a forum for the publication
of high quality manuscripts concerning the interaction between
accounting/auditing and their socio-economic and political environments. It
therefore encourages critical analysis of policy and practice in these areas.
Analysis could explore policy alternatives and provide new perspectives for
the accounting discipline.

ACCOUNTING AUDITING & ACCOUNTABILITY JOURNAL

The problems of concern are international (in varying degree) and may have differing cultural, social and institutional structures. Analysis can be international, national or organization specific. It can be from a single, multi- or inter-disciplinary perspective.

EDITORIAL CRITERIA
Major criteria used to evaluate papers are: (1) Subject matter: must be of importance to the accounting discipline;(2) Research question: must fall within the journal's scope; (3) Research: well designed and executed, and (4) Presentation: well written and conforming to the journal's style.

THE REVIEWING PROCESS
Each paper submitted is subject to the following review procedures:
(1) It is reviewed by the editor for general suitability for this publication.
(2) If it is judged suitable two reviewers are selected and a double blind review process takes place.
(3) Based on the recommendations of the reviewers, the editors then decide whether the particular article should be accepted as it is, revised or rejected.

ARTICLE FEATURES AND FORMATS REQUIRED OF AUTHORS
There are a number of specific requirements with regard to article features and formats which authors should note carefully:

1. Word length
Articles should be between 4,000 and 7,000 words in length.

2. Title
A title of not more than eight words in length should be provided.

3. Autobiographical note
A brief autobiographical note should be supplied including full name, appointment, name of organization and e-mail address.

4. Word processing
Please submit to the Editor three copies of the manuscript in double line spacing with wide margins.

5. Headings and sub-headings
These should be short and to-the-point, appearing approximately every 750 words. Headings should be typed in capitals and underlined; sub-headings should be typed in upper and lower case and underlined. Headings should not be numbered.

6. References
References to other publications should be in Harvard style. They should contain full bibliographical details and journal titles should not be abbreviated. For multiple citations in the same year use a, b, c immediately following the year of publication. References should be shown as follows:

* Within the text - author's last name followed by a comma and year of publication all in round brackets, e g. (Fox, 1994).

* At the end of the article a reference list in alphabetical order as follows:

ACCOUNTING AUDITING & ACCOUNTABILITY JOURNAL

(a) For books:
   surname, initials, year of publication, title, publisher, place of
   publication, e.g. Casson, M. (1979), Alternatives to the Multinational
   Enterprise, Macmillan, London.
(b) For chapter in edited in book:
   surname, initials, year, title, editor's surname, initials, title,
   publisher, place, pages, e.g.
   Bessley, M. and Wilson, P. (1984), "Public policy and small firms in
   Britain", in Levicki, C. (Ed.), Small Business Theory and Policy, Croom
   Helm, London, pp. 111-26.
(c) For articles:
   surname, initials, year, title, journal, volume, number, pages, e.g.
   Fox, S. (1994), "Empowerment as a catalyst for change: an example from
   the food industry", Supply Chain Management, Vol. 2 No. 3, pp. 29-33.

If there is more than one author list surnames followed by initials. All
authors should be shown.
Electronic sources should include the URL of the electronic site at which they
may be found.

Notes/Endnotes should be used only if absolutely necessary. They should be
identified in the text by consecutive numbers enclosed in square brackets and
listed at the end of the article.

7. Figures, charts, diagrams

Use of figures, charts and diagrams should be kept to a minimum and
information conveyed in such a manner should instead be described in text
form. Essential figures, charts and diagrams should be referred to as figures
and numbered consecutively using arabic numerals. Each figure should have a
brief title and labelled axes. Diagrams should be kept as simple as possible
and avoid unnecessary capitalization and shading In the text, the position of
the figure should be shown by typing on a separate line the words "take in
Figure 1".

8. Tables

Use of tables should be kept to a minimum. Where essential, these should be
typed on a separate sheet of paper and numbered consecutively and
independently of any figures included in the article. Each table should have a
number in roman numerals, a brief title, and vertical and horizontal headings.
In the text, the position of the table should be shown by typing on a separate
line the words "take in Table 1". Tables should not repeat data available
elsewhere in the paper.

9. Photos, illustrations

Half-tone illustrations should be restricted in number to the minimum
necessary. Good glossy bromide prints should accompany the manuscripts but not
be attached to manuscript pages. Illustrations unsuitable for reproduction,
e.g. computer-screen capture, will not be used. Any computer programs should
be supplied as clear and sharp print outs on plain paper. They will be
reproduced photographically to avoid errors.

10. Emphasis

Words to be emphasized should be limited in number and italicized. Capital
letters should be used only at the start of sentences or in the case of proper
names.

ACCOUNTING AUDITING & ACCOUNTABILITY JOURNAL

11. Abstracts

Authors must supply an abstract of 100-150 words when submitting an article. It should be an abbreviated, accurate representation of the content of the article. Major results, conclusions and/or recommendations should be given, followed by supporting details of method, scope or purpose. It should contain sufficient information to enable readers to decide whether they should obtain and read the entire article.

12. Keywords

Up to six keywords should be included which encapsulate the principal subjects covered by the article. Minor facets of an article should not be keyworded. These keywords will be used by readers to select the material they wish to read and should therefore be truly representative of the article's main content.

PREPARATION FOR PUBLICATION

13. Final submission of the article

Once accepted by the Editor for publication, the final version of the article should be submitted in manuscript accompanied by a 3.5" disk of the same version of the article marked with: disk format; author name(s); title of article; journal title; file name. This will be considered to be the definitive version of the article and the author should ensure that it is complete, grammatically correct and without spelling or typographical errors.

In preparing the disk, please use one of the following formats:
- for text prepared on a PC - AMI Pro, FrameMaker, Office Writer, Professional write, RTF, Word or WordPerfect;
- for text prepared on a Macintosh system - FrameMaker, MacWrite, MS Works, Nisus 3, RTF, Word, WordPerfect WriteNow or ASCII
- for graphics, figures, charts and diagrams, please use one of the following formats:

File type	Programs	File extension
Windows Metafile	Most Windows programs	.wmf
WordPerfect Graphic	All WordPerfect software	.wpg
Adobe Illustrator	Adobe Illustrator	.ai
	Corel Draw	
	Macromedia Freehand	
Harvard Graphics	Harvard Graphics	.cgm
PIC	Lotus graphics	.pic
Computer/Graphics Metafile	Lotus Freelance	.cgm
DXF	Autocad	.dxf
	Many CAD programs	
GEM	Ventura Publisher	.gem
Macintosh PICT	Most Macintosh Drawing	

Only vector type drawings are acceptable, as bitmap files (extension .bmp, .pcx or .gif) print poorly. If graphical representations are not available on disk, black ink line drawings suitable for photographic reproduction and of dimensions appropriate for reproduction on a journal page should be supplied with the article.

If you require technical assistance in respect of submitting an article please consult the relevant section of MCB's World Wide Web Literati Club on http://www.mcb.co.uk/literati/nethome.htm or contact Mike Massey at MCB, e-mail: mmassey@mcb.co.uk

ACCOUNTING AUDITING & ACCOUNTABILITY JOURNAL

14. Journal Article Record Form
Each article should be accompanied by a completed and signed Journal Article Record Form. This form is available from the Editor or can be downloaded from MCB's World Wide Web Literati Club on
http://www.mcb.co.uk/literati/nethome.htm

15. Author proofs
Where author proofs are supplied, they will be sent to corresponding authors who will be expected to correct and return them within five days of receipt or the article will be published without author corrections. The publisher is not responsible for any error not marked by the author on the proof Corrections on the proof are limited to typesetting errors; no substantial author changes are allowed at this stage.

COPYRIGHT
Authors submitting articles for publication warrant that the work is not an infringement of any existing copyright and will indemnify the publisher against any breach of such warranty. For ease of dissemination and to ensure proper policing of use, papers and contributions become the legal copyright of the publisher unless otherwise agreed.

ACCOUNTING, AUDITING & ACCOUNTABILITY is published by MCB University Press, 60/62 Toller Lane, Bradford, West Yorkshire BD8 9BY, UK. Tel: +44 1274 777700, Fax: +44 1274 785200 or 785201.

ACCOUNTING BUSINESS AND FINANCIAL HISTORY

ADDRESS FOR SUBMISSION :

JOHN RICHARD EDWAREDS, EDITOR
ACCOUNTING BUSINESS AND FINANCIAL
  HISTORY
CARDIFF BUSINESS SCHOOL
BUSINESS HISTORY RESEARCH UNIT
COLUM DRIVE
CARDIFF, CF1 3EU
UK
0 1222 874197
0 1222 874419 (Fax)
E-Mail : edwardsjr@cardiff.ac.uk

CIRCULATION DATA :

Reader : Academic

Frequency of Issue : 3 Times/Year

Copies Per Issue : Less than 1000

Subscription Price : 85.00 US$
  Institution : 222.00 US$

Sponsorship : Profit Oriented Corp.

PUBLICATION GUIDELINES :

Manuscript Length : 30-40

Copies Required : Three

Computer Submission : No

Format : N/A

Fees to Review : 0.00 US$

REVIEW INFORMATION :

Type of Review : Blind Review

No. of External Reviewers : Two

No. of In House Reviewers : One

Acceptance Rate : 40 %

Time To Review : 2-3 months

Reviewer's Comments : Yes

Fees to Publish : 0.00 US$

Invited Articles : 31-50%

MANUSCRIPT TOPICS : COST ACCOUNTING; ECONOMIC HISTORY;
  ACCOUNTING, BUSINESS & FINANCIAL HISTORY

PUBLICATION GUIDELINES :

MANUSCRIPT GUIDELINES/COMMENTS :

1. Authors should submit three complete copies of their text, tables and figures, with any original illustrations, to: John Richard Edwards, Business History Research Unit, Cardiff Business School, Colum Drive, Cardiff CFI 3EU.

2. The submission should include a cover page showing the author's name, the department where the work was done, an address for correspondence, if different, and any acknowledgements.

3. Submissions should be in English, typed in double spacing with wide margins, on one side only of the paper, preferably of A4 size. The title, but not the author's name should appear on the first page of the manuscript.

4. Articles should normally be as concise as possible and preceded by an abstract of not more than 100 words and a list of up to 6 keywords for on-line searching purposes.

5. Within the manuscript there may be up to three levels of heading.

ACCOUNTING BUSINESS AND FINANCIAL HISTORY

6. Tables and figures should not be inserted in the pages of the manuscript but should be on separate sheets. They should be numbered consecutively in Arabic numerals with a descriptive caption. The desired position in the text for each table and figure should be indicated in the margin of the manuscript.

7. Use the Harvard system of referencing which gives the name of the author and the date of publication as a key to the full bibliographical details which are set out in the list of references. When the author's name is mentioned in the text, the date is inserted in parentheses immediately after the name, as in 'Aldcroft (1964)'. When a less direct reference is made to one or more authors, both name and date are bracketed, with the references separated by a semi-colon, as in 'several authors have noted this trend (Rimmer, 1960; Pollard, 1965; Mckendrick, 1970)'. Where appropriate, page numbers should also be provided (Robert, 1980: 56). When the reference is to a work of dual or multiple authorship, use 'Harvey and Press (1988)' or 'Yamey et al. (1963)' respectively. If an author has two references published in the same year, add lower case letters after the date to distinguish them, as in 'Johnson (1984a, 1984b)'. Always use the minimum number of figures in page numbers dates etc, e.g. 22-4, 105-6 (but 112-13 for 'teen numbers) and 1968-9.

8. Direct quotations of 40 words or more should start on a separate line and be indented.

9. Footnotes should be used only where necessary to avoid interrupting the continuity of the text. They should be numbered consecutively using superscript arabic numerals. They should appear at the end of the main text, immediately before the list of references.

10. Submissions should include a reference list, in alphabetical order, at the end of the article. The content and format should conform to the following examples.

Kennedy, William P. (1987) Industrial Structure: Capital Markets and the Origins of British Economic Decline, Cambridge: Cambridge University Press.

Chapman, S.D. (1985) 'British-based investment groups before 1914', The Economic History Review, 38: 230-51.

Hunt, Bishop Carleton (1936) The Development of the Business Corporation in England 1800 1867, Cambridge, Mass.: Harvard University Press. Reprinted (1969) New York: Russell & Russell.

Davenport-Hines, R.P.T. and Geoffrey Jones (eds) (1989) British Business in Asia since 1860, Cambridge: Cambridge University Press.

11. Page proofs will be sent for correction to a first-named author, unless otherwise requested. The difficulty and expense involved in making amendments at the page proof stage make it essential for authors to prepare their typescripts carefully: any alteration to the original text is strongly discouraged.

ACCOLLUNTING, BUSINESS AND FINANCIAL HISTORY is published by E & FN SPON, (an imprint of Chapman & Hall), 2-6 Boundary Row, London SE1 8HN, UK. Tel: 0171-865-0066, Fax: 0171-522-99623. E-mail: spon@chall.co.uk

ACCOUNTING EDUCATION: A JOURNAL OF THEORY, PRACTICE AND RESEARCH

ADDRESS FOR SUBMISSION :

BILL SCHWARTZ, CO-EDITOR (NON-EMPIRICAL)
ACCOUNTING EDUCATION: A JOURNAL OF
  THEORY, PRACTICE AND RESEARCH
VIRGINIA COMMONWEALTH UNIVERSITY
SCHOOL OF BUSINESS
1015 FLOYD AVENUE
RICHMOND, VA 23284-4000
804-828-7194
804-828-8884 (Fax)
E-Mail : bschwartz@busnet.bus.vcu.edu

CIRCULATION DATA :

Reader : Academic

Frequency of Issue : 2 Times/Year

Copies Per Issue :

Subscription Price : 70.00 US$

Sponsorship : Profit Oriented Corp.

PUBLICATION GUIDELINES :

Manuscript Length : 21-25

Copies Required : Three

Computer Submission : No

Format : N/A

Fees to Review : 35.00 US$

REVIEW INFORMATION :

Type of Review : Blind Review

No. of External Reviewers : Two

No. of In House Reviewers : One

Acceptance Rate : 11-20%

Time To Review : 2-3 months

Reviewer's Comments : Yes

Fees to Publish : 0.00 US$

Invited Articles : 6-10%

MANUSCRIPT TOPICS : ACCOUNTING THEORY & PRACTICE; COST ACCOUNTING;
  ACCOUNTING EDUCATION

PUBLICATION GUIDELINES : Chicago Manual of Style

MANUSCRIPT GUIDELINES/COMMENTS :

DAVID E. STOUT, CO-EDITOR (EMPIRICAL)
ACCOUNTING EDUCATION: A JOURNAL OF THEORY, PRACTICE AND RESEARCH
COLLEGE OF COMMERCE & FINANCE
VILLANOVA UNIVERSITY
VILLANOVA, PA 19085-1678
TEL: (610)519-4048
FAX: (610) 519-7864
INTERNET: stout@ucis.vill.edu

STATEMENT OF PURPOSE
ACCOUNTING EDUCATION: A JOURNAL OF THEORY, PRACTICE AND RESEARCH is a
refereed, academic journal whose purpose is to meet the needs of individuals
interested in the educational process. We plan to publish thoughtful,
well-developed articles that are readable, relevant and reliable.
Articles may be non-empirical or empirical. Our emphasis is pedagogy, and
articles MUST explain how teaching methods or curricula/programs can be
improved.

ACCOUNTING EDUCATION: A JOURNAL OF THEORY, PRACTICE AND RESEARCH

NON-EMPIRICAL manuscripts should be academically rigorous. They can be theoretical syntheses, conceptual models, position papers, discussions of methodology, comprehensive literature reviews grounded in theory, or historical discussions with implications for current and future efforts. Reasonable assumptions and logical development are essential. Most manuscripts should discuss implications for research.

For EMPIRICAL reports sound research design and execution are critical. Articles should have well articulated and strong theoretical foundations. In this regard, establishing a link to the non-accounting literature is desirable. Replications and extensions of previously published works are encouraged. As a means for establishing an open dialogue, responses to or comments on articles published previously are welcomed.

REVIEW PROCEDURES

ACCOUNTING EDUCATION: A JOURNAL OF THEORY, PRACTICE AND RESEARCH will provide authors with timely reviews clearly indicating the review status of the manuscript. The results of initial reviews normally will be reported to authors within eight weeks. Authors will be expected to work with an Editor who will act as a liaison between the authors and the reviewers to resolve areas of concern.

EDITORIAL POLICY AND MANUSCRIPT GUIDELINES

1. Manuscripts should be typewritten and double-spaced on 8 1/2" by 11" white paper. Only one side of the page should be used.

2. Manuscripts should include a cover page which indicates the author's name, address, affiliation and any acknowledgements. The author should NOT be identified anywhere else in the manuscript.

3. Manuscripts should include on a separate lead page an abstract not exceeding 250 words. The author's name and affiliation should NOT appear on the abstract. It should contain a concise statement of the purpose of the manuscript, the primary methods or approaches used (if applicable), and the main results, conclusions, or recommendations.

4. Topical headings should be in caps and centered. Subheadings should be flush with the left margin, underlined, and NOT in caps. Headings and subheadings should NOT be numbered.

5. Tables, figures and exhibits should appear on separate pages. Each should be numbered and have a title.

6. Footnotes and references should appear at the end of the manuscript. However, every effort should be made to incorporate material into the body of the paper. The list of references should include only works actually cited.

7. In order to be assured of an anonymous review, authors should NOT identify themselves directly or indirectly in the text of the paper. Reference to unpublished working papers and dissertations should be avoided. If necessary, authors may indicate the reference is being withheld for the reasons cited here.

8. Every effort should be made to use a spell check and a grammar check. Accepted manuscripts ultimately must be submitted on an IBM compatible disk.

ACCOUNTING EDUCATION: A JOURNAL OF
THEORY, PRACTICE AND RESEARCH

9. Manuscripts currently under review by other publications or manuscripts that already have been published (including proceedings from regional or national meetings) should NOT be submitted. Please include a statement to that effect in the cover letter accompanying your submission. Complete reports of research presented at a regional or national meeting, which have not been published in the proceedings, are acceptable for submission.

10. THREE copies of each manuscript should be submitted.

11. The author should send a check for $35.00 made payable to ACCOUNTING EDUCATION as a submission fee.

ACCOUNTING EDUCATION: AN INTERNATIONAL JOURNAL

ADDRESS FOR SUBMISSION :

RICHARD M. S. WILSON, EDITOR
ACCOUNTING EDUCATION: AN INTERNATIONAL
   JOURNAL
LOUGHBOROUGH UNIVERSITY BUSINESS SCHOOL
ASHBY ROAD
LOUGHBOROUGH
LEICESTERSHIRE, LE11 3TU
UK
44 1509 223139
44 1509 223961 (Fax)
E-Mail : R.M.Wilson@lboro.ac.uk

CIRCULATION DATA :

Reader : Academic

Frequency of Issue : Quarterly

Copies Per Issue : Less than 1000

Subscription Price : 62.00 US$
   Institutional : 267.00 US$

Sponsorship : Profit Oriented Corp.

PUBLICATION GUIDELINES :

Manuscript Length : 21-25

Copies Required : Four

Computer Submission : No

Format : N/A

Fees to Review : 0.00 US$

REVIEW INFORMATION :

Type of Review : Blind Review

No. of External Reviewers : Three

No. of In House Reviewers : Two

Acceptance Rate : 21-30%

Time To Review : 2-3 months

Reviewer's Comments : Yes

Fees to Publish : 0.00 US$

Invited Articles : 5% or less

MANUSCRIPT TOPICS : COST ACCOUNTING; ACCOUNTING EDUCATION

PUBLICATION GUIDELINES :

MANUSCRIPT GUIDELINES/COMMENTS :

In USA: Bruce A. Baldwin, Associate Editor
        Accounting Education: An International Journal
        Arizona State University
        P.O. Box 37100
        Phoenix, AZ 85069-7100
        Tel: 602-543-6200 Fax: 602-543-6221
        E-mail: icbab@asuvm.inre.asu.edu

ACCOUNTING EDUCATION has the following major aims:
(i) to enhance the educational base of accounting practice by providing a
forum for identifying, exploring and assessing issues relating to the academic
and professional preparation of future accounting practitioners;

(ii) to promote excellence in accounting education and training by acting as a
catalyst to facilitate improvements via such means as curriculum development,
innovative learning methods, and new teaching materials;

(iii) to stimulate research in accounting education and training and to
disseminate the results of enquiries into the effectiveness of alternative
teaching methods, etc.;

ACCOUNTING EDUCATION: AN INTERNATIONAL JOURNAL

(iv) to provide a means of highlighting the contribution IT has to make to developing better accounting education and training both in respect of relevant content and effective delivery;

(v) to build links among those who teach, train and employ accounting/finance students and to offer a platform for the exchange of views reflecting the priorities to be attached by different parties to issues in accounting education and training;

(vi) to stimulate and develop the European and international dimensions of accounting education and training;

(vii) to assist in integrating the various elements in the overall process of accounting education and training into a coherent whole.
Notes for contributors

NOTES FOR CONTRIBUTORS

ACCOUNTING EDUCATION is a quarterly international journal devoted to publishing research-based papers and other information on key aspects of accounting education and training of relevance to practitioners, academics, trainers, students and professional bodies.

It is a forum for the exchange of ideas, experiences, opinions and research results relating to (a) the preparation of students/trainees for careers in public accounting, managerial accounting, financial management, corporate accounting, controllership, treasury management, financial analysis, internal auditing, and accounting in government and other non-commercial organizations; and (b) the continuing professional education of practitioners.

The coverage includes aspects of accounting education and training policy, curriculum issues, computing matters, and accounting research as it impinges on educational or training issues.

The journal seeks to make available innovative teaching resource material that can be used by readers in their own institutions. As a necessary corollary to this, the journal seeks to publish papers dealing with the effectiveness of accounting education or training.

In addition to publishing original papers the journal also includes exemplars and reviews relating to what we teach, how we teach it, and how effective our endeavours are in providing an adequate educational and training base for accounting practice.

SUBMISSION OF PAPERS

Manuscripts should be submitted (four copies) with original figures to the Editor, Professor Richard M. S. Wilson.

The Editor will be pleased to deal with enquiries from potential authors about papers they may be considering writing or submitting to ACCOUNTING EDUCATION. However, comments will not be given on drafts that have not been formally submitted.

All submissions will be subject to refereeing by experts in the field. There is no submission fee and no page charges.

ACCOUNTING EDUCATION: AN INTERNATIONAL JOURNAL

If a paper appears to be generally suitable and in line with the aims of the Journal it will be passed on by the Editor to an Associate Editor with arrangements being made for at least two appropriate referees to comment on the paper via a double-blind review.

The Editor will reach a decision on publishability after taking into account the reports from referees and Associate Editors. Authors will be provided with referees' reports and publishing decisions within as short a period as possible.

In certain circumstances (e.g. when papers are submitted directly to the Associate Editors in either Hong Kong or the USA) a variation on the above procedure may be employed.

Manuscripts will only be considered for ACCOUNTING EDUCATION if they are unpublished and not being submitted for publication elsewhere. If previously published tables, illustrations or text exceeding 200 words are to be included then the copyright holder's written permission should be obtained, and included with the submission. A clear statement should appear in the text if any material has been published elsewhere in a preliminary form.

Copies of questionnaires and other research instruments should be included with manuscripts to facilitate editorial review. As a result of space limitations these may not be published.

The Editor will be pleased to deal with enquiries from potential authors about papers they may be considering writing or submitting to ACCOUNTING EDUCATION. However, detailed comments will not be given on drafts that have not been formally submitted.

EVALUATIVE CRITERIA

The principal criteria by which submissions to ACCOUNTING EDUCATION will be assessed are: relevance, novelty, usefulness, readability, house style, clarity, conciseness, linkages to existing literature, substance, rigour, validity, readability, ethical aspects and quality relative to the aims of the Journal.

MANUSCRIPT PREPARATION

FORMAT AND STYLE

Manuscripts should be in English and be typed (double-spaced) with a generous margin (at least 2.5 cm) at each edge of each page on one side of international A4 bond paper.

The first page (title page) should contain the title of the paper, authors' names and institutional affiliations. The address, telephone number, fax number, telex number and E-mail code (if available) of the author to whom decisions, proofs and offprints should be sent should also be given.

Authors should enclose a brief biographical outline with their submissions.

ABSTRACT

The second page should include the paper's title and an abstract (up to 150 words). The abstract should be an accurate representation of the paper's contents. Major results, conclusions, and/or recommendations should be given with brief details of methods, etc. There should be no indication (other than on the title page) of the identity of the author(s) or the author's (or authors') affiliations.

KEYWORDS
Up to six keywords or descriptors that clearly describe the subject matter of the paper should be provided. These keywords will facilitate indexing as well as help in describing the subject matter for prospective readers.

REFERENCES
Citations in the text should follow the Harvard scheme (i.e. name(s) of authors(s) followed by the year of publication and page numbers where relevant, ail in parenthesis). Where a source has more than two authors cite the first author's name and et al. For multiple citations in the same year use a, b, and c immediately following the year of publication.

The reference section should only contain references cited in the text. These should be arranged in alphabetical order by surname of the first author (then chronologically). Each reference should contain full bibliographic details; journal titles should not be abbreviated. The following style is expected:

Gray, R.H. and Helliar, C. (eds) (1992) The British Accounting Review Research Register. London: Academic Press 5th ed..

Novin, A.M., Pearson, M.A. and Senge, S.V. (1990) Improving thc curriculum for aspiring management accountants: the practitioner's point of view. Journal of Accounting Education 6 (2) Fall, 207-24.

Walsh, A.J. (1988) The making Of the chartered accountant. In D. Rowe (ed.) The Irish Chartered Accountant, pp.155-73. Dublin: Gill and Macmillan.

FIGURES AND TABLES
All figures and tables should be given titles, numbered consecutively in arabic numerals, and referred to within the text. Labelling should be clear and of sufficient size to be legible after any necessary reduction. Lettering on line figures should usually be prepared with a 2:1 reduction in mind.

Permission to reproduce illustrations from other published work must be obtained by the author before submitting an article and any acknowledgement should be included in the figure captions.

Tables should be titled, numbered consecutively and independently of any figures, and referred to within the text.

ACKNOWLEDGEMENTS
Should appear at the end of the paper before the list of references.

FOOTNOTES
Should be kept to a minimum and appear at the end of the paper on a separate page.

MATHEMATICAL NOTATION
Mathematics should only be used if this contributes significantly to the clarity and economy of presentation, or is essential to the argument of a paper. Whenever possible authors should put mathematics in an appendix. The

ACCOUNTING EDUCATION: AN INTERNATIONAL JOURNAL

conclusions of articles using mathematics should be summarized in a form that is intelligible to non-mathematical readers of the Journal.

PROOFS AND OFFPRINTS

The designated author will receive proofs which should be corrected and returned within three days. Alterations to the proofs which were not in the original manuscript are not permitted. Such revisions may be charged for as they are expensive and time consuming.

Offprints can be ordered via the form that will accompany the proofs. The designated author will receive 25 free offprints following publication. Additional copies will be charged for.

COPYRIGHT MATTERS

Manuscripts will only be considered for ACCOUNTING EDUCATION if they are unpublished and not being submitted for publication elsewhere. If previously published tables, illustrations or text exceeding 200 words are to be included then the copyright holder's written permission should be obtained, and included with the submission. A clear statement should appear in the text if any material has been published elsewhere in a preliminary form.

Authors submitting articles with a view to publication warrant that the work is not an infringement of any existing copyright and agree to indemnify the publisher against any breach of such warranty.

Upon acceptance of a paper by ACCOUNTING EDUCATION the author(s) will be asked to transfer copyright, via a supplied form, to the publisher, Chapman and Hall, 2-6 Boundary Row, London SE1 8HN, UK. Telephone: 071-865 0066, Facsimile: 071-522 9624, Email: journal@chall.mhs.com.compuserve

REFEREEING CRITERIA

Submissions relating to one or more of ACCOUNTING EDUCATION'S aims will be refereed in accordance with the criteria specified below (in no significant order):

		SUMMARY ASSESSMENT		
		Yes	No	See comments
* Relevance:	Is the topic apt and relevant to the journal's aims? Is it topical? Will it be of interest to the journal's readers?	___	___	___
* Novelty:	Does the submission contain originality or otherwise make a new contribution? Innovative styles of presentation (e.g. use of diaries, annotated dialogues) are to be encouraged.	___	___	___
* Usefulness:	Can the ideas/results be put into effect?	___	___	___
* Readability:	Is the submission well written (to suit the journal's readership of practitioners and academics)?	___	___	___

ACCOUNTING EDUCATION: AN INTERNATIONAL JOURNAL

* Clarity: Is the main message apparent and the grammar correct? Is the submission comprehensible to those who may not be specialists in the particular field? Are the figures suitable?   ___ ___ ___

* House style: Is the paper presented in accordance with the journal's house style? Is the title accurate and informative? Are the key words adequate? Is the abstract appropriate?   ___ ___ ___

* Conciseness: Is the submission sharply focused?   ___ ___ ___

* Linkages: Does the paper take sufficient account of, and make appropriate reference to, previous work in the area?   ___ ___ ___

* Substance: Is the subject matter important? Is the treatment given to the subject matter comprehensive? Are the messages/results significant? Is the paper's length appropriate? Should specific parts be expanded or reduced?   ___ ___ ___

* Rigour: Is the work in question well-designed and executed? Is the analysis appropriate to the problem and correctly used? If the statistical analysis is really necessary could it be relegated to an appendix?   ___ ___ ___

* Validity: Do the results stem from the causes? Can the results be generalized?   ___ ___ ___

* Reliability: Is the submission authoritative, consistent with prior work, and replicable?   ___ ___ ___

* Ethics: What are the ethical implications of this paper? Are they identified?   ___ ___ ___

* Quality: Bearing in mind that some submissions will not be of a 'research' nature, hence not all the criteria given above will apply, is it the case that the submission is good (of its type) relative to achieving the journal's aims? If the paper represents an authoritative summary or synthesis of a developing branch of accounting knowledge that has a clear pedagogic flavour please deal with it in a sympathetic manner.   ___ ___ ___

ACCOUNTING EDUCATORS' JOURNAL

ADDRESS FOR SUBMISSION :

JEFFREY L. HARKINS, EDITOR
ACCOUNTING EDUCATORS' JOURNAL
UNIVERSITY OF IDAHO
DEPARTMENT OF ACCOUNTING
MOSCOW, ID 83843
USA
208-885-6453
208-882-8939 (Fax)
E-Mail : jeffh@uidaho.edu

PUBLICATION GUIDELINES :

Manuscript Length : 11-15

Copies Required : Four

Computer Submission : Yes

Format : For Final Draft Only

Fees to Review : 40.00 US$

CIRCULATION DATA :

Reader : Academic

Frequency of Issue : 2 Times/Year

Copies Per Issue : Less than 1000

Subscription Price : 30.00 US$
  Institution : 40.00 US$
  Foreign : 50.00 US$

Sponsorship :

REVIEW INFORMATION :

Type of Review : Blind Review

No. of External Reviewers : Two

No. of In House Reviewers : Zero

Acceptance Rate : 21-30%

Time To Review : 4-6 months

Reviewer's Comments : Yes

Fees to Publish : 0.00 US$

Invited Articles : 5% or less

MANUSCRIPT TOPICS : ACCOUNTING INFORMATION SYSTEMS;
  ACCOUNTING THEORY & PRACTICE; ACCOUNTING EDUCATION

PUBLICATION GUIDELINES :

MANUSCRIPT GUIDELINES/COMMENTS :

Manuscripts should be double-spaced on white 8-1/2 x 11" paper. The cover page should include the title of manuscript, authors' full names, affiliations and complete mailing address. The second page should include the title of the manuscript and an abstract of not more than 200 words. The third page should include the manuscript title and the first page of text.

Instruments, cases of forms used to gather data should be included at the back of the paper. They need not be referenced nor published, but should be available for the reviewers to evaluate.

References to other works should be in square brackets in the body of the text and include author's name and year of publication. Include page numbers when references are to works of over 25 pages. The list of references should be in alphabetical order at the end of the text and include all referenced literature. Footnotes should be used for discussions that would disrupt the flow of the text. They should be numbered sequentially and be placed at the end of the text. Authors are encouraged to include materials that will assist the reviewers, such as copies of difficult to locate materials referenced in

ACCOUNTING EDUCATORS' JOURNAL

the text and discussions of essential issues that would be excessive if included in the text. The inclusion of these materials will facilitate the review process.

Tables and figures should appear on separate pages and be placed at the end of the text. They should be numbered at the top of the page and referenced in the text. Indicate in the text where tables should be placed. Tables and figures included in manuscripts accepted for publication must be submitted in camera-ready form. Normally proportional spacing and printing on a laser printer is adequate.

Authors should send three copies of their manuscripts to the Editor.

POLICY ON REPRODUCTION
Permission is hereby granted to reproduce any of the contents of the ACCOUNTING EDUCATOR'S JOURNAL for classroom use by faculty members. Please indicate the source and our copyright on any reproduction.

Written permission is required to reproduce any of these copyright material in other publications.

Mail requests for subscriptions to the Editor.

ACCOUNTING ENQUIRIES

ADDRESS FOR SUBMISSION :

STANLEY C.W. SALVARY, EDITOR
ACCOUNTING ENQUIRIES
CANISIUS COLLEGE
WEHLE SCHOOL OF BUSINESS
BUFFALO, NY 14208
USA
(716) 888-2869
(716) 888-2248 (Fax)
E-Mail : SALVARY@CCVMSA

CIRCULATION DATA :

Reader : Academic

Frequency of Issue : 2 Times/Year

Copies Per Issue : Less than 1000

Subscription Price : 40.00 US$
   Institution : 80.00 US$

Sponsorship : Profit Oriented Corp.

PUBLICATION GUIDELINES :

Manuscript Length : 40 or less

Copies Required : Four

Computer Submission : No

Format : N/A

Fees to Review : 25.00 US$

REVIEW INFORMATION :

Type of Review : Blind Review

No. of External Reviewers : Two

No. of In House Reviewers : One

Acceptance Rate : 33 %

Time To Review : 4-6 months

Reviewer's Comments : Yes

Fees to Publish : 0.00 US$

Invited Articles : 6-10%

MANUSCRIPT TOPICS : ACCOUNTING INFORMATION SYSTEMS;
   ACCOUNTING THEORY & PRACTICE; AUDITING; CAPITAL BUDGETING; COST ACCOUNTING;
   GOVERNMENT & NON-PROFIT ACCOUNTING; TAX ACCOUNTING; ACCOUNTING HISTORY

PUBLICATION GUIDELINES : Accounting Enquiries

MANUSCRIPT GUIDELINES/COMMENTS :

EDITORIAL POLICY
ACCOUNTING ENQUIRIES is devoted to the study of accounting and accounting
related issues. This journal will publish articles in, but not limited to, the
following areas: accounting theory and practice, accounting history, auditing
theory and practice, standard setting, and behavioral issues in accounting and
auditing. The journal should prove to be a forum for scholarly debate and
exchange of ideas. No paradigm will be espoused by this journal: competing
theories are to be examined; contradictions are to be exposed for scrutiny;
and ideas are to be explored for the purpose of theory building.

Articles will be refereed double blind. Only well researched, logically
developed and properly articulated articles will be considered for
publication. Both theoretical and empirical research are equally acceptable
and highly desirable. Mathematical papers will be considered if those papers
either demonstrate applications for solving real problems rather than assume
away the problems that they are to solve, or are pedagogical notes which
demonstrate for classroom purposes means of solving accounting problems.
Papers which are designed to demonstrate mathematical elegance of particular

ACCOUNTING ENQUIRIES

models are not acceptable, since they are better suited for publication in mathematics journals. Of interest would be historical research that traces the origins of accounting ideas and examines the causes of divergence from their original conceptualization and the effect of such divergence on current day accounting practice.

SUBMISSIONS
Four copies of manuscripts should be submitted to the editor at the editor's location. An abstract must accompany the manuscript. The review period takes from twelve to sixteen weeks. Manuscript style-instructions are mailed upon request.

STYLE INSTRUCTIONS
AUTHOR INFORMATION: Provide the following information: On the first page of the manuscript, (1) title, (2) author, (3) institutional affiliation, (4) address, and (5) telephone number. Reviewers will not receive this page. On the next page of the manuscript, include the title and the abstract.

ABSTRACT: A single paragraph abstract of no more than 100 words must be included. Do not include references, footnotes, or abbreviations in the abstract.

TYPING FORMAT: The text, the footnotes, and the references are to be double-spaced. Leave wide margins for ease of editing and of typesetting.

HEADINGS AND SUBHEADINGS: No more than three levels of headings should be used. Center first-level headings and capitalize. Second-level headings are to be indented five spaces from the left margin and capitalize the first letter of the first word and of major words. Third-level headings are to be indented five spaces from the left margin and capitalize the first letter, and end these with a period. Do not use letters or numbers before headings (e.g., I, II, or A, B, etc.).

FOOTNOTES: The initial footnote, identifying the author's(s') affiliation, should be marked with an asterisk. AVOID FOOTNOTES IN THE TEXT. USE ENDNOTES.

EQUATIONS: Only those equations that are referenced in the text are to be numbered consecutively. Indent equations and place numbers at the right margin. Type equations clearly with one space before and after mathematical function signs except in subscripts and superscripts. Type the main components, the equal signs, and the fraction bar on the main line of typing. Spell out in the right margin any handwritten Greek letters used in equations. Write on one line mathematical expressions used within a paragraph.

NUMBER OF SIGNIFICANT DIGITS: In results of calculations, keep numbers of significant digits constant, not exceeding four.

TABLES: Tables are to appear immediately in the text of the paper after they have been introduced. Center the word "TABLE" followed by an arabic numeral above the body of the table. Separate headings in a table from the title of the table and from the body of the table with solid lines. Use a solid line to end the table or to separate the body of the table from table footnotes. Mark table footnotes with asterisks. Capitalize only the first letter of the word "Table" (e.g., Table 1) when referring to a specific table in the text of the paper.

ACCOUNTING ENQUIRIES

FIGURES: Camera-ready form of a professional quality for figures should be provided. Photocopies are acceptable at the initial stage. In the text when referring to specific figures, capitalize only the first letter (e.g., Figure 1). When labeling figures, capitalize the first letter in the word and number with arabic numerals (e.g., Figure 1). In the title of each figure, capitilize the first letter of the first word and of major words.

REFERENCES: List references alphabetically by author's last name at the end of the paper.
Include only those references cited in the text. Cite references in the text by enclosing the last name of the author, year, and page(s) number(s).

STYLE OF REFERENCES: The following facts are to be included in the list of references:
    BOOKS: (1) full name of author(s), editor(s), or institution/business responsible for writing the book; (2) full title; (3) series (if any); (4) volume number; (5) edition; (6) city of publication; (7) publisher's name; and (8) date of publication.
    ARTICLES: (1) full name of author(s), (2) title, (3) name of periodical, (4) volume number and date, and (5) pages occupied by article. Use FULL NAME rather than initials whenever possible.

PRESENTATION: To minimize editorial changes, check the manuscript for clarity, grammar, spelling, punctuation, and consistency of references.

ACCOUNTING FORUM

ADDRESS FOR SUBMISSION :

GLEN LEHMAN, JOINT CHIEF EDITOR
ACCOUNTING FORUM
UNIVERSITY OF SOUTH AUSTRALIA
SCHOOL OF ACCOUNTING
NORTH TERRACE
ADELAIDE, SA 5000
AUSTRALIA
+61 08-302-2309
+61 08-302-2102 (Fax)
E-Mail : Glen.Lehman@UniSA.edu.au

CIRCULATION DATA :

Reader : Business Persons &
         Academic

Frequency of Issue : Quarterly

Copies Per Issue : Less than 1000

Subscription Price : 45.00 A.U.$
  Institution/Company : 55.00 A.U.$
  Library : 80.00 A.U.$

Sponsorship : University

PUBLICATION GUIDELINES :

Manuscript Length : Open

Copies Required : Two

Computer Submission : Yes

Format : Word for Windows/IBM compat

Fees to Review : 0.00 US$

REVIEW INFORMATION :

Type of Review : Blind Review

No. of External Reviewers : Three

No. of In House Reviewers : Zero

Acceptance Rate : 11-20%

Time To Review : 2-3 months

Reviewer's Comments : Yes

Fees to Publish : 0.00 US$

Invited Articles : 5% or less

MANUSCRIPT TOPICS : ACCOUNTING INFORMATION SYSTEMS;
  ACCOUNTING THEORY & PRACTICE; AUDITING; GOVERNMENT & NON-PROFIT ACCOUNTING;
  SOCIAL AND ENVIRONMENTAL ACCOUNTING

PUBLICATION GUIDELINES :

MANUSCRIPT GUIDELINES/COMMENTS :

TONY TINKER, JOINT CHIEF EDITOR
CITY UNIVERSITY OF NEW YORK
BARUCH COLLEGE BOX E 0723
17 LEXINGTON AVENUE
NEW YORK, NY 10010   USA

ACCOUNTING FORUM is a quarterly journal covering all aspects of accounting.
ACCOUNTING FORUM is a vehicle for scholastic papers of quality which have the
potential to advance the knowledge of theory and practice in all areas of
accounting, business finance and associated areas.

1. Only manuscripts not currently under consideration by another publisher
will be considered.

2. A maximum length of 5,000 words will generally be required and the Editor
reserves the right to modify articles to increase readability. Articles will
also be considered in sections for consecutive issues of AF.

ACCOUNTING FORUM

3. Authors should indicate their position and affiliation and provide an address to which two complimentary copies of AF will be posted.

4. Three copies of each manuscript (and on IBM Compatible Word for Windows 6.0 disk if possible) should be typed, double-spaced and have wide margins. AN ABSTRACT NOT EXCEEDING 50 WORDS SHOULD BE INCLUDED.

5. All diagrams and graphs should be prepared on separate sheets and be of a professional quality ready for reproduction.

6. The Harvard (author-date) System should be used:

    (1) In citing works quote the author followed by the date of publication, and if relevant, page numbers eg. (Brown 1988, p.3).

    (2) A list of references is required, containing only cited references, in alphabetical order by author. This should include the author's name, year of publication in round brackets, the publisher and place of publication. For articles, the periodical, volume number, month of issue and page numbers are required.

7. Address all contributions to Glen Lehman, Joint Chief Editor.

SUBSCRIPTION RATES: Australia, add $5 for postage
                       International, add $15 for postage

ACCOUNTING HISTORIANS JOURNAL

ADDRESS FOR SUBMISSION :

BARBARA D. MENINO, EDITOR
ACCOUNTING HISTORIANS JOURNAL
UNIVERSITY OF NORTH TEXAS
P.O. BOX 13677
DENTON, TX 76205
USA
817-565-3094
817-565-3803 (Fax)
E-Mail : Merino@COBAF.unt.edu

CIRCULATION DATA :

Reader : Academic

Frequency of Issue : 2 Times/Year

Copies Per Issue : 1001-2000

Subscription Price : 36.00 US$

Sponsorship : Professional Assoc.

PUBLICATION GUIDELINES :

Manuscript Length : 16-20

Copies Required : Three

Computer Submission : No

Format : N/A

Fees to Review : 36.00 US$
 Members/Acad.of Acc. 15.00 US$

REVIEW INFORMATION :

Type of Review : Blind Review

No. of External Reviewers : Two

No. of In House Reviewers : Zero

Acceptance Rate : 11-20%

Time To Review : 2-3 months

Reviewer's Comments : Yes

Fees to Publish : 0.00 US$

Invited Articles : 5% or less

MANUSCRIPT TOPICS : ACCOUNTING INFORMATION SYSTEMS;
  ACCOUNTING THEORY & PRACTICE; ACCOUNTING HISTORY

PUBLICATION GUIDELINES :

MANUSCRIPT GUIDELINES/COMMENTS :

MANUSCRIPTS should be in English and of acceptable style and organization for
clarity of presentation. Submit three copies, typewritten, double spaced on
one side of 8 1/2 X 11 inch (approx. 28.5 cm X 28.0 cm) white paper;
paragraphs should be indented. The manuscript should not exceed 7,000 words
and margins should be wide enough to facilitate editing and duplication. All
pages, including bibliographic pages, should be serially numbered. Manuscripts
should be run through a spellcheck software program or similar review prior to
submission.

COVER SHEET. The cover sheet should state the title of the paper, name(s) of
author(s), affiliation(s), the address for future correspondence and the FAX
number or EMAIL address (or both) of the author designated as the contact
person for the manuscript.

ABSTRACT. An abstract of not more than 100 words should accompany the
manuscript on a separate page. The title, but not the name(s) of the author(s)
should appear on the abstract page and on the first page of the manuscript.

ACCOUNTING HISTORIANS JOURNAL

SUBMISSION FEE. A submission fee of $36 (U.S.) for non Academy members or a reduced fee of $15 (U.S.) for Academy members should accompany all submissions. Manuscripts currently under review by other publications should not submitted.

MAJOR HEADINGS within the manuscript should be centered, underlined, and unnumbered with the first letter of major words capitalized. Subheadings should be on a separate line beginning flush with the left margin and underlined with the first letter of major words capitalized. Third level headings should lead into the paragraph, be underlined and followed by a period; text should follow immediately on the same line.

TABLES, FIGURES AND EXHIBITS should be numbered (arabic), titled, and, when appropriate, referenced. Limited use of original documents can be accommodated in the Journal if authors can provide glossy black and white prints at least 5 X 7. Important textual materials may be presented in both the original language and the English translation. Tables, and similar items must be discussed in the text and will not be included unless they lend support to the text.

LITERATURE REFERENCES
Footnotes should not be used for literature references. The work cited should be referenced using the author's name and date of publication in the body of the text, inside square brackets, i.e., Garner [1954, p. 33], [Mills, Fall 1979, p. 52]. If the author's name is mentioned in the text, it need not be repeated, i.e., Garner [1954, p. 33] concluded.... If a reference has more than three authors, only the first name and 'et al' should be used in the text citation. References to statutes, legal treatise or court cases should follow the accepted form of legal citation. All references, whether to direct quotations or to paraphrased material, should contain page numbers.

CONTENT FOOTNOTES
Content footnotes may be used sparingly to expand upon or comment upon the text itself. These should numbered consecutively throughout the manuscript and should appear at the bottom of page on which the reference appears.

BIBLIOGRAPHY
A bibliography of works cited should appear at the end of the manuscript. The works cited should be listed alphabetically according to the surname of the first author. Information about books and journals should include the following information--Books, author(s), title underlined, place of publication, name of publisher, date of publication; Journals, author(s), article title with quotation marks, Journal, title underlined, date of issue in parenthesis, page numbers. Multiple works by an author should be listed in chronological order; if multiple works appear in a single year, the suffix a, b, etc. should be used to identify each work.

For questions of style not covered above, authors should consult a style manual such as Turabian, Kate L. A MANUAL FOR WRITERS OF TERM PAPERS, THESES AND DISSERTATIONS, published by the University of Chicago Press.

DISKETTE. When a manuscript has been accepted for publication, authors will be asked to submit a diskette (either 5 1/4 or 3 1/2 inch) with the final manuscript. The diskette should be prepared in IBM compatible ASCII file format.

ACCOUNTING HISTORIANS JOURNAL

GALLEY PROOFS will be sent to the author(s) as permitted by scheduling; however, additions of new material must be strictly limited.

COMPLEMENTARY COPIES AND REPRINTS. Author(s) will be provided with 3 copies of the Journal issue in which the manuscript is published. Reprints may be ordered from the printer; the minimum order is 100. The printer will establish the price and bill the author(s) directly for the cost of the reprints.

ACCOUNTING HISTORY

ADDRESS FOR SUBMISSION :

GARRY D. CARNEGIE, EDITOR
ACCOUNTING HISTORY
DEAKIN UNIVERSITY
SCHOOL OF ACCOUNTING AND FINANCE
GEELONG VICTORIA, 3217
AUSTRALIA
+61 3 5227 2733
+61 3 5227 2264 (Fax)
E-Mail : carnegie@deakin.edu.au

CIRCULATION DATA :

Reader : Academic

Frequency of Issue : 2 Times/Year

Copies Per Issue : Less than 1000

Subscription Price : 60.00 AUS.$
  Airmail : 72.00 AUS.$

Sponsorship : Professional Assoc.

PUBLICATION GUIDELINES :

Manuscript Length : 26-30

Copies Required : Three

Computer Submission : No

Format : N/A

Fees to Review : 0.00 US$

REVIEW INFORMATION :

Type of Review : Blind Review

No. of External Reviewers : Two

No. of In House Reviewers : Zero

Acceptance Rate : 21-30%

Time To Review : 2-3 months

Reviewer's Comments : Yes

Fees to Publish : 0.00 US$

Invited Articles : 11-20%

MANUSCRIPT TOPICS : COST ACCOUNTING; ECONOMIC HISTORY;
   SPECIFICALLY ACCOUNTING HISTORY

PUBLICATION GUIDELINES :

MANUSCRIPT GUIDELINES/COMMENTS :

ACCOUNTING HISTORY is sponsored by Accounting History Special Interest Group
of the Accounting Association of Australia and New Zealand.

EDITORIAL POLICIES
ACCOUNTING HISTORY aims to publish quality historical papers. These could be
concerned with exploring the advent and development of accounting bodies,
conventions, ideas, practices and rules. They should attempt to identify the
individuals and also the local, time-specific environmental factors which
affected accounting, and should endeavour to assess accounting's impact on
organisational and social functioning.

EDITORIAL PROCEDURES
1. Address copies of all manuscripts and editorial correspondence to the
Editor.

2. The cover of the manuscript should contain the following:
    (i)   Title of manuscript.
    (ii) Name of author(s).

(iii) Institutional affiliation of author(s) including telephone, fax and email address(es).
(iv) Month of submission.
(v) Any acknowledgment, not exceeding 50 words. An acknowledgment should not be included in the consecutive number of other notes.

3. An abstract of no more than 150 words should be presented on a separate page immediately preceding the text of the manuscript.

4. Three copies of all manuscripts should be submitted for review. Manuscripts should be typed on one side of the paper only, double-spaced and all pages should be numbered. Manuscripts currently under review for publication in other outlets should not be submitted.

5. Headings should be formatted so that major headings are flush left, bold, lower case and two font sizes larger than the main text. Second level headings should be flush left, bold, lower case and same size as main text. Third level headings should be flush left, italics, lower case and same size as main text. For example:

1. Flush left, bold, lower case, two font sizes larger than main text
2. Flush left, bold, lower case, same size font as main text
3. Flush left, italics, lower case, same size font as main text.

6. Figures, tables, diagrams and appendices should be numbered consecutively and tided.

7. Notes should appear as endnotes and be numbered consecutively. They should begin on a separate page at the end of the manuscript.

8. References should appear in the text as Smith (1970) or Smith (1970, p.l20). The full references should be typed on separate sheets and appear after any notes at the end of the manuscript. The following rules should be adopted:

Books
Smith, X.Y., (1970), Advanced Accounting, Sydney: Cobb Publishing Co.

Periodicals
Smith, X.Y. and Smyth, A.B., (1970), "The Current Cost Controversy-Again", Journal of the New School, Vol.6, No.1, May, pp.10-32.

9. When a paper is accepted for publication the authors are requested to provide a copy of the paper on a 3 1/2" diskette as well as a printed copy of the accepted version of the paper. Submissions saved in text format (specifically ASCII text) are preferred. Microsoft Word or WordPerfect (for Macintosh or PC compatibles) are the preferred wordprocessing formats.

10. Two copies of books to be considered for review should be forwarded to the Book Review Editor.

ACCOUNTING HORIZONS

ADDRESS FOR SUBMISSION :

HELEN GERNON, EDITOR
ACCOUNTING HORIZONS
UNIVERSITY OF OREGON
COLLEGE OF BUSINESS ADMINISTRATION
DEPARTMENT OF ACCOUNTING
EUGENE, OR 97403-1208
USA
541-346-5127

PUBLICATION GUIDELINES :

Manuscript Length : 7000 Words Maximum

Copies Required : Five

Computer Submission : Yes

Format : WordPerfect,ASCII,Microsoft

Fees to Review : 75.00 US$
  Nonmembers of AAA 100.00 US$

CIRCULATION DATA :

Reader : Business Persons &
        Academic

Frequency of Issue : Quarterly

Copies Per Issue : Over 25,000

Subscription Price : 60.00 US$

Sponsorship : Professional Assoc.

REVIEW INFORMATION :

Type of Review : Blind Review

No. of External Reviewers : Two

No. of In House Reviewers : One

Acceptance Rate : 11-20%

Time To Review : 2-3 months

Reviewer's Comments : Yes

Fees to Publish : 0.00 US$

Invited Articles : 6-10%

MANUSCRIPT TOPICS : ACCOUNTING INFORMATION SYSTEMS;
  ACCOUNTING THEORY & PRACTICE; AUDITING; COST ACCOUNTING;
  GOVERNMENT & NON-PROFIT ACCOUNTING; TAX ACCOUNTING

PUBLICATION GUIDELINES : Chicago Manual of Style

MANUSCRIPT GUIDELINES/COMMENTS :

EDITORIAL POLICIES
In general, HORIZONS publishes carefully edited, articulately written,
practice-based papers. The journal's focus is applied. Practitioners are
widely used in the review process as their views as to what is relevant are
invaluable. Horizons represents a partnership between the accounting
profession and academia. This is what makes HORIZONS successful and able to
fulfill its unique mission.

ACCOUNTING HORIZONS publishes articles and other items of interest to
practicing accountants in industry, public accounting and government;
educators; students; and others who have a strong interest in contemporary
accounting theory, practice and policy. The views of thoughtful and
knowledgeable accountants from all disciplines, regarding the application of
accounting ideas are invited. Articles shall explore a substantive research
question that is practice oriented, and include methodologically supported
conclusions or recommendations. Priority is given to those articles which have
the most potential to make a difference to society and to accountancy.

ACCOUNTING HORIZONS

The common thread among all articles published in ACCOUNTING HORIZONS is that they are applied, in the contexts described above. All manuscripts should present innovative ideas and apply appropriate methodology for the question at hand. All articles should be written so that nonspecialists can read and understand them. For example, in situations where complex methodology is utilized, technical materials should be placed in an appendix to enhance readability. Similarly, if a research instrument, such as a questionnaire, is involved, that instrument should be included in an appendix.

Commentaries from practice, policy setting and academia are invited on a regular basis. This section is used to publish specific topical statements which are not readily available to accountants elsewhere. From time to time, a joint commentary by a practitioner and an academic may be commissioned. This section of the journal is used to help bridge any gap between practice and theory. Horizons is also receptive to uninvited commentary submissions, which may be edited for their appropriateness and relevance to the readership. The criteria against which "Commentaries" will be evaluated include the originality of the ideas and concepts and the underlying support provided for them.

SUBMISSION OF MANUSCRIPTS
Authors should note the following guidelines for submitting manuscripts:

1. Manuscripts currently under consideration by another journal or other publisher should not be submitted. The author must state that the work is not submitted or published elsewhere.

2. In the case of manuscripts reporting on field surveys or experiments, five copies of the instrument (questionnaire, case, interview plan or the like) should be submitted.

3. Five copies should be submitted together with a check in U.S. funds for $75.00 for members or $100.00 for nonmembers of the AAA made payable to the American Accounting Association and sent to Helen Gernon, Department of Accounting, College of Business Administration, University of Oregon, Eugene, OR 97403-1208. The submission fee is nonrefundable.

4. The author should retain a copy of the paper.

5. Revisions must be submitted within 12 months from request, otherwise they will be considered new submissions.

COMMENTS
Comments on articles previously published in ACCOUNTING HORIZONS will be reviewed (anonymously) by two reviewers in sequence. The first reviewer will be the author of the original article being subjected to critique. If substance permits, a suitably revised comment will be sent to a second reviewer to determine its publishability in ACCOUNTING HORIZONS. If a comment is accepted for publication, the original author will be invited to reply. All other editorial requirements, as enumerated above, also apply to proposed comments.

MANUSCRIPT PREPARATION AND STYLE
The ACCOUNTING HORIZONS manuscript preparation guidelines follow (with a slight modification) documentation 2 of the CHICAGO MANUAL OF STYLE (14th ed.;

University of Chicago Press). Another helpful guide to usage and style is The ELEMENTS OF STYLE, by William Strunk, Jr., and E. B. White (Macmillan). Spelling follows WEBSTER'S INTERNATIONAL DICTIONARY.

FORMAT

1. All manuscripts should be typed on one side of 8 1/2 x 11" good quality paper and be double spaced, except for indented quotations.

2. Manuscripts should be as concise as the subject and research method permit, generally not to exceed 7,000 words.

3. Margins should be at least one inch from top, bottom and sides to facilitate editing and duplication.

4. To assure anonymous review, authors should not identify themselves directly or indirectly in their papers. Single authors should not use the editorial "we."

5. A cover page should include the title of the paper, the author's name, title and affiliation, any acknowledgments, and a footnote indicating whether the author would be willing to share the data (see last paragraph in this statement).

6. All pages, including tables, appendices and references, should be serially numbered.

7. Spell out numbers from one to ten, except when used in tables and lists, and when used with mathematical, statistical, scientific or technical units and quantities, such as distances, weights and measures. For example: three days; 3 kilometers; 30 years. All other numbers are expressed numerically. Generally when using approximate terms spell out the number, for example, approximately thirty years.

8. In nontechnical text use the word percent; in technical text the symbol % is used. (See the CHICAGO MANUAL for discussion of the correct usage.)

9. Use a hyphen to join unit modifiers or to clarify usage. For example: a well-presented analysis; re-form. See WEBSTER'S for correct usage.

10. Headings should be arranged so that major headings are centered, bold and capitalized. Second level headings should be flush left, bold, and both upper and lower case. Third level headings should be flush left, bold, italic, and both upper and lower case. Fourth level headings should be paragraph indent, bold and lower case. Headings and subheadings should not be numbered. For example:

A CENTERED, BOLD, ALL CAPITALIZED, FIRST LEVEL HEADING
A Flush Left, Bold, Upper and Lower Case, Second Level Heading
A Flush Left, Bold, Italic, Upper and Lower Case, Third Level Heading
   A paragraph indent, bold, lower case, fourth level heading. Text starts...

SYNOPSIS

A synopsis of about 150-200 words should be presented on a separate page immediately preceding the text. The synopsis should be nonmathematical and include a readable summary of the research question, method, and the significance of the findings and contribution. The title, but not the author's name or other identification designations, should appear on the synopsis page.

TABLES AND FIGURES
The author should note the following general requirements:

1. Each table and figure (graphic) should appear on a separate page and should be placed at the end of the text. Each should bear an arabic number and a complete title indicating the exact contents of the table or figure.

2. A reference to each table or figure should be made in the text.

3. The author should indicate by marginal notation where each table or figure should be inserted in the text, e.g., (Insert Table X here).

4. Tables or figures should be reasonably interpreted without reference to the text.

5. Source lines and notes should be included as necessary.

6. Figures must be prepared in a form suitable for printing.

MATHEMATICAL NOTATION
Mathematical notation should be employed only where its rigor and precision are necessary, and in such circumstances authors should explain in the narrative format the principal operations performed. Notation should be avoided in footnotes. Unusual symbols, particularly if handwritten, should be identified in the margin when they first appear. Displayed material should clearly indicate the alignment, superscripts and subscripts. Equations should be numbered in parentheses flush with the right-hand margin.

DOCUMENTATION
Citations: Work cited should use the "author-date system" keyed to a list of works in the reference list (see below). Authors should make an effort to include the relevant page numbers in the cited works.

1. In the text, works are cited as follows: author's last name and date, without comma, in parentheses: for example (Jones 1987); with two authors: (Jones and Freeman 1973); with more than two: (Jones et al. 1985); with more than one source cited together: (Jones 1987; Freeman 1986); with two or more works by one author: (Jones 1985, 1987).

2. Unless confusion would result, do not use "p." or "pp." before page numbers, for example (Jones 1987, 115).

3. When the reference list contains more than one work of an author published in the same year, the suffix a, b, etc. follows the date in the text citation: for example (Jones 1987a) or (Jones 1987a; Freeman 1985b).

4. If an author's name is mentioned in the text, it need not be repeated in the citation: for example "Jones (1987, 115) says..."

5. Citations to institutional works should use acronyms or short titles where practicable: for example, (AAAASOBAT 1966); (AICPA Cohen Commission Report

1977). Where brief, the full title of an institutional work might be shown in a citation: for example (ICAEW The Corporate Report 1975).

6. If the manuscript refers to statutes, legal treatises or court cases, citations acceptable in law reviews should be used.

REFERENCE LIST: Every manuscript must include a list of references containing only those works cited. Each entry should contain all data necessary for unambiguous identification. With the author-date system, use the following format recommended by the CHICAGO MANUAL:

1. Arrange citations in alphabetical order according to surname of the first author or the name of the institution responsible for the citation.

2. Use authors' initials instead of proper names.

3. Dates of publication should be placed immediately after authors' names.

4. Titles of journals should not be abbreviated.

5. Multiple works by the same author(s) should be listed in chronological order of publication. Two or more works by the same author(s) in the same year are distinguished by letters after the date.

Sample entries are as follows:

American Accounting Association, Committee on Concepts and Standards for External Financial Reports. 1977. Statement on Accounting Theory and Theory Acceptance. Sarasota, FL: AAA.

Becker, H., and D. Fritsche. 1987. Business ethics: A cross-cultural comparison of managers' attitudes. Journal of Business Ethics 6: 289-295.

Bowman, R. 1980a. The importance of market-value measurement of debt in assessing leverage. Journal of Accounting Research 18 (Spring): 617-630.

_____. 1980b. The debt equivalence of leases: An empirical investigation. The Accounting Review 55 (April): 237-253.

Cohen, C. 1991. Chief or indians-Women in accountancy. Australian Accountant (December): 20-30.

Harry, J., and N. S. Goldner. 1972. The null relationship between teaching and research. Sociology of Education 45 (1): 47-60.

Jensen, M. C., and C. W. Smith. 1985. Stockholder, manager, and creditor interests: Applications of agency theory. In Recent Advances in Corporate Finance, edited by E. Altman and M. Subrahmanyam. Homewood, IL: Richard D. Irwin.

Munn, G. G., F. L. Garcia, and C. J. Woelfel, eds. 1991. Encyclopedia of Banking and Finance, 9th ed. Chicago, IL: St. James Press.

ACCOUNTING HORIZONS

Ohlson, J. A. 1991. Earnings, book values, and dividends in security
valuation. Working paper, Columbia University.

FOOTNOTES: Footnotes are not to be used for documentation. Textual footnotes
should be used only for extensions and useful excursions of information that
if included in the body of the text might disrupt its continuity. Footnotes
should be consecutively numbered throughout the manuscript with superscript
Arabic numerals. Footnote text should be double-spaced and placed at the end
of the article.

POLICY ON REPRODUCTION
An objective of ACCOUNTING HORIZONS is to promote the wide dissemination of
the results of systematic scholarly inquiries into the broad field of
accounting.

Permission is hereby granted to reproduce any of the contents of HORIZONS for
use in courses of instruction, as long as the source and American Accounting
Association copyright are indicated in any such reproductions.

Written application must be made to the Editor for permission to reproduce any
of the contents of HORIZONS for use in other than courses of instruction e.g.,
inclusion in books of readings or in any other publications intended for
general distribution. In consideration for the grant of permission by HORIZONS
in such instances, the applicant must notify the author(s) in writing of the
intended use to be made of each reproduction. Normally, HORIZONS will not
assess a charge for the waiver of copyright.

Except where otherwise noted in articles, the copyright interest has been
transferred to the American Accounting Association. Where the author(s) has
(have) not transferred the copyright to the Association, applicants must seek
permission to reproduce (for all purposes) directly from the author(s).

POLICY ON DATA AVAILABILITY
The following policy has been adopted by the Executive Committee in its April
1989 meeting. "An objective of (THE ACCOUNTING REVIEW, ACCOUNTING HORIZONS,
ISSUES IN ACCOUNTING EDUCATION) is to provide the widest possible
dissemination of knowledge based on systematic scholarly inquiries into
accounting as a field of professional, research and educational activity. As
part of this process, authors are encouraged to make their data available for
use by others in extending or replicating results reported in their articles.
Authors of articles which report data dependent results should footnote the
status of data availability and, when pertinent, this should be accompanied by
information on how the data may be obtained."

ACCOUNTING INSTRUCTORS' REPORT

ADDRESS FOR SUBMISSION :

BELVERD E. NEEDLES, JR., EDITOR
ACCOUNTING INSTRUCTORS' REPORT
DEPAUL UNIVERSITY
SCHOOL OF ACCOUNTANCY
1 EAST JACKSON BLVD.
CHICAGO, IL 60604-2287
USA
312-362-5130
312-362-6208 (Fax)
E-Mail : bneedles@condor.depaul.edu

CIRCULATION DATA :

Reader : Academic

Frequency of Issue : 2 Times/Year

Copies Per Issue : 5001-10,000

Subscription Price :

Sponsorship : Profit Oriented Corp.

PUBLICATION GUIDELINES :

Manuscript Length : 1-5

Copies Required : Two

Computer Submission : Yes

Format : N/A

Fees to Review : 0.00 US$

REVIEW INFORMATION :

Type of Review : Blind Review

No. of External Reviewers : One

No. of In House Reviewers : One

Acceptance Rate : 21-30%

Time To Review : 4-6 months

Reviewer's Comments : No

Fees to Publish : 0.00 US$

Invited Articles : 6-10%

MANUSCRIPT TOPICS : ACCOUNTING THEORY & PRACTICE; AUDITING;
   ACCOUNTING EDUCATION

PUBLICATION GUIDELINES :

MANUSCRIPT GUIDELINES/COMMENTS :

ACCOUNTING MANAGEMENT & INFORMATION TECHNOLOGIES

ADDRESS FOR SUBMISSION :

PROFESSOR RICHARD BOLAND, EDITOR
ACCOUNTING MANAGEMENT & INFORMATION
  TECHNOLOGIES
CASE WESTERN UNIVERSITY
WEATHERHEAD SCHOOL OF MANAGEMENT
CLEVELAND, OH 44106
USA
216-368-6022
216-368-4776 (Fax)
E-Mail : rjb7@po.cwru.edu

CIRCULATION DATA :

Reader : Academic

Frequency of Issue : Quarterly

Copies Per Issue :

Subscription Price :

Sponsorship : Profit Oriented Corp.

PUBLICATION GUIDELINES :

Manuscript Length : Any

Copies Required : Four

Computer Submission : No

Format : N/A

Fees to Review : 0.00 US$

REVIEW INFORMATION :

Type of Review : Blind Review

No. of External Reviewers : Three

No. of In House Reviewers : Zero

Acceptance Rate : 11-20%

Time To Review : 2-3 months

Reviewer's Comments : Yes

Fees to Publish : 0.00 US$

Invited Articles : 5% or less

MANUSCRIPT TOPICS : ACCOUNTING INFORMATION SYSTEMS;
  ACCOUNTING THEORY & PRACTICE; COST ACCOUNTING; STRATEGIC MANAGEMENT POLICY;
  COMMUNICATION;TECHNOLOGY IMPACT

PUBLICATION GUIDELINES :

MANUSCRIPT GUIDELINES/COMMENTS :

Advances in information technologies shape and are shaped by practices of
accounting and managing. New information technologies affect social and
economic affairs across the industrial, service and financial sectors as well
as in education, health and government. Patterns of management and decision
making within and across organizations are being changed, challenging
traditional meanings of authority, and shifting the relative effectiveness of
different ways of organizing. The world that accountants account for is being
altered, as are their methods and measures for doing so. Understanding the
relation of information technologies to emerging practices in the management
and control of enterprise is an urgent scholarly and policy concern.

ACCOUNTING, MANAGEMENT AND INFORMATION TECHNOLOGIES is an international
journal offering a forum for research on the interrelations of information
technologies with accounting and control systems and with management practices
and policies.

The journal invites a broad range of analyses of these interrelated
technologies as well as critical questioning of them from such fields as

ACCOUNTING MANAGEMENT & INFORMATION TECHNOLOGIES

philosophy, anthropology, law, and social and political theory. Of special concern is the design, deployment and use of information technologies in the practice of accounting of management, including, but not limited to, expert systems, integrated manufacturing, individual and group decision support, performance monitoring and collaborative work. Topics of special interest within this overall scope include:

* Evaluating changes in economic relations, governance structures, and accounting systems accompanying applications of information technologies.

* Exploring the relationship of information technologies to management decision processes and their organizational and human consequences.

* Understanding associated changes in the design of the workplace and in patterns of human communication, dialogue and interpretation.

* Analyzing the impacts of information technologies and global networks on financial markets and management practices.

* Arguing questions of ethics, privacy and individual rights raised by the use of information technologies in accounting and management.

* Changing concepts and practices of management, auditing and accounting associated with advances in information technologies.

The journal invites a broad spectrum of contemporary and historical scholarship, including theoretical, empirical, analytical and interpretive studies, as well as action research.

Submissions in four copies to Professor Richard Boland.

INSTRUCTIONS TO AUTHORS

The contribution of the author(s) should be an original one and it should in no way violate any existing copyright, and it should contain nothing of a libelous or scandalous nature.

MANUSCRIPTS: Four copies of the manuscript should be submitted to the Editor. They should be typed in double spacing on one side of the paper. A cover page should give the title of the manuscript, the author's name, position and institutional affiliation, and an acknowledgement if desired. The title of the manuscript, but not the author's name should appear on the first page of the text. If the manuscript refers to questionnaire or other research instruments which are not fully reproduced in the text, authors must also submit three copies of the complete research instrument.

ABSTRACTS AND INDEX: Four copies of an abstract not exceeding 150 words should accompany each manuscript submitted. Authors are also asked to supply a maximum of 10 'key' words or phrases which will be useful for indexing purposes.

TABLES AND FIGURES: Each table and figure should have a number and brief title. The author should clearly indicate where he or she would like each table and figure to be placed. Each table and figure should accompany the manuscript on a separate sheet and, wherever possible, should be drawn in

ACCOUNTING MANAGEMENT & INFORMATION TECHNOLOGIES

India ink on good white paper board, SUITABLE FOR DIRECT REPRODUCTION. Captions to figures should be typed consecutively on a separate page at the end of the paper.

LITERATURE CITATIONS: No footnotes should be used for literature citations. The work should be cited by author's name and year of publication in the body of the text, e.g. (Zuboff, 1988); or when reference is made to a specific page (Rorty, 1989, p. 44-46). Where the author's name is included in the text, the name should not be repeated in the reference citation: e.g. "Johnson (1989, p. ix) says...". For identification purposes, the suffix a, b, etc., should follow the date when the bibliography contains more than one work published by an author in a single year.

BIBLIOGRAPHY: The manuscript should include a bibliography containing only those references cited in the text. The references should be arranged in alphabetical order according to the surname of the first author. Works by the same author should be listed in order of publication. Each reference should contain full bibliographical details. The author's name should be as it appear in the publication and journal titles should not be abbreviated, e.g.

Huber, George P., "The Nature and Design of Post-Industrial Organizations", Management Science (1984) 30: 928-951.
Bijker, Wiebe E., Thomas P. Hughes and Trevor Pinch (eds). The Social Construction of Technological Systems (Cambridge: MIT Press,1987).

FOOTNOTES: Footnotes for clarification or elaboration should be used sparingly. Where used, they should be numbered consecutively with superscript Arabic numerals.

RESEARCH INSTRUMENTS: Because of space limitations, questionnaires and other research instruments sometimes may not be fully reproduced in the published paper. When they are not fully reproduced a note must be inserted in the text of the paper indicating the address from which copies of the complete instrument are available.

ACCOUNTING ORGANIZATIONS & SOCIETY

ADDRESS FOR SUBMISSION :

ANTHONY G. HOPWOOD, EDITOR-IN-CHIEF
ACCOUNTING ORGANIZATIONS & SOCIETY
UNIVERSITY OF OXFORD
SCHOOL OF MANAGEMENT STUDIES
THE RADCLIFFE INFIRMARY
WOODSTOCK ROAD
OXFORD, OX2 6H3
UK
+44 01865-228470, -228479
+44 01865-228471 (Fax)
E-Mail : Anthony.Hopwood@obs.ox.ac.uk

CIRCULATION DATA :

Reader : Academic

Frequency of Issue : 8 Times/Year

Copies Per Issue : 1001-2000

Subscription Price : 897.00 US$
  Associated Personal : 222.00 US$
  Europe $564 and : 139.00 U.K.$

Sponsorship :

PUBLICATION GUIDELINES :

Manuscript Length : Any

Copies Required : Three

Computer Submission : No

Format : N/A

Fees to Review : 0.00 US$

REVIEW INFORMATION :

Type of Review : Blind Review

No. of External Reviewers : Two

No. of In House Reviewers : Zero

Acceptance Rate : 11-20%

Time To Review : 2-3 months

Reviewer's Comments : Yes

Fees to Publish : 0.00 US$

Invited Articles : 5% or less

MANUSCRIPT TOPICS : ACCOUNTING INFORMATION SYSTEMS;
  ACCOUNTING THEORY & PRACTICE; AUDITING; COST ACCOUNTING; ECONOMIC HISTORY;
  GOVERNMENT & NON-PROFIT ACCOUNTING; INTERNATIONAL & ECONOMIC DEVELOPMENT;
  ORGANIZATIONAL & SOCIAL ANALYSIS OF ACCOUNTING

PUBLICATION GUIDELINES :

MANUSCRIPT GUIDELINES/COMMENTS :

ASSOCIATE EDITORS
PETER MILLER, Department of Accounting and Finance, London School of Economics
and Political Science, Houghton Street, London WC2A 2AE, UK.
JACOB G. BIRNBERG, Graduate School of Business, University of Pittsburg, PA,
USA.
MICHAEL SHIELDS, Fogelman College of Business, The University of Memphis, TN,
USA.

AIMS AND SCOPE
ACCOUNTING, ORGANIZATIONS & SOCIETY is a major international journal concerned
with all aspects of the relationship between accounting and human behaviour,
organizational structures and processes, and the changing social and political
environment of the enterprise. Its unique focus covers such topics as: the
social role of accounting, social accounting, social audit and accounting for
scarce resources; the provision of accounting information to employees and
trade unions and the development of participative information systems;

ACCOUNTING ORGANIZATIONS & SOCIETY

processes influencing accounting innovations and the social and political aspects of accounting standard setting; behavioural studies of the users of accounting information; information processing views of organizations, and the relationship between accounting and other information systems and organizational structures and processses; organizational strategies for designing accounting and information systems; human resource accounting; cognitive aspects of accounting and decision-making processes, and the behavioural aspects of budgeting, planning and investment appraisal.

AUDIENCE:
Researchers and students involved in behavioural, organisational and social aspects of accounting, personnel managers, information technologists.

ABSTRACTED/INDEXED IN:
Current Contents, Social/Biobehavioral Science, Research Alert, Social Sciences Citation Index.

Published material will range from original theoretical and empirical contributions to review articles describing the state of the art in specific areas. Shorter critical assessments of experiments related to the behavioural and social aspects of accounting will also be published. Other features of the journal are book reviews and other bibliographical materials. The objectives of the journal are:

1. To provide a specialized forum for the publication of research on the behavioural, organizational and social aspects of accounting.

2. To foster new thinking, research and action on the social and behavioural aspects of accounting.

3. To report on experiments on the behavioural and social aspects of accounting in a way that explains how the experiment was developed, the process by which it was implemented and its consequences, both planned and unplanned. The journal is particularly interested in discussions of the interplay between theory, practice and social and individual values.

4. To accelerate the transfer from research to practice by promoting an international dialogue between researchers, accountants, managers and administrators.

The journal will be concerned with all aspects of the relationship between accounting and human behaviour, organizational structures and processes, and the changing social and political environment of the enterprise. Its unique focus will cover such topics as:

* the social role of accounting, social accounting, social audit and accounting for scarce resources
* the provision of accounting information to employees and trade unions and the development of participative information systems
* processes influencing accounting innovations and the social and political aspects of accounting standard setting
* behavioural studies of the users of accounting information
* information processing views of organizations, and the relationship between accounting and other information systems and organizational structures and processes

ACCOUNTING ORGANIZATIONS & SOCIETY

* organizational strategies for designing accounting and information systems
* human resource accounting
* cognitive aspects of accounting and decision-making processes
* the behavioural aspects of budgeting, planning and investment appraisal.

INSTRUCTIONS TO AUTHORS

The contribution of the author(s) should be an original one and it should in no way violate any existing copyright, and it should contain nothing of a libelous or scandalous nature.

MANUSCRIPTS. Three copies of the manuscript should be submitted to the Editor-in-Chief or, in the case of the papers dealing with cognitive aspects of accounting, to Barry Lewis, the Associate Editor responsible for this area. They should be typed in double spacing on one side of the paper. A cover page should give the title of the manuscript, the author's name, position and institutional affiliation, and an acknowledgement, if desired. The title of the manuscript, but not the author's name, should appear on the first page of the text. If the manuscript refers to questionnaires of other research instruments which are not fully reproduced in the text, authors must also submit three copies of the complete research instrument.

ABSTRACTS AND INDEX. Three copies of an abstract not exceeding 80 words should accompany each manuscript submitted. Authors are also asked to supply a maximum of 10 "key" words or phrases for indexing purposes.

TABLES AND FIGURES. Each table and figure should have a number and brief title. The author should clearly indicate where he or she would like each table and figure placed. Each table and figure should accompany the manuscript on a separate sheet, and wherever possible, should be drawn in India ink on good white board, SUITABLE FOR DIRECT REPRODUCTION. Captions to figures should be typed consecutively on a separate page at the end of the paper.

LITERATURE CITATIONS. No footnotes should be used for literature citations. The work should be cited by author's name and year of publication in the body of the text, e.g. (Watson, 1975); or when reference is made to a specific page (Wilkes & Harrison, 1975, p. 21). Where the author's name is included in the text, the name should not be repeated in the reference citation: e.g. "Angrist (1975, p. 79) says...." For identification purposes, the suffix, a, b, etc. should follow the date when the bibliography contains more than one work published by an author in a single year.

BIBLIOGRAPHY. The manuscript should include a bibliography containing only those references cited in the text. The references should be arranged in alphabetical order according to the surname of the first author. Works by the same author should be listed in order of publication. Each reference should contain full bibliographical details and journal titles should not be abbreviated, e.g.

King, P., Is the Emphasis of Capital Budgeting Theory Misplaced?, Journal of Business Finance and Accounting (Spring 1975) pp. 69-82.

LeBreton, P.P., Administrative Intelligence -- Information Systems (Boston: Houghton Mifflin, 1969).

ACCOUNTING ORGANIZATIONS & SOCIETY

FOOTNOTES. Footnotes for clarification or elaboration should be used sparingly. Where used, they should be numbered consecutively with superscript Arabic numerals.

RESEARCH INSTRUMENTS. Because of space limitations, questionnaires and other research instruments sometimes may not be fully reproduced int he published paper. when they are not fully reproduced, a note must be inserted in the text of the paper indicating the address from which copies of the complete instrument are available.

PROOFS AND COPIES. Proofs of paper should be checked by the author(s) and returned to the publisher with corrections within 48 hours. At this stage, only printer's typographical errors should be corrected, and any substantial changes other than these will be charged to the author. Twenty-five copies of each paper are provided free of charge and additional copies may be ordered when proofs are returned.

CONTRIBUTIONS: Manuscripts should be sent to the Editor-in-Chief of ACCOUNTING, ORGANIZATIONS AND SOCIETY.

ACCOUNTING, ORGANIZATIONS AND SOCIETY is published by Pergamon, and imprint of Elsevier Science Ltd., The Boulevard, Langford Lane, Kidington, Oxford OX5 1GB, UK. Tel: +44 (0) 1865 843479/843781, Fax: +44 (0) 1865 843952; or Elsevier Science Ltd., 660 White Plains Road, Tarrytown, NY 10591-5153, USA. Tel: +1-914-524-9200, Fax: +1-914-333-2444.

E-mail: freesamples@elsevier.co.uk (quoting journal title and your full name and postal address).

ACCOUNTING PERSPECTIVES

ADDRESS FOR SUBMISSION :

JAMES R. HASSELBACK, EDITOR
ACCOUNTING PERSPECTIVES
P.O. BOX 10867
TALAHASSE, FL 32302
904-894-2244
904-894-2244 (Fax)
E-Mail jhassel@cob.fsu.edu

Change in Editor's Address
  May Occur in : 12/31/99

CIRCULATION DATA :

Reader : Academic

Frequency of Issue : 2 Times/Year

Copies Per Issue : Less than 1000

Subscription Price : 30.00 US$

Sponsorship : Profit Oriented Corp.

PUBLICATION GUIDELINES :

Manuscript Length : 21-25

Copies Required : Four

Computer Submission : No

Format : N/A

Fees to Review : 40.00 US$

REVIEW INFORMATION :

Type of Review : Blind Review

No. of External Reviewers : Two

No. of In House Reviewers : Zero

Acceptance Rate : 21-30%

Time To Review : 4-6 months

Reviewer's Comments : Yes

Fees to Publish : 0.00 US$

Invited Articles : 5% or less

MANUSCRIPT TOPICS : ACCOUNTING INFORMATION SYSTEMS;
   ACCOUNTING THEORY & PRACTICE; AUDITING; CAPITAL BUDGETING; COST ACCOUNTING;
   GOVERNMENT & NON-PROFIT ACCOUNTING; TAX ACCOUNTING; ACCOUNTING EDUCATION

PUBLICATION GUIDELINES : American Psychological Association

MANUSCRIPT GUIDELINES/COMMENTS :

ACCOUNTING PERSPECTIVES is a double-blind refereed journal that will publish
articles of interest to Accounting faculty members. Initial publications of
the journal will focus on faculty issues such as research productivity,
promotion, movement, and gender issues related to those topics.

The Journal is published twice a year.
Subscription to ACCOUNTING PERSPECTIVES is $30 per year ($40 for foreign).

EDITORIAL POLICY AND MANUSCRIPT GUIDELINES
1. The Journal solicits unpublished manuscripts not currently under
consideration by another publication. Papers submitted in connection with a
formal program may be submitted provided the manuscript does not appear in
whole or in part (other than a brief abstract). In the proceedings of the
event. Each author must provide the Editor with a statement that the
manuscript or a similar one has not been published and is not, nor will be,
under consideration for publication elsewhere while being reviewed by
ACCOUNTING PERSPECTIVES. Manuscripts with more than four authors are
discouraged.

ACCOUNTING PERSPECTIVES

2. Manuscripts should be typed on 8 1/2" by 11" good quality white paper and be double spaced, except for indented quotations. Only one side of the page should be used. Margins of at least one inch from top, bottom, and sides should facilitate editing and duplication. Do not fax copies of manuscripts.

3. Manuscripts should include a cover page which indicates the author's name, address, affiliation, and any acknowledgements. The author should not be identified anywhere else in the manuscript.

4. Manuscripts should include a separate abstract page not exceeding 250 words. The title but not the author's name and affiliation should appear on the abstract. The abstract should contain a concise statement of the purpose of the manuscript, the primary methods or approaches used, and the significance of the findings and contribution.

5. In order to be assured of an anonymous review, authors should not identify themselves directly or indirectly in the text of the paper. Reference to unpublished working papers and dissertations should be avoided. If necessary, authors may indicate the reference is being withheld because of self citation.

6. Tables, figures, and exhibits should appear on separate pages. Each should be numbered and have a title.

7. Footnotes and should appear at the end of the manuscript. However, every effort should be made to incorporate material into the body of the paper.

8. Accepted manuscripts ultimately must be submitted on an IBM compatible disk; preferably in WordPerfect 5.1, however an ASCII file format is acceptable. Manuscript copyright will be transferred to ACCOUNTING PERSPECTIVES.

9. Four copies of each manuscript should be submitted along with a $40 check made payable to Aviso Publications as a submission fee.

ARTICLE FORMATTING REQUIREMENTS

Articles will be printed in the journal using WordPerfect. Diskettes of the article using WordPerfect 5.1 would be appreciated but are otherwise acceptable in ASCII format.

    Use one inch margin for top, bottom, and sides.
    Use he or she rather than he/she or (s)he; better yet--change wording.
    Use of commas--Smith, Smith, and Smith.
    Place two spaces between each sentence.
    Indent all new paragraphs; use the tab command.
    Place periods and commas within closing single or double quotations marks.
    Place other punctuation marks inside quotation marks only when they are
        part of the of the quoted material.
    Place all footnotes or endnotes at the end of the paper.
    In the References use: Adams, J.A., M.B. Brown, and G.K. Cassel.
    Use "and" rather than "&" between multiple authors in References.
    Format all charts using DEC TAB on each column or place a ? between
        columns in ASCII.

ACCOUNTING PERSPECTIVES

Author's name - the preferred form is first name, middle initial, and last name because this reduces the likelihood of mistaken identity. Use the same form for publication throughout your career.

Clauses - "that" clauses are essential to the meaning of the sentence; "which" clauses can merely add further info or be essential, set off with commas if nonrestrictive.

Who/Whom - if you can substitute he or she, who is correct; if you can substitute him or her, whom is the correct pronoun.

If it is necessary to sent your articles overnight, your must use the U.S. Postal Service since private courier services (UPS, Federal Express, etc.) do not deliver to a post office box number.

ACCOUNTING RESEARCH JOURNAL

ADDRESS FOR SUBMISSION :

ROBERT FAFF, JOINT EDITOR
ACCOUNTING RESEARCH JOURNAL
RMIT BUSINESS
DEPARTMENT OF ECONONICS AND FINANCE
GPO BOX 2476V
MELBOURNE, VIC, 3001
03 9660 5905
03 9660 5986 (Fax)
E-Mail : robertf@oak.bf.rmit.edu.au

CIRCULATION DATA :

Reader : Academic

Frequency of Issue : 2 Times/Year

Copies Per Issue : Less than 1000

Subscription Price : 30.00 AUD.$
   Australia,NewZealand : 25.00 AUD.$

Sponsorship :

PUBLICATION GUIDELINES :

Manuscript Length : N/A

Copies Required : Three

Computer Submission : Yes

Format : 3.5 disk

Fees to Review : 0.00 US$

REVIEW INFORMATION :

Type of Review : N/A

No. of External Reviewers : Two

No. of In House Reviewers : One

Acceptance Rate : 21-30%

Time To Review : 2-3 months

Reviewer's Comments : Yes

Fees to Publish : 0.00 US$

Invited Articles : 5% or less

MANUSCRIPT TOPICS : ACCOUNTING INFORMATION SYSTEMS;
   ACCOUNTING THEORY & PRACTICE; AUDITING;
   FINANCE, COMMERCIAL LAW, COGNATE DISCIPLINES

PUBLICATION GUIDELINES :

MANUSCRIPT GUIDELINES/COMMENTS :

JOINT EDITOR: Scott Holmes
                  University of Newcastle
                  Department of Commerce
                  University Drive
                  Callaghan NSW 2308
                  Phone: (049) 215 036
                  Fax: (049) 216 905

EDITORIAL POLICY
The objective of the ACCOUNTING RESEARCH JOURNAL is to provide a valuable
forum for communication between the profession and academics on the research
and practice of accounting, finance, auditing, commercial law and cognate
disciplines. The editors would encourage submissions in any of the above
areas, which have a practical and/or applied focus. However, this policy does
not exclude the publication of theoretical works. The journal is committed to
the dissemination of research findings to as wide an audience as possible. As
a result, we strongly encourage authors to consider a wide and varied
readership when writing papers.

ACCOUNTING RESEARCH JOURNAL

Three types of articles are published in the ACCOUNTING RESEARCH JOURNAL: (1) Main articles; (2) Notes and Comments; and (3) Educational articles.

* MAIN ARTICLES. These papers are written in an academic style, providing considerable detail about the issues at hand. The paper may be either theoretical or empirical or a combination of both. Work involving a case study approach is acceptable. In addition, well balanced review articles covering fundamental and/or topical areas relevant to the accounting and finance disciplines will be encouraged.

* NOTES AND COMMENTS. These papers are shorter pieces of work that, for example, focus on a specific topical issue or critique a previously published paper.

* EDUCATIONAL ARTICLES. These papers would involve issues or experiments which have accounting education (broadly defined) as their central focus. While these papers would normally be shorter than main articles, longer pieces may be justified depending on the specific topic area.

MANUSCRIPT AWARD
An annual prize of $500 and a certificate will be awarded to the best manuscript published in the ACCOUNTING RESEARCH JOURNAL.

PREPARATION OF MANUSCRIPTS
1. Manuscripts should be typed on one side of the paper only, double-spaced; all pages should be numbered.

2. Headings, Figures, Tables and Diagrams should be numbered consecutively and titled.

3. Footnotes should be numbered consecutively with superscript arabic numerals. Footnotes must appear on the page they refer to and not on a separate sheet at the end of the manuscript.

4. References should appear in the text as Brown (1988) or Brown (1988, p. 120). The full references should be typed on separate sheets at the end of the manuscript. The following rules should be adopted:

MONOGRAPHS
Brown, X.Y. (1988), Advanced Commercial Law, Brett Publishing Co., Brisbane.

PERIODICALS
Brown, X.Y. and Black, A.B. (1988), 'The Current Tax Law,' Journal of Taxation, June, vol. 1, pp. 15-50.

ACCOUNTING REVIEW

ADDRESS FOR SUBMISSION :

GERALD L. SALAMON, EDITOR
ACCOUNTING REVIEW
INDIANA UNIVERSITY
SCHOOL OF BUSINESS
BLOOMINGTON, IN 47405
USA
812-855-2612
812-855-8679 (Fax)
E-Mail : areview @indiana.edu

CIRCULATION DATA :

Reader : Academic

Frequency of Issue : Quarterly

Copies Per Issue : 5001-10,000

Subscription Price : 100.00 US$

Sponsorship : Professional Assoc.

PUBLICATION GUIDELINES :

Manuscript Length : 26-30

Copies Required : Four

Computer Submission : No

Format : N/A

Fees to Review : 75.00 US$
    Nonmembers of AAA 100.00 US$

REVIEW INFORMATION :

Type of Review : Blind Review

No. of External Reviewers : Two

No. of In House Reviewers : Zero

Acceptance Rate : 11-20%

Time To Review : 2-3 months

Reviewer's Comments : Yes

Fees to Publish : 0.00 US$

Invited Articles : 5% or less

MANUSCRIPT TOPICS : ACCOUNTING THEORY & PRACTICE; AUDITING;
  COST ACCOUNTING; TAX ACCOUNTING

PUBLICATION GUIDELINES :

MANUSCRIPT GUIDELINES/COMMENTS :

EDITORIAL POLICY
According to the policies set by the Publications Committee (which were
endorsed by the Executive Committee and were published in the ACCOUNTING
EDUCATION NEWS, June 1987), THE ACCOUNTING REVIEW "should be viewed as the
premier journal for publishing articles reporting the results of accounting
research and explaining and illustrating related research methodology. The
scope of acceptable articles should embrace any research methodology and any
accounting-related subject, as long as the articles meet the standards
established for publication in the journal.... No special sections should be
necessary. The primary, but not exclusive, audience should be -as it is now-
academicians, graduate students, and others interested in accounting
research."

The primary criterion for publication in THE ACCOUNTING REVIEW is the
significance of the contribution an article makes to the literature.

The efficiency and effectiveness of the editorial review process is critically
dependent upon the actions of both authors submitting papers and the

reviewers. Authors accept the responsibility of preparing research papers at a level suitable for evaluation by independent reviewers. Such preparation, therefore, should include subjecting the manuscript to critique by colleagues and others and revising it accordingly prior to submission. The review process is not to be used as a means of obtaining feedback at early stages of developing the research.

Reviewers and associate editors are responsible for providing critically constructive and prompt evaluations of submitted research papers based on the significance of their contribution and on the rigor of analysis and presentation. Associate editors also make editorial recommendations to the editor.

MANUSCRIPT PREPARATION AND STYLE

The ACCOUNTING REVIEW'S manuscript preparation guidelines follow (with a slight modification) the B-format of the CHICAGO MANUAL OF STYLE (14th ed.; University of Chicago Press). Another helpful guide to usage and style is THE ELEMENTS OF STYLE, by William Strunk, Jr., and E. B. White (Macmillan). Spelling follows WEBSTER'S INTERNATIONAL DICTIONARY.

FORMAT

1 . All manuscripts should be typed on one side of 8 1/2 x 11" good quality paper and be double spaced, except for indented quotations.

2. Manuscripts should be as concise as the subject and research method permit, generally not to exceed 7,000 words.

3. Margins of at least one inch from top, bottom and sides should facilitate editing and duplication.

4. To assure anonymous review, authors should not identify themselves directly or indirectly in their papers. Single authors should not use the editorial "we."

5. A cover page should show the title of the paper, the author's name, title and affiliation, any acknowledgments, and a footnote indicating whether the author would be willing to share the data (see last paragraph in this statement).

PAGINATION: All pages, including tables, appendices and references, should be serially numbered. The first section of the paper should be untitled and unnumbered. Major sections may be numbered in Roman numerals. Subsections should not be numbered.

NUMBERS: Spell out numbers from one to ten, except when used in tables and lists, and when used with mathematical, statistical, scientific, or technical units and quantities, such as distances, weights and measures. For example: three days; 3 kilometers; 30 years. All other numbers are expressed numerically. Generally when using approximate terms spell out the number, for example, approximately thirty years.

PERCENTAGES AND DECIMAL FRACTIONS: In nontechnical copy use the word percent in the text; in technical copy the symbol % is used. (See the CHICAGO MANUAL for discussion of these usages.)

HYPHENS: Use a hyphen to join unit modifiers or to clarify usage. For example: a well-presented analysis; re-form. See WEBSTER's for correct usage.

KEY WORDS: The abstract is to be followed by four key words that will assist in indexing the paper.

ABSTRACT / INTRODUCTION
An Abstract of about 100 words should be presented on a separate page immediately preceding the text. The Abstract should concisely inform the reader of the manuscript's topic, its methods and its findings. Keywords and the Data Availability statements should follow the Abstract. The text of the paper should start with a section labeled "I. Introduction," which provides more details about the paper's purpose, motivation, methodology and findings. Both the abstract and the introduction should be relatively non-technical, yet clear enough for an informed reader to understand the manuscript's contribution. The manuscript's title, but neither the author's name nor other identification designations, should appear on the Abstract page.

TABLES AND FIGURES
The author should note the following general requirements:

1. Each table and figure (graphic) should appear on a separate page and should be placed at the end of the text. Each should bear an Arabic number and a complete title indicating the exact contents of the table or figure.

2. A reference to each graphic should be made in the text.

3. The author should indicate by marginal notation where each graphic should be inserted in the text.

4. Graphics should be reasonably interpreted without reference to the text.

5. Source lines and notes should be included as necessary.

EQUATIONS: Equations should be numbered in parentheses flush with the right-hand margin.

DOCUMENTATION
CITATIONS: Work cited should use the "author-date system" keyed to a list of works in the reference list (see below). Authors should make an effort to include the relevant page numbers in the cited works.

1. In the text, works are cited as follows: authors' last name and date, without comma, in parentheses: for example, (Jones 1987); with two authors: (Jones and Freeman 1973); with more than two: (Jones et al. 1985); with more than one source cited together (Jones 1987; Freeman 1986); with two or more works by one author: (Jones 1985, 1987).

2. Unless confusion would result, do not use "p." or "pp." before page numbers: for example, (Jones 1987, 115).

3. When the reference list contains more than one work of an author published in the same year, the suffix a, b, etc. follows the date in the text citation: for example, (Jones 1987a) or (Jones 1987a; Freeman 1985b).

ACCOUNTING REVIEW

4. If an author's name is mentioned in the text. it need not be repeated in the citation; for example, "Jones (1987, 115) says...."

5. Citations to institutional works should use acronyms or short titles where practicable; for example, (AAA ASOBAT 1966); (AICPA Cohen Commission Report 1977). Where brief, the full title of an institutional work might be shown in a citation: for example, (ICAEW The Corporate Report 1975).

6. If the manuscript refers to statutes, legal treatises or court cases, citations acceptable in law reviews should be used.

REFERENCE LIST: Every manuscript must include a list of references containing only those works cited. Each entry should contain all data necessary for unambiguous identification. With the author-date system, use the following format recommended by the CHICAGO MANUAL:

1. Arrange citations in alphabetical order according to surname of the first author or the name of the institution responsible for the citation.

2. Use author's initials instead of proper names.

3. Dates of publication should be placed immediately after author's name.

4. Titles of journals should not be abbreviated.

5. Multiple works by the same author(s) should be listed in chronological order of publication. Two or more works by the same author(s) in the same year are distinguished by letters after the date.

6. Inclusive page numbers are treated as recommended in CHICAGO MANUAL section 8.67. Sample entries are as follows:

American Accounting Association, Committee on Concepts and Standards for External Financial Reports. 1977. Statement on Accounting Theory and Theory Acceptance. Sarasota, FL: AAA.

Demski, J. S., and D. E. M. Sappington. 1989. Hierarchical structure and responsibility accounting. Journal of Accounting Research 27 (Spring): 40-58.

Dye, R., B. Balachandran, and R. Magee. 1989. Contingent fees for audit firms. Working paper, Northwestern University, Evanston, IL.

Fabozzi, F., and I. Pollack, eds. 1987. The Handbook of Fixed Income Securities. 2d ed. Homewood, IL: Dow Jones-Irwin.

Kahneman, D., P. Slovic, and A. Tversky, eds. 1982. Judgment Under Uncertainty: Heuristics and Biases. Cambridge, United Kingdom: Cambridge University Press.

Porcano, T. M. 1984a. Distributive justice and tax policy. The Accounting Review 59 (October): 619-36.

_____. 1984b. The perceived effects of tax policy on corporate investment intentions. The Journal of the American Taxation Association 6 (Fall): 7-19.

ACCOUNTING REVIEW

Shaw, W. H. 1985. Empirical evidence on the market impact of the safe harbor leasing law. Ph.D. Dissertation, University of Texas at Austin.

Sherman, T. M., ed. 1984. Conceptual Framework for Financial Accounting. Cambridge, MA: Harvard Business School.

FOOTNOTES: Footnotes are not used for documentation. Textual footnotes should be used only for extensions and useful excursions of information that if included in the body of the text might disrupt its continuity.

Footnotes should be consecutively numbered throughout the manuscript with superscript Arabic numerals.

Footnote text should be doubled-spaced and placed at the end of the article.

SUBMISSION OF MANUSCRIPTS
Authors should note the following guidelines for submitting manuscripts:

1 . Manuscripts currently under consideration by another journal or publisher should not be submitted. The author must state that the work is not submitted or published elsewhere.

2. In the case of manuscripts reporting on field surveys or experiments. four copies of the instrument (questionnaire, case, interview plan or the like) should be submitted.

3. Four copies should be submitted together with a check in U.S. funds for $75.00 for members or $100.00 for nonmembers of the AAA made payable to the American Accounting Association. Effective January 1990, the submission fee is nonrefundable.

4. The author should retain a copy of the paper.

5. Revisions must be submitted within 12 months from request, otherwise they will be considered new submissions.

COMMENTS
Comments on articles previously published in The Accounting Review will be reviewed (anonymously) by two reviewers in sequence. The first reviewer will be the author of the original article being subjected to critique. If substance permits, a suitably revised comment will be sent to a second reviewer to determine its publishability in The Accounting Review. If a comment is accepted for publication, the original author will be invited to reply. All other editorial requirements, as enumerated above, also apply to proposed comments.

POLICY ON REPRODUCTION
An objective of THE ACCOUNTING REVIEW is to promote the wide dissemination of the results of systematic scholarly inquiries into the broad field of accounting.

Permission is hereby granted to reproduce any of the contents of the Review for use in courses of instruction, as long as the source and American Accounting Association copyright are indicated in any such reproductions.

ACCOUNTING REVIEW

Written application must be made to the Editor for permission to reproduce any of the contents of the Review for use in other than courses of instruction--e.g., inclusion in books of readings or in any other publications intended for general distribution. In consideration for the grant of permission by the Review in such instances, the applicant must notify the author(s) in writing of the intended use to be made of each reproduction. Normally, the Review will not assess a charge for the waiver of copyright.

Except where otherwise noted in articles, the copyright interest has been transferred to the American Accounting Association. Where the author(s) has (have) not transferred the copyright to the Association, applicants must seek permission to reproduce (for all purposes) directly from the author(s).

POLICY ON DATA AVAILABILITY
The following policy has been adopted by the Executive Committee in its April 1989 meeting.

"An objective of (THE ACCOUNTING RECIEW, ACCOUNTING HORIZONS, ISSUES IN ACCOUNTING EDUCATION) is to provide the widest possible dissemination of knowledge based on systematic scholarly inquiries into accounting as a field of professional research, and educational activity. As part of this process, authors are encouraged to make their data available for use by others in extending or replicating results reported in their articles. Authors of articles which report data dependent results should footnote the status of data availability and, when pertinent, this should be accompanied by information on how the data may be obtained."

ACCOUNTING TRENDS AND TECHNIQUES

ADDRESS FOR SUBMISSION :

COLLEN KATZ, EDITOR
ACCOUNTING TRENDS AND TECHNIQUES
AMERICAN INSTITUTE OF CPAS
HARBOR SIDE FINANCIAL
201 PLAZA 3
JERSEY CITY, NJ 07311
201-938-3456

PUBLICATION GUIDELINES :

Manuscript Length :

Copies Required :

Computer Submission : N/A

Format : N/A

Fees to Review : 0.00 US$

CIRCULATION DATA :

Reader :

Frequency of Issue :

Copies Per Issue :

Subscription Price :

Sponsorship :

REVIEW INFORMATION :

Type of Review : N/A

No. of External Reviewers :

No. of In House Reviewers :

Acceptance Rate :

Time To Review :

Reviewer's Comments :

Fees to Publish : 0.00 US$

Invited Articles :

MANUSCRIPT TOPICS : ACCOUNTING INFORMATION SYSTEMS;
   ACCOUNTING THEORY & PRACTICE; AUDITING; COST ACCOUNTING;
   GOVERNMENT & NON-PROFIT ACCOUNTING; TAX ACCOUNTING

PUBLICATION GUIDELINES :

MANUSCRIPT GUIDELINES/COMMENTS :

This Journal is published once a year and surveys annual reports. It is
published by the staff at the Institute and does not solicit manuscripts.

ACQUISITION REVIEW QUARTERLY

ADDRESS FOR SUBMISSION :

DR. JAMES PRICE, EDITOR
ACQUISITION REVIEW QUARTERLY
DEFENSE SYSTEMS MANAGEMENT COLLEGE
ATTN: AS-VAP
9820 BELVIOR ROAD, STE. G38
FORT BELVIOR, VA 22060-5565
703-805-4290
703-805-2917 (Fax)
E-Mail : wittmeyerj@dsmc.dsm.mil

CIRCULATION DATA :

Reader : Academic

Frequency of Issue : Quarterly

Copies Per Issue : 10,001-25,000

Subscription Price : 12.00 US$
  Gov't Employ - Free : 0.00 US$

Sponsorship :

PUBLICATION GUIDELINES :

Manuscript Length : 21-25

Copies Required : Two

Computer Submission : Yes

Format : MSWord 6.0,WP 6.0,MSPowerp

Fees to Review : 0.00 US$

REVIEW INFORMATION :

Type of Review : Blind Review

No. of External Reviewers : Three

No. of In House Reviewers : One

Acceptance Rate : 11-20%

Time To Review : 4-6 months

Reviewer's Comments : Yes

Fees to Publish : 0.00 US$

Invited Articles : 5% or less

MANUSCRIPT TOPICS : ACCOUNTING INFORMATION SYSTEMS;
  GOVERNMENT & NON-PROFIT ACCOUNTING; WEAPONS ACQUISITION (PROCUREMENT)

PUBLICATION GUIDELINES : American Psychological Association

MANUSCRIPT GUIDELINES/COMMENTS :

ADVANCES IN ACCOUNTING

ADDRESS FOR SUBMISSION :

PHILIP M. J. RECKERS, EDITOR
ADVANCES IN ACCOUNTING
ARIZONA STATE UNIVERSITY
COLLEGE OF BUSINESS
TEMPE, AZ 85287
USA
602-965-2283
602-965-8392 (Fax)
E-Mail : iepmr@asuvm.inre.asu.edu

CIRCULATION DATA :

Reader : Academic

Frequency of Issue : 1 Times/Year

Copies Per Issue : Less than 1000

Subscription Price : 28.25 US$

Sponsorship : Profit Oriented Corp.

PUBLICATION GUIDELINES :

Manuscript Length : Any

Copies Required : Four

Computer Submission : No

Format : N/A

Fees to Review : 25.00 US$

REVIEW INFORMATION :

Type of Review : Blind Review

No. of External Reviewers : Two

No. of In House Reviewers : One

Acceptance Rate : 11-20%

Time To Review : 2-3 months

Reviewer's Comments : Yes

Fees to Publish : 0.00 US$

Invited Articles : 5% or less

MANUSCRIPT TOPICS : ACCOUNTING INFORMATION SYSTEMS;
   ACCOUNTING THEORY & PRACTICE; AUDITING; COST ACCOUNTING;
   GOVERNMENT & NON-PROFIT ACCOUNTING; TAX ACCOUNTING

PUBLICATION GUIDELINES :

MANUSCRIPT GUIDELINES/COMMENTS :

ADVANCES IN ACCOUNTING (AIA) is a professional publication whose purpose is to
meet the information needs of both practitioners and academicians. We plan to
publish thoughtful, well-developed articles on a variety of current topics in
financial and management accounting, accounting education and auditing.

Articles may range from empirical to analytical, from practice-based to the
development of new techniques. Articles must be readable, relevant, and
articles must be understandable and concise. To be relevant, articles must be
related to problems facing the accounting and business community. To empirical
reports, sound design and execution are critical. For theoretical treatises,
reasonable assumptions and logical development are essential.

AIA welcomes all comments and encourages articles from practitioners and
academicians. Editorial correspondence pertaining to manuscripts should be
sent to Bill N. Schwartz.

EDITORIAL POLICY AND MANUSCRIPTS FORM GUIDELINES
1. Manuscripts should be typewritten and double-spaced on 8" x 11" white

ADVANCES IN ACCOUNTING

paper. Only one side of a page should be used. Margins should be set to facilitate editing and duplication except as noted:

    A. Tables, figures and exhibits should appear on a separate page. Each should be numbered and have a title.

    B. Footnotes should be presented by citing the author's name and the year of publication in the body of the text, e.g., Schwartz [1981]; Reckers and Pany [1980].

2. Manuscripts should include a cover page which indicated the author's name and affiliation.

3. Manuscripts should include on a separate lead page an abstract not exceeding 200 words. The author's name and affiliation should not appear on the abstract.

4. Topical headings and subheadings should be used. Main headings in the manuscript should be centered, secondary headings should be flush with the left-hand margin. (As a guide to usage and style, refer to William Strunk, Jr. and E.B. White, THE ELEMENTS OF STYLE.)

5. Manuscripts must include a list of references which contain only those works actually cited. (As a helpful guide in preparing a list of references, refer to Kate L. Turabian. A MANUAL FOR WRITERS OF TERM PAPERS, THESES, AND DISSERTATIONS.)

6. In order to be assured of an anonymous review, authors should not identify themselves directly or indirectly. Reference to unpublished working papers and dissertations should be avoided. If necessary, authors may indicate that the reference is being withheld for the reasons cited above.

7. The author will be provided one complete volume of the AIA issue in which his or her manuscript appears and ten off-prints of the article.

8. Manuscripts currently under review by other publications should not be submitted. Complete reports of research presented at a national or regional conference of a professional association (e.g. AAA, DSI, etc.) and "State of the Art" papers are acceptable.

9. FOUR copies of each manuscript should be submitted to the Editor-in-Chief at the Virginia Commonwealth University address. Copies of any and all research instruments also should be included.

For additional information regarding the type of manuscripts that are desired, see AIA Statement of Purpose.

ADVANCES IN ACCOUNTING INFORMATION SYSTEMS

ADDRESS FOR SUBMISSION :

STEVE G. SUTTON, EDITOR
ADVANCES IN ACCOUNTING INFORMATION
   SYSTEMS
BRYANT COLLEGE
1150 DOUGLAS PIKE
SMITHFIELD, RI 02917-1284
USA
401-232-6129
401-232-6319 (Fax)
E-Mail : SSUTTON@RESEARCH1.BRYANT.EDU

CIRCULATION DATA :

Reader : Academic

Frequency of Issue : 1 Times/Year

Copies Per Issue : 1001-2000

Subscription Price : 37.50 US$
   Institution : 63.50 US$

Sponsorship : Profit Oriented Corp.

PUBLICATION GUIDELINES :

Manuscript Length : 21-25

Copies Required : Four

Computer Submission : Yes

Format : ASCII w/hard copy

Fees to Review : 0.00 US$

REVIEW INFORMATION :

Type of Review : Blind Review

No. of External Reviewers : Two

No. of In House Reviewers : One

Acceptance Rate : 21-30%

Time To Review : 2-3 months

Reviewer's Comments : Yes

Fees to Publish : 0.00 US$

Invited Articles : 5% or less

MANUSCRIPT TOPICS : ACCOUNTING INFORMATION SYSTEMS;
   ACCOUNTING THEORY & PRACTICE; COST ACCOUNTING;
   GOVERNMENT & NON-PROFIT ACCOUNTING; TAX ACCOUNTING; INFORMATION SYSTEMS

PUBLICATION GUIDELINES : In Journal

MANUSCRIPT GUIDELINES/COMMENTS :

AiAIS STATEMENT OF PURPOSE
Statement of purpose ADVANCES IN ACCOUNTING INFORMATION SYSTEMS (AiAIS) is a
professional publication whose purpose is to meet the information needs of
both practitioners and academicians. We plan to publish thoughtful,
well-developed articles that examine the rapidly evolving relationship between
accounting and information technology. Articles may range from empirical to
analytical, from practice-based to the development of new techniques. Articles
must be readable and logically integrated. To be reliable, conclusions must
follow logically from the evidence and arguments presented. For empirical
reports sound design and execution are critical. For theoretical treatises,
reasonable assumptions and logical development are essential. Relevant
articles must be related to problems facing the integration of accounting and
information technology. Specific issues that the journal will address include,
but are not limited to, the following:

* Control and auditability of information systems
* Management of information technology
* Artificial intelligence research in accounting

ADVANCES IN ACCOUNTING INFORMATION SYSTEMS

* Development issues in accounting and information systems
* Human factors issues related to information technology
* Development of theories related to information technology
* Methodological issues in information technology research
* Information systems validation
* Human-computer interaction research in accounting information systems.

AiAIS welcomes all comments and encourages articles from practitioners and academicians.

Editorial correspondence pertaining to manuscripts should be forwarded to the Editor.

EDITORIAL POLICY AND MANUSCRIPT FORM GUIDELINES
1. Manuscripts should be typewritten and double-spaced on 8 1/2" x 11" white paper. Only one side of a page should be used. Margins should be set to facilitate editing and duplication except as noted:

   a. Tables, figures, and exhibits should appear on a separate page. Each should be numbered and have a title.
   b. Footnotes should be presented by citing the author's name and the year of publication in the body of the text, for example, Sutton (1990) and Hale, etal. (1991).

2. Manuscripts should include a cover page which indicates the author's name and affiliation.

3. Manuscripts should include on a separate lead page an abstract not exceeding 200 words. The author's name and affiliation should not appear on the abstract.

4. Topical headings and subheadings should be used. Main headings in the manuscript should be centered, secondary headings should be flush with the left-hand margin. (As a guide to usage and style, refer to William Strunk, Jr. and E.B. White, THE ELEMENT OF STYLE.)

5. Manuscripts must include a list of references which contain only those works actually cited. (As a helpful guide in preparing a list of references, refer to Kate L. Turabian, A MANUAL FOR WRITERS OF TERM PAPERS, THESES, AND DISSERTATIONS.)

6. In order to be assured of an anonymous review, authors should not identify themselves directly or indirectly. Reference to unpublished working papers and dissertations should be avoided. If necessary, authors may indicate that the reference is being withheld for the reasons cited above.

7. The author will be provided one complete volume of the AiAIS issue in which his or her manuscript appears and the senior author will receive twenty-five off prints of the article.

8. Manuscripts currently under review by other publications should not be submitted. Complete reports and research presented at a national or regional conference of a professional association (e.g., AAA, DSI, etc.) and "State of the Art" papers are acceptable.

ADVANCES IN ACCOUNTING INFORMATION SYSTEMS

9. FOUR copies of each manuscript should be submitted to the Editor. Copies of any and all research instruments also should be included.

10. For additional information regarding the type of manuscripts that are desired, see AiAIS STATEMENT OF PURPOSE.

ADVANCES IN INTERNATIONAL ACCOUNTING

ADDRESS FOR SUBMISSION :

TIMOTHY J. SALE, EDITOR
ADVANCES IN INTERNATIONAL ACCOUNTING
UNIVERSITY OF CINCINNATI
DEPARTMENT OF ACCOUNTING INFORMATION
  SYSTEMS
MAIL LOCATION 211
CINCINNATI, OH 45221-0211
USA
513-556-6062
513-556-4891 (Fax)
E-Mail : tim.sale@uc.edu

CIRCULATION DATA :

Reader : Academic

Frequency of Issue : 1 Times/Year

Copies Per Issue : Less than 1000

Subscription Price : 63.00 US$

Sponsorship : Profit Oriented Corp.

PUBLICATION GUIDELINES :

Manuscript Length : 26-30

Copies Required : Two

Computer Submission : Yes

Format : ASCII/only on acceptance

Fees to Review : 0.00 US$

REVIEW INFORMATION :

Type of Review : Blind Review

No. of External Reviewers : Two

No. of In House Reviewers : One

Acceptance Rate : 50 %

Time To Review : 2-3 months

Reviewer's Comments : Yes

Fees to Publish : 0.00 US$

Invited Articles : 5% or less

MANUSCRIPT TOPICS : ACCOUNTING INFORMATION SYSTEMS;
  ACCOUNTING THEORY & PRACTICE; AUDITING; COST ACCOUNTING;
  GOVERNMENT & NON-PROFIT ACCOUNTING; INTERNATIONAL FINANCE; TAX ACCOUNTING

PUBLICATION GUIDELINES :

MANUSCRIPT GUIDELINES/COMMENTS :

AUTHOR'S RESPONSIBILITIES
The author is responsible for correct spelling and punctuation, accurate
quotations with page numbers, complete and accurate references, relevant
content, coherent organization, legible appearance, and so forth. The author
must proofread the manuscript after it is typed, making all corrections and
changes before submitting the manuscript. Before submitting the manuscript to
the editor please use the checklist to be sure all necessary material is
included.

The author is also responsible for preparing the manuscript on a word
processor. Just as word processing eliminates a good amount of retyping,
submitting a disk provides an opportunity to eliminate duplicate keyboarding
by the typesetter. One key to success is compatibility. Therefore, the
following steps should be followed closely.

1. Use a word processing program that is able to create an IBM compatible
   ASCII file.
2. Use 5 1/4 inch, double density disks.

3. Structure manuscript to follow guidelines.
4. Print one (1) copy for styling/copy-editing purposes.
5. Save one (1) copy of file in ASCII format.
    * Follow instructions in your word processing program.
    * Keep entire manuscript on one (1) file (no more than 75,000 characters per file).
    * Eliminate manuscript page numbers and identifying abbreviated title.
    * DO NOT use a 27 ASCII value line ending.
    * Use a 13 ASCII value at end of a paragraph.
    * DO NOT include tabular material on the file: all tabular text will be keyboarded from your printed copy.
    * DO NOT use codes for heads, bullet lists, number lists, etc.
6. Submit the file in ASCII format with your printed copy.

VOLUME EDITOR'S RESPONSIBILITY
The volume editor is responsible for reviewing all printed manuscripts and disks before submission for publication.

Printed manuscripts should be checked for original artwork, tables, and, where necessary, letters of permission to reprint. The manuscript checklist is a good guide to ensure a complete manuscript.

The disk should be checked for proper format. If it is not a file in ASCII format, it is the volume editor's responsibility to either return the disk to the author for reformatting in ASCII or to have it done him/herself.

GENERAL INSTRUCTIONS

PAPER
Type the manuscript on one side of standard-sized (8 1/2 x 11 in.) heavy white bond paper. DO NOT use half sheets or strips of paper glued, taped, or stapled to the pages.

ABSTRACT
Begin the abstract on a new page. Type the word "ABSTRACT" in all uppercase letters, centered at top of page. Type the abstract itself as a single paragraph, double-spaced, indent 5 spaces from the left margin and 5 spaces from the right margin.

TEXT
Begin the text on a new page. The sections of the text follow each other without a break.

APPENDICES
Double-space the appendices and begin each on a separate page. Type the word "APPENDIX" in all uppercase letters and identifying capital letters in the order in which they are mentioned in text, centered at the top of the page. If there is only one appendix, do not use an identifying letter.

AUTHOR ACKNOWLEDGMENT NOTES
This note is neither numbered nor is it mentioned in text. Type the word "ACKNOWLEDGMENT" in all uppercase letters, centered at top of a new page. Type the acknowledgment itself as a double-spaced single paragraph.

NOTES
Notes that are mentioned in text are numbered consecutively throughout the
chapter. Double-space the notes and begin on a separate page. Center the word
"NOTES" in all uppercase letters at the top of the page. Indent the first line
of each note 5 spaces and type the notes in the order in which they are
mentioned in text.

REFERENCES
Each series has it's own individual style, whether it be APA, ASA, reference
notes, or a style unique to their discipline. For the style that you must
follow, consult the PUBLICATION MANUAL OF THE AMERICAN PSYCHOLOGICAL
ASSOCIATION (Third Edition), THE CHICAGO MANUAL OF STYLE (13th Edition), or a
previous published volume in the series.

References cited in test MUST appear in the reference list; conversely, each
entry in the reference list MUST be cited in text. It is the author's
responsibility to make certain that each source referenced appears in both
places and that the text citation and reference list are identical.

IMPORTANT: (1) Foreign language volumes, parts, numbers, editions, and so on
MUST be translated into their English equivalents. (2) JAI Press does not use
either op. cit. or loc. cit. A short-title form is required. Ibid. is
acceptable.

Items to be included in a full reference are
BOOK: Author's full name
      Complete title of the book
      Editor, compiler, or translator, if any
      Series, if any, and volume or number in series
      Edition, if not the original
      Number of volumes
      Facts of publication--city where published, publisher, date of
        publication
      Volume number, if any
      Page number(s) of the particular citation

ARTICLE IN PERIODICAL:
      Author's full name
      Title of the article
      Name of the periodical
      Volume (and number) of the periodical
      Date of the volume or issue
      Page number(s) of the particular citation

UNPUBLISHED MATERIAL;
      Title of document, if any, and date
      Folio number or other identifying material
      Name of collection
      Depository, and city where it is located

TABLES
Tables are numbered consecutively in the order in which they are first
mentioned in text and are identified by the word "Table" and an arabic
numeral. Double-space each table, regardless of length, and begin each table
on a separate page. Type the short title of the manuscript and the page number

in the upper right-hand corner of every page of a table. Tables are complicated to set in type and more expensive to publish than text. Therefore, they should be reserved for important data directly related to the content of the paper. Refer to every table and its data in text. Do not write "the table above/below" or "the table on p. 32" because the position and page number of a table cannot be determined until the text is typeset. In text, indicate the approximate placement of each table by a clest break in the text, inserting:

TABLE 1 ABOUT HERE

set off double-spaced above and below. Do not abbreviate table headings. Limit the use of rules to horizonatal rules only. Draw all rules in pencil.

FIGURES
Figures are also numbered consecutively in the order in which they are first mentioned in text. Use the word "Figure" and an arabic numeral. Indicate the location of each figure by a clear break, inserting:

INSERT FIGURE 1 ABOUT HERE

set off doubled-spaced above and below.

All figures, charts, illustrations, halftones, and chemical structures are figures and must be submitted in a form suitable for reproduction by the printer without redrawing or retouching. Careful adherence to the following instructions will ensure the high quality appearance of your paper.

1. All figures must be submitted as glossy prints or original ink drawings.

2. All lettering must be done professionally. Three methods of lettering are acceptable: professional lettering, stencil, or dry-transfer sheets. Freehand and typewritten lettering is not acceptable. It is best not to use all capital lettering. Lettering should be large enough so that it is completely legible after photo reduction. Lettering should be large enough so that it is completely legible after photo reduction. Lettering in all figures should be the same size.

3. When planning a figure, take into consideration that all published figures must fit the dimemsions of a book page. Figures should be no larger than 4 1/2 x 7 inches. If a figure exceeds this size, it should be large enough andsharp enough to be legible when reduced to fit page. Please remember that reducing the width of a figure will reduce the length by the same percentage.

4. Graphs and charts: Keep lines clean and simple and eliminate all extraneous detail. Graph paper, if used, should be ruled in faint blue.

5. Illustrations: Illustrations should be prepared by a professional artist. The least amount of detail necessary should be used.

6. Halftones: Original photos of professional quality are a necessity. Place overlays on all halftones to prevent scratches and damage from handling. Please keep in mind that halftones require a complicated printing process, which makes them more expensive than line drawings to reproduce.

ADVANCES IN INTERNATIONAL ACCOUNTING

Important: Color halftones are very costly to print. If color halftones are submitted, they will be printed in black and white. If any halftones MUST be printed in color, the cost will be charged to the author.

7. Chemical structures: Computer generated chemical structures are only acceptable and encourages if prepared on a system such as Chemdraw or Wimp and output on high quality paper by a printer such as Apple Laserwriter or a Plotter such as HP7550A. Schemes must be sized so as not to exceed the 4 1/2 x 7 inch specifications.

8. Unlike the figure, which is reproduced from the glossy print, the figure number and legend is typeset and placed outside the figure. Therefore, type al figure numbers and legends double-spaced on a separate page.

9. For identification by the production editor and printer, please indicate on the back of each photo the author, title of paper, number and figure legend. All information should be written lightly in soft pencil, using as little pressure as possible. "Top" should be written on any illustration that might accidentally be reproduced wrong side up. Submit the same number of photocopies of figures as the printed copy of the manuscript.

10. Staples, of course, should never be used on any illustration copy, nor should paper clips unless they are well padded with several thicknesses of paper to prevent scratching and identation.

11. Prints should never be folded. They should be put in a separate envelope and protected by a sheet or sheets of stiff cardboard.

12. The author is responsible for obtaining permission to reproduce a figure from a copyrighted source. A photocopy of the permission must be submitted with the manuscript.

13. We will naturally assume that the print(s) have been thoroughly checked for accuracy before submission to JAI Press.

14. All prints will be considered final.

15. No corrections will be allowed.

16. All prints will be returned to the author.

TYPE ELEMENT
The type MUST be dark, clear, and readable. A typeface that is made up of dots, as generated by some printers, is acceptable only if it is clear and legible.

DOUBLE SPACING
Double space between ALL lines of the manuscript, which includes the title, headings, footnotes, quotations, references, figure captions, and ALL parts of tables. NEVER use single-spacing or one-and-a-half spacing.

MARGINS
Leave uniform margins of 1 1/2 in. at the top, bottom, right, and left of every page. The length of each typed line is 5 1/2 inch. Do not justify lines; leave the right margin uneven. DO NOT hyphenate words at the end of a line;

ADVANCES IN INTERNATIONAL ACCOUNTING

let a line run short or long rather than break a word. Type no more than 25 lines of text on a manuscript page.

HEADINGS
Most manuscripts use from one to four headings. The four levels should appear as:
CENTERED ALL UPPERCASE HEADING
Centered Uppercase and Lowercase Heading
Flush Left, Underlined, Uppercase and Lowercase Side Heading
    Indented, underlined, lowercase paragraph heading ending with a period.

PARAGRAPHS AND INDENTATION
Indent the first line of every paragraph and the first line of every footnote five spaces. Thpe the remaining lines of the manuscript to a uniform left-hand margin.

QUOTATIONS
Direct quotations must be accurate. Quotations of 40 words or less should be incorporated into the text and enclosed by double quotation marks ("). Display quotations of more than 40 words should appear as a double-spaced block with no quotation marks. DO NOT single-space. Indent 5 spaces from the left margin and 5 spaces from the right margin.

PERMISSION TO QUOTE
Any direct quotation, regardless of length must be accompanied by a reference citation that includes the author, year of publication, and page number(s). If you quote at length from a copyrighted work, you will also need written permission from the owner of the copyright. It is the author's responsibility to obtain permission. A copy of the letter of permission must accompany the manuscript.

STATISTICAL AND MATHEMATICAL COPY
Type all signs and symbols in mathematical copy that you can. Either type a character that resembles the symbol or draw the symbol in by hand. Identify symbols that may be hard to read or ambiguous to the copy editor or typesetter. The first time the ambiguous symbol appears in the manuscript, spell out and circle the name next to the symbol. Space mathematical copy as you would space words. Align signs and symbols carefully. Type subscripts half a line below the symbol and superscripts half a line above the symbol. Display a mathematical equation by setting it off from the text by double-spacing twice above and below the equation. If the equation is identified by a number, type the number in parenthesis flush against the right margin. Do not underline (1) greek letters, subscripts, and superscripts that function as identifiers, and (2) abbreviations that are not variables. Mark symbols for vectors with a wavy line. Underline all other statistical symbols.

PARTS OF A MANUSCRIPT
Order of manuscript pages: Number all pages consecutively. Arrange the pages of the manuscript as follows:
    title page (page1)
    abstract (page 2)
    text (page 3)
    appendixes (start each on a separate page)
    author acknowledgement notes

notes (start on a new page)
references (start on a new page)
tables (start each on a separate page)
figures (start each on a separate page)

This arrangement is not the way the printed paper will appear; it is necessary for handling by the copy editor and the typesetter.

After the manuscript pages are arranged in the correct order, number them consecutively, beginning with the title page. Number ALL pages. Type the number in the upper right-hand corner using arabic numerals. Identify each manuscript page by typing an abbreviated title above the page number.

TITLE PAGE
The title page includes 4 elements:
* The title in uppercase letters.
* The Author(s) in uppercase and lowercase letters.
* An abbreviated title to be used as a running head. The running head should be a maximum of 70 characters, which includes all letters, punctuation, and spaces between words.
* Complete mailing address and phone number of each author.

ADVANCES IN PUBLIC INTEREST ACCOUNTING

ADDRESS FOR SUBMISSION :

CHERYL R. LEHMAN, PH.D.
ADVANCES IN PUBLIC INTEREST ACCOUNTING
HOFSTRA UNIVERSITY
SCHOOL OF BUSINESS
HEMPSTEAD, NY 11550
USA
516-463-6986 OR 5684
516-564-4834 (Fax)
E-Mail : ACTCRL@VAXD.HOFSTRA.EDU

CIRCULATION DATA :

Reader : Academic

Frequency of Issue : 1 Times/Year

Copies Per Issue : Less than 1000

Subscription Price : 27.50 US$
  Institution : 54.50 US$

Sponsorship : Profit Oriented Corp.

PUBLICATION GUIDELINES :

Manuscript Length : Any

Copies Required : Five

Computer Submission : No

Format : N/A

Fees to Review : 0.00 US$

REVIEW INFORMATION :

Type of Review : Editorial Review

No. of External Reviewers : Two

No. of In House Reviewers : Zero

Acceptance Rate : 21-30%

Time To Review : 2-3 months

Reviewer's Comments : Yes

Fees to Publish : 0.00 US$

Invited Articles : 21-30%

MANUSCRIPT TOPICS : ACCOUNTING THEORY & PRACTICE; COST ACCOUNTING

PUBLICATION GUIDELINES :

MANUSCRIPT GUIDELINES/COMMENTS :

1. ADVANCES IN PUBLIC INTEREST ACCOUNTING is a publication with two major
aims. First to provide a forum for the growing body of researchers who are
concerned with critically appraising and radically transforming conventional
accounting theory and practice. And second, to increase the social
self-awareness of accountants and encourage them to assume a greater
responsibility for the profession's social role.

2. We are seeking original manuscripts that explore all facets of this broad
agenda. For example, we would welcome manuscripts from authors who are tyring
to:

* expand accounting's focus beyond the behavior of individual corporate
  entities;

* explore alternatives to the neo-classical economic model that currently
  grounds much of accounting theory;

* find alternatives to conventional effcency and profitability measures of
  corporate performance;

* investigate the ways accounting contributes to the allocative, distributive, social and ecological consequesces of corporate activities;

* incorporate into the reporting system the costs that corporations externalize by imposing them on their employees, their communities, and future generations;

* explore the ways in which both financial and managerial accounting participate in resolving the social tensions that surround corporate activities;

* expand the profession's reporting responsibilities beyond investors and creditors to encompass the broader set of those who interact with and are acted upon by the corporation;

* recognize the heterogeneity of interests and conflicts within investors and creditor groups;

* Address the implications of the changing market structure of the accounting profession and the diminution of auditing services in relation to tax and consulting practices.

3. Send five copies of prospective manuscripts to Cheryl Lehman, Hofstra University.

4. All manuscripts should be typewritten and double-spaced on 8-1/2" x 11" white paper. Only one side of a page should be set to facilitate editing and publication except as noted:
    a. Tables, figures and exhibits should appear on a separate page. Each should be numbered and have a title,
    b. Footnotes should be presented by citing the author's name and the year of publication in the body of the text, e.g. Schwartz (1981); Reckers and Pany (1980).

6. Manuscripts should include a cover page which indicates the author's name and affiliation.

7. Manuscripts should include on a separate lead page an abstract not exceeding 200 words. The author's name and affiliation should not appear on the abstract. 8. Topical headings and subheadings should be used. Main headings in the manuscript should be centered, secondary headings should be flush with the left-hand margin. (As a guide to usage and style, refer to William Strunk Jr. and E.B. White, THE ELEMENTS OF STYLE.)

9. Manuscripts must include a list of references which contain only those works actually cited. (As a helpful guide in preparing a list of references, refer to Kate L. Turabian, A MANUAL FOR WRITERS OF TERM PAPERS, THESES, AND DISSERTATIONS.)

10. In order to be assured of an anonymous review, authors should not identify themselves directly or indirectly. Reference to unpublished working papers and dissertations should be avoided. If necessary, authors may indicate that the reference is being withheld for the reasons cited above. 11. The author will be provided one complete volume of the issue in which his or her manuscript appears and ten off-prints of the article.

ADVANCES IN PUBLIC INTEREST ACCOUNTING

11. Manuscripts currently under review by other publications should not be submitted. Complete reports of research presented at a national or regional conference of a professional association (e.g. AAA, AIDS etc.) and "State of the Art" papers are acceptable. 13. Five copies of each manuscript should be submitted to the General Editor, Cheryl R. Lehman. Ph.D. 14. Copies of any and all research instruments should be included.

ADVANCES IN TAXATION

ADDRESS FOR SUBMISSION :

PROFESSOR THOMAS M. PORCANO, EDITOR
ADVANCES IN TAXATION
MIAMI UNIVERSITY
RICHARD T. FARMER SCH. OF BUS. ADMIN.
DEPARTMENT OF ACCOUNTANCY
OXFORD, OH 45056
USA
513-529-6200
513-529-4740 (Fax)
E-Mail : TPORCANO@SBA-LAWS.SBS.MUOHIO.EDU

CIRCULATION DATA :

Reader : Academic

Frequency of Issue : 1 Times/Year

Copies Per Issue : Less than 1000

Subscription Price : 29.25 US$
   Institution : 58.50 US$

Sponsorship :

PUBLICATION GUIDELINES :

Manuscript Length : More than 20

Copies Required : Three

Computer Submission : No

Format : N/A

Fees to Review : 30.00 US$

REVIEW INFORMATION :

Type of Review : Blind Review

No. of External Reviewers : Two

No. of In House Reviewers : Zero

Acceptance Rate : 21-30%

Time To Review : 2-3 months

Reviewer's Comments : Yes

Fees to Publish : 0.00 US$

Invited Articles : 5% or less

MANUSCRIPT TOPICS : COST ACCOUNTING; PUBLIC POLICY ECONOMICS;
   TAX ACCOUNTING

PUBLICATION GUIDELINES :

MANUSCRIPT GUIDELINES/COMMENTS :

Editor's E-mail: TPORCANO@SBA - LAWS.SBA.MUOHIO.EDU

ADVANCES IN TAXATION is a refereed academic tax journal published annually.
Academic articles on any aspect of federal, state, or local taxation will be
considered. These include, but are not limited to, compliance, computer usage,
education, law, planning, and policy. Interdisciplinary research
involvingeconomics, finance, or other areas also is encouraged. Acceptable
research methodologies include any analytical, behavioral, descriptive, legal,
quantitative, survey, or theoretical approach appropriate to the project.

Manuscripts must be readable, relevant, and reliable. To be readable, articles
must be understandable and concise. To be relevant, articles must be directly
related to problems inherent in systems of taxation. To be reliable,
conclusions must follow logically from the evidence and arguments presented.
For empirical papers, sound research design and execution are critical. For
theoretical papers, reasonable assumptions and logical development are
essential.

Three copies of the typed manuscript should be submitted together with a check

ADVANCES IN TAXATION

for $30.00 in U.S. funds made payable to ADVANCES IN TAXATION. The manuscript should be double spaced on 8 1/2" x 11" paper. The submission fee is nonrefundable. On the cover page the author(s) should include name, affiliation, address, phone number, fax number, and e-mail address (if available). In the case of manuscripts reporting on field surveys or experiments, three copies of the instrument also should be submitted. Manuscripts currently under consideration by another journal or publisher should not be submitted.

ADVANCES IN TAXATION is published by JAI Press, which is a well-regarded publisher of academic literature in a number of business and non-business fields. Subscription information may be obtained by calling the publisher at (203) 661-7602.

1. Manuscripts should be typewritten and double-spaced on 8-1/2" x 11" white paper. Only one side of a page should be used. Margins should be set to facilitate editing and duplication except as noted:

   A. tables, figures and exhibits should appear on a separate page. Each should be numbered and have a title.

   b. literature citations should be presented by citing the author's name and the year of publicatin in the body of the text, for example, Schwartz (1981); Reckers and Pany (1980).

   c. textual footnotes should be used only for extensions, the inclusion of which in the text might disrupt its continuity. Footnotes should be numbered consecutively throughout the manuscript with subscript Arabic numbers, and placed at the end of the text.

2. Manuscripts should include a cover page which indicates the author's name and affiliation.

3. Manuscripts should include on a separate lead page an abstract not exceeding 200 words. The author's name and affiliation should not appear on the abstract.

4. Topical headings and subheadings should be used. Main headings in the manuscript should be centered and typed in uppercase, secondary headings should be centered with initial capital letters, tertiary headings should be lefthand justified, italicized (underlined), with capital letters. (As a guide to usage and style, refer to William Strunk, Jr. and E.B. White, THE ELEMENTS OF STYLE.)

5. Manuscripts must include a list of references which contain only those works actually cited. The entries should be arranged in alphabetical order according to the surname of the first author. Samples of entries are as follows:

Swenson, C.W., and M.L. Moore, "Use of Input-Output Analysis in Tax Research". Advances in Taxation, Vol. 1 (1987), pp. 49-84.

Pocano, T.M., "The Perceived Effects of Tax Policy on Corporate Investment Intentions", The Journal of the American Taxation Association, (Fall 1984), pp. 7-19.

ADVANCES IN TAXATION

6. In order to be assumed of an anonymous review, authors should not identify themselves directly or indirectly. Reference to unpublished working papers and dissertations should be avoided. If necessary, authors may indicate that the reference is being withheld for the reasons cited above.

7. The author will be provided one complete volume of the AIT volume which his or her manuscript appears and ten offprints of the article.

8. Manuscripts currently under review by other publications should not be submitted. Complete reports of research presented at a national or regional conference of a professional association (e.g., AAA, AIDS, etc.) and "State of the Art" papers are acceptable.

9. Three copies of each manuscript should be submitted to the Editor. Copies of any and all research instruments should be included.

10. For additional information regarding the type of manuscripts that are desired, see AIT Statement of Purpose.

AFRICAN ECONOMIC AND BUSINESS REVIEW

ADDRESS FOR SUBMISSION :

UCHENNA N. AKPOM, EDITOR-IN-CHIEF
AFRICAN ECONOMIC AND BUSINESS REVIEW
P.O. BOX 71302
TUSCALOOSA, AL 35407
205-652-3473
E-Mail : livuna01@uwamail.sestal.edu

CIRCULATION DATA :

Reader : Academic

Frequency of Issue : 2 Times/Year

Copies Per Issue : Less than 1000

Subscription Price : 20.00 US$
   Institutions : 40.00 US$

Sponsorship : Non Profit Corp. &
              University

PUBLICATION GUIDELINES :

Manuscript Length : 16-20

Copies Required : Three

Computer Submission : Yes

Format : WordPerfect, MicrosoftWord

Fees to Review : 20.00 US$

REVIEW INFORMATION :

Type of Review : Blind Review

No. of External Reviewers : Two

No. of In House Reviewers : One

Acceptance Rate :

Time To Review :

Reviewer's Comments : Yes

Fees to Publish : 0.00 US$

Invited Articles :

MANUSCRIPT TOPICS : ACCOUNTING THEORY & PRACTICE; ECONOMETRICS;
   INTERNATIONAL & ECONOMIC DEVELOPMENT; INTERNATIONAL FINANCE;
   PUBLIC POLICY ECONOMICS; ALL AREAS OF ECONOMICS, BUSINESS, AND MARKETING

PUBLICATION GUIDELINES : American Psychological Association

MANUSCRIPT GUIDELINES/COMMENTS :

The AFRICAN ECONOMIC AND BUSINESS REVIEW invites submission of original,
scholarly empirical and theoretical articles in all areas of economics and
business. Though the emphasis is on Africa, articles based on any other region
will be considered. Send your manuscript to Dr. Uchenna N. Akpom.

Submit three (3) copies of the manuscript, double-spaced, on standard 8 1/2 x
11 paper. Enclose a submission fee of $20.00 (which includes a one-year
subscription) payable to "African Economic and Business Review."

Since the journal uses the blind-review process, only the title of the article
should appear on the manuscript. The author's name, title, institutional
affiliation, and all other identifying materials should be written on a
separate cover page.

Include an abstract of 150 words or less.

Present all tables, and diagrams, on separate pages and place at the end of
the manuscript following references. Locate placement in text by a phrase such

AFRICAN ECONOMIC AND BUSINESS REVIEW

as "TABLE 1 ABOUT HERE" set off in parentheses from the rest of the text.

All charts and illustrations must be camera-ready, not needing further artwork or typesetting.

Notes should be sequentially numbered in the text. They should all be placed as ENDNOTES in a separate appendix titled "Notes." Notes should be kept to a minimum. Citations or references should not be included in notes.

All source references should be identified at the appropriate point in the text by author and date in parentheses. List all references alphabetically by author in a separate appendix titled, "References," following the format described in THE PUBLICATION MANUAL OF THE AMERICAN PSYCHOLOGICAL ASSOCIATION,3rd. edition. See examples below:

Abootalebi, A R (1995). Democratization in developing countries: 1980-1989. Journal of Developing Areas, 29(4): 507-29.
Ezumah, N.N., and DiDomenico, C.M. (1995). Enhancing the role of women in crop on: A case study of igbo women in Nigeria. World Development, 23(10): 1731-44.
Dinham, B. Agribusiness in Africa. London: Earth Resources Research, 1987.
Kasfir, N. Class, Political domination and the African state. In Z. Ergas (Ed.), The African state in transition (pp. 45-60). London: Macmillan Press, 1987.

AGRICULTURAL ECONOMICS
(J. OF INTL. ASSN. OF AGRI. ECONOMIST)

ADDRESS FOR SUBMISSION :

STANLEY R. JOHNSON, EDITOR-IN-CHIEF
AGRICULTURAL ECONOMICS
  (J. OF INTL. ASSN. OF AGRI. ECONOMIST)
IOWA STATE UNIVERSITY
CENTER FOR AGRICULTURAL AND RURAL
  DEVELOPMENT
578 HEADY HALL
AMES, IA 50011-1070
USA
515-294-6638
515-294-5179 (Fax)
E-Mail : ecbalm@iastate.edu

Change in Editor's Address
  May Occur in : 12/31/97

CIRCULATION DATA :

Reader : Academic

Frequency of Issue : Bi-Monthly

Copies Per Issue :

Subscription Price :

Sponsorship : Profit Oriented Corp. &
              Professional Assoc.

PUBLICATION GUIDELINES :

Manuscript Length :

Copies Required : Three

Computer Submission : Yes

Format : See Guidelines

Fees to Review : 0.00 US$

REVIEW INFORMATION :

Type of Review : Blind Review

No. of External Reviewers : Two

No. of In House Reviewers : One

Acceptance Rate : 11-20%

Time To Review : 2-3 months

Reviewer's Comments : Yes

Fees to Publish : 0.00 US$

Invited Articles : 5% or less

MANUSCRIPT TOPICS : ECONOMETRICS;
  INTERNATIONAL & ECONOMIC DEVELOPMENT; PUBLIC POLICY ECONOMICS;
  AGRICULTURAL ECONOMICS

PUBLICATION GUIDELINES : Chicago Manual of Style

MANUSCRIPT GUIDELINES/COMMENTS :

The Editor and Editorial Board, under the general direction of the IAAE
President, Executive Committee and Council, are charged with implementing
Journal policy to serve members of IAAE around the world.

SUBMISSION OF MANUSCRIPTS
Submission of an article is understood to imply that the article is original
and is not being considered for publication elsewhere. Upon acceptance of the
article to the publisher. This transfer will ensure the widest possible
dissemination of information.

Papers for consideration should be submitted to the Editor-in-Chief.

Book reviews will be included in the journal on a range of relevant books that
are not more than two years old. Book reviews will be solicited by the Book

AGRICULTURAL ECONOMICS
(J. OF INTL. ASSN. OF AGRI. ECONOMIST)

Review Editor. Unsolicited reviews will be included in the journal on a range of relevant books that are not more than two years old. Book reviews will be solicited by the Book Review Editor. Unsolicited reviews will not usually be accepted, but suggestions for appropriate books for review may be sent to the Book Review Editor:

C.L. Delgado
International Food Policy Research Institute
1200 17th Street, N.W., Washington, DC 20036-3006, USA

ELECTRONIC MANUSCRIPTS
Electronic manuscripts have the advantage that there is no need for the rekeying of text, thereby avoiding the possibility of introducing errors and resulting in reliable, and fast delivery of proofs.

For the initial submission of manuscripts for consideration, hard copies are sufficient. For the processing of ACCEPTED PAPERS, electronic versions are preferred. After FINAL ACCEPTANCE, your disk plus three final and exactly matching printed versions should be submitted together. Double density (DD) or high density (HD) diskettes (3.5 or 5.25 inch) are acceptable. It is important that the file seved is in the native format of the word processor program used. Label the disk with the name of the computer and word processing package used, your name, and the name of the file on the disk. Further information may be obtained from the Publisher.

PREPARATION OF MANUSCRIPTS
1. Manuscripts should be written in English. Authors whose native language is not English are strongly advised to have their manuscripts checked by an English-speaking colleague prior to submitting.

Authors in Japan, please note: Upon request, Elsevier Science Japan will provide authors with a list of people who can check and improve the English on their paper (before submission). Please contact our Tokyo office: Elsevier Science Japan, 20-12 Yushima 3-chome, Bunkyo-ku, Tokyo 113; tel. (03)3833-03821; fax (03) 3836-3064.

2. Submit the original of your manuscript plus two copies omitting author names (for the double blind referee process). Enclose the original illustrations and two sets of photocopies (three prints of any photographs).

3. Manuscripts should be typewritten, typed on one side of the paper, with wide margins and double spacing throughout, i.e., also for abstracts, footnotes and references. Every page of the manuscript, including the title page, references, tables, etc. should be numbered in the upper right-hand corner. However, in the text no reference should be made to page numbers, if necessary, one may refer to sections. Underline words that should be in italics, and do not underline any other words. Avoid excessive usage of italics to emphasize part of the text.

4. Manuscripts in general should be organized in the following order:

Title (should be clear, descriptive, and not too long)
Name(s) of author(s)
Affiliation(s)
Present address(es) of author(s)
Complete correspondence address to which the proofs should be sent

AGRICULTURAL ECONOMICS
(J. OF INTL. ASSN. OF AGRI. ECONOMIST)

Any (short) additional information concerning research grants, etc., may be included on the title page under the address(es). If this information is long, please include it in the text, either at the end of the introduction or in a separate acknowledgment section preceding the references.
Abstract
Introduction
Material studies, area descriptions, methods, techniques
Results
Discussion
Conclusion
Acknowledgments
References
Tables
Figure captions

5. In typing the manuscript, titles and subtitles should not be run within the text They should be typed on a separate line, without indentation. Use lower case letter type.

6. SI units should be used.

7. If a special instruction to the copyeditor or typesetter is written on the copy, it should be encircled. The typesetter will then know that the enclosed matter is not to be set in type. When a typewritten character may have more than one meaning (e.g., the lower case letter l may be confused with the numeral 1), a note should be inserted in a circle in the margin to make the meaning clear to the typesetter. If Greek letters or uncommon symbols are used in the manuscript, they should be written very clearly and if necessary a note such as "Greek lowercase chi" should be put in the margin and encircled.

8. Elsevier reserves the privilege of returning accepted manuscripts and illustrations to the author for revision if the manuscripts or illustrations are not in the proper form specified by this guide.

ABSTRACTS
The abstract should be clear, descriptive, and not longer than 400 words.

TABLES
1. Authors should take notice of the limitations set by the size and layout of the journal. Large tables should be avoided. Reversing columns and rows will often reduce the dimensions of a table.

2. If many data are to be presented, an attempt should be made to divide them over two or more tables.

3. Drawn tables from which blocks need to be made should not be folded.

4. Tables should be numbered according to their sequence in the text. The text should include references to all tables.

5. Each table should be typewritten on a separate page of the manuscript Tables should never be included in the text.

6. Each Table should have a brief and self-explanatory title.

AGRICULTURAL ECONOMICS
(J. OF INTL. ASSN. OF AGRI. ECONOMIST)

7. Column headings should be brief, but sufficiently explanatory. Standard abbreviations of units of measurement should be added between parentheses.

8. Vertical lines should not be used to separate columns. Leave some extra space between the columns instead.

9. Any explanation essential to the understanding of the table should be given as a footnote at the bottom of the table.

ILLUSTRATIONS
1. All illustrations (line drawings and photographs) should be submitted separately, unmounted and not folded.

2. Illustrations should be numbered according to their sequence in the text. References should be made in the text to each illustration.

3. Each illustration should be identified on the reverse side (or-in the case of line drawings-on the lower front side) by its number and the name of the author. An indication of the top of the illustrations is required in photographs of profiles, thin sections, and other cases where doubt can arise.

4. Illustrations should be designed with the format of the page of the journal in mind. Illustrations should be of such a size as to allow a reduction of 50%

5. Lettering should be in Indian ink or by printed labels. Make sure that the size of the lettering is big enough to allow a reduction of 50% without becoming illegible. The lettering should be in English. Use the same kind of lettering throughout and follow the style of the journal.

6. If a scale should be given, use bar scales on all illustrations instead of numerical scales that must be changed with reduction.

7. Each illustration should have a caption. The captions to all illustrations should be typed on a separate sheet of the manuscript.

8. Explanations should be given in the typewritten legend. Drawn text in the illustrations should be kept to a minimum.

9. Photographs are only acceptable if they have good contrast and intensity Sharp and glossy copies are required. Reproductions of the photographs already printed cannot be accepted.

10. Color illustrations cannot usually be included, unless the cost of their reproductions is paid for by the author.

REFERENCES
1. All publications cited in the test should be presented in a list of references following the text of the manuscript. The manuscript should be carefully checked to ensure that the spelling of author's names and dates are exactly the same in the text as in the reference list.

2. In the text refer to the author's name (without initial) and year of publication, followed - if necessary - by a short reference to appropriate pages. Examples. "Since Peterson (1993) has shown that..." "This is in agreement with results obtained later (Peterson and Kramer, 1994, pp. 12-16)."

AGRICULTURAL ECONOMICS
(J. OF INTL. ASSN. OF AGRI. ECONOMIST)

3. If reference is made in the text to a publication written by more than two authors the name of the first author should be used followed by "et al." This indication, however, should never be used in the list of references. In the list of references names of first author and coauthors should be mentioned.

4. References cited together in the text should be arranged chronologically. The list of references should be arranged alphabetically on authors' names, and chronologically per author. If an author's name in the list is also mentioned with coauthors the following order should be used: publications of the single author, arranged according to publication dates; publications of the same author with one coauthor; publications of the author with more than one coauthor. Publications by the same author(s) in the same year should be listed as 1994a, 1994b, etc.

5. Use the following system for arranging your references:
a. For periodicals
Arnade, C.A., 1994. Testing two trade models in Latin American agriculture. Agric. Econ., 10: 49-159.
b. For books
Polopolus, L.C. and Alvarez, J., 1991. Marketing sugar and other sweeteners. Developments in Agricultural Economics, 9. Elsevier Amsterdam, 361 pp.
c. For edited symposia
Edwards, F. and Spawton, T., 1991. Pricing in the Australian wine industry: a marketing perspective. In E P. Botos (editor), Vine and Wine Economy. Proc. Int. Symp., 95-29 June 1990, Kecskemet, Hungary. Developments in Agricultural Economics, 8. Elsevier, Amsterdam, pp. 203-212.
d. For multi-author books
Grinnell, G.E., 1992. Economics of Energy in Agriculture. In R.C. Fluck (Editor), Energy in Farm Production. Energy in World Agriculture, 6. Elsevier, Amsterdam, pp. 33-46.
e. For unpublished reports, departmental notes, etc.
Setzinger, A.H. and Paarlberg, P.L., 1990. The export enhancement program: How has it affected wheat exports? Agric. Inf. Bull. 575, U.S. Department of Agriculture, Washington, DC.

6. Do not abbreviate the titles of periodicals mentioned in the list of references; alternatively use the International List of Periodical Title Word Abbreviations.

7. In the case of publications in any language other than English, the original title is to be retained. However, the titles of publications in non-Latin alphabets should be transliterated, and a notation such as "(in Russian)" or "(in Greek with English abstract)" should be added.

8. In referring to a personal communication, the two words are followed by the year, e.g. "J. McNary, personal communication, 1984."

FORMULAE
1. Formulae should be typewritten if possible. Leave ample space around the formulae.

2. Subscripts and superscripts should be clear.

3. Greek letters and other non-Latin or handwritten symbols should be explained in the margin where they are first used. Take special care to show

AGRICULTURAL ECONOMICS
(J. OF INTL. ASSN. OF AGRI. ECONOMIST)

clearly the difference between zero (0) and the letter (O), and between one (1) and the letter (l).

4. Give the meanlng of all symbols immediately after the equation in which they are first used.

5. For simple fractions use the solidus (/) instead of a horizontal line, e.g. $I_p/2_m$ rather than $\frac{I_p}{2_m}$.

6. Equations should be numbered serially at the right-hand side in parentheses. In general only equations explicitly referred to in the text need be numbered.

7. The use of fractional powers instead of root signs is recommended. Also, powers of E are often more conveniently denoted by exp.

8. Levels of statistical significance that can be mentioned without further explanation are $*P < 0.05$, $**P < 0.01$ and $***P < 0.001$.

9. In chemical formulae, valence of ions should be given as, e.g., Ca and CO not as Ca^{++} or CO_3^{--}.

10. Isotope numbers should precede the symbols, e.g., ^{18}O .

11. The repeated writing of chemical formulae in the text is to be avoided where reasonably possible; instead, the name of the compound should be given in full. Exceptions may be made in the case of a very long name occurring very frequently or in the case of a compound being described as the end product of a gravimetric determination (e.g., phosphate as P_2O_5).

FOOTNOTES
1. Footnotes should only be used if absolutely essential. In most cases it will be possible to incorporate the information in normal text.

2. If used, footnotes should be numbered in the text, indicated by superscript numbers) and should be kept as short as possible.

NOMENCLATURE
1. Authors and editors are, by general agreement, obliged to accept the rules governing biological nomenclature, as laid down in the International Code of Botanical Nomeclature of Bacteri, and the International Code of Zoological Nomenclature.

2. All biotica (crops, plants, insects, birds, mammals, etc.) should be identified by their scientific names when the English term is first used, with the exception of common domestic animals.

3. All biocides and other organic compounds must be identified by their Geneva names when first used in the text. Active ingredients of all formulations should be likewise identified.

4. For chemical nomenclature, the conventions of the International Union of Pure and Applied Chemistry and the official recommendations of the IUPAC-IUB Combined Commission of Biochemical Nomenclature should be followed.

AGRICULTURAL ECONOMICS
(J. OF INTL. ASSN. OF AGRI. ECONOMIST)

COPYRIGHT
1. An author, when quoting from someone else's work, or when considering reproducing an illustration or table from a book or journal article, should make sure that such a quote or reproduction does not infringe a copyright.

2. Although in general an author may quote from other published works, the author should obtain permission from the holder of the copyright if the author wishes to make substantial extracts or to reproduce tables, plates, or other illustrations. If the copyright-holder is not the author of the quoted or reproduced material, it is recommended that the permission of the author should also be sought.

3. Material in unpublished letters and manuscripts is also protected and must not be published unless permission has been obtained.

4. A suitable acknowledgment of any borrowed material must always be made.

PROOFS
1. Copyediting of manuscripts is performed by the staff of Elsevier. The author is asked to check the galley proofs for typographical errors and to answer queries from the copyeditor.

2. Elsevier, at its discretion, is entitled to recover from the author of any paper or report published in the journal, any cost occasioned by alterations made by the author in the printer's proofs other than correction of typesetting errors and essential additions that update information in the paper; the latter preferably as sentences at the end of existent paragraphs or as new paragraphs.

OFFPRINTS
1. Fifty offprints will be supplied free of charge.
2. Additional offprints can be ordered on an offprint order form, which is included with the proofs.
3. UNESCO coupons are acceptable in payment of extra offprints.

AGRICULTURAL ECONOMICS HAS NO PAGE CHARGES

AMERICAN ECONOMIC REVIEW

ADDRESS FOR SUBMISSION :

ORLEY ASHENFELTER, EDITOR
AMERICAN ECONOMIC REVIEW
209 NASSAU STREET
PRINCETON, NJ 08542-4607
USA
609-921-0301/0304
609-921-1870 (Fax)

PUBLICATION GUIDELINES :

Manuscript Length :

Copies Required : Four

Computer Submission : No

Format : N/A

Fees to Review : 0.00 US$

CIRCULATION DATA :

Reader : Academic

Frequency of Issue : Quarterly

Copies Per Issue : Over 25,000

Subscription Price :

Sponsorship : Professional Assoc.

REVIEW INFORMATION :

Type of Review : N/A

No. of External Reviewers :

No. of In House Reviewers : One

Acceptance Rate : 6-10%

Time To Review :

Reviewer's Comments : No

Fees to Publish : 0.00 US$

Invited Articles : 5% or less

MANUSCRIPT TOPICS : CAPITAL BUDGETING; COST ACCOUNTING;
 ECONOMETRICS; INSURANCE; INTERNATIONAL & ECONOMIC DEVELOPMENT;
 PUBLIC POLICY ECONOMICS; MARKETING THEORY & APPLICATIONS; ECONOMICS;
 FINANCE & INVESTMENTS; SMALL BUSINESS ENTREPRENEURSHIP;
 STRATEGIC MANAGEMENT POLICY; AS RELATED TO FIELD OF ECONOMICS

PUBLICATION GUIDELINES :

MANUSCRIPT GUIDELINES/COMMENTS :

Type of Review: 50% Blind, 50% Editorial
No. of External Reviewers: Varies
Time to Review: Varies
Invited Articles: None

1. A SUBMISSION FEE must accompany each manuscript. Effective May 1, 1987, the
fee is $50 for members of The American Economic Association, $100 for
nonmembers. (Please pay with a check or money order payable in United States
dollars. Canadian and foreign payments must be in the form of a draft or check
drawn on a United State Bank payable in United States dollars.

2. REPLICATION OF EMPIRICAL MATERIAL: It is the policy of the AMERICAN
ECONOMIC REVIEW to publish papers only where the data used in the analysis are
clearly and precisely documented, are readily available to any researcher for
purposes of replication, and where details of the computations sufficient to
permit replication are provided. The Managing Editor should be notified at the

time of submission if the data used in a paper are proprietary, or if, for some other reason, the above requirements cannot be met.

3. FORMAT: Submit four (4) copies to the above address. Text should be typed on one side of sheet only. DOUBLE SPACE ALL MATERIAL including abstracts, footnotes, and table headings. One-inch margins on both sides are required. (Accepted manuscripts should be typed in final form on good quality bond paper and the ORIGINAL should be submitted to be sent to the printer.) The first page of a paper should contain only three items: title of article, author byline, and the abstract, respectively.

4. TEXTUAL DIVISIONS: The introductory section needs no heading or number; SUBSEQUENT SECTION HEADINGS SHOULD BE GIVEN ROMAN NUMERALS: SUBSECTIONS SHOULD BE LETTERED A,B, ETC.

5. FOOTNOTES should be numbered consecutively, double spaced, beginning on a new page at the end of the manuscript, following references. INITIAL FOOTNOTE GIVING AUTHOR(S) COMPLETE ADDRESS(ES) SHOULD BE MARKED WITH AN ASTERISK.

6. TABLES should be placed on separate pages - not incorporated with text; numbered consecutively with Arabic numerals. Sources of data should be double spaced and placed at the end of the table. (Full citation of the sources is to be included in the references.) Footnotes are also double spaced, following source or notes, keyed by lower case letters ONLY.

7. FIGURES on diagrams should be numbered consecutively with Arabic numerals. Legends, if any, should be typed on a covering sheet of paper. Figures for ACCEPTED manuscripts MUST be in black India ink on heavy white 8-1/2" x 11" paper, with large enough lettering to survive photo reduction (rough drawings may be submitted initially). Typewriter labels are not acceptable.

8. MATHEMATICAL should be typed on separate lines and numbered consecutively at LEFT MARGIN, using Arabic numerals in parentheses. Use Greek letters only when necessary. Ambiguities may arise between capital and lower case letters; zero and o (O); and letters ETA and N; NU and V, the subscript letter "el" and number 1.

9. SYMBOLIC NOTATION: when used, notation should be listed, summarized, and briefly identified in a separate table.

10. USE OF MATHEMATICAL APPENDIX: Authors are encouraged to use an appendix for technical proofs and derivations that can be separated from the main text. The appendix would begin on a new page to follow text and precede references.

11. QUOTATIONS must correspond exactly with the original in wording, spelling, and punctuation. Page numbers must be given. Changes must be indicated: Use brackets to identify insertions; use dots ... to show omissions. Also indicate where emphasis has been added. Quotations beginning or ending in the middle of a sentence should begin or end with dots ... Only quotations of over 50 words should be separated from the text; also double spaced; indented at beginning margin, and page number to be shown in brackets.

12. SPELLING: Authority for spelling, capitalization, and hyphenation of words is WEBSTER'S COLLEGIATE DICTIONARY. Avoid overcapitalization and excessive underlining or italics for emphasis. Use "quotation marks" only for FIRST

occurrence of terms with special meaning. A priori, ex officio, per se, for example, are not underlined, but EX POST, POST HOC, LAISSEZ-FAIRE are, showing they are to italics when printed.

13. REFERENCE TO INDIVIDUALS in the text should include the first name (or initials, if the individual does not use his first name). Subsequent references should be by last name only. Do not refer to individuals as Mister, Doctor, Professor, etc.

14. REFERENCE TO ORGANIZATIONS or governmental agencies should give the name in full, followed by abbreviation in parentheses -- subsequent references should give abbreviation only. For example: Social Research Council (SSRC) ... second usage, SSRC.

15. REFERENCE TO ARTICLES AND BOOKS in the text: Give author(s') full name and year of publication the first time cited, with page number where appropriate. When more that one work by a particular author is cited, give year of publication in parentheses each time cited.

16. REFERENCE SECTION: Double space and begin on a new page following text, giving full information. Authors of articles and books (surname first) are to be listed alphabetically, A to Z -- followed by material without specific authors or editors, such as government documents, bulletins, or newspapers. Note: List these alphabetically by issuing department or title. (Please see sample below.)
    A. BOOKS: List author or editor, title, place of publication, publisher and year.
    B. ARTICLES: List author, Utitle of article", Journal, month and year of issue, vol. in Arabic numerals, inclusive page numbers.

Samples:

Bailey, Martin Neal, "Productivity and the Services of Capital and Labor", Brookings Papers on Economic Activity, 1:1981, 1-50.

Kerr, Clark and Siegel, Abraham, "The Interindustry Propensity to Strike--An International Comparison", in A. Korhauser et al., eds., Industrial Conflict, New York: McGraw Hill, 1954, ch. 15.

Maitland, F.W., _____ Constitutional History of England, Cambridge: Cambridge University Press, 1908.

_____ and Montague, F.C., A Sketch of English Constitutional History, New York: G. P. Putnam's Sons, 1915.

Ostroy, Joseph M., "The Informational Efficiency of Monetary Exchange," American Economic Review, September 1973, 63, 597-610.

Parnes, Herbert S. et al., (1972a) The Pre-retirement Years: A Longitudinal Study of the Labor Market Experience of Men, Vol. 2, Center for Human Resource Research, Ohio State University, 1972.

_____, (1972b) The Pre-retirement Years: A Longitudinal Study of the Labor Market Experience of Men, vol. 3, Center for Human Resource Research, Ohio State University, 1972.

AMERICAN ECONOMIC REVIEW

Van Ypersele de Strihou, Jacques, "Sharing the Defense Burden Among Western
    Allies, "Review of Economics and Statistics", November 1967, 49, 527-36.

California State Personnel Board, Job Specification Sheets, Sacramento,
irregular.

Quarterly Economic Trends, Federal Reserve Bank of St. Louis, March 9, 1973.
    U.S. Department of Commerce, Bureau of Census, Historical Statistics of
    the United States, Part 1, Series D, Washington: USGPO, 1975, 986-1021.

AMERICAN ECONOMIST

ADDRESS FOR SUBMISSION :

MICHAEL SZENBERG, EDITOR-IN-CHIEF
AMERICAN ECONOMIST
PACE UNIVERSITY
LUBIN GRADUATE SCHOOL OF BUSINESS
NEW YORK, NY 10038
USA
212-346-1921
212-346-1573 (Fax)

CIRCULATION DATA :

Reader : Academic

Frequency of Issue : 2 Times/Year

Copies Per Issue : 5001-10,000

Subscription Price : 15.00 US$
    For 3 years : 30.00 US$

Sponsorship : Professional Assoc.

PUBLICATION GUIDELINES :

Manuscript Length : 11-15

Copies Required : Three

Computer Submission : No

Format : N/A

Fees to Review : 0.00 US$

REVIEW INFORMATION :

Type of Review : Blind Review

No. of External Reviewers : Two

No. of In House Reviewers : Two

Acceptance Rate : 11-20%

Time To Review : 4-6 months

Reviewer's Comments : Yes

Fees to Publish : 25.00 US$

Invited Articles : 6-10%

MANUSCRIPT TOPICS : COST ACCOUNTING; ECONOMETRICS; ECONOMIC HISTORY;
    INTERNATIONAL & ECONOMIC DEVELOPMENT; INTERNATIONAL FINANCE;
    PORTFOLIO & SECURITY ANALYSIS; PUBLIC POLICY ECONOMICS

PUBLICATION GUIDELINES : Chicago Manual of Style

MANUSCRIPT GUIDELINES/COMMENTS :

1. Copies. Submit three copies of the manuscript. Recommended length: 10-15
pages. Use white, standard weight 8-1/2" x 11" paper.

2. Double space all material throughout, including footnotes, references, and
quoted matter. Leave 1-inch margin on all sides.

3. Place all references (no more than ten), alphabetized by author, in a
numbered list at the end of the paper in a section titled "References". See
article in this journal for the style to be followed. When you refer in the
text to a publication on this list, insert its number in brackets, including
specific page numbers if necessary. Place it at the end of the sentence or
quoted matter. Example (5, pp. 76089).

4. Number footnotes (no more than fifteen) consecutively throughout the paper,
not page by page. Footnotes should be substantive and typed on separate sheets
following the last page of the article.

AMERICAN ECONOMIST

5. Place tables and figures on separate page. Tables and figures are to be numbered in Arabic. Graphs are considered to be figures.

6. Prepare all figures and graphs on heavy white paper, acetate sheeting, or tracing cloth. Use suitable paper for black-and-white reproduction by a photographic process.

7. Equations should be typed on separate lines and should be identified by consecutive Arabic numbers (in parentheses) at the conclusion of the equation. Use Greek letters only when necessary.

8. Abstract your article to a maximum length of 100 words on a separate page. The abstract are considered for publication in the JOURNAL OF ECONOMIC LITERATURE. The order of the abstract should be:

    Author's surname, followed by initials
    Title of article in English
    Text of abstract
    Name of journal
    Location of author if known, e.g. institution, city, state

Suggested source for style and language usage: MANUAL OF STYLE, University of Chicago Press, 1969.

AMERICAN ENTERPRISE (THE)

ADDRESS FOR SUBMISSION :

SCOTT WALTER, SENIOR EDITOR
AMERICAN ENTERPRISE (THE)
1150 17TH STREET, N.W.
WASHINGTON, DC 200326
USA
202-862-5887
202-862-7178 (Fax)
E-Mail : 75272.1226@compuserve.com

CIRCULATION DATA :

Reader : Business Persons,
         Academic, &
         Government

Frequency of Issue : Bi-Monthly

Copies Per Issue : 3001-4000

Subscription Price : 28.00 US$
  Organization : 49.00 US$

Sponsorship : Non Profit Corp.

PUBLICATION GUIDELINES :

Manuscript Length : 16-20

Copies Required : Three

Computer Submission : No

Format : N/A

Fees to Review : 0.00 US$

REVIEW INFORMATION :

Type of Review : Blind Review

No. of External Reviewers : Two

No. of In House Reviewers : Two

Acceptance Rate : 21-30%

Time To Review : 2-3 months

Reviewer's Comments : No

Fees to Publish : 0.00 US$

Invited Articles : 21-30%

MANUSCRIPT TOPICS : COST ACCOUNTING; PUBLIC POLICY ECONOMICS;
    BUSINESS LAW & PUBLIC RESPONSIBILITY; GOVERNMENT REGULATION OF BUSINESS

PUBLICATION GUIDELINES : Chicago Manual of Style

MANUSCRIPT GUIDELINES/COMMENTS :

We seek articles that are scholarly in content, but written to be accessible
to a more general readership.

AMERICAN JOURNAL OF AGRICULTURAL ECONOMICS

ADDRESS FOR SUBMISSION :

MICHAEL K. WOHLGENANT, EDITORS
AMERICAN JOURNAL OF AGRICULTURAL
  ECONOMICS
NORTH CAROLINA STATE UNIVERSITY
DEPT. OF AGRICULTURAL & RESOURCE ECON.
RALEIGH, NC 27695-8109
USA
919-515-4673
919-515-1794 (Fax)
E-Mail : sclarke@iastate.edu

CIRCULATION DATA :

Reader : Academic

Frequency of Issue : 5 Times/Year

Copies Per Issue : 5001-10,000

Subscription Price : 90.00 US$

Sponsorship : Professional Assoc.

PUBLICATION GUIDELINES :

Manuscript Length : Less than 30

Copies Required : Four

Computer Submission : No

Format : N/A

Fees to Review : 0.00 US$

REVIEW INFORMATION :

Type of Review : Blind Review

No. of External Reviewers : Two

No. of In House Reviewers : One

Acceptance Rate : 21-30%

Time To Review : 2-3 months

Reviewer's Comments : Yes

Fees to Publish : 0.00 US$

Invited Articles : 11-20%

MANUSCRIPT TOPICS : COST ACCOUNTING;
  INTERNATIONAL & ECONOMIC DEVELOPMENT; PUBLIC POLICY ECONOMICS; ECONOMICS;
  AGRICULTURAL ECONOMICS

PUBLICATION GUIDELINES : Chicago Manual of Style

MANUSCRIPT GUIDELINES/COMMENTS :

SUBMITTING FOR CONSIDERATION AND REVIEW
1. COVER LETTER. In a cover letter, the author(s) must state (a) that the
material in the manuscript has not been published, is not being published or
considered for publication elsewhere, and will not be submitted for
publication elsewhere unless rejected by the Journal editor or withdrawn by
the author(s); (b) that the material in the manuscript, so far as the
author(s) knows, does not infringe upon other published material covered by
copyright; (c) that the author's (s') employer, if any, either does not assert
an ownership interest in the manuscript or is willing to convey such interest
to the American Agricultural Economics Association (AAEA); and (d) that
submission of the manuscript gives the AAEA exclusive right to publish, to
copyright, and to allow or deny reproduction of it, in whole or in part. If
the applicability of point (a) is unclear, the author(s) must explain.

2. AUTHOR'S IDENTIFICATION. To protect their anonymity in the review process,
authors should not identify themselves in the manuscript. Attach a separate
page that includes names of the author(s) and appropriate biographical
information, as well as the title of the manuscript. Include only the title on

the first page of the text.

3. TEXT PREPARATION. Double-space all material, including footnotes, tables, and references, on 8-1/2-by-11 inch standard weight white paper with 1-1/4 inch margins. Use 12 point Times or a similar type style and size. (Also see electronic preparation guidelines below.) The A JAE does not ordinarily consider for publication any manuscript exceeding thirty double-spaced pages, including footnotes, tables, figures, and references. In addition, model documentation and other supporting materials may be submitted with the manuscript to facilitate the review process.

4. STYLE. Follow A MANUAL OF STYLE by the University of Chicago Press, as well as previous issues of A JAE.

5. DATA AND DOCUMENTATION. Authors are expected to document their data sources, models, and estimation procedures as thoroughly as possible, and to make data used in their analyses available to other researchers for replication purposes. If, for legal or proprietary reasons, the data cannot be made available to all potential users, this limitation should be noted.

6. MATHEMATICAL NOTATION. Use only essential mathematical notation. Mathematical notation is costly to typeset and may limit the readership. Avoid using the same character for both superscripts and subscripts or using capital letters for such, and avoid overbars, tildes, carets, and other modifications of standard type. Asterisks, primes, and small English letter superscripts are suitable. (See guidelines below for math typesetting.)

7. FOOTNOTES. Number footnotes consecutively throughout the paper, not page by page. Type all footnotes, double-spaced, on a separate page following the article. Footnotes should be only explanatory and not for citations or for directing the reader to a particular work. Such information can be incorporated into the text. A first unnumbered footnote should include names, titles, and institutions of affiliation for each author, and any miscellaneous information pertaining to the published work.

8. REFERENCES AND CITATIONS. Place "References," alphabetized by author, in a list at the end of the paper. Only cited works may be included in the reference list. AJAE article information should include month as well as year of publication; e.g., Amer. J. Agr. Econ. 73(May 1991):345 60. All citations should appear in the text and contain the author's name and page numbers when necessary. Citations can be inserted parenthetically; e.g. (Doe, p. 5). Specify the date of publication if the same author appears more than once in the reference list; e.g. (Doe 1971, p. 5). If the author's name appears as part of a sentence, a parenthetical reference is unnecessary unless page numbers or a date are needed. Use "et al." only with four or more authors. Do not use "et al." in the reference section. A reference/citation style sheet is available from the technical editor.

9. TABLES. Place each table on a separate page; double-space all material; omit vertical rules.

10. FIGURES. Send high-resolution (1200 dpi or higher) hard copy originals of figures. Each figure should be placed on a separate page, and each must have a title.

AMERICAN JOURNAL OF AGRICULTURAL ECONOMICS

11. FOUR COPIES. Send four fully legible copies to the editor. All copies should be inspected for completeness and quality of reproduction.

12. ABSTRACT. Instructions for the preparation of an abstract will be sent when a manuscript is accepted for publication.

13. PAGE CHARGE. Major support for this journal comes from page charges of $65 per printed page or a fraction thereof, payable by the supporting institution or granting agency. Payment does not affect acceptance, scheduling, or form of publication. Instructions for payment are sent with galley proofs.

ELECTRONIC PREPARATION OF MANUSCRIPTS FOR PUBLICATION
1. WORD PROCESSING. Text should be submitted in popular word-processing formats for ease of translation. A JAE prefers Microsoft Word 5 (Macintosh or PC). We cannot accommodate TeX-based manuscripts at this time.

2. FORMATTING. Do use character formatting - i.e., formatting you can do on single characters or words (bold for vectors and matrices, italic for variables, superscript, subscript), but do not use your processor's other special features (auto footnote placement, table editors, etc.) Tables are most translatable when created manually with tabs, rather than formatted with a table editor.

3. MATH TYPESETTING. If possible, use Symbol font for the mathematical notation in the manuscript. Refrain from use of embellished letters (dots, bars, tildes, carets). Run equations into text if at all possible (rather than displaying). Simplify notation to avoid costly typesetting; e.g. a stacked fraction is preferably changed to a one-line form (such as a = bx/n). For more complex mathematical notation, the journal prefers use of the Microsoft Word Equation Editor or Math Type. Other methods of math typesetting may be used, but will be reset by AJAE for publication, and thus must be carefully proofread.

4. FIGURES. Figures must be presented in hard copy form at a high resolution (1200 dpi or higher). Figures will be scanned for electronic placement in the layout.

EDITOR: Michael K. Wohlgenant

BOOK REVIEW EDITOR: Jim Hite, Department of Agricultural Economics, clemson university, 225 Barre Hall, Clemson, SC 29634. Tel: 803-656-3374, Fax: 803-656-4780.

TECHNICAL EDITOR: Sandra Clarke, 1110 Buckeye Avenue, Ames, Iowa 50010-8063. Tel: 515-223-3234, Fax: 515-223-3101.

AMERICAN JOURNAL OF ECONOMICS AND SOCIOLOGY

ADDRESS FOR SUBMISSION :

DR. FRANK GENOVESE, EDITOR
AMERICAN JOURNAL OF ECONOMICS
  AND SOCIOLOGY
BABSON COLLEGE
BABSON PARK, MA 02157-0310
USA
617-239-4339
617-239-6465 (Fax)
E-Mail : GENOVESE@BABSON.EDU

CIRCULATION DATA :

Reader : Academic

Frequency of Issue : Quarterly

Copies Per Issue : 2001-3000

Subscription Price : 25.00 US$
  For 2 years : 45.00 US$

Sponsorship : Non Profit Corp.

PUBLICATION GUIDELINES :

Manuscript Length : 25

Copies Required : Four

Computer Submission : Yes

Format : Prefer MS DOS/final copy

Fees to Review : 0.00 US$

REVIEW INFORMATION :

Type of Review : N/A

No. of External Reviewers :

No. of In House Reviewers : Two

Acceptance Rate : 21-30%

Time To Review : 2-3 months

Reviewer's Comments : Yes

Fees to Publish : 0.00 US$

Invited Articles : 5% or less

MANUSCRIPT TOPICS : COST ACCOUNTING; ECONOMIC HISTORY;
  INTERNATIONAL & ECONOMIC DEVELOPMENT; PUBLIC POLICY ECONOMICS; REAL ESTATE;
  RESOURCE USE & TAXATION; INCOME & WEALTH DISTRIBUTION; FREE TRADE

PUBLICATION GUIDELINES : Modern Language Association (MLA Style Manual)

MANUSCRIPT GUIDELINES/COMMENTS :

If possible, send final edited copy of manuscript in ASCII on MS DOS disk.
Reviewer's comments are sent blind to authors.

1. A group of specialists in the social sciences and in moral and social
philosophy, in association with men of affairs, founded the Journal to
encourage interdisciplinary research by providing for its publication. The
four philosophers, four economists, and four sociologists in the group sought
to further the useful recognition by scientists and scholars of their social
responsibilities for human betterment. It is a venture in cooperation between
the social sciences and related disciplines towards constructive synthesis in
social thought. It provides an ample voice to many specialists who are trying
to cope with the challenge that modern society presents to them.

As a scientific journal it sets no ideological standards for collaborators or
contributors. It embraces the widest freedom consistent with scientific
integrity as defined by the American Professional Learned Societies in the
fields it covers.

AMERICAN JOURNAL OF ECONOMICS
AND SOCIOLOGY

2. Contents consists of articles (under 5000 words); notes (preferably under 3000 words); comments (preferably under 1000 words); book reviews (under 1000 words); book notices and comment on significant periodical and pamphlet literature (up to 200 words); and brief announcements and commentary on meetings and matters of significance to the academic and research communities.

3. Succinct and clear presentation should be sought. Many readers will not be specialists in the authors' fields. Quotations should be sparse and short. When, in the rare case, they exceed 100 words the publisher's permission must be obtained and acknowledged. The seeking and consideration of suggestions from colleagues regarding manuscripts before their submission are advised. An unnecessary plethora of citations impedes reading.

4. The MLA STYLE MANUAL published by the Modern Language Association, 10 Astor Place, New York, NY 10003, is followed with the following exceptions:

    1. All copy except for tabular material) should be double-spaced with generous margins. Notes should be signalled by superscripted numbers (and appear in paragraph form with the first line indented) at the end of the text. The call number will not be superscripted in this position.
    2. The 2nd Edition of the MERRIAM-WEBSTER DICTIONARY is the standard for spelling.
    3. Bibliographic notes should be in the form (place, publisher, date). Names of journals cited should be spelled out as an aid to non-U.S. readers.
    4. Periodical volume numbers should be in Arabic numerals.

5. Photographic reproduction requires the careful preparation of figures and tables, (one to a page at the end of the manuscript). A notation in the text should show their desirable approximate printed positioning.

6. The author(s) must assign all ownership rights (on a form it will provide) to the non-profit corporate publishers. The author(s) will be given the right to make any further use of the material without fee to the corporation. The copyright clearance center controls copying. Its fees are applied to the Journal's deficit.

7. No payment is made for contributions. Two copies of the Journal and 50 reprints of articles are provided. Manuscripts submitted should be for sole consideration by this one journal. Manuscripts are evaluated for their suitability as soon as possible.

8. A single page abstract of less than 150 words should set forth the findings and conclusions.

9. Articles submitted should be well-documented, the data used easily available to any researcher for replication, and the manner of computation sufficiently well-explained to permit such replication unless these conditions are modified in writing by the Editor-in-Chief.

10. Authors of accepted articles are charged a fee equal to the annual individual subscription price and will receive a year's subscription to the Journal.

ANNALS OF REGIONAL SCIENCE

ADDRESS FOR SUBMISSION :

T. J. KIM, CO-EDITOR
ANNALS OF REGIONAL SCIENCE
UNIVERSITY OF ILLINOIS, URBANA-CHAMPAIGN
DEPARTMENT OF URBAN AND REGIONAL
  PLANNING
611 EAST LORADO TAFT DRIVE
CHAMPAIGN, IL 61820
USA

PUBLICATION GUIDELINES :

Manuscript Length :
Copies Required : Three
Computer Submission : Yes
Format : After Acceptance
Fees to Review : 0.00 US$

REVIEW INFORMATION :

CIRCULATION DATA :

Reader : Academic

Frequency of Issue : Quarterly

Copies Per Issue : Less than 1000

Subscription Price : 301.00 US$

Sponsorship : University

Type of Review : Editorial Review
No. of External Reviewers : Three
No. of In House Reviewers : Two
Acceptance Rate : 21-30%
Time To Review : 2-3 months
Reviewer's Comments : Yes
Fees to Publish : 0.00 US$
Invited Articles : 5% or less

MANUSCRIPT TOPICS : ECONOMETRICS;
  INTERNATIONAL & ECONOMIC DEVELOPMENT; PUBLIC POLICY ECONOMICS

PUBLICATION GUIDELINES :

MANUSCRIPT GUIDELINES/COMMENTS :

EDITORS
B. Johansson, Regional Planning, Royal Institute of Technology, S-10044
Stockholm, Sweden.

T. J. Kim, Department of Urban and Regional Planning, University of Illinois-
Urbana-Champaign, 611 East Lorado Taft Drive, Champaign, IL 61820, USA.

R. R. Stough, The Center for Regional Analysis, The Institute of Public
Policy, George Mason University, Fairfax, VA 22030-4444, USA.

BOOK REVIEW EDITOR
W.P. Anderson, Department of Geography, 1280 Main Street West, McMaster
University, Hamilton, Ontario, Canada L8S 5K1.

PURPOSE
This journal is a quarterly in the interdisciplinary field of regional and
urban studies. Its purpose is to promite high quality scholarship on the
importantant theoretical and empirical issues in regional science. The journal
publishes papers which ake a new or substantial contribution to the body of

knowledge in which the spatial dimension plays a fundamental role, such as regional economics, resource management, location theory, urban and regional planning, transportation and ocmmunication, human geography, population distribution, and environmental quality.

INSTRUCTIONS FOR AUTHORS

1. SUBMITTED MANUSCRIPTS should make a new or substantial contribution to the body of knowledge. Policy-oriented articles should meet the test of feasibility and effectiveness of the proposed measures. Commissioned articles should focus on technical insights or important lessons to be learned from a specific body of research.

2. Please submit one original manuscript typed on one side of the sheet only plus two copies photocopies on both sides to keep postage charges to a minimum. In order to reduce mailing costs, rejected manuscripts will not normally be returned. Simultaneous submission to other journals is not permissible, nor should the paper have been accepted or published elsewhere.

3. MANUSCRIPTS should be typewritten on one side of the paper only, doublespaced with wide margins. All pages should be numbered consecutively. Titles and subtitles should be short. References, tables and legends for figures should be typed on separate pages.

4. The FIRST PAGE of the manuscript should contain: (i) the title; (ii) the name(s), institutional affiliation(s) and address(es) of the author(s); (iii) an abstract of not more than 15 lines. A footnote on the same sheet should give the name and present address of the author to whom proofs should be addressed. To facilitate communication between the authors, editors and publisher, the author should furnish a telex or fax number on the title page of the manuscript.

5. ACKNOWLEDGEMENTS and information on grants received can be given in a first footnote, which should not be included in the consecutive numbering of footnotes.

6. IMPORTANT FORMULAE (displayed) should be numbered consecutively throughout the manuscript as (1), (2), etc. on the right-hand side of the page.

7. FOOTNOTES should be kept to a minimum and be numbered consecutively throughout the text with superscript arabic numerals.

8. The list of REFERENCES should include only publications cited in the text. The references should be cited in alphabetical order under the first author's name. Citations in the text should be by author and year.

JOURNAL PAPERS: 1. names and initials of all authors; 2. year of publication in parentheses; 3. full title of cited paper; 4. full title of journal;

ANNALS OF REGIONAL SCIENCE

5. arabic volume numbers; 6. first and last page numbers, e.g.:
Ermisch J (1990) European women's employment and fertility again. J Popul Econ
3:3-18.

BOOKS: 1. Names and initials of all authors; 2. year of publication in
parentheses; 3. full title; 4. edition; 5. publisher; 6. place of publication,
e.g.:
Verbon H (1988) The evolution of public pension schemes. Springer, Berlin
Heidelberg New York.

9. FIGURES are to be numbered consecutively and should be submitted
separately. For line drawings, good-quality glossy prints in the desired final
size are preferred. Computer printouts are acceptable, provided they are
legible and reproducible.

10. TABLES are to be numbered separately from the illustrations. Each table
should have a short title.

Authors using COMMON WORD-PROCESSING SYSTEMS are requested to follow the
Technical Instructions printed in this issue.

Authors preparing their papers with TEX are encouraged to ask for Springer-
Verlag's TEX macropackages, called PJour 1 g (plain-TEX) and LJour 1 (LATEX),
either by letter to Springer-Verlag or by e-mail to svserv@vax.ntp.springer.de
- Springer-Verlag's e-mail server address. This message must contain one
(several) of the following commands
for PJour 1 g: get /tex/plain/pjourlg.zip
for LJour 1:   get /tex/latex/1jour1.zip

Authors who wish to submit disks to the editor should do do only after the
manuscript has been accepted for publicaiton. They must then include any macro
definitions they have used together with a printout for reference. It is
important to ensure that the text is identical in the hard copy and in the
soft copy. Authors who have written their papers in TEX but have not, for
whatever reasons, used Springer-Verlag's macros should likewise send in a disk
and corresponding copy. Springer-Verlag will then decide on a case-by-case
basis whether it makes sense economically to work from the TEX files.

11. PAGE PROOFS will be sent to the author(s). Corrections should be limited
to printer's errors, since the costs involved in making in any other
alterations are substantial and may be charged to the author. When returning
proofs, the author(s) must agree to transfer copyright of the manuscript to
the publisher. Fifty (50) reprints of each paper will be supplied free of
charge. Additional reprints can be ordered at cost price when the proofs are
returned.

COPYRIGHT. Submission of a manuscript implies: that the work described has not
been published before (except in the form of an abstract or as part of a
published lecture, review, or thesis); that it is not under consideration for
publication elsewhere; that its publication has been approved by all
coauthors, if any, as well as by the responsible authorities at the institute
where the work has been carried out: that, if and when the manuscript is
accepted for publication, the authors agree to automatic transfer of the
copyright to the publisher; and that the manuscript will not be published
elsewhere in any language without the consent of the copyright holders.

ANNALS OF REGIONAL SCIENCE

APPLICATION OF FUZZY LOGIC AND THE THEORY OF EVIDENCE IN ACCOUNTING

ADDRESS FOR SUBMISSION :

PHILIP H. SIEGEL, EDITOR
APPLICATION OF FUZZY LOGIC AND THE
  THEORY OF EVIDENCE IN ACCOUNTING
MONMOUTH UNIVERSITY
SCHOOL OF BUSINESS
DEPARTMENT OF ACCOUNTING/BUSINESS LAW
WEST LONG BRANCH, NJ 07764-1898
USA
732-571-7523
732-263-5290 (Fax)
E-Mail : psiegel@mondec.monmouth.edu

PUBLICATION GUIDELINES :

Manuscript Length : 21-25
Copies Required : Three
Computer Submission : No
Format : N/A
Fees to Review : 45.00 US$

REVIEW INFORMATION :

Type of Review : Blind Review
No. of External Reviewers : Two
No. of In House Reviewers : One
Acceptance Rate : 21-30%
Time To Review : 4-6 months
Reviewer's Comments : Yes
Fees to Publish : 0.00 US$
Invited Articles : 5% or less

CIRCULATION DATA :

Reader : Academic
Frequency of Issue : 1 Times/Year
Copies Per Issue : 1001-2000
Subscription Price : 45.00 US$
  Institution : 75.00 US$
Sponsorship : University

MANUSCRIPT TOPICS : ACCOUNTING INFORMATION SYSTEMS;
  ACCOUNTING THEORY & PRACTICE; AUDITING; CAPITAL BUDGETING; COST ACCOUNTING;
  PORTFOLIO & SECURITY ANALYSIS; TAX ACCOUNTING

PUBLICATION GUIDELINES : American Psychological Association

MANUSCRIPT GUIDELINES/COMMENTS :

AUTHOR'S RESPONSIBILITIES
The author is responsible for correct spelling and punctuation, accurate
quotations with page numbers, complete and accurate references, relevant
content, coherent organization, legible appearance, and so forth. The author
must proofread the manuscript after it is typed, making all corrections and
changes before submitting the manuscript. Before submitting the manuscript to
the editor please use the checklist on last page of pamphlet to be sure all
necessary material is included.

The author is also responsible for preparing the manuscript on a computer.
Just as word processing eliminates a good amount of retyping, submitting a
disk provides an opportunity to eliminate duplicate keyboarding by the
typesetter. One key to success is COMPATIBILITY. Therefore, the following
steps should be followed closely.

1. Use a word processing program that is able to create an IBM compatible
file. For technical material (math, etc.) Macintosh files are acceptable.
(Macintosh files should be submitted on HIGH DENSITY disks only.)

APPLICATION OF FUZZY LOGIC AND THE
THEORY OF EVIDENCE IN ACCOUNTING

2. Use either 5 1/4 or 3 1/2 inch, double (low) density or high density disks. NOTE: If you use double (low) density disks, be sure that the disk is formatted for double (low) density. If you use high density, be sure that the disk is formatted for high density. Unformatted or incorrectly formatted disks are unusable.

3. Structure the manuscript according to the Guidelines. Print one (1) copy of the manuscript for copy editing/styling purposes. Be sure to DOUBLE-SPACE this copy. That includes the notes and references.

4. Keep each chapter on one (1) file if possible. Do not make separate files for text, notes, and references. Tables may go in a separate file. A single file should contain no more than 200,000 characters. Please do not store in subdirectories.

5. DO NOT use a footnote feature. All notes should be typed in a separate section at the end of the chapter.

6. Eliminate manuscript page numbers and identifying abbreviated title from disk AFTER the chapter has been printed out.

7. Submit the word processing file with your printed copy. Please indicate on the disk which word processing program and version you have used (e.g., WordPerfect 4.0, 5.1, 6.0; Word Star; WordPerfect for Windows 5.1, 6.0; Microsoft Word for Windows, etc.).

8. If using a graphics program (for art only), please put in a SEPARATE file in either: .tiff
            eps image (encapsulated post script)
            .ps (post script)
Please DO NOT include tables in the graphics program.

9. PLEASE be sure that the manuscript and disk submitted match. If the material on the disk has been updated, please print out a new copy of the manuscript to be sure you are submitting the correct version.

VOLUME EDITOR'S RESPONSIBILITY
The volume editor is responsible for reviewing all printed manuscripts and disks before submission for publication.

Printed manuscripts should be checked for original artwork, tables, and, where necessary, letters of permission to reprint.

GENERAL INSTRUCTIONS

PAPER
Type or print the manuscript on one side of standard-sized (8 1/2 x 11"), or European equivalent, paper. Do not use onionskin or erasable paper. All pages must be of the same size. Do not use half sheets or strips of paper glued, taped, or stapled to the pages.

TYPE ELEMENT
The type must be dark, clear, and readable. A typeface that is made up of dots, as generated by some printers, is acceptable only if it is clear and legible.

APPLICATION OF FUZZY LOGIC AND THE THEORY OF EVIDENCE IN ACCOUNTING

DOUBLE SPACING
Double space between all lines of the manuscript, which includes the title, headings, notes, quotations, and references, figure captions. Never use single-spacing or one-and-a-half line spacing except on tables.

MARGINS
Leave uniform margins of 1 1/2" at the top, bottom, right, and left of every page. The length of each typed line is 5 1/2". Do not justify lines; leave the right margin uneven. Do not hyphenate words at the end of a line; let a line run short or long rather than break a word. Type no more than 25 lines of text on a manuscript page.

HEADINGS
Most manuscripts use from one to four headings. The four levels should appear as:

CENTERED ALL UPPERCASE HEADING

Centered Uppercase and Lowercase Heading

Flush Left, Underlined, Uppercase and Lowercase Side Heading

Indented, underlined, lowercase paragraph heading ending with a period.

PARAGRAPHS AND INDENTATION
Indent the first line of every paragraph and the first line of every note five spaces. Type the remaining lines of the manuscript to a uniform left-hand margin.

QUOTATIONS
Direct quotations must be accurate. Quotations of 40 words or less should be incorporated into the text and enclosed by double quotation marks ("). Display quotations of more than 40 words should appear as a double-spaced block with no quotation marks. Do not single-space. Indent 5 spaces from the left margin and 5 spaces from the right margin.

PERMISSION TO QUOTE
Any direct quotation, regardless of length must be accompanied by a reference citation that includes the author, year of publication, and page number(s). If you quote at length from a copyrighted work, you will also need written permission from the owner of the copyright. It is the author's responsibility to obtain the reprint permission. A copy of the letter of permission must accompany the manuscript.

STATISTICAL AND MATHEMATICAL COPY
Type all signs and symbols in mathematical copy that you can. Either type a character that resembles the symbol or draw the symbol in by hand. Identify symbols that may be hard to read or ambiguous to the copy editor or typesetter. The first time the ambiguous symbol appears in the manuscript, spell out and circle the name next to the symbol. Space mathematical copy as you would space words. Align signs and symbols carefully. Type subscripts half a line below the symbol and superscripts half a line above the symbol. Display a mathematical equation by setting it off from the text by double-spacing twice above and below the equation. If the equation is identified by a number, type the number in parentheses flush against the right margin. Do not

APPLICATION OF FUZZY LOGIC AND THE
THEORY OF EVIDENCE IN ACCOUNTING

underline: (1) greek letters, subscripts, and superscripts that function as identifiers, and (2) abbreviations that are not variables. Mark symbols for vectors with a wavy line to indicate bold typeface. Underline all other statistical symbols.

PARTS OF A MANUSCRIPT

Order of manuscript pages: Number all pages consecutively. Arrange the pages of the manuscript as follows:

> title page (page 1)
> abstract (page 2)
> text (page 3)
> appendices (start each on a separate page)
> author acknowledgment
> notes (start on a new page)
> references (start on a new page)
> tables (start each on a separate page)
> figures (start each on a separate page)

This arrangement is not the way the printed paper will appear; it is necessary for handling by the copy editor and the typesetter.

After the manuscript pages are arranged in the correct order, number them consecutively, beginning with the title page. Number all pages. Type the number in the upper right-hand corner using arabic numbers. Identify each manuscript page by typing an abbreviated title above the page number.

TITLE PAGE

The title page includes 4 elements:

* The title in uppercase (capital) letters.
* The author(s) in uppercase and lowercase letters.
* An abbreviated title to be used as a running head. The running head should be a maximum of 70 characters, which includes all letters, punctuation, and spaces between words.
* Complete mailing address, phone, and fax numbers of each author.

ABSTRACT
Begin the abstract on a new page. Type the word "ABSTRACT" in all uppercase letters, centered at top of page. Type the abstract itself as a single paragraph, double-spaced, indent 5 spaces from the left margin and 5 spaces from the right margin.

TEXT
Begin the text on a new page. The sections of the text follow each other without a break.

APPENDICES
Begin each Appendix on a separate page. Type the word "APPENDIX" in all uppercase letters and identifying capital letters in the order in which they are mentioned in text, centered at the top of the page. If there is only one Appendix, it is not necessary to use an identifying letter.

APPLICATION OF FUZZY LOGIC AND THE
THEORY OF EVIDENCE IN ACCOUNTING

AUTHOR ACKNOWLEDGMENT
This note is neither numbered nor is it mentioned in text. In all uppercase
letters, type the word "ACKNOWLEDGMENT" centered at top of a new page. Type
the acknowledgment itself as a double-spaced single paragraph.

NOTES
Notes that are mentioned in text are numbered consecutively throughout the
chapter. Double-space the notes and begin on a separate page. Center the word
"NOTES" in all uppercase letters at the top of the page. Indent the first line
of each note 5 spaces and type the notes in the order in which they are
mentioned in text.

REFERENCES
Each series has its own individual style, whether it be APA, ASA, reference
notes, or a style unique to its discipline. For the style that you must
follow, consult the PUBLICATION MANUAL OF THE AMERICAN PSYCHOLOGICAL
ASSOCIATION (Fourth Edition), THE CHICAGO MANUAL OF STYLE (14th Edition), or a
previously published volume in the series.

References cited in text MUST appear in the reference list; conversely, each
entry in the reference list must be cited in text. It is the author's
responsibility to make certain that each source referenced appears in both
places and that the text citation and reference list are identical.

IMPORTANT: (1) Foreign language volumes, parts, numbers, editions, and so on
MUST be translated into their English equivalents. Both the original language
and the English translation will appear in the references. Authors MUST
transliterate or romanize languages that do not use Latin characters (e.g.,
Greek, Russian, Chinese, Arabic, etc.), along with their English translation.
A comprehensive resource for this is a publication issued by the Library of
Congress, titled ALA-LC ROMANIZATION TABLES: TRANSLITERATION SCHEMES FOR
NON-ROMAN SCRIPTS. (2) JAI Press does not use either op. cit. or loc. cit. A
short-title form is required. Ibid. is acceptable.

Items to be included in a full reference are:

BOOK:
    Author's full name
    Complete title of the book
    Editor, compiler, or translator, if any
    Series, if any, and volume or number in series
    Edition, if not the original
    Number of volumes
    Facts of publication: city where published, publisher, date of publication
    Volume number, if any
    Page number(s) of the particular citation

ARTICLE IN A PERIODICAL:
    Author's full name
    Title of the article
    Name of the periodical
    Volume (and number) of the periodical
    Date of the volume or issue
    Page number(s) of the particular citation

APPLICATION OF FUZZY LOGIC AND THE
THEORY OF EVIDENCE IN ACCOUNTING

UNPUBLISHED MATERIAL:
    Title of document, if any, and date
    Folio number or other identifying material
    Name of collection
    Depository and city where it is located

TABLES
Tables are numbered consecutively in the order in which they are first
mentioned in text and are identified by the word "Table" and an arabic
numeral. Begin each table on a separate page. Type the short title of the
manuscript and the page number in the upper right-hand corner of every page of
a table. Tables are complicated to set in type and more expensive to publish
than text. Therefore, they should be reserved for important data directly
related to the content of the paper. Refer to every table and its data in
text. Do not write "the table above/below" or "the table on p. 32" because the
position and page number of a table cannot be determined until the text is
typeset. In text, indicate the approximate placement of each table by a clear
break in the text, inserting:

TABLE 1 ABOUT HERE

set off double-spaced above and below. Do not abbreviate table headings. Limit
the use of rules to horizontal rules only. Draw all rules in pencil.

FIGURES
Figures are also numbered consecutively in the order in which they are first
mentioned in text. Use the word "Figure" and an arabic numeral. Indicate the
location of each figure by a clear break, inserting:

INSERT FIGURE 1 ABOUT HERE

set off double-spaced above and below.

All figures, charts, illustrations, and halftones are figures and must be
submitted in a form suitable for reproduction by the printer without redrawing
or retouching. Careful adherence to the following instructions will ensure the
high quality appearance of your paper.

1. All figures must be submitted as either camera-ready original ink drawings
or laser quality copy.

2. All lettering must be done professionally. Three methods of lettering are
acceptable: professional lettering, stencil, or dry-transfer sheets. Freehand
and typewritten lettering is not acceptable. It is best not to use all capital
lettering. Lettering should be large enough so that it is completely legible
after photo reduction. Lettering in all figures should be the same size.

3. When planning a figure, take into consideration that all published figures
must fit the dimensions of a book page. Figures should be no larger than 4 x
6" If a figure exceeds this size, it should be large enough and sharp enough
to be legible when reduced to fit the page. Please remember that reducing the
width of a figure will reduce the length by the same percentage.

4. Graphs and charts: Keep lines clean and simple and eliminate all extraneous
detail. Graph paper should never be used.

APPLICATION OF FUZZY LOGIC AND THE
THEORY OF EVIDENCE IN ACCOUNTING

5. Illustrations: Illustrations should be prepared by a professional artist. The least amount of detail necessary should be used.

6. Halftones: Original photos of professional quality are a necessity. Place overlays on all halftones to prevent scratches and damage from handling. Please keep in mind that halftones require a complicated printing process, which makes them more expensive than line drawings to reproduce.

> IMPORTANT: Color halftones are very costly to print. If color halftones are submitted, they will be printed in black and white. If any halftones must be printed in color, the cost will be charged to the author.

7. Unlike the figure, which is reproduced from the glossy print, the figure number and legend is typeset and placed outside the figure. Therefore, type all figure numbers and legends double-spaced on a separate page.

8. When enclosing a figure in a box, do not include figure caption within the box. The figure number and captions are set separately.

9. For identification by the production editor and printer, please indicate on the back of each photo the author, title of paper, number and figure legend. All information should be written lightly in soft pencil, using as little pressure as possible. "Top" should be written on any illustration that might accidentally be reproduced wrong side up.

10. Staples, of course, should never be used on any illustration copy, nor should paper clips unless they are well padded with several thicknesses of paper to prevent scratching and indentation. Scotch tape should never be used to attach illustration copy to another page as tape edges show up as black lines in reproduction.

11. Prints should never be folded. They should be put in a separate envelope and protected by a sheet or sheets of stiff cardboard.

12. The author is responsible for obtaining permission to reproduce a figure from a copyrighted source. A photocopy of the permission must be submitted with the manuscript.

13. We will naturally assume that the print(s) have been thoroughly checked for accuracy before submission to JAI Press.

14. All prints will be considered final and no corrections will be allowed.

15. Unless otherwise indicated, prints will not be returned to the author.

MANUSCRIPT CHECKLIST

__ Is the manuscript typed on 8 1/2 X 11" paper?

__ Is the entire manuscript-including quotations, references, notes, figure captions, and all parts of tables- double-spaced?

__ Is the manuscript neatly prepared and clean?

__ Are the margins 1 1/2 inch?

APPLICATION OF FUZZY LOGIC AND THE
THEORY OF EVIDENCE IN ACCOUNTING

_ Are the title page, abstract, notes, references, tables, and figures on separate pages?

_ Are all pages numbered in sequence, starting with the title page?

_ Are all headings of the same level typed in the same format?

_ Are Greek letters and all but the most common mathematical symbols indentified?

_ Are all non-Greek letters that are used as statistical symbols or algebraic variables underlined?

_ Are all notes indicated in text and are the note numbers correctly located?

_ Are references cited both in text and in the reference list?

_ Do the text citations and reference list entries agree both in spelling and in date?

_ Are journal titles in the reference list spelled out fully?

_ Are inclusive page numbers for all articles or chapters in books provided in the reference list?

_ Does every table column have a heading?

_ Are tables horizontally ruled with light pencil lines only?

_ Have all vertical table rules been omitted?

_ Have all figures been submitted as camera-ready?

_ Are the elements in the figures large enough to remain legible after the figure has been reduced to fit a printed page?

_ Is each figure labeled on its back with the author's name, title of paper, figure number, and figure legend?

_ Are all figures and tables mentioned in text?

_ Is the placement of each table and figure indicated in text?

_ Is written permission to use previously published text, tables, or figures enclosed with the manuscript?

_ Are page numbers provided in text for all quotations?

APPLIED ECONOMICS

ADDRESS FOR SUBMISSION :

MAURICE H. PESTON, EDITOR
APPLIED ECONOMICS
11 NEW FETTER LANE
LONDON, EC4P 4EE
UK
0 171 583 9855
0 171 842 2302 (Fax)

CIRCULATION DATA :

Reader : Academic

Frequency of Issue : Monthly

Copies Per Issue :

Subscription Price :
  Institution : 1254.00 US$

Sponsorship :

PUBLICATION GUIDELINES :

Manuscript Length : 7000 Words

Copies Required : Three

Computer Submission : Yes

Format : Standard Wordprocessing

Fees to Review : 0.00 US$

REVIEW INFORMATION :

Type of Review : N/A

No. of External Reviewers : Two

No. of In House Reviewers : One

Acceptance Rate :

Time To Review : 4-6 months

Reviewer's Comments : Yes

Fees to Publish : 0.00 US$

Invited Articles :

MANUSCRIPT TOPICS : ECONOMETRICS;
   INTERNATIONAL & ECONOMIC DEVELOPMENT; PUBLIC POLICY ECONOMICS

PUBLICATION GUIDELINES :

MANUSCRIPT GUIDELINES/COMMENTS :

AIMS AND SCOPE
The primary purpose of APPLIED ECONOMICS is to encourage the application of
economic analysis to specific problems in both the private and public sector.
It particularly hopes to foster quantitative studies, the results of which
promise to be of use in the practical field and help to bring economic theory
nearer to the realities of life.

Contributions which make use of the methods of mathematics, statistics and
operations research will be welcomed, provided the conclusions are factual and
properly explained.

INSTRUCTIONS TO AUTHORS
1. SUBMISSION. Authors should submit three copies of their papers along with
an abstract to Professor M. Peston, 11 New Fetter Lane, London EC4P 4EE, UK.
Submission of manuscripts on disc is encouraged. These should be prepared
using a standard word processing package. Three printed copies are to be
supplied with the disc, these matching the contents of the discs exactly. The
contents of the papers shall be the sole responsibility of the authors and
publication shall not imply the concurrence of editors or publishers.

APPLIED ECONOMICS

2. THE MANUSCRIPT. Manuscripts must be typed with double spacing throughout on one side of A4 paper only, with a 4 cm left-hand margin. The text and references should be checked thoroughly for errors before submission. It is the responsibility of the author to ensure that the typescript is correct in style, syntax and spelling (Shorter Oxford English Dictionary).

Papers should normally be divided into headed sections.

3. TITLE PAGE. The first page of the typescript must contain: the full title; the affiliation and full address of the author(s); a running title of not more than 75 letters and spaces; an abstract of not more than 200 words; the name and full postal address of the author who will be responsible for correspondence and correcting of proofs.

4. ABBREVIATIONS. Any word or words to be abbreviated should be written in full when first mentioned followed by the abbreviation in parentheses.

5. ILLUSTRATIONS. Illustrations should not be inserted in the pages of the manuscript but supplied separately with the typescript. Line drawings should be drawn clearly in Indian ink on tracing paper and at about double the intended size. Lettering should be stencilled either in Indian ink or Letraset, again large enough for any necessary reduction; typewritten annotations are not acceptable. The captions should be typed on a separate page at the end of the manuscript and not included in the text or under the illustrations.

6. TABLES. Tables should be numbered and headed with short titles. They should be typed on separate sheets at the end of the manuscript.

7. ACKNOWLEDGEMENTS. Acknowledgements should appear at the end of the text.

8. REFERENCES. The Harvard system is used. When quoted in the text the style is: ...Smith (1972)... or (Brown and Jones, 1972) or ...Smith et al. (1972a). References are listed alphabetically after the text. Journal and book titles should be written out in full. Examples are:

> Brigham, E. F. (1965) The determinants of residential land values, Land Economics, 41, 325-34.

> Phelps-Brown, H. (1981) Labour market policy, in Changing Perceptions of Economic Policy (Ed.) F. Cairncross, Methuen, London, pp. 68-113.

9. FOOTNOTES. These should be numbered consecutively in the text and gathered on a separate sheet of the typescript.

10. PROOFS. Proofs will be sent to the 'corresponding' author for correction. These must be corrected and returned within three weeks otherwise publication may be delayed. Alterations to proofs other than correction of printer's errors may be charged to the authors.

11. OFFPRINTS. Each corresponding author will receive 25 free offprints. Extra copies can be purchased on request.

12. COPYRIGHT. Submission of a paper to APPLIED ECONOMICS will be taken to imply that it presents original unpublished work, not under consideration for

APPLIED ECONOMICS

publication elsewhere. A copyright assignment form will be sent to the authors of submitted papers prior to refereeing. This publishing agreement should be completed and returned to the editorial office. The agreement becomes void if the paper is not accepted for publication in the journal. The copyright covers the exclusive rights to reproduce and distribute the article, including reprints, photographic reproductions, microfilm or any other reproductions of similar nature, and translations.

Permission to publish illustrations must be obtained by the author before submission and any acknowledgements should be included in the captions.

APPLIED FINANCIAL ECONOMICS

ADDRESS FOR SUBMISSION :

PROFESSOR MARK P. TAYLOR, EDITOR
APPLIED FINANCIAL ECONOMICS
UNIVERSITY OF LIVERPOOL
EDITORIAL OFFICE OF AFE
DEPARTMENT OF ECONOMICS
LIVERPOOL, L69 3BX
UK
+44 151 794 3036
+44 151 794 3068 (Fax)
E-Mail : afe@liv.ac.uk

CIRCULATION DATA :

Reader : Academic

Frequency of Issue : Bi-Monthly

Copies Per Issue : 1001-2000

Subscription Price : 290.00 US$
  European : 172.00 L EU
  Rest of World : 185.00 L ROW

Sponsorship :

PUBLICATION GUIDELINES :

Manuscript Length : 21-25

Copies Required : Three

Computer Submission : No

Format : N/A

Fees to Review : 0.00 US$

REVIEW INFORMATION :

Type of Review : Blind Review

No. of External Reviewers : Two

No. of In House Reviewers : Zero

Acceptance Rate : 21-30%

Time To Review : 2-3 months

Reviewer's Comments : Yes

Fees to Publish : 0.00 US$

Invited Articles : 5% or less

MANUSCRIPT TOPICS : COST ACCOUNTING; ECONOMETRICS;
  INTERNATIONAL FINANCE; PORTFOLIO & SECURITY ANALYSIS; FINANCE

PUBLICATION GUIDELINES :

MANUSCRIPT GUIDELINES/COMMENTS :

AIMS AND SCOPE
APPLIED FINANCIAL ECONOMICS is a refereed companion journal to APPLIED
ECONOMICS. It publishes research papers, short articles, notes and comments on
financial economics, banking and monetary economics, with a particular bias
towards practical aspects and applied topics. Particular attention is paid to
the actual operations of financial institutions and financial markets.

APPLIED FINANCIAL ECONOMICS is important reading for financial economists,
financial institutions, economists in banks and specialists in accountancy,
management and economics.

INSTRUCTIONS TO AUTHORS
1. SUBMISSION. Authors should submit three copies of their papers along with
an abstract to the Editor. Submission of manuscripts on disc is encouraged.
These should be prepared using a standard word processing package. Three
printed copies are to be supplied, these matching the contents of the discs
exactly. The contents of the papers shall be the sole responsibility of the
authors and publication shall not imply the concurrence of editors or
publishers.

APPLIED FINANCIAL ECONOMICS

2. THE MANUSCRIPT. Manuscripts must be typed with double spacing throughout on one side of A4 paper only, with a 4 cm left-hand margin. The text and references should be checked thoroughly for errors before submission. It is the responsibility of the author to ensure that the typescript is correct in style, syntax and spelling (Shorter Oxford English Dictionary).

Papers should normally be divided into headed sections.

3. TITLE PAGE. The first page of the typescript must contain: the full title; the affiliation and full address of the author(s); a running title of not more than 75 letters and spaces; an abstract of not more than 200 words; the name and full postal address of the author who will be responsible for correspondence and correcting of proofs.

4. ABBREVIATIONS. Any word or words to be abbreviated should be written in full when first mentioned followed by the abbreviation in parentheses.

5. ILLUSTRATIONS. Illustrations should not be inserted in the pages of the manuscript but supplied separately with the typescript. Line drawings should be drawn clearly in Indian ink on tracing paper and at about double the intended size. Lettering should be stencilled either in Indian ink or Letraset, again large enough for any necessary reduction; typewritten annotations are not acceptable. The captions should be typed on a separate page at the end of the manuscript and not included in the text or under the illustrations.

6. TABLES. Tables should be numbered and headed with short titles. They should be typed on separate sheets at the end of the manuscript.

7. ACKNOWLEDGEMENTS. Acknowledgements should appear at the end of the text.

8. REFERENCES. The Harvard system is used. When quoted in the text the style is: ...Smith (1972) ...or (Brown and Jones, 1972) or ...Smith et al. (1972a). References are listed alphabetically after the text. Journal and book titles should be written out in full. Examples are:

> Brigham, E. F. (1965) The determinants of residential land values, Land Economics, 41, 325-34.
> Phelps-Brown, H. (1981) Labour market policy, in Changing Perceptions of Economic Policy (Ed.) F. Cairncross, Methuen, London, pp. 68-1 13.

9. FOOTNOTES. These should be numbered consecutively in the text and gathered on a separate sheet of the typescript.

10. PROOFS. Proofs will be sent to the 'corresponding' author for correction. These must be corrected and returned within three weeks otherwise publication may be delayed. Alterations to proofs other than correction of printer's errors may be charged to the authors.

11. OFFPRINTS. Copies can be purchased using the Offprint Order Form provided with the proofs.

12. COPYRIGHT. Submission of a paper to APPLIED FINANCIAL ECONOMICS will be taken to imply that it presents original unpublished work, not under consideration for publication elsewhere. A copyright assignment form will be

APPLIED FINANCIAL ECONOMICS

sent to the authors of submitted papers prior to refereeing. This publishing agreement should be completed and returned to the editorial office. The agreement becomes void if the paper is not accepted for publication in the journal. The copyright covers the exclusive rights to reproduce and distribute the article, including reprints, photographic reproductions, microfilm or any other reproductions of similar nature, and translations.

Permission to publish illustrations must be obtained by the author before submission and any acknowledgements should be included in the captions.

APPRAISAL JOURNAL

ADDRESS FOR SUBMISSION :

DONNA O'LOUGHLIN, MANAGING EDITOR
APPRAISAL JOURNAL
875 NORTH MICHIGAN AVENUE
CHICAGO, IL 60611-1980
USA
312-335-4445
312-335-4400 (Fax)

PUBLICATION GUIDELINES :

Manuscript Length : 16-20

Copies Required :

Computer Submission : No

Format : N/A

Fees to Review : 0.00 US$

CIRCULATION DATA :

Reader : Business Persons

Frequency of Issue : Quarterly

Copies Per Issue : Over 25,000

Subscription Price : 35.00 US$

Sponsorship : Professional Assoc.

REVIEW INFORMATION :

Type of Review : Blind Review

No. of External Reviewers : Zero

No. of In House Reviewers : Three

Acceptance Rate : 21-30%

Time To Review : One month or less

Reviewer's Comments : No

Fees to Publish : 0.00 US$

Invited Articles : 5% or less

MANUSCRIPT TOPICS : COST ACCOUNTING; REAL ESTATE;
   REAL ESTATE APPRAISAL

PUBLICATION GUIDELINES : Chicago Manual of Style

MANUSCRIPT GUIDELINES/COMMENTS :

Submit SIX copies of the manuscript.

1. THE APPRAISAL JOURNAL retains its preeminence in real estate appraisal by
keeping abreast of the latest issues of importance and interest to appraisers.
Fresh ideas are always welcome. We invite you to write for THE APPRAISAL
JOURNAL. Each year THE APPRAISAL JOURNAL awards two cash prizes: the Robert
H. Armstrong Award for the best article published that year in the Journal,
and the Sanders A. Kahn Award for the best article based on a practical
application. Authors of articles accepted for publication receive six
complimentary copies; authors of shorter features receive three.

2. REVIEW. For the purposes of review, each manuscript submitted is considered
anonymously. Reviews are conducted by at least three members of the Appraisal
Journal Board, and by outside specialists when deemed appropriate. A
manuscript approved "with revisions" may be returned to the author with
specific recommendations. No other manuscript will be returned to authors.
Authors of manuscripts that are not accepted for publication in THE APPRAISAL
JOURNAL will receive notification by letter.

APPRAISAL JOURNAL

3. THE MANUSCRIPT. Writing is always received best when it is succinct, interesting, and lucid. The editors believe that this is the case even in technical matters and hope that it is reflected in THE APPRAISAL JOURNAL.

THE APPRAISAL JOURNAL shall be entitled to make the manuscript conform to Appraisal Institute style of capitalization, punctuation, spelling and usage; for clarity of presentation; and for errors in grammar and spelling. However, THE APPRAISAL JOURNAL shall not be free, in the process of editing, to make substantive changes in the manuscript.

4. Specifics for Authors to Include:
1. SIX copies of the manuscript, typewritten, and double or triple spaced on one side of plain white 8-1/2 x 11 inch paper, including quoted matter, footnotes, and bibliographies

2. Anonymous title page for reviewing purposes - include a cover letter with complete address and telephone number of author(s)

3. Abstract of 75-100 words

4. Brief professional biography, including present employment, title, degrees, designations, and publishing accomplishments

5. Accurate mathematics and statistics for which the author is responsible

6. Brief major and secondary headings to emphasize divisions

7. Footnotes (where needed), numbered consecutively along with all facts of publication or sources of quotations

EXAMPLES:
BOOKS
1. American Institute of Real Estate Appraisers. The Appraisal of Real Estate, 8th ed. (Chicago: American Institute of Real Estate Appraisers, 1983), 49-50.

2. George Bloom and Henry Harrison. Appraising the Single Family Residence (Chicago: American Institute of Real Estate Appraisers, 1978), 240.

ARTICLES
3. John B. Corgel, Paul R. Goebel, and Charles E. Wade. "Measuring Energy Efficiency for Selection and Adjustment of Comparable Sales." The Appraisal Journal (January 1983): 71-78.

4. Robert H. Zerbst and William B. Brueggeman. "FHA and VA Mortgage Discount Points and Housing Prices." The Journal of Finance, vol. 32, no. 5 (December 1977): 17701771.

5. Ibid., 1773. [Zerbst and Brueggeman, same article as in immediately preceding note, different pages]

6. Corgel, Goebel, and Wade, 77-78. [Reference to note 3, but interrupted by a different source reference]

LEGAL CITATIONS
7. Suess Builders Co. v. City of Beaverton, 245, 656 p. 2d 306 (1982).

8. United States v. Blankinship, 543 F. 2d 1272 (9th Cir. 1976).

9. United States v. 97.19 Acres of Land, 511 F. Supp. 565.

10. 543 F. 2d 1272. [second reference to note 8]

COLLOQUIUMS, WORKING PAPERS, AND DISSERTATIONS
11. James H. Boykin, "Development of Value Theory to its Present State." 1984 Real Estate Valuation Colloquium (Cambridge, Mass.: Lincoln Inst. for Land Policy, 1984).

12. Kenneth T. Rosen, "Creative Financing and Housing Prices: A Study of Capitalization Effect." Working Paper 82-85 (Berkeley: Univ. of California, Center for Real Estate and Urban Economics, August 1982).

13. James R. DeLisle, "Toward a Formal Statement of Residential Real Estate Appraisal Theory: A Behavioral Approach" (Ph.D. diss., University of Wisconsin, 1981), 55-60.

DISSERTATIONS ON MICROFILM
14. James R. DeLisle, Toward a Formal Statement of Residential Real Estate Appraisal Theory:A Behavioral Approach (Ann Arbor, Mich.: University Microfilms,1981),55-60.

8. Always write out individual names and acronyms in full in the first text citation, e.g. net operating income (NO1); short forms or acronyms may be used thereafter.

9. Original charts, tables, maps, drawings, and photographs, if appropriate, indicating where these are to appear and accompanied by titles or captions.

10. Joint authors' preferences for order of bylines and biographies; these will appear alphabetically unless otherwise specified.

Additional information on accepted style and organization may be found in THE CHICAGO MANUAL OF STYLE, 14th edition, revised and expanded. Chicago: University of Chicago Press, 1993.

ATLANTIC ECONOMIC JOURNAL

ADDRESS FOR SUBMISSION :

JOHN M. VIRGO, PH D., MANAGING EDITOR
ATLANTIC ECONOMIC JOURNAL
SOUTHERN ILLINOIS UNIVERSITY
BOX 1101
EDWARDSVILLE, IL 62026-1101
USA
618-692-2291
618-692-3400 (Fax)
E-Mail : jvirgo@eniac.ac.siue.edu

CIRCULATION DATA :

Reader : Academic

Frequency of Issue : Quarterly

Copies Per Issue : 1001-2000

Subscription Price : 147.00 US$
  Overseas : 162.00 US$

Sponsorship : Professional Assoc.

PUBLICATION GUIDELINES :

Manuscript Length : 16-20

Copies Required : Two

Computer Submission : Yes

Format : Low density/WordPerfect6.01

Fees to Review : 70.00 US$
  Atlan.Eco.Soc.Member 45.00 US$

REVIEW INFORMATION :

Type of Review : Blind Review

No. of External Reviewers : Two

No. of In House Reviewers : One

Acceptance Rate : 6-10%

Time To Review : 2-3 months

Reviewer's Comments : Yes

Fees to Publish : 0.00 US$

Invited Articles : 5% or less

MANUSCRIPT TOPICS : COST ACCOUNTING; ECONOMETRICS; ECONOMIC HISTORY; INTERNATIONAL & ECONOMIC DEVELOPMENT; PUBLIC POLICY ECONOMICS; ECONOMICS; FINANCE & INVESTMENTS

PUBLICATION GUIDELINES :

MANUSCRIPT GUIDELINES/COMMENTS :

1. COPIES AND JEL CATEGORY. Submit two copies of the manuscript, indicating the primary area of interest that your paper falls under on the first page of the manuscript. Use white, standard weight 8-1/2 x 11 inch paper.

2. TYPING. Double space all material throughout, including footnotes, references, and quoted matter. Leave a 1-inch margin on all sides.

3. REFERENCES VS. FOOTNOTES. Be certain to separate references from footnotes. References are works cited within the text. Footnotes are explanatory remarks about a specific point in the text.

Examples:
  Reference
  John M. Virgo, "Changing Regulatory Agencies and Decision Making in the Federal Government", Health Care: An International Perspective, International Health Economics and Management Institute, January 1984.

ATLANTIC ECONOMIC JOURNAL

Footnote
1 For a more detailed explanation of faculty unionization, see Virgo [1977, pp. 3-21].

4. REFERENCES. Place all references, alphabetized by author's last name (with first name first), on separate pages at the end of the paper in a section titled "References".

Example:
E. J. Mishan, "What is Producers' Surplus?" American Economic Review, 58, December 1968.

When you refer in the text to a publication on this list, insert the author's last name and year of publication in brackets, including specific page numbers where necessary. Place it at the end of the sentence or before quoted matter. If reference is made to two or more works by the same author in the same year, designate them as follows: 1986(a), 1986(b), etc.

Example:
This form of analysis has received some attention in the literature [Spengler, 1978(b), pp. 20-7].

5. FOOTNOTES. Number footnotes consecutively throughout the paper, not page by page. Type footnotes on separate pages following the last page of the article. Footnotes should be limited in number and short in length.

6. TABLES. Place all tables on separate pages. Tables are to be numbered in Arabic numerals using the following format:

TABLE 1
Title of Table
Table

7. FIGURES. Place all figures on separate pages. Graphs are considered to be figures. Figures are to be numbered in roman numerals using the following format:

FIGURE 1
Title of Figure
Figure

8. FIGURE AND GRAPH PREPARATION. Upon acceptance for publication, all figures and graphs must be prepared on heavy white paper, acetate sheeting, or tracing cloth. Use appropriate paper for black-and-white reproduction by a photographic process. Label all axes and curves where applicable. Axes should be labeled by title rather than by notation.

All graphs and figures are to be professionally drawn using Press or Times Roman type style for reproduction on a width of 16 or 33 picas.

If graphic facilities are not available, the ATLANTIC ECONOMIC JOURNAL can have the work done by an outside company with the author billed our cost (about $50.00 per graph).

9. CAPITALIZATION. Capitalize full names of schools, departments, and divisions within a university; School of the Arts, School of Nursing, but history department, medical school.

Capitalize academic titles only when preceding the name: Professor Jones, but Kenneth Jones, professor of biology.

Capitalize the names of legislative, judiciary, and administrative bodies and government departments: Congress, House of Representatives, Department of Justice, Office of Equal Employment Opportunity.

Do not capitalize the words government, federal, or state unless they are part of a proper name: State of Illinois, but "The state changed its policy".

Capitalize and underline to indicate italics in titles of books; plays; poems; and songs: Gone with the Wind, A Streetcar Named Desire, How Do I Love Thee? The words a, in, of, etc. are capitalized only at the beginning or end of a title.

10. COMMA. Separate the day of the month and year, but do not use commas when only the month and year are given without a day: August 28, 1983, but August 1983.

11. NUMERALS. General rule: Spell out numbers through nine except in statistical matter; use figures for 10 or more.

Spell out a figure when beginning a sentence even though numerals are used elsewhere in the text.

Always use figures with abbreviations of measurements and for decimals and percentages (always spell out percent): 3 ft., 2 in., 4.5 km; 6 percent.

Dimensions, degrees, distances, weights, measures, sums of money, and like matter should be expressed in figures when appearing in mathematical, statistical, or scientific text: a board 1 -1 /2 inches thick by 18 inches wide was used; 45 miles; 3 cubic feet; 9 pounds.

12. SUBMISSION: A handling fee of $27.00 for members of the Atlantic Economic Society and $45.00 for non-members is required at the time of submission. Your checks should be made payable to: ATLANTIC ECONOMIC JOURNAL. All manuscripts should be submitted to the Managing Editor.

ATLANTIC JOURNAL OF INTERNATIONAL
ACCOUNTING AND MULTI-NATIONAL BUSINESS

ADDRESS FOR SUBMISSION :

MARY MCCABE, EDITOR
ATLANTIC JOURNAL OF INTERNATIONAL
  ACCOUNTING AND MULTI-NATIONAL BUSINESS
4725 DORSEY HALL DRIVE
SUITE A-807
ELLICOTT CITY, MD 21042

CIRCULATION DATA :

Reader : Academic

Frequency of Issue : 1 Times/Year

Copies Per Issue : Less than 1000

Subscription Price : 100.00 US$
  Academic : 50.00 US$

Sponsorship : Non Profit Corp.

PUBLICATION GUIDELINES :

Manuscript Length : 21-25

Copies Required : Three

Computer Submission : No

Format : N/A

Fees to Review : 30.00 US$
  Subscriber 10.00 US$

REVIEW INFORMATION :

Type of Review : Blind Review

No. of External Reviewers : Two

No. of In House Reviewers : Zero

Acceptance Rate : 11-20%

Time To Review : 2-3 months

Reviewer's Comments : Yes

Fees to Publish : 0.00 US$

Invited Articles : 5% or less

MANUSCRIPT TOPICS : ACCOUNTING THEORY & PRACTICE; COST ACCOUNTING;
  INTERNATIONAL & ECONOMIC DEVELOPMENT

PUBLICATION GUIDELINES : Chicago Manual of Style

MANUSCRIPT GUIDELINES/COMMENTS :

We seek submissions that address real business problems or situations.

AUDIT: THE AUDIT AUTOMATION MAGAZINE

ADDRESS FOR SUBMISSION :

KEN EBBAGE,EDITOR
AUDIT: THE AUDIT AUTOMATION MAGAZINE
PENTANA LTD.
GATE HOUSE
FRETHERNE ROAD
WELWYN GARDEN CITY
HERTS,   AL8 6NS
IRELAND
+01707 373335
+01707-372922 (Fax)

CIRCULATION DATA :

Reader : Business Persons

Frequency of Issue : Bi-Monthly

Copies Per Issue : Less than 1000

Subscription Price : 225.00 US$

Sponsorship : Profit Oriented Corp.

PUBLICATION GUIDELINES :

Manuscript Length : 11-15

Copies Required : One

Computer Submission : Yes

Format : MS-DOS/prefer Winword 2.0

Fees to Review : 0.00 US$

REVIEW INFORMATION :

Type of Review : Blind Review

No. of External Reviewers : Zero

No. of In House Reviewers : One

Acceptance Rate : 90 %

Time To Review : One month or less

Reviewer's Comments : No

Fees to Publish : 0.00 US$

Invited Articles : Over 50%

MANUSCRIPT TOPICS : ACCOUNTING INFORMATION SYSTEMS;
   ACCOUNTING THEORY & PRACTICE; AUDITING

PUBLICATION GUIDELINES :

MANUSCRIPT GUIDELINES/COMMENTS :

AUDITING: A JOURNAL OF PRACTICE AND THEORY

ADDRESS FOR SUBMISSION :

WILLIAM L. FELIX, JR., EDITOR
AUDITING: A JOURNAL OF PRACTICE
  AND THEORY
UNIVERSITY OF ARIZONA
DEPARTMENT OF ACCOUNTING
TUSCON, AZ 85721
USA
520-621-2443
520-621-3742 (Fax)
E-Mail : wfelix@bpa.arizona.edu

CIRCULATION DATA :

Reader : Academic &
       Auditing
Frequency of Issue : 2 Times/Year
Copies Per Issue : 1001-2000
Subscription Price : 25.00 US$
  With AAAA Dues : 0.00 US$
Sponsorship : Professional Assoc.

PUBLICATION GUIDELINES :

Manuscript Length : 20+
Copies Required : Four
Computer Submission : No
Format : N/A
Fees to Review : 50.00 US$

REVIEW INFORMATION :

Type of Review : Editorial Review
No. of External Reviewers : Two
No. of In House Reviewers : Zero
Acceptance Rate : 11-20%
Time To Review : 2-3 months
Reviewer's Comments : Yes
Fees to Publish : 0.00 US$
Invited Articles : 5% or less

MANUSCRIPT TOPICS : AUDITING; COST ACCOUNTING

PUBLICATION GUIDELINES :

MANUSCRIPT GUIDELINES/COMMENTS :

EDITORIAL PHILOSOPHY
The purpose of this journal is to contribute to improving the theory and
practice of auditing. The term "auditing" is to be interpreted broadly. Thus
this journal invites articles on internal and external auditing as well as
comprehensive and financial (attest) audits. Practices and developments in
auditing in different countries, either in corporate or governmental contexts,
are appropriate topics, and so are uses of auditing in new ways and for
different purposes. Discussion and analysis of current problems and issues in
auditing will constitute an important part of the journal's contents. This
will include surveys which summarize and evaluate developments in related
fields which have an important bearing on auditing. Papers reporting results
or original research which have improvements in auditing theory or auditing
methodology as a central focus are also invited. The objective is to promote a
two-way flow between research and practice which will influence developments
in auditing education as well as auditing research and auditing practice.

MANUSCRIPT PREPARATION AND STYLE
AUDITING: A JOURNAL OF PRACTICE & THEORY's manuscript preparation guidelines
follow closely that used in THE ACCOUNTING REVIEW, another American Accounting
Association publication. These guidelines follow (with slight modification)

AUDITING: A JOURNAL OF PRACTICE AND THEORY

the B-format of the CHICAGO MANUAL OF STYLE (13th ed.; University of Chicago Press). Another helpful guide to usage and style is THE ELEMENTS OF STYLE, by William Strunk, Jr., and E.B. White (Macmillan). Spelling follows WEBSTER'S INTERNATIONAL DICTIONARY.

FORMAT

1. All manuscripts should be typed on one side of 8 1/2 x 11" paper and be double-spaced, except for indented quotations, footnotes, and references.

2. Manuscripts should be as concise as the subject and research method permit, and as a general rule, should not exceed 7,000 words.

3. Margins of at least one inch on top, bottom, and sides will facilitate editing and duplication.

4. A cover page should show the title of the paper, the author's name, title, affiliation, complete mailing address, and any acknowledgements. The title of the paper, but not the author's name, should appear on the Summary page and on the first page of the text.

5. All pages, including tables, appendices, and references, should be serially numbered.

6. When not in lists, numbers from one through ten should be spelled out, except where decimals are used. All others should be written numerically.

7. Hyphens are preferred to the compounding or to the coining of words. Authors should avoid using first person.

8. Mathematical notation should be employed only where its rigor and precision are indispensable, and in such circumstances authors should explain in narrative format the principal operations performed. Notation should be avoided in footnotes. Unusual symbols, particularly if handwritten, should be identified in the margin when they first appear. Displayed material should clearly indicate the alignment, superscripts, and subscripts. Equations should be numbered in parentheses flush with the right-hand margin.

9. headings should be arranged so that major headings are centered and capitalized. Second level headings should be flush with the side of the page and subsequent levels appropriately indented. For example:

A CENTERED, ALL CAPITALIZED, FIRST LEVEL HEADING

A flush Side Second Level Heading
   A Third Level Heading
      A Fourth Level Heading

TABLES AND FIGURES
Each table and figure should appear on a separate page and bear an arabic number and a complete title indicating the exact contents. A reference to each table or figure should appear in the text. The author should indicate by marginal notation where each table or figure is to be inserted in the text, e.g., [Insert table X here].

AUDITING: A JOURNAL OF PRACTICE AND THEORY

SUMMARY
A summary, of approximately (but not in excess of) 300 words, should be on a separate page immediately preceding the text. This summary should be non-mathematical and easily readable, with an emphasis on the significant findings or conclusions of the article. The intent is to enable the target audience--practitioners and academics--to quickly determine the relevance of the article to their own interests. Thus, the language should be less formal than that used in the article itself, and discussion of method should be brief, unless that is the main focus of the article.

DOCUMENTATION
LITERATURE CITATIONS: Work cited should be in the body of the text, by the author's name and the year of publication.

1. With one author, use author's last name and date, without comma, in parentheses: for example (Shank 1975); with two authors: (Storey and Moonitz 1976); with more than two: (Jones et al. 1985); with more than one source cited together: (Shank 1975; Chambers 1976); with two or more works by one author: (Jones 1985, 1987).

2. Citations to institutional works should employ acronyms or short titles, where practicable; for example (AAAASOBAT 1966) or (AICPA Cohen Commission Report 1977). Where brief, the full title of an institutional work may be used; for example (ICAEW The Corporate Report 1975).

3. Unless confusion would result, do not use "p." or "pp." before page numbers; for example (Khun 1970, 20).

4. If an author's name is mentioned in the text, it need not be repeated in the citation; for example, "Khun (1970, 20) says...."

5. When the reference list contains more than one work of an author published in a single year, the suffix a, b, etc. follows the date in the text citation; for example (Demski 1973a).

6. If the manuscript refers to statutes, legal treaties, or court cases, citations acceptable in law reviews should be used.

FOOTNOTES: Textual footnotes are used only for extensions and explanations whose inclusion in the body of the manuscript might disrupt the continuity. Footnotes should be numbered consecutively throughout the manuscript with superscript arabic numbers. Footnotes are placed at the end of the text.

REFERENCE LIST: The list of references follows the text, and contains only those works actually cited. Each entry should contain all of the data necessary for unambiguous identification, in the following format

1. Arrange citations in alphabetical order according to the surname of the first author, or the name of the institution responsible for a work with no author listed.

2. Multiple works by the same author(s) should be listed in chronological order of publication: two or more works by the same author(s) in the same year are distinguished by letters after the date.

AUDITING: A JOURNAL OF PRACTICE AND THEORY

3. Use authors' initials instead of proper names.

4. Do not abbreviate titles of journals.

5. Dates of publication should be placed immediately after author's name.

Sample entries:

American Accounting Association, Committee on Concepts and Standards for External Financial Reports. 1977. Statement on Accounting Theory and Theory Acceptance. Sarasota, FL: AAA.

Dye, R., B. Balachandran, and R. Magee. 1989. Contingent fees for audit firms. Working paper, Northwestern University, Evanston, IL.

Garrison, R. 1988. Managerial Accounting. Homewood, IL: BPI/Irwin.

Revsine, L. 1970a. Data expansion and conceptual structure. The Accounting Review (October): 704-11.

_____, 1970b. Change in budget pressure and its impact on supervisor behavior. Journal of Accounting Research (Autumn): 90-91.

AUSTRALIAN ECONOMIC REVIEW

ADDRESS FOR SUBMISSION :

DR. D. JOHNSON, JOINT EDITOR
AUSTRALIAN ECONOMIC REVIEW
UNIVERSITY OF MELBOURNE
INST. OF APPLIED ECONOMIC & SOCIAL RES.
PARKVILLE, VICTORIA, 3052
AUSTRALIA
61-03-9344-5330
61-03-9344-5630 (Fax)
E-Mail : johnson@iaesr.unimelb.edu.au

CIRCULATION DATA :

Reader : Academic

Frequency of Issue : Quarterly

Copies Per Issue : Less than 1000

Subscription Price : 90.00 AUS.$
   Inst., Co., Library : 180.00 AUS.$
   In Australia $70 and : 160.00 AUS.$

Sponsorship : University

PUBLICATION GUIDELINES :

Manuscript Length : 26-30

Copies Required : Four

Computer Submission : Yes

Format : Macintosh

Fees to Review : 0.00 US$

REVIEW INFORMATION :

Type of Review : Editorial Review

No. of External Reviewers : Two

No. of In House Reviewers : One

Acceptance Rate : 21-30%

Time To Review : 2-3 months

Reviewer's Comments : Yes

Fees to Publish : 0.00 US$

Invited Articles : 6-10%

MANUSCRIPT TOPICS : ECONOMETRICS; ECONOMIC HISTORY;
   INTERNATIONAL & ECONOMIC DEVELOPMENT; PUBLIC POLICY ECONOMICS;
   SOCIAL ECONOMICS

PUBLICATION GUIDELINES :

MANUSCRIPT GUIDELINES/COMMENTS :

The REVIEW is published four times each year. It contains contributed and
commissioned articles on applied economic and social topics. There are several
regular sections of the REVIEW: the 'Contributed Articles' section which
contains unsolicited articles on economic and social matters; 'Policy Forum'
which deals with major issues of economic policy; 'Data Surveys' which
outlines the main features of databases available to researchers; 'For the
Student' which address matters of interest to students in schools and
universities; and 'Region at a Glance' a statistical section which contains a
compilation of recent economic and social statistics for Australia and the
Asia-Pacific region.

SUBMISSIONS
The Institute invites submissions of articles particularly on topics of
interest to an Australian audience. The editors are particularly interested in
articles associated with the causes and consequences of differences in
economic performance at the national, local, enterprise, individual and group
levels. Contributed articles are subjected to normal refereeing processes. The
length of articles should not normally exceed 30 double-spaced A4 pages or its

equivalent. Authors are requested to supply four copies of manuscripts
submitted for publication. Authors of accepted articles are required to send
an unformatted (ASCII) copy on computer disc. Authors should request a style
guide.

GUIDE TO AUTHORS
Articles submitted for publication in the REVIEW should focus on presenting
the results of applied economic research on economic and social issues in
Australia, or where a wider topic is examined, the implications for Australia
should be given central emphasis. The techniques used and results attained
should be explained in a way that can be understood by the generalist
economist, but the article should contain, or be accompanied by, sufficient
information on techniques, programs, assumptions, and data to enable a
specialist referee to assess the work. Avoid specialist terminology.

Submit four copies of the typed manuscript (single-sided and double-spaced) to
the Editor, accompanied by an abstract of up to 200 words summarising the
central argument or findings; and a short description of the article (less
than 24 words) which will be included on the contents page if the article is
accepted. The article should not exceed 30 A4 pages. If the article is
accepted for publication the authors are requested to provide a copy of the
paper on a diskette.

1. HEADINGS

* The use of subheadings to break up the text is encouraged. Consecutive
Arabic numerals should be used to number sections and subsections. Headings
should be typed in upper and lower case; e.g., 1. Government Intervention 1.1
Policy Instruments 1.1.1 Prices

* All sections should be titled; including the introductory paragraphs (eg 1.
Introduction)

2. ITALICS, QUOTES, NUMBERS, YEARS, SHORTENED FORMS, CAPITALISATION, SPELLING

ITALICS
* Underline words that are to be set in italics. (Use italics rather than bold
for emphasis.)

QUOTES, QUOTATION MARKS
* Quote extracts meticulously, preserving the punctuation and spelling of the
extract quoted. Run short quotes (less than 30 words) in the text. Longer
quotes should be indented and set separately (with a para indent only if there
was one in the original).

* Give a source for each quotation and for data, opinions or conclusions that
are not your own.

* Obtain written permission to quote copyright material, e.g. a continuous
excerpt of more than 500 words. It is a courtesy to ask permission of both the
copyright owner and the author, if not the same, and to mention both in the
acknowledgement.

* Use single quotation marks for words or phrases placed in quote marks. Quote
marks are not required for long quotes which have been set separately. Use

double quotation marks for quotes within quotes (e.g., 'The growth in "long-term unemployment" was described...').

NUMBERS, YEARS
* From one to ten are written in words except when referring to measurements or percentages. Large numbers have a space rather than a comma between groups of three digits to the right or left of the decimal (e.g. 42 000); this also applies to money. However, four-digit numbers have no space (e.g 2000) unless they are to be aligned with larger numbers (greater than four digits) in a table.

* References to spans of numbers (other than years) should use as few figures as possible (e.g. 402-5, 421-39, 440-553). An exception is made for numbers between 10 and 19 in each each hundred (e.g. 10-11, 13-14, 115-16).

* Use an en rule for financial years (1995-96; not 1995/96).

* No apostrophe is required in spans of years (e.g. l990s).

* Use 'l990s' rather than 'Nineties'. Use '1 January' rather than 'January 1st'/'January 1'.

* When numbers begin a sentence they should be written in words rather than figures.

SHORTENED FORMS, CAPITALISATION
* Shortened forms: spell out the term the first time it is mentioned, followed by the shortened form in brackets. Use as few as possible. When shortened forms are not possessive, no apostrophe is needed (e.g. NIEs not NIE's).

* Spell out abbreviations: cf, e.g., i.e., US, UK, %, $m, $b, pa ('cf' should be 'compare with', e.g. should be 'for example', etc.)

* An initial capital should be used when referring to a specific chart, table, figure, section, appendix (e.g. Table 1, Chart A, Subsection 2.3, Appendix 1); but lowercase when non-specific (e.g. this section presents data).

* When using an initial capital for a word, ensure consistency in its usage throughout the article.

* p., pp., ch., vol., s. can be used in the text when providing reference details in brackets.

SPELLING
* The Macquarie dictionary is used as a spelling reference.
* Spelling: when there's a choice use 's' rather than 'z'
* Data are (not Data is). Per cent (not percent).

3. MATHEMATICAL FORMULATIONS

* Write equations in as simple a form as possible and construct them so as to fit into a one-column width (66mm). They should be numbered using consecutive Arabic numerals in brackets at the end of the equation. Lengthy mathematical formulations should be placed in appendices.

AUSTRALIAN ECONOMIC REVIEW

* Ambiguities should be avoided e.g. between zero and the letter o; the partial derivative sign and lower case delta; the letters n and eta; lower case and capital letters. Subscripts and superscripts should be located clearly.

* Letters used as symbols should be set in italics, unless they represent vector quantities, in which case the typeface should be bold. The abbreviations for math functions (such as cos, sin, tan, ln) should be set in roman type, similarly numerals and the greek alphabet should be in roman typeface (not italics). There should be spaces around the functions (+ = - / > <, etc.).

* The hierarchy of brackets is parentheses within square brackets within braces { [()] } .

ENDNOTES
* An asterisk should be used for an endnote attached to the main heading/author; superscripted Arabic numerals should be used in the text for indicating endnotes. The endnotes should be located at the end of the manuscript and listed by consecutive Arabic numerals.

* Avoid lengthy endnotes. Do not use endnotes to list references.

TABLES AND DIAGRAMS
* Tables, Charts and Figures must have a caption. The caption should be typed in upper and lower case (e.g. Table 1 Growth, Wages and Unions). Label tables and figures using consecutive Arabic numerals (Table 1, Figure 1); label charts with consecutive letters of the Roman alphabet (Chart A).

* A source (author, year, and if necessary page) should be listed at the bottom of charts and tables. The full citation of the reference should be given in the References (exception: ABS Catalogue publications can be listed in full at the foot of the table or chart).

* Tables: Appendix A shows examples of the format required for Review tables. Note the short length of headings. Notes in tables should be marked using consecutive Roman letters (a,b,c) to avoid confusion with the numbers in the table.

* Diagrams: Illustrations should be provided as both hard copy and data Spreadsheets/data should be supplied so that charts can be reproduced using DeltaGraph. A diagram constructed from data should be labelled 'Chart'; a diagram not constructed from data should be labelled 'Figure'.

REFERENCES
* References in the text: give the authors name and year of publication, with a page reference if necessary. Surnames only are used. The ampersand is used when listing sources in brackets; e.g. (see Brown, Blandy & Grey 1994, p. 6; Kenyon 1994; Johnson & Blandy 1992). Note no commas between the author and year, and the use of the semicolon to separate references. ONLY LIST THOSE REFERENCES THAT HAVE BEEN CITED IN THE ARTICLE.

* Do not use endnotes to list references. References should be cited in the text and should be fully listed in alphabetical order (by author surname) at the end of the article in a Reference section (after the Endnotes). If there

are two articles by the same author in the same year, use a, b etc. to differentiate (e.g. Tan, A. l991a, Unemployment...; Tan, A. l991b, Wages...).

* Legislation does not appear in the Reference list. First references to legislation should cite the title of the Act/Ordinance, in italics, exactly and in full; in subsequent references a descriptive title, presented in roman type and with the date omitted, may be used: e.g., Interstate Road Transport Act 1985 (Cwlth), then Interstate Road Transport Act.

* Legal authorities do not appear in the Reference list. The details necessary for full citation of legal authorities are: name of case, (date) or volume number, or both, abbreviated name of report series, beginning page of reference e.g. West v. The Commonwealth (1960) 103 CLR 182. If a specific page number is necessary: West v. The Commonwealth (1960) 103 CLR 182 at 183. Upon first reference in the text, an authority must be cited in full. An abbreviated form (or the name the case is commonly known as) may be given in brackets following the formal citation. Thereafter the abbreviated/common form may be used e.g. West v. The Commonwealth (1960) 103 CLR 182 (the Sugar Case).

* Please ensure reference sections are complete and presented in the following style:

ABS Publication
Australian Bureau of Statistics 1994, Australian National Accounts: National income, Expenditure and Product, Cat. no. 5206.0, ABS, Canberra.

Book
Brannen, J. & Wilson, G. (eds) 1987, Give and Take with Families: Studies in Resource Distribution, Allen & Unwin, London.
Grubel, H. G. & Lloyd, P. J. 1975, Intra Industry Trade, Allen & Unwin, Sydney.

Article/Chapter in Book
Blank, R. M. & Blinder, R. S. 1986, 'Macroeconomics, income distribution and poverty', in Fighting Poverty, vol. 1, eds S. H. Danzinger & D. H. Weinberg, Harvard University Press, Cambridge, Massachusetts.

Published P.roceedings
Evans, R. 1973, 'Labor market information in Japanese labor markets', in Industrialization and Manpower Policy in Asian Countries: Proceedings of the Asian Regional Conference on Industrial Relations, Tokyo, Japan, Japan Institute of Labor, Tokyo, pp. 157-72.

Journal Article
Chapman, B. J., Junankar, P. N. & Kapuscinski, C. A. 1992, 'Projections of long-term unemployment', Australian Bulletin of Labour, vol. 18, no. 3, pp. 195-207.
Hart, P. E. 1976, 'The comparative statics and dynamics of income distributions', Journal of the Royal Statistical Society, ser. A. (General), vol. 139, pt 1, pp. 108-25.

Newspaper/Magazine Article
Forman, D. 1992, 'The new heroes who make and export', Business Review Weekly, 2 Oct., pp. 45-6.

Working Papers/Research Papers
Adams, P. D. 1984, 'The typical year database for the agricultural sector of
ORANI 78', IMPACT Centre Working Paper no. OP-45, University of Melbourne.
Dwyer, J., Kent, C. & Pease, A. 1993, 'Exchange rate pass-through: Different
responses of importers and exporters', Reserve Bank of Australia Research
Discussion Paper no. 9304, Sydney.

Mimeo
Brown, J. A. C. 1967, The life cycle in income, mimeo, Department of
Economics, University of Bristol.

Conference Paper
Suzuki, R. 1982, Workers' attitudes towards compensation, paper presented to
10th World Congress of Sociology, Mexico City, 16-21 Aug.

Thesis
Crowley, F. K. 1949, Working class conditions in Australia, PhD thesis,
University of Melbourne.

CORRECTIONS TO PROOFS
Proofs are for the purpose of detecting errors in the typesetting. Do not
alter the article unless it is absolutely necessary. When you receive page
proofs please read and check them carefully.

Appendix 1
Examples of One-Column and Two-Column Width Tables

Note the use of upper and lower case.

Table 4 The Green Paper Growth
and Unemployment Projections

	Base growth	High growth
Unemployment rate 1992–93 (per cent)	11.0	11.0
Real GDP growth, average (per cent per annum)	3.5	4.75
Labour productivity (per cent per annum)	1.0	1.75
Labour force growth (per cent per annum)	1.9	2.25
Unemployment rate 2000–01 (per cent)	7.0	5.0

Source: Committee on Employment Opportunities (1993, p. 52).

Table 1 National Accounts

	GDP ($million current, seasonally adjusted)	GDP ($million 1989–90, seasonally adjusted)	GDP growth rate (per cent)	Household disposable income ($million current, seasonally adjusted)
1990–91	379 253	367 619	-0.6	245 699
1991–92	387 325	368 749	0.7	257 111
1992–93	403 852	380 683	3.0	267 311
1993–94	425 566	396 858	3.7	279 113
1993 June quarter	103 469	97 133	1.9	67 887
September quarter	104 221	97 608	0.5	67 869
December quarter	104 794	97 971	0.4	68 590
1994 March quarter	107 450	100 043	2.1	70 531
June quarter	108 702	100 716	0.7	71 204

Sources: ABS, *Australian National Accounts: National Income, Expenditure and Product*, Cat. no. 5206.0; *Australian Economic Indicators*, Cat. no. 1350.0.

Table 5 GDP Growth Rates for Selected Asian and OECD Economies
(per cent per annum)

Nation	1992	1993	1994[a]	1995[a]
Asia				
South Korea	5.0	5.6	7.0	7.0
Taiwan	6.0	5.9	6.0	6.5
Hong Kong	5.3	5.5	5.0	5.0
Singapore	5.8	9.9	8.0	7.0
Malaysia	7.8	8.5	8.4	8.0
OECD				
United States	2.6	3.0	4.0	3.0
Germany	2.1	−1.3	1.8	2.6
France	1.2	−0.9	1.8	2.9
Italy	0.7	−0.7	1.5	2.6
United Kingdom	−0.6	1.9	2.8	3.2
Australia	2.1	4.0	4.0	4.3
OECD average	1.7	1.2	2.6	2.9

Note: (a) Estimate.

Source: OECD (1994, p. 119, Table A4).

B-QUEST (BUSINESS QUEST)

ADDRESS FOR SUBMISSION :

CAROLE SCOTT, EDITOR
B-QUEST (BUSINESS QUEST)
STATE UNIVERSITY OF WEST GEORGIA
COLLEGE OF BUSINESS
WEST GEORGIA COLLEGE
CARROLLTON, GA 30118-3020
770-836-6477
770-836-6774 (Fax)
E-Mail : cscott@sbf.bus.westga.edu

CIRCULATION DATA :

Reader : Academic

Frequency of Issue : Quarterly

Copies Per Issue :

Subscription Price :

Sponsorship : University

PUBLICATION GUIDELINES :

Manuscript Length : 16-20

Copies Required : One

Computer Submission : Yes

Format : Dos, Windows Word, WordPerfect

Fees to Review : 0.00 US$

REVIEW INFORMATION :

Type of Review : Blind Review

No. of External Reviewers : One

No. of In House Reviewers : One

Acceptance Rate :

Time To Review : 2-3 months

Reviewer's Comments : Yes

Fees to Publish : 0.00 US$

Invited Articles :

MANUSCRIPT TOPICS : ACCOUNTING INFORMATION SYSTEMS;
   ACCOUNTING THEORY & PRACTICE; AUDITING; CAPITAL BUDGETING; COST ACCOUNTING;
   GOVERNMENT & NON-PROFIT ACCOUNTING; INSURANCE;
   INTERNATIONAL & ECONOMIC DEVELOPMENT; INTERNATIONAL FINANCE;
   PORTFOLIO & SECURITY ANALYSIS; PUBLIC POLICY ECONOMICS; REAL ESTATE;
   TAX ACCOUNTING; BUSINESS INFORMATION SYSTEMS; CONSUMER ECONOMICS

PUBLICATION GUIDELINES : MLA Writers Handbook

MANUSCRIPT GUIDELINES/COMMENTS :

B-QUEST is a new publication; there is no data yet (on acceptance rates and circulation). Some articles are invited.

We accept computer submission or a 3.5 inch disk (one of these is a must), formatted in DOS or Windows Word or WordPerfect. It should be noted that this is an electronic journal; there is no paper version. It will be archived.

   World Wide Web address (URL): http://www.westga.edu/~bquest/

B-QUEST (BUSINESS QUEST), a new, World Wide Web, academic journal of applied topics in business and economics, invites you to submit manuscripts in the following and closely related fields: advertising, auditing, banking, business information systems, business law, consumer economics, corporate finance, cost accounting, economics, entrepreneurship, forecasting, government relations, investment analysis, management accounting, marketing research, risk management, and sales management. Although manuscripts of 2,500 to 3,500 words are preferred, up to 5,000 words are acceptable.

In order to serve as an interface between different academic disciplines and between academicians and practitioners, B-QUEST will publish on the World Wide Web highly readable articles in the various business disciplines and economics whose subject matter is of interest to either or both academicians and practitioners. Particularly welcome are articles of an interdisciplinary nature. B-QUEST is exclusively an electronic journal.

Manuscripts are invited from both academic and non-academic sources. Manuscripts previously published or under consideration for publication elsewhere are not acceptable. Mathematical notation should be kept to the minimum necessary for understanding. Do not include jargon, higher mathematics, or advanced statistical techniques in the body of the manuscript. Purely theoretical topics are not acceptable. A summary of the manuscript should be provided. Copyright to B-QUEST's contents is vested in the publisher, State University of West Georgia, College of Business.

MANUSCRIPT GUIDELINES

Submissions may be made at any time. Manuscripts should be sent either on a three and one-half-inch disk in Dos or Windows WordPerfect or as a WordPerfect attachment to an E-mail message. Query before submitting a manuscript in any other form. Please follow the MLA (Modern Language Association) WRITER'S GUIDE, 4th edition. Send manuscripts and address queries to the editor.

Each submission should have a title page on which also appears the name(s) of the author(s), the author(s)' institutional affiliation and position, mailing address, voice mail number, and, if available, a FAX number and E-mail address. (This information should appear nowhere else in the manuscript.) Inquire about graphical material's format before sending it.

Manuscripts should be in English and written in a clear and concise style suitable for an international audience of academicians and practitioners. Footnotes should be held to a minimum. Tables and graphs should have titles which make clear what they contain and be numbered consecutively. Terms should be written out when first used along with their abbreviations, which can subsequently be used in place of the terms.

REVIEW PROCESS

Receipt of manuscripts will be acknowledged; subsequently there will be notification of their acceptance or rejection. After being reviewed by the editor for general acceptability, non-invited articles submitted by academicians will be blind reviewed by two reviewers, at least one of whom is an outside reviewer. (Blind-reviewed articles will be identified as such in the journal.) The acceptability of other manuscripts will be determined by the editor. Manuscripts will either be accepted as they are; returned with reviewers' comments for revision; or rejected. Turn around time will probably be much shorter than that of the average non-electronic academic journal. Manuscripts will be published on the World Wide Web (WWW or Web) as they are accepted. A new issue will be published every quarter.

BANK ACCOUNTING & FINANCE

ADDRESS FOR SUBMISSION :

CLAIRE GREENE, EDITOR
BANK ACCOUNTING & FINANCE
130 BELKNAP STREET
CONCORD, MA 01742
USA
508-369-6285
508-371-2961 (Fax)
E-Mail : 200-4466@mcimail.com

CIRCULATION DATA :

Reader : Business Persons

Frequency of Issue : Quarterly

Copies Per Issue : 2001-3000

Subscription Price : 220.00 US$
    Academics : 66.00 US$

Sponsorship : Profit Oriented Corp.

PUBLICATION GUIDELINES :

Manuscript Length : 16-25

Copies Required : Two

Computer Submission : Yes

Format : IBM PC Compat, WordPerfect

Fees to Review : 0.00 US$

REVIEW INFORMATION :

Type of Review : Blind Review

No. of External Reviewers : Two

No. of In House Reviewers : One

Acceptance Rate : 50 %

Time To Review : 1-2 months

Reviewer's Comments : Yes

Fees to Publish : 0.00 US$

Invited Articles : Over 50%

MANUSCRIPT TOPICS : ACCOUNTING INFORMATION SYSTEMS;
   ACCOUNTING THEORY & PRACTICE; AUDITING; COST ACCOUNTING;
   INTERNATIONAL FINANCE; PORTFOLIO & SECURITY ANALYSIS; BANKING

PUBLICATION GUIDELINES : Chicago Manual of Style

MANUSCRIPT GUIDELINES/COMMENTS :

HOW TO SUBMIT A MANUSCRIPT
Bank ACCOUNTING & FINANCE welcomes articles to be considered for publication.
BANK ACCOUNTING & FINANCE is the first in-depth, practical journal for bank
accounting and financial officers. Readers are CFOs, treasurers controllers,
accountants, auditors, cashiers, and financial VPs.

Readers are interested in articles on topics including, but not limited to,
the following:

* financial accounting,
* management accounting,
* capital planning,
* profitability measurement,
* asset/liability management,
* liquidity issues, * treasury management and investment policy,
* new financial instruments and capital markets products,
* bank stock analysis,
* risk management,

BANK ACCOUNTING & FINANCE

* portfolio management,
* cost control,
* mergers and acquisitions,
* technology,
* reporting systems,
* auditing and internal control,
* regulation,
* taxes.

For example, the following types of articles would be appealing to the practitioners who read BANK ACCOUNTING & FINANCE:

* Description and analysis of implementation issues for new standards and rules issued by FASB, the EITF , bank regulators, the SEC, and the IRS.

* Case studies showing how a particular bank designed a new management accounting system, implemented new techniques of A/L management, combined operations after a merger, or improved controls for derivatives.

* Surveys showing how a group of banks implemented a new accounting standard or correlating banks' stock prices to strategy or reporting practices.

Articles should be practical, with concrete advice, illustrative anecdotes and examples, and a description of results readers might expect if they follow the author's recommendations. Articles generally run from 3,000 to 7,500 words (12 to 30 double-spaced typewritten pages). The how and case study approach is particularly appropriate for BANK ACCOUNTING & FINANCE.

SUBMISSION GUIDELINES
To propose an article, please contact editor Claire Greene before you start to write (voice 508-369-6285; fax 508-371-2961. She will enjoy talking over your idea with you and can help you tailor it to BANK ACCOUNTING & FINANCE'S specific needs for manuscripts.

BANK ACCOUNTING & FINANCE is published by Institutional Investor, Inc., 488 Madison Avenue, New York, NY 10022. Tel: 212-224-3545 Fax: 212-224-3527.

BANKER'S MAGAZINE

ADDRESS FOR SUBMISSION :

SUSAN L. GORDON, MANAGING EDITOR
BANKER'S MAGAZINE
WARREN GORHAM & LAMONT
1 PENN PLAZA, 42ND FLOOR
NEW YORK, NY 10119
USA
212-971-5821
212-971-5215 (Fax)
E-Mail : sgordon@ny.wgl.com

CIRCULATION DATA :

Reader : Business Persons

Frequency of Issue : 6 Times/Year

Copies Per Issue :

Subscription Price : 135.00 US$

Sponsorship : Profit Oriented Corp.

PUBLICATION GUIDELINES :

Manuscript Length : 11-15

Copies Required : One

Computer Submission : Yes

Format : WordPerfect

Fees to Review : 0.00 US$

REVIEW INFORMATION :

Type of Review : Editorial Review

No. of External Reviewers :

No. of In House Reviewers : Two

Acceptance Rate : 11-20%

Time To Review : One month or less

Reviewer's Comments : Yes

Fees to Publish : 0.00 US$

Invited Articles : Over 50%

MANUSCRIPT TOPICS : AUDITING; ECONOMETRICS; INTERNATIONAL FINANCE;
  ECONOMICS; FINANCE & INVESTMENTS; BANKING

PUBLICATION GUIDELINES : Chicago Manual of Style

MANUSCRIPT GUIDELINES/COMMENTS :

1. CHICAGO MANUAL OF STYLE

2. THE BANKER'S MAGAZINE provides practical, topical articles for executives
in commercial banks, savings and loans, credit unions, brokerage houses, and
related financial services institutions.

3. We encourage authors to write from first-hand experience in a practical,
"how to" manner, avoiding lengthy, academic articles on theoretical subjects.
Our readership consists of senior bank executives who are interested in
learning from the experiences of other bankers in the various areas of
banking.

4. We publish articles on an exclusive basis. Articles will not be accepted if
they have appeared or have been accepted for publication elsewhere.

5. While the utmost care will be given all manuscripts, we cannot accept
responsibility for returning unsolicited manuscripts. Articles accepted for
publication are subject to editorial revision.

BANKER'S MAGAZINE

6. Full-length manuscripts should run between 10-12 typed, double-spaced pages, including exhibits and footnotes (1500 to 2000 words). Columns should be somewhat shorter, approximately 7 to 10 pages (1000 to 1600 words).

7. Manuscripts muat be submitted on computer disks in WordPerfect, in addition to hard copy.

8. Write in the active voice in the third person. Avoid all personal references, such as "I" or "you".

9. Use heads and subheads to emphasize points and break up the copy. Type all heads flush with the left-hand margin, underlining the main heads.

10. Exhibits or charts accompanying manuscripts should be drawn or printed in black ink.

11. Place references and footnotes at the end of the article, separate from the text. These citations should follow the CHICAGO MANUAL OF STYLE and also be typed double-spaced.

12. Include a brief biographical sketch of yourself, including your firm affiliation and your title.

BEHAVIORAL RESEARCH IN ACCOUNTING

ADDRESS FOR SUBMISSION :

DON FINN, EDITOR
BEHAVIORAL RESEARCH IN ACCOUNTING
TEXAS TECH UNIVERSITY
COLLEGE OF BUSINESS ADMINISTRATION
AMERICAN ACCOUNTING ASSOCIATION
BOX 42101
LUBBOCK, TX 79409-2101
806-742-2038
806-742-2099 (Fax)
E-Mail : oddon@coba2.ttv.edu

CIRCULATION DATA :

Reader : Academic

Frequency of Issue : 2 Times/Year

Copies Per Issue : 1001-2000

Subscription Price :
  AAA + ABO Membership : 20.00 US$

Sponsorship : Professional Assoc.

PUBLICATION GUIDELINES :

Manuscript Length : 21-25

Copies Required : Four

Computer Submission : No

Format : N/A

Fees to Review : 50.00 US$

REVIEW INFORMATION :

Type of Review : Blind Review

No. of External Reviewers : Two

No. of In House Reviewers : Zero

Acceptance Rate : 11-20%

Time To Review : 4-6 months

Reviewer's Comments : Yes

Fees to Publish : 0.00 US$

Invited Articles : 5% or less

MANUSCRIPT TOPICS : ACCOUNTING THEORY & PRACTICE; AUDITING;
   COST ACCOUNTING; TAX ACCOUNTING; BEHAVIORAL ACCOUNTING RESEARCH

PUBLICATION GUIDELINES :

MANUSCRIPT GUIDELINES/COMMENTS :

EDITORIAL POLICIES
BEHAVIORAL RESEARCH IN ACCOUNTING is published by the Accounting, Behavior and
Organizations Section of the American Accounting Association. Original
research relating to accounting and how it affects and is affected by
individuals and organizations will be considered by the journal. Theoretical
papers and papers based upon empirical research (e.g., field, survey, and
experimental research) are appropriate. Replications of previously published
studies will be considered. The primary audience of the journal is the
membership of the Accounting, Behavior and Organizations Section of the
American Accounting Association.

For a manuscript to be acceptable for publication, the research question
should be of interest to the intended readership, the research project should
be well-designed and well executed, and arguments or findings should be
presented effectively and efficiently.

THE REVIEW PROCESS
Each manuscript submitted to BEHAVIORAL RESEARCH IN ACCOUNTING is subject to
the following review procedures:

BEHAVIORAL RESEARCH IN ACCOUNTING

REVIEW PROCESS
1. Each manuscript is reviewed by the editor for general suitability for this journal.

2. For those that are judged suitable, at lease two reviewers are selected and a double blind review process takes place.

3. Using the recommendations of the reviewers, the editor will decide whether the particular manuscript should be accepted as is, revised, or rejected for publication.

The process described above is a general process. In any particular case, deviations may occur from the steps described.

SUBMISSION OF MANUSCRIPTS
Authors should note the following guidelines for submitting manuscripts:

1. Manuscripts currently under consideration by another journal or other publisher should not be submitted. The author must state that the work is not submitted or published elsewhere.

2. In the case of manuscripts reporting on field surveys or experiments, four copies of the instrument (questionnaire, case, interview plan, or the like) should be submitted.

3. Four copies should be submitted together with a check for $50.00 in U.S. funds payable to the American Accounting Association and sent to Don W. Finn, Texas Tech University, COBA, P.O. Box 42101, Lubbock Texas 79409-2101. The submission fee is nonrefundable.

4. The author should retain a copy of the paper.

5. Revisions must be submitted within 12 months from request, otherwise they will be considered new submissions.

MATHEMATICAL NOTATION
Mathematical notation should be employed only where its rigor and precision are necessary, and in such circumstances authors should explain in the narrative format the principal operations performed. Notation should be avoided in footnotes. Unusual symbols, particularly if handwritten, should be identified in the margin when they appear. Displayed material should clearly indicate the alignment, superscripts, and subscripts. Equations should be numbered in parentheses flush with the right-hand margin.

DOCUMENTATION
CITATIONS: Work cited should use the "author-date system" keyed to a list of works in the reference list (see below). Authors should make an effort to include the relevant page numbers in the cited works.

1. In the text, works are cited as follows: author's last name and date, without comma, in parentheses: for example (Jones 1987); with two authors: (Jones and Freeman 1973); with more than two: (Jones et al. 1985): with more than one source cited together (Jones 1987; Freeman 1986); with two or more works by one author: (Jones 1985, 1987).

BEHAVIORAL RESEARCH IN ACCOUNTING

2. Unless confusion would result, do not use "p." or "pp." before page numbers, for example Jones 1987, 115).

3. When the reference list contains more than one work of an author published in the same year, the suffix a, b, etc. follows the data in the text citation, for example (Jones 1987a) or Jones 1987a; Freeman 1985b).

4. If an author's name is mentioned in the text, it need not be repeated in the citation, for example "Jones (1987, 115) says . . ."

5. Citations to institutional works should use acronyms or short titles where practicable, for example (AAA ASOBAT 1966); (AICPA Cohen Commission Report 1977). Where brief, the full title of an institutional work might be shown in a citation, for example (ICAEW The Corporate Report 1975).

6. If the manuscript r refers to statutes, legal treatises, or court cases, citations acceptable in law reviews should be used.

REFERENCE LIST: Every manuscript must include a list of references containing only those works cited. Each entry should contain all data necessary for unambiguous identification. With the author-date system, use the following format recommended by the Chicago Manual:

1. Arrange citations in alphabetical order according to surname of the first author or the name of the institution responsible for the citation.

2. Use author's initials instead of proper names.

3. In listing more than one name in references (Rayburn, L., and B. Harrelson,...), there should always be a comma before "and."

4. Dates of publication should be placed immediately after author's names.

5. Titles of journals should not be abbreviated.

6. Multiple works by the same author(s) should be listed in chronological order of publication. Two or more works by the same author(s) in the same year are distinguished by letters after the date.
Sample entries are as follows:

American Accounting Association, Committee on Concepts and Standards for External Financial Reports. 1977. Statement on Accounting Theory and Theory Acceptance. Sarasota, FL: AAA.

Bohrnstedt, G. W. 1970. Reliability and Validity Assessment in Attitude Measurement. In Attitude Measurement, edited by G. Summers, 80-99. Chicago, IL: Rand McNally.

Burgstahler,D. 1987. Inference from Empirical Research The Accounting Review 62 (January): 203-214. Chow, C. 1983. The impacts of Accounting Regulation on Bondholder and Shareholder Wealth: The Case of the Securities Act. The Accounting Review 58 (3): 4845-520.

Hunt, S. D.; L. B. Chonko and J. B. Wilcox. 1984. Ethical Problems of Marketing Researchers. Journal of Marketing Research (August):304-324.

Maranell, G., ed. 1974. Scaling A Sourcebook of Behavioral Scientist. Chicago, IL: Aldine Publishing Company.

Saaty, T. L., and L. G. Vargas. 1984a. The Legitimacy of Rank Reversal. Omega 12: 513-516.

_____and_____. 1984b. Inconsistency and Rank Reversal. Journal of Mathematical Psychology 28: 205-214.

Waterhouse, J., and A. Richardson. 1989. Behavioral Research Implications of the New Management Accounting Environment. Working paper, University of Alberta.

FOOTNOTES: Footnotes are not to be used for documentation. Textual footnotes should be used only for extensions and useful excursions of information that, if included in the body of the text, might disrupt its continuity. Footnotes should be double-spaced and numbered consecutively throughout the manuscript with superscript Arabic numerals. Footnotes are placed at the end of the text.

POLICY ON REPRODUCTION
An objective of BEHAVIORAL RESEARCH IN ACCOUNTING is to promote the wide dissemination of the results of systematic scholarly inquires into the broad field of accounting.

Permission is hereby granted to reproduce any of the contents of BRIA for use in courses of instruction, as long as the source and American Accounting Association copyright are indicated in any such reproductions.

Written application must be made to the Editor for permission to reproduce any of the contents of BRIA for use in other than courses of instruction-e.g., inclusion in books of readings or in any other such instances, the applicant must notify the author(s) in writing of the intended use of each reproduction. Normally, BRIA will not assess a charge for the waiver of copyright.

Except as otherwise noted in articles, the copyright has been transferred to the American Accounting Association for all items appearing in this journal. Where the author(s) has (have) not transferred the copyright to the American Accounting Association, applicants must seek permission to reproduce (for all purposes) directly from the author(s).

MANUSCRIPT PREPARATION AND STYLE

BEHAVIORAL RESEARCH IN ACCOUNTING's manuscript preparation guidelines follow (with a slight modification) documentation 2 of the CHICAGO MANUAL OF STYLE (14th ed.; University of Chicago Press). Another helpful guide to usage and style is THE ELEMENTS OF STYLE, by William Strunk, Jr., and E. B. White (Macmillan). Spelling follows WEBSTER'S INTERNATIONAL DICTIONARY.

FORMAT
1. All manuscripts should be typed on one side of 8 1/2 x 11" good quality paper and be double-spaced, except for indented quotations.

2. Manuscripts should be as concise as the subject and research method permit, generally not to exceed 7,000 words.

3. Margins should be at least one inch from top, bottom, and sides to facilitate editing and duplication.

4. To assure anonymous review, authors should not identify themselves directly or indirectly in their papers. Single authors should not use the editorial "we."

BEHAVIORAL RESEARCH IN ACCOUNTING

5. A cover page should include the title of the paper, the author's name, title, and affiliation, any acknowledgments, and a footnote indicating whether the author would be willing to share the data (see last paragraph in this statement).

6. All pages, including tables, appendices, and references, should be serially numbered.

7. Spell out numbers from one to ten, except when used in tables and lists, and when used with mathematical, statistical, scientific, or technical units and quantities, such as distances, weights, and measures. For example: three days; 3 kilometers; 30 years. All other numbers are expressed numerically. Generally, when using approximate terms, spell out the number, for example, approximately thirty years.

8. In nontechnical text use the word percent; in technical text the symbol% is used (See the CHICAGO MANUAL for discussion of the correct usage.

9. a. Use a hyphen (-) to join unit modifiers or to clarify usage. For example: a well-presented analysis; re-form. See WEBSTER'S for correct usage.
    b. En dash (-) is used between words indicating a duration, such as hourly time or months or years. No space on either side.
    c. Em dash(--) is used to indicate an abrupt change in thought, or where a period is strong and a comma is too weak. No space on either side.

10. The following will be Roman in all cases: i.e., e.g., ibib., et al., op.cit.
11. Initials: A. B. Smith (space between): States, etc.: U.S., U.K. (no space)

12. When using "Big 6" or "Big 8" use Arabic figures (don't spell out).

13. Ellipsis should be used not periods, example: .... not. . . .

14. Use "SAS" No. #" no "SAS #."

15. Use only one space after periods, colons, exclamation points, question marks, quotation marks--any punctuation that separates two sentences.

16. a. Use real quotation marks--never inch marks: "and" not and.
    b. Use apostrophes, not footmarks: 'not'.

17. Punctuation used with quote marks:
    a. Commas and periods are always placed inside the quotation marks.
    b. Colons and semicolons go outside the quotation marks.
    c. Question marks and exclamation points go in or out, depending on whether they belong to the material inside the quote or not. If they belong to the quoted material, they go inside the quote marks, and vice versa.

18. Punctuation and parentheses: Sentence punctuation goes after the closing parenthesis if what is inside the parentheses is part of the sentence (as this phrase is). This also applies to commas, semicolons, and colons. If what is inside the parentheses is an entire statement of its own, the ending punctuation should also be inside the parentheses.

BEHAVIORAL RESEARCH IN ACCOUNTING

19. Headings should be arranged so that major headings are centered, bold, and capitalized. Second level headings should be flush left, bold, and both upper and lower case. Third level headings should be flush left bold, italic, and both upper and lower case. Fourth level headings should be paragraph indent, bold, and lower case.
Headings and subheadings should not be numbered. For example:

A CENTERED, BOLD, ALL CAPITALIZED, FIRST LEVEL HEADING
A Flush Left, Bold, Upper and Lower Case, Second Level Heading
A Flush Left, Bold, Italic, Upper and Lower case, Third Level Heading
   A paragraph indent, bold, lower case, fourth level heading. Text starts...

ABSTRACT
An abstract of about 100-150 words should be presented on a separate page immediately preceding the text. The abstract should be nonmathematical and include a readable summary of the research question, method, and the significance of the findings and contribution. The title, but not the author's name or other identification designations, should appear on the abstract page.

TABLES AND FIGURES
The author should note the following general requirements:
1. Each table and figure (graphic) should appear on a separate page and should be placed at the end of the text. Each should bear an Arabic number and a complete title indicating the exact contents of the table or figure.

2. A reference to each table or figure should be made in the text.

3. The author should indicate by marginal notation where each table or figure should be inserted in the text, e.g., (Insert Table X here).

4. Tables or figures should be reasonably interpreted without reference to the text.

5. Source lines and notes should be included as necessary.

6. When information is not available, use "NA" capitalized with no slash between.

7. Figures must be prepared in a form suitable for printing.

POLICY ON DATA AVAILABILITY
The following policy, adopted by the Executive Committee of the AAA in April 1989, is applicable to all manuscripts submitted to BEHAVIORAL RESEARCH IN ACCOUNTING:

> ...authors are encouraged to make their data available for use by others .... Authors of articles which report data dependent results should footnote the status of data availability and, when pertinent, this should be accomplished by information on how the data may be obtained.

BEST'S REVIEW LIFE AND HEALTH

ADDRESS FOR SUBMISSION :

LEE MCDONALD, EDITOR
BEST'S REVIEW LIFE AND HEALTH
A.M. BEST COMPANY
AMBEST ROAD
OLDWICK, NJ 08858
USA
908-439-2200 EXT 5561
908-439-3363 (Fax)
E-Mail : mcdonal@ambest.com

CIRCULATION DATA :

Reader : Insurance Agents,Brokers & Per

Frequency of Issue : Monthly

Copies Per Issue : Over 25,000

Subscription Price : 22.00 US$

Sponsorship : Profit Oriented Corp.

PUBLICATION GUIDELINES :

Manuscript Length : 4-6

Copies Required : One

Computer Submission : Yes

Format : ASCII or Any Usual

Fees to Review : 0.00 US$

REVIEW INFORMATION :

Type of Review : Editorial Review

No. of External Reviewers : Zero

No. of In House Reviewers : Two

Acceptance Rate : 11-20%

Time To Review : 1-2 months

Reviewer's Comments : No

Fees to Publish : 0.00 US$

Invited Articles : 11-20%

MANUSCRIPT TOPICS : INSURANCE

PUBLICATION GUIDELINES :

MANUSCRIPT GUIDELINES/COMMENTS :

BEST'S REVIEW LIFE AND HEALTH is published primarily for insurance agents and
brokers as well as home office executives. We welcome original articles
discussing trends, problems and controversies affecting the professionals in
this audience. When submitting an article for consideration, please keep these
guidelines in mind:
1. Only articles written exclusively for BEST'S REVIEW LIFE AND HEALTH will be
published. Material that has been sent to other publications will not be
considered.

2. We rely on the author's integrity in submitting original work. Any material
derived from other sources should be clearly identified within the text (see
item 11). Prior to publication, authors must sign a statement verifying
originality and acknowledging our copyright.

3. The article should be based on the knowledge/experience of the author.
Since BEST'S REVIEW LIFE AND HEALTH considers the author as the expert, he or
she must not interview other individuals or quote from academic and other
opinion pieces. In certain cases, background research and supporting data may
be appropriate, and as indicated above, these sources must be properly
identified.

BEST'S REVIEW LIFE AND HEALTH

4. We do not publish articles that promote the author's company, products or services.
5. Articles should focus on a specific issue, not several tangential matters. Authors should explain technical terms clearly and simply so they can be understood by a broad segment of readers.

6. Authors are strongly encouraged to discuss article ideas with an editor and submit an outline for review before investing a substantial amount of time in writing. Articles will not be accepted until they are received and evaluated by the editors.

7. All articles are edited by our staff. Editors will contact authors when questions arise during the editing process. Due to the volume of material we publish, we are unable to provide authors with edited manuscripts or galleys for review.

8. Articles should be between 1,500 words (approximately six double-spaced pages) and 2,000 (approximately eight double-spaced pages) in length. As a general rule, tell the story in as few words as possible.

9. All articles should be typed double-spaced with one-inch margins around the page. Avoid outline form or all caps. Number the pages at the bottom. If the article was prepared on a word-processing system, send a 5 1/4-inch or 3 1/2-inch diskette that is double-sided and, preferably, high-density (1.2 meg). The material should be in flat ASCII format, although we can accept virtually any word processing format. Be sure to write the author's name and article title on the label.

10. Write your full name and any pertinent professional designations that should appear in the author's ID. Be sure to include your current business affiliation, showing the name, location and type of business.

11. Articles should not contain footnotes, endnotes or bibliographies. Authors must cite sources (full name, location and, if necessary, a brief description of person and/or company) within the text. Since most of our readers are not lawyers, legal citations should consist of case, court and date.

12. Articles should be written in narrative style, in paragraph form.
13. Include only essential charts, tables and diagrams, labeling them clearly and completely, and showing the source of the material at the bottom.

14. Articles should be mailed to BEST'S REVIEW LIFE AND HEALTH at the A.M. Best Company, Ambest Road, Oldwick, N.J. 08858 or faxed to 908-439-3363, or e-mailed to bestreview@ambest.com.

15. Authors will receive five complimentary copies of the magazine in which their article appears. Reprints are available to authors in quantities of 100 or more at cost.
16. Since each issue of BEST'S REVIEW LIFE AND HEALTH is copyrighted by the A.M. Best Company, publications wishing to use the article after it has appeared in our magazine must obtain permission to do so.
Thank you for your interest in our publication. We look forward to working with you.

BEST'S REVIEW PROPERTY AND CASUALITY

ADDRESS FOR SUBMISSION :

LEE MCDONALD, EDITOR
BEST'S REVIEW PROPERTY AND CASUALITY
A.M. BEST COMPANY
AMBEST ROAD
OLDWICK, NJ 08858
USA
908-439-2200 EXT 5561
908-439-3363 (Fax)
E-Mail : mcdonal@ambest.com

CIRCULATION DATA :

Reader : Insurance Agents, Brokers, Per

Frequency of Issue : Monthly

Copies Per Issue : Over 25,000

Subscription Price : 22.00 US$

Sponsorship : Profit Oriented Corp.

PUBLICATION GUIDELINES :

Manuscript Length : 4-6

Copies Required : One

Computer Submission : Yes

Format : ASCII or Any Usual

Fees to Review : 0.00 US$

REVIEW INFORMATION :

Type of Review : Editorial Review

No. of External Reviewers : Zero

No. of In House Reviewers : Two

Acceptance Rate : 11-20%

Time To Review : 1-2 months

Reviewer's Comments : No

Fees to Publish : 0.00 US$

Invited Articles : 11-20%

MANUSCRIPT TOPICS : INSURANCE

PUBLICATION GUIDELINES :

MANUSCRIPT GUIDELINES/COMMENTS :

BEST'S REVIEW PROPERTY AND CASUALTY is published primarily for insurance
agents and brokers as well as home office executives. We welcome original
articles discussing trends, problems and controversies affecting the
professionals in this audience. When submitting an article for consideration,
please keep these guidelines in mind:
1. Only articles written exclusively for BEST'S REVIEW PROPERTY AND CASUALTY
will be published. Material that has been sent to other publications will not
be considered.

2. We rely on the author's integrity in submitting original work. Any material
derived from other sources should be clearly identified within the text (see
item 11). Prior to publication, authors must sign a statement verifying
originality and acknowledging our copyright.

3. The artide should be based on the knowledge/experience of the author. Since
BEST'S REVIEW PROPERTY AND CASUALTY considers the author as the expert, he or
she must not interview other individuals or quote from academic and other
opinion pieces. In certain cases, background research and supporting data may
be appropriate, and as indicated above, these sources must be properly
identified.

BEST'S REVIEW PROPERTY AND CASUALITY

4. We do not publish articles that promote the author's company, products or services.

5. Articles should focus on a specific issue, not several tangential matters. Authors should explain technical terms clearly and simply so they can be understood by a broad segment of readers.

6. Authors are strongly encouraged to discuss article ideas with an editor and submit an outline for review before investing a substantial amount of time in writing. Articles will not be accepted until they are received and evaluated by the editors.

7. All articles are edited by our staff. Editors will contact authors when questions arise during the editing process. Due to the volume of material we publish, we are unable to provide authors with edited manuscripts or galleys for review.

8. Articles should be between 1,500 words (approximately six double-spaced pages) and 2,000 (approximately eight double-spaced pages) in length. As a general rule, tell the story in as few words as possible.

9. All articles should be typed double-spaced with one-inch margins around the page. Avoid outline form or all caps. Number the pages at the bottom. If the article was prepared on a word-processing system, send a 5 1/4-inch or 3 1/2-inch diskette that is double-sided and, preferably, high-density (1.2 meg). The material should be in flat ASCII format, although we can accept virtually any word processing format. Be sure to write the author's name and article title on the label.

10. Write your full name and any pertinent professional designations that should appear in the author's ID. Be sure to include your current business affiliation, showing the name, location and type of business.

11. Articles should not contain footnotes, endnotes or bibliographies. Authors must cite sources (full name, location and, if necessary, a brief description of person and/or company) within the text. Since most of our readers are not lawyers, legal citations should consist of case, court and date.

12. Articles should be written in narrative style, in paragraph form.

13. Include only essential charts, tables and diagrams, labeling them clearly and completely, and showing the source of the material at the bottom.

14. Articles should be mailed to BEST'S REVIEW PROPERTY AND CASUALTY at the A.M. Best Company, Ambest Road, Oldwick, N.J. 08858 or faxed to 908-439-3363 or e-mailed to bestreview@ambest.com.

15. Authors will receive five complimentary copies of the magazine in which their article appears. Reprints are available to authors in quantities of 100 or more at cost.

16. Since each issue of BEST'S REVIEW PROPERTY AND CASUALTY is copyrighted by the A.M. Best Company, publications wishing to use the article after it has appeared in our magazine must obtain permission to do so.

Thank you for your interest in our publication. We look forward to working with you.

BRITISH ACCOUNTING REVIEW

ADDRESS FOR SUBMISSION :

PROF. TREVOR HOPPER, EDITOR
BRITISH ACCOUNTING REVIEW
UNIVERSITY OF MANCHESTER
DEPT. OF ACCOUNTING & FINANCIAL MGT.
ROSCOW BUILDING
MANCHESTER, M13 9PL
UK
+44 1712 674466
+44 1714 822293 (Fax)
E-Mail : apsubs@acad.com

CIRCULATION DATA :

Reader : Academic

Frequency of Issue : Quarterly

Copies Per Issue : 1001-2000

Subscription Price : 195.00 US$
   Brit.Acct.Assn.Mem. : 40.00 US$

Sponsorship : University

PUBLICATION GUIDELINES :

Manuscript Length : Up to 8,000 Words

Copies Required : Four

Computer Submission : No

Format : N/A

Fees to Review : 0.00 US$

REVIEW INFORMATION :

Type of Review : Blind Review

No. of External Reviewers : Two

No. of In House Reviewers : Zero

Acceptance Rate : 21-30%

Time To Review : 2-3 months

Reviewer's Comments : Yes

Fees to Publish : 0.00 US$

Invited Articles : 5% or less

MANUSCRIPT TOPICS : ACCOUNTING INFORMATION SYSTEMS;
   ACCOUNTING THEORY & PRACTICE; AUDITING; CAPITAL BUDGETING; COST ACCOUNTING;
   GOVERNMENT & NON-PROFIT ACCOUNTING; INTERNATIONAL FINANCE;
   PORTFOLIO & SECURITY ANALYSIS; TAX ACCOUNTING; FINANCE & INVESTMENTS

PUBLICATION GUIDELINES :

MANUSCRIPT GUIDELINES/COMMENTS :

TELEX: 25775 ACPRES G
URL: http://www.hbuk.co.uk/ap/journals/ba.htm
The BRITISH ACCOUNTING REVIEW is published by Academic Press Ltd. (a
subsidiary of Harcourt Brace U Company Ltd.) 24-28 Oval Road, London NW1 7DX,
England. Phone, Fax, Telex, E-mail and URL are above.

EDITORIAL POLICY
The BRITISH ACCOUNTING REVIEW is pleased to publish original scholarly papers
across the whole spectrum of Accounting and Finance. Papers should be
comprehensible to colleagues with a specialism or informed interest in the
general area to which the paper relates but who may, however, not be experts
in the specific issues dealt with in the paper. Prospective authors are
requested to bear in mind that there is an international readership of BAR but
that currently, over 50% of the readers are British, a proportion of whom are
undergraduate and postgraduate students.

BRITISH ACCOUNTING REVIEW

In addition to research reports, papers with a pedagogic, reflective or polemical emphasis are particularly welcomed. These might include authoritative state-of-art and review articles, comments and notes, papers which give guidance on research methods, reports on innovative teaching methods and/or articles concerned with educational issues. Essays prompted by the publicatin of a significant text or monograph are also welcomed. Additionally, studies which seek to replicate, develop and reinterpret previously published research (in, for example, a different national or organisational context) are encouraged.

The editors are pleased to receive any enquiries from authors about papers they are considering submitting to BAR, but the editors will not read and comment upon papers prior to their submission to the journal. Manuscripts should not normally be longer than 8,000 words. Manuscripts of more than 10,000 words will normally not be considered without the prior agreement of the editors. The editors reserve the right to return manuscripts directly to authors without being put through the refereeing process. Reasons for this will include situations in which, in the editors' judgement, for example: the manuscript is more appropriate to other more specialist journals; the manuscript falls outside the editorial policy; the author(s) have not complied with the NOTES TO CONTRIBUTORS.

NOTES FOR CONTRIBUTORS
Four copies of any manuscripts for consideration by BAR should be sent to the Co-editors.

ACCEPTANCE CRITERIA. BAR is particularly concerned with the readability of papers. Prospective authors are asked to pay particular attention to the clarity of their communication. Authors are reminded that the most common root causes for the rejection of a manuscript are the failure to expose the material as widely as possible before submission and failure to comply with the EDITORIAL POLICY and NOTES FOR CONTRIBUTORS. Authors are asked to use mathematics only if it contributes to the clarity and economy of presentation, or is an essential part of the argument. Authors are encouraged to put the mathematics in an appendix whenever possible. The conclusions of mathematical articles should be summarised in a form intelligible to the non-mathematical reader.

Submission of a paper to BAR automatically implies that the manuscript is not concurrently under consideration for publication elsewhere. All papers submitted to BAR will normally only be published subject to review by double blind referee. In the interests of a fair review, authors should try and avoid the use of anything which would make their indentity obvious. Referees are asked to comment upon the ORIGINALITY, AUTHORITY, COMPREHENSIVENESS, CONTRIBUTION, INTEREST and USEFULNESS of a submitted paper. All papers are also subjected to editorial review shich, whilst covering style and quality of communication, may also cover academic and scholarly content. The editors make every effort to give a decision on manuscripts as soon as possible.

PREPARATION OF COPY. Manuscripts must be typed in journal style on one side only of the paper (preferably A4 or 8 1/2 x 11 in.), double spaced (including notes and references), with a margin of at least 1 1/2 in. on the left-hand side. Essential notes should be indicated by superscript figures in the text and collected in a single section placed before the references under a heading 'Notes'. Tables and figures should be attached on separate sheets at the end of the manuscript: their position should be indicated in the text. A short abstract should be included at the head of the paper.

Citations in the text should read thus: Brown & Smith (1975), or (Brown & Smith, 1975), or, for specific quotations, (Brown & Smith, 1975, pp. 63-64). The conventions White (1975a), White (1975b) should be used if more than one publication by the same author(s) in a particular year is cited. Where there are three authors or more, all names should be given in the first citation; subsequently us et al. References should be listed in full, alphabetically at the end of the paper in the following style:

Arnold, J., Carsberg, B. & Scapens, R. (1980). Topics in Management Accounting, Oxford, Philip Allan.

Benston, G. (1981). 'Are accounting standards necessary?' In R. Leach & E. Stamp (eds), British Accounting Standards, The First 10 Years, pp. 201-214. Cambridge, Woodhead-Faulkener.

Bromwich, M. (1977). 'The use of present value valuation models in published accounting reports', The Accounting Review, July, pp. 587-596.

PROOFS AND OFFPRINTS. Authors are expected to correct proofs quickly and not to make revisions on proofs; revisions made on proofs may be charged for by the editors. No payments are made to authors.

Authors submitting a manuscript do so on the understanding that if it is accepted for publication, exclusive copyright in the paper shall be assigned to the Publisher. In consideration for the assignment of copyright, the Publisher will supply 50 offprints of each paper. Further offprints may be ordered at extra cost; the copyright assignment/offprint order form will be sent with the proofs. The Publisher will not put any limitation on the personal freedom of the author to use material contained in the paper in other works which may be published.

BUSINESS CREDIT

ADDRESS FOR SUBMISSION :

MEGAN SNYDER, EDITOR
BUSINESS CREDIT
CREDIT RESEARCH FOUNDATION
8815 CENTRE PARK DRIVE, SUITE 200
COLUMBIA, MD 21045-2158
USA
410-740-5560
410-740-5574 (Fax)
E-Mail (Web Address): http://www.nacm.org

CIRCULATION DATA :

Reader : Business Persons

Frequency of Issue : Monthly

Copies Per Issue : Over 25,000

Subscription Price : 22.00 US$
  Assn. Membership : 75.00 US$

Sponsorship : Professional Assoc.

PUBLICATION GUIDELINES :

Manuscript Length : 16-20

Copies Required : Two

Computer Submission : Yes

Format : WordPerfect 5.1

Fees to Review : 0.00 US$

REVIEW INFORMATION :

Type of Review : Editorial Review

No. of External Reviewers :

No. of In House Reviewers : One

Acceptance Rate : 50 %

Time To Review : 2-3 months

Reviewer's Comments : No

Fees to Publish : 0.00 US$

Invited Articles : 31-50%

MANUSCRIPT TOPICS : ACCOUNTING INFORMATION SYSTEMS; AUDITING;
   CAPITAL BUDGETING; COST ACCOUNTING; INTERNATIONAL FINANCE;
   PORTFOLIO & SECURITY ANALYSIS

PUBLICATION GUIDELINES : AP Style Manual

MANUSCRIPT GUIDELINES/COMMENTS :

1. Contributions to BUSINESS CREDIT should be geared for top credit management
executives--for those who already know the basics of information having to do
with commercial credit and finance.
2. Our readers are interested in data processing, bank services, insurance
opportunities, factoring, cash flow and application, leasing, accounts
receivable management, inventory control, management techniques, new office
equipment, fraud prevention, productivity, motivation, personal health,
bankruptcy laws and other legislation, and economic forecasts.
3. Articles should be written adapted to the point of view of the NACM-member
credit executive who is interested in such topics as those listed above. Facts
should be presented objectively, giving both advantages and disadvantages of
services, techniques or merchandise, and pros and cons of issues and theories.

4. Manuscripts should be between 8 and 20 double-spaced, typewritten pages.
All manuscripts should be original. No photocopies please. We can also accept
files on MS-DOS diskettes, or via telecommunication. Sidebar or filler pieces
that are 1 to 3 pages in length are also accepted. Please include a short
biography with any submission.

BUSINESS ECONOMICS

ADDRESS FOR SUBMISSION :

EDMUND MENNIS, EDITOR
BUSINESS ECONOMICS
P.O. BOX 1146
PALOS VERDES ESTATES, CA 90274
USA
310-373-3270
310-373-4788 (Fax)

CIRCULATION DATA :

Reader : Business Persons

Frequency of Issue : Quarterly

Copies Per Issue : 5001-10,000

Subscription Price : 55.00 US$

Sponsorship : Professional Assoc.

PUBLICATION GUIDELINES :

Manuscript Length : 16-20

Copies Required : Three

Computer Submission : Yes

Format : If Accepted for Pub.

Fees to Review : 0.00 US$

REVIEW INFORMATION :

Type of Review : Blind Review

No. of External Reviewers : Two

No. of In House Reviewers : One

Acceptance Rate : 11-20%

Time To Review : 1-2 months

Reviewer's Comments : Yes

Fees to Publish : 0.00 US$

Invited Articles : 31-50%

MANUSCRIPT TOPICS : CAPITAL BUDGETING; ECONOMETRICS;
  INTERNATIONAL & ECONOMIC DEVELOPMENT; INTERNATIONAL FINANCE;
  PUBLIC POLICY ECONOMICS; BUSINESS EDUCATION; ECONOMICS;
  FINANCE & INVESTMENTS; STRATEGIC MANAGEMENT POLICY; GENERAL BUSINESS;
  ORGANIZATIONAL BEHAVIOR AND THEORY;
  LABOR RELATIONS & HUMAN RESOURCE MGT (HRM);
  MANAGEMENT INFORMATION SYSTEMS (MIS); OPERATIONS RESEARCH/STATISTICS;
  ORGANIZATIONAL DEVELOPMENT; PRODUCTION/OPERATIONS;
  PROBLEMS IN FUNDING, GATHERING

PUBLICATION GUIDELINES : Chicago Manual of Style

MANUSCRIPT GUIDELINES/COMMENTS :

BUSINESS ECONOMICS welcomes unsolicited manuscripts to be considered for
publication. Manuscripts will be reviewed by the Editor and one or more of the
Associate Editors, and every effort will be made to give the author a decision
within five weeks. No submission fee is charged. The following guidelines for
authors are offered.

1. Please keep in mind the objectives of BUSINESS ECONOMICS as stated on the
inside front cover. Articles will be judged primarily for clarity, timeliness
andj particultarly for interest to our membrship. An early paragraph should
_comment briefly on the significance and usefulness of the material in the
article for the practicing business economist.

BUSINESS ECONOMICS

2. Manuscript length should be about 4,500 words, reduced by space needed for any charts andtables. Charts and tables should be essential for the exposition in the article, and charts should be provided in a camera-ready copy format.

3. Footnotes and references should be placed at the end of the text. Mathematical exposition should be kept to a minimum and if considered necessary should be placed in an appendix to the article if at all possible. A summary of not more than 100 qords should be included at the beginning of the article. Divisions and subdivisions should be indicated with appropriate headings.

4. To facilitate review, please forward three double spaced typewritten copies of each manuscript. The author's name and affiliation should be on a cover sheet but not included directly in the manuscript itself. The manuscripts should be sent directly to the Editor.

CA MAGAZINE

ADDRESS FOR SUBMISSION :

NELSON LUSCOMBE, EDITOR
CA MAGAZINE
CANADIAN INST. OF CHARTERED ACCOUNTANTS
277 WELLINGTON STREET, W.
TORONTO, ONTARIO, M5V 3H2
CANADA
416-204-3246
416-204-3409 (Fax)

CIRCULATION DATA :

Reader : Canadian Chartered Accountants

Frequency of Issue : 10 Times/Year

Copies Per Issue : Over 25,000

Subscription Price : 47.00 Can.$
  Member,Stud.,Faculty : 37.00 Can.$
  Outside Canada : 72.00 Can.$

Sponsorship : Professional Assoc.

PUBLICATION GUIDELINES :

Manuscript Length : 11-15

Copies Required : One

Computer Submission : Yes

Format : Wd for Win,WdPer,Text only

Fees to Review : 0.00 US$

REVIEW INFORMATION :

Type of Review : Editorial Review

No. of External Reviewers : One

No. of In House Reviewers : Two

Acceptance Rate : 6-10%

Time To Review : 1-2 months

Reviewer's Comments : No

Fees to Publish : 0.00 US$

Invited Articles : Over 50%

MANUSCRIPT TOPICS : ACCOUNTING INFORMATION SYSTEMS;
  ACCOUNTING THEORY & PRACTICE; AUDITING; CAPITAL BUDGETING; COST ACCOUNTING;
  ECONOMETRICS; INSURANCE; PORTFOLIO & SECURITY ANALYSIS; TAX ACCOUNTING;
  BUSINESS LAW & PUBLIC RESPONSIBILITY

PUBLICATION GUIDELINES :

MANUSCRIPT GUIDELINES/COMMENTS :

Material must be of specific interest to Canadian Chartered Accountants.

CANADIAN BANKER

ADDRESS FOR SUBMISSION :

SIMON HALLY, EDITOR
CANADIAN BANKER
P.O. BOX 348
COMMERCE COURT POSTAL STATION
TORONTO, ON M5L 1G2
CANADA
416-362-6092
416-362-5658 (Fax)
E-Mail : inform@cba.ca

CIRCULATION DATA :

Reader : Business Persons

Frequency of Issue : 6 Times/Year

Copies Per Issue : Over 25,000

Subscription Price : 32.10 US$

Sponsorship : Professional Assoc.

PUBLICATION GUIDELINES :

Manuscript Length : 6-10

Copies Required : One

Computer Submission : No

Format : N/A

Fees to Review : 0.00 US$

REVIEW INFORMATION :

Type of Review : Editorial Review

No. of External Reviewers : Three

No. of In House Reviewers : Two

Acceptance Rate : 21-30%

Time To Review : 4-6 months

Reviewer's Comments : No

Fees to Publish : 0.00 US$

Invited Articles : 11-20%

MANUSCRIPT TOPICS : ACCOUNTING THEORY & PRACTICE; AUDITING;
  INTERNATIONAL FINANCE; PORTFOLIO & SECURITY ANALYSIS; REAL ESTATE;
  TAX ACCOUNTING

PUBLICATION GUIDELINES : Canadian Press Stylebook

MANUSCRIPT GUIDELINES/COMMENTS :

Above is the address for submission of ARTICLE OUTLINES.

1. CANADIAN PRESS STYLEBOOK

2. CANADIAN BANKER is a forum for the presentation of authoritative and
stimulating information about banking and other subjects pertinent to the
industry. The Journal is designed, first, for the communication of information
to employees of the Canadian banks to assist in their career development and
further their general knowledge. Additionally, it presents viewpoints on
Canadian banking to external audiences at home and abroad, and has been
regarded as the industry's journal of record since its establishment in 1893.
The Journal is a forum for discussion, not a medium of official pronouncement,
so the range of content is wide and varied.

LENGTH OF MANUSCRIPT: 2000 words or less.

CANADIAN JOURNAL OF AGRICULTURAL ECONOMICS

ADDRESS FOR SUBMISSION :

D.GORDON, T.HORBULYK, W.KERR, EDITORS
CANADIAN JOURNAL OF AGRICULTURAL
  ECONOMICS
UNIVERSITY OF CALGARY
DEPARTMENT OF ECONOMICS
CALGARY, ALBERTA, T2N 1N4
CANADA
403-220-8137
403-220-8137 (Fax)
E-Mail : cjae@acs.ucalgary.ca

Change in Editor's Address
  May Occur in : 07/31/98

CIRCULATION DATA :

Reader : Academic

Frequency of Issue : Quarterly

Copies Per Issue : Less than 1000

Subscription Price : 50.00 US$

Sponsorship : Professional Assoc.

PUBLICATION GUIDELINES :

Manuscript Length : 21-30

Copies Required : Four

Computer Submission : Yes

Format : N/A

Fees to Review : 0.00 US$

REVIEW INFORMATION :

Type of Review : Blind Review

No. of External Reviewers : Three

No. of In House Reviewers : Zero

Acceptance Rate : 21-30%

Time To Review : 1-2 months

Reviewer's Comments : Yes

Fees to Publish : 65.00 US$

Invited Articles : 6-10%

MANUSCRIPT TOPICS : ECONOMETRICS; ECONOMIC HISTORY;
  PUBLIC POLICY ECONOMICS

PUBLICATION GUIDELINES : Chicago Manual of Style

MANUSCRIPT GUIDELINES/COMMENTS :

COVERING LETTER: Papers should be submitted to the Editors, whose address may
be found on the inside front cover of the journal. In a covering letter, the
author should state: (a) why the material submitted would be of interest of
the readers of the CJAE; b) that the material contained in the manuscript has
not been published and is not being considered for publication elselwhere; and
(c) that-the material contained in the manuscript does not infringe upon other
copyright material. When the applicability of any of these points is unclear,
please explain fully.

CONDITION OF SUBMISSION: It is a condition of submission that the manuscript
is not being considered for publication elsewhere without the knowledge of the
Editors, and that it will not be sent for such consideration without prior
notification of the Editors. Authors are advised that (a) copyright for any
material published in the CJAE is held by the Canadian Agricultural Economics
and Farm Management Society, and (b) the CJAE is supported by a page charge of
$45 per printed page, payable by the author or supporting agency or
institution.

CANADIAN JOURNAL OF AGRICULTURAL ECONOMICS

COVER PAGE: Since manuscripts are sent anonymously to reviewers, the name and affiliation of the author should not be identified in the manuscript; instead, on a separate cover page, include the name and affiliation of the author, along with acknowledgement (if any) and the title of the manuscript.

LENGTH: Although no specific length for a manuscript is required and no page limit is imposed, a manuscript should be written clearly and concisely.

NUMBER OF COPIES: Five clean copies of a manuscript are required.

TYPE: Type rnanuscripts double-spaced on one side of standard 8 1/2 by 11 inch paper, using 1 1/4 inch margins. Equations should be numbered at the right hand margin.

TITLE: The manuscript's title appears at the top of the page following the cover page and should be as short as possible.

ABSTRACT: Include English and French versions of a nonmathematical abstract of not more than 200 words.

SECTIONS: A lengthy paper may be divided into sections, each with an appropriate short heading. Do not number sections.

TABLES: Type each table on a separate page and identify it with a numbered heading (e.g. Table 1. Growth in agricultural productivity in Canada, l951-8l). Use superior letters (not numbers) for footnotes to tables.

ILLUSTRATIONS: Line drawings may be submitted in their original form or as high-quality photographs of the drawings. They should generally be not more than twice final size. Lettering should be of one size throughout in upper and lower case and should be at least 1.5 mm high when reduced. Labelling on graphs should be parallel to the graph's axes. Abbreviations, units, etc. should follow journal style. Single illustrations should not be mounted, but composite figures may be mounted on art board forming a rectangular block. Use uppercase letters to mark subdivisions. All illustrations should be labelled on the back in pencil with the senior author's name and the figure number. High quality figures produced on a computer and printed on a laser printer are encouraged. Illustrations produced on dot-matrix printers are not acceptable.

REFERENCES: List references alphabetically by author, double-spaced, on a separate page at the end of the manuscript. Include only the works cited. The following examples illustrate the style of these references for a book, an article, a monogaph or bulletin and a thesis or unpublished work, respectively.

McNair, D. K. 1980. Taxation of Farmers and Fishermen. Toronto: Richard de Boo Limited.

Goyette, Lacroix and Patenaude. 1982. A predictive model of the cost of farm-to-plant milk assembly by contract haulers. Canadian Journal of Agricultural Economics 30 (July): 187-200.

Funk, T. F. and A. T. Vincent. 1978. The farmer decision process in purchasing corn herbicides. Research Bulletin AEERE/78/2. Guelph: University of Guelph, School of Agricultural Economics and Extension Education, January.

CANADIAN JOURNAL OF AGRICULTURAL ECONOMICS

McCartney, L. K. 1979. An evaluation of price and sensory preference for retailer and manufacturer brands of food. MSc. thesis. Montreal: McGill University.

Note that the following information is required: full names (as printed) of all authors; title; and full publication details (for books, list place of publication, publisher, and date of publication; for articles. List volume, month and year, and page numbers).

To cite a work in the text, use the author's name and year of publication in parentheses in the appropriate place with the citation taking the following form: (Doe 1982) or (Doe 1982, 10-14)

NOTES: Notes are for informative material only, not for references. Number them consecutively and type double-spaced on a separate sheet at the end of the manuscript preceding references.

OTHER MATTERS: For further information on matters of style and mechanics, see: Turabian, Kate L. 1973. A MANUAL FOR WRITERS OF PAPERS, THESES AND DISSERTATIONS, 4th ed. rev. Chicago: University of Chicago Press. For spelling, consult WEBSTER'S THIRD NEW INTERNATIONAL DICTIONARY.

REVIEW: A submission to the CJAE is sent to three or more reviewers who determine the manuscript's suitability for publication. However, authors, are encouraged to have manuscripts reviewed by their peers prior to submission. This, along with editorial assistance, will greatly improve the chances of publication and will usually shorten the time between submission and publication.

POLICY ON DATA DOCUMENTATION: Authors are expected to provide complete documentation of empirical models, estimation techniques and data sets used in the manuscript. Data sets should be made available to other researchers for replication purposes only. If, for whatever reason, data can not be made available this should be noted in the covering letter on first submission. Incases where empirical modelling or data sets are too voluminous to fit reasonably in an article or publishable Appendix, this material can be sent with the manuscript for use by the editor and referees for review purposes.

Mailing: Address correspondence concerning accepted papers in press, proofs, and invoices to:

Tim Fenton
Agricultural Institute of Canada
Suite 1112, 141 Laurier Avenue West
Ottawa, Ontario, Canada K1P 5J3
Fax: (613)594-5190

CANADIAN JOURNAL OF ECONOMICS
REVUE CANADIENNE D'ECONOMIQUE

ADDRESS FOR SUBMISSION :

B. CURTIS EATON, EDITOR
CANADIAN JOURNAL OF ECONOMICS
  REVUE CANADIENNE D'ECONOMIQUE
SIMON FRASER UNIVERSITY
DEPARTMENT OF ECONOMICS
BURNABY, BC V5A 1S6
CANADA
604-291-5462
604-291-5944 (Fax)
E-Mail : cje_econ@sfu.ca

Change in Editor's Address
  May Occur in : 06/30/99

CIRCULATION DATA :

Reader : Academic

Frequency of Issue : Quarterly

Copies Per Issue : 4001-5000

Subscription Price :
  Assn. Member Fee : 55.00 US$
  +$5 Postage Foreign : 60.00 US$

Sponsorship : Professional Assoc.

PUBLICATION GUIDELINES :

Manuscript Length : 16-20

Copies Required : Four

Computer Submission : No

Format : N/A

Fees to Review : 55.00 CAN.$

REVIEW INFORMATION :

Type of Review : Editorial Review

No. of External Reviewers : Two

No. of In House Reviewers :

Acceptance Rate : 21-30%

Time To Review : 4-6 months

Reviewer's Comments : Yes

Fees to Publish : 0.00 US$

Invited Articles : 5% or less

MANUSCRIPT TOPICS : ACCOUNTING INFORMATION SYSTEMS; ECONOMETRICS;
  ECONOMIC HISTORY; INTERNATIONAL & ECONOMIC DEVELOPMENT;
  PUBLIC POLICY ECONOMICS

PUBLICATION GUIDELINES :

MANUSCRIPT GUIDELINES/COMMENTS :

1. The CANADIAN JOURNAL OF ECONOMICS is interested in publishing papers that
are significant contributions to knowledge in all areas of economics, with the
exception of extremely narrow papers addressed to small specialist audiences.

2. Manuscript submissions and all correspondence relating to the contents of
the Journal should be sent to the Editor. Manuscripts should be sent in four
copies. Detailed styles guidelines are available to authors on request.

3. Authors who are not members of the Canadian Economics Association must
enclose with the manuscript either a submission fee of $35 Canadian or a
membership fee on the terms indicated on the inside front cover, as
applicable.

4. Papers should be literate, should reveal a knowledge of the relevant
literature, should contain no errors, and should, in addition, contain at

least one of the following:
  A. A new theoretical result;
  B. A new empirical interpretation of received theory;
  C. New empirical findings which are likely to be of use or interest to other scholars;
  D. A replication of important foreign work with Canadian data (these papers should be quite short);
  E. High level of criticism or evaluation of the work of others.

5. In manuscripts with mathematical proofs the authors should submit with the manuscripts separate statements on the full mathematical workings which lead to the conclusions. These are required for the assistance of the referees and will help speed up the appraisal of the manuscripts. Any ancillary material available from the author on request should be enclosed for the referees.

6. Manuscripts may be typed, Xeroxed, or mimeographed, but must be double-spaced on 8-1/2" x 11" paper. Tables and diagrams should be submitted on separate pages. Footnotes, including the lead footnote, also double-spaced should be placed in a single listing at the end of the paper.

7. References to other work should also be incorporated in a separate list of references typed doublespaced. These references should be listed alphabetically with name of author, title, and date of publication, in the following forms as appropriate.

References

   Head, J.G. and C.S. Shoup (1969) Public Goods, Private Goods, and Ambiguous Goods, Economic Journal 79, 567-72.

   Marsh, D.B. (1960) Foreign Trade and Investment (New York: Norton)

Items in the list of references should be referred to either in the text or in footnotes by naming the author and date. For example:

  A. Head and Shoup (1969, 568);
  B. Marsh (1960, 4);
  C. Marsh (1960, 7) (not op cit);
  D. (ibid., 12)

8. Diagrams should be provided in a form suitable for reproduction. Ideally, diagrams should be done professionally in India ink (black) on strong white paper and one and one-half times the size that the figure is to be when printed.

9. The author will be asked to incorporate least-cost mathematical notation as far as possible, and to provide a separate listing of numbered equations. Please try to avoid letters and L and O as symbols, because these can be confused with numbers. Avoid circumflexes, bars, dots, and tildes, so far as possible, because these must be set by hand: Superscripts or subscripts are to be preferred. Fractions should, whenever possible, be written in the form $(B + MQ) / (3J)$, not in the form

$$\frac{B + M^Q}{3J}$$

Roots should be written as fractional powers--for instance, $(x/y + m/n)^{1/3}$, not

$$\sqrt[3]{\frac{x}{y} + \frac{m}{n}}$$

10. Statistical tables should be included only when the data are not readily available elsewhere and when they are actually used in the paper's analysis.

11. The detailed results of regressions and similar calculations should be included only to the extent that these results:

A. Are actually discussed in the paper, or
B. Will be of definitive use to other scholars.

GUIDELINES FOR REFEREES

12. The CANADIAN JOURNAL OF ECONOMICS is interested in publishing papers in all areas of economics which are significant contributions to knowledge. Papers should be literate, should reveal a knowledge of the relevant literature, should contain no errors and should, in addition, contain at least one of the following:

A. A new theoretical result
B. A new empirical interpretation of received theory
C. New empirical findings which are likely to be of use or interest to other scholars
D. A replication of important foreign work with Canadian data (these paper should be quite short)
E. High level criticism or evaluation of the work of others.

CANADIAN JOURNAL OF REGIONAL SCIENCE

ADDRESS FOR SUBMISSION :

WILLIAM J. MILNE, EDITOR
CANADIAN JOURNAL OF REGIONAL SCIENCE
UNIVERSITY OF NEW BRUNSWICK
DEPARTMENT OF ECONOMICS
FREDERICTON
NEW BRUNSWICK, E3B 5A3
CANADA
506-453-4828
506-453-4514 (Fax)
E-Mail : WMILNE@UNB.CA

CIRCULATION DATA :

Reader : Academic

Frequency of Issue : 3 Times/Year

Copies Per Issue : Less than 1000

Subscription Price : 50.00 US$

Sponsorship : Professional Assoc. &
              University

PUBLICATION GUIDELINES :

Manuscript Length : 3000-5000 wds.

Copies Required : Three

Computer Submission : No

Format : N/A

Fees to Review : 0.00 US$

REVIEW INFORMATION :

Type of Review : Blind Review

No. of External Reviewers : Two

No. of In House Reviewers : Zero

Acceptance Rate : 37 %

Time To Review : 2-3 months

Reviewer's Comments : Yes

Fees to Publish : 0.00 US$

Invited Articles : 31-50%

MANUSCRIPT TOPICS : ECONOMETRICS; PUBLIC POLICY ECONOMICS;
  REGIONAL ECONOMICS; URBAN ECONOMICS

PUBLICATION GUIDELINES :

MANUSCRIPT GUIDELINES/COMMENTS :

The CANADIAN JOURNAL OF REGIONAL SCIENCE invites submission, in English or
French, of articles (3000 - 5000 words), research notes and comments
(notexceeding 2000 words), and book reviews concerned with regional and urban
issues, especially those of relevance to Canada. Only original material, not
previously published, will be considered. Manuscripts should be submitted to
the Editor.

MANUSCRIPTS should be typed double spaced, on one side of a 8-1/2 x 11 inch
paper, and submitted in triplicate. The author's name, affiliation and full
mailing address should appear on a separate title page.

HEADINGS should be in upper and lower case. First order headings are centred.
Second order headings should begin at the left margin. Third order headings
begin at the left margin and are underlined.

REFERENCES, in parentheses, should consist of the author's last name and the
year of publication, with page number included where appropriate (Martin 1983,
50-53). Reference list should be arranged in alphabetical order, with the date

following immediately after authors' names. Persons submitting papers are requested to limit the number of references to one per 300 words of text.

FOOTNOTES, restricted to explanation or provision of further information, should be numbered consecutively. The number of footnotes should be limited to one per 1000 words of text. Although the footnotes will appear at the bottom of individual pages, for typesetting purposes they should be typed on a separate sheet which follows the REFERENCES section.

ABSTRACTS in both English and French of about 100 words must accompany articles.

ILLUSTRATIONS should be clear and legible but need not be prepared for production before acceptance of article, when originals or high quality of photographic reproductions will be required. Dimensions of figures, including title, should not exceed 11 x 16 inches.

CANADIAN TAX JOURNAL

ADDRESS FOR SUBMISSION :

LAUREL AMALIA, EDITOR-IN-CHIEF
CANADIAN TAX JOURNAL
ONE QUEEN STREET EAST, STE. 1800
TORONTO, M5C 2Y2
CANADA
416-863-9784
416-863-9585 (Fax)

PUBLICATION GUIDELINES :

Manuscript Length : Any

Copies Required : Three

Computer Submission : Yes

Format : Any

Fees to Review : 0.00 US$

CIRCULATION DATA :

Reader : Academic &
          Tax Professionals;Gov't Offic.

Frequency of Issue : Bi-Monthly

Copies Per Issue : 5001-10,000

Subscription Price : 120.00 CAN.$
  Free/Indv Membership : 210.00 CAN.$
  Free/Corp Membership : 450.00 CAN.$

Sponsorship : Non Profit Corp.

REVIEW INFORMATION :

Type of Review : Blind Review

No. of External Reviewers : Two

No. of In House Reviewers : Zero

Acceptance Rate : 21-30%

Time To Review : 1-2 months

Reviewer's Comments : Yes

Fees to Publish : 0.00 US$

Invited Articles : 5% or less

MANUSCRIPT TOPICS : COST ACCOUNTING; INSURANCE; REAL ESTATE;
   TAX ACCOUNTING; ACCOUNTING; ECONOMICS; FINANCE & INVESTMENTS;
   INTERNATIONAL BUSINESS; THESE TOPICS RE: TAXATION;
   BUSINESS LAW; SMALL BUSINESS & ENTREPRENEURSHIP

PUBLICATION GUIDELINES :

MANUSCRIPT GUIDELINES/COMMENTS :

The Canadian Tax Foundation invites interested readers to submit manuscripts
for possible publication in the CANADIAN TAX JOURNAL, a forum for the
dissemination of research in and informed comment on taxation and public
finance, with PARTICULAR RELEVANCE TO CANADA.

Manuscripts may be written in either French or English, should present an
ORIGINAL ANALYSIS of the topic, and should not have been published elsewhere.
All manuscripts submitted are subject to review by an editorial committee.
Manuscripts may be (1) accepted outright, (2) accepted if recommended
revisions are made, or (3) rejected, with reasons.

It is recommended that a detailed draft proposal be submitted before writing
commences toensure that the topic has not already been committed to another
author. Proposals that are accepted are not to be viewed as a commitment on
the foundation's part to publish the resulting manuscripts; these manuscripts
are subject to the same review procedures as are all other manuscripts.

CANADIAN TAX JOURNAL

Contributors are responsible for submitting detailed abstracts of their manuscripts, for providing complete and accurate citations to reference materials used, and for preparing manuscripts in the prescribed format. A style and format guide for literature citation and manuscript preparation may be obtained from the editor.

Prospective contributors should submit a current curriculum vitae and three copies of their draft proposals or manuscripts to Ms. Laurel Amalia, Editor. Telephone or written inquiries are welcome.

STYLE AND FORMAT GUIDE FOR PAPERS SUBMITTED
Please submit three (3) copies PLUS original typescript and a copy of your disk.

MANUSCRIPT FORMAT
SPACING: Typed double spaced for text AND FOR FOOTNOTES on 8-1/2 x 11 inch bond paper. (Footnotes should be included as a group at the back of the paper.)

WORD-PROCESSING: If the manuscript is being prepared on a word processor, use triple spacing if the double spacing is narrower than double spacing on a nmormal typewriter. Manuscripts must be printed out on a letter-quality printer (i.e., laser, ink jet, or daisy wheel, but NOT dot matrix) with an unjustified righthand margin. Do NOT use a proportional type face.

MARGINS: 1-1/2 inches at top, bottom, and lefthand margins; 1 inch at right.

NUMBERING: Paged consecutively, upper righthand corner.

TITLE PAGE: Title page should include title of paper; author's name; name of firm, institution, or affiliation; and , if applicable, name of conference at which the paper was presented.

HEADINGS: Differentiate levels of headings so that the organization of the content of the paper is apparent. (You may or may not require all the heading levels given below.)

MAIN HEADINGS--all capital letters; centred on page.

FIRST ORDER OF SUBHEADINGS--type in capital and lower case letters; centre on the page; underline the subheading.

SECOND ORDER OF SUBHEADINGS--type in capital and lower case letters; start the subheading flush with the lefthand margin; underline the subheading.

THIRD ORDER OF SUBHEADINGS--capitalize only the first letter of the first word and type all other words in lower case letters; start the subheading flush left with the lefthand margin.

FOURTH ORDER OF SUBHEADINGS--begin the subheading with an arabic numeral enclosed on the right with a xlosing parenthesis [for example, 1), 2), 3)]; capitalize only the first letter of the first word as above; start the subheading flush with the lefthand margin; underline the subheading.

FIFTH ORDER OF SUBHEADING--begin the subheading with a lower case letter enclosed on the right with a closing parenthesis [for example, a), b), c)]; capitalize only the first letter of the first word; start the subheading flush left with the lefthand margin; underline the subheading.

SIXTH ORDER OF SUBHEADING--capitalize only the first letter of the first word; start the subheading flush left with the lefthand margin; underline the subheading and end with a period; start the first sentence of the paragraph after the period on the same line as the subheading.

ABSTRACT
Papers submitted for publication in the CANADIAN TAX JOURNAL are to include a detailed abstract.

REFERENCES TO LITERATURE
Contributors are responsible for providing complete and accurate quotations and citations to references. A traditional system for footnoting is used for foundation publications. Specific-discipline citation systems that include, say, parenthetical abbreviated references in the text to a bibliographical list of references are not acceptable for publication.

1) Double check all quoted material for absolute accuracy. Cite the reference work and the page number for the quotation in a footnote.

2) Provide all details for complete citations to references including, where applicable, complete case title, case reporter, court where heard, starting page, and specific page(s); authorship for books, complete title underlined, volume or editon, city where published, publisher, date of publication, and specific page(s); authorship for periodical articles or parts of books, complete title in quotation marks, title of periodical or whole work underlined (plus author of whole work), date of issue, volume, issue number, or edition, inclusive page numbers, and specific page(s).

If you are in doubt about what to include, provide the editor will ALL details from the title page.

PLEASE DIRECT ANY QUERIES TO LAUREL AMALIA, EDITOR.

CERTIFIED ACCOUNTANT

ADDRESS FOR SUBMISSION :

BRIAN O'KANE, EDITOR
CERTIFIED ACCOUNTANT
GRANARY HOUSE4
RUTLAND STREET
CORK,
IRELAND
+353-21-313855
+353-21-313496 (Fax)
E-Mail : mail@cork-publishing.com

CIRCULATION DATA :

Reader : Business Persons
Frequency of Issue : Monthly
Copies Per Issue : Over 25,000
Subscription Price : 80.00 U.K.$
Sponsorship : Professional Assoc.

PUBLICATION GUIDELINES :

Manuscript Length : 6-10
Copies Required : One
Computer Submission : Yes
Format : MS-DOS/prefer Winword 2.0
Fees to Review : 0.00 US$

REVIEW INFORMATION :

Type of Review : Blind Review
No. of External Reviewers : Zero
No. of In House Reviewers : Two
Acceptance Rate : 90 %
Time To Review : One month or less
Reviewer's Comments :
Fees to Publish : 0.00 US$
Invited Articles : Over 50%

MANUSCRIPT TOPICS : ACCOUNTING INFORMATION SYSTEMS;
   ACCOUNTING THEORY & PRACTICE; AUDITING; CAPITAL BUDGETING; COST ACCOUNTING;
   GOVERNMENT & NON-PROFIT ACCOUNTING; INTERNATIONAL & ECONOMIC DEVELOPMENT;
   INTERNATIONAL FINANCE; PUBLIC POLICY ECONOMICS; TAX ACCOUNTING;
   SMALL BUSINESS ENTREPRENEURSHIP

PUBLICATION GUIDELINES :

MANUSCRIPT GUIDELINES/COMMENTS :

CERTIFIED ACCOUNTANT is published by Cork Publishing Ltd, Mary Rose
O'Sullivan, Marketing Manager, 19 Rutland Street, Cork, Ireland. Tel: +353 21
313855, Fax: +363 21 313496.

CGA MAGAZINE

ADDRESS FOR SUBMISSION :

LESLEY WOOD, PUBLISHER/EDITOR
CGA MAGAZINE
CERTIFIED GEN. ACCOUNTANTS' ASSN OF CAN.
700-1188
WEST GEORGIA STREET
VANCOUVER, BC V6E 4A2
CANADA
604-669-3555
604-689-5845 (Fax)
E-Mail : editcga@cga.canada.org

CIRCULATION DATA :

Reader : Business Persons &
         Professional Accountants

Frequency of Issue : Monthly

Copies Per Issue : Over 25,000

Subscription Price : 45.00 US$

Sponsorship : Professional Assoc.

PUBLICATION GUIDELINES :

Manuscript Length : 6-10

Copies Required : Two

Computer Submission : Yes

Format : Does not matter

Fees to Review : 0.00 US$

REVIEW INFORMATION :

Type of Review : Blind Review

No. of External Reviewers : One

No. of In House Reviewers : One

Acceptance Rate : 5% or less

Time To Review : 2-3 months

Reviewer's Comments : Yes

Fees to Publish : 0.00 US$

Invited Articles : Over 50%

MANUSCRIPT TOPICS : ACCOUNTING INFORMATION SYSTEMS;
ACCOUNTING THEORY & PRACTICE; AUDITING; COST ACCOUNTING; INSURANCE;
TAX ACCOUNTING

PUBLICATION GUIDELINES :

MANUSCRIPT GUIDELINES/COMMENTS :

BACKGROUND
CGA Magazine is the official publication of the Certified General Accountants'
Association of Canada (CGA-Canada). Published monthly, the bilingual magazine
reaches an audience of over 40,000 CGAs and CGA students across Canada, in the
Caribbean, Hong Kong and Macau.

CONTENT
Articles published deal with topics of interest to professional accountants --
accounting, auditing, taxation, law, finance, business and aspects of
computers. A certain number of background, general interest articles are
included from time to time. Frequent "focus" issues contain several articles
dealing with different aspects of a special topic.

QUERIES
Potential authors should send a query letter to the editor discussing the
proposed article. Your letter should explain the relevance of the topic,
include a brief outline of the areas to be covered and explain how the article

CGA MAGAZINE

will differ from others published on the same topic. Queries should state whether an article is original or has been previously published. A length should also be proposed.

In your letter, tell us a bit about yourself. What makes you the right person to do this article? Have you published before, and if so, for whom? If you have published previously, you might want to include a sample of your work.

The editorial team generally considers article ideas during our monthly meeting, so it may be a few weeks before you receive a response to your query.

Queries should be sent to Editor, CGA Magazine 700 1188 West Georgia St., Vancouver V6E 4A2.

WRITING

If your query is successful, the editor will commission you to write the article. At this point, a deadline will be established and a target length determined.

Once an article has been approved, do not change the topic without consulting with the editor. Your new topic may not fit into editorial plans or may have already been assigned to someone else.

Any article that you write for CGA Magazine should not be shown to anyone else prior to publication. This includes the manufacturer of any product you may review, the subject of an interview or any other publication. Should you encounter difficulties with this policy, refer the matter to your editor.

"I Prefer to write in French"

Not a problem! Our French editor will be happy to work with you.

STYLE

All articles must be thoroughly researched and you are ultimately responsible for accuracy. Use graphs, tables or charts and examples where appropriate. Remember that the readers are professionals with good grounding in all accounting and many business areas -- writing at too low a level is inappropriate. However, esoteric jargon should always be avoided. First and second person ("I", "you") can be used, providing the resulting tone is not condescending. The best way to get a "feel" for the magazine's style is to study a few back issues.

All articles are edited, and some changes are inevitable. When you write an article, it becomes your "baby" -- it is often difficult to view it objectively. The "outside" eye of an editor can sometimes see ways of making your presentation even clearer. Remember that writing a magazine article is a joint effort -- you and the editor are a team! You will be contacted should any points require clarification, and the article, after editing, will be returned to you for final approval before publication.

DEADLINES

Deadlines are sacred. We need enough time to edit the article, obtain your final approval and do a translation. Always give the editor plenty of notice if you anticipate problems meeting the deadline.

CGA MAGAZINE

WHAT TO SUBMIT
Please submit your article both on diskette in any version of WordPerfect and in "hard copy." At this time, send along a head and shoulders style photo and a one or two-sentence biography, both of which will be published with the article.

RIGHTS
Our acceptance of your original material assumes first-time world rights in French and English. After that, you are free to republish your original article elsewhere. As a courtesy, we ask that, on republication, mention be made of the CGA Magazine issue in which the article first appeared. If you choose to republish the edited version, mention of prior publication in CGA Magazine is essential.

CGA Magazine is sent to universities, colleges and professional associations across Canada. We often get requests to reprint material for educational purposes. You will be contacted for approval before such a request is granted whenever possible. If we cannot reach you, however, we will grant permission ourselves. Please note that no money exchanges hands in these arrangements, so you will not miss out on any revenues!

Likewise, requests to reprint in another publication will be referred back to you, though again, we will co-ordinate the permission-granting process. Anyone reprinting material from CGA Magazine is required to credit the magazine and author, and indicate that reprint permission was obtained.

Thank you for your interest in CGA Magazine.

CHARTERED ACCOUNTANT'S JOURNAL OF NEW ZEALAND

ADDRESS FOR SUBMISSION :

ANGUS MC LEOD, EDITOR
CHARTERED ACCOUNTANT'S JOURNAL
  OF NEW ZEALAND
NEW ZEALAND SOCIETY OF ACCOUNTANTS
CIGNA HOUSE
P.O. BOX 11-342, 40 MERCER STREET
WELLINGTON,
NEW ZEALAND
011 64 4 474 7842
011 64 4 499 033 (Fax)
E-Mail : angus_m@nzsa.co.nz

CIRCULATION DATA :

Reader : Business Persons

Frequency of Issue : 11 Times/Year

Copies Per Issue : 10,001-25,000

Subscription Price : 72.50 N.Z.$
  Single copy : 17.80 N.Z.$

Sponsorship : Professional Assoc.

PUBLICATION GUIDELINES :

Manuscript Length : 6-10

Copies Required : Two

Computer Submission : Yes

Format : E-mail as per Guidelines

Fees to Review : 0.00 US$

REVIEW INFORMATION :

Type of Review : Editorial Review

No. of External Reviewers : Two

No. of In House Reviewers : Two

Acceptance Rate : 50 %

Time To Review : 2-3 months

Reviewer's Comments : No

Fees to Publish : 315.00 N.Z.$
  Depending on Length   420.00 N.Z.$

Invited Articles : 21-30%

MANUSCRIPT TOPICS : ACCOUNTING INFORMATION SYSTEMS;
  ACCOUNTING THEORY & PRACTICE; AUDITING; CAPITAL BUDGETING; COST ACCOUNTING;
  GOVERNMENT & NON-PROFIT ACCOUNTING; TAX ACCOUNTING

PUBLICATION GUIDELINES :

MANUSCRIPT GUIDELINES/COMMENTS :

COPIES PER ISSUE: 13,500; SUBSCRIPTION PRICE: Postage not included.

NUMBER OF REVIEWERS: The number of internal reviewers varies from one to two,
as does the number of external reviewers. A copy of the reviewer's comments is
not sent unless the author asks to be contacted.

For information on author guidelines and publication style for manuscripts see
previously published articles in the journal and the following guidelines.

Thank you for your interest in contributing to the CHARTERED ACCOUNTANTS
JOURNAL OF NEW ZEALAND, the monthly publication of the New Zealand Society of
Accountants.

Before you commence work, or as you consider the suitability of an article you
have already written, you will need to consider your potential audience
carefully.

CHARTERED ACCOUNTANT'S JOURNAL
OF NEW ZEALAND

You should be aware that under the Society's new structure, members have elected which of the three "Colleges" they will belong to. Their interests are separate and distinct in some ways, and overlap in others.

Briefly, the College structure can be described as follows:

* The College of Chartered Accountants-Society members working in all sectors whose primary focus is accounting, including holders of Public Practice Certificates.

* The College of Associate Chartered Accountants-Members whose primary focus is other than accounting-general management and education, for example.

* The College of Accounting Technicians-A new group of members who are trained to provide accounting support services in all types of organisations. Their work is largely of practical, "hands-on" nature.

Like the Society as a whole, the Journal seeks to cater for the interests of all three groups as fully as possible.

Further information on the College structure and ways in which the Journal seeks to meet the different markets is available from the Editor.

Your first task in preparing an article will therefore be to decide which target group or groups your material is aimed at, and to write accordingly.

Our reviewers (see below) will consider the potential audience(s) of submitted material as an important part of their function in deciding suitability for publication. A copy of the reviewers' evaluation guidelines is attached.

Respondents to our recent readership survey emphasised strongly that they seek in the Journal practical information of direct value to their work.

If appropriate, case studies, worked examples and brief summaries are very popular with readers. These can be presented apart from the main flow of the text.

Some further pointers:
1. Articles should not exceed 1200 words (or if they do, they should be divided into parts).

2. If the article has not yet been written, a brief synopsis should be forwarded to the Editor for consideration and comment.

3. Manuscripts should preferably be typed double-spaced on one side of A4 paper.

4. Disks are also acceptable, particularly if graphs or tables are included. The followings points should be noted if forwarding material on disk:

* Indicate whether the disk is high or medium density.
* Indicate the programme it is written in (Microsoft Word is preferred).
* Do not use typist's return at the end of lines.
* Do not space paragraphs.
* Do not use Microsoft Word table for tables but tab limited text.

CHARTERED ACCOUNTANT'S JOURNAL
OF NEW ZEALAND

* If you are using PC file, save in RTF format and also send the original text.
* If you are sending graphs or figures, also forward the data on which the illustration is based.
* E-mail is available.

Further information is available from the Production Manager.

5. Provide a brief, preferably bullet-pointed, summary at the head of the article to indicate its content.

6. Layout and style - see previous issues for examples.

7. Deadlines fall in the middle of each month for publication in the second succeeding month - for example, a 15 June deadline for publication in the first week of August (subject to time taken for review - see (9), below).

8. If a deadline is looming, articles should be faxed with original script plus disks and any additional material being sent by post.

9. All articles are subject to a formal review procedure, which is likely to take between 2 and 6 weeks. Reviewers consider (among other things) level of coverage - see above, topicality, readability and accessibility.

Articles will be accepted for publication (always subject to editorial input, however), returned for amendment or rejected (with reasons).

10. Photographs (preferably 6 x 4 colour prints), graphs and other illustrations are welcome so long as they are high-quality.

11. Payment - whether articles are paid for is by negotiation with the Editor. There are two flat rates, depending on length.

Please contact the Editor for further information. We look forward to working with you.

CHINA ECONOMIC REVIEW

ADDRESS FOR SUBMISSION :

BRUCE REYNOLDS, EDITOR
CHINA ECONOMIC REVIEW
CORNELL UNIVERSITY
EAST ASIA PROGRAM
140 URIS HALL
ITHACA, NY 14853
USA
607-255-5929
607-255-2818 (Fax)
E-Mail : blr1@cornell.edu

CIRCULATION DATA :

Reader : Academic

Frequency of Issue : 3 Times/Year

Copies Per Issue : Less than 1000

Subscription Price : 55.00 US$
   Institution : 110.00 US$

Sponsorship : Professional Assoc.

PUBLICATION GUIDELINES :

Manuscript Length : 20-40

Copies Required : Three

Computer Submission : No

Format : N/A

Fees to Review : 0.00 US$

REVIEW INFORMATION :

Type of Review : Blind Review

No. of External Reviewers : Two

No. of In House Reviewers : One

Acceptance Rate : 21-30%

Time To Review : One month or less

Reviewer's Comments : Yes

Fees to Publish : 0.00 US$

Invited Articles : 5% or less

MANUSCRIPT TOPICS : ECONOMETRICS; ECONOMIC HISTORY;
   INTERNATIONAL & ECONOMIC DEVELOPMENT; INTERNATIONAL FINANCE;
   PORTFOLIO & SECURITY ANALYSIS; PUBLIC POLICY ECONOMICS

PUBLICATION GUIDELINES : China Economic Review

MANUSCRIPT GUIDELINES/COMMENTS :

EDITORIAL POLICY
1. The CHINA ECONOMIC REVIEW seeks to publish original scholarship which adds
   to understanding of the economy of China and East Asia, in particular
   papers dealing with policy, performance or institutional change.
   Submissions are subjected to double-blind peer review.

2. Submission of a manuscript to CER implies a commitment by the author to
   publish in it. Articles previously published and those under consideration
   by another journal may not be submitted.

3. Manuscripts and editorial communications should be addressed to the Editor.

MANUSCRIPT PREPARATION
1. Initial submission in typescript: three copies, on 8 1/2" by 11" paper with
   1" margins. Manuscripts will not be returned.

2. Final revisions on 5 1/2" disk (plus two hard copies), ASCII file based on
   WordPerfect (or Microsoft Word).

3. Include an abstract of no more than 150 words with JEL numbers.

4. All copy - including the abstract, quotations, tabular material, notes and references - must be double-spaced.

5. Type all tables on separate pages, numbered consecutively, with brief descriptive titles, and place them at the end of the manuscript following references. Indicate the appropriate placement within the text by using [Insert Table 1 here].

6. Artwork (illustrations, charts) should be referred to in the text as "Figures". It must be camera-ready, not needing further artwork or typesetting. If it is computer-generated, please save to a TIF, CGM, PCX or similar disk file.

7. An alphabetical list of references should follow the endnotes. Authors should ensure that there is a complete reference for every citation in the text, following the form illustrated below:

Becker, G.S. 1981. A treatise on the family. Cambridge: Harvard University Press.
Czinkota, M.R. 1982. Conclusion: The state of the art. In M. Czinkota & G. Tesar, eds., Export management: an international context. New York: Pergamon.
Wang, M.L. 1971. The evolution of reciprocal trade. Quarterly Journal of Asian Trade, 46:35-57.

SUBSCRIPTIONS
Correspondence on subscriptions, change of address, back-orders, and advertising should be sent to: JAI Press Inc., 55 Old Post Road-No. 2, P.O. Box 1678, Grenwich, Connecticut 06836-1678.

CMA MAGAZINE

ADDRESS FOR SUBMISSION :

D.R. HICKS, PUBLISHER
CMA MAGAZINE
SOCIETY OF MGMT. ACCOUNTANTS OF CANADA
PO BOX 176
HAMILTON, ON L8N 3C3
CANADA
905-525-4100
905-525-4533 (Fax)
E-Mail : dan.hicks@resonet.com

CIRCULATION DATA :

Reader : Financial Executives

Frequency of Issue : 10 Times/Year

Copies Per Issue : Over 25,000

Subscription Price : 40.00 US$
  Overseas : 60.00 US$

Sponsorship : Professional Assoc.

PUBLICATION GUIDELINES :

Manuscript Length : 11-15

Copies Required : Two

Computer Submission : Yes

Format : N/A

Fees to Review : 0.00 US$

REVIEW INFORMATION :

Type of Review : Blind Review

No. of External Reviewers : One

No. of In House Reviewers : One

Acceptance Rate : 21-30%

Time To Review : 2-3 months

Reviewer's Comments : No

Fees to Publish : 0.00 US$

Invited Articles : Over 50%

MANUSCRIPT TOPICS : ACCOUNTING INFORMATION SYSTEMS; COST ACCOUNTING;
  GOVERNMENT & NON-PROFIT ACCOUNTING; PORTFOLIO & SECURITY ANALYSIS;
  ACCOUNTING; ECONOMICS; FINANCE & INVESTMENTS; INTERNATIONAL BUSINESS;
  SMALL BUSINESS ENTREPRENEURSHIP; STRATEGIC MANAGEMENT POLICY;
  GENERAL BUSINESS; LABOR RELATIONS & HUMAN RESOURCE MGT (HRM);
  MANAGEMENT INFORMATION SYSTEMS (MIS);
  ORGANIZATIONAL DEVELOPMENT; PRODUCTION/OPERATIONS

PUBLICATION GUIDELINES : Canadian Press Style Book

MANUSCRIPT GUIDELINES/COMMENTS :

1. Management accountants are involved in most aspects of business from an
accounting and managerial prospective.

2. Articles should be brief (about 1500 words), readable and practical,
illustrating how organizations can do things better (more cheaply, with good
quality and economy of personnel). Management accountants are members of the
management team providing information (not necessarily financial) for
strategic, tactical and operational decisions. Their contribution is based on
in-depth knowledge about what information is required and how it must be
organized and presented to improve such decisions. Therefore, most aspects of
business are of interest to them.

3. We especially like case study types of articles, featuring interviews with
management, accounting and other authorities; articles of new developments in

CMA MAGAZINE

computers and software, management methods, accounting practices, etc.; articles on news and trends in management accounting and management, taxes, legislation, etc.

4. Articles should be readable and interesting, with the minimum of footnotes and references, as well as business jargon.

COMMERCIAL INVESTMENT REAL ESTATE JOURNAL

ADDRESS FOR SUBMISSION :

CATHERINE A. SIMPSON, EDITOR
COMMERCIAL INVESTMENT REAL ESTATE
  JOURNAL
430 N.MICHIGAN AVENUE, SUITE 600
CHICAGO, IL 60611-4092
USA
312-321-4464
312-321-4530 (Fax)
E-Mail :csimpson@cirei.mhs.compuserve.com

CIRCULATION DATA :

Reader : Commercial Real Estate Profess
Frequency of Issue : Bi-Monthly
Copies Per Issue : 5001-10,000
Subscription Price : 38.00 US$
Sponsorship : Professional Assoc.

PUBLICATION GUIDELINES :

Manuscript Length : 6-12
Copies Required : One
Computer Submission : Yes
Format : Microsoft Word
Fees to Review : 0.00 US$

REVIEW INFORMATION :

Type of Review : Blind Review
No. of External Reviewers : Three
No. of In House Reviewers : Two
Acceptance Rate : 50 %
Time To Review :
Reviewer's Comments : Yes
Fees to Publish : 0.00 US$
Invited Articles : Over 50%

MANUSCRIPT TOPICS : COST ACCOUNTING; REAL ESTATE;
   FINANCE & INVESTMENTS; COMMERCIAL REAL ESTATE TRENDS AND TECHNIQUES

PUBLICATION GUIDELINES : Chicago Manual of Style

MANUSCRIPT GUIDELINES/COMMENTS :

1. CHICAGO MANUAL OF STYLE

2. COMMERCIAL INVESTMENT REAL ESTATE JOURNAL, published bimonthly, keeps
brokers, investors, developers, lenders, attorneys, and other practitioners up
to date on issues of importance in the commercial-investment real estate
field. The JOURNAL not only covers trends, but also presents how-to
information needed to carry out commercial-investment real estate
transactions.

3. JOURNAL readers are interested in a variety of topics including: taxation,
development, brokerage, leasing, asset management, software applications,
financing tools, and institutional investment. If you need help in selecting a
topic, contact the Editor at 312-321-4464.

4. All articles should be submitted in typewritten form on plain 8-1/2" x 11"
paper. Send one original and the file on disk. Article length should be
between 6 and 12 double-spaced, typewritten pages. Supply a brief professional
biography, including present title, designations, place of employment,
publishing accomplishments and expertise in the subject you are writing about.

COMMERCIAL INVESTMENT REAL ESTATE
JOURNAL

Furnish footnotes where needed and supply complete, accurate information.

5. Include charts, graphs, photographs, and illustrations whenever possible to emphasize and clarify points in your article. Follow these guidelines when selecting and preparing graphics:

1. Photographs should be black and white glossies.
2. All hand-drawn graphics, such as floor plans, should be done neatly and legibly in black ink and should be suitable for reproduction (camera-ready) as submitted.
3. Identify all graphics on the back in pencil or on tape. Graphics will not be returned unless specifically requested.

6. All articles are reviewed by our Editorial Review Board, composed of commercial-investment real estate professionals. The board decides whether an article is appropriate for publication in the JOURNAL. A manuscript approved by the Editorial Board "with revisions" may be returned to the author with specific recommendations for further information or clarification. After the editor receives the revised article, an approximate date of publication will be discussed.

7. Aim for clear, concise and lively writing, even if your topic is technical in nature. When appropriate, include case studies - real life examples - to illustrate your points. Overly promotional material is not acceptable and will be edited out of your article.

8. The JOURNAL is interested in original, unpublished material and owns the copyright for all of its content. If your manuscript has been published elsewhere, please provide us with full information about the publication in which it appeared. Please inform us if your manuscript is currently under consideration or scheduled for publication elsewhere.

9. Writing for the JOURNAL gives you the opportunity to share your expertise, as well as to receive national recognition in your field. Authors receive five complimentary copies of the issue in which their article appears. In addition, reprints of articles are available at a minimal cost and make excellent handouts to current and potential clients.

COMMERCIAL LENDING REVIEW

ADDRESS FOR SUBMISSION :

CLAIRE GREENE, EDITOR
COMMERCIAL LENDING REVIEW
130 BELKNAP STREET
CONCORD, MA 01742
USA
508-369-6285
508-371-2961 (Fax)
E-Mail 200-4466@mcimail.com

CIRCULATION DATA :

Reader : Business Persons

Frequency of Issue : Quarterly

Copies Per Issue : 1001-2000

Subscription Price : 180.00 US$
  Academics : 54.00 US$

Sponsorship : Profit Oriented Corp.

PUBLICATION GUIDELINES :

Manuscript Length : 11-25

Copies Required : Two

Computer Submission : Yes

Format : IBM PC Compat, WordPerfect

Fees to Review : 0.00 US$

REVIEW INFORMATION :

Type of Review : Blind Review

No. of External Reviewers : Two

No. of In House Reviewers : One

Acceptance Rate : 50 %

Time To Review : 1-2 months

Reviewer's Comments : Yes

Fees to Publish : 0.00 US$

Invited Articles : Over 50%

MANUSCRIPT TOPICS : ACCOUNTING INFORMATION SYSTEMS;
   ACCOUNTING THEORY & PRACTICE; AUDITING; COST ACCOUNTING;
   INTERNATIONAL FINANCE; REAL ESTATE; COMMERCIAL BANKING

PUBLICATION GUIDELINES : Chicago Manual of Style

MANUSCRIPT GUIDELINES/COMMENTS :

The COMMERCIAL LENDING REVIEW welcomes articles to be considered for
publication. The REVIEW is a quarterly journal covering all aspects of
commercial lending. It is designed to provide practical, useful information
for loan and credit officers, as well as top lending management. Attorneys,
accountants, regulators, and other professionals in banking also read the
REVIEW.

Readers are interested in articles on topics including, but not limited to,
the following:

* marketing and market research,
* pricing and negotiating,
* credit analysis,
* profitability measurement,
* loan structuring,
* documentation,
* loan review,
* accounting,

COMMERCIAL LENDING REVIEW

* asset sales and securitization,
* technology and other tools to improve and streamline the credit process,
* commercial real estate,
* environmental and lender liability,
* cash management and other fee-based services for commercial customers,
* lending to particular industries,
* leasing,
* determining the loan-loss allowance,
* human resources issues including incentives and productivity bench-marking,
* portfolio and risk management,
* regulation,
* secured lending,
* workouts and bankruptcy.

Articles should be practical, with concrete advice, illustrative anecdotes and examples, and a description of results readers might expect if they follow the author's recommendations. Articles generally run from 2,500 to 6,000 words (10 to 24 double-spaced typewritten pages). The how-to and case study approach is particularly appropriate for the REVIEW.

SUBMISSION GUIDELINES
To propose an article, please contact editor claire Greene before you start to write (voice 508-369-6285; fax 508-371-2961). She will enjoy talking over your ida with you and can help you tailor it to the REVIEW'S needs for manuscripts.

COMMERCIAL LENDING REVIEW is published by Institutional Investor, Inc., 488 Madison Avenue, New York, NY 10022. Tel: 212-224-3545 Fax: 212-224-3527.

COMPARATIVE ECONOMIC STUDIES

ADDRESS FOR SUBMISSION :

SUSAN J. LINZ, EDITOR
COMPARATIVE ECONOMIC STUDIES
MICHIGAN STATE UNIVERSITY
DEPARTMENT OF ECONOMICS
MARSHALL HALL
EAST LANSING, MI 48824-1038
USA
517-353-7280
517-432-1068 (Fax)

CIRCULATION DATA :

Reader : Academic

Frequency of Issue : Quarterly

Copies Per Issue : 1001-2000

Subscription Price : 25.00 US$

Sponsorship : Professional Assoc.

PUBLICATION GUIDELINES :

Manuscript Length : 21-25

Copies Required : Three

Computer Submission : No

Format : N/A

Fees to Review : 25.00 US$
   If ACES Member 0.00 US$

REVIEW INFORMATION :

Type of Review : Blind Review

No. of External Reviewers : Two

No. of In House Reviewers : One

Acceptance Rate : 11-20%

Time To Review : 2-3 months

Reviewer's Comments : Yes

Fees to Publish : 0.00 US$

Invited Articles : 5% or less

MANUSCRIPT TOPICS : COST ACCOUNTING;
   INTERNATIONAL & ECONOMIC DEVELOPMENT; ECONOMICS; COMPARATIVE ECONOMICS

PUBLICATION GUIDELINES :

MANUSCRIPT GUIDELINES/COMMENTS :

COMPENSATION & BENEFITS REVIEW

ADDRESS FOR SUBMISSION :

LINDA J. BENNETT, MANAGING EDITOR
COMPENSATION & BENEFITS REVIEW
AMERICAN MANAGEMENT ASSOCIATION
135 WEST 50TH STREET
NEW YORK, NY 10020
USA
212-903-8069
212-903-8083 (Fax)
E-Mail : L_bennett@amanet.org

CIRCULATION DATA :

Reader : Compensation & Benefits Mgrs.

Frequency of Issue : Bi-Monthly

Copies Per Issue : 5001-10,000

Subscription Price : 89.00 US$

Sponsorship : Professional Assoc.

PUBLICATION GUIDELINES :

Manuscript Length : 16-20

Copies Required : Two

Computer Submission : Yes

Format : WP 5.1

Fees to Review : 0.00 US$

REVIEW INFORMATION :

Type of Review : Editorial Review

No. of External Reviewers : One

No. of In House Reviewers : One

Acceptance Rate : 21-30%

Time To Review : 2-3 months

Reviewer's Comments : Yes

Fees to Publish : 0.00 US$

Invited Articles : 21-30%

MANUSCRIPT TOPICS : COMPENSATION/BENEFITS;
   PUBLIC POLICY ANALYSIS AND MANAGEMENT;
   LABOR RELATIONS & HUMAN RESOURCE MGT (HRM)

PUBLICATION GUIDELINES : Chicago Manual of Style

MANUSCRIPT GUIDELINES/COMMENTS :

Thank you for your interest in wanting to submit an article for our
COMPENSATION & BENEFITS REVIEW journal.

Feature articles should target the information needs of compensation and
benefits specialists, including new laws and regulations affecting
compensation and benefits plans, compensation and benefits strategies, new
trends, plan design, executive compensation trends, and so on. Whenever
possible, include tables, graphs, and sidebars. We also welcome case studies,
opinion pieces, research findings, and interviews.

REQUIREMENTS FOR ALL SUBMITTED ARTICLES
Articles are to be in Wordperfect 5.1, 3 1/2*" disk. (We can translate other
word processing programs, if necessary, or accept a file transfer by
modem--call the number below for instructions.) Include two double-spaced hard
copies. PRIOR TO SENDING YOUR DISK, PLEASE CHECK IT FOR DEFECTS AND TO ENSURE
THAT YOUR ARTICLE IS, INDEED, RETRIEVABLE.

We ask that you present feature articles as follows:

COMPENSATION & BENEFITS REVIEW

1. Length: 4,200 to 10,500 words.
2. Font: Courier 10cpi.
3. Style:
   a. Enhance the article with BOLDFACE, italic, and BOLD ITALIC commands only. Keep software commands simple--i.e., don't use complicated publishing programs.
   b. Use the small letter "o" in place of bullets; two hyphens for a long dash.

4. Put all tables, graphs, and sidebars, etc. at the end of the article, each on a separate page, and label as Exhibit 1, 2, 3, etc. Include appropriate references to each exhibit in the text.

5. Exhibits may be submitted on disk or hard copy. We will have complex exhibits set by our compositor. NOTE: PLEASE SUPPLY DATAPOINTS FOR GRAPHS AND CHARTS THAT WE MUST SET. Submit original drawings, if possible, for reproduction of artwork.

6. Include a one-to-two paragraph executive summary with each article. Additional presentation suggestions:

* Maintain a lively, readable style. Use subheads and vivid verbs. Make sentences active, not passive (e.g., instead of "Employees were asked what they thought about their compensation program," write "The company asked employees what they thought...."). Always identify who is doing the asking, planning, etc.

* Spell out all acronyms at least once.

* Avoid literature citations in text and footnotes. If one seems indispensable, place it in parentheses within the text, not at the bottom of the page.

* Please include the full first names of any authors referenced.

SPECIFIC PERMISSION TO QUOTE FROM COPYRIGHTED MATERIAL is to be included on a separate page or in the cover letter. Permission is required for quotations of more than 150 words, for tables or exhibits previously published elsewhere, and for shorter material quoted in substantial part.

As we do not have a fact-checking department, authors are responsible for verifying the accuracy of the information in their articles--including any math as well as spelling and style of company names and individual names and titles cited.

We take submission of a manuscript to be the author's representation that the manuscript is not currently under consideration by another periodical and that it has not been published or accepted for publication elsewhere.

The review process takes approximately 4-6 weeks. Upon publication, we provide the author with two copies of the issue in which the article appears and 100 reprints of the article.
For further information, call the editor at 212-903-8069 or
                              e-mail to L_BENNETT@AMANET.ORG

COMPUTATIONAL ECONOMICS

ADDRESS FOR SUBMISSION :

H. M. AMMAN, EDITOR-IN-CHIEF
COMPUTATIONAL ECONOMICS
UNIVERSITY OF AMSTERDAM
DEPARTMENT OF ECONOMICS
ROETERSSTRAAT 11, E-G13
AMSTERDAM - NL,
THE NETHERLANDS
+31 20 5254 203
+31 20 5254 254 (Fax)
E-Mail : amman@fee.uva.nl

CIRCULATION DATA :

Reader : Academic

Frequency of Issue : 5 Times/Year

Copies Per Issue : Less than 1000

Subscription Price : 299.00 US$
  Members : 62.00 US$

Sponsorship : Profit Oriented Corp.

PUBLICATION GUIDELINES :

Manuscript Length : 16-20

Copies Required : Four

Computer Submission : Yes

Format : LATEX, TEX

Fees to Review : 0.00 US$

REVIEW INFORMATION :

Type of Review : Editorial Review

No. of External Reviewers : Two

No. of In House Reviewers : One

Acceptance Rate : 21-30%

Time To Review : 4-6 months

Reviewer's Comments : Yes

Fees to Publish : 0.00 US$

Invited Articles : 11-20%

MANUSCRIPT TOPICS : ACCOUNTING INFORMATION SYSTEMS; ECONOMETRICS;
  COMPUTATIONAL ECONOMICS

PUBLICATION GUIDELINES : American Math. Society (AMITEX)

MANUSCRIPT GUIDELINES/COMMENTS :

COMPUTATIONAL ECONOMICS serves as an interface for work which integrates
computer science with economic or management science. Work published in the
journal falls in the fields of symbolic information processing, numerical
procedures, computational aspects of mathematical programming, hardware
developments, operational research, artificial intelligence, user interfaces,
database interfaces, and software research.

The topics of interest to COMPUTATIONAL ECONOMICS include: - computational
statistics and econometrics

* decision theory and optimal control theory
* applications and methodology of artificial intelligence in economics and
  management
* computer software developments and modelling languages
* operational research techniques in economics and management - computer
  hardware developments, array processing and parallel processing and their
  applications
* database interfaces, query procedures and user interfaces in economics and
  management.

COMPUTATIONAL ECONOMICS

COMPUTATIONAL ECONOMICS also publishes state of the art reports by invited authors, brief software reports, critical reviews and special issues devoted to the depth study of a particular topic.

COMPUTATIONAL ECONOMICS is required reading for all those in the business field for whom the computer is more than just a desk-top executive toy.

COMPUTATIONAL ECONOMICS is surveyed by Computer and Information Systems Abstract Journal; INSPEC Information Services; ACM Computing Reviews; Current Mathematical Publications; Mathematical Reviews; MathSci; Journal of Economic Literature; The International Bibliography of the Social Sciences; Engineering Index; COMPENDEX PLUS; Ei Page One; Zentralblatt fur Mathematik; Computer Literature Index; Economic Literature Index; Econlit; International Current Awareness Service; ACM Guide to Computing Literature; International Development Abstracts

CONSTITUTIONAL POLITICAL ECONOMY

ADDRESS FOR SUBMISSION :

RICHARD E. WAGNER, CO-EDITOR
CONSTITUTIONAL POLITICAL ECONOMY
GEORGE MASON UNIVERSITY
CENTER FOR STUDY OF PUBLIC CHOICE
MSN 1D3 - GEORGE'S HALL
4400 UNIVERSITY DRIVE
FAIRFAX, VA 22030-4444
703-993-2324
703-993-2323 (Fax)
E-Mail : r.wagner@vms1.gmu.edu

CIRCULATION DATA :

Reader : Academic

Frequency of Issue : Quarterly

Copies Per Issue : Less than 1000

Subscription Price : 60.00 US$
    Institution : 232.00 US$

Sponsorship : Profit Oriented Corp.

PUBLICATION GUIDELINES :

Manuscript Length : 26-30

Copies Required : Three

Computer Submission : No

Format : N/A

Fees to Review : 0.00 US$

REVIEW INFORMATION :

Type of Review : Editorial Review

No. of External Reviewers : One

No. of In House Reviewers : Two

Acceptance Rate : 11-20%

Time To Review : 2-3 months

Reviewer's Comments : Yes

Fees to Publish : 0.00 US$

Invited Articles : 5% or less

MANUSCRIPT TOPICS : ACCOUNTING INFORMATION SYSTEMS;
    PUBLIC POLICY ECONOMICS; CONSTITUTIONAL LAW & ECONOMICS

PUBLICATION GUIDELINES : Chicago Manual of Style

MANUSCRIPT GUIDELINES/COMMENTS :

Co-editor: Viktor J. Vanberg
            Albeat-Ludwigs-Universitat Freiburg
            Abteilung Fur Wiatschafts Politik
            D-79085 Freiburg 1. Br.
            Germany

CONSTITUTIONAL POLITICAL ECONOMY is published by Kluwer Academic Press, P.O.
Box 17, 3300 AH Dordrecht, The Netherlands. Phone (31) 78 524400, Fax (31) 78
524474.

CONSTRUCTION MANAGEMENT AND ECONOMICS

ADDRESS FOR SUBMISSION :

DR. WILL P. HUGHES, EDITOR
CONSTRUCTION MANAGEMENT AND ECONOMICS
UNIVERSITY OF READING
DEPARTMENT OF CONSTRUCTION MANAGEMENT
 AND ENGINEERING
P.O. BOX 219, WHITEKNIGHTS
READING, RG6 6AW
UK
+44 118 931 8201
+44 118 931 3856 (Fax)
E-Mail : W.P.Hughes@reading.ac.uk

CIRCULATION DATA :

Reader : Academic

Frequency of Issue : Bi-Monthly

Copies Per Issue : Less than 1000

Subscription Price : 500.00 US$
   Member/ASCC and CIB : 179.00 US$
   Student Share Rate : 48.00 US$

Sponsorship :

PUBLICATION GUIDELINES :

Manuscript Length : 11-15

Copies Required : Four

Computer Submission : Yes

Format : Microsoft Wd / Wd Perfect

Fees to Review : 0.00 US$

REVIEW INFORMATION :

Type of Review : Blind Review

No. of External Reviewers : Over 3

No. of In House Reviewers : Zero

Acceptance Rate : 50 %

Time To Review : 2-3 months

Reviewer's Comments : Yes

Fees to Publish : 0.00 US$

Invited Articles : 5% or less

MANUSCRIPT TOPICS : COST ACCOUNTING; REAL ESTATE;
   CONSTRUCTION MANAGEMENT

PUBLICATION GUIDELINES :

MANUSCRIPT GUIDELINES/COMMENTS :

1. SUBMISSION
Authors should submit four copies of their papers to facilitate refereeing
with original artwork to: Professor Ranko Bon or Dr Will Hughes, Department of
Construction Management and Engineering, University of Reading, PO Box 219,
Whiteknights, Reading RG6 6AW, UK. It will be assumed that the authors will
keep a copy. Papers will be anonymously refereed by acknowledged experts in
the subject. Only those receiving favourable recommendations from the referees
will be accepted for publication. If an author is uncertain about whether a
paper is suitable for publication in the Journal, it is acceptable to submit a
synopsis first.

2. EFFECTIVE COMMUNICATION
The paper should be written and arranged in a style that is succinct and
easily followed. An informative but short title, a concise abstract with
keywords, and a well-written introduction will help to achieve this. Simple
language, short sentences and a good use of headings all help to communicate
information more effectively. Discursive treatment of the subject matter is
discouraged. Figures should be used to aid the clarity of the paper. The
reader should be carefully guided through the paper. Think about your reader.

3. MANUSCRIPT - PAPERS

(a) Length: although there is no length limitation, papers should fall within
the range of 2000-5000 words. Authors are requested to state how many words
their paper contains. The manuscript must be in English, typed in double
spacing on one side of A4 paper only, with a 4 cm margin on the left-hand
side. The pages should be numbered consecutively. There should be no loose
addenda or notes or other explanatory material. The manuscript should be
arranged under headings and subheadings.

(b) Title page: the first page of the manuscript must contain the full title,
the affiliation(s) and address(es) of the author(s), a running title of not
more than 75 characters and spaces, and the name and address of the author who
will be responsible for correspondence and correcting proofs.

(c) Abstract and keywords: an abstract and up to five keywords for the
purposes of indexing should be included, preferably on the title page. The
abstract must not exceed 200 words and must precis the paper giving a clear
indication of the conclusions it contains. Keywords must be carefully selected
to facilitate readers' search.

(d) Illustrations: illustrations must accompany the manuscript but should not
be included in the text. Photographs, standard forms, and charts should be
referred to as 'Fig. 1', 'Fig. 2' etc. They should be numbered in the order in
which they are referred to in the text.

Illustrations should be submitted in a form ready for reproduction. Diagrams
and drawings should be drawn in black indian ink on white card or tracing
paper. Figures will normally be reduced in size on reproduction and authors
should draw with this in mind. With a reduction scale of 2:1 in mind the
authors should use lines not less than 0.25 mm thick, and upper and lower case
lettering, the capital of which should be 4 mm high. To keep within the type
area of the Journal, drawings for a 2:1 reduction should not exceed 280 mm in
width. If you draw for any reduction other than 2:1 please indicate your
intentions. Stecil lettering or Letraset should be used; typewritten
annotations are not acceptable.

Forms should be completed in black indian ink. Photographs should be black and
white glossy prints Each should have written lightly on the back the author's
name, the figure number and an indication of which is top. Where lettering is
to appear on the photograph, two prints should be supplied, one of which
should be left unlettered.

(e) Measurements: metric units should be used; if other units are used then
metric equivalents should be given in parentheses.

(f) References: the Harvard system is used. References in the text should be
quoted in the following manner: Smith (1975) or (Brown and Green, 1976) or if
there are more than two authors, Jones et al. (1980). References should be
collected at the end of the paper in alphabetical order by the first author's
surname. If references to the same author have the same year, they should be
differentiated by using 1980a and 1980b etc. The style should follow the
examples below:

Ranasinghe, M. and Russell, A.D. (1993) Elicitation of subjective
    probabilities for economic risk analysis. Construction Management and
    Economics, 11, 326-40.
Stone, P.A. (1980) Building Design Evaluation: Costs-in-use. E & FN Spon,
    London.
Barrett, S. (1981) Implementation of public policy. In Policy and Action
    Barrett, S. and Fudge, C. (eds), Chapman & Hall, London, pp. 1-33.

If no person is named as the author the body should be used - for example:
Royal Institution of Chartered Surveyors (1980) Report on Urban Planning
Methods, London.

(g) Endnotes: a limited number of explanatory endnotes is permissible. These
should be numbered 1, 2, 3, consecutively in the text and denoted by
superscripts. They should be typed on a separate sheet of paper at the end of
the text. Endnotes should not be used for academic or project citations.

4. MANUSCRIPTS - SHORT PAPERS OR NOTES
Short papers or notes should be as short as possible, and should not be longer
than 2000 words. The specifications from the previous section apply in all
respects. Short papers or notes may offer comments on other papers published
by this Journal, as well as offer original contributions.

5. PROOFS
Proofs will be sent to the corresponding author for correction. The difficulty
and expense involved in making amendments at proof stage makes it essential
for authors to prepare their manuscript carefully: any alterations to the
original text are strongly discouraged. Our aim is rapid publication: this
will be helped if authors provide good copy following the above instructions,
and return their proofs as quickly as possible.

6. OFFPRINTS
Offprints may be ordered when returning proofs. Free offprints will not be
provided.

7. COPYRIGHT
Submission of an article to this Journal is taken to imply that it represents
original, unpublished work, not under consideration for publication elsewhere.
Authors will be asked to transfer the copyright for their papers to the
publisher if and when the article is accepted for publication, using the form
provided. The copyright covers the exclusive rights to reproduce and
distribute the article, including reprints, photographic reproductions,
microfilm or any reproduction of a similar nature, and translations.
Permission to publish illustrations must be obtained by the author before
submission and any acknowledgements should be included in the figure captions.

CONSTRUCTION MANAGEMENT AND ECONOMICS is published by E & FN SPON (an imprint
of Chapman & Hall), 2-6 Boundary Row, London SE1 8HN, UK. Tel: 0171-865-0066,
Fax: 0171-522-9623. E-mail: spon@chall.co.uk

CONTEMPORARY ACCOUNTING RESEARCH

ADDRESS FOR SUBMISSION :

EDITORIAL ASSISTANT
CONTEMPORARY ACCOUNTING RESEARCH
UNIVERSITY OF ALBERTA
FACULTY OF BUSINESS
3-23 BUSINESS BUILDING
EDMONTON, ALBERTA, T6G 2R6
CANADA
403-492-7513
403-492-3325 (Fax)

CIRCULATION DATA :

Reader : Academic

Frequency of Issue : 2 Times/Year

Copies Per Issue : 1001-2000

Subscription Price : 75.00 US$
  Institution : 100.00 US$

Sponsorship : Professional Assoc.,
              University

PUBLICATION GUIDELINES :

Manuscript Length :

Copies Required : Three

Computer Submission : No

Format : N/A

Fees to Review : 100.00 US$
  C.A.Acc.Assn. Member 50.00 US$

REVIEW INFORMATION :

Type of Review : Blind Review

No. of External Reviewers : Two

No. of In House Reviewers : Zero

Acceptance Rate : 11-20%

Time To Review : 2-3 months

Reviewer's Comments : Yes

Fees to Publish : 0.00 US$

Invited Articles : 5% or less

MANUSCRIPT TOPICS : ACCOUNTING INFORMATION SYSTEMS;
  ACCOUNTING THEORY & PRACTICE; AUDITING; CAPITAL BUDGETING; COST ACCOUNTING;
  GOVERNMENT & NON-PROFIT ACCOUNTING; TAX ACCOUNTING

PUBLICATION GUIDELINES : Chicago Manual of Style

MANUSCRIPT GUIDELINES/COMMENTS :

FINAL MANUSCRIPT PRESENTATION
(1) Margins should be at least 1/2 inches around the body of the text to
facilitate editing and duplication.
(2) All pages including endnotes, tables, figures, illustrations, appendices
and references, should be numbered consecutively.

(3) The cover page should contain the following information:
    * title
    * author's name (in all capital letters) and university affiliation
      (institution only & in italicized upper and lower case letters)
    * acknowledgements and information on grants received
    * contact author address, phone, fax, and email.

(4) Please ensure that the various elements of the paper are in this order on
the disk:
    * Title/Author
    * Acknowledgments

CONTEMPORARY ACCOUNTING RESEARCH

* Abstract (see note 5)
* Body of Text (see note 6)
* Appendix (if applicable)
* Endnotes (if applicable)
* References
* Tables (if applicable)
* Figures (if applicable)

(5) An abstract of NOT MORE THAN 250 WORDS should be presented on the second page immediately preceding the text. The abstract should include the following information:
* the research question
* the method of examination
* the principal findings

Please ensure that the abstract is within the requested guidelines. Extensive abstracts disrupt the continuity of the article both in comprehension and written form.

(6) Please do not use the word INTRODUCTION to begin the "body" of the text. It is redundant, and the text will be sufficiently set apart from the abstract to indicate the beginning.

(7) All endnotes should be numbered consecutively, in full size numbers, and presented on a separate page immediately following the text.

(8) An original and two photocopies of each drawing will be required for publication. The original must be either professionally drawn in black ink, or laser printed on white bond paper. The cost of redrawing illustrations of insufficient quality will be charged to the author.

(9) The abbreviations e.g., i.e., and etc., should be used only within parentheses. If they are not in parentheses, then they must be spelled out: for example, that is, and and so on.

(10) Equations are set (with variables italicized) flush left, with the number, in parentheses, set flush right.
$$E=MC2 \tag{1}$$

(11) All formal capitalization rules should be followed. CAR will NO LONGER present titles with an initial capital letter only. Nothing in the manuscript should be in all capital letters except the author name(s) following the title of the paper and the word TABLE in table titles (see note 12).

TABULAR MATTER
(12) The word "table" appears in all capitals, Roman text and left justified, followed by an arabic numeral. The title follows on the next line, again in Roman text with an initial capital letter only.
TABLE 1

(13) The word "figure" appears with an initial capital only, bolded and left justified, followed by an Arabic numeral. The title appears on the same line in Roman text with an initial capital letter only.
Figure 1

(14) Each table, figure, or illustration should be presented on a separate page and bear an arabic number AND a title. Table headings should be typed with the first word only capitalized, except for proper words that are in the title, or the first word following a colon or dash.

(15) The author should indicate by legible marginal notation where a table, figure, or illustration should be inserted in the text.

(16) Please do NOT use spaces instead of tabs to separate the items in columns in tables. The spaces must be stripped individually which is a time-consuming process. It is helpful if only one tab can separate each column.

(17) If vertical lines are necessary in a table, please draw them in separately on a hard copy and make a special note of them. Please do not put them in on the computer - they often will not convert from disk to disk. Tables should not be enclosed in boxes.
EXAMPLE:

TABLE 1 Results by category: Periods 1 and 2

Explanatory variables	Predicted sign	Coefficient	t-statistic	One-tailed probability
Ratio	xxx	xv	xvv	xvx
Mean	yxv	yyx	yyx	yxv
Earnings per share	yxy	yxx	yxx	yx
Total				

TEXT HEADINGS
(18) Headings should NOT be numbered or lettered. The style of type will indicate the level of the heading.

First level heads are boldface, initial letter only capitalized except for proper words, flush left. (Signified in my editing by I.)
This is a first level head

Second level heads are italicized, initial letter only capitalized except for proper words, flush left. (Signified in my editing by ll.)
This is a second level head (italicize)

Third level heads are roman, initial letter only capitalized except for proper words, flush left. (Signified in my editing by lll.)
This is a third level head

Fourth level heads are boldface, run into the text line, followed by a period, and first letter only capitalized. (Signified in my editing by IV.)
This is a fourth level head (bold). Text follows on the same line.

(19) The first line of text after a heading is flush left. Thereafter, all paragraphs are indented. This rule holds true for the first three types of heads.

DECIMALS, VARIABLES AND EQUATIONS

(20) Decimal fractions should be preceded by a zero (0.25, not .25).
Exception: Do not use a zero before a decimal fraction when the number cannot be greater than 1 (e.g., correlations, proportions, and levels of statistical significance:
$p < .05$).

(21) CAR styles uses the following:
* Variables in text and equations are typed in italics.
* Vectors in text and equations are typed in nonitalics (both Greek and Arabic).
* Matrices in text and equations are typed in bold.
* Scalars in text and equations are typed in italics.

** If the printer cannot print italics, please DO NOT substitute underlines for italics. Instead, please highlight the items which are to be italicized on the hard copy you send to the copy editor. We assume that underlines below letters indicate that the letters are to have bars below them.

TEXT FORMATION

(22) In the text, when not in lists, numbers from one through nine should be written out in full, except where decimals are used.

(23) In the BODY of the text, please write out the word percent (%).

(24) Endnotes should be referred to in the body of the text in superscript arabic numerals.

(25) Where the derivation of formulas has been abbreviated, a full derivation should be presented an the appendix.

(26) Hyphenation should be kept to a minimum, but be careful to avoid ambiguous expressions that may arise from lack of hyphens. DO NOT hyphenate words at the end of lines.

(27) Avoid referring to elements that appear "above" or "below". Instead, refer to a named element ("TABLE 4"), or refer to the "preceding" or "following" element. The same problem holds true when referring to previous pages throughout the text. The "printed" pages will not have the same numbers as the "typed" pages.

(28) Titles, names of organizations, and so on must be spelled out in full the first time they appear in the text. Thereafter abbreviations are appropriate.

BIBLIOGRAPHIC INFORMATION
(29) IN-TEXT REFERENCES

In-text references should be placed in parentheses with NO COMMA between the author name and the year. If a page number is given, it should follow a comma, after the year (no p. or pp. is needed). The date need be given only once per paragraph unless confusion could result.
References made in the text should appear as follows:

"Riddell (1983) noted that..."
"This was also observed by previous writers (e.g., Levi and Dexter 1983; Rosen 1981)...'

"During the rule of Augustus, many extravagant buildings were constructed (Richley 1992, 453)..."

(30) At the end of the manuscript a complete list of references should be presented following the guidelines set out on below. PLEASE ensure that all "references" have been referred to in the manuscript. Any found to be extraneous will be deleted during the editing process. Check also that the date of each reference in text is the same as that in the reference section. Also check that the spelling of the name(s) of the author(s) is the same both in the text and the reference section.

(31) During the editing process, only the FORM of your references is checked. You must ensure that the references given are both complete and correct.

(32) When citing work by two authors in the text, both names must be listed. If the work is authored by three or more authors, all authors must be named in the first reference to the work. Thereafter, it is appropriate to use "et al.".

(33) Multiple works by an author should be cited chronologically in the reference list.

(34) Unpublished work should be cited only rarely, and if any such work has been published since the last version of the manuscript, the reference should be updated.

(35) HANGING INDENTS
In references and endnotes, and in any other copy in the text, if the computer will not automatically create hanging indents (indentations that follow a line of copy that begins flush left, as shown in the example), DO NOT use carriage returns and tabs to create the effect.

ex. Altman, E. Financial Ratios, Discriminant Analysis and the Prediction of Corporate Bankruptcy. Journal of Finance (September 1968), 587-609.

If equipment will not automatically create a hanging indent, submit copy that simply wraps from line to line with no carriage return.

ex. Altman, E. Financial Ratios, Discriminant Analysis and the Prediction of Corporate Bankruptcy. Jouna/ of Finance (September 68), 587-609.

(36) CAPITALIZATION AND PUNCTUATION
Please note the capitalization and punctuation guidelines of the references in note 39. CAR has been simplified by deleting the use of quotation marks around article titles. Standard capitalization is still used. Periods separate the items in the reference. For scholarly journals, the volume and/or number is not necessary if the issue is identified by month/season and year.

(37) PLACEMENT OF ENDNOTES
A problem has occurred with previous papers where the endnotes have been "suppressed" on the diskette. The endnotes print out fully on the hard copy but cannot be accessed on the computer. Please type endnotes as regular text at the end of the paper.

(38) EXAMPLES
PLEASE BE SURE TO FOLLOW THIS INFORMATION CLOSELY. THE EXAMPLES LISTED BELOW REFLECT THE CURRENT TREND IN CITING BIBLIOGRAPHIC REFERENCES

Author, Initial, and Initial Author. Article Title. Publication (Month and Year), 489-499.

Author, Initial. Publication. Publisher, Year, 489-499.

Author, Initial, Initial Author, and Initial Author. Publication. Publisher, Year, 489-499.

Author, Initial. Article Title. In Publication, ed. Initial Editor. Publisher, Year, 489-499.

Author, Initial, Initial Author, and Initial Author. Publication, 2nd ed. Publisher, Year, 489-499.

Author, Initial. Paper Title. Working paper. Affiliation, Year.

Author, Initial. Dissertation Title. Ph.D. Dissertation. University, Year.

Author, Initial. Paper Title. Paper presented at Conference Name. City, Year.

(39) SPECIAL NOTES
Page indicators (i.e. p. or pp.) are not necessary in the references. The page numbers should stand alone.

In situations where two or more authors names appear in a reference, the first name is recorded last name first, followed by the first initial and a comma, then the first initial of the second author, followed by his/her surname.

CORPORATE CASHFLOW

ADDRESS FOR SUBMISSION :

RICHARD H. GAMBLE, EDITOR
CORPORATE CASHFLOW
6155 POWERS FERRY ROAD, N.W.
ATLANTA, GA 30339
404-618-0918

CIRCULATION DATA :

Reader : Treasury Managers
Frequency of Issue : Monthly
Copies Per Issue : Over 25,000
Subscription Price : 78.00 US$
Sponsorship : Profit Oriented Corp.

PUBLICATION GUIDELINES :

Manuscript Length : 6-10
Copies Required : One
Computer Submission : Yes
Format : N/A
Fees to Review : 0.00 US$

REVIEW INFORMATION :

Type of Review : N/A
No. of External Reviewers : Zero
No. of In House Reviewers : Two
Acceptance Rate : 11-20%
Time To Review : 2-3 months
Reviewer's Comments : No
Fees to Publish : 0.00 US$
Invited Articles : Over 50%

MANUSCRIPT TOPICS : AUDITING; CAPITAL BUDGETING;
  INTERNATIONAL FINANCE; TREASURY MANAGEMENT

PUBLICATION GUIDELINES :

MANUSCRIPT GUIDELINES/COMMENTS :

COPIES PER ISSUE: 40,000

CORPORATE CONTROLLER

ADDRESS FOR SUBMISSION :

STEPHEN COLLINS, MANAGING EDITOR
CORPORATE CONTROLLER
RIA GROUP
395 HUDSON STREET
NEW YORK, NY 10014
212-367-6398
212-367-6718 (Fax)

CIRCULATION DATA :

Reader : Business Persons

Frequency of Issue : Bi-Monthly

Copies Per Issue : 5001-10,000

Subscription Price : 125.00 US$

Sponsorship : Profit Oriented Corp.

PUBLICATION GUIDELINES :

Manuscript Length : 11-20

Copies Required : Two

Computer Submission : Yes

Format : WordPerfect 5.1

Fees to Review : 0.00 US$

REVIEW INFORMATION :

Type of Review : Blind Review

No. of External Reviewers : Two

No. of In House Reviewers : Two

Acceptance Rate : 50 %

Time To Review : 1-2 months

Reviewer's Comments : No

Fees to Publish : 0.00 US$

Invited Articles : 31-50%

MANUSCRIPT TOPICS : ACCOUNTING INFORMATION SYSTEMS;
  ACCOUNTING THEORY & PRACTICE; CAPITAL BUDGETING; TAX ACCOUNTING

PUBLICATION GUIDELINES : Chicago Manual of Style

MANUSCRIPT GUIDELINES/COMMENTS :

COST ENGINEERING

ADDRESS FOR SUBMISSION :

KATHY DEWEESE, MANAGING EDITOR
COST ENGINEERING
AACE INTERNATIONAL
209 PRAIRIE AVENUE, SUITE 100
MORGANTOWN, WV 26505
USA
304-296-8444/800-858-COST
304-291-5728 (Fax)
E-Mail : 74757.2636@compuserve.com

CIRCULATION DATA :

Reader : Academic &
        Construction/Engineering

Frequency of Issue : Monthly

Copies Per Issue : 5001-10,000

Subscription Price : 52.00 US$
  All Non-US Countries : 68.00 US$
  Airmail : 90.00 US$

Sponsorship : Professional Assoc. &
            Non Profit Corp.

PUBLICATION GUIDELINES :

Manuscript Length : 11-15

Copies Required : Four

Computer Submission : No

Format : N/A

Fees to Review : 0.00 US$

REVIEW INFORMATION :

Type of Review : Blind Review

No. of External Reviewers : Three

No. of In House Reviewers : One

Acceptance Rate : 60 %

Time To Review : 2-3 months

Reviewer's Comments : Yes

Fees to Publish : 0.00 US$

Invited Articles : 5% or less

MANUSCRIPT TOPICS : ACCOUNTING INFORMATION SYSTEMS;
  CAPITAL BUDGETING; COST ACCOUNTING; ECONOMETRICS;
  INTERNATIONAL & ECONOMIC DEVELOPMENT; INTERNATIONAL FINANCE;
  COST/PROJECT MANAGEMENT

PUBLICATION GUIDELINES : Chicago Manual of Style

MANUSCRIPT GUIDELINES/COMMENTS :

ABOUT COST ENGINEERING MAGAZINE AND THE MANUSCRIPT REVIEW PROCESS . . .

COST ENGINEERING magazine is a monthly publication of the AACE International.
The first issue was published in 1958 and served as a forum for the accumulation and exchange of cost engineering knowledge ;i.e., cost estimating, cost
control, business planning and management science, profitability analysis,
project management, and planning and scheduling. COST ENGINEERING magazine
continues to invite manuscripts on these topics.

COST ENGINEERING is a highly respected, refereed, technical journal. The
technical articles published in the magazine serve as a reference for the
magazine's 6,000+ subscribers. COST ENGINEERING's Board of Reviewers consists
of international consultants; professors and researchers; AACE's technical
directors and committee chairs; and professional cost engineers with many
Canadian, American, and international firms. Many of the reviewers are well-
Known authors themselves.

COST ENGINEERING

Approximately 30 to 35 technical articles are published each year in the magazine. The review process for each manuscript takes an average of 3 to 4 months. Everyone who submits a manuscript will be notified of its receipt and of its acceptance or rejection when the review is complete. If a paper is accepted for publication, it is scheduled on the magazine's editorial calendar. Publication, then, is within 1 year of acceptance. COST ENGINEERING will rarely consider publishing more than one manuscript by any author in one year's volume of the magazine. COST ENGINEERING does not pay for manuscripts, nor is it interested in commercial or marketing-type articles on a particular product, method, or company. Please follow the enclosed author guidelines when preparing and submitting your manuscript to COST ENGINEERING magazine.

If you have any questions about COST ENGINEERING magazine or would like to talk with an editor about preparing your manuscript, call (304) 296-8444.

ABOUT THE MAGAZINE
COST ENGINEERING is published 12 times a year by AACE International. Technical papers go through a blind review process.

The review process takes at least 3 months to complete.

PREPARING YOUR MANUSCRIPT
* Since we use a blind review process, DO NOT use your name in the paper. The title page should contain your name and address.

* PREVIOUSLY-PUBLISHED WORK - you must notify us if the work you are submitting has previously been published elsewhere.

* FORMAT - please submit a clean, professional-looking copy, either a good xerox or a clear computer printout. Only print on the front page. Please number all pages.

* REFERENCES - we require proper credit and documentation of any information that is not the author's original work. Include complete bibliographic information for every reference in your paper. References should be numbered and listed at the end of the paper, in alphabetical order, by the author's last name. Include the title, publisher, place of publication, publication date, and page numbers (if necessary). When something mentioned in your paper must be referenced, cite the reference by its number in the reference section, and enclose the number in brackets. We follow the CHICAGO MANUAL OF STYLE, 14th edition.

* EQUATIONS - All equations must be typed or included in your software program. Do not hand-letter equations.

* ILLUSTRATIONS - All tables and figures must be laser-printed or typeset. We cannot accept hand-drawn figures. Your figures and tables must be legible and integrated with the text, not lumped together in an appendix at the end.

* UNITS OF MEASURE - We use metric units. If other units are used, metric equivalents must be given in parenthesis.

* ABBREVIATIONS AND ACRONYMS - spell out the words the first time you use an abbreviation or acronym. Make sure that any "jargon" or special terms are

defined.
SUBMITTING YOUR MANUSCRIPT
* Send 4 (FOUR) copies of your manuscript, along with an IBM-compatible disk
(preferably WordPerfect 5.2, Microsoft Word for Windows 2.0, or ASCII).

* CLEARANCES - all papers dealing with subjects containing information that
could be construed as company confidential or private must be accompanied by
written clearance from the author's company.

* Manuscripts and disks cannot be returned.

* You will be notified by mail when we have received your manuscript and on
its status.

IF YOUR PAPER IS ACCEPTED
An editor will contact you about the specifics of the production and
scheduling of your work.

* TITLE AND COPYRIGHT - you will be sent a copyright form to sign and have
notarized. Title and copyright of your paper become vested in AACE
International upon acceptance of the paper. Once a paper is accepted for
publication in COST ENGINEERING and the author(s) signs the publication
agreement, the paper may not be published elsewhere unless authorized by AACE
International Reproduction elsewhere in whole or in part is welcomed, provided
that proper credit is given to the author and to AACE International. If COST
ENGINEERING publishes a manuscript that has previously been copyrighted, the
copyright must be transferred to AACE International.

* RESPONSIBILITY - statements and opinions expressed are the responsibility of
the author. AACE international publishes articles in COST ENGINEERING for the
benefit of its members and to make public and preserve skills and knowledge of
cost engineering and cost management. Publication does not necessarily imply
endorsement by AACE International.

IF YOUR ARE ASKED TO REVISE YOUR PAPER
If revisions are deemed necessary, an editor will contact you.

* MINOR REVISIONS - you will be asked to supply one copy of the revised paper.
If our editor determines that the revisions have been made, you will be
notified.

* MAJOR REVISIONS - if the reviewers feel that your paper needs substantial
reworking, four copies of the revised paper must be submitted. The paper will
then go out to the same reviewers. You will be notified of the result.

IF YOUR PAPER IS REJECTED
If your work is rejected, you will be notified by mail.

SEND YOUR MANUSCRIPTS TO: AACE International (see address above).

CPA JOURNAL

ADDRESS FOR SUBMISSION :

JAMES L. CRAIG, JR., CPA, MANAGING ED.
CPA JOURNAL
530 FIFTH AVENUE
NEW YORK, NY 10036-5101
USA
212-719-8300
212-719-3364 (Fax)
E-Mail : JCRAIG@LUCAONLINE.COM

CIRCULATION DATA :

Reader : Business Persons &
        CPAs

Frequency of Issue : Monthly

Copies Per Issue : Over 25,000

Subscription Price : 42.00 US$

Sponsorship : Professional Assoc.

PUBLICATION GUIDELINES :

Manuscript Length : 2500-4000 Words

Copies Required : Three

Computer Submission : Yes

Format : WP 5.1, 6.1 or ASCII Text

Fees to Review : 0.00 US$

REVIEW INFORMATION :

Type of Review : Blind Review

No. of External Reviewers : Over 3

No. of In House Reviewers : Three

Acceptance Rate : 21-30%

Time To Review : 2-3 months

Reviewer's Comments : No

Fees to Publish : 0.00 US$

Invited Articles : 6-10%

MANUSCRIPT TOPICS : ACCOUNTING INFORMATION SYSTEMS;
  ACCOUNTING THEORY & PRACTICE; AUDITING; COST ACCOUNTING;
  GOVERNMENT & NON-PROFIT ACCOUNTING; INSURANCE; TAX ACCOUNTING;
  BUSINESS LAW & PUBLIC RESPONSIBILITY; ECONOMICS; FINANCE & INVESTMENTS;
  GENERAL BUSINESS; TECHNOLOGY; INTERNET; ONLINE SERVICES;
  PERSONAL FINANCIAL PLANNING; ESTATE PLANNING

PUBLICATION GUIDELINES : Chicago Manual of Style

MANUSCRIPT GUIDELINES/COMMENTS :

1. CHICAGO MANUAL OF STYLE

2. We publish original articles of interest to practitioners, those in
business, and in educational fields. Submitted articles should offer: Help in
resolving questions that arise in practice, advice in implementing published
standards and guides, insight to problems with, preferably, workable
solutions, or report on the status of developing issues. Our articles should
be of broad interest, although some could relate to specific industries or
techniques. Article should be of immediate interest and timely to the
profession. The Journal also allots space to theoretical discussion and
viewpoints and will consider brief articles of this genre.

3. Please write clearly, concise and to the point--avoid numerous footnotes
and citations. What we look for is originality and logic. We reserve the right
to edit manuscripts for lucidity and grammar.

CPA JOURNAL

4. Manuscripts of 2500-4000 words are desireable. Shortr articles may be considered for use in our monthly departments (accounting, auditing, etc.) All major headings should be flush left, with initial uppercase letters. Subheads should also be flush left, with initial uppercase letters. Subheads are a writer's tool to logically present thought and introduce ideas in a minimal amount of space. Use subheads wisely.

5. Tables and figures should be numbered, titled so references made within the text can refer to the key. Tables and figures should be on separate sheets. Please submit clear and accurate renderings of the tables and figures.

6. Include a brief biography (about 25 words) with your name, title, affiliation, address, and telephone number.

7. Authors are notified when an article is accepted as a feature or department article. The acceptance letter also serves as a copyright permission form which grants THE CPA JOURNAL copyright privileges, including the right to authorize reprints.

8. Manuscripts should be submitted typed, double-spaced on 8-1/2" x 11" white paper. We ask that three copies be submitted along with the computer disk. Send manuscript package, including two copies and bio to the above address. Manuscripts will be returned upon written request. Any question re: topic, idea development, presentation, etc., please contact The JOURNAL.

CPCU JOURNAL

ADDRESS FOR SUBMISSION :

MICHELE IANETTI, MANAGING EDITOR
CPCU JOURNAL
P.O. BOX 3009
720 PROVIDENCE ROAD
MALVERN, PA 19355-0709
USA
610-251-2766
610-251-2761 (Fax)

CIRCULATION DATA :

Reader : Business Persons &
        Academic

Frequency of Issue : Quarterly

Copies Per Issue : Over 25,000

Subscription Price : 25.00 US$
  Members/part of dues : 0.00 US$

Sponsorship : Professional Assoc.

PUBLICATION GUIDELINES :

Manuscript Length : 16-30

Copies Required : Three

Computer Submission : Yes

Format : Microsoft Word

Fees to Review : 0.00 US$

REVIEW INFORMATION :

Type of Review : Blind Review

No. of External Reviewers : Two

No. of In House Reviewers : One

Acceptance Rate : 21-30%

Time To Review : 2-3 months

Reviewer's Comments : Yes

Fees to Publish : 0.00 US$

Invited Articles : 6-10%

MANUSCRIPT TOPICS : INSURANCE; TRANSPORTATION/PHYSICAL DISTRIBUTION

PUBLICATION GUIDELINES : Chicago Manual of Style

MANUSCRIPT GUIDELINES/COMMENTS :

The Editor is Barry D. Smith, Ph.D., CPCU, CLU, FLMI, Associate Professor, New Mexico State University.

1. The CHICAGO MANUAL OF STYLE, The University of Chicago Press, Thirteenth Edition.

2. We publish articles primarily of interest to practitioners. Our goal is to provide an interface between those with new ideas or newly developed information and those who can implement the ideas. Articles of a highly technical nature are acceptable if the author has explained the concepts in a manner that is accessible to practitioners. Articles should pertain to the insurance industry in general, or to property and casualty insurance in particular.

3. Facts which are not commonly known as well as quotations should be cited in endnote form. We prefer that citations not be extensive.

4. Manuscripts should be submitted in article form. We encourage a liberal use of sub-headings.

CPCU JOURNAL

5. Tables and figures should be numbered and titled. Reference should be made in the manuscript to the point of insertion. They can be submitted on separate pages.

6. Include a two to three sentence biography of the author(s) as well as a three to four sentence abstract.

7. Authors will be asked to state that the article has not been published elsewhere, and that proper credit has been given where necessary.

8. Articles submitted by academics will generally be reviewed by two assistant editors, who are all professors and CPCUs. A "double-blind" system is used, whereby the author's identity is not known to the reviewer, and the reviewers' identities are not known to the author. Reviewers comments are generally shared with the authors. Other submissions are generally reviewed by the editor.

9. Deadlines for acceptance of articles are three months prior to the publication date (June 1 for the September issue, e.g.).

CREDIT AND FINANCIAL MANAGEMENT REVIEW

ADDRESS FOR SUBMISSION :

MICHAEL DURANT, EXECUTIVE EDITOR
CREDIT AND FINANCIAL MANAGEMENT REVIEW
CREDIT RESEARCH FOUNDATION
8815 CENTRE PARK DRIVE, SUITE 200
COLUMBIA, MD 21045
USA
410-740-5499
410-740-4620 (Fax)
E-Mail : mwdurant@aol.com

CIRCULATION DATA :

Reader : Business Persons &
         Academic

Frequency of Issue : Quarterly

Copies Per Issue : Less than 1000

Subscription Price :
  Part of Assoc. Mem. : 80.00 US$

Sponsorship : Profit Oriented Corp. &
              Professional Assoc.

PUBLICATION GUIDELINES :

Manuscript Length : 11-15

Copies Required : Four

Computer Submission : Yes

Format : WP 5.1 or Microsoft Word

Fees to Review : 0.00 US$

REVIEW INFORMATION :

Type of Review : Blind Review

No. of External Reviewers : Two

No. of In House Reviewers : Two

Acceptance Rate : 50 %

Time To Review : 2-3 months

Reviewer's Comments : Yes

Fees to Publish : 0.00 US$

Invited Articles : 31-50%

MANUSCRIPT TOPICS : ACCOUNTING THEORY & PRACTICE;
  PORTFOLIO & SECURITY ANALYSIS; PUBLIC ADMINSTRATION

PUBLICATION GUIDELINES :

MANUSCRIPT GUIDELINES/COMMENTS :

Research papers may address any of the following topics: corporate finance,
credit policy, credit scoring, export credit, liquidity analysis, portfolio
management, working capital management, creating customer value, international
business management, management information systems, organizational structure,
reengineering, total quality management, or work team.

Case studies may address these practices within corporations and/or the
specific credit and collection functions of credit policy, sales maximization,
customer contacts, billing, cash application, or collections.

Research articles and case studies should be submitted to CRF, to be reviewed
by at least two members of the editorial review board or other parties
designated by the CRF director of research. Please submit articles on disk.
Attach a one paragraph abstract of the article on a separate page.

Tables, charts, and graphs should appear on separate pages in numerical order
at the end of the test as exhibits. All notes should appear as endnotes on
separate pages following the exhibits, using CHICAGO MANUAL OF STYLE format.
References should be listed alphabetically at the end of the manuscript.

CRITICAL PERSPECTIVES ON ACCOUNTING

ADDRESS FOR SUBMISSION :

PROFESSOR TONY TINKER, EDITOR
CRITICAL PERSPECTIVES ON ACCOUNTING
BARUCH COLLEGE - BOX E-723
17 LEXINGTON AVENUE
NEW YORK, NY 10010
USA
212-802-6436
212-802-6436 (Fax)
E-Mail : atibb@cunyvm.cuny.edu

CIRCULATION DATA :

Reader : Academic

Frequency of Issue :   6 Times/Year

Copies Per Issue : Less than 1000

Subscription Price : 137.00 US$

Sponsorship : Profit Oriented Corp. &
University

PUBLICATION GUIDELINES :

Manuscript Length : 20+

Copies Required : Four

Computer Submission : Yes

Format : N/A

Fees to Review : 0.00 US$

REVIEW INFORMATION :

Type of Review : Blind Review

No. of External Reviewers : Three

No. of In House Reviewers : Three

Acceptance Rate : 6-10%

Time To Review : 2-3 months

Reviewer's Comments : Yes

Fees to Publish : 0.00 US$

Invited Articles : 5% or less

MANUSCRIPT TOPICS : ACCOUNTING INFORMATION SYSTEMS;
  ACCOUNTING THEORY & PRACTICE; AUDITING; CAPITAL BUDGETING; COST ACCOUNTING;
  ECONOMIC HISTORY; GOVERNMENT & NON-PROFIT ACCOUNTING;
  INTERNATIONAL & ECONOMIC DEVELOPMENT; INTERNATIONAL FINANCE;
  PUBLIC POLICY ECONOMICS; ACCOUNTING; BUSINESS LAW & PUBLIC RESPONSIBILITY;
  ECONOMICS; FINANCE & INVESTMENTS; INTERNATIONAL BUSINESS;
  STRATEGIC MANAGEMENT POLICY;
  PHILOSOPHICAL ISSUES/ETHICS,EPISTEMOLOGY,RESEARCH; PUBLIC ADMINISTRATION;
  ORGANIZATIONAL BEHAVIOR AND THEORY;
  LABOR RELATIONS & HUMAN RESOURCE MGT (HRM);
  ORGANIZATIONAL BEHAVIOR AND THEORY; POETRY

PUBLICATION GUIDELINES : Chicago Manual of Style

MANUSCRIPT GUIDELINES/COMMENTS :

CRITICAL PERSPECTIVES ON ACCOUNTING aims to provide a forum for the growing
number of accounting researchers and practitioners who realize that
conventional theory and practice is ill-suited to the challenges of the modern
environment, and that accounting practices and corporate behaviour are
inextricably connected with many allocative, distributive, social and
ecological problems of our era. From such concerns, a new literature is
emerging that seeks to reformulate corporate, social and political activity,
and the theoretical practical means by which we apprehend and affect that
activity.

CRITICAL PERSPECTIVES ON ACCOUNTING

Specific issues that the journal will address include, but are not limited to, the following:

* Studies involving the political economy of accounting, critical accounting, radical accounting, and accounting's implication in the exercise of power
* Financial accounting's role in the processes of international capital formation, including its impact on stock market stability and international banking activities
* Management accounting's role in organizing the labour process
* The relationship between accounting and the state in various social formations
* Studies of accounting's historical role, as a means of "remembering" the subject's social and conflictual character
* The role of accounting in establishing "real" democracy at work and other domains of life
* Accounting's adjudicative function in international exchanges, such as that of the third world debt
* Antagonisms between the social and private character of accounting, such as conflicts of interest in the audit process
* The identification of new constituencies for radical and critical accounting information
* Accounting's involvement in gender and class conflicts in the workplace
* The interplay between accounting, social conflict, industrialization, bureaucracy and technocracy
* Reappraisals of the role of accounting as a science and technology
* Accounting's implication in the management conflict around state enterprises
* Critical reviews of "useful" scientific knowledge about organizations

INSTRUCTIONS TO AUTHORS

NOTES OF GUIDANCE TO CONTRIBUTORS
Authors submitting papers for publication warrant that the work does not infringe any existing copyright and does not contain material of a libelous or scandalous nature. Further, the author indemnifies the publisher and editors against any branch of such warranty.

FORMAT AND STYLE

CHICAGO MANUAL OF STYLE
Manuscripts are to be typewritten double spaced on one side (preferably international-size A4). Authors should include four copies of:

* an abstract not exceeding 150 words - it should summarize the purpose, methodology, and major conclusions of the article;
* 10 key words or phrases that can be used for indexing purposes;
* a short biographical sketch for each of the authors, together with their addresses and phone numbers.

The cover page of the manuscript should include the title, the authors name(s), position and institutional affiliation, and any acknowledgements. Only the title should appear on the next page of the manuscript and on the abstract. Footnotes, identified in the text by a numeral that is superscripted, should not include literature citations, and should be listed at the end of the paper, before the bibliography.

CRITICAL PERSPECTIVES ON ACCOUNTING

Literature citations in the text should include the author's name, the year of publication, and the specific page numbers if required (e.g., Mickey and Donald, 1968; p. 24). For more than two authors, the citation should be abbreviated as follows: (Kramdon et al., 1988, p. 1). Multiple citations of the same author(s) in the same year should be distinguished in the text (and in the bibliography) by a, b, c, etc. and followed by the year of publication. The bibliography should only include references cited in the text and should be arranged in the alphabetical order according to the surname of the first author. Full bibliographical details are required. The following style is required for

1. articles;
2. books;
3. citations from edited books;
4. translated books;
5. reference to a report.

1. DuBoff, R.B., and Herman, E.S., "Alfred Chandler's New Business History: A Review", Politics & Society, Vol. 10, No. 1, 1980, pp. 87-110.
2. Anderson, P., CONSIDERATIONS ON WESTERN MARXISM (London: New Left Review Books,1976).
3. Hall, S., "The Little Caesars of Social Democracy", in Hall, S. and Jacques, M., (eds) The Politics of Thatcherism, pp. 309-322, (London: Lawrence & Wishart, 1983).
4. Adorno, T.W., Negative Dialektic (Frankfurt: Suhrkamp, 1968). Negative Dialectics, E.B. Ashton (trans) (New York: Seabury Press,1973).
5. Joint WHO Committee on Multinational Expansion. THE ROLE OF THE MULTINATIONAL IN HEALTH AND SAFETY DEVELOPMENTS (Geneva: World Health Organisation, 1982, Technical Report Series 503).

CHARTS, DIAGRAMS AND FIGURES
These should all be called figures, numbered consecutively in Arabic numerals, with a brief title in capitals and labelled axes. The text should clearly indicate where the figure is to appear. Each figure should be submitted on a separate sheet of paper and be suitable for direct reproduction.

TABLES
Tables should be numbered consecutively and independently of figures. Tables should be labelled with Roman numerals, a brief descriptive title, and headings down and across. The text should indicate clearly where each table is to appear. Each table should be submitted on a separate sheet of paper and be suitable for direct reproduction.

PROOFS AND COPIES
Page proofs should be checked by the author and returned to the publisher within 48 hours. Only printer's typographical errors should be corrected at this stage; any substantive changes other than these will be charged to the author. The Editors reserve the right to publish a paper without the author's own corrections in cases of undue delay in returning the proofs.

NOTES FOR REVIEWERS AND AUTHORS
The journal aims to provide a prompt and informative response to authors. Manuscripts that pass an initial preliminary screening will be sent to two blind reviews. It is policy to offer authors constructive and supportive reviews and thus, as far as possible, reviewers will be encouraged to stress

in their review what additional work would be necessary to bring a submission to publication standard.

REPRINTS
50 reprints of each paper are supplied free of charge. In the case of multiple authored papers, they will be sent to the first named author. Additional quantities may be ordered at the time the proofs are checked, on the form provided. There are no page charges.

SUBMISSION REQUIREMENTS
Only manuscripts not under consideration elsewhere should be submitted. Copies of questionnaires and other research instruments should be included with the submission. However, space limitations may preclude the publication of this material. When they are not reproduced a note should be included indicating an address where readers may obtain a complete copy of the instruments should be included with the submission. However, space limitations may preclude the publication of this material. When they are not reproduced a note should be include indicating an address where readers may obtain a complete copy of the instrument.

Four copies of each manuscripts should be submitted to the Editor.

DE ECONOMIST

ADDRESS FOR SUBMISSION :

PROFESSOR S.K. KUIPERS, MANAGING EDITOR
DE ECONOMIST
UNIVERSITY OF GRONINGEN
DEPARTMENT OF ECONOMICS
W.S.N. - GEBOUW
BOX 802
9700 AV GRONINGEN,
THE NETHERLANDS
0 50 3633762
0 50 3637337 (Fax)
E-Mail : S.K.Kuipers@eco.RUG.nl

CIRCULATION DATA :

Reader : Business Persons,
   Academic, &
   Civil Servants

Frequency of Issue : Quarterly

Copies Per Issue : 3001-4000

Subscription Price : 178.00 US$
 Membership Fee : 30.00 US$

Sponsorship :

PUBLICATION GUIDELINES :

Manuscript Length : 21-25

Copies Required : Three

Computer Submission : No

Format : N/A

Fees to Review : 0.00 US$

REVIEW INFORMATION :

Type of Review : Editorial Review

No. of External Reviewers : One

No. of In House Reviewers : Two

Acceptance Rate : 40 %

Time To Review : 1-2 months

Reviewer's Comments : Yes

Fees to Publish : 0.00 US$

Invited Articles : 5% or less

MANUSCRIPT TOPICS : COST ACCOUNTING;
 INTERNATIONAL & ECONOMIC DEVELOPMENT; INTERNATIONAL FINANCE;
 PUBLIC POLICY ECONOMICS; MICRO-,MACRO-, LABOR- ECONOMICS; MONETARY THEORY

PUBLICATION GUIDELINES :

MANUSCRIPT GUIDELINES/COMMENTS :

DE ECONOMIST, QUARTERLY REVIEW OF THE ROYAL NETHERLANDS ECONOMIC ASSOCIATION

INSTRUCTIONS FOR AUTHORS
1. AIMS AND SCOPE
Since 1852 DE ECONOMIST has provided an outlet for high quality research in
economics. It reflects studies dealing with theoretical issues as well as
applied work, preferably with a European flavour. Surveys of current research
are also initiated and published with some regularity.

2. MANUSCRIPTS
Manuscripts intended for publication in DE ECONOMIST should be written in
English and submitted in duplicate to the Managing Editor:

Prof. S.K. Kuipers Department of Economics, University of Groningen
W.S.N.-Building, P.O. Box 800, 9700 AV Groningen, The Netherlands Phone: (50)
633 731; Fax: (50) 637 337.

DE ECONOMIST

Articles submitted for publication in DE ECONOMIST cannot be submitted for publication in other journals at the same time. Articles which have been, or will be published in other journals in a slightly different or condensed form or in a different language should not be submitted for publication in DE ECONOMIST.

In general, articles should not exceed 20 pages, i.e. about 8,000 words.

Manuscripts should be typewritten on A4 (210 x 297 mm) or US Letter (8 1/2" x 11") bond paper, one side only, leaving 30 mm (or 1 ") margins on all sides. Please double-space all materials, including footnotes, endnotes, and references.

Number pages consecutively with the first page containing the title, the author(s) and the affiliation(s).

Quoted passages of more than 40 words should be set off from the text by indenting the left-hand margin five spaces, as a block quotation.

Symbols representing variables should be italicized or underlined.

A short summary of up to 100 words should be included at the end of the manuscript following the references.

3. ILLUSTRATIONS
Submit only clear reproductions of artwork. Authors should retain original artwork until a manuscript has been accepted in its final version. All figures must be in a form suitable for reproduction (reduction). Original inked drawings of laserprinter output reproduce best, but if they are not available, same-sized glossies or matt photostats are acceptable. Photographs should be in black and white on glossy paper. Computer printout is acceptable for figures only if it is done on a high quality laserprinter.

4. NUMBERING OF FIGURES AND TABLES
Each figure and table should be mentioned in the text and should be numbered consecutively using Arabic numbers in order of appearance in the text. On the reverse side of each figure, write the name of the (first) author and the figure number. The figures should be integrated into the text as much as possible rather than being inserted at the end of the document.

5. HEADLINES AND CAPTIONS
Headlines and captions should be identified by the use of numbers separated by decimals to indicate sections and subsections:
4 REFORM AND RETREAT OF THE WELFARE STATE
4.1 The Financing of the Welfare State

6. FOOTNOTES
Explanatory footnotes should be used sparingly and indicated by consecutive superscript numbers in the text. Footnotes should appear at the end of the document in the manuscript, and will appear at the foot of the page in the printed version. In tables, footnotes are preferable to long explanatory material in either the heading or body of the table. Such explanatory footnotes identified in superscript letters should be placed under the table.

Acknowledgements, grant numbers, a reprint request address and any change of address should be given in a separate, asterisked (not numbered) footnote, which will appear on the opening page.

7. CROSS REFERENCES
Do not cross reference to page numbers. Cross references should refer to a section number:

e.g.: See section 2.2

8. REFERENCES
References to books, journal papers, articles in collections and conference or workshop proceedings, and reports should be collected in a list at the end of the paper and listed in alphabetical order.

References to books should include the authors' name; year of publication; title in full, underlined or in italics; place of publication, publisher; page numbers, if relevant. For example:

Cardoso, E. and A. Helwege (1992), Latin America's Economy, Diversity, Trends, and Conflicts, Cambridge, MA / London, MIT Press.

References to essays in an edited collection should include the author's name; year of publication; title of essay; editor's name; title of volume, underlined or in italics; place of publication, publisher; first and last page numbers. For example:

Hergert, M. and D. Morris (1988), 'Trends in international Collaborative Agreements,' in: F.J. Contractor and P. Lorange (eds.), Cooperative Strategies in International Business, Lexington, MA, Lexington Books, pp. 99-1 10.

References to essays in conference proceedings should include the author's name; year of publication; title of essay; title of proceedings underlined or in italics; place of conference, publisher and/or organization from whom proceedings can be obtained; first and last page numbers. For example:

Obstfeld, M. (1986), 'Capital Mobility in the World Economy, Theory and Measurement,' in: K. Brunner and A. Meltzer (eds.), The National Bureau Method, International Capital Mobility and Other Essays, Carnegie-Rochester Conference Series on Public Policy, 24, pp.55-104.

References to articles in periodicals should include the author's name; year of publication; title of article; full title of periodical, underlined or in italics; volume; number where appropriate; and first and last page numbers.

Becker, G. (1983), 'A Theory of Competition among Pressure Groups for Influence,' Quarterly Journal of Economics, 48, pp. 371 400.

References to technical reports or doctoral dissertations should include the author's name; year of publication; title of article, underlined or in italics; identifying number or description, department, institution, and location of institution. For example:

Meyer, B. (1988), Unemployment Insurance and Unemployment Spells, NBER working paper nr. 2546, Washington D.C.

DE ECONOMIST

9. CITATION TO REFERENCES
In the text a reference already identified by the author should be followed by the date of the reference in brackets and the page number where appropriate. Otherwise the reference should be enclosed within brackets including the name of the author followed by the date and page number. In the event that the author has had two or more works published during the same year, the citation and the reference should contain a lower case letter after the date to distinguish the works.

Groot (1990)
(Nickell (1979a))
(Nickell (1979b))
(Groot (1990), Kerckhoffs et al. (1992))
(Kooreman and Ridder (1983))

10. REPRINTS
50 Reprints of each article will be provided free of charge. Additional reprints can be ordered when proofs are returned to the publisher (Kluwer Academic Publishers, P.O. Box 17, 3300 AA Dordrecht, The Netherlands).

11. COPYRIGHT
Copyright will be established in the name of Kluwer Academic Publishers.

12. PERMISSIONS
It is the responsibility of the author to obtain written permission for a quotation from unpublished material, or for all quotations in excess of 250 words in one extract or 500 words in total from any work still in copyright, and for the reprinting of illustrations or tables from unpublished or copyrighted material.

13. ADDITIONAL INFORMATION
Alterations in proof (as distinct from the correction of printer's errors) entail serious financial and technical difficulties. We, therefore, request authors whose articles are accepted for publication not to make alterations in proof, or at any rate to keep these down to a minimum. The original typescript must be regarded as definitive, and we reserve the right to charge authors for alterations made in proof.

No fee is paid for either articles or book reviews.

More information and advice on the suitability of manuscripts in other formats (e.g. electronic or disk submission) can be obtained from:

the Publisher:
Kluwer Academic Publishers, ECOT, P.O.Box 17, 3300 AA Dordrecht, The Netherlands. Fax: (31) 78 392254, Email: EDITDEPT@WKAP.NL

DEMOGRAPHY

ADDRESS FOR SUBMISSION :

ROBERT D. MARE, EDITOR
DEMOGRAPHY
UNIVERSITY OF WISCONSIN, MADISON
CENTER FOR DEMOGRAPHY AND ECOLOGY
4412 SOCIAL SCIENCE BUILDING
1180 OBSERVATORY DRIVE
MADISON, WI 53706-1393
USA
608-262-5391
608-262-8400 (Fax)
E-Mail : DERMOGRAPHY@ssc.wisc.edu

CIRCULATION DATA :

Reader : Academic

Frequency of Issue : Quarterly

Copies Per Issue : 3001-4000

Subscription Price : 85.00 US$

Sponsorship : Professional Assoc.

PUBLICATION GUIDELINES :

Manuscript Length : 30-40

Copies Required : Four

Computer Submission : No

Format : N/A

Fees to Review : 20.00 US$

REVIEW INFORMATION :

Type of Review : Blind Review

No. of External Reviewers : Three

No. of In House Reviewers :

Acceptance Rate : 11-20%

Time To Review : 2-3 months

Reviewer's Comments : Yes

Fees to Publish : 0.00 US$

Invited Articles : 5% or less

MANUSCRIPT TOPICS : ECONOMETRICS;
   INTERNATIONAL & ECONOMIC DEVELOPMENT; PUBLIC POLICY ECONOMICS

PUBLICATION GUIDELINES : Chicago Manual of Style

MANUSCRIPT GUIDELINES/COMMENTS :

EDITORIAL POLICY
The editors welcome submissions that contribute to the scientific literature
and that are of general interest to demographers. DEMOGRAPHY publishes
research conducted in several disciplines including the social sciences,
geography, history, biology, statistics, business, epidemiology, and public
health. Research studies as well as review papers of commentaries will be
considered for publication. Specialized research papers, theoretical
developments, and improvements in models or methods, policy evaluations,
applications of demographic principles or techniques, assessments of
demographic data, comparative studies, historical studies, and studies of
developed and developing countries are welcome. Brief commentaries on articles
previously published in DEMOGRAPHY will also be considered. Comments should
present reanalyses that generate new substantive conclusions. Revisions of
papers published in proceedings not under copyright will be considered; the
volume of the proceedings should be noted in the submission letter.

Manuscripts submitted to DEMOGRAPHY will be judged in part by whether they
have reconciled their results with already-published research on the same
topic. Further, authors of accepted manuscripts will be asked to preserve the

DEMOGRAPHY

data used in their analysis and to make the data available to others at
reasonable cost from a date six months after the publicaiton date for the
paper and for a period of three years thereafter. Authors wishing to request
manuscript submission after receiving this notice; otherwise, authors will be
assumed to accept the requirement. The use of proprietary data sets, for
example, may prompt an exemption request.

DEMOGRAPHY is a peer-reviewed journal. All manuscripts considered appropriate
for the journal are reviewed externally. To preserve anonymity, authors and
referees should avoid self-identifying references. Submission of a manuscfript
to DEMOGRAPHY is taken to indicate the author's commitment to publish in the
journal. A paper submitted to DEMOGRAPHY while it is under review by another
journal will not be accepted for review.

PREPARATION OF MANUSCRIPTS
1. Submit four copies of the paper, three printed back to back, and retain the
original for your files. To ensure anonymity, include only the title on the
manuscript. Attach a separate page with the title of the manuscript, your
name, and your affiliatin.

2. Be sure to include a self-address stamped postcard or a reliable e-mail
address to be used in confirming that your manuscript reached the DEMOGRAPHY
office. Also be sure to include the non-refundable $20.00 manuscript
submission fee payable to the Population Association of America.

3. Print all copy (including indented material, references, footnotes and
acknowledgments) in Courier 12-point font, double-spaced, with 1-1/2-inch
margins all around. Underline all material to be italicized.

4. Incude an abstract ofno more than 100 words.

5. Indentify all symbols in the margins. Circle these and all other
explanatory notes not inteded for printing.

6. Type each table on a separate page. Cite each table in the test.

7. All figures artwork must be clear, sharp, black, and able to withstand
reduction.

MANUSCRIPT PAGES should be numbered consecutively, and the manuscript should
be organized as follows:
1. title page
2. Abstract
3. Text of paper (no tables or figures)
4. Notes
5. Appendices
6. Acknowledgements
7. References
8. Tables
9. Figure titles
10. Camera-ready artwork for figures

Please retain an exact copy of all submitted materials.

DEMOGRAPHY

TITLE PAGE
The title page should contain the title of the manuscript and the names, places of employment, and complete addresses of all authors as they want them to appear in the published journal.

ABSTRACT
The author should include on a separate page an abstract of not more than 100 words. The abstract should summarize the research and results and highlight the importance of the findings. It should not include details about data sources or methods (unless the paper's primary contribution is in its use of sources or methodology), nor should it contain lengthy mathematical expressions or complicated notation.

TEXT
The text should be typed double-spaced, using Courier 12-point font, with 1 1/2 inch margins on all sides. Use a five character or 1/2-inch indent for paragraphs. Underline all material to be italicized.

HEADINGS. The main body of the article should be divided by appropriate section and subsection headings. No headings should be numbered. Primary headings, including those for notes, appendices, acknowledgments, and references, should be typed in upper- and lowercase letters and centered. Subheadings should not be used unless a section can be divided into two or more subsections. Secondary headings should be typed on a separate line, flush left with the margin, in upper- and lowercase letters; capitalize the first letter of all words of four or more letters. If tertiary headings are used, they should be at the beginning of a paragraph, indented, in upper and lowercase letters, underlined, and followed by a period; capitalize the first letter of all words of four or more letters.

REFERENCE CITATIONS. All references included in the References at the end of the manuscript must be cited in the text. Reference citations must include the author's surname and the year of publication, according to the following style.

1. A direct citation of a reference places only the date within parentheses: for example, Cupples (1985).

2. An indirect citation of a reference places both the name and the date within parentheses, using no punctuation between them, for example, (Smith 1980).

3. Citation of a particular page or pages of a chapter follows the date and is preceded by a comma. Use sec., chap., app., eq., p., and pp. in such citations: for example, (Cupples 1985, pp. 26-27); (Cupples 1985, chap. 5).

4. References following direct quotations must include the page number(s) of the quote: for example, "This was found to be fallacious thinking upon closer investigation" (Smith and Smith 1958, p. 209).

5. For works with multiple authors: Use the full form of citation at all times for two authors. Use the full form the first time only for three to five authors; thereafter use the first author's surname followed by the phrase "et al." for citations of references with six or more authors.

6. When two or more works by the same author are cited together, do not repeat the name(s) and separate the years by commas: for example, (Condran 1984, 1985).

7. When citing several references within parentheses, place them in alphabetical order and separate them with semicolons: for example, (Condran 1984; Cupples 1985; Smith 1980).

8. With more than one reference to an author in the same year, distinguish those works by attaching lower case letters (a, b) to the year of publication: (1992a, 1992b).

NUMBERS. Spell out numbers one through nine, use numerals for numbers 10 and above. When referring to millions, numerals may be used before the word "million": for example, 3 million; 45 million. Percentages are always indicated with numerals followed by the symbol "%". Page numbers should be indicated in full, as should years: for example, pages 481-495; years 1972-1976.

MATHEMAICAL MATERIAL. Long mathematical expressions should be centered on a separate line and identified by consecutive Arabic numerals in parentheses flush with the right margin. Short expressions should remain in text unless there is a need to refer to them elsewhere in the text. Indicate break points for equations likely to exceed the width of the journal column. the numerator and denominator of a fraction appearing in the text should be separated with a solidus (/) rather than a divisions bar: for example, $(a+b)/(c+d)$. It is not necessary to underline mathematical material for italics, since such material will be typeset in italics unless otherwise indicated and underlining may be mistaken for boldface. Indicate boldface by placing a wavy line below the symbol, A.

Mathematical notation not to be typeset in italics or boldface should be explained in the margin. Superscripts and subscripts should be typed as such. Identify in the margin any handwritten Greek letters and other unusual or difficult to read symbols. Differentiate between easily confused symbols such as the letter I and the numeral 1 and the letter O (o) and the numeral 0. Do not use an asterisk to indicate multiplication.

NOTES
Notes to the text appear in a list at the end of the manuscript. They are identified in text by superscript numbers. The list of Notes should be typed double-spaced in consecutive order on a new page at the end of the body of the manuscript. Each note should have a paragraph indent and the number should be typed in superscript position.

APPENDICES
Appendices, if used, should include material that is helpful to readers but not essential to the text. They should not be simply a table; such an appendix will be incorporated in text as a regular table. If more than one appendix is used, label them with uppercase letters. The Appendices should be placed after the Notes and before the Acknowledgments.

ACKNOWLEDGMENTS
If appropriate, authors may acknowledge financial assistance in the form of grants or university funding, assistance by individual colleagues, and any

other pertinent information, in this sequence, in the Acknowledgments. Do not place acknowledgments in a numbered note or on the title page; rather, place them in a separate section headed "Acknowledgments" and typed double-spaced on a new page preceding the References section.

REFERENCE LIST
The parts of a reference are author, date of publication, and title and publication information. All parts must be included in a complete reference.

AUTHOR. Author names are typed in upper- and lowercase letters, surname first followed by a comma and initials with periods and a space between all; for multiple-author works, separate all authors' names with commas and precede the last with the symbol "&": for example, DaVanzo J. (single author reference); Bumpass, L.L., & Sweet, J.A. (multi-author reference). An editor (editors) is identified by the abbreviation within parentheses, (ed.) [(eds.)], following the name. The reference list is alphabetized by authors' surnames, with work by a single author preceding that authors' work in collaboration with others. Works by multiple authors should include all authors' names, never simply the first author's name followed by "et al". when more than one work is listed for the same author or team of authors, replace the name(s) with a short line preceding the date for second and subsequent works, which are listed in ascending chronological order. If there is no author listed for a reference, use the title of the work being listed in this position and alphabetize according to the first word (other than "A" and "The").

DATE OF PUBLICATION. The date of publication follows the author name(s), within parentheses and followed by a period: for example, Anderson, T.W. (1974). If two or more works by the same author or team of authors have the same publication date, list them alphabetically by article title and distinguish them by lowercase "a," "b," and so on, after the date: for example, (1970a). Works accepted for publication but not off press are listed as "in press"; this may be changed on proofs if the work comes off press by that time.

TITLE AND PUBLICATION INFORMATION FOR A JOURNAL ARTICLE. The title of an article in a journal is typed in upper- and lowercase letters and enclosed in quotation marks, with a period at the end, inside the closing quotation mark. The full title of the journal is used, typed in upper- and lowercase letters, underlined, and followed by a comma. This is followed by the series designation, if any (e.g., Ser. A,), which is closed with a comma; the volume number in Arabic numerals, followed by a comma (e.g., 35,); the issue number (if the page numbering for each issues starts with 1), underlined, within parentheses, and preceding the comma closing the volume information [e.g., (3)]; and the inclusive, full page numbers (e.g., 209-244). The following is an example of this type of reference:

Kasarda, J.D. (1980). "The Implications of Contemporary Distribution Trends for National Urban Policy." Social Science Quarterly, 61, 373-400.

TITLE AND PUBLICATION INFORMATION FOR A BOOK OR A CHAPTER IN A BOOK. The title of a book is typed in upper- and lowercase letters and underlined. A period is placed at the end of the title. This is followed by the location an name of the publisher, separated by a colon (e.g., New York: Academic Press). If only a chapter is being listed, type the title in upper- and lowercase letters, within quotations marks, with a period at the end before the closing quotation mark. The title of the book comes next, preceded by the word "In". If the book is an edited volume, close the title with a comma and give the name(s) of the editor(s), following the abbreviation "ed", and close with a period: for example, ed. J. Smith. Then give the location and name of the publisher followed by a comma and the inclusive page numbers. The following is an example of this type of reference:

Jain, A.K., Hermalin, A.I., & Sun, T.H. (1979). "Lactation and Natural Fertility." In Natural Fertility, eds. H. Leridon & J. Menken. Liege, Belgium: Ordina, p.p. 149-163.

UNPUBLISHED OR OBSCURE WORKS. DEMOGRAPHY discourages references to unpublished or obscure works. If reference to an unpublished manuscript is necessary, however, the title is typed in upperand lowercase letters, within quotation marks, and closed with a period before the closing quotation mark. Next, note the type of document (e.g., unpublished Ph.D. dissertation, unpublished technical report, Technical Report 721, unpublished manuscript) and the sponsoring body or repository. If a university is this body or repository, include the department or division name; if a corporation or other institution, include the location. The following is an example of this type of reference:

Haveman, R., Wolfe, B., & Warlick, J. (1985). "Behavioral Responses to Social Security Retrenchment: Estimates from a Trichotomous Choice Model." Discussion Paper 789-85 presented at the Institute for Research on Poverty, University of Wisconsin.

Personal communications are not included in the list but are cited in text as follows: (P. Smith, personal communication, March 2, 1984).

Personal communications are not included in the list but are cited in text as follows: (P. Smith, personal communication, March 2, 1984).

Following are some examples of correct format for different types of references commonly found in articles published in DEMOGRAPHY.

Bean, F.D., & Tienda, M. (1987). The Hispanic Population of the United States. New York: Russell Sage.

Brass, W. (1974). "Perspectives in Population Prediction, lllustrated by the Statistics of England and Wales." Journal of the Royal Statistical Society, Ser. A, 137, 532-583.

Duncan, O.D., & Duncan, B. (1955). "A Methodological Analysis of Segregation Indices." American Sociological Review, 20, 210-217.

Heuser,R.L.,(1976). Fertility Tables for Birth Cohorts by Color: 1917-1973. Washington,D.C.: U.S. Government Printing Office. [DHEW Publication No. (HRA) 76-1152].

Institute for Research on Poverty. (1980). Wisconsin Absent Parent Income Study (WAPS) [machine readable data files]. Madison: University of Wisconsin, Institute for Research on Poverty.

James, DR., & Taeuber, K.E. (1985). "Measures of Segregation." In Sociological Methodology 1985, ed. N. Tuma, San Francisco: Joseey-Bass, pp. 1-32.

Kenya Fertility Survey.1978: Standard Recode (version 3). (1977). London: International Statistical Institute (producer and distributor).

Kidane, A. (1983). "Estimating Streams of Immigrants to Addis Ababa." Unpublished manuscript, Addis Ababa University, Dept. of Statistics.

Miller, A.R., Treiman, D.J., Cain, P.S., & roos, P.A. (eds.). (1980). Work. Jobs. Occupations: A Critical Review of the Dictionary of Occupational Titles, Final Report to the U.S. Dept. of Labor by the Committee on Occupational Classification and Analysis. Washington, D.C.: National Academy Press.

National Center for Health Statistics. (1985a). Vital Statistics of the United States. 1980 (Vol. 2): Mortality. Part B. Washington, D.C.: U.S. Dept. of Health and Human Services.

_____(1985b). Advance Report of Final Natality Statistics. 1983, Monthly vital Statistics Report, Vol. 34, No. 6 (Suppl.) Hyattsville, MD: Public Health Service. [DHHS Pub. No. (PHS) 85-1120.]

Pratt, W., Mosher, W., Bachrach, C., & Horn, M. (1984). "Understanding U.S. Fertility." Population Bulletin. 39(5).

Rindfuss, R. & Parnell, A. (1986). "How Much Does Marriage Matter Anyhow?" Paper presented at the Annual Meeting of the Population Association of America, San Francisco.

U.S. Bureau of the Census. (1976). Child Support and Alimony: 1981, Current Population Reports, Ser. P-23, No. 124. Washington, D.C.: U.S. Government Printing Office.

_____. (1983). General Population Characteristics. Part 1: United States Summary. 1980 Census Population. Washington, D.C.: U.S. Government Priting Office.

TABLES

NUMBERING AND CITING. Tables are numbered consecutively in the order in which they are cited. Thus each table must be cited. In page layout tables are placed in sequence as close as possible to their first citation in text.

TITLE. Each table must have a brief descriptive title: for example, Table 1. Indices of Urban and Metropolitan Concentration for the United States (%): 1950-1980. The title should not duplicate information in the headings of the table.

COLUMN HEADINGS. Every column must have a heading that identifies the content, including the stub column. A heading should be brief and should not be much wider than the longest entry in the column. Standard abbreviations may be used without explanation (e.g., "no" for number, "%" for percent), but abbreviations of technical terms and the like must be explained in a note to the table. Sometimes a straddle heading may be appropriate to avoid repeating the same word in two or more column heads:

Migration interval
1935-1940 1955-1960 1965-1970 1970-1975

DEMOGRAPHY

Headings are separated from the title by a double horizontal rule covering the entire width of the table, straddle heads are separated from column heads by a single horizontal rule straddling only the pertinent columns, and column heads are separated from the body by a single rule covering the entire width of the table. No vertical rules are used.

BODY. No horizontal or vertical rules are used in the body of the table. Rows in a table should be single-spaced, with occasional gaps for bid tables (e.g., every fifth line). Columns should be fairly close together, to help the eye move from one to the other. Only like items should be included in the same column. If the bottom part of a table requires different column headings, it should be presented as a separate table. Within columns decimal points should be aligned. If values are also given parenthetically, align those values separately. Close the body with a single horizontal rule covering the entire width.

NOTES AND FOOTNOTES TO TABLES. When additional information must be given (e.g., explanations of abbreviations, descriptions of procedures, and anything applicable to the general comprehension table), it should be presented as a note immediately beneath the rule closing the body. The word "Note" should be typed flush left, underlined, and followed by a colon and the text of the note. The source of the data or the table itself should be noted in a separate footnote following the Note. The word "Source" should be typed flush left, underlined, and followed by a colon and the text of the footnote. If a particular entry in a column or an entire column requires explanation, use a footnote designated by a superscript lowercase letter next to the entry or column head. The footnote follows the Note and Source and has a paragraph indent. Asterisks are used to denote significance levels. When more than one level appears in a table, use an asterisk, for the lowest level, two for the next level, and so on: for example, *p<.05. **p<.01.

FIGURES
FIGURE TITLES. Each figure must have a title and legend, including the figure number. Figures are numbered consecutively as they are cited in text. The titles are typed double-spaced on a single sheet of paper and are placed after the tables. They will be typeset and placed beneath the figures. Figures must be clearly described. The combined information of the figure legend and the text of the body of the paper should provide a clear, complete description of everything on the figure. Detailed legends can often be of great help to the reader. First, describe completely what is graphed in the display; then draw the reader's attention to salient features of the display, and briefly state the importance of these features. Generally, it is a good idea to include the key to symbols in the legend as well, to avoid cluttering the display. Abbreviations must be defined in the legend.

FIGURE ARTWORK. Figures must be visually clear and capable of withstanding reduction. They are reduced at least to the size of the journal column and sometimes as small as half of the width of the journal column. It is best to prepare artwork so that when reduced to this size, the letters and symbols will be no smaller than the type used for tables and figure titles. All lines, lettering, and plotting symbols must be sharp and dark enough to bear reduction without loss of clarity. A reducing photocopier is often useful in judging how well the original can stand reduction. If you do not want a figure reduced, prepare the artwork to the appropriate size, with lettering and symbols no larger than journal text type.

DEMOGRAPHY

The preferable form for camera-ready artwork is a glossy black-and-white print of professionally prepared artwork (or the actual artwork)-that is, typeset words, symbols, and numbers with bars and rules done in black tape or India ink. Hand-lettered and drawn artwork is acceptable only when neatly executed in India ink. Typed or pencil-drawn and -lettered artwork is never acceptable because these media do not reproduce well; computer output is sometimes only marginally better and can be much worse. Photocopies are never acceptable. The main criterion is that everything be sharp and black. To aid legibility of words, use upper- and lowercase letters-not all uppercase letters-for axis labels and any other labeling necessary. Decimal fractions should not have a zero before the decimal point: for example, .05 or -.05.

COMPUTER-GENERATED ARTWORK. Because of the technological advances that have occurred over the past few years, some computer-generated artwork is now comparable in quality to professionally prepared art. If you have access to the proper equipment (preferably a laser printer or Linotype imagesetter), this is obviously the most economical way to prepare your figures. Be sure that you will get solid black lines and symbols; the contrast must be a sharp, dark black on white. Plotters often do not give a sufficiently dark black line. No colors other than black should be used. If the black is not dark enough, your figures will be returned to be redone.

DERIVATIVES QUARTERLY

ADDRESS FOR SUBMISSION :

TODD PETZEL, EDITOR
DERIVATIVES QUARTERLY
THE COMMON FUND
450 POST ROAD EAST, P.O. BOX 909
WESTPORT, CT 06881-0909
USA
203-341-2000
203-221-7722 (Fax)

CIRCULATION DATA :

Reader : Business Persons

Frequency of Issue : Quarterly

Copies Per Issue : 1001-2000

Subscription Price : 300.00 US$
    Academics : 75.00 US$

Sponsorship : Profit Oriented Corp.

PUBLICATION GUIDELINES :

Manuscript Length : 16-20

Copies Required : Three

Computer Submission : Yes

Format : WordPerfect

Fees to Review : 0.00 US$

REVIEW INFORMATION :

Type of Review : Editorial Review

No. of External Reviewers : Two

No. of In House Reviewers : Zero

Acceptance Rate :

Time To Review : 2-3 months

Reviewer's Comments : No

Fees to Publish : 0.00 US$

Invited Articles : Over 50%

MANUSCRIPT TOPICS : PORTFOLIO & SECURITY ANALYSIS

PUBLICATION GUIDELINES :

MANUSCRIPT GUIDELINES/COMMENTS :

SUBMISSION OF MANUSCRIPTS
Please refer to the following guidelines when submittig a manuscript for
publication. We may return any paper to the author for revisions that does not
follow these instructions. The editors reserve the right to make changes for
clarity and consistency.

1. Submit three copies of the manuscript double-spaced with wide margins and
pages numbered. The front page should include the authors' full names, titles,
addresses, zipcodes, and phone/fax numbers. The authors should also supply a
diskette copy of the paper. Please note the type of word processing software
used and securely attach the article title, author's name, and address to the
diskette.

2. References, endnotes, tables, and figures should appear on separate pages
at the end of the text.

3. Limit references to works cited in the text and list them alphabetically.
Citations in the text should appear as "Smith [1990] suggests that..." Use
page numbers for quotes.

DERIVATIVES QUARTERLY

4. Minimize the number of endnotes. Use periods instead of commas between authors' names and titles of references. Use superscript Arabic numbers in the text and on the endnote page.

5. Number and title all exhibits, with one to a page. Write out the column heads and legends; they should be understandable without reference to the text. Submit graphs in camera-ready form and as large as possible because they will be shrunk for the text. Note: we cannot draw graphs for you.

6. Center each equation on a separate line, numbered consecutively with Arabic numbers, in parentheses in the right margin. Identify Greek letters or equations into the text.

7. DERIVATIVES QUARTERLY'S copyright agreement form must be signed prior to publication.

SEND 2 COPIES TO:
Todd Petzel
Editor, Derivatives Quarterly
Executive Vice President and
  Chief Investment Officer
The Common Fund
450 Post Road East
P.O. Box 909
Westport, CT 06881-0909

SEND 1 COPY (WITH DISKETTE) TO:
Noelle Schultz
Editorial Production Director
Derivatives Quarterly
Institutional Investor, Inc.
488 Madison Avenue
New York, NY 10022

DERIVATIVES QUARTERLY is published by Institutional Investor, Inc., 488 Madison Avenue, New York, NY 10022. Tel: 212-224-3545 Fax: 212-224-3527.

DERIVATIVES RISK MANAGEMENT SERVICE
(DRMS)

ADDRESS FOR SUBMISSION :

G. TIMOTHY HAIGHT, GENERAL EDITOR
DERIVATIVES RISK MANAGEMENT SERVICE
  (DRMS)
DERIVATIVES RISK MANAGEMENT SERVICE
1 BLENMONT COURT
PHOENIX, MD 21131
USA
410-592-9877
410-592-9877 (Fax)
E-Mail : Thaight@charm.net

CIRCULATION DATA :

Reader : Business Persons

Frequency of Issue : Quarterly

Copies Per Issue : 1001-2000

Subscription Price : 225.00 US$

Sponsorship : Non Profit Corp.

PUBLICATION GUIDELINES :

Manuscript Length : 16-20

Copies Required : Two

Computer Submission : No

Format : N/A

Fees to Review : 0.00 US$

REVIEW INFORMATION :

Type of Review : Blind Review

No. of External Reviewers : One

No. of In House Reviewers : One

Acceptance Rate : 11-20%

Time To Review : 2-3 months

Reviewer's Comments : Yes

Fees to Publish : 0.00 US$

Invited Articles : 31-50%

MANUSCRIPT TOPICS : ACCOUNTING INFORMATION SYSTEMS;
  ACCOUNTING THEORY & PRACTICE; PORTFOLIO & SECURITY ANALYSIS; TAX ACCOUNTING;
  DERIVATIVES

PUBLICATION GUIDELINES :

MANUSCRIPT GUIDELINES/COMMENTS :

Manuscripts should be submitted in duplicate to the General Editor.
Please send the manuscript on a 3.5" disk in Wordperfect format. Authors
should also retain an exact copy of their manuscript for future reference.

The following guidelines should be kept in mind.

1. Articles should be at least 15 manuscript pages (double spaced) in length
and include a complete bibliography. Papers must be original, timely and
unpublished.

2. The DERIVATIVES RISK MANAGEMENT SERVICE is intended to provide end-users
with a reference guide for the proper use of derivative instruments as a
hedging device. Therefore, the articles should be oriented along the lines of
a "how to" guide, if applicable, so that the reader can both identify and
apply the concepts and methods covered in each tab. This would involve the use
of a step-by-step approach, consisting of numerous subheads, paragraphs,
numbered and bulleted items. Graphs, tabular materials and charts are also
welcomed. Authors may want to use descriptive case histories to illustrate or

DERIVATIVES RISK MANAGEMENT SERVICE
(DRMS)

emphasize specific points, ideas or recommendations.

3. Place footnotes at the end of the article on a separate sheet of paper. An alphabetical list of references cited in the text should also be located at the end of the article. Citations to references are designated by inserting the names of the authors and the years of publication in brackets throughout the article.

As a general proposition, authors should be aware that the general goal of this publication is to assist subscribers in (1) understanding the nature of derivative instruments and arrangements; (2) structuring appropriate derivatives strategies and policies; (3) interpreting recent legal and regulatory developments affecting derivatives markets; and (4) establishing suitable internal operating systems for derivatives, including accounting, disclosure and tax procedures.

Papers are accepted on the basis of their contribution to the field, clarity, and timeliness. In order to assure the integrity of the review process, authors are requested to provide biographical information on a separate piece of paper. Do not include names of the author(s) on the manuscript itself.

CHAPTER TOPICS

Tab 1 Derivatives Developments - Industry Trends

Tab 2 Legal and Regulatory Update

Tab 3 Derivative Products and Arrangements

Tab 4 Derivatives Strategies and Policies

Tab 5 Risk Management/Measurement

Tab 6 Internal Operating Procedures

Tab 7 End-user Experience

    a. Financial Institutions

    b. Other Financial Services Industries

    c. Non-Financial Corporations

Tab 8 Tax Issues

Tab 9 Accounting and Disclosure Issues

DERIVATIVES: TAX, REGULATION, FINANCE

ADDRESS FOR SUBMISSION :

JOHN ENSMINGER, LL.M., EDITOR
DERIVATIVES: TAX, REGULATION, FINANCE
RIA GROUP
90 FIFTH AVENUE
NEW YORK, NY 10011
212-807-2189
212-337-4186 (Fax)
E-Mail www.jensminger@riag.com

CIRCULATION DATA :

Reader : Business Persons

Frequency of Issue : Bi-Monthly

Copies Per Issue : 1001-2000

Subscription Price : 175.00 US$

Sponsorship : Profit Oriented Corp.

PUBLICATION GUIDELINES :

Manuscript Length : 16-20

Copies Required : One

Computer Submission : Yes

Format : Word, WordPerfect, etc.

Fees to Review : 0.00 US$

REVIEW INFORMATION :

Type of Review : Editorial Review

No. of External Reviewers : One

No. of In House Reviewers : One

Acceptance Rate : 21-30%

Time To Review : One month or less

Reviewer's Comments : No

Fees to Publish : 0.00 US$

Invited Articles : 31-50%

MANUSCRIPT TOPICS : ACCOUNTING INFORMATION SYSTEMS;
    ACCOUNTING THEORY & PRACTICE; INTERNATIONAL FINANCE; TAX ACCOUNTING

PUBLICATION GUIDELINES : Harvard Blue Book

MANUSCRIPT GUIDELINES/COMMENTS :

EDITOR IN CHIEF: Lewis Steinberg.

Editorial Guidelines for Authors are available from editor on request.
Generally editor edits manuscripts into journal style.

Here's the only periodical that delivers in-depth, analytical coverage of new
and existing types of derivatives from tax, accounting and regulatory
perspectives. It reports on how leading practitioners in the field
successfully manage risk with these complex, yet increasingly popular
instruments.

DERIVATIVES: TAX, REGULATION, FINANCE gives you the best advice possible in
concise articles and columns that explore:

* Tax strategies, plus accounting, banking, financial engineering, and U.S.
  regulatory aspects

* Cross-border trading, currency exchange products, and the treatment of
  foreign currency transactions

DERIVATIVES: TAX, REGULATION, FINANCE

* IRS, SEC, and major financial center regulation of derivatives

* Trading of derivatives, OTC derivatives, and embedded derivatives on established and emerging markets

* New financial instruments categorized as derivatives

* and much more.

Order Code: JDER.
Published six times annually.

ECONOMETRIC REVIEWS

ADDRESS FOR SUBMISSION :

ESFANDIAR MAASOUMI, EDITOR
ECONOMETRIC REVIEWS
SOUTHERN METHODIST UNIVERSITY
DEDMAN COLLEGE
DEPARTMENT OF ECONOMICS
DALLAS, TX 75275-0496
USA
214-768-4298
214-768-1891 (Fax)
E-Mail : MAASOUMI@MAIL.CIS.SMU.EDU

Change in Editor's Address
  May Occur in : 01/01/01

CIRCULATION DATA :

Reader : Academic

Frequency of Issue : Quarterly

Copies Per Issue : 2001-3000

Subscription Price : 40.00 US$
  Organizations : 450.00 US$

Sponsorship : Profit Oriented Corp.

PUBLICATION GUIDELINES :

Manuscript Length : Any

Copies Required : Four

Computer Submission : No

Format : N/A

Fees to Review : 0.00 US$

REVIEW INFORMATION :

Type of Review : Blind Review

No. of External Reviewers : Two

No. of In House Reviewers : One

Acceptance Rate : 11-20%

Time To Review : 4-6 months

Reviewer's Comments : Yes

Fees to Publish : 0.00 US$

Invited Articles : 5% or less

MANUSCRIPT TOPICS : ACCOUNTING INFORMATION SYSTEMS; ECONOMETRICS;
  PUBLIC POLICY ECONOMICS; APPLIED ECONOMICS

PUBLICATION GUIDELINES : Any issue of ER

MANUSCRIPT GUIDELINES/COMMENTS :

ECONOMETRIC THEORY

ADDRESS FOR SUBMISSION :

PETER C.B. PHILLIPS, EDITOR
ECONOMETRIC THEORY
YALE UNIVERSITY
COWLES FOUNDATION FOR RESEARCH
IN ECONOMICS
P.O. BOX 208281 YALE STATION
NEW HAVEN, CT 06520-8281
USA
203-432-3695
203-432-6167 (Fax)
E-Mail : pcb@yalevm.cis.yale.edu

CIRCULATION DATA :

Reader : Academic

Frequency of Issue : Quarterly

Copies Per Issue : Less than 1000

Subscription Price : 89.00 US$
  Institution : 182.00 US$
  Single Parts : 39.00 US$

Sponsorship :

PUBLICATION GUIDELINES :

Manuscript Length : 16-20

Copies Required : Four

Computer Submission : No

Format : N/A

Fees to Review : 0.00 US$

REVIEW INFORMATION :

Type of Review : Editorial Review

No. of External Reviewers : Two

No. of In House Reviewers : One

Acceptance Rate : 11-20%

Time To Review : 4-6 months

Reviewer's Comments : Yes

Fees to Publish : 0.00 US$

Invited Articles : 6-10%

MANUSCRIPT TOPICS : ECONOMETRICS; STATISTICS

PUBLICATION GUIDELINES : Chicago Manual of Style

MANUSCRIPT GUIDELINES/COMMENTS :

CONTRIBUTIONS. Contributions are welcomed from all countries. They should be
be written in English.

MANUSCRIPTS. Four copies of manuscripts should be submitted to the Editor.
Manuscripts are accepted for review on the understanding that the same work
has not been published not is presently submitted elsewhere. While under
editorial review, it is the responsibility of the authors to keep the Editor
informed about submissions, publication plans and actual publication of
related research or abstracts thereof in other outlets, including letters,
journals, review publications, journals in other disciplines, conference
proceedings and published dissertations. It is further understood that all
persons listed as authors have given their approval for the submission of the
paper and that any person cited as a source of personal communication has
approved such citation; written authorization may be required at the Editor's
discretion. Authors are responsible for obtaining written permission to
publish material for which they do not own the copyright. Articles and other
material published in ECONOMETRIC THEORY represent the opinions of the authors
and should not be construed to reflect the opinions of the Editor, Advisory
Board, Editorial Board or the Publisher.

ECONOMETRIC THEORY

PROBLEMS AND SOLUTIONS SERIES. This series will publish student exercises in econometrics and research level problems. All problems must be submitted in triplicate with a clear title, relevant references and a complete solution to:

Dr. Juan J. Dolado
Servicio de Estudios
Banco de Espana
Alcala 50
E-28014
Madrid, Spain

After publication of a problem, solutions are invited for publication in the following issue and will be selected on a competitive basis that takes into account the correctness, conciseness and elegance of the solution. All problems and solutions will be refereed.

Readers are also encouraged to write to the Editor with interested unsolved problems for which only partial results are currently available, and to advise the Editor if they discover a published problem for which a solution already exists in the literature.

PREPARATION OF MANUSCRIPT. The ENTIRE manuscript (including notes and references) should be typed double-spaced on 8-1/2" x 11" or A4 white paper, with wide margins to accommodate copy editing. Manuscript pages should be numbered consecutively. PAGE 1 should provide the article title, author's (s') name(s) in the form preferred for publication), complete affiliations and telephone numbers. At the bottom of page 1 place any footnotes to the title or authors, indicated by superscripts *, **, etc. PAGE 2 should contain a proposed running head (abbreviated form of the title) of 40 characters or less, and the name and mailing address of the author to whom proofs should be sent. PAGE 3 should contain a short abstract of the paper in less than 150 words. The abstract will appear at the head of the article when published in the Journal.

EQUATIONS. All equations should be typewritten and the numbers for displayed equations should be placed in parentheses in the right margin. References to equations should simply use the form "(3)". Superscripts and subscripts should be typed clearly above and below the line, respectively. Theorem, lemma and proposition statements should appear in italic print. End of proof signposts should appear as such: ∎
Authors are encouraged to use the following order for parentheses: {[(...)]}

TABLES AND FIGURES: Tables and figures should be numbered consecutively in a separate series. Every table or figure should have a title or caption and at least one referencecin the text to indicate its appropriate location. Figures (charts, graphs, or other artwork) should be ready for photographic reproduction; they cannot be redrawn by the printer. All figure labels and details should be clearly printed and large enough to remain legible after a reduction to half size.

10. REFERENCES: Beginning in 1995, with Volume 11, references should be cited in the text by the author's last name and the date. Complete bibliographic information for each citation should be included in the list of references. References should be typed in alphabetical order in the style of the following examples:

ECONOMETRIC THEORY

Bergstrom, A.R. (1976) Statistical Inference in Continuous Time Economic Models. Amsterdam: North Holland.

Granger, C.W.J. (1983) Generating Mechanisms, Models and Causality. In. W. Hildenbrand (ed.), Advances in Econometrics, pp. 237-253. New York: Cambridge University Press.

Herz, C.S. (1955) Bessel Fluctions of Matrix Argument. Annals of Mathematics 61, 474-523.

Sargan, J.D. and A. Bhargava (1982) Maximum likelihood estimation of regression models with first order moving average errors when the root lies on the unit circle. Econometrica 51, 799-820.

Woolridge, J.M. (in press) On the limits of GLM for specification testing: A comment of Gurmu and Trivedi, Economitric Theory.

Journal names should not be abbreviated.

FOOTNOTES. When more than a simple source citation is called for, footnotes may used. These should be numbered consecutively throughout the text and typed together at the end of the page before the references. Source citations within footnotes follow the same style as citations in the text.

COPYEDITING AND PROOFREADING. The Publisher reserves the right to copyedit and proofread all articles accepted for publication, but authors will be asked to review their manuscripts if changes have been substantial. Page proof of articles will be sent to authors for corrections of typographical errors only.

OFFPRINTS. Authors receive 25 offprints of their articles free of charge; additional numbers may be purchased if ordered at proof stage (an order form will be sent with proofs). Contributors will be asked to assign their copyrights, on certain conditions, to Cambridge University Press.

EDITORIAL POLICY. Since its inception ECONOMETRIC THEORY aimed to endow econometrics with an innovative and authoritative journal dedicated to advance theoretical research in econometrics. It provides a centralized professional outlet for original theoretical contributions in all of the major areas of econometrics and seeks to foster the multidisciplinary features of econometrics that extend beyond the subject of econometrics. Among the many aspects of econometrics to come within the scope of ET are the statistical theory of estimation, testing, prediction and decision procedures in traditionally active areas of research such as linear and nonlinear modeling, simultaneous equations theory, time series, studies of robustness, nonparametric methods, inference under misspecification, finite sample econometrics, limited dependent variable models, the treatment of panel data, and models of discrete choice. ET provides a receptive arena for theoretical studies which open up new fields of research in econometrics and whose application potential is on a longer term horizon. Particularly welcome are papers which promote original econometric research in relation to modern developments in mathematical statistics and probability theory. Contributions which exposit methodological and technical advances in these fields and which illustrate their potential in econometric research are actively encouraged. Articles which unify earlier econometric work either in productive ways or by the use of more elegant methods also lie within the scope of the Journal.

ECONOMETRIC THEORY

As well as articles that embody original theoretical research, ET publishes historical studies on the evolution of econometrics through and on the subject's major scholars. ET serves an educational role in econometrics by the inclusion of a "Problems and Solutions Series" and by the publication of pedagogical paper that deal explicitly with educational issues.

ECONOMETRIC THEORY is published five times a year. Institutional orders may be sent to a book seller, subscription agent, or direct to Cambridge University Press, 40 West 20th Street, New York, NY 10011-4211, or outside the USA, Canada, and Mexico to Cambridge University Press, The Edinburgh Building, Shaftesbury Road, Cambridge CB2 2RU, England.

ECONOMETRICA

ADDRESS FOR SUBMISSION :

DREW FUDENBERG, EDITOR
ECONOMETRICA
HARVARD UNIVERSITY
DEPARTMENT OF ECONOMICS
CAMBRIDGE, MA 02138
USA
617-496-5895
617-495-4341 (Fax)
E-Mail : fudenberg@fas.harvard.edu

CIRCULATION DATA :

Reader : Academic

Frequency of Issue : Bi-Monthly

Copies Per Issue : 5001-10,000

Subscription Price :
  Free with Membership : 52.00 US$

Sponsorship : Professional Assoc.

PUBLICATION GUIDELINES :

Manuscript Length :

Copies Required : Four

Computer Submission : No

Format : N/A

Fees to Review : 0.00 US$

REVIEW INFORMATION :

Type of Review : Editorial Review

No. of External Reviewers : Two

No. of In House Reviewers : Zero

Acceptance Rate :

Time To Review : 2-3 months

Reviewer's Comments : Yes

Fees to Publish : 0.00 US$

Invited Articles : 5% or less

MANUSCRIPT TOPICS : ECONOMETRICS; OPERATIONS RESEARCH/STATISTICS

PUBLICATION GUIDELINES : Chicago Manual of Style

MANUSCRIPT GUIDELINES/COMMENTS :

1. Four copies of the original manuscript should be sent to the Editor.
They must be accompanied by a letter of submission and be written in either
French or English. Submission of a paper is held to imply its contents
represent original and unpublished work, and that it has not bee submitted for
publication elsewhere. If the author has submitted work elsewhere, or if he
does so during the term in which ECONOMETRICA is considering the manuscript,
then it is his responsibility to provide ECONOMETRICA with details. Normally,
the review process is expected to take no more than four months. There is
neither a submission charge nor page fee; nor is any payment made to the
authors.

2. Papers may be rejected, returned for specified revision, or accepted.
Currently, a paper will appear approximately ten months from date of
acceptance.

3. All submitted manuscripts should be typed on bond paper of standard size,
preferably 8.5 by 11 inches, and should have margins of at least on inch on
all sides. Double space all material in the manuscript, including captions,
headnote, footnotes, references, and so forth. Please submit only high-quality
reproductions (not Ditto, Thermofax, or Verifax).

4. Except as noted below, specific instructions on the form in which to prepare the manuscript can be found in the "Manual for ECONOMETRICA Authors", written by Hugo Sonnenschein and Dorothy Hodges, and published in the July, 1980 issue of ECONOMETRICA. The Manual describes how footnotes, diagrams, tables, etc. should be prepared. In addition, it explains editorial policy regarding style and standards of craftsmanship.

From Volume 54, on, beginning with the July 1986 issue, papers should be cited by author (date) e.g., Grandmont (1985), rather than by number as in previous issues. Apart from this, papers accepted for publication must be prepared in the form laid out in the Manual; moreover, it will facilitate the submission and review process for both the author and referees if all submitted manuscripts conform as closely as possible to these guidelines.

5. Papers should be accompanied by a summary that is suitable as a headnote. The headnote should be full enough to convey the main results of the paper. On the same sheet as the headnote should appear the title of the paper, the name(s) and full address(es) of the author(s), together with a list of keywords to appear at the end of the headnote.

6. If you plan to submit a comment on an article which has appeared in ECONOMETRICA, please follow the following guidelines. First, send a copy to the author and explain that you are considering submitting the comment to ECONOMETRICA. Second, when you submit your comment, please include any response that you have received form the author. Comments on published articles will be considered only if they state you have been through this process. If an author does not respond to your letter after a reasonable amount of time, then this should be explained in your submission. Authors will be invited to submit for consideration a reply to any published comment of this kind that is accepted.

7. Introduction

The purpose of this article is to explain current editorial procedures and policies of ECONOMETRICA. The content should be of particular interest to authors who plan to submit manuscripts to the journal. Section 2 deals briefly with clarity in writing and exposition. Section 3 explains our organization and how submissions are handled. Section 4 covers details concerning the preparation of manuscripts.

In Section 1 of our constitution, the purpose of the Econometric Society is defined: "The Econometric Society is an international society for the advancement of economic theory in its relation to statistics and mathematics ... Its main object is to promote studies that aim at the unification of the theoretical-quantitative and the empirical-quantitative approach to economic problems and that are penetrated by constructive and rigorous thinking. ECONOMETRICA has no tightly controlled policy towards subject matter. No paper is rejected because it is "too mathematical" or "too quantitative", but because our membership includes economists with a variety of research interest, it is necessary that full length contributions be prepared so that the non-specialist is informed of what they are about and told why the results are important. This is the major way in which ECONOMETRICA tries to distinguish its offerings from those in the more specialized journals.

ECONOMETRICA

8. Writing for ECONOMETRICA

For publication in ECONOMETRICA, manuscripts should meet the highest
scientific standards. This means they should be novel, important, and correct;
in addition, they should be well presented. For a more specialked journal,
good presentation might reduce to a matter of craftsmanship; however, for
ECONOMETRICA this should imply, for full-length articles, a careful
explanation of the results and their importance, including relationships with
other literature and (wherever possible) applications to related areas.

Avoid definitions in the first paragraphs or pages; try to avoid formulae and
specialized terminology in the introduction. Write crisply but clearly; the
editors will provide the space for you to explain the results in an attractive
manner. Authors of papers concerned with high abstract theoretical analysis
should keep in mind that our membership includes economists whose own work is
rather applied. Similarly, authors of applied papers should make their results
accessible to members who have little acquaintance with the institutions being
considered.

Expository writing for professional journals is an exciting business. It
consists of two separate tasks:

i. the elimination of bad writing, by assuring that the article is
    grammatically correct and conveys precisely the thoughts to be expressed,
    and
ii. the cultivation of good writing, by reworking the manuscript again and
    again, sentence by sentence, until the ideas are put forward with the
    maximum amount of clarity.

The combination of these two in the preparation of a manuscript will ensure
that the finished paper will receive the attention it deserves for its
theoretical insights and empirical findings.

In our opinion, there are three types of reference work which the prospective
author will find useful. The first is a dictionary; precise word meaning is
important in accurately conveying ideas. The second is a grammar book; proper
use of punctuation and grammar is vital in attaining clarity in exposition. (A
good reference grammar in English is Allen's LIVING ENGLISH STRUCTURE, and
there are many comparable French titles.) The third reference work, which we
strongly recommend for its tips on mathematical writing and its examples of
"do's and don'ts", is the "Manual for Monthly Authors" by Harley Flanders.
This appeared in the January 1971 issue of the AMERICAN MATHEMATICAL MONTHLY
(Volume 78, No. 1), and reprints are available on request from the
Mathematical Association of America, 1225 Connecticut Avenue, N.W.,
Washington, D.C. 20036. Adherence to the fundamental rules of exposition as
set forth in these references will help the prospective author to eliminate
bad writing.

Avoiding grammatical and notational errors, though important, is only the
first step. Good writing, especially good mathematical writing, calls for
something more -- the extra effort stressed in (ii) above. To quote Harley
Flanders'"Manual":

Good writing requires constant empathy with the potential reader, skill,
self-criticism, and above all, hard work. After your paper is finished and a

draft typed, then you must challenge every single word, sentence, phrase, paragraph, and section. Is the order right? Why this choice of words? Can excess verbiage be trimmed? Can explanations and proofs be made clearer?

Write crisply; never be satisfied with the first draft. As mentioned above, the varied readership of ECONOMETRICA necessitates a careful exposition of the importance of technical results; this makes the "good writing" component of an artide especially important. No paper will be rejected because it is "too mathematical" or "too numerical", but for a journal such as ours to remain viable, papers must be written so that the non-specialist is informed of their contents and the importance of their findings. A good test of the "readability" of a paper is to pass the completed manuscript to a colleague in another specialty; his comments should enlighten you to problems in comprehension which our heterogeneous group of readers might face.

9. Consideration of Submitted Papers

All papers should be sent to the Editor.

Four high-quality copies of the original paper (not the original) should be submitted. They must be accompanied by a letter of submission and be written in either English or French. The Editor will reply with a card which acknowledges receipt of the manuscript and indicates which Co-editor will have charge of the paper. Submission of a paper is help to imply that its contents represent original and unpublished work, and that it has not been submitted for publication elsewhere. If the author has submitted related work elsewhere, or H he does so during the term in which ECONOMETRICA is considering the manuscript, then it is his responsibility to provide ECONOMETRICA with details.

9.1 The Review Process

Normally, the review process is expected to take no more than three months. (The yearly Editor's Report contains statistics regarding our present performance.) A paper is ordinarily sent to two referees, one of whom is often an Associate Editor. Referees are informed that it is not their responsibility to decipher poorly prepared manuscripts. A submission may be rejected solely because typographical errors and imprecise definitions make it hard to appraise.

The volume of papers submitted to ECONOMETRICA is such that the Editors must rely heavily on the referees' reports. What happens if you disagree with those reports and the Editor's decision? The general principle (but not inflexible rule) is that our decision is final. Rarely is it the case that referees ar convinced by the arguments of the author. Sometimes the problem in one of communication; for example, the referee doe snot understand what the author really means. However, the fact that such a problem exists for a supposedly expert (but sometimes unsympathetic) referee is important information. Referees expect authors to say exactly what they mean. They are often openly hostile when asked to return a paper in which they have discovered a major error, ill-defined term, impenetrable style, etc. Here is a quote from a letter which I recently received from a referee. "I dislike the idea that the publication process is a repeated game where the author first presents some vague notes and then gradually invests more effort when forced by a referee." While I find this view somewhat stern, especially when applied to "young" authors, it is not without merit. In any case, I judge that many (most?) of our most experienced referees would express similar feelings. If an author believes that a referee is incompetent (a strong word) for his task, then, assuming the author is correct, the blame must lie with the Editor who chose the referee. A rebuttal, directed at the referee, is most likely to be fruitful when the matter at issue is a simple fact. For example, the referee says that "Theorem A in the paper is a trivial consequence of the well known result B"; however, B does not apply since one of its conditions is easily seen not to be satisfied.

There are many journals which publish econometrics, mathematical economics, and theory. We are not final arbiters. When we reject a paper, it can be (and usually is) submitted to another independent journal. This is the "appeal procedure" which is built into the system; our policy that rejections are normally definitive relies upon this type of initiative by authors who disagree with the reports of referees.

9.2 Following Acceptance of a Paper

Papers may be rejected, returned for specified revision, or accepted. Currently papers appear approximately one year from the date of acceptance. (The yearly Editor's Report provides information concerning the current backlog.) When an article is accepted, it is sent to the Managing Editor, who immediately schedules the manuscript for publication. A letter is sent to the author indicating a TENTATIVE issue assignment, approximately when proofs may be received and any missing materials that may be required before the paper can be processed for publication. The manuscript is then turned over to a copymarker who prepares it for the printer. Grammar and spelling are corrected, the manuscript is checked for consistency in notation and references, and various copy-marking symbols are added to instruct the printer on type sizes and styles to be used, special spacing and indentation requirements, and placement of figures and tables.

A final review of the copymarked manuscript is made by the Managing Editor before the paper is forwarded to the printer. If minor ambiguities are noted, a query is addressed to the author on the front of the manuscript, so the matter may be corrected at proof stage.

Once the paper has been received by the printer, it is typeset and page proofs are pulled and sent directly to the author and Managing Editor. Accompanying the author's proofs are the original manuscript, instructions for correction and return of the proofs, and instructions for ordering reprints. The author should take special note of any queries on the front of the manuscript, the deadlines for return of proofs, and reprint order, and the different addresses to which each should be returned, as set out in the instructions sent with the proofs. PROOFS SHOULD BE RETURNED AS SOON AS POSSIBLE, since the issue to which a paper is finally assigned depends on the date corrected proofs are received from an author.

When the Managing Editor receives the corrected proofs, all author and printer corrections are compiled on a single set of proofs, which are returned to the printer following a thorough review for any additional errors. At this time a letter is sent to the author of each full length article soliciting an abstract suitable for publication in the JOURNAL OF ECONOMIC LITERATURE. Complete instructions for the abstract accompany the letter.

ECONOMETRICA

As soon as the correct proofs and a compilation of reprint orders for an issue are received by the printer, preparation and distribution of the completed issue are undertaken. Reprints are produced and distributed to authors by the printer after the issue itself has been completed and distributed.

10. MANUSCRIPT PREPARATION FOR ECONOMETRICA

The final manuscript submitted to the Managing Editor should be typed on bond paper of standard size (one side only and preferably 8.5 by 11 inches), with margins of at least one inch on all sides. Double space ALL material in the manuscript including captions, headnote, footnotes, references, and so forth. Please do not submit Ditto, Thermofax, or Verifax reproductions.

10.1 The title to the manuscript should be centered and typed in all capitals. If it exceeds one line, it should be double-spaced. Avoid superfluous words in titles, such as "SOME" in "SOME RECENT CONTRIBUTIONS TO..." or "unless they serve as important qualifications. The author's name, introduced by the word "By" is typed in upper and lower case and is centered below the title as shown in the following illustration:

DEMAND EQUATIONS FOR HOUSING

By John Doe and Mary Smith

If the manuscript is an article, the author by-line should be followed by a headnote (a paragraph of less than 100 words describing for the reader the nature of the article). The headnote is indented on both margins, typed in paragraph style, and double-spaced. Headnotes are not published for notes and comments.

10.2 Footnotes

Footnote numbering is consecutive throughout the paper, beginning with the number "1" rather than any other symbol. If the first footnote of the article related to the paper (e.g., this article was prepared under the auspices of ONR Project 123, the footnote should appear at the end of the title. If the first footnote expresses acknowledgments or refers to the author, the footnote number should appear at the end of the author by-line. Author affiliation should not be included in footnotes or on the title page; it always follows the text of the manuscript. All footnote numbers should be superscripts (not in parentheses) and should follow (not precede) punctuation in the text. Although all footnotes will be printed at the bottom of relevant pages in the final publication, they should not be placed thus in the manuscript. Instead, all footnotes should be typed together (double-spaced) on a separate page at the end of the manuscript (following references).

10.3 Text

If the main body of the manuscript is divided into sections, the section titles are centered, given Arabic numerals, and typed in upper and lower case. Subordinate section headings are italicized upper and lower case, and may be centered, flush left, or at the beginning of the paragraph with the subsequent text following on the same line if each subsection is one paragraph in length. Subsection headings may be unnumbered, or may be assigned Roman letters or Arabic numerals such as 1.1, 1.2, etc.

The first line of the FIRST paragraph of the text should be typed flush left rather than indented in usual paragraph form. Sections of the text to be highlighted are italicized in publication; authors should indicate those phrases which they wish to italicize by underlining them.

There are a few additional points of style to which ECONOMETRICA adheres: If the paper is in English, use American rather than British spelling. Except in certain footnote or reference situations, spell out words that are not standard Latin abbreviations (e.g., Section, not Sec.; if and only if, not iff; right hand side, not r.h.s.). Spell our numerals in text passages if they occur infrequently and are not too involved. The word per cent is always two words. Capitalize "Section", "Chapter", "Theorem", "Lemma", etc. when reference is made to a particular one. Names of persons should NOT be typed in all capitals. Abbreviations such as GNP and CES are typed without periods. Avoid unnecessary hyphenation; many hyphenated words can be treated as two words or as one compound word. Do not italicize common Latin terms such as i.e., e.g., a priori, etc. In the enumeration of three or more items, use a comma before "and" (e.g., Smith, Jones, and Brown). Commas and periods ALWAYS precede closing quotation marks rather than following them. Quotations of approximately five lines or more should be set off from the text and indented on both margins. AvoW starting a sentence with lower case mathematical symbols or equation numbers not preceded by the word "Equation". Minimize the use of "however" as the first word of a sentence.

Theorems, lemmas, corollaries, propositions, and assumptions, when presented formally, should be set out as separate paragraphs using the following style.

LEMMA 3: If there exists...

They should be italicized (as shown) unless they occur so often that the pages are filled with italics (in this event italicize only theorems). Proofs should not be italicized, but should be set out as separate paragraphs using the same style illustrated above. If the proof concludes with "Q.E.D." this should be italicized and typed flush right on the last line of the proof. Definitions are also presented in the same styles as theorems, lemmas, etc., but only defined terms are italicized. The sentence preceding a theorem, lemma, corollary, etc. should end with a period or colon.

A mathematical formula should be presented in the line of text (rather than displayed) unless it
i.   is numbered for later reference,
ii. is over half a line long, or
iii. involves matrices or other expressions which require extra vertical spacing when printed.

Fairly short and simple fractions may be included in the text if presented on a single line as in the following example: (a + b) / (c + d). Care should be taken, however, to avoid ambiguity in presentation of such fractions. The fraction (a/b + c) can be misread. Present such an expression as (a/(b + c)) or ((a/b) + c) to resolve the ambiguity. Parentheses within parentheses are acceptable. More complex equations should be displayed; i.e., they should be written on a new line and indented. For example:

$$P_u X_u = P_u (K_{12} \frac{1}{T_u P_u} + K_{13} \frac{1}{T_{u\text{-}1} P_{u\text{-}1}})$$

ECONOMETRICA

For displayed equations, equation numbers are Arabic, are enclosed in parentheses, and are placed flush left. Equations may be numbered consecutively throughout the article or throughout the section (in the latter case the number would appear as (2.3) meaning third equation in Section 2). Use lower case Roman numerals in parentheses for other enumerations in the text so no confusion arises between references to equation numbers and other enumerations in the article. Displayed equations are indented. Indications of the range of an index, such as (i = 1 ,...,n) should be placed flush right and should appear in parentheses. Other conditions, such as i j, need not be flush right, but should be preceded by extra spacing and would not originally appear in parentheses. Unless essential, avoid inclusion of words in displayed mathematics. If an equation is followed by "where", and definitions, "where" should begin a new line. If a symbol is defined in words, avoid the equality sign: use "means", "represents", "is", or another expression.

All mathematical material must be punctuated. Colons at the end of phrases preceding formulas are often unnecessary and should be used only when required. An ellipsis always consists of exactly three dots, though it may be followed by a period. Indexes on summation, product, integration, maximization, and other such symbols should appear in subscript position when occurring in lines of text; otherwise they appear directly below and above the appropriate symbols. For example, in displayed material $\sum_{i=1}^{n} x_i$

Is appropriate, while in a line of text $\sum_{i=1}^{n} x_i$, is used. Avoid large braces covering multiple lines if possible.

All material appearing in ECONOMETRICA is italicized (with the exception of mathematical expressions such as ln, cos var, min, max, lim, tr), but the author should NOT underline mathematics in his manuscript. The printer has standing instructions about italicized mathematical material.

To eliminate confusion of symbols (such as 1 (one) and l (ell), x (ex) and x (times), ϵ (Epsilon) and $\in$ (is an element of), ϕ (phi) and γ (null set), O (oh) and 0 (zero); use proper and distinctive fonts in the manuscript or make marginal notes on the manuscript regarding the intended symbols. In addition, a list of the symbols used should be included on a separate sheet of paper. ECONOMETRICA uses the symbols $\leq$ and $\geq$ rather than $\leqq$ and $\geqq$ or $\leqslant$ and $\geqslant$. If a distinction between $\leq$ and $\leqq$ is employed in the manuscript, both symbols will be used.

Please avoid the use of bold face symbols unless absolutely necessary.

In reporting estimation results (whether in equation or table format) parenthetical expressions presented below estimates should contain standard errors rather than t ratios. Expressions

using "th", as "i^{th}" of "j^{th}", for example, should be typed with the "th" on the main line: "ith" or "jth". In the printed version "i" and "j" will be italicized and "th" will be Roman.

Papers should be submitted in the form in which they are to be published; referees and editors should not be expected to do any shortening on text or proofs, but this may sometimes be requested. If an obvious but tedious proof has been omitted form the text, four copies should be forwarded along with the manuscript to aid the referees. Tedious but not obvious proofs can often be printed as working papers which are available to the reader on request; if this is done, four copies of the working paper should also be forwarded.

10.4 Author Affiliation and Appendixes

The author's (permanent) affiliation at the time of publication appear in upper and lower case italics on a separate line (to the left and indented) following the conclusion of the text material, as shown in the following illustration for a single author.

University of Chicago

In the case of two authors, the affiliations should be presented as follows: *University of Chicago and Northwestern University*

The affiliation is followed by the Appendix, if these is one. The caption APPENDIX (all capitals) should be centered. If there are several appendixes, they may be titled APPENDIX A, APPENDIX B, etc.

10.5 References

References in most articles are gathered together in a reference list at the end of the article, arranged alphabetically, and preceded by boldface numbers in brackets. (Boldface is indicated to the printer by a wavy line under a symbol.) References in the text make use of these boldface numbers in brackets, and all internal references, such as chapter numbers, also appear within the brackets. If several reference numbers occur together, they are separated by commas within a single set of brackets. Consider the examples in the following excerpt:

... as shown in [5]. Similar remarks occur in [3, 16]. This contracts with the views expressed in [6, Ch. 2; 7; 8; and 9]. The essential point made by Smith [20, p. 162 and pp. 195-197] is that...

Occasionally we deviate from this standard reference practice for good cause.

The caption REFERENCES (all capitals) should be centered at the top of the reference list. The references should be arranged alphabetically by last name. In alphabetizing, names beginning with Mc are placed between Mb and Md. Names beginning with lower case words are placed according to the first letter of the lower case word (von Huas would go under the V's). If there are two or more references by the same author, these may appear in alphabetical order by title or chronological order. The second and subsequent items do not reproduce the author's name; a dash is used instead. If an author appears alone and as a co-author, the co-authored items appear lower in the alphabetical order and the dash in not used for the first appearance of any set of co-authors, as shown in the following example:

Adams, A.B.:

_____:
Adams, A.B., and C.D. Black

_____:
Adams, A.B., C.D. Black, and E.F. Carter

Authors' names should be typed in upper and lower case with the last name first (but ONLY for the first of coauthors), and should be followed by a colon. Second and subsequent lines of a reference should be indented. All references should be followed by a period. Titles of unpublished manuscripts are in quotes; books and periodicals are italicized. All major words in a title are capitalized. References to books should include place of publication. Titles of journals or books should not be abbreviated. Some examples follow; please note the punctuation.

Diewert, W.E. (1974): "Intertemporah Consumer Theory and the Demand for Durables", Econometrica, 42, 497-516.

Houthakker, H.S. and I.D. Taylor (1970): Consumer Demand in the United States: Analyses and Projections. Cambridge, Mass.: HaNard University Press.

Muth, R.J. (1960) "The Demand for Non-Farm Housing", in The Demand for Durable goods, ed by A.C. Harberger, Chicago: University of Chicago Press.

The reference list should only contain items to which text references are made.

10.6 Tables

Tables should be gathered on separate sheets at the end of the manuscript (following references and footnotes). They should never be incorporated in the body of the text. They should be numbered with Roman numerals. Explicit reference is not made to each table by number in the text, make marginal notes on the manuscript to indicate the approximate location desired for each table.

The caption to the table should appear at the top as shown in the accompanying example (Table 1). The top rule is a double rule; all other rules are single. Vertical rules are avoided unless absolutely necessary. Footnotes to tables are designated by Roman letter superscripts and the footnotes should appear together at the bottom of each table (see Table 1).

TABLE I

Average Annual Costs

Policy	TotalCosts[a]	Size of Deduction
A	135.00	0
B	116.00	0
C	23.70	900

[a]The entries are above annual costs where r = .0005.

10.7 Figures

Figures, no matter how small, should never be run into the text. They should be gathered at the end of the manuscript and numbered with Arabic numerals. If the text does not explicitly refer to a figure by number, use a marginal note to indicate the approximate location desired for the figure.

ECONOMETRICA

Professional drawings of ALL illustrations (no matter how simple) must be provided by the author. These should be FINAL as even minor revisions of figures in proof may be costly. The drawings should be camera-ready and should include all labels and keys appearing in the figures and on the axes. The drawings should be done in India ink with professional lettering (no typewritten labels, please).

Figure captions need not be included in the drawings; simply note each figure number on the back of the drawing. Figure captions will be typeset by the printer and will appear below the figures. Gather the captions together on a separate sheet for the printer. Titles may be incorporated in the captions or omitted. See the following examples, which illustrate punctuation and capitalization:

Figure 1

Figure 2 -- Comparison of Results.

11. Conclusion

This manual is an attempt to explain ECONOMETRICA's publication process to prospective authors. To that end, we have described the special demands of writing for ECONOMETRICA. Also, we have discussed in detail our procedures for the consideration of submitted manuscripts, and given the form in which paper should be submitted.

It is our privilege to serve as the Editor and Managing Editor of ECONOMETRICA; the breadth of material covered in the journal and the importance of the theoretical and empirical results reported make the task of editing both interesting and challenging. This manual is a product of our experience, and is intended to serve both authors and readers. Authors should find the submission of manuscript to be an easier process; readers should benefit from more rapid publication of papers and the increased "readability" of the published work.

ECONOMIC AFFAIRS

ADDRESS FOR SUBMISSION :

PROF.COLIN ROBINSON,EDITOR
ECONOMIC AFFAIRS
THE INSTITUTE OF ECONOMIC AFFAIRS
2 LORD NORTH STREET
LONDON,   SW1P 3LB
ENGLAND
44-71-799-3745
44-71-799-2137 (Fax)

CIRCULATION DATA :

Reader : Business Persons &
         Academic

Frequency of Issue : Bi-Monthly

Copies Per Issue : 3001-4000

Subscription Price : 24.00 US$
   Institutional : 44.00 US$

Sponsorship : Non Profit Corp.

PUBLICATION GUIDELINES :

Manuscript Length : 1-15

Copies Required : Two

Computer Submission : No

Format : N/A

Fees to Review : 0.00 US$

REVIEW INFORMATION :

Type of Review : Blind Review

No. of External Reviewers : One

No. of In House Reviewers : Two

Acceptance Rate : 50 %

Time To Review : 2-3 months

Reviewer's Comments : No

Fees to Publish : 0.00 US$

Invited Articles : Over 50%

MANUSCRIPT TOPICS : ECONOMETRICS;
   INTERNATIONAL & ECONOMIC DEVELOPMENT; PUBLIC POLICY ECONOMICS

PUBLICATION GUIDELINES :

MANUSCRIPT GUIDELINES/COMMENTS :

1. ECONOMIC AFFAIRS offers a platform for market economists (and their
critics) to present analysis of current and impending trends in economic
thinking and policy.

2. ECONOMIC AFFAIRS is read by politicians, industrialists, teachers and
non-specialists in many other walks of life and in over 40 countries. The
material should thus be SCHOLARLY in tone but SIMPLE and clear enough in prose
for non-economists.

3. In the effort to combine scholarships with topicality, ECONOMIC AFFAIRS
will be working within tight limits--even tyrannies--of time and space. Since
the aim is to include as large a numbr of contributions as possible in each
issue, texts should be written CRISPLY and tautly.

4. Articles (1000-3000 words) should be strong in CONCLUSIONS for policy.

5. To attract maximum attention, NEW insights and implicatins for policy
should be stated concisely, explicitly and wherever possible QUANTITATIVELY,
even as substantially SUPPORTABLE estimates.

ECONOMIC AFFAIRS

6. The material should, whenever possible, include photographic illustrations (especially), tables and charts. A small number of footnotes is admissible, but most references should be confined to the text.

7. Authors are asked to supply an INFORMAL head-and-shoulders photograph of themselves (smiling) and around 150 words of biographical detail.

8. Owing to the timetable, we hope authors will allow us editorial discretion in putting their texts into our house style and, where necessary, to shorten the texts to fit the space. Where possible, we shall telephone to obtain agreement.

9. Where the argument at several key points can be summarized in concise, graphic sentences, they could be included in the press release to help attract attention.

10. Manuscripts should be typed on A4 paper in double spacing, leaving wide margins.

ECONOMIC DEVELOPMENT AND
CULTURAL CHANGE

ADDRESS FOR SUBMISSION :

LIA GREEN, MANAGING EDITOR
ECONOMIC DEVELOPMENT AND
  CULTURAL CHANGE
UNIVERSITY OF CHICAGO
1130 EAST 59TH STREET
CHICAGO, IL 60637
USA
773-702-7951

CIRCULATION DATA :

Reader : Academic

Frequency of Issue : Quarterly

Copies Per Issue : 3001-4000

Subscription Price : 30.00 US$

Sponsorship :

PUBLICATION GUIDELINES :

Manuscript Length : 16-20

Copies Required : Two

Computer Submission : No

Format : N/A

Fees to Review : 0.00 US$

REVIEW INFORMATION :

Type of Review : Editorial Review

No. of External Reviewers : Two

No. of In House Reviewers :

Acceptance Rate : 6-10%

Time To Review : 4-6 months

Reviewer's Comments : Yes

Fees to Publish : 0.00 US$

Invited Articles : 5% or less

MANUSCRIPT TOPICS : ECONOMETRICS;
  INTERNATIONAL & ECONOMIC DEVELOPMENT; PUBLIC POLICY ECONOMICS

PUBLICATION GUIDELINES : Chicago Manual of Style

MANUSCRIPT GUIDELINES/COMMENTS :

1. Two copies of each manuscript must be submitted. Carbons will be accepted
for the second copy only. All manuscripts must be double-spaced (text, notes,
tables, etc.). Allow right- and left-hand margins of at least 1 1/2 inches
each. Do not justify right-hand margins. Manuscripts will be returned only if
specifically requested, and if a self-addressed, stamped envelope is enclosed.

2. First page of manuscript:
    a. The title should be at least 2 inches from the top edge of the paper.
    b. Allow 1-inch space, and on a separate line, type the name(s) of the
       author(s). On the next line, type the affiliation(s).
    c. Type in upper and lower case letters. Do NOT use all capitals.

3. Notes to each article will appear in a separate section, "Notes", at the
end of the article. The first note in that section will be the acknowledgement
or explanatory note, if any, indicated by an asterisk (*) to the article
title. Note numbers in text should be superscripts:

(Text) ...in that study.[4] Notes should be numbered on the line, followed by a
    period. Each note is a separate single paragraph:

ECONOMIC DEVELOPMENT AND
CULTURAL CHANGE

(Note) 3. John Jones, "Rice Farming Techniques...", Notes should be typed double-spaced on pages separated from and following the text.

Some examples follow:

1. John D. Jones, "Organizational Effectiveness", Economic Theory 9, ed. G. H. Green, trans. F. L. Lauterbach (New York: Macmillan Co., 1962).

2. E.F. Brown, "Basic Business Problems", Harvard Business Review 42 (April 1981): 64-73, esp. 65.

3. C.D. Miller, Problems of the retailer, 2d ed., Harvard Series in Management, no. 1 (Cambridge, Mass., Harvard University Press, 1986).

4. Peter Wells, "Problems of Undergraduates" (Ph.D. diss., University of Chicago, 1965).

5. John Smith, "Distribution of Corn" (Discussion Paper no. 1, Jamestown University, Institute of Anglo-lndian Relations, 1620).

6. P.F. Wilson, "Management Policy", mimeographed (Chicago: University of Chicago, Department of Economics, 1980).

7. World Bank, Struggle for Power (Washington, D.C.: World Bank, 1981).

In subsequent references to a work, repeat the author's last name. If more than one work by the same author is cited, repeat author and title of the work being clted. Do not use op. Cit. Use ibid. only to refer to a work in the preceding note (NOT for earlier citations within the same note).

4. Any equation of mathematical material of two levels or more should be typed on a line by itself in the text with extra space above and below it. Equation numbers should be at the right-hand side of the line and should be in parentheses.

5. Tabular material and computer printouts: Each table should be on a separate sheet of paper, and should follow the Notes. Each table should be numbered and should be referred to IN ORDER in the text. If tables have more than 8 columns excluding the stub column, or more than 50 row entries, special arrangements for production may be necessary. Computer printouts must be reducible to page size. If computer printouts are unable to be reduced to the specified size, they may be left out of the journal and replaced by a note informing the reader to contact the author for details.

6. Illustrations: Each illustration (figure) should be on a separate sheet of paper, and should follow the tabular material. Legends for the illustrations should be typed in order on a sheet of paper which should accompany the illustrations. All illustrations should be referred to in order in text, as figure 1, figure 2, etc. Maps, line drawings, and diagrams should be prepared with India ink on white drawing paper, or tracing paper. Several drawings grouped on a page as one figure are distinguished as A, B, C, etc. Figures must be able to be reduced to page size or smaller. Authors may submit original drawings (if small enough) or very clear, glossy photographs of them. The smallest symbols or letters used should not be less than 1.5 mm high after reduction. The author should supply two copies of each figure suitable for

ECONOMIC DEVELOPMENT AND CULTURAL CHANGE

sending to reviewers (photocopies, offset reproductions, etc., folding to less than 8 1/2 X 11 inches).

7. Miscellaneous: Any unusual symbols or abbreviations in the text or tabular material should be identified in the margin (in lead pencil).

8. Any foreign language spellings and transliterations are the responsibility of the author. On matters of spelling and Style, refer to WEBSTER'S NEW INTERNATIONAL DICTIONARY (3d ed.) and the University of Chicago Press MANUAL OF STYLE (13th ed.).

ECONOMIC DEVELOPMENT HORIZONS
(SURVEY OF REGIONAL LITERATURE)

ADDRESS FOR SUBMISSION :

R.D. NORTON, EDITOR
ECONOMIC DEVELOPMENT HORIZONS
  (SURVEY OF REGIONAL LITERATURE)
BRYANT COLLEGE
CENTER FOR REGIONAL ANALYSIS
SMITHFIELD, RI 02917
USA
401-232-6307
401-232-6720 (Fax)
E-Mail : cscott@acad.bryant.edu

CIRCULATION DATA :

Reader : Academic

Frequency of Issue : Quarterly

Copies Per Issue : Less than 1000

Subscription Price : 45.00 US$
  Foreign : 60.00 US$

Sponsorship : University

PUBLICATION GUIDELINES :

Manuscript Length :

Copies Required :

Computer Submission : No

Format : N/A

Fees to Review : 0.00 US$

REVIEW INFORMATION :

Type of Review : Blind Review

No. of External Reviewers :

No. of In House Reviewers :

Acceptance Rate :

Time To Review :

Reviewer's Comments : No

Fees to Publish : 0.00 US$

Invited Articles :

MANUSCRIPT TOPICS : ECONOMETRICS;
  INTERNATIONAL & ECONOMIC DEVELOPMENT; PUBLIC POLICY ECONOMICS

PUBLICATION GUIDELINES :

MANUSCRIPT GUIDELINES/COMMENTS :

We DO NOT solicit manuscripts.

ECONOMIC DEVELOPMENT QUARTERLY

ADDRESS FOR SUBMISSION :

EDWARD W. HILL, EDITOR
ECONOMIC DEVELOPMENT QUARTERLY
CLEVELAND STATE UNIVERSITY
LEVIN COLLEGE OF URBAN AFFAIRS
CLEVELAND, OH 44115
USA
216-687-2174
216-687-9277 (Fax)
E-Mail : ned@wolf.csuohio.edu

CIRCULATION DATA :

Reader : Business Persons &
        Academic

Frequency of Issue : Quarterly

Copies Per Issue : 1001-2000

Subscription Price : 63.00 US$
  Institution : 186.00 US$
  For Outside USA, Add : 8.00 US$

Sponsorship : Professional Assoc.

PUBLICATION GUIDELINES :

Manuscript Length : 15-30

Copies Required : Five

Computer Submission : No

Format : N/A

Fees to Review : 0.00 US$

REVIEW INFORMATION :

Type of Review : Blind Review

No. of External Reviewers : Three

No. of In House Reviewers : Zero

Acceptance Rate : 21-30%

Time To Review : 2-3 months

Reviewer's Comments : Yes

Fees to Publish : 0.00 US$

Invited Articles : 11-20%

MANUSCRIPT TOPICS : ACCOUNTING INFORMATION SYSTEMS; ECONOMETRICS;
  INTERNATIONAL & ECONOMIC DEVELOPMENT; PUBLIC POLICY ECONOMICS

PUBLICATION GUIDELINES : American Psychological Association

MANUSCRIPT GUIDELINES/COMMENTS :

MANUSCRIPTS should be submitted to Edward W. Hill, Editor. Full length
manuscripts should be approximately 25 double-spaced, typewritten pages,
although longer manuscripts will not be excluded from consideration. The
review process for EDQ requires that five (5) copies of each manuscript be
submitted. One copy should have a title page giving the title of the
submission and the name(s), institutional affiliation(s), mailing address(es),
and office telephone number(s) of the author(s). The four remaining copies
should have no markings that would allow the author(s) to be identified.
All articles are peer reviewed by both practitioners and academics.

The body of the manuscript should bear only the title of the article on the
first page. All manuscripts must include an abstract of 100-150 words typed on
a separate sheet of paper, and a short (less than 50 words) biographical
statement including affiliation, research interests, and/or recent
publications. All copy should be typed, double-spaced, on standard white paper
and should follow the style suggested in the publication manual of the
AMERICAN PSYCHOLOGICAL ASSOCIATION (APA, 4th ed.), with notes and references
in separate sections at the end of the article. Artwork should appear on

separate pages and figures should be camera-ready. Manuscripts will not be returned to the authors.

The editors assume that manuscripts are for the exclusive consideration of EDQ and have not been submitted elsewhere, nor should manuscripts have been published elsewhere in substantially similar form or with substantially similar content. Authors in doubt about what constitutes prior publication should consult the editor. In addition to traditional peer-reviewed articles (submission process described above) EDQ has several other featured sections with different procedures for submissions. A copy of the final revised manuscript saved on IBM-compatible disk should be included with the final revised hard copies. Submission of a manuscript implies commitment to publish in the journal.

Review essays are to make available to our readers concise presentations of the literature within a specialized area within the field of economic defelopment. Reviews will describe and summarize debates within particular fields in nontechnical, jargon-free language, but will not enter into the debate itself. To prevent unnecessary overlap in the reviews, potential contributors are encouraged to consult with the editors prior to preparing submissions. For any reviews, whether based on books, articles, consultancy reports, "fugitive" materials, or other unpublished documents, please contact either of the following: Marie Howland, Dept. of Urban Studies & Planning, University of Maryland-College Park, College Park, MD 20742 (301/405-6790); or Wim Wiewel, Great Cities Institute (M/C 107), The University of Illinois-Chicago, 322 South Greet Street, Suite 108, Chicago, IL 60607-3502 (312/996-8700).

Industry Studies are designed to bring the readers up to date on the problems and prospects for continued development of growth industries and/or industries which have a substantial impact on the economy. Potential contributors should contact Marie Howland or Wim Wiewel (address above).

Forum provides readers with the opportunity to comment on articles published in previous issues of EDQ. Comments for the Forum and letters to the Editors should be directed to Edward W. Hill, Editor (address above).

REFERENCES

Newspaper Articles
Daily newspaper:
> Hopey, D. (1986, February 28). Steel valley authority rolls up its
>   sleeves. The Pittsburgh Press, p. C6.
>
> (If no author is given, begin with the title and alphabetize by the first
> significant word in the title. In text, use a short title for the
> parenthetical citation and quotation marks: ("Steel valley authority,"
> 1986)

Unpublished Paper Presented at a Meeting
> Vogel, D. (1986, Setember). Coercion versus consultation: A comparison of
>   environmental protection policy in the United States and Great
>   Britain. Paper presented at the annual meeting of the American
>   Political Science Association, Washington, DC.

Report
  Ross, S. (1994). Women's labor force participation (Working Paper No. 30).
    New York: National Bureau of Economic Research, Center for Economic
    Analysis.
Unpublished Dissertation
  Morgan, W. (1964). The effects of state and local tax and financial
    inducements on industrial location. Unpublished doctoral dissertation,
    University of Colorado [city if known].

ECONOMIC GEOGRAPHY

ADDRESS FOR SUBMISSION :

SUSAN HANSON & RICHARD PEET, EDITORS
ECONOMIC GEOGRAPHY
CLARK UNIVERSITY
GRADUATE SCHOOL OF GEOGRAPHY
950 MAIN STREET
WORCESTER, MA 01610
USA
508-793-7311
508-793-8881 (Fax)
E-Mail : econman@clarku.edu

CIRCULATION DATA :

Reader : Academic

Frequency of Issue : Quarterly

Copies Per Issue : 2001-3000

Subscription Price : 35.00 US$
    Library/Institution : 45.00 US$
    Student : 20.00 US$

Sponsorship : University

PUBLICATION GUIDELINES :

Manuscript Length : 26-30

Copies Required : Four

Computer Submission : No

Format : N/A

Fees to Review : 0.00 US$

REVIEW INFORMATION :

Type of Review : Blind Review

No. of External Reviewers : Three

No. of In House Reviewers : Zero

Acceptance Rate : 6-10%

Time To Review : 1-2 months

Reviewer's Comments : Yes

Fees to Publish : 0.00 US$

Invited Articles : 21-30%

MANUSCRIPT TOPICS : ECONOMETRICS;
    INTERNATIONAL & ECONOMIC DEVELOPMENT; PUBLIC POLICY ECONOMICS;
    LOCATIONAL ASPECTS OF ECONOMIC ACTIVITY

PUBLICATION GUIDELINES :

MANUSCRIPT GUIDELINES/COMMENTS :

The editors of ECONOMIC GEOGRAPHY invite articles that will contribute to
theoretical advances and debates in economic geography, broadly conceived.

Contributors should submit manuscripts to the Editors. Because each manuscript
will be sent to at least two reviewers, authors should provide four copies of
the manuscript and illustrations (three sets of illustrations may be in
xeroxed form). High mailing costs preclude returning manuscripts to authors.

Manuscripts should be in the English language (American spelling) and should
be typed double spaced, with wide margins, do NOT justify the right margin.
The abstract, list of references, tables, and a list of figure captions should
be typed double spaced on separate sheets.

The letter of transmittal accompanying a manuscript should contain a statement
affirming that neither the whole article nor substantial portions of it have
been submitted or published elsewhere. Should portions of the article be
submitted elsewhere, please send a copy of this submission.

ECONOMIC GEOGRAPHY

TITLE PAGE.--On the title page provide the full names of authors, academic or other professional affiliations, and the complete address of the author with whom the editors should correspond.

ABSTRACT.--Each paper should be accompanied by an abstract of no more than 250 words. The abstract should summarize the purpose, methods, and major findings of the paper. Key words should appear at the end of the abstract.

FOOTNOTES.--Because footnotes are expensive and especially where lengthy are awkward to typeset, they should be brief and used sparingly. In many cases, such information can be accommodated in the body of the text.

When a footnote is essential, it should be brief and limited to explaining a point in the manuscript. Footnotes (not endnotes) should be typed DOUBLE SPACE at the bottom of the page.

REFERENCES.--cite references in the text by typing in parentheses the last name(s) of author(s), followed by the year the work was published. Two or more cited publications by the same author(s) that appeared in the same year should be distinguished by a, b, c, etc., after the year, for example (Jones 1967b). Immediately after the text (and following the "Notes" section, if any), under the heading "References," list complete reference citations alphabetically by senior author's last name. A reference to "in press" implies that the paper has been accepted for publication. Titles of periodicals should be given in full. Examples of correct citations appear in this issue. For further guidance, refer to A MANUAL OF STYLE, The University of Chicago Press.

UNITS OF MEASURE.--Authors must use the International System of units (metric) but may show other units in parentheses.

EQUATIONS.--Equations should be numbered sequentially in parentheses in the right-hand margin. Authors should provide instructions in the margin for any special type required (Greek letters, boldface, etc.) the first time the symbol is used. Authors should be careful to differentiate between capital and lower-case letters, Latin and Greek characters, and letters and numerals. For example, the numeral 1 and the letter l are often confused.

TABLES.--Each table should be discussed in the text, but readers should be able to understand tables without reference to the text. Type all tables on separate sheets, double spaced, and number them sequentially with Arabic numerals. For each table provide a descriptive title and informative column heading. Table titles should be concise and should summarize the relationship or pattern presented by the table. Please keep tabular material to a minimum --it is expensive to typeset.

ILLUSTRATIONS.--Illustrations should be discussed in the text and should be numbered sequentially with Arabic numerals (for example, Figure 1). The editors will not return original illustrations. Captions for illustrations should be typed on a separate sheet. Illustrations must be of professional quality and should be in the form of camera-ready positive photographic prints (not matte finish). All labels and symbols must be proportioned for printing at single- or double-column width. Size of illustration should be in proportion to complexity of graphic content. All photographs should be in the form of glossy prints and should be cropped to appropriate size for publication.

ECONOMIC GEOGRAPHY

Readers should be able to understand all illustrations without reference to the text.

PERMISSIONS.--If previously published material (including illustrations) of substantial extent is included in a manuscript, the author is obliged to obtain written permission from the copyright holder.

ECONOMIC HISTORY REVIEW

ADDRESS FOR SUBMISSION :

FORREST CAPIE, CO-EDITOR
ECONOMIC HISTORY REVIEW
CITY UNIVERSITY BUSINESS SCHOOL
DEPARTMENT OF BANKING & FINANCE
FROBISHER CRESENT, BARBICAN CENTRE
LONDON, EC2Y 8HB
UK
0171 477 8730
0171 477 8880 (Fax)
E-Mail : F.H.Capie@City.ac.uk

CIRCULATION DATA :

Reader : Academic

Frequency of Issue : Quarterly

Copies Per Issue : 4001-5000

Subscription Price : 30.00 US$
    Institution : 102.00 US$

Sponsorship : Professional Assoc.

PUBLICATION GUIDELINES :

Manuscript Length : 21-25

Copies Required : Two

Computer Submission : No

Format : N/A

Fees to Review : 0.00 US$

REVIEW INFORMATION :

Type of Review : Blind Review

No. of External Reviewers : Two

No. of In House Reviewers : Two

Acceptance Rate : 33 %

Time To Review : 4-6 months

Reviewer's Comments : Yes

Fees to Publish : 0.00 US$

Invited Articles : 5% or less

MANUSCRIPT TOPICS : ECONOMETRICS; ECONOMIC HISTORY; SOCIAL HISTORY

PUBLICATION GUIDELINES :

MANUSCRIPT GUIDELINES/COMMENTS :

These notes indicate the main literary and typographical conventions of the
ECONOMIC HISTORY REVIEW. All corrections and alterations to contributions at
proof stage (apart from the correction of misprints) are extremely expensive.
It is very important, therefore, that authors should adhere to the Review
conventions. If a typescript is accepted, a copy-edited version of the text
will be sent to the author some months before publication. This is the last
stage at which any change proposed by the author will be considered. When
submitting a typescript the author should ensure that it is complete in all
respects and that it includes a summary (see section I below) and lists of
data points for any graphs (see section I.6 below). In case of doubt or
ambiguity the Editors follow the ruling of three related publications:

    The concise Oxford dictionary (8th edition, 1990)
    The Oxford dictionary for writers and editors (1981)
    Hart's rules for compositors and readers at the University Press, Oxford
        (39th edition, 1983)

General advice to authors: authors are asked to bear in mind when writing that
their work should be accessible to non-specialists. They should use clear
language, avoid specialized technical terms as far as possible, and relegate

lengthy discussions of method, or collections of data, if these are needed at all, to appendices. Titles of articles should be simply worded, as brief as possible, and should convey to the reader the content of the article.

1. PRESENTATION

TWO copies of each article should be submitted. Authors should retain additional copies for their own use as the cost of postage prevents the Editors from returning scripts not accepted for publication.

A SUMMARY of the article, not exceeding 100 words, should also be submitted, specifying its principal conclusions in the context of currently accepted views on the subject.

1.1 PAPER AND TYPING: articles should be typed, in double-spacing, on one side only of international A size paper, widh a wide margin. Pages should be numbered consecutively.

1.2 LENGTH: articles should not normally exceed 8,000 words, including footnotes; notes and comments should not exceed 2,500 words. Authors should inform the Editors of the exact length of articles and comments.

1.3 SUBSECTIONS major articles should be divided into subsections designated with roman numerals (I Il, Ill, etc.), but without subtitles.

1.4 FOOTNOTES: these should be double-spaced, numbered consecutively throughout the article; they should not be typed at the foot of each page but typed separately from the text at the end of the article. Footnotes should be confined, as far as possible, to necessary references. Acknowledgements should appear as footnote 1 to the title or first sentence.

1.5 TABLES: check tables carefully both for their contents and their final form. For references to notes in tables use a, b, c, etc. (See section 5 below). Authors should double-check that figures in tables do add up to the totals given. In the case of tables which occupy less than a whole page, the position which they are to occupy in the text should be indicated. Tables are printed without vertical rules but horizonal rules should be used to secure clarity: an example of good practice will be found in section 5 below. Sources for tables should always be provided, using the same conventions for source references as in footnotes.

1.6 GRAPHS AND MAPS: these should be supplied clearly drawn. They will be redrawn professionally. Where a graph or map is to occupy a full page, care should be taken to ensure that the proportions of the figure match those of a page in the Review 7 7/8" x 4 7/8", or 20.0 cm x 12.4 cm). In the case of maps, the outlines of the area represented and all geographical features included (rivers, boundaries, town sites, etc.) MUST be drawn or placed accurately, and the scale of the map indicated. In the case of graphs, the co-ordinates of all points to be plotted must be supplied on a separate sheet (e.g. year and annual output data). Consider carefully whether the scales should be natural on each axis, or whether, say, a logarithmic scale is preferable, given the nature of the information to be conveyed (as, for example, where the rate of growth is the key variable).

2. REFERENCES

2.1 CONSOLIDATED LIST

A consolidated alphabetical list of all books, articles, essays, and theses referred to should be provided. It will be printed at the end of the article. The following points should be noted:

2.1.1. Publications should be listed, that is all articles, books, and theses in alphabetical order, giving the author's surname first followed by initials. If more than one publication by the same author is listed, the items should be given in chronological order. Newspapers and manuscripts (including 'working papers', 'research papers', etc.) should not be listed. Any official publications should be listed at the end, in chronological order, under the separate heading OFFICIAL PUBLICATIONS.

2.1.2 Initial capitals are used only for the first word in each book or article title, for proper names, and for adjectives derived from the name of a country (e.g. Australian wool).

2.1.3 Dates in the titles of books and articles are preceded by a comma, and subtitles separated by a colon.

2.1.4 References to volume numbers of books and journals are given in roman or arabic as IN THE ORIGINAL SOURCE.

2.1.5 In the case of articles or contributions to collections of essays, IT IS ESSENTIAL TO GIVE COMPLETE PAGE REFERENCES.

2.1.6 Journal titles are capitalized and should be given in an abbreviated form (see section 4 below).

Some examples are given below:

2.1.7 BOOKS: place of publication to be given in all cases except London. Style as follows:

> Church, R., The history of the British coal industry, 1: 1830-1913, Victorian pre-eminence (Oxford, 1986).
> Cunningham, W., Alien immigrants to England (1879).
> Halevy, E., A history of the English people in the nineteenth century, 6 vols. (1913-34).
> Heaton, H., The Yorkshire woollen and worsted industries from the earliest times up to the industrial revolution (Oxford, 2nd edn. 1965).
> Kirby, J.L., ed., Abstracts of feet of fines relating to Wiltshire, 1377--509 (Wilts. Rec. Soc., XLI, 1985).
> Supple, B. E., The Royal Exchange Assurance: a history of British insurance, 1720-1970 (1970).

Where a volume is one of a series, or where a chapter from a collective work is cited, give the editor(s) of the individual volume in the following form:

> Chambers, J. D., 'Population change in a provincial town: Nottingham, 700-1800', in L. S. Pressnell, ed., Studies in the industrial revolution presented to T. S. Ashton (1960), pp. 97-124.

Landes, D., 'Technological change and development in western Europe, l750-1914', in H. J. Habakkuk and M. M. Postan, eds., Cambridge economic history of Europe, VI, pt. I, The industrial revolution and after (Cambridge, 1965), pp. 274-60l.

Foreign titles follow the conventions of their own languages. Thus in German capitalization is more extensive:

Imhof, A. E., ed., Historische Demographie als Sozialgeschichte: Giessen und Umgebung vom 17. zum 19. Jahrhundert, 2 vols. (Darmstadt, 1975).

2.1.8 ARTICLES: omit the definite article in journal titles; give the date of publication as year only, unless the series has no numbered volumes; note the sequence of volume number, year of publication, and page references. GIVE COMPLETE PAGE REFERENCES:

Ashworth, W., 'Economic aspects of late Victorian naval administration', Econ. Hist. Rev., 2nd ser., XXII (1969), pp. 491-505.

Whyte, I. D. and Whyte, K. A., 'Continuity and change in a seventeenth-century Scottish farming community', Agric. Hist. Rev., 32 (1984), pp. 159-69.

2.1.9 OFFICIAL PAPERS: Parliamentary Papers are always abbreviated as P.P. Give full title, year of publication, volume number. Thus:

Select Committee on Manufactures, Commerce, and Shipping (P.P. 1833, Vl).

Accounts and Papers (P.P. 1890, XLV), Dockyard expense accounts, 1888-9. The command paper number is not required.

2.1.10 THESES: no italics (i.e. not underlined in the typescript)-for titles of unpublished theses:

Vamplew, W., 'Railways and the transformation of the Scottish economy' (unpub. Ph.D. thesis, Univ. of Edinburgh, 1969).

2.2. FOOTNOTES

In the footnotes, books, articles, essays, theses, and ofmcial publications should be referred to in abbreviated form, with the precise page reference if applicable. IF THE REFERENCE IS TO THE WHOLE ARTICLE, OR TO A BOOK IN GENERAL, NO PAGINATION SHOULD BE PROVIDED. If a work is cited in more than one consecutive footnote, use 'ibid.', unless the previous note contains more than one source. When more than one work by the same author is cited in a footnote, use 'idem'. 'Op.cit.' and 'loc.cit.' should not be used.

Some examples are given below:

2.2.1 BOOKS:

Cunningham, Alien immigrants, pp. 4-6.
Halevy, History of the English people, II, pp. 64-7.
Supple, Royal Exchange Assurance, p. 230.
Landes, 'Technological change', p. 382.
Kirby, ed., Feet of fines relating to Wiltshire, p. 19.

2.2.2 ARTICLES:

Whyte and Whyte, 'Continuity and change', p. 163.
Ashworth, 'Economic aspects', p. 503.

2.2.3 OFFICIAL PAPERS

S.C. on Manufactures (P.P. 1833, Vl), Q.456 or QQ.457-8. Where a page reference is used, the continuous pagination for the whole volume and NOT the pagination for the individual report must be given.
Hansard (Commons), 4th ser., XXXVI, 22 Aug. 1896, cols. 641-2.
H. of C. Journals, LXXX (1824), p. 110.
H. of L. journals, LXX (1824), 18 June.

2.2.4 THESES:

Vamplew, 'Railways', pp. 10-9.

Newspapers and manuscripts will NOT appear in the consolidated list. The following conventions should be followed:

2.2.5 NEWSPAPERS: omit the definite article in newspaper titles, with the traditional exception of The Times. Note the sequence of title of newspaper and day, month, and year of publication:

'The officious official' in Morning Post, 15 Sept. 1921.
Report in The Times, 30 Oct. 1918, p. 11, col. 1.
Economist, 11 Dec. 1920, p. 1032.

2.2.6 MANUSCRIPT REFERENCES: the Public Record Office and the British Library are always accorded standardized abbreviations as P.R.O. and B.L. respectively:

P.R.O., King's Remembrancer's Memoranda Roll, EI59/68, m. 78.
B.L., Add. MS 36,042, fo. 2 (plural fos.).

Give titles of other record repositories, and names of collections of papers, in full in first reference (including location where necessary):

Scottish Record Office (hereafter S.R.O.), Airlie Papers, G.D. 16, section 38/82, 5 April 1844.
Compton Papers, kept at the estate office of the Marquess of Northampton, Castle Ashby (hereafer C.A.), bundle 1011, no. 29.
Northampton County Record Office (hereafter N.R.O.), Brudenell of Deene Papers, i.x.37, Peter Morlet to Thomas Lord Brudenell, 27 June 1652.

Note that manuscript is abbreviated to MS not MSS; manuscripts MSS.

3. LITERARY CONVENTIONS

3.1 FIGURES: all figures up to and including nine in words ('six women', 'seven years') and above nine in numbers ('88 feet', '17 weeks') except where a series is given. Thus '8 sheep, 12 horses, and 36 goats'. Use 'eighteenth century' not '18th century'. Use 'l930s' not 'l930's'. Give all percentages in figures, not words. 'Per annum' and 'per cent' should be used in text; 'p.a.' and '%' should be used in tables and footnotes. Avoid numbers of more than five figures in the text whenever possible: '5 5 million' rather than '5,500,000', '5-5m.', or 'five and a half million'. In both text and tables use commas for numbers with four or more figures. Thus 879, but 3,602, 15,827. Fractions with hyphens: 'two-thirds'.

3.2 YEARS: use 1801-4 when from 1801 to 1804 is meant; use 1801/ 2 when a calendar year (or part thereof) occurring over two adjacent years is meant. Use 1852-72, not 1852-1872. In general, when referring to numbers in sequence, avoid unnecessary repetition: thus 10-3, 20-6, 101-7, 151-7.

3.3 DATES: wherever possible, give dates in full, as '30 January 1938'. In footnotes, abbreviate the months from August to February inclusive, with full stops.

3.4 QUOTATIONS: use single quotation marks ''. For quotations within quotations, use double quotation marks, as '. . .". . ."'. . .'. When a sentence ends with a quotation, the full stop should be included in the quotation marks when a whole sentence is quoted; when a phrase is quoted, the full stop should be outside the quotation marks. In general follow HART'S RULES. Quotations of five lines of type (more than c.55 words) should be broken off from the text and should not be enclosed by quotation marks.

3.5 ITALIC AND ROMAN: commonly used abbreviations should be in roman type, thus: ibid., et al., i.e., e.g. Foreign words and phrases, when used, should be in italics (i.e. underlined in the typescript), as should names of journals, newspapers, and books. Thus passim, Wirtschaftswunder, The Times.

3.6 PUNCTUATION: insert a comma before 'and' in a sequence of three or more items: 'red, white, and blue' NOT 'red, white and blue'.

3.7 ALTERNATIVES: where there is an alternative follow the practice of HART'S RULES. Use 'f., ff.' not 'sq., sqq.'. Number should be abbreviated to 'no.' not 'nr.'. In footnotes, part should be abbreviated to 'pt.', appendix to 'app.', chapter to 'ch.', figure to 'fig.', table to 'tab.', column to 'col.'. Use 'above' and 'below' in footnote references, not 'supra' and 'infra'.

3.8 CAPITALS: use initial lower case for geographical divisions, as opposed to political ones ('eastern Europe', 'south Wales', 'north-western England', but 'North Dakota'); initial lower case when referring to titled people generally, but capitals when referring to one specific individual by title ('kings, dukes, mayors' but 'the King of England, the fifth Duke of Norfolk, the Mayor of Wandsworth'); similarly initial capitals for 'Act' or 'Bill' when a specific measure is referred to, but otherwise lower case. Currencies, e.g. dollars, francs, should be lower case.

3.9 HYPHENS: when two words are used adjectivally (provided one of the two is not an adverb) the two words should be hyphenated; thus: 'working-class housing', 'nineteenth-century urbanization', 'short-term change', but 'very rapid municipalization', 'newly independent country'. In general, hyphens should be used as sparingly as possible; the following compound words are now deemed not to need a hyphen: 'prewar', 'interwar', 'postwar', 'macroeconomic'.

3.10 ABBREVIATIONS: well-known abbreviations should be used when appropriate. Thus give 'Professor' as 'Prof.', 'Company' as 'Co.', and 'Limited' as 'Ltd.'. Abbreviated words should be followed by a full stop, with the exception of abbreviations in very common use; thus: 'jr.', 'ed.' but 'Dr.', 'Mr.', and 'Mrs.'. Use '&' in titles of firms, not 'and'. Full stops are not needed in commonly used abbreviations such as UK, GDP, etc., or in acronyms, but should be used, for example, in D.C., N.U.M.

3.11 USE OF ACADEMIC TITLES: avoid including academic titles in references to individual scholars; the surname alone will normally suffice.

ECONOMIC HISTORY REVIEW

ARTICLES WHICH RELY HEAVILY ON UNPUBLISHED DISCUSSION OR RESEARCH PAPERS AND MAKE EXTENSIVE REFERENCE TO THEM WILL NOT NORMALLY BE ACCEPTED FOR PUBLICATION.

4. ABBREVIATION OF JOURNAL TITLES

The following abbreviations should be used for journal titles:

Agricultural History Review	Agric. Hist. Rev.
American Historical Review	Amer. Hist. Rev
Bulletin of the Institute of Historical Research	Bull. Inst. Hist. Res.
Bulletin of the Sociey for the Study of Labour History	Bull. Soc. Study Lab. Hist.
Business History	Bus. Hist.
Comparative Studies in Sociey and History	Comp. Stud. Soc. & Hist.
Economic History Review	Econ. Hist. Rev.
English Historical Review	Eng. Hist. Rev.
Economic Journal	Econ. J.
Explorations in Economic History	Exp. Econ. Hist.
Historical Journal	Hist. J.
Historical Research	Hist. Res.
History	Hist.
International Review of Social History	Int. Rev. Soc. Hist.
Journal of Economic History	J. Econ. Hist
Journal of European Economic History	J. Eur. Econ Hist.
Journal of Historical Geography	J. Hist. Geog.
Journal of Medieval History	J. Med. Hist.
Journal of Political Economy	J. Pol. Econ
Journal of Transport History	J. Transp. Hist.
Journal of the Royal Statistical Sociey	J.R.S.S.
Lloyds Bank Review	Lloyds Bank Rev.
Manchester School	Man. School
Medical History	Medic. Hist.
Midland History	Midland Hist.
Northern History	Northern Hist.
Oxford Economic Papers	Oxf. Econ. Pap.
Past and Present	P. & P.
Quarterly Journal of Economics	Qu. J. Econ.
Social History	Soc. Hist.
Scottish Journal of Political Economy	Scot. J. Pol. Econ.
Scandinavian Economic History Review	Scand. Econ. Hist. Rev.
Textile History	Text. Hist.
Transactions of the Royal Historical Sociey	Trans. Roy. Hist. Soc.
Transactions of the Historic Sociey of Cheshire	Trans. Hist Soc. Lancs. & Chesh.
Victorian Studies	Vict. Stud.
Welsh History Review	Welsh Hist. Rev.
Yorkshire Bulletin	Yorks. Bull.

For other titles, follow the above practice.

5. TABLE DESIGN

Table 7. Capital stock utilization

	Based on capital-output ratio		Based on capital-labour ratio [a]		
	in industry	in industry plus trade			
	(1)	(2)	(3)	(4)	(5)
1925	75[b]	80.9[b]	91.4	89.9	83.6
1926	72	72.5	79.8	79.1	75.2
1927	89	87.8	89.9	89.5	87.4
1928	86	85.2		89.6	
1929	86	84.5		88.0	
1930	74	76.5		76.5	

Notes: col. 3 assumes that the capital-labour ratio was constant 1925-8; col. 4 that it was increasing at o.5% p.a.; col. 5 that it was increasing at 3%p.a.
  a defined as percentage of normal capital stock utilization.
  b pardy based on estimated data.

Sources: col. 1, Krengel, Anlagevermogen, p. 87; col. 2, Hoffman, Wachstum, p. 245, cols. 3-5, for 1925-7, Balderston, 'German economy', app. v, tab. C; col. 4, for 1928-30, Mester, Eine Zeitreihe, p. 81.

August 1992

[a,b used above in table and notes should be in superscript.]

CO-EDITOR: JOHN HATCHER
              CORPUS CHRISTI COLLEGE
              CAMBRIDGE
              CB2 1RH

ECONOMIC INQUIRY

ADDRESS FOR SUBMISSION :

FRANK G. WYKOFF, EDITOR
ECONOMIC INQUIRY
POMONA COLLEGE
109 SEAVER NORTH
645 NORTH COLLEGE AVENUE
CLAREMONT, CA 91711-6363
USA
909-621-8303
909-621-8668 (Fax)
E-Mail : CWilliams@POMONA.EDU

Change in Editor's Address
  May Occur in : 07/01/99

CIRCULATION DATA :

Reader : Academic

Frequency of Issue : Quarterly

Copies Per Issue : 3001-4000

Subscription Price : 35.00 US$

Sponsorship : Professional Assoc.

PUBLICATION GUIDELINES :

Manuscript Length : 40 Typed Pgs. Max.

Copies Required : Four

Computer Submission : No

Format : N/A

Fees to Review : 155.00 US$
  WEA Member 100.00 US$

REVIEW INFORMATION :

Type of Review : Blind Review

No. of External Reviewers : Two

No. of In House Reviewers : Zero

Acceptance Rate : 6-10%

Time To Review : 4-6 months

Reviewer's Comments : Yes

Fees to Publish : 0.00 US$

Invited Articles : 5% or less

MANUSCRIPT TOPICS : COST ACCOUNTING; ECONOMETRICS; ECONOMIC HISTORY;
   INTERNATIONAL & ECONOMIC DEVELOPMENT; INTERNATIONAL FINANCE;
   PUBLIC POLICY ECONOMICS; ALL ASPECTS OF ECONOMICS

PUBLICATION GUIDELINES : Chicago Manual of Style

MANUSCRIPT GUIDELINES/COMMENTS :

ECONOMIC INQUIRY believes that published articles must be readable. The
inclusion of Donald McCloskey's paper "Economical Writing" as lead article in
the April 1985 issue indicates our commitment to this end. Perusing this
article prior to preparing your final draft would be time well spent.

Refer to the CHICAGO MANUAL OF STYLE, University of Chicago Press, for
questions not answered in this style guide. The Manual also contains useful
information on mathematical style. If you have any specific questions call Ms.
Carolyn Williams, ECONOMIC INQUIRY, (909) 621-8303.

I.   COMPUTER PROCESSING
Disk and three hard copies are required for all accepted manuscripts. Use IBM
compatible Microsoft Word or WordPerfect. Indicate which software program you
have used and whether it is for DOS or Windows. Text the disk to be sure the
file has been copied.

ECONOMIC INQUIRY

II. TITLE PAGE

A. Title. Typed in upper and lower case letters, centered.

B. Author's name. Upper and lower case.

C. Asterisk. Following the last author's name (see footnote section VIII, page 8).

D. Running heads. Left running head is always ECONOMIC INQUIRY. Author supplies right running head. It consists of author's last name in upper case and a shortened title in upper case LIMITED TO 50 CHARACTERS. Three authors should separate names by a comma and an ampersand (&). More than three authors use first author's surname, followed by et al. See example below for two authors.

Example of title page:

Compensating Wage Differentials for Mandatory Overtime
Ronald G. Ehrenburg
and
Paul L. Schuman*
RRH: EHRENBURG & SCHUMAN: WAGE DIFFERENTIALS

III. ABSTRACT

A. EI requires an abstract of all articles published except speeches, addresses and comments.

B. Work hard on your abstract. The reader's decision to tackle your article will often be based on its contents. Give a clear idea of the main conclusion of the article, the methods employed and a clear indication of the line of reasoning. The opening sentence should indicate the major conclusion of the article.

C. Abstracts must not contain equations, diagrams, or footnotes.

D. Abstracts are limited to 100 words. NO EXCEPTIONS.

E. Put JOURNAL OF ECONOMIC LITERATURE categories to which paper belongs in upper right corner of abstract page. If there is more than one category, list the principal one first. Center the title below using upper and lower case.

F. Put names, affiliation and location in upper and lower case flush left below the abstract.

IV. TEXT

A. Double space. Never use both sides of the paper. Use 8 1/2 x 11-inch paper, Times Roman 12 point type or the equivalent, one-inch margins all around making a 6.5-inch maximum line length and 27 lines of type per double-spaced page. Paper is not to exceed 45 pages.

B. Dividing the manuscript into sections. Number section headings with Roman numerals in upper case, centered. Subheadings are upper and lower case and underlined, flush left. Further subheadings are flush left, underlined, upper and lower case, and followed by a period. The text then begins on the same line, immediately following the subheading.

ECONOMIC INQUIRY

Example of text layout

I. INTRODUCTION

Text, text, text, ... text, text, text, text, text, text, text.

II. EXCHANGE RESERVE ACTION

Seasonal Opportunity [underlined]

Text, text, text, ... text, text, text, text, text, text, text.

Core Male Unemployment Rate [underlined]. This subject of study throughout is a . . . text, text, text, text, text.

C. Location of figures and tables. See section VI for instructions. Indicate the position of the figures and tables in the text by a hand-written note in the margin.

D. Footnote citations in the text
  1. Show the footnote citations within the text in this manner:
        Note the effects of this recent policy on the price of tea in China.

  2. Provide footnotes in a separate listing at the back of the paper, following the references. Do not place them at the bottom of text pages.

  3. Footnotes in figures and tables. Do not use numbers to identify, as they might appear to be exponents and would probably be out of order with the numerical sequence of numbers in the text. Figures and tables are often not placed exactly where the author indicates. We suggest you use a,b,c, or *,**,***. Be sure that sources cited on tables are included in your list of references.

  4. Footnotes in appendices. Number them consecutively with the numbers in the text. Many appendices are simply tables. In that case, use the instructions for table footnotes.

F. Reference citations
Refer in the text to listed references by author with date and, if necessary, page numbers, placed in brackets. Separate year references to different articles within brackets by semicolons. A comma indicates that the next number is a page number. If a reference comes at the end of a sentence, the period follows the bracket. List in the reference list and cite every publication or unpublished manuscript mentioned.

    Sample citation
        Adams [1980a, 43-49, 1980b, 962-69] has examined this issue in recent publications.

ECONOMIC INQUIRY prefers that cited author's name not be placed inside the brackets in text. Please try to reword your sentence so that the author's name can be gracefully worked into the text; instead of "(see Adams [1976] and Jones [1920])" say "as in Adams [1976] and Jones [1920]." A footnote is another way to handle this, especially when the number of references is large. Initials of cited authors may be omitted if this introduces no ambiguity.

ECONOMIC INQUIRY

V. MATHEMATICS

A. Math symbols

1. Variables. Underline variables so that the typesetter knows that they should be italicized. Underline in blue ink. Only exception, variables in equations set apart from the text do not have to be blue-lined. Do not use an italic typeface to indicate variables in the manuscript.

2. Please differentiate between math symbols in the text and mere abbreviations that are not math symbols. Note in the margin any characters that are not completely clear without reading the paper. For example, identify:
   a. upper vs. lower-case theta and pi
   b. upper vs. lower-case subscripts and superscripts
   c. upper and lower case o (oh) vs. zero
   d. one vs. "ell" (l)
   e. cap sigma and cap chi vs. summation and product signs
   f. any handwritten characters

3. Use English and avoid computerese in text. Example: "The change in personal income, occasioned by the fall in the taxes..." If you feel there may be confusion, put variables in parentheses after each word describing the variable. Example: "The relationship of primary exports (E) to domestic prices (P) and foreign prices (P)..."

B. Equations

1. EI requires that equations be written in linear style, using a solidus (/) to denote fractions. Examples can be found in the CHICAGO MANUAL OF STYLE. Undesirable form of equation:

$$\ln K_t' = \delta_K \frac{\ln\beta_0^K + \beta_3^K[\ln\frac{1}{0}(1-b-c)]}{1+\beta_3^K} + \frac{\delta_K\beta_1^K}{1+\beta_3^K}\ln P_L$$

This equation should be done like this:

$$\ln K_t' = \delta_K \{\ln\beta_0^K + \beta_3^K[\ln 1/0(1-b-c)]\}/(1+\beta_3^K)$$
$$+ [\delta_K\beta_1^K/(1+\beta_3^K)]\ln P_L$$

2. Note enclosure rules used above, from the Chicago Manual, 13th edition, page 357:

$$\left\{\left[\left(\{[()]\}\right)\right]\right\}$$

C. Mathematical notation (Refer to THE CHICAGO MANUAL OF STYLE)

These rules reduce printing costs and delays.

1. Avoid unusual symbols where common ones will do (e.g., use A' rather than $\tilde{A}$). Distinguishing marks after symbols rather than above them aids typesetting (e.g., B* rather than $\hat{B}$).

2. Avoid notation which requires setting in small fonts (e.g., where both subscripts and superscripts are used). Avoid the $e^{f(x)}$ form where f(x) is complicated; exp [f(x)] reduces small font setting. Avoid the $\partial^2 f(x,y)/\partial x\partial y$ notation for partial derivatives where f_{xy} will serve without ambiguity.

3. Minimize mathematical footnotes; we prefer lemmas in the text or mathematical appendices preferable.

4. Try to substitute a symbol for a frequently used expression with subscripts (which require another fraction of a line below); e.g.,   use ω instead of $\omega = (1 - \varepsilon_h - \varepsilon_f)$.

5. Use special care in distinguishing between symbols. Take care with w and , v and , and numbers 0 and 1 and letters O and l where the same typed symbol is used.

6. Avoid repeated use of time or sectorial subscripts and supescripts where these can be suppressed without ambiguity; avoid repeated listing of the arguments of functions where these can be omitted without confusion.

7. Check type, size, and position of the brackets carefully.

V.   TABLES AND FIGURES

A. Tables
    1. EI will typeset your tables, but they must be neat and legible.
    2. Submit original and one of each table on separate sheets of paper.
    3. Place Table I, Table II, etc., centered above the table. Do not use all upper case for titles.
    4. Place tables at the back of the manuscript.
    5. Only camera ready art or laser output orignals are accepted.
    6. Tables must contain no vertical lines, and a minimum horizontal lines.
    7. For footnotes in tables, see section IV.
    8. Indicate placement of tables by hand-written notes in the margins of the text.
    9. TABLES MUST BE SUBMITTED ERROR FREE! This is the most expensive type of alteration. You will be billed for your errors.
   10. Tables should use English and not computerese; e.g., write Personal Income, not PersInc.

B. Figures and Diagrams
    1. Place each figure or diagram on a separate sheet.
    2. Each figure or diagram must be camera-ready original artwork of professional quality or laser output; 5 x 8 inches for full page and 5 x 4 inches for a half page.
    3. Center Figure number (Figure 1, Figure 2, etc.) above each figure. Figures are given Arabic numbers. Do not abbreviate "Fig."
    4. A further title is optional, but do not use all upper case letters.
5. Indicate placement of each figure or diagram in the margin of the text.

VI. REFERENCES

A. Place the refereoce sheet immediately following the text.
B. List only those references which are actually cited in the text or footnotes. The EI reference section is not a bibliography.
C. Double-space references alphabetically, author's last name first.
D. First line is flush left. Indent spaces on each line after the first of a reference.
E. In the event of multiple articles by the same author, arrange them chronologically, oldest first.

F. Book listing. Author's Name. Title. Place of publication: Name of publisher, year of publication. See examples 4-8 below.
G. Article listing. Author's Name. Title. Name of journal, month and year of publication, pages of the article. See example 1 below. Volume and number of the journal are not necessary unless the journal provides no month or season of publication. In such a case, specify journal title, comma, volume numberr with issue number in parentheses after it, comma, year, comma, pages. See example 2 below.
H. Unpublished works. See example 10 below.
K. Unauthored work. List by publishing agency and insert alphabetically in references.

REFERENCES

(Ex. 1)   Billings, Bradley B. and Wanda J. D. Watkins. "The Relative Quality of Economics Journals.' Western Economic Journal, December 1972, 467-69.
(Ex. 2)   Bungus, Jane. "Revealed Preference among Economists." Journal Title 39(4), 1923, 162-73. (Use this form only if month or season is not available.)
(Ex. 3)   California Coastal Commission. Offshore Drilling Rights. Sacramento, 1980.
(Ex. 4)   Doe, Doris and Calvin Coauthor. Title of Book. Boston: Brown and Company, 1978.
(Ex. 5)   Doe, Doris, ed. Book She Edited. Boston: Brown and Company, 1976.
(Ex. 6)   Flamingo, James. Flamingo's Collected Works, edited by Jevons Marshall. Boston: etc....
(Ex. 7)   Gregious, Marvin. His Book in a Series, Title of Series. Boston: etc....
(Ex. 8)   _____. His Work in a Later Edition, 2nd. ed. Boston: etc....
(Ex. 9)   Gregious, Marvin and Sam Strange. "Chapter in a Cooperative Work," in Title of Work, edited by M. Sams. Boston: Brown and Company, 1979, 26-40.
(Ex. 10)   Boy, Sue. "Her Unpublished Work." Ph.D. dissertation (or Photocopy or Working paper), University of Oklahoma, 1972.
(Ex. 11)   New York Times. "Man Bites Dog," 25 July 1981, Sec.A, p.6.
(Ex. 12)   Blonder, Alice. "Interest Rates Now and Then." National Bureau of Economic Research Working Paper No. 1429, 1983. (Or Brookings Papers on Economic Activity 2, 1979.)

VII. FOOTNOTE PAGE AT END OF TEXT

A. Place the footnote sheet, or sheets, at the back of paper, after the references.
B. Author asterisk foonote should be first (including author's title or position, institutional affiliation and any acknowledgements). DO NOT PLACE ON TITLE PAGE.
C. DOUBLE SPACE ALL FOOTNOTES.
D. Sample footnotes.
    * Assistant Professor, University of the Yukon, and Professor, Albatross College. We wish to thank Harry Marshall and Rudolpho Blanco for helpful discussions. Two anonymous referees made useful suggestions.
    1. Sinclair [1980] surveys empirical studies of the demand for electric power.

VIII. MISCELLANEOUS
A. Spelling and hyphenation. Refer to WEBSTER'S NEW COLLEGIATE DICTIONARY and
   THE CHICAGO MANUAL OF STYLE.
   B. EI preferences:

	Don't Use
75 percent	seventy five percent, 75%
1920s	1920's
June 1930	June, 1930
21 June 1930	June 21, 1930
Hicks's	Hicks'
Mass.	MA., Massachusetts

Sample of page numbers:

50-54	50-4
169-70	169-170
100-103	100-03
101-4	101-04
109-17	109-117
1049-75	1049-1075

FINAL CHECK LIST

1. Are the figures, if any, laser quality or professionally drawn? Have you
   included the original and 2 copies of each?
2. Is every footnote citation in the text found in the footnote list?
3. Is every reference listed in the reference list at the back of the paper
   cited somewhere in the text or footnotes?
4. Are all references complete? (author's names, page #'s, dates, etc.)
5. Are ALL mathematical formulas in LINEAR style? Absolutely no exceptions!!!
6. Are the footnotes in a separate file from the text?
7. Have all requirements on page 2 been met?

ECONOMIC JOURNAL

ADDRESS FOR SUBMISSION :

M. WICKENS, MANAGING EDITOR
ECONOMIC JOURNAL
UNIVERSITY OF YORK
DEPARTMENT OF ECON. & RELATED STUDIES
HESLINGTON, YORK, YO1 5DD
UK
44 1904 433575
44 1904 433759 (Fax)

Change in Editor's Address
  May Occur in : 12/31/99

CIRCULATION DATA :

Reader : Academic

Frequency of Issue : 6 Times/Year

Copies Per Issue : 5001-10,000

Subscription Price : 76.00 US$
  Under 30 years : 38.00 US$

Sponsorship : Professional Assoc.

PUBLICATION GUIDELINES :

Manuscript Length : 16-20

Copies Required : Four

Computer Submission : No

Format : N/A

Fees to Review : 0.00 US$
  Member/Royal Eco.Soc 0.00 US$
  Author must join Soc 0.00 US$

REVIEW INFORMATION :

Type of Review : Editorial Review

No. of External Reviewers : Two

No. of In House Reviewers : Zero

Acceptance Rate : 6-10%

Time To Review : 2-3 months

Reviewer's Comments : Yes

Fees to Publish : 0.00 US$

Invited Articles : 5% or less

MANUSCRIPT TOPICS : ACCOUNTING INFORMATION SYSTEMS; ECONOMETRICS;
  INTERNATIONAL & ECONOMIC DEVELOPMENT; PUBLIC POLICY ECONOMICS

PUBLICATION GUIDELINES :

MANUSCRIPT GUIDELINES/COMMENTS :

1. The ECONOMIC JOURNAL is uniquely pre-eminent as a general economics
journal serving the whole of the international community of economists. It is
the official journal of the Royal Economic Society, available free to
members, with a long and distinguished history and a proud record of
fostering communication amongst economists. It publishes articles, notes,
book reviews and book notes across the broad spectrum of economics, covering
both theoretical and empirical aspects, and it aims to encourage the
dissemination of new ideas and new results across specialist divisions both
within economics and between economics and other disciplines.

2. In order to make the reading and typesetting of the ECONOMIC JOURNAL as
straightforward as possible, we have evolved a common house style which we
apply to all articles and notes. Our main general requirements are set out in
the "Notes to Contributors" which you will find on the inside of the back
cover of any recent issue of the JOURNAL. Our preferred style is set out in
greater detail in the checklist below -- if this leaves you in any doubt,
please refer to recent issues of the JOURNAL or contact the Managing Editor.

ECONOMIC JOURNAL

3. We would like to emphasize that articles should not, in general, exceed fifteen JOURNAL pages (approximately 7,500 words), and in view of the extreme competition for space, the Editor will not normally consider for publication papers of more than twenty JOURNAL pages (approximately 10,000 words).

4. Please send three copies of your typescript.

5. Sections:
   1. should be consecutively numbered in Roman numerals;
   2. should preferably have short titles;
   3. The first few paragraphs by way of introduction do not usually require any section number or title;
   4. The first level of sub-section is displayed in italics beginning at the left-hand side of the line. If "numbering" is required, please use letters;
   5. The second level of sub-section is in italics but not displayed. (The sub-section will follow on the same line as the title.) If numbering is required, use (i), (ii), etc.

6. Tables:
   1. should have titles (short);
   2. should be consecutively numbered, 1, 2, 3, etc.;
   3. should not require vertical lines.

7. Figures:
   1. should be abbreviated as "fig." in both headings and the text;
   2. should be very clear and accurate - they will be copied directly AND REDUCED;
   3. Hand-written instructions or clarifications should not be written on the fig. itself, but on a copy;
   4. should have titles (short);
   5. should be numbered consecutively, 1, 2, 3, - etc.

8. Mathematics:
   1. Numbers less than 1 but great than -1 must have 0 before the decimal point;
   2. Equations should be numbered in a single sequence (1), (2), on the right-hand side of the page;
   3. Algebra should include punctuation;
   4. Make sure expressions are correctly aligned, especially fractions, "=", subscripts and superscripts; please do not cramp algebra;
   5. The order of precedence of brackets is $(\{[(\ldots)]\})$ and so on;
   6. If matrix algebra is employed, please use capitals for matrices, lower case for vectors and Greek lower case for scalars (matrices and vectors will be denoted in bold and scalars in italic). Transposition is denoted by prime "A";
   7. Use obliques where convenient in fractions.

9. English Usage:
   1. English spelling, labour, specialisation, etc. should be used;
   2. While it is impossible to make any comment on style, please try to avoid such examples as hyphens instead of adjectives, conjunctions as the first word in sentences, split infinitives, etc.

ECONOMIC JOURNAL

10. References:
    1. In the text these should be Brown (1964), (Brown, 1964) or Brown (1964;1965). The title, etc., of the article/book should occur in a list of references;
    2. The list of references should be in alphabetical order of author's name and in chronological order for each author. For subsequent publications of the same author, use instead of repeating his name;
    3. The form of the entries in the list should be:

For Books
Name, Initials. (date), Title in italics with liberal use of capital letters but no quotation marks. Place of publication: Publisher.

For Articles
Name, Initials, (date). Title in Roman with single quotes and no capitals after the first except for proper nouns'. Title of journal in full italics except the ECONOMIC JOURNAL in capitals, vol. no., (month of quarter) pp. abcd-3.

11. Multiple authors names in full in the list of references, e.g. Name, A., Name, B. and Name, C., but for more than two authors use Name, A. et al. (date) in the text.

An example of the JOURNAL system is given below:

REFERENCES

Amacher, R., Tollison, R. and Willett, T. (1975). 'Budget size in a democracy: a review of the arguments'. Public Finance Quarterly, vol. 3, pp. 99-120.

Brennan, G. and McGuire, T. (1975). 'Optimal policy choice under uncertainty'. Journal of Public Economics, vol. 4 (February), pp. 205-9.

Bucanan, J., Tollison, R. and Tullock, G. (1980). Toward a Theory of the Rent-Seeking Society. College Station, Texas: A & M Presss.

_____ and Tullock, G. (1962). The Calculus of Consent. Ann Arbor: University of Michigan Press.

Cowling, K. and Mueller, D. (1978). 'The social costs of monopoly power'. ECONOMIC JOURNAL   (December) vol. 88, pp. 727-48.

Downs, A. (1960). 'Why the government is too small in a democracy'. World Politics, vol. 13, pp. 541-63.

Harberger, A. (1954). 'Monopoly and resource allocation'. American Economic Review, vol. 44 (May), pp. 77-87.

_____ (1971). 'Three basic postulates for applied welfare economics: an interpretive essay'. Journal of Economic Literature (September), vol. 9, no. 3, pp. 785-97.

Ladd, H. and Tideman, N. (1981). Tax and Expenditure Limitations. Washington: Urban Institute Press.

Musgrave, R. (1981). 'Leviathan cometh -- or does he?' In Ladd and Tideman (1981), pp. 77-117.

Niskanen,W.(1971). Bureaucracy and Representative Government. Chicago: Aldine Press.

Worcester, D. (1973). 'New estimates of the welfare losses due to monopoly'. Southern Economic Journal, vol. 40 (October), pp. 234-45.

12. Footnotes. Please avoid using more than a minimum of footnotes; most can be avoided by either incorporation in the text or judicious use of the list of references.

13. Please pay careful attention to these requirements, particularly those relating to the use of mathematics and the ECONOMIC JOURNAL system for references and footnotes. ARTICLES WHICH HAVE BEEN ACCEPTED FOR PUBLICATION BUT DO NOT COMPLY WITH THESE REQUIREMENTS WILL HAVE TO BE RETURNED TO AUTHORS FOR CORRECTION BEFORE THEY CAN BE SENT TO THE PRINTERS.

ECONOMIC MODELLING

ADDRESS FOR SUBMISSION :

PROF.SEAN HOLLY,EDITOR
ECONOMIC MODELLING
UNIVERSITY OF CAMBRIDGE
DEPT. OF APPLIED ECONOMICS
CAMBRIDGE, CB3 9DE
UK
+44-1223-335251
+44-1223-335299 (Fax)
E-Mail : s.holly@econ.cam.ac.uk

CIRCULATION DATA :

Reader : Academic

Frequency of Issue : Quarterly

Copies Per Issue : Less than 1000

Subscription Price : 200.00 U.K.$
  EUROPE : 200.00 U.K.$
  REST OF WORLD : 215.00 U.K.$

Sponsorship : Profit Oriented Corp.

PUBLICATION GUIDELINES :

Manuscript Length : MORE THAN 20
Copies Required : Three
Computer Submission : No
Format : N/A
Fees to Review : 0.00 US$

REVIEW INFORMATION :

Type of Review : Editorial Review
No. of External Reviewers : Two
No. of In House Reviewers : One
Acceptance Rate : 50 %
Time To Review : 2-3 months
Reviewer's Comments : Yes
Fees to Publish : 0.00 US$
Invited Articles :

MANUSCRIPT TOPICS : CAPITAL BUDGETING; ECONOMETRICS;
   INTERNATIONAL & ECONOMIC DEVELOPMENT; INTERNATIONAL FINANCE;
   PORTFOLIO & SECURITY ANALYSIS; PUBLIC POLICY ECONOMICS

PUBLICATION GUIDELINES :

MANUSCRIPT GUIDELINES/COMMENTS :

1. Manuscripts must be submitted in triplicate to Prof.Sean Holly,editor.
Submission of a manuscript is held to imply that it is original work, that a
significant part of it has not already been published, and that it is not
being submitted elsewhere. Translated material, which has not been published
in English, will also be considered. If a figure, table, or part of a text
from previously published work is included, the author should obtain written
permission to reproduce from the copyright holder. All papers will be
published in English and should be submitted in that language. The editors
reserve the right to edit or otherwise alter all contributions, but authors
will receive a proof for approval before publication.

2. Manuscripts should be typed in journal style, double-spaced (including
footnotes and references) with wide margins, on one side only of good quality
paper (preferably A4 size).

3. Manuscripts should be arranged in the following order of presentation:
First sheet: Title, subtitle (if any), author's name, affiliation, full postal
address and telephone number. Respective affiliations and addresses of

co-authors should be clearly indicated.
Second sheet: A self-contained abstract of up to 100 words, three keywords, acknowledgements (if any), article title abbreviated appropriately for use as a running headline.

Subsequent sheets: Main body of text: List of references, appendixes, tables (on separate sheets), footnotes (numbered consecutively), captions to illustrations (on a separate sheet), illustrations. The text should be organized under appropriate section headings which, ideally, should not be more than 600 words apart.

4. Authors are urged to write as concisely as possible, but not at the expense of clarity. The main title of the article should be kept short, up to 40 characters including spaces, but may be accompanied by a subtitle if further clarification is desired. Descriptive or explanatory passages, necessary as information but which tend to break the flow of the main text should be put into footnotes or appendixes. Sl units should be used throughout with other units in parentheses if required.

5. Particular care should be taken in identifying symbols used in equations. Expressions should be lined up accurately and subscripts and superscripts properly located. Greek letters and unusual symbols should be identified in the margin. Distinction should be made between the letter l, the numeral 1 and prime between the letter o and zero, and between upper and lower case letters. Important equations should be identified by consecutive Arabic numbers in parentheses at the right hand side of the column. Matrices should be constructed so that they will fit into the width of the printed column.

6. Footnotes should be typed double spaced and grouped together at the end of the manuscript. They should be designated in the text by superscript numerals in continuous sequence.

7. All references should be typed double spaced, alphabetically by author, at the end of the main text, numbered consecutively in Arabic numerals. They should follow journal style, e.g. for journals:

1.   Richard Stone. "A Simple Growth Process Tending to Stationarity". The Economic Journal, Vol 90, No 359, September 1980, pp. 593-97.

or for books:
2.   L.F. Pearce. "The Southampton Econometric Model of the UK and Its Trading Partners" in K. Hilton and D.F. Heathfield, eds. The Econometric Study of the United Kingdom, Macmillan, London, 1970.

Journal titles should be given in full.

References should be quoted in the text or in footnotes by giving the author's name, followed by the reference number within square brackets, and page numbers if relevant.

8. Tables should be numbered consecutively in Arabic numerals and given a suitable caption. Notes and references within tables should be included with the tables, separately from the main text. Notes should be referred to by superscript letters. All tables columns should have an explanatory heading. Tables should no repeat the data available elsewhere in the article, e.g. in

an illustration.

9. All graphs, diagrams, and other drawings should be referred to as figures, which should be numbered consecutively in Arabic numerals and placed on separate sheets at the end of the manuscript. Their position should be indicated in the text. All illustrations must have captions, which should be typed on a separate sheet.

10. Articles may be published more quickly if illustrations are supplied to the required standards. However, authors should not be deterred from submitting articles because their illustrations do not meet the required standards, as they can be redrawn in our studio.

11. Illustrations should be drawn in black ink on tracing cloth or paper. For lettering, Standard graph or similar stencils should be used (template size nos. 203/3.5 and 203/2.5) using the appropriate pen sizes. Lower case (small) letters should be used throughout, with initial capital letter for the first word only. If suitable stencils are not available, lettering should be drawn in soft pencil only and left for our studio to insert in ink.

12. Illustrations should be drawn to either 160 or 340 mm width, including lettering. The maximum height at drawn size should not exceed 440 mm.

13. As all illustrations will be photographically reduced in size, lines must be drawn proportionally thicker and symbols larger than required in the printed version. Preferably, the axes of graphs should be drawn with a No. 0.3 rotring or similar pen and the curves with pen no. 0.5. Two photocopies of each drawing should be supplied in addition to the originals and the lettering could be printed in ink on these copies. Authors are asked to use a selection of the following symbols on graphs, since these are already available to the printer: x + △ □ ○ ▽ ■ ● ▲ ▼

14. Authors should minimize the amount of descriptive matter on graphs and drawings to refer to curves, points, etc., by their symbols and to place descriptive matter in the caption. Scale grids should not be used in graphs unless required for actual measurements.

15. Before publication authors are requested to assign copyright to Heinemann. This allows Heinemann to sanction reprints and photocopies and to authorize the reprint complete issues of volumes according to demand. Authors' traditional rights will not be jeopardized by assigning copyright in this manner, as they will retain the right to re-use and a veto over third-party publication. The appropriate copyright transfer form will be sent to authors when their paper has been approved for publication.

16. Authors are responsible for ensuring that all manuscripts (whether original or revised) are accurately typed before final submission. One set of proofs will be sent to authors before publication, which should be returned PROMPTLY (by Express Air Mail if outside UK). The publishers reserve the right to charge for any changes made at the proof stage (other than printers errors) since the insertion or deletion of a single word may necessitate the resetting of whole paragraphs.

17. Fifty offprints of each paper will be provided free of charge. Further offprints in minimum quantities of 100 can be purchased from the publisher.

ECONOMIC PLANNING - JOURNAL FOR AGRICULTURAL AND RELATED INDUSTRIES

ADDRESS FOR SUBMISSION :

DR. PETER HARSANY, EDITOR
ECONOMIC PLANNING - JOURNAL FOR
  AGRICULTURAL AND RELATED INDUSTRIES
ACADEMIC PUBLISHING CO.
P.O. BOX 145
MOUNT ROYAL, GNE, H3P 3B9
CANADA
514-738-5255

CIRCULATION DATA :

Reader : Academic

Frequency of Issue : Bi-Monthly

Copies Per Issue : 1001-2000

Subscription Price : 17.00 US$

Sponsorship :

PUBLICATION GUIDELINES :

Manuscript Length : 6-10

Copies Required : Two

Computer Submission : No

Format : N/A

Fees to Review : 0.00 US$

REVIEW INFORMATION :

Type of Review : Editorial Review

No. of External Reviewers : Zero

No. of In House Reviewers : Two

Acceptance Rate : 50 %

Time To Review : 2-3 months

Reviewer's Comments : No

Fees to Publish : 0.00 US$

Invited Articles : Over 50%

MANUSCRIPT TOPICS : CAPITAL BUDGETING;
  INTERNATIONAL & ECONOMIC DEVELOPMENT; PUBLIC POLICY ECONOMICS;
  AGRICULTURAL ECONOMICS; ECONOMIC PLANNING'

PUBLICATION GUIDELINES :

MANUSCRIPT GUIDELINES/COMMENTS :

1. ECONOMIC PLANNING - JOURNAL FOR AGRICULTURAL AND RELATED INDUSTRIES is an international magazine to fill the gap between highly sophisticated, specialized scientific papers and the popular farm publications. Its essential goal is to provide information on:

Theory of economic planning; effects of planning on farm industry; role of manufacturing industries in the adjustment process projected; evaluation of current research projects and institutional activities; information on marketing and general agricultural science.

ECONOMIC RECORD

ADDRESS FOR SUBMISSION :

PROFESSOR R. A. WILLIAMS, EDITOR
ECONOMIC RECORD
UNIVERSITY OF MELBOURNE
DEPARTMENT OF ECONOMICS
MELBOURNE, VIC, 3052
AUSTRALIA
61-3-344-7426
61-3-344-6899 (Fax)
E-Mail : g.isgro@ecomfac.unimelb.edu.au

CIRCULATION DATA :

Reader : Business Persons &
          Academic

Frequency of Issue : Quarterly

Copies Per Issue : 3001-4000

Subscription Price :

Sponsorship : Professional Assoc.

PUBLICATION GUIDELINES :

Manuscript Length : Less than 30

Copies Required : Three

Computer Submission : No

Format : N/A

Fees to Review : 60.00 US$
    Subscribers 0.00 US$

REVIEW INFORMATION :

Type of Review : Editorial Review

No. of External Reviewers : Two

No. of In House Reviewers : Zero

Acceptance Rate : 21-30%

Time To Review : 4-6 months

Reviewer's Comments : Yes

Fees to Publish : 0.00 US$

Invited Articles : 5% or less

MANUSCRIPT TOPICS : COST ACCOUNTING; ECONOMETRICS; ECONOMIC HISTORY;
  INTERNATIONAL & ECONOMIC DEVELOPMENT; PUBLIC POLICY ECONOMICS;
  ECONOMIC/APPLIED ANALYSIS, METHODOLOGY, BANKING

PUBLICATION GUIDELINES :

MANUSCRIPT GUIDELINES/COMMENTS :

1. All submissions should be in the English language, typed on one side of the
page only, doublespaced and with wide margins. Articles should not normally
exceed a total length of 30 pages of A4 or its equivalent and should be
accompanied by an Abstract not exceeding 70 words. Abstracts will appear at
the commencement of published articles and will also be forwarded to the
JOURNAL OF ECONOMIC LITERATURE.

2. Submission of a paper will be held to imply that it is original work, that
a significant part of it has not already been published, and that it is not
being submitted for publication elsewhere.

3. All manuscripts must be sent in triplicate to the Editor.

4. All articles and comments submitted by persons who are not financial
members of the Economic Society of Australia must be accompanied by a
submission fee of $A60. Members submitting articles or comments should
indicate the Branch of which they are a current financial member.

5. Authors are expected to include an introduction indicating the nature of their enquiry, the principal findings and the economic significance of their findings. The introduction and Abstract should be written for the non-specialist. Lengthy mathematical presentations should, whenever possible, be located in appendices. Articles will not usually be published if they are minor variations of existing analyses or of interest only to very small and specialized audiences, or if they are mainly descriptive.

6. Footnotes should be typed double-spaced at the end of the article. Any footnote attached to the main heading should be designated by an asterisk. All other footnotes must be designated by numerals in continuous sequence.

7. A condition of acceptance for publication is that illustrations should be of professional quality and ready for reproduction. if possible they should be suitable for reduction to single column width.

8. Mathematical notation should be as simple as possible. Abbreviating symbols should be used for expressions which occur frequently. Important equations should be identified by consecutive Arabic numbers (in parentheses) at the conclusion of the equation. Expressions should be lined up accurately and superscripts and subscripts properly indicated. Use Greek letters only where they are necessary. Ambiguities should be avoided, for example, between capital and lower- case letters, zero and the letter O, the letters eta and n, the sign for a partial derivative and lower-case delta. Matrices should be constructed so that they will fit into the width of a single column.

Wherever possible fractions should be expressed as a/b and $a/(b + c)$ rather than b and $b + c$.

9. All references should be typed double-spaced, alphabetically by author, at the end of the manuscript. They must include the author's name as it appears on the cited work, the year of publication (in brackets), the title of the work, and (in the case of books) publisher and the place of publication, or (in the case of articles) the periodical, volume number, and pages.

10. References in the text should be made by giving the author's name, followed by the year of publication in brackets and, if relevant, page numbers; e.g. Jones (1968, p. 10). If more than one cited work by an author was published in the one year, these should be referred to in the text and list of references as (1968a), (1968b) etc.

11. If major sections of papers are numbered, the numbering should be in Roman numerals. Figures and tables should be numbered in Arabic numerals.

ECONOMICA

ADDRESS FOR SUBMISSION :

HUGH WILLS, MANAGING EDITOR
ECONOMICA
LONDON SCHOOL OF ECONOMICS
HOUGHTON STREET
LONDON, WC 2A 2AE
ENGLAND
44 0171 9557855
44 0171 2422357 (Fax)

CIRCULATION DATA :

Reader : Academic

Frequency of Issue : Quarterly

Copies Per Issue : 2001-3000

Subscription Price : 32.00 US$
    Institution : 88.00 US$

Sponsorship : University

PUBLICATION GUIDELINES :

Manuscript Length : 16-20

Copies Required : Three

Computer Submission : No

Format : N/A

Fees to Review : 32.00 US$

REVIEW INFORMATION :

Type of Review : N/A

No. of External Reviewers : Three

No. of In House Reviewers : Two

Acceptance Rate : 6-10%

Time To Review : 4-6 months

Reviewer's Comments : Yes

Fees to Publish : 0.00 US$

Invited Articles : 5% or less

MANUSCRIPT TOPICS : ACCOUNTING INFORMATION SYSTEMS; ECONOMETRICS;
    ECONOMIC HISTORY; INTERNATIONAL & ECONOMIC DEVELOPMENT;
    PUBLIC POLICY ECONOMICS

PUBLICATION GUIDELINES :

MANUSCRIPT GUIDELINES/COMMENTS :

1. All papers should be sent to the Managing Editor, Economica Publishing
Office, London School of Economics, Houghton Street, London WC2A 2AE. Two
copies must be submitted; these will normally not be returned. The author will
be notified in due course whether the paper has been accepted for publication,
and whether revision is necessary. Papers which would exceed 20 pages of
ECONOMICA when printed will rarely be accepted without considerable
modification. There is now a submission fee, for details see recent issues of
ECONOMICA.

2. The Editors reserve the right to make minor grammatical and other changes
at any stage before publication. These are sometimes necessary to make the
paper conform to the general style of ECONOMICA and should not be construed as
a criticism of the author's style.

3. The author of a paper accepted for publication will receive a galley proof
for correction. The correction of proofs must NOT be used as an opportunity to
revise the paper. Alterations at proof state are extremely costly, and any new
material should, if the Editors agree to its inclusion, be inserted as an

extra note at the end of the paper.

4. A schedule of charges for offprints is sent to the author with the proofs.

5. Papers published in ECONOMICA become the copyright of the London School of Economics and Political Science, which will always be glad to consider applications for reproduction in full or part elsewhere. Any permission fee charged for reproduction will be shared equally between the School and the author.

6. The submission of a well-prepared typescript which conforms as nearly as possible to the style used by ECONOMICA will greatly aid the ease and speed of publication. A glance at current issues of ECONOMICA will show the style adopted, but the main features are described below. SINCE A CARELESSLY WRITTEN AND PRESENTED PAPER CAN INVOLVE BOTH THE AUTHOR AND THE EDITORS IN MUCH EXTRA WORK AND CAUSE DELAYS, THE EDITORS SUGGEST THAT BEFORE SUBMITTING A PAPER THE AUTHOR SHOULD CHECK THESE POINTS, further details of which are given in subsequent paragraphs:

    a. Is the paper in its final form?
    b. Are the sections, tables, and figures correctly and consecutively
       numbered and provided with suitable headings and legends?
    c. Are the figures adequately prepared for reproduction?
    d. Has the use of footnotes been reduced to a minimum?
    e. Does the list of references correspond to those in the text, and are
       they in the approved form?
    f. Are the mathematical portions presented as clearly as possible for the
       printer?

7. Papers should be typewritten on one side of the paper, with ample margins and double spacing throughout (quotations, references and appendices as well as text). If a paper is divided into sections, the introductory one usually requires no heading or number; subsequent sections should be given Roman numerals, and the section heading should be typed in capitals and centered. Headings of subsections (if any) should be flush with the left margin.

8. Tables should be numbered consecutively with Arabic numerals, and a descriptive heading typed above each table. Tables should, as far as possible, be self-explanatory without reference to the text. Small tables may be typed with the text, but large tables should be typed on separate sheets and the position of each table in the text indicated by an instruction such as-- "Table 2 here". Vertical rules should not be used in tables.

9. Figures should be numbered consecutively with Arabic numerals, and should have an explanatory legend or title. Figures should be submitted on separate sheets. The use of mathematical symbols or complicated notations WITHIN the figure should be avoided. The final preparation of figures for press is done by our own artist, who would appreciate an indication of any special geometric features, such as tangencies or parallelism.

10. ECONOMICA strongly discourages the use of footnotes. It is the Editors' experience that their elimination causes little difficulty and reduces printing costs. Where the use of notes in unavoidable (e.g. in articles on economic history), they will be placed at the end of the article: they should be consecutively numbered throughout, reference numbers in the text being typed superscript, without brackets.

11. Acknowledgments of financial support, technical advice, computational assistance, priorty and so forth should be made in a section headed 'Acknowledgements', placed at the end of the text.

12. References should be set out in alphabetical order of the author's name, in a list at the end of the paper. The list of references should contain only those papers refereed to in the text, and references to unpublished reports or to personal communications should be avoided. References should be given in standard form, as in the following examples:

HAHN, F.H. (1973). The winter of our discontent. Economica, 40, 322-330.

JOHNSON, H.G. (1964a). The international competitive position of the United States and the balance of payments prospect for 1968. Review and Economics and Statistics, 46, 14-32.

_____(1964b). Money. Trade and Economic Growth (2nd ed.). London: Allen and Unwin.

_____(1972). Uncertainty and probability in international economics. In Uncertainty and Expectations in Economics (C.F. Carter and J.L. Ford, eds.), pp. 148-159. Oxford Blackwell.

JOHNSON, H.G. AND NOBAY, A.R. (eds.) (1971). The Current Inflation. London: Macmillan.

MINISTRY OF TRANSPORT AND CIVIL AVIATION (1959). The Transport of Goods by Road. London: HMSO.

The following points should be noted:
 a. The first and last page numbers of a paper must be given.
 b. Journal titles should not be abbreviated.
 c. Series and part numbers should not be used unless their omission causes ambiguity; they are rarely needed. A series number, where necessary, should precede the volume number; a part number, where necessary, should be placed in parentheses immediately after the volume number. Two common cases in which such information is needed are illustrated in the following examples (in approved style): American Economic Review, 53 (Papers and Proceedings), 247-259. Journal of the Royal Statistical Society, A, 122, 145-174.

13. References in the text should be by author's surname and year of publication, as in the following examples:

    "Brown (1970) in a paper on..."
    "Brown (1970, p.12) has shown that..."
    "This method has been criticized (Jones, 1969a,b; Brown and Smith, 1970."
    "A proof is given by Jones et al. (1968)."

The following points should be noted:
 a. When more than two collaborating authors are quoted the first surname only should be given followed by et al., e.g. Jones et al. (1968), not Jones, Smith and White (1968). In the list of references, however, all names must be given in full.

b. The word 'and' is used in preference to '&'.
c. When a book is quoted, references to a particular page, section or chapter is nearly always necessary.
d. Ibid., op. cit., loc. cit. must not be used.

In particular papers where the above system of citing references is awkward, the Editors are prepared to consider any reasonable alternative.

14. It is important to distinguish symbols that cannot be typed, and in particular to distinguish carefully between

a. capitals and small letters,
b. ordinary and bold-faced letters,
c. certain Greek letters and similar Roman letters,
d. subscripts, superscripts, and "ordinary" symbols,
e. numbers 0 and 1 and letters o and l where the same symbol is used.

Boldfaced symbols should be underlined with a wiggly line in pencil. Mathematical symbols are automatically set in italics, and need not be underlined except to prevent ambiguity, e.g. when an isolated letter, such as a, occurs in the text. However, certain standard abbreviations are set in Roman fount, not italic fount, e.g. Iog, lim, exp, (but not e), max, min, sup, inf, var, cov, sin, cos.

15. Small fount setting is technically difficult, expensive, and sometimes impossible. To reduce the use of small founts:

a. Avoid elaborate notations involving multiple suffices.
b. Avoid the simultaneous use of both subscripts and superscripts where possible.
c. Do not use subscripts or superscripts on quantities which are limits of summation or integration, or which in turn become subscripts or superscripts: define a fresh symbol.
d. Use the expression "exp" for the exponential function when the argument is longer than a single compact group of symbols, e.g. $\exp (a + bt + ct^2)$ but e^t.
e. Avoid the notation for partial derivatives where f_{xy} will serve without ambiguity. Note than F_{12}, if unambiguous, is preferred. See note c.

16. Equations and long formulae should be displayed (i.e. shown on a separate line), where necessary being numbered at the left of the page. Short isolated formulae should usually be left in the text and then must be arranged so as not to be more than one line high. For example, $i = 1 \sum x_i$ must not be left in the text, it should be written $\sum x_i$ (if the limits of summation are obvious) or X = ... + X , otherwise it should be displayed.

17. The solidus sign (/) should be used for fractions in the text. Note than it is essential to bracket a group of symbols to the right of the solidus if they are to be included in the denominator; $(a + b)/(c + d) (h + k)$ is wrong, being ambiguous without a special contention. However, simple fractions 1/2, ... should be written as one-line fractions, thus $1/2t$ is preferred to $t/2$, while $\frac{t}{2}$ must not be used in the text.

18. Equations involving complicated expressions should, where possible, be avoided by introducing abbreviating symbols, e.g.,

$$w = (1 - 3_h - 3_f) \text{ or } u = \frac{1}{(1 - 3_h - 3_f)},$$ which saves a fraction line as well.

19. Equations must be punctuated in the usual way.

20. Some further details:

a. Where several sets of brackets occur inside one another in the same formula, the other should be [{0}].

b. Square roots should be denoted by the sine or the superscript /12, the former being used in simple expressions, the latter in complicated ones.

c. The range of running variables should be given as in the following example:

$$P_i + 1 = ap_i + bp_{i-1}$$

$(i = I, \ldots, n).$

21. Failure to follow these rules, especially the rules concerning the presentation of references, is likely to lead to considerable delays in the publication of a paper.

ECONOMICS LETTERS

ADDRESS FOR SUBMISSION :

ERIC MASKIN, EDITOR
ECONOMICS LETTERS
HARVARD UNIVERSITY
LITTAUER CENTER
DEPARTMENT OF ECONOMICS
CAMBRIDGE, MA 02138
617-495-4560
617-495-7730 (Fax)
E-Mail : ppreston@arrow.harvard.edu

CIRCULATION DATA :

Reader : Academic

Frequency of Issue : Monthly

Copies Per Issue : 1001-2000

Subscription Price : 285.00 US$
    Institution : 1295.00 US$

Sponsorship : Profit Oriented Corp.

PUBLICATION GUIDELINES :

Manuscript Length : 6-10

Copies Required : Two

Computer Submission : No

Format : N/A

Fees to Review : 0.00 US$

REVIEW INFORMATION :

Type of Review : Editorial Review

No. of External Reviewers : One

No. of In House Reviewers : One

Acceptance Rate : 11-20%

Time To Review : 1-2 months

Reviewer's Comments : Yes

Fees to Publish : 0.00 US$

Invited Articles : 5% or less

MANUSCRIPT TOPICS : ECONOMETRICS;
    GOVERNMENT & NON-PROFIT ACCOUNTING;
    MACROECONOMICS, APPLIED & THEORETICAL ECONOMICS

PUBLICATION GUIDELINES :

MANUSCRIPT GUIDELINES/COMMENTS :

AIMS AND SCOPE
Many economists today are concerned by the proliferation of journals and the
concomitant labyrinth of research to be conquered in order to reach the
specific information they require. To combat this tendency, ECONOMICS LETTERS
has been conceived and designed outside the realm of the traditional economics
journal. As a letter journal, it is:

* Concise: Contributions are limited to a maximum of 4 printed pages, allowing
readers to determine their potential interest in a letter very quickly, and to
digest a large amount of material in a usable form

* Rapid: Monthly publication ensures a brief manuscript turnover time (maximum
of 4 months from submission to final publication)

* Efficient: A quick way to stay up-to-date with developments in all areas of
economics.

The only letter journal in its field, ECONOMICS LETTERS is a valuable addition

ECONOMICS LETTERS

to the specialist literature in offering quick dissemination and easy accessibility of new results, models and methods in all fields of economic research.

Each article in ECONOMICS LETTERS is classified according to the JEL Classification System, and an author and subject index is published in the last issue of each volume to facilitate reference. A complete index of volumes 1 - 25 covering 10 years of economic literature is available from the publisher upon request. It provides author, title and subject indexes and thus constitutes a handy reference work for researchers and information officers alike.

INSTRUCTIONS TO AUTHORS
(1) Papers must be in English and should not exceed 4 printed pages (or 1600 words) including diagrams, figures, tables, etc.

(2) Papers for publication should be sent in duplicate to the Editor.

Submission of a paper will be held to imply that it contains original unpublished work and is not being submitted for publication elsewhere. All papers submitted will be refereed by the Board of Editors. The Editor does not accept responsibility for damage or loss of papers submitted.

Upon acceptance of an article, author(s) will be asked to transfer copyright of the article to the publisher. This transfer will ensure the widest possible dissemination of information.

(3) Manuscripts should be double spaced, with wide margins, and printed on one side of the paper only. All pages should be numbered consecutively. Titles and subtitles should be short. References, tables, and legends for figures should be printed on separate pages. The legends and titles on tables and figures must be sufficiently descriptive such that they are understandable without reference to the text. The dimensions of figure axes and the body of tables must be clearly labeled in English. ECONOMICS LETTERS encourages the use of recycled paper for all manuscript submissions.

(4) The first page of the manuscript should contain the following information: (i) the title; (ii) the name(s) and institutional affiliation(s) of the author(s); (iii) an abstract of not more than 40 words. A footnote on the same sheet should give the name, address and telephone and fax numbers of the corresponding author [as well as an e-mail address].

(5) The first page of the manuscript should also contain at least one classification code according to the Classification System for Journal Articles as used by the JOURNAL OF ECONOMIC LITERATURE; in addition, up to five keywords should be supplied.

(6) Acknowledgements and information on grants received should be given in a footnote on the first page of the manuscript or before the references.

(7) Footnotes should be kept to a minimum and numbered consecutively throughout the text with superscript Arabic numerals. They should be double spaced and not include displayed formulae or tables.

(8) Displayed formulae should be numbered consecutively throughout the

manuscript as (1), (2), etc. against the right-hand margin of the page. In cases where the derivation of formulae has been abbreviated, it is of great help to the referees if the full derivation can be presented on a separate sheet (not to be published).

(9) References to publications should be as follows: "Smith (1992) reported that . . ." or "This problem has been studied previously (e.g., Smith et al., 1969)". The author should make sure that there is a strict one-to-one correspondence between the names and years in the text and those on the list. The list of references should appear at the end of the main text (after any appendices, but before tables and legends for figures). It should be double spaced and listed in alphabetical order by author's name. References should appear as follows:

For monographs
Hawawini, G. and I. Swary, 1990, Mergers and acquisitions in the U.S. banking industry: Evidence from the capital markets (North-Holland, Amsterdam).

For contributions to collective works
Brunner, K. and A.H. Meltzer, 1990, Money supply, in: B.M. Friedman and F.H. Hahn, eds., Handbook of monetary economics, Vol. 1 (North-Holland, Amsterdam) 357-396.

For periodicals
Griffiths, W. and G. Judge, 1992, Testing and estimating location vectors when the error covariance matrix is unknown, Journal of Econometrics 54, 121-138.

Note that journal titles should not be abbreviated.

(10) Illustrations will be reproduced photographically from originals supplied by the author; they will not be redrawn by the publisher. Please provide all illustrations in duplicate (one high-contrast original and one photocopy). Care should be taken that lettering and symbols are of a comparable size. The illustrations should not be inserted in the text, and should be marked on the back with figure number, title of paper, and author's name. All graphs and diagrams should be referred to as figures, and should be numbered consecutively in the text in Arabic numerals.

Illustrations can be printed in colour when they are judged by the Editor to be essential to the presentation. The publisher and the author will each bear part of the extra costs involved. Further information concerning colour illustrations and the costs to the author can be obtained from the publisher.

(11) Tables should be numbered consecutively in the text in Arabic numerals and printed on separate sheets. All unessential tables should be eliminated from the manuscript.

Any manuscript which does not conform to the above instructions may be returned for the necessary revision before publication. Contributors are reminded that once their contribution has been accepted, all further correspondence should be sent directly to Elsevier Editorial Services, Mayfield House, 256 Banbury Road, Oxford OX2 7DH, UK, tel (+44) (0) 1865 314900, fax (+44) (0) 1865 314990. As all proofreading will be done by the Publisher's staff and no proofs will be sent to the Author, the presentation of the manuscript should be very clear.

ECONOMICS LETTERS

USING THE ELSEVIER STYLE FILE FOR MICROSOFT WORD 6.0

Elsevier has produced a template document for Microsoft Word 6.0 which will allow authors to produce manuscripts that can be brought directly into the Elsevier production process, preserving a lot of their structuring. This will enable the more accurate production of proofs, reducing your need during proofreading to locate typographic mistakes.

INSTALLING THE STYLE FILE
The Elsevier styles are located in a template document called elsevier.dot. Download this and place it in your default templates/styles directory (this will normally be something like c:\winword\templates). The template document contains a list of Word styles which can then be applied to your document in the normal way, i.e. at the start of a paragraph choose the appropriate style for that paragraph. If you are not familiar with the use of Word styles, please consult your Word documentation.

USING THE STYLE FILE
The style file can be used in two ways, you can either create a new document using the template file, or attach the template document to an existing document.

To create a new document, choose New from the File menu, then select ELSEVIER in the TEMPLATE list box before clicking on OK.

To attach the template to an existing document, first open the document, and then select Templates from the File menu. Press the attach button in the Templates and Add-ins dialogue and double click on elsevier.dot in the file selector. Then ensure that the Automatically Update Document Styles check box is crossed before clicking on OK in the Templates and Add-ins dialogue.

Whichever method you have used, the Elsevier styles will then be available in the Styles list box on the tool bar, and in the STYLE dialogue box on the format menu.

APPLYING ELSEVIER STYLES TO YOUR DOCUMENT
The Elsevier styles are listed below. To use a style, first select the text to which you would like to attach the style, then choose the style name from the styles list box on the tool bar, or choose Style from the Format menu, then choose the style name from the Styles list box.

STYLE NAME	APPLY TO
Abstract	The whole of the abstract.
Acknowledgements	The whole of the acknowledgements.
Address	Each authors' address.
Appendix	Each appendix heading.
Author	The whole author address block.
Caption	Each figure or table caption.
City	The city in each authors' or correspondence address.
Collaborators	Any collaborators' address.
Correspondence address	Any correspondence address.
Country	The country in each authors' or correspondence address.
Endnote reference	The main text reference to any endnote.
Endnote text	The actual text of each endnote.

ECONOMICS LETTERS

Footnote reference	The main text reference to any endnote.
Footnote text	The actual text of each footnote.
Heading 1...9	Section headings, level 1 to 9.
Keywords	The whole keywords or abbreviations section.
List (Bulleted)	The whole of a bulleted list (separate the bulleted items by pressing Return).
List (Numbered)	The whole of a numbered list (separate the numbered items by pressing Return).
List (Un-numbered)	The whole of an un-numbered list (separate the items by pressing Return).
Quotation	A 'displayed' quotation.
Subtitle	The whole of any article subtitle.
Title	The whole of the article title.

It is important that the elements in your article are presented in the following order: title; subtitle; authors; collaborators; correspondence address; abstract; keywords; main body of article (containing section headings, lists, footnotes, endnotes and displayed quotations as required); acknowledgements; appendices; bibliography of reference list. In addition, use the table and equation facilities available in Microsoft Word as required.

The styles in the template document will apply some simple visual formatting to your article. There is no need to add further complex visual formatting by hand, as this will be stripped out in our conversion process. Only use facilities such as bold or italic where this contributes to the meaning of your article (for example to signify variables or matrices in mathematics.)

For help with the use of the Elsevier Microsoft Word style file, please e-mail b.cobb@elsevier.co.uk.

Elsevier Science Complete Catalogue
Use the search engine provided to find full descriptive details about any of our publications, together with ordering information.

Elsevier Science Tables of Contents (ESTOC)
The tables of contents for Elsevier Science journals since January 1995.

Elsevier Science Home Page
http://www.elsevier.com/homepage/about/styles/

ECONOMICS OF EDUCATION REVIEW

ADDRESS FOR SUBMISSION :

ELCHANAN COHN, PH.D.,EDITOR
ECONOMICS OF EDUCATION REVIEW
UNIVERSITY OF SOUTH CAROLINA
COLLEGE OF BUSINESS ADMINISTRATION
DEPARTMENT OF ECONOMICS
COLUMBIA, SC 29208
803-777-2714
803-777-6876 (Fax)
E-Mail : feu00004@darla.badm.sc.edu

CIRCULATION DATA :

Reader : Academic

Frequency of Issue : Quarterly

Copies Per Issue : Less than 1000

Subscription Price : 291.00 US$

Sponsorship : Profit Oriented Corp. &
                University

PUBLICATION GUIDELINES :

Manuscript Length : 16-25

Copies Required : Four

Computer Submission : No

Format : N/A

Fees to Review : 0.00 US$

REVIEW INFORMATION :

Type of Review : Blind Review

No. of External Reviewers : Two

No. of In House Reviewers : Zero

Acceptance Rate : 21-30%

Time To Review : 4-6 months

Reviewer's Comments : Yes

Fees to Publish : 0.00 US$

Invited Articles : 5% or less

MANUSCRIPT TOPICS : PUBLIC POLICY ECONOMICS; ECONOMICS OF EDUCATION

PUBLICATION GUIDELINES :

MANUSCRIPT GUIDELINES/COMMENTS :

Individuals will receive lower rates where institution subscribes.

1. Papers submitted for publication should be submitted in quadruplicate to
the Editor. Proposals for book reviews should be sent to William H. Phillips,
Book Review Editor, Department of Economics, University of South Carolina,
Columbia, SC 29208, USA.

2. Manuscripts must be typed on one side of the page only and must be
double-spaced, with two-inch (five-centimetre) margins on all sides.

3. Manuscripts will not be considered for publication if they have been
published before or if they are concurrently under review by another journal
or publisher. Papers accepted for publication must not be published elsewhere
without the consent of the Editor and Publisher.

4. All manuscripts should be prepared in accordance with the journal's style,
which is outlined below.

5. The title page should contain: (i) the title of the article, which should
clearly outline the nature of the subject; (ii) a short running head of no

more than 40 characters (including spaces), placed at the bottom of the title page and identified; (iii) the names and addresses of all authors; (iv) the name and adress of the author responsible for correspondence and to whom requests for reprints should be addressed; and (v) any source(s) of support in the form of grants.

6. Papers must contain an abstract briefly summarizing the essential contents, followed by the relevant JEL classification; this should not exceed 150 words.

7. Illustrations should accompany the typescript but should not be inserted in the text. All figures. charts and diagrams should be referred to as Figures' and should be numbered consecutively in the order that they are referred to in the text. All figures should be submitted in a form suitable for direct reproduction: therefore original figures or glossy prints should be provided. It is not possible to reproduce from prints with weak lines. Illustrations submitted should normally be about twice the final size required. A list of the figure captions should be typed on a separate sheet at the end of the manuscript.

8. Tables should be so constructed as to be intelligible without reference to the text. with every table and column being provided with a heading. The approximate location of figures and tables in the text must be clearly indicated.

9. Acknowledgements should appear on a separate sheet at the end of the written section before the notes.

10. Short footnotes may be included at the foot of a manuscript page. Longer notes should be numbered and grouped together in a 'Notes' section at the end of the text. The note number (1,....5, etc.) should be inserted in the text where appropriate.

11. All references to other papers, books, etc. should be listed in alphabetical order at the end of the paper. In the text the author(s)' name(s) and date of publication should be given, e.g. (Jones, 1975): (Jones and Smith, 1974): (Jones et al., 1979): (Smith. 1980a): (Smith. 1980b): ...as shown by Dale (1982).

In the reference list all references to articles in journals should contain: the names and initials of all authors, the year of publication, the title of the paper, the name of the journal abbreviated according to the World List of Scientific Periodicals (4th Edn) (1963-1965). 3 vols. London: Butterworths, the volume number and page numbers: for articles within books the Editor(s)' name(s) and the town and name of the Publisher should also be given:

Treiman, D.J. and Terrell, K. (1975). The process of status attainment in the United States and Great Britain. Am. J. Sociol. 81. 563-583.

Kay, J.A. and King, M.A. (1980) The British Tax System. Oxford: Oxford University Press.

Hansen, W.L. and Weisbrod, B.A. (1971c) A new approach to higher education finance. In Financing Higher Education: Alternatives for the Federal Government (Edited by Orwig. M.O.). pp. 206-236. Iowa City: American College Testing Program.

ECONOMICS OF EDUCATION REVIEW

12. Submission of manuscripts on disk: Authors are encouraged to submit a computer disk (5.25" or 3.5" HD/DD disk) containing the final version of the paper along with two (2) hard copies of the final manuscript to the editorial office. Please observe the following criteria:

(a) Send only hard copy when first submitting your paper.

(b) When your paper has been refereed, revised if necessary and accepted, send a disk containing the final version with the final hard copy. Make sure that the disk and the hard copy match exactly.

(c) Specify what software was used, including which release (e.g. WordPerfect 5.1).

(d) Specify what computer was used (either IBM compatible PC or Apple Macintosh).

(e) Text, tables, and illustrations (if available on disk) should be supplied as separate files.

(f) The file should follow the general instructions on style/arrangement and, in particular, the reference style.

(g) The file should use the wrap-around end-of-line feature (i.e. no returns at the end of each line). All textual elements should begin flush left, no paragraph indents. Place two returns after every element such as title, headings, paragraphs, figure and table callouts.

(h) Keep a back-up disk for reference and safety.

13. Authors of accepted papers are responsible for proofreading and must return the proofs directly to Elsevier Science Ltd without delay. Delayed return of proofs may result in the manuscript being dropped from the scheduled issue. Corrections to proofs must be restricted to printer's errors; any substantial changes other than these may be charged to the author.

14. Twenty-five reprints of each paper will be supplied free of charge. Additional reprints can be obtained a a reasonable price provided that they are ordered when the proofs are returned, using the form provided.

15. All material will be discarded I month after publication unless specifically requested by the author to be returned.

ECONOMICS OF PLANNING

ADDRESS FOR SUBMISSION :

EDITORIAL OFFICE
ECONOMICS OF PLANNING
KLUWER ACADEMIC PUBLISHERS
SPUILBOULEVARD 50
P.O. BOX 17
3300 AA DORDRECT,
THE NETHERLANDS

617-871-6528 (Fax)
E-Mail : zrolnik@wkap.com

CIRCULATION DATA :

Reader : Academic

Frequency of Issue : Quarterly

Copies Per Issue : 1001-2000

Subscription Price : 156.00 USD.$
   Institution : 96.50 US$

Sponsorship : Professional Assoc. &
   University

PUBLICATION GUIDELINES :

Manuscript Length : 20+

Copies Required : Three

Computer Submission : No

Format : N/A

Fees to Review : 0.00 US$

REVIEW INFORMATION :

Type of Review : Blind Review

No. of External Reviewers : Two

No. of In House Reviewers : One

Acceptance Rate : 21-30%

Time To Review : 2-3 months

Reviewer's Comments : Yes

Fees to Publish : 0.00 US$

Invited Articles : 11-20%

MANUSCRIPT TOPICS : ACCOUNTING INFORMATION SYSTEMS;
   PUBLIC POLICY ECONOMICS; COMPARATIVE ECONOMICS

PUBLICATION GUIDELINES : American Psychological Association

MANUSCRIPT GUIDELINES/COMMENTS :

SCOPE. ECONOMICS OF PLANNING is an international journal devoted to the study
of comparative economics, planning and development and economic transition,
especially in developing countries and economies previously identified as
centrally planned economies. The journal provides a world wide forum for
scholarly discussion of both theoretical and empirical issues. ECONOMICS OF
PLANNING accepts only original material, not previously published elsewhere.

SUBMISSION OF MANUSCRIPTS. Manuscripts intended for publication should be
written in English and submitted in quadruplicate to: Economics of Planning
Editorial Office, P.O. Box 17, 3300 AA Dordrecht, The Netherlands.
NorthAmerican Authors may submit manuscripts to: Economics of Planning
Editorial Office, P.O. Box 230, Accord, MA 02018-0230. All copies of the
manuscript must be of a reasonable quality; manuscripts with unreadable parts
will not be considered. There is no strict length limit for manuscripts, but
authors are reminded that excessively long papers can be returned to the
authors for shortening. The advisable length limit for manuscripts is not more
than 30 typewritten double-spaced A4 pages.

The English can be either British or American spelling variants, but not a

mixture.
The entire manuscript (including abstract, keywords, references, captions, and notes) should be typed double-spaced on 21 x 29 cm (A4) paper or on 8 1/2 x 11 inch white bond paper. Liberal margins (2.5 cm) should be left at the top and the bottom, as well as the sides of each page.

A leaflet containing INFORMATION FOR AUTHORS is available from the Editor, or from the Humanities and Social Sciences Division, Kluwer Academic Publishers, P.O. Box 17, 3300 AA Dordrecht, The Netherlands. Also see Vol.26, No. 3, pp. 289-293.

OFFPRINTS. Twenty-five offprints of each article will be provided free of charge. Additional offprints can be ordered when proofs are returned to the publisher.

NO PAGE CHARGES are levied on authors or their institutions.

EDITOR
Wojciech W. Charemza
University of Leicester
Department of Economics
University Road, Leicester LE1 7RH, U.K.

AMERICAN EDITOR
David M. Kemme
Robert C. Wang Center for International Business
University of Memphis
Memphis, TN 38152, U.S.A.

EMERGING MARKETS QUARTERLY

ADDRESS FOR SUBMISSION :

BRIAN BRUCE, EDITOR
EMERGING MARKETS QUARTERLY
1900 PRESTON ROAD, SUITE 267-310
PLANO, TX 75093
USA
972-608-0658
972-378-3918 (Fax)

PUBLICATION GUIDELINES :

Manuscript Length : 16-20

Copies Required : Three

Computer Submission : Yes

Format : WordPerfect

Fees to Review : 0.00 US$

CIRCULATION DATA :

Reader : Business Persons

Frequency of Issue : Quarterly

Copies Per Issue : Less than 1000

Subscription Price : 325.00 US$
    Academics : 81.00 US$

Sponsorship : Profit Oriented Corp.

REVIEW INFORMATION :

Type of Review : Editorial Review

No. of External Reviewers : Two

No. of In House Reviewers : Zero

Acceptance Rate :

Time To Review : 2-3 months

Reviewer's Comments : No

Fees to Publish : 0.00 US$

Invited Articles : Over 50%

MANUSCRIPT TOPICS : PORTFOLIO & SECURITY ANALYSIS

PUBLICATION GUIDELINES :

MANUSCRIPT GUIDELINES/COMMENTS :

SUBMISSION OF MANUSCRIPTS
Please refer to the following guidelines when submitting a manuscript for
publication. We may return any paper to the author for revisions that does not
follow these instructions. The editors reserve the right to make changes for
clarity and consistency.

1. Submit two copies of the manuscript double-spaced with wide margins and
pages numbered. The front page should include the authors' full names, titles,
addresses, zip codes, and phone/fax numbers. If the paper is accepted for
publication, the authors must supply a diskette copy of the paper. Please note
the type of word processing software used and securely attach the article
title, author's name, and address to the diskette.

2. References, endnotes, tables, and figures should appear on separate pages
at the end of the text.

3. Limit references principally to works cited in the text and list them
alphabetically. Citations in the text should appear as "Smith [1990] suggests
that..." Use page numbers for quotes. Use periods instead of comas between
authors' names and titles of references.

4. Minimize the number of endnotes. Use superscript Arabic numbers in the text and on the endnote page.

5. Number and title all exhibits, with one to a page. Write out the column heads and legends; they should be understandable without reference to the text. Submit graphs in camera-ready form; we cannot draw graphs for you.

6. Center any equations on a separate line, numbered consecutively with Arabic numbers in parentheses in the right margin. Identify Greek letters in the margin for the typesetter. Please make clear markings when inserting Greek letters or equations into the text.

7. EMERGING MARKETS QUARTERLY'S copyright agreement form must be signed prior to publication.

8. After a manuscript has been accepted for publication, further changes can only be made at the galley stage.

SEND 2 COPIES TO:
Brian R. Bruce
Emerging Markets Quarterly
1900 Preston Road
Suite 267-310
Plano, TX 75093
Phone: (972) 608-0658
Fax: (972) 378-3918

SEND 1 COPY TO:
Ms. Noelle Schultz
Editorial Production Director
Institutional Investor, Inc.
488 Madison Avenue, 12th Floor
New York, NY 10022
Phone: (212) 224-3193
Fax: (212) 224-3527

EMERGING MARKETS QUARTERLY is published by Institutional Investor, Inc., 488 Madison Avenue, New York, NY 10022. Tel: 212-224-3545 Fax: 212-224-3527.

EMPIRE STATE REALTOR

ADDRESS FOR SUBMISSION :

SALVATORE I. PRIDIDERA, JR., EDITOR
EMPIRE STATE REALTOR
NEW YORK STATE ASSOCIATION OF REALTORS
130 WASHINGTON AVENUE
ALBANY, NY 12210-2298
USA
518-463-0300
518-462-5474 (Fax)
E-Mail : nysar@albany.net

CIRCULATION DATA :

Reader : Business Persons &
        REAL ESTATE PROFESSIONALS

Frequency of Issue : Monthly

Copies Per Issue : Over 25,000

Subscription Price : 12.00 US$
    Members : 2.00 US$

Sponsorship : Professional Assoc.

PUBLICATION GUIDELINES :

Manuscript Length : 500 wds.

Copies Required : One

Computer Submission : Yes

Format : DOS/PM4

Fees to Review : 0.00 US$

REVIEW INFORMATION :

Type of Review : Editorial Review

No. of External Reviewers : Zero

No. of In House Reviewers : Three

Acceptance Rate : 50 %

Time To Review : One month or less

Reviewer's Comments : No

Fees to Publish : 0.00 US$

Invited Articles : Over 50%

MANUSCRIPT TOPICS : REAL ESTATE

PUBLICATION GUIDELINES :

MANUSCRIPT GUIDELINES/COMMENTS :

1. The EMPIRE STATE REALTOR is published 12 times each year by the New York State Association of Realtors. We welcome the submission of articles by non-members relating to the real estate and housing industries. All manuscripts submitted are reviewed by the ESR Editorial Board and will not be returned. Only authors of those manuscripts accepted for publication in the EMPIRE STATE REALTOR will be notified by return mail or phone. The following guidelines are designed to assist in the preparation of manuscripts to be considered for publication.

2. The EMPIRE STATE REALTOR is a tabloid newspaper, 20 pages, published 12 times annually.

3. All articles submitted must be typewritten, double-spaced on 8 1/2" x 11" white paper. Clear photocopies are acceptable.

4. Authors should enclose a brief biography with all articles submitted. Black and white photographs will be accepted for review, with the understanding that they will not be returned and no guarantee of being printed.

EMPIRE STATE REALTOR

5. All articles will be carefully reviewed if they are determined to relate to any aspect of the real estate and housing industries. The spectrum of articles suitable for publication range from factual, "hard news" stories to creative feature articles.

6. Submission of articles by authors will be considered permission to publish same. All articles published become the property of NYSAR.

7. The New York State Association of Realtors is not responsible for statements, opinions, ideas or comments written by others and published in the EMPIRE STATE REALTOR. The publication of an article does not necessarily constiture an official endorsement.

8. The EMPIRE STATE REALTOR does not offer any financial remuneration for articles or manuscripts published in any of its issues.

9. All articles are to be submitted to the Editor.

EMPIRICAL ECONOMICS

ADDRESS FOR SUBMISSION :

BALDEV RAJ, CANADIAN EDITOR
EMPIRICAL ECONOMICS
WILFRID LAURIER UNIVERSITY
SCHOOL OF BUSINESS AND ECONOMICS
WATERLOO, ONTARIO, N2L 3C5
CANADA
519-884-1970 EXT 2550
519-884-0201 (Fax)

CIRCULATION DATA :

Reader :

Frequency of Issue : Quarterly

Copies Per Issue : Less than 1000

Subscription Price : 464.00 US$

Sponsorship : Profit Oriented Corp. &
Non Profit Corp.

PUBLICATION GUIDELINES :

Manuscript Length : 11-30

Copies Required : Three

Computer Submission : N/A

Format : N/A

Fees to Review : 0.00 US$

REVIEW INFORMATION :

Type of Review : N/A

No. of External Reviewers : Two

No. of In House Reviewers : One

Acceptance Rate : 21-30%

Time To Review : 2-3 months

Reviewer's Comments : Yes

Fees to Publish : 0.00 US$

Invited Articles : 11-20%

MANUSCRIPT TOPICS : ACCOUNTING INFORMATION SYSTEMS;
CAPITAL BUDGETING; ECONOMETRICS; INSURANCE;
INTERNATIONAL & ECONOMIC DEVELOPMENT; PORTFOLIO & SECURITY ANALYSIS;
PUBLIC POLICY ECONOMICS; REAL ESTATE

PUBLICATION GUIDELINES :

MANUSCRIPT GUIDELINES/COMMENTS :

EDITORS

WINFRIED POHLMEIER, University of Konstanz, Faculty of Economics and
Statistics, P.O. Box 5560, D124, D-78434 Konstanz, Germany. Phone (07531)
88-2660, Fax (07531) 44-4450, e-mail: winfried.pohlmeier@uni-konstanz.de

BALDEV RAJ, School of Business and Economics, Wilfrid Laurier University,
Waterloo, Ontario, Canada N2L 3C5. Phone (519) 884-1970, Fax (519) 884-0201,
e-mail: braj@mach1.wlu.ca

ANDREAS WORGOTTER, Institute for Advanced Studies, Department of Economics,
Stumpergasse 56, A-1060 Vienna, Austria (Coordinating Editor). Phone (431) 5
99 91, Fax (431) 599 91-163, e-mail: woergoet@ihssv.wsr.ac.at

EMPIRICAL ECONOMICS publishes papers of high quality dealing with the
confrontation of relevant economic theory with observed data through the use
of adequate econometric methods. Papers cover topics like estimation of

established relationships between economic variables, testing of hypotheses derived from economic theory, policy evaluation, simulation, forecasting, methodology, econometric methods and measurement. Preference is given to contributions on industrialized market economies. Contributions dealing with developing and non-market economies should be of interest for non-specialists in these fields. Papers including international comparisons are given high priority. Shorter papers, notes and comments are also welcome. Authors are expected to cooperate in case readers, editors or referees should want to replicate results reported in submitted contributions. Both positive and negative results of replication efforts may be published in EMPIRICAL ECONOMICS.

INSTRUCTIONS TO AUTHORS
Manuscripts are accepted for review with the understanding that the same work has not been published, and is not under consideration for publication elsewhere.

Four copies of every manuscript should be submitted to one of the editors.

When preparing manuscripts for the journal please note the following items.

1. Form and content of the manuscript should be carefully checked to exclude the need for later corrections, as papers will be made up to pages immediately after typesetting. Any subsequent changes in the text will be charged to the authors.

The desired positions of figures and tables must be marked in the margin of the manuscript. Manuscripts must be typed on one side of the paper only and with wide margins. References and legend should be typed on separate sheets. The author receives page proofs (2 sets) of his paper with provisional page numbers. These provisional numbers may be referred to during correction. The final page numbers are inserted by the publisher when an issue is ready for press.

2. The first manuscript page should provide the title, name of all authors, names of institutes or firms, any footnotes to the title, address to which proofs are to be sent, and running title.

3. Each paper is to be be preceded by a short summary in English, which should not exceed 12 typewritten lines.

4. Words to be set in italics for emphasis should be underlined.

5. Footnotes to the text should be avoided.

6. Figures are to be numbered consecutively. For direct reproduction, lettered ink drawings are required. Computer printouts are accepted, provided they are black enough. Do not paste the illustrations in the manuscript; enclose them on separate sheets.

7. Tables are to be numbered separately from the illustrations and each table should have a title.

8. Formulas are to be typewritten whenever possible. Special signs are to be marked in colour. Formulas should be numbered consecutively on the right-hand

EMPIRICAL ECONOMICS

side of the page.
9. The list of references should include only publications cited in the text.
The references should be listed in alphabetical order under the first author's
name. Citations in the text should be by author and year.

EXAMPLES FOR REFERENCES
Bennett E, Wooders M (1979) Income distribution and firm formation. J of
Comparative Economics 3: 304-317

Basar T (1986) A tutorial on dynamic and differential games. In Basar T
(ed) Dynamic games and applications in economics, Springer-Verlag, Berlin
Heidelberg New York Tokyo pp 1-25

A total of 30 offprints of each paper will be supplied free of charge.
Additonal reprints can be ordered at cost price.

Copyrights of the submitted article are transferred by the author(s) to
Physica-Verlag if and when the article is accepted for publication. The
copyright covers the exclusive and unlimited rights to reproduce and
distribute the article in any form of reproduction (printing, electronic media
or any other form); it also covers translation rights for all languages and
countries. For U.S. authors the copyright is transferred to the extent
transferable. It is a fundamental condition that submitted papers have not
been published and will not be published elsewhere without the publisher's
permission.

ENTREPRENEURSHIP & REGIONAL DEVELOPMENT

ADDRESS FOR SUBMISSION :

GERALD SWEENEY, EDITOR
ENTREPRENEURSHIP & REGIONAL
  DEVELOPMENT
C/O SICA INNOVATION CONSULTANTS LTD
ONE DUN EMER PARK
DUBLIN, 16
IRELAND
+353 1295 6612
+353 1294 1458 (Fax)
E-Mail : sica@iol.ie

Change in Editor's Address
  May Occur in : 01/07/99

CIRCULATION DATA :

Reader : Academic

Frequency of Issue : Quarterly

Copies Per Issue : Less than 1000

Subscription Price : 40.00 US$

Sponsorship : Profit Oriented Corp.

PUBLICATION GUIDELINES :

Manuscript Length : 11-15

Copies Required : Three

Computer Submission : No

Format : N/A

Fees to Review : 0.00 US$

REVIEW INFORMATION :

Type of Review : Blind Review

No. of External Reviewers : Two

No. of In House Reviewers : One

Acceptance Rate : 11-20%

Time To Review : 2-3 months

Reviewer's Comments : Yes

Fees to Publish : 0.00 US$

Invited Articles : 11-20%

MANUSCRIPT TOPICS : INTERNATIONAL & ECONOMIC DEVELOPMENT;
  PUBLIC POLICY ECONOMICS

PUBLICATION GUIDELINES : American Psychological Association

MANUSCRIPT GUIDELINES/COMMENTS :

ENTREPRENEURSHIP & REGIONAL DEVELOPMENT is a journal for the 1990s. The last
decade has witnessed the worldwide recognition of the key role of the
entrepreneur in economic development, prosperity and vitality.
ENTREPRENEURSHIP & REGIONAL DEVELOPMENT was launched in 1989 as THE forum for
international interest in this field. It is oriented towards empirical
research on entrepreneurship and brings together such factors as networking,
innovation, venture capital and social culture. In addition to this, the
journal focuses on evaluation of new technology, education and local
development programmes and the role of the public and private sectors.

ENTREPRENEURSHIP & REGIONAL DEVELOPMENT is a spirited, challenging journal
that offers and international insight into the changing face of the world
economy. Complete details on submission can be obtained from the inside back
cover of the Journal.

ESSAYS IN ECONOMIC AND BUSINESS HISTORY

ADDRESS FOR SUBMISSION :

WILLIAM R. CHILDS, EDITOR
ESSAYS IN ECONOMIC AND BUSINESS HISTORY
OHIO STATE UNIVERSITY
DEPARTMENT OF HISTORY
106 DULLES HALL
230 W. 17TH STREET
COLUMBUS, OH 43210-1367
614-292-7014
614-292-2282 (Fax)
E-Mail Childs.1@osu.edu

CIRCULATION DATA :

Reader : Academic

Frequency of Issue : 1 Times/Year

Copies Per Issue : Less than 1000

Subscription Price : 25.00 US$

Sponsorship : Professional Assoc. &
University

PUBLICATION GUIDELINES :

Manuscript Length : 21-25

Copies Required : One

Computer Submission : Yes

Format : IBM Compatible

Fees to Review : 0.00 US$

REVIEW INFORMATION :

Type of Review : Editorial Review

No. of External Reviewers : Two

No. of In House Reviewers : Two

Acceptance Rate :

Time To Review : 2-3 months

Reviewer's Comments : Yes

Fees to Publish : 25.00 US$

Invited Articles : 6-10%

MANUSCRIPT TOPICS : ECONOMETRICS; ECONOMIC HISTORY;
   INTERNATIONAL & ECONOMIC DEVELOPMENT; PUBLIC POLICY ECONOMICS;
   BUSINESS HISTORY

PUBLICATION GUIDELINES :

MANUSCRIPT GUIDELINES/COMMENTS :

The EBHS publishes selected papers from its annual meetings in the Society's
journal, ESSAYS IN ECONOMIC AND BUSINESS HISTORY. In the spring of the
following year, all members receive a copy of the journal, which is indexed in
JOURNAL OF ECONOMIC LITERATURE, JOURNAL OF AMERICAN HISTORY, and AMERICA:
HISTORY AND LIFE, and several other sources.

Your paper will be peer reviewed and the Editors may decline to publish it if
the reviewers believe it does not meet the standards of EEBH.

Only papers published in the EEBH are eligible for the annual Charles Kennedy
Award of $250 for the best paper delivered at the meeting.

SPECIFIC REQUIREMENTS
Your paper must be no longer than 25 pages, double-spaced (text and
endnotes/references), type size 11pt or larger.

Please include at the beginning of your essay, after the title and your name,
an Abstract of 75 to 100 words describing the contents of your article.

ESSAYS IN ECONOMIC AND BUSINESS HISTORY

To be considered, we must receive BOTH A HARD COPY and a DISK COPY. In order to cut down on production time and eliminate errors, please note the following:

> All disks should be IBM compatible. (MAC users: convert your file!)
> Please do not embed your endnotes--remove them to the end of the file.
> Include the following information with your disk: high or low capacity;
>   word processing program and version number; and, the file name.

PUBLICATION FEES
A modest publication fee is mandatory for each accepted paper and is due when you return your proof pages. For members, the cost is $25.00 and for non-members, the cost is $40.00 ($15.00 of which covers a one-year membership in EBHS). This modest fee helps defray a portion of the cost the Society incurs in publishing the EEBH.

STYLE SHEET for ESSAYS IN ECONOMIC AND BUSINESS HISTORY

Before submitting your essay for consideration, please be sure that your work conforms with the styles noted below. Adherence to these guidelines will reduce the number of errors and enhance the quality of your journal.

The Editors prefer Endnotes, but you may choose to use References. In either case, all citations will conform to the examples below.

Note: Bibliographies usually repeat the sources already listed in the Endnotes or References, so they are superfluous. You may, however, include a brief section, "Additional Bibliography," which includes works not cited.

ENDNOTES
For books:
    8. Alfred Crosby, The Columbian Exchange: Biological and Cultural Consequences of 1492 (Westport, 1972) and Ecological Imperialism: The Biological Expansion of Europe, 9001900 (New York, 1986).

All subsequent citations will include the author's last name(s) and a short title of the work:
    9. Crosby, The Columbian Exchange, 68-72, 90-98.

For articles:
    5. Andre Gunder Frank, "A Plea for World System History," Journal of World History, 2(Spring 1991), 1-28. Note that "p. " and "pp." are not used.

For edited works:
    21. Wilfried Feldenkirchen, "Concentration in German Industry 1870-1939," in Hans Pohl (ed), The Concentration Process in the Entrepreneurial Economy Since the Late 19th century (Stuttgart, 1988), 124.

For manuscripts:
    23. John S. Smith to Pete Doe, January 30, 1909, Box 121, folder 11, John Smith Papers, Virginia Historical Society Archives, Charlottesville, Virginia [hereafter cited as Smith Papers]. Once a correspondent has been identified by his/her full name, then use only the last name in subsequent citations.

Other style issues:
Ibid. (no italics) will be used only when there was only one citation in the previous note. Otherwise, use the short title format.
For all dates, spell-out the months: January 21, 1909.

REFERENCES
All References will be numbered and placed in alphabetical order at the end of the essay:
25. "Russian oil outlook grows gloomier," Oil and Gas Journal, December 7, 1992, 33-35.

References will follow the examples for books, articles, edited works, and manuscripts noted above.

Reference citations within the essay will appear within brackets [ ] and include the number and page numbers, if appropriate:
He attributes the rapid depletion of the most productive oil wells to the irrational and wasteful exploitations years ago. [25, p. 34] (Only in references will you use "p." or "pp.")

LAYOUT AND PRINTING
CHARTS & TABLES & ILLUSTRATIONS: Please (1) place all charts, tables, and illustrations at the end of your essay, and (2) be sure that you use the best printer available. Use Times Roman print. The Editors will place the charts and tables within the text at the appropriate place; since they xerox the original, they need the clearest print available. Illustrations should enhance the prose and not be just "window dressing."

LAYOUT
Please layout your essay in the format of the 1996 volume of EEBH. Use the minimum number of word processing commands. Please do not justify the righthand margin; please delete hyphenation.

EUROPEAN ACCOUNTING REVIEW

ADDRESS FOR SUBMISSION :

ANNE LOFT, EDITOR
EUROPEAN ACCOUNTING REVIEW
COPENHAGEN BUSINESS SCHOOL
HOWITZVEJ 60, DK 2000F
DEMARK
0045 38152343
0045 38152321 (Fax)
E-Mail : al.aa@ cbs.dh

Change in Editor's Address
  May Occur in : 01/04/00

CIRCULATION DATA :

Reader : Academic

Frequency of Issue : Quarterly

Copies Per Issue : 1001-2000

Subscription Price : 215.00 US$

Sponsorship : Professional Assoc.

PUBLICATION GUIDELINES :

Manuscript Length : No Limit

Copies Required : Three

Computer Submission : No

Format : N/A

Fees to Review : 0.00 US$

REVIEW INFORMATION :

Type of Review : Blind Review

No. of External Reviewers : Two

No. of In House Reviewers : Zero

Acceptance Rate : 11-20%

Time To Review : 2-3 months

Reviewer's Comments : Yes

Fees to Publish : 0.00 US$

Invited Articles : 6-10%

MANUSCRIPT TOPICS : ACCOUNTING THEORY & PRACTICE; AUDITING;
  COST ACCOUNTING; TAX ACCOUNTING; INTERNATIONAL ACCOUNTING

PUBLICATION GUIDELINES :

MANUSCRIPT GUIDELINES/COMMENTS :

CO-EDITOR: Peter Walton
Manuscripts are accepted for review in all major European languages.

SUBMISSION OF ARTICLES
Authors should submit three complete copies of their paper, with any original
illustrations. It will be assumed that the authors will keep a copy of their
paper.

Submission of a paper to the journal will be taken to imply that it presents
original, unpublished work not under consideration for publication elsewhere.
By submitting a manuscript, the authors agree that the copyright has been
assigned to the Association.

Articles should be submitted to Anne Loft, Copenhagen Business School,
Howitzvej 60, DK 2000F, Denmark.

Authors should specify the section of the journal for which they are
submitting their work.

EUROPEAN ACCOUNTING REVIEW

THE MANUSCRIPT

Submissions should be in English, typed in double spacing with wide margins, on one side only of the paper, preferably of A4 size. The title, but not the author's name, should appear on the first page of the manuscript. Furthermore, to assist objectivity, the author should avoid any reference to himself or herself which would enable identification by referees.

Articles should normally be as concise as possible and preceded by an abstract of not more than 200 words.

Tables and figures should not be inserted in the pages of the manuscript but should be on separate sheets. They should be numbered consecutively in arabic numerals with a descriptive caption. The desired position in the text for each table and figure should be indicated in the margin of the manuscript. Permission to reproduce copyright material must be obtained by the authors before submission and any acknowledgements should be included in the typescript or captions as appropriate.

Notes should be used only where necessary to avoid interrupting the continuity of the text. They should be numbered consecutively and placed at the end of the article before the bibliographic references.

If an article is accepted for publication, authors are requested to send an electronic version of their paper on disk. They are asked to ensure that the typescript is an exact printout of what is on the disk and provide details of the make and model of the computer and the name and version of the work processing package used.

REFERENCES

The Harvard system uses the name of the author and the date of publication as a key to the full bibliographical details which are set out in the references.

When the author's name is mentioned in the text, the date is inserted in parentheses immediately after the name, as in 'Fitchew (1990)'. When a less direct reference is made to one or more authors, both name and date are bracketed, with the references separated by a semi-colon, as in 'several authors have noted this trend (Roberts, 1990; Brunsson, 1990; Johnson, 1987)'.

When the reference is to a work of dual or multiple authorship, use only surnames or the abbreviated form, as in 'Johnson and Kaplan (1987)' or 'Jones et al. (1976)'. If an author has two references published in the same year, add lower-case letters after the date to distinguish them, as in 'Roberts (1990a, 1990b)'.

The date of publication used is the date of the source you have referred to. However, when using a republished book, a translation or a modern edition of an older edition, also give the date of the original publication, as in Flint (1988/1988), in order to place the work chronologically and locate it in the reference list. When using a reprinted article, cite date of original publication only, as this both places the work chronologically and locates it in the reference list. (See Format of reference for forms of citation in reference list.)

Page numbers are indicated by inserting the relevant numbers after the date, separated from the date by a colon and with no other punctuation, as in

'Provasoli (1989: 56)' or 'Casey and Bartczak (1985: 423)'. Always use the minimum number of figures in page numbers, dates, etc., e.g. 22-41, 101-2, 1968-9; but for 'teen numbers use 13-14, 1914-18, etc.

When an article is to be published in English, but references are made to institutions or works whose official title is not English, the following procedure should apply.

(a) institutions should always be referred to by their full official native title when first mentioned in the text, and by that title or an abbreviation of it thereafter. An English translation may be included, if appropriate, at the first mention, e.g. standard setting is the responsibility of the Conseil National de la Comptabilite (CNC - national accounting council). The CNC consists of...';

(b) articles, book titles, etc., which have been published other than in English should be referred to, where appropriate, using their original title;

(c) where a quotation is used in the text, this should be an English translation, with the foreign language appended as a footnote if this is essential for an understanding of the point, e.g. 'It is a little different to the extent that it does not consider accounting exclusively as a technique of capturing, recording and manipulating information' (Colasse, 1991 translation).

FORMAT OF REFERENCE LISTS AND BIBLIOGRAPHIES
Submissions should include a reference list whose content and format conforms to the following examples. Note: secondary lines are indented; authors' names are given in full; page numbers are required for articles in readers, journals and magazines; where relevant, translator and date of first publication of a book, and original date of reprinted article, are noted.

Book
> Bromwich, M. (1985) The Economics of Standard Setting. London: Prentice-Hall/ICAEW.

Multiple author
> Bruns, W. J. and Kaplan, R. S. (eds) (1987) Accounting and Management: Field Study Perspectives. Boston: Harvard Business School Press.

Article in edited volume
> Kaplan, R. S. (1985) 'Accounting lag: the obsolescence of cost accounting systems', in Clark, K. and Lorenze, C. (eds) Technology and Productivity: the Uneasy Alliance. Boston, MA: Harvard Business School Press, pp. 195-226.

Article in journal
> Ordelheide, D. (1993) 'The true and fair view: impact on and of the Fourth Directive', European Accounting Review, 2(1): 81-90.

Report
> Fitchew, G. E. (1990) 'Summing up', in Commission of the European Communities, The Future of Harmonization of Accounting Standards Within the European Communities. Brussels.

Article in newspaper
> The Times Literary Supplement (1991) 'The year that shook the world', 23 August 1991: 9.

EUROPEAN ACCOUNTING REVIEW

Unpublished

> Zito, A. (1994) 'Epistemic communities in European policy-making', Ph.D. dissertation, Department of Political Science, University of Pittsburgh.

NB: If referring to a revised or second edition, cite only edition used.

PROOFS

Page proofs will be sent for correction to a first-named author, unless otherwise requested. The difficulty and expense involved in making amendments at the page-proof stage make it essential for authors to prepare their typescript carefully: any alteration to the original text is strongly discouraged. Authors should correct printers' errors in red; minimal alterations of their own should be in black. Conference reports and doctoral summaries will be proofread by the editors.

OFFPRINTS

25 offprints and a copy of the journal will be supplied free of charge for each main article. In the case of joint authorship, offprints must be shared.

EUROPEAN ECONOMIC REVIEW

ADDRESS FOR SUBMISSION :

PROFESSOR FRANCOIS BOURGUIGNON, EDITOR
EUROPEAN ECONOMIC REVIEW
DELTA, 48 BD JOURDAN
PARIS, 75014
FRANCE
331-4581-4302
331-4432-2123 (Fax)
E-Mail : BOURG@Delta.eus.fr

CIRCULATION DATA :

Reader : Academic

Frequency of Issue : 8 Times/Year

Copies Per Issue : 2001-3000

Subscription Price : 600.00 US$

Sponsorship : Professional Assoc.

PUBLICATION GUIDELINES :

Manuscript Length : 11-20

Copies Required : Three

Computer Submission : No

Format : N/A

Fees to Review : 40.00 US$

REVIEW INFORMATION :

Type of Review : Editorial Review

No. of External Reviewers : Two

No. of In House Reviewers : Zero

Acceptance Rate : 11-20%

Time To Review : 4-6 months

Reviewer's Comments : Yes

Fees to Publish : 0.00 US$

Invited Articles : 5% or less

MANUSCRIPT TOPICS : COST ACCOUNTING;
   INTERNATIONAL & ECONOMIC DEVELOPMENT; INTERNATIONAL FINANCE;
   PUBLIC POLICY ECONOMICS

PUBLICATION GUIDELINES :

MANUSCRIPT GUIDELINES/COMMENTS :

1. Papers must be in English.

2. Papers for publication should be sent in triplicate to the Editor.

Submission of a paper will be held to imply that it contains original
unpublished work and is not being submitted for publication elsewhere. The
Editor does not accept responsibility for damage or loss of papers submitted.

Upon acceptance of an article, author(s) resident in the USA will be asked to
transfer copyright of the article to the publisher. This transfer will ensure
the widest possible dissemination of information under U.S. copyright law.

3. Manuscripts should be typewritten on one side of the paper only,
double-spaced with wide margins. All pages should be numbered consecutively.
Titles and subtitles should be short. References, tables and legends for
figures should be typed on separate pages. The legends and titles on tables
and figures must be sufficiently descriptive such that they are understandable
without reference to the text. The dimensions of figure axes and the body of

tables must be clearly labeled in English.
4. The first page of the manuscript should contain the following information:
     I.   The title;
     Il.   The name(s) and institutional affiliation(s) of the author(s);
     Ill. An abstract of not more than 100 words.

A footnote on the same sheet should give the name and present address of the author to whom proofs and reprint order form should be addressed.

5. Acknowledgements and information on grants received can be given before the references or in a first footnote, which should be included in the consecutive numbering of footnotes.

6. Important formulae (displayed) should be numbered consecutively throughout the manuscript as (1), (2), etc. on the right-hand side of the page. Where the derivation of formulae has been abbreviated, it is of great help to referees if the full derivation can be presented on a separate sheet (not to be published).

7. Footnotes should be kept to a minimum and be numbered consecutively throughout the text with superscript Arabic numerals.

8. The references should include only the most relevant papers. In the text, references to publication should appear as follows: "Smith (1969) reported that..." or "this problem has been a subject in literature before [e.g., Smith (1969, p. 102]". The author should make sure that there is a strict "one-to-one correspondence" between the names (years) in the text and those on the list. At the end of the manuscript (after any appendices), the complete references should be listed as:

For monographs
Tobin, James, 1971, Essays in economics, vol. 1, Macroeconomics
(North-Holland, Amsterdam).

For contributions to collective works
Glesjer, Hebert, 1970, Predictive world models, in: Colette Duprez and Etienne Sadi Kirschen, eds., Megistos, A world income and trade model for 1975
(North-Holland, Amsterdam) 3-16.

For periodicals
Goldfeld, Stephen M. and Richard E. Quandt, 1973, A Markov model for switching regressions, Journal of Econometrics, 1, 3-15.

Note that journal titles should not be abbreviated.

9. Illustrations should be provided in triplicate (1 original drawn in black ink on white paper plus 2 photocopies). Care should be taken that lettering and symbols are of a comparable size. The drawings should not be inserted in the text and should be marked on the back with figure numbers, title of paper, and name of author. All graphs and diagrams should be referred to as figures and should be numbered consecutively in the text in Arabic numerals. Graph paper should be ruled in blue and any grid lines to be shown should be inked black. Illustrations of insufficient quality which have to be redrawn by the publisher will be charged to the author.

EUROPEAN ECONOMIC REVIEW

10. All unessential tables should be eliminated from the manuscript. Tables should be numbered consecutively in the text in Arabic numerals and typed on separate sheets.

Any manuscript which does not conform to the above instructions may be returned for the necessary revision before publication.

PAGE PROOFS WILL BE SENT TO THE AUTHORS. CORRECTIONS OTHER THAN PRINTER'S ERRORS MAY BE CHARGED TO THE AUTHOR. TWENTY-FIVE REPRINTS OF EACH PAPER ARE SUPPLIED FREE; AVAILABLE AT COST IF THEY ARE ORDERED WHEN THE PROOF IS RETURNED.

EUROPEAN JOURNAL OF FINANCE

ADDRESS FOR SUBMISSION :

C. J. ADCOCK, EDITOR
EUROPEAN JOURNAL OF FINANCE
UNIVERSITY OF WESTMINISTER
309 REGENT STEET
LONDON, W1R 8AL
UK
+44 171 911 5000 EXT 2079
+44 181 402 0755 (Fax)
E-Mail : EJF@WMIN.AC.UK

CIRCULATION DATA :

Reader : Academic

Frequency of Issue : Quarterly

Copies Per Issue : Less than 1000

Subscription Price : 305.00 US$

Sponsorship :

PUBLICATION GUIDELINES :

Manuscript Length : 21-25

Copies Required : Four

Computer Submission : No

Format : N/A

Fees to Review : 65.00 US$
    EURO 50.00 US$

REVIEW INFORMATION :

Type of Review : Blind Review

No. of External Reviewers : Two

No. of In House Reviewers : Zero

Acceptance Rate :   50 %

Time To Review : 2-3 months

Reviewer's Comments : Yes

Fees to Publish : 0.00 US$

Invited Articles : 5% or less

MANUSCRIPT TOPICS : CAPITAL BUDGETING; COST ACCOUNTING;
   ECONOMETRICS; INSURANCE; INTERNATIONAL FINANCE;
   PORTFOLIO & SECURITY ANALYSIS; FINANCIAL ECONOMICS

PUBLICATION GUIDELINES :

MANUSCRIPT GUIDELINES/COMMENTS :

The emphasis of EUROPEAN JOURNAL OF FINANCE is primarily on research and
current issues in finance which reflect European interests and concerns.
Relevance to real world problems is a paramount concern.

(1) SUBMISSION OF PAPERS. Authors should submit four copies of their paper,
typed with double spacing on one side only of A4 sheets with a wide left hand
margin (30mm). The pitch should not exceed 12 characters per inch and the
character height must be at least 10 points. Papers must be written in English
and spelling should follow the Oxford English Dictionary.

(2) COVER PAGE. The cover page should contain only the the title of the paper
and the name(s) and affiliation(s) of the author(s). This page is removed
before the paper is sent to referees. For papers with more than one author,
this page must clearly designate one author to whom correspondence and proofs
are to be sent. A full postal address must be provided for the designated
author.

(3) FIRST PAGE. The first page should contain only the title of the paper, an abstract of about 100 words and a list of up to 6 keywords. The abstract should be a summary in words of the content of the paper and should not include references or equations.

(4) TEXT should be arranged in sequentially numbered sections using Arabic numerals. The first section should be the INTRODUCTION. Where appropriate for the content, sub-sections are allowed and these should be titled and numbered with a second digit (2.1, 2.2 and so on).

(5) SUMMARY AND/OR CONCLUSIONS The paper should end with a short non-technical summary or set of conclusions. Where appropriate this should include an indication of on-going work, or research that is required in the area. Acknowledgement of assistance and funding should appear here.

(6) TABLES AND FIGURES should be typed on separate pages. Their location in the paper should be indicated in the text. They must be self contained in the sense that they can be understood by a reader without the need to refer to the main text. Tables and figures should have a title followed by a descriptive legend. Authors should ensure that all table column headings and titling are clear and brief. Tables and figure should be separately and sequentially numbered. Authors must ensure that there is a reference to each table and figure in the text of the paper.

(7) EQUATIONS. All but very short mathematical expressions should be displayed on a separate line and centred. Equations should be sequentially numbered and punctuated in the usual way. Authors must ensure that their notation is unambiguous (for example o (oh) and 0 (zero). The use of bold to indicate vector matrix quantities should be noted in the margin. All mathematical terms must be clearly defined and it is sometimes useful to remind the reader if a technical term appears in a subsequent section.

(8) DEVELOPMENT OF MATHEMATICAL EXPRESSIONS should be presented in appendices with only the relevant results appearing in the text. Where results are being quoted from specialist mathematical journals or texts authors should ensure that the development is comprehensible to the a non-specialist reader and that sources are adequately cited, but should avoid unnecessary repetition of standard material.

(9) ABBREVIATIONS. All abbreviations should be clearly defined when they first appear in the text, for example as in European Journal of Finance(EJF). The definition may be omitted for abbreviations which are ubiquitous, for example EC, ECU.

(10) FOOTNOTES in the text should be numbered consecutively. The footnotes should appear at the end of the paper, after the summary/conclusions, but before appendices.

(11) REFERENCES should be listed in alphabetical order of surnames at the end of the paper after any appendices. References to books, monographs, collected works and conference papers should be prepared in the standard way:

For papers in journals and periodicals:
    Solnik B(1974) An Equilibrium Model of the International Capital Market, Journal of Economic Theory,8, 500 -524.

For books and monographs:
> Clark E, Levasseur M & Rousseau P(1993) International Finance, Chapman & Hall, London.

and for contributions to collected works:
> Harris L(1988) Intra-Day Stock Return Patterns in Dimson E Stock Market Anomalies, CUP, Cambridge.

A new references in the text should appear as ... Smith and Jones(1985) .... When a reference is to be cited a number of times, it is useful to define it, for example .. Smith and Jones(1985) (henceforth SJ85) ....

Multiple citations to an author in the same year should be identified by l lower case letter, as in Smith & Jones(199la), Smith and Jones(199lb) and so on.

(12) SUBMISSION CONDITIONS. It is a condition of submission to EJF that the paper contains original work and has not been submitted for publication in another journal or another form such as a monograph or book. Authors of submitted are expected not to submit their work for publication elsewhere until an editorial decision has been reached.

(13) SUBMISSION FEE. A cheque for 50ECU (or equivalent in any EC currency) to cover the submission fee should accompany each new paper submitted to EJF.

(14) REFEREEING AND PROOF READING. The receipt of all papers will be acknowledged by the managing editors. The aim of the editors of EJF is to reach a decision on all submitted papers in at most four months from submission. For accepted papers, the designated author is responsible for checking galley proofs, which will be sent to him directly by the publisher, and for returning them in the indicated timescale.

(15) CORRESPONDENCE OR COMMENTARY relating to published papers should be received within one year of the publication of the paper to which it refers. Commentary papers are expected to be brief and will be refereed in the normal way. Letters should be typed double spaced, follow the layout and style conventions for papers and should be limited to 400 words. The editors reserve the right to referees and/or to shorten letters.

EUROPEAN JOURNAL OF FINANCE is published by E & FN SPON (an imprint of Chapman & Hall), 2-6 Boundary Row, London SE1 8HN, UK. Tel: 0171-865-0066, Fax: 0171-522-9623. E-mail: spon@chall.co.uk

EUROPEAN JOURNAL OF LAW AND ECONOMICS

ADDRESS FOR SUBMISSION :

DR. JURGEN G. BACKHAUS, EDITOR
EUROPEAN JOURNAL OF LAW AND ECONOMICS
UNIVERSITY OF LIMBURG
DEPARTMENT OF ECONOMICS
P.O. BOX 616
6200 MD MAASTRICHT,
THE NETHERLANDS
031 433 883652
031 433 258440 (Fax)

CIRCULATION DATA :

Reader : Business Persons &
        Academic

Frequency of Issue : Quarterly

Copies Per Issue : Less than 1000

Subscription Price : 115.00 US$
  Institution : 280.00 US$

Sponsorship : Profit Oriented Corp.

PUBLICATION GUIDELINES :

Manuscript Length : 26-30

Copies Required : Three

Computer Submission : No

Format : N/A

Fees to Review : 0.00 US$

REVIEW INFORMATION :

Type of Review : Editorial Review

No. of External Reviewers : Two

No. of In House Reviewers : Two

Acceptance Rate : 21-30%

Time To Review : 1-2 months

Reviewer's Comments : Yes

Fees to Publish : 0.00 US$

Invited Articles : 5% or less

MANUSCRIPT TOPICS : ACCOUNTING INFORMATION SYSTEMS;
  PUBLIC POLICY ECONOMICS; LAW AND ECONOMICS, JEL. CODE: K

PUBLICATION GUIDELINES : Chicago Manual of Style

MANUSCRIPT GUIDELINES/COMMENTS :

AIMS AND SCOPE
The EUROPEAN JOURNAL OF LAW AND ECONOMICS publishes analytical work on the
impact of legal interventions into economic processes by legislators, courts
and regulatory agencies. There is an emphasis on European Community Law and
the comparative analysis of legal structures and legal problem solutions in
member states of the European Community. The editors are particularly
interested in papers discussing the institutional (and) legal prerequisites
for efficient market operation both in the European Community and in the new
European market economies.

The editors provide readers with high quality and empirical research in law
and economics. Case studies are welcome, as are the analyses of proposed
legislation and court cases. The EUROPEAN JOURNAL OF LAW AND ECONOMICS also
publishes literature surveys, review articles, and book reviews and notes.
Finally, important developments and topics in law and economics analysis will
be documented and examined in special issues dedicated to that subject.

EDITORIAL POLICY
The EUROPEAN JOURNAL OF LAW AND ECONOMICS is a peer-reviewed, quarterly

journal. Reviewers are asked to evaluate submissions with respect to both analytical rigor and practical usefulness. Work published here must be original and the analytical results must be reproducible. Authors must be prepared to have their (analytical) work challenged through academic discourse, and authors will be given an opportunity to respond to any challenges.

ADDRESS FOR CONTRIBUTORS
Submissions (with cover letters) of 3 copies of your contribution should be sent to the Editor.

MANUSCRIPT PREPARATION
Final versions of accepted manuscripts (including notes, references, tables, and legends) should be typed double-spaced on 8.5" x 11" (22 cm x 29 cm) white paper with 1" (2.5 cm) margins on all sides. Sections should appear in the following order: title page, abstract, text, notes, references, tables, figure legends, and figures. Comments or replies to previously published articles should also follow this format with the exception of abstracts, which are not required.

TITLE PAGE. The title page should include the article title, author's names and permanent affiliations, and the name, current address, and telephone number of the person to whom page proofs and reprints should be sent.

ABSTRACT. The following page should include an abstract of not more than 100 words and a list of two to six keywords. Also include JEL subject category number.

TEXT. The text of the article should begin on a new page. The introduction should have no heading or number. Subsequent headings (including appendices) should be designated by arabic numerals (1, 2, etc.) and subsection headings should be numbered 1.1, 1.2, etc. Figures, tables, and displayed equations should be numbered consecutively throughout the text (1, 2, etc.). Equation numbers should appear flush left in parentheses and running variables for equations (e.g. $i + 1, ..., n$) flush right in parentheses.

NOTES. Acknowledgements and related information should appear in a note designated by an asterisk after the last author' s name, and subsequent notes should be numbered consecutively and designated by superscripts in the text. All notes should be typed double-spaced beginning on a separate page following the text.

REFERENCES. References in the text should follow the author-date format (e.g. Brown (1986), Jones (1978a, 1978b), Smith and Johnson (1983)). References should be typed double-spaced beginning on a separate page following the notes, according to the following samples (journal and book titles may be underlined rather than italicized). References with up to three authors should include the names of each authors, references with four or more authors should cite the first author and add "et al.". It is the responsibility of the authors to verify all references.

Sample References
Machlup, F. (1969). "Positive and Normative Economics: An Analysis of the Ideas." In R. L. Heilbronner, (ed.), Economic Means and Social Ends, Englewood Cliffs, NJ, Prentice-Hall.

EUROPEAN JOURNAL OF LAW AND ECONOMICS

Stephen, F.H. (1986). "Decisions Making under Uncertainty: In Defence of Shackle." Journal of Economic Studies 13, 45-57.

Shavell, S. (1987). Economic Analysis of Accident Law, Cambridge, MA: Harvard University Press.

TABLES. Tables should be titled and typed double-spaced, each on a separate sheet, following the references. Notes to tables should be designated by superscripted letters within each table and typed double-spaced on the same page as the table. Use descreptive labels rather than computer acronyms, and explain all abbreviations. When tables are typed on oversized paper, please submit both the original and a reduced copy.

FIGURES. Figures for accepted manuscripts should be submitted in camera-ready form, i.e., clear glossy prints or drawn in India ink on drafting paper or high quality white paper. Lettering in figures should be large enough to be legible after half-size reduction. Authors should submit one 5" x 7" (13 cm x 18 cm) original and two photocopies of each figure, with author's names, manuscript title, and figure number on the back of each original and copy (use gummed labels if necessary to avoid damaging originals). Figures should be enclosed in a separate envelope backed by cardboard and without staples or paper clips. Figure legends should be typed double-spaced on a separate sheet following the tables.

PAGE PROOFS AND REPRINTS
Corrected page proofs must be returned within three days of receipt, and alterations other than corrections may be charged to the authors. Authors will receive 50 free reprints, and may order additional copies when returning the corrected proofs.

EUROPEAN JOURNAL OF LAW AND ECONOMICS is published by Kluwer Academic Press, P.O. Box 17, 3300 AH Dordrecht, The Netherlands. Phone (31) 78 524400, Fax (31) 78 524474.

EUROPEAN JOURNAL OF POPULATION

ADDRESS FOR SUBMISSION :

DANIEL CORGEAU, DAVID COLEMAN, EDITORS
EUROPEAN JOURNAL OF POPULATION
INSTITUT NATIONAL D'ETUDES
 DEMOGRAPHIQUES (INED)
27, RUE DU COMMADEUR
75675 PARIS CEDEX 14,
FRANCE
0142182107
0142132195 (Fax)
E-Mail : courgeau@ined.fr

CIRCULATION DATA :

Reader : Academic

Frequency of Issue : Quarterly

Copies Per Issue : Less than 1000

Subscription Price : 109.00 US$
    Institution : 264.00 US$

Sponsorship : Professional Assoc.

PUBLICATION GUIDELINES :

Manuscript Length : 26-30

Copies Required : Four

Computer Submission : No

Format : N/A

Fees to Review : 0.00 US$

REVIEW INFORMATION :

Type of Review : Blind Review

No. of External Reviewers : Two

No. of In House Reviewers : Two

Acceptance Rate : 21-30%

Time To Review : 1-2 months

Reviewer's Comments : Yes

Fees to Publish : 0.00 US$

Invited Articles : 5% or less

MANUSCRIPT TOPICS : ACCOUNTING INFORMATION SYSTEMS;
  PUBLIC POLICY ECONOMICS; POPULATION STUDIES

PUBLICATION GUIDELINES :

MANUSCRIPT GUIDELINES/COMMENTS :

SCOPE AND AIMS
The EUROPEAN JOURNAL OF POPULATION addresses a broad public of researchers,
policy-makers and others concerned with population processes and their
consequences. Its aim is to improve understanding of population phenomena by
giving priority to work that contributes to the development of theory and
method, and which spans the boundaries between demography and such disciplines
as sociology, anthropology, economics, geography, history, political science
and epidemiology and other sciences contributing to public health.

Published under the auspices of the EUROPEAN ASSOCIATION FOR POPULATION
STUDIES (EAPS), the Journal seeks to bring out similarities and contrasts in
demographic experience, in theoretical explanations, in research strategies
and in policy implications and formulation both within Europe as a region and
between Europe and other regions.

REVIEW PROCEDURE
All papers are submitted to expert referees for review. Their reports are
fully considered in selecting material for publication. The names of specific
referees are never divulged to the author; however, review comments may be

provided to assist the author in revising his paper. Letters are reviewed by the Editor for appropriateness and content. If it has been necessary to shorten or otherwise edit material submitted, this fact will be clearly indicated.

MANUSCRIPTS

ORGANIZATION OF THE PAPER AND STYLE OF PRESENTATION

All contributions are to be prepared in a style which maximizes information content, usefulness and relevance to a wide spectrum of readers. Papers should not require from the reader too specialized a background and should be generally understandable. In case supporting details of greater interest to the specialist are needed to complete the paper, these should be prepared in the form of an appendix. Authors are encouraged to make maximum use of figures, drawings, photographs and tabular presentations. It is a basic policy of this journal to let the content of the material covered establish the maximum length allowed for papers. Prospective authors should, however, make every effort to write concisely and succinctly, avoiding unnecessary detail.

It is recognized that there may be some situations where exceptions to the requested uniformity in style are appropriate, and the editors and publisher are ready to work with the author on any special problems. It is, however, in the best interests of producing a good journal in a timely manner to require adherence to certain standards of style for the preparation of typescripts as well as published papers.

1. Manuscripts should be written in impeccable English or French.

2. Submit the original and three copies of your manuscript. Enclose the original illustrations and two sets of photocopies (three prints of any photographs).

3. Manuscripts should be typed on one side of the paper, with wide margins and double spacing throughout, i.e., also for the abstract, footnotes and references. Every page of the manuscript, including the title page, references, tables, etc., should be numbered in the upper right-hand corner. However, in the text no reference should be made to page numbers; if necessary, one may refer to sections. Underline words that should be in italics, and do not underline any other words. Avoid the excessive use of italics as well as bold typeface to emphasize parts of the text.

4. SI (Systeme International) metric units should be used.

5. If a special instruction to the copy editor or typesetter is written on the copy it should be encircled. The typesetter will then know that the instruction is not to be set in type. When a typewritten character might have more than one meaning (e.g. the lowercase letter l may be confused with the numeral 1), a note should be inserted in a circle in the margin to make the meaning clear to the typesetter. If Greek letters or uncommon symbols are used in the manuscript, they should be written very clearly, and if necessary a note such as 'Greek lowercase chi' should be put in the margin and encircled.

6. Manuscripts should be organized in the following order:
   Title
   Name(s) of author(s)

EUROPEAN JOURNAL OF POPULATION

> Complete address of affiliation(s)
> Correspondence address
> Abstract
> Introduction
> **Main body of text subdivided by subheadings**
> Conclusion
> Appendix (if there is one)
> Acknowledgements
> References
> Tables   Illustrations and figure captions

7. Kluwer reserves the right to return to the author for revision accepted manuscripts and illustrations which are not in the proper form given in this guide.

TITLE PAGE
The first page should include:
> Title (clear, descriptive and not too long)
> Name(s) of author(s)
> Complete address of affiliation(s) - including a direct telephone/fax
>   number if possible
> Correspondence address, if different from affiliation
> Abstract (complete, self-explanatory and preferably not longer than 100
>   words)

Any short information concerning research grants, etc., may be included at the bottom of the title page but if this information is long, please include it in the 'Acknowledgements' section preceding the references.

ABSTRACT
(1) The abstract should be clear, descriptive, self-explanatory and/not longer than 100 words. It should also be suitable for publication elsewhere.

(2) At the beginning of each abstract provide the bibliographic entry by which the paper will be referenced, as follows:
> [name, initials], [year], [title paper], European Journal of Population.

MAIN BODY OF TEXT
Indicate headings and subheadings as follows: 1, 1.2, 1.3.1 etc. This makes it easier for the typesetter to set the headings, avoid misunderstandings about their relative importance and also has the advantage that you can easily refer to a section in other parts of the paper ('.. . as discussed in section 2.2 ...' etc.).

TABLES
1. Authors should take notice of the limitations set by the size and layout of the journal. Large tables should be avoided. Reversing columns and rows will often reduce the dimensions of a table.

2. If many data are to be presented, an attempt should be made to divide them over two or more tables.

3. Drawn tables intended for direct reproduction should not be folded.

4. Tables should be numbered according to their sequence in the text. The text should include references to all tables.

5. Each table should be typewritten on a separate page of the manuscript. Tables should never be included in the text.

6. Each table should have a brief and self-explanatory title.

7. Column headings should be brief, but sufficiently explanatory. Standard abbreviations of units of measurement should be added between parentheses.

8. Vertical lines should not be used to separate columns. Leave some extra space between the columns instead.

9. Any explanations essential to the understanding of the table should be given in footnotes at the bottom of the table.

ILLUSTRATIONS
1. Illustrations (line drawings and photographs) should be on separate sheets of paper, not pasted on pages and not folded.

2. Illustrations should be numbered according to their sequence in the text, and labelled fig. 1, fig. 2, etc. References should be made in the text to each illustration

3. Each illustration should be identified on the reverse side (or, in the case of line drawings, on the lower front side) by its number and the name of the author. An indication of the top of the illustrations is required in those cases where doubts may arise.

4. Illustrations should be designed with the format of the page of the journal in mind. Illustrations should be of such a size as to allow a reduction of 50%.

5. Lettering should be done using transfer letters or Indian ink. Make sure that the size of the lettering is big enough to allow a reduction of 50% without becoming illegible. The text in the illustration should be in English or in French. Use the same kind of lettering on every illustration.

6. On maps and other illustrations where a scale is needed, use bar scales rather than numerical ones, i.e., do not use scales of the type 1:10,000. This avoids problems if the illustration needs to be reduced.

7. Each illustration should have a self-explanatory caption. The captions to all illustrations should be typed on a separate sheet of the manuscript.

8. Explanations should be given in the typewritten legend. The text in the illustration itself should be kept to a minimum.

9. Photographs are only acceptable if they have good contrast and intensity. Only sharp and glossy original photographs without screen can be satisfactorily reproduced. Reproductions of photographs which have already appeared in print cannot be accepted.

10. Colour illustrations cannot usually be included, unless the cost of their reproduction is paid for by the author.

COMPUTER OUTPUT
Computer-produced output is only acceptable for photographic reproduction if
the original copies, on unruled paper in black ink, are produced by
high-quality (carbon ribbon) typewriters or other comparable impact-type
devices. Photo-composition output is normally acceptable.

MATHEMATICAL EXPRESSIONS
1. All formulae in a manuscript should be presented in a consistent and clear
way, with respect to the meaning of each symbol and its correct position.
Please type formulae throughout. Only if unavoidable should symbols be put in
by hand, but be careful that everything is clear and unambiguous.

2. All handwritten and unusual symbols must be collected in a separate list
giving a clear explanation of each symbol and identified in the manuscript at
its first occurrence.

3. Do not use special typefonts if there is no need to.

4. Do not use complicated juxtapositions of symbols, especially in the text.
Also try to avoid complicated subscripts and superscripts; second-order
indices especially may present difficulties and third-order indices are taboo.

5. All formulae which are to be referred to later on must be displayed and
numbered consecutively (1), (2) etc. on the right-hand side of the page.

REFERENCES
1. In the text, refer to the author's name (without initial, unless more than
one author has the same surname) and year of publication; if it is considered
helpful, a short reference may be made to the appropriate pages. Examples:
'[name] ([year]) suggested that...'; '...as was clearly the case ([name],
[year], pp. [first page]-[last page]).'

2. Refer to a personal communication as follows: ([name], personal
communication, [year]).

3. If reference is made in the text to a publication written by more than two
authors, the name of the first author should be used followed by 'et al.' This
indication, however, should never be used in the list of references: in this
list the names of the first author and all co-authors should be mentioned.

4. References cited together in the text should be arranged chronologically.

5. All publications cited in the text should be presented in a list of
references following the text of the manuscript. The manuscript should be
carefully checked to ensure that the spelling of the author's names and the
dates are exactly the same in the text as in the reference list, and that the
reference list is complete.

6. The list of references should be arranged alphabetically by authors' names,
and chronologically per author. If an author's name is mentioned separately as
well as with one or more co-authors, the following order should be used:
publications of a single author, arranged in chronological order -
publications of the author with one co-author - publications of the author
with more than one coauthor. Publications by the same author(s) in the same

year should be listed as 1985a, 1985b, etc.
7. Use the following system for arranging your references:
a. For periodicals
   [name, initials], [year], [title paper], [title periodical] [volume],
   [first page]-[last page].
b. For edited symposia, special issues, etc., published in a periodical
   [name, initials], [year], [title paper], in: [title issue], special issue
   of [title periodical] [volume], [first page]-[last page].
c. For books
   [name, initials], [year], [title book] ([publisher], [place of
   publication]).
d. For multi-author books
   name, initials], [year], [title paper], in: [initials + names of editors]
   [eds.], [title book] ([publisher], [place of publication])
   [first page]-[last page].
e. For unpublished reports, departmental notes, etc.
   [name, initials], [year], [title paper], Unpublished [description] ([name
   of institute, department, etc.]).
f. For papers not yet published
   [name, initials], [year], [title paper], Submitted for publication in (or:
   Accepted for publication in) [title periodical].

8. Do not abbreviate the titles of periodicals in the list of references.

9. In the case of publications in any language other than English, the
original title is to be retained. However, the titles of publications in
non-Latin alphabets should be transliterated, and a notation such as '(in
Russian)' or '(in Greek, with English abstract)' should be added.

FOOTNOTES
1. Footnotes should only be used if absolutely essential. In most cases it
will be possible to incorporate the information in the text.

2. If used, they should be numbered in the text, indicated by superscript
numbers and kept as short as possible.

MANUSCRIPTS ON DISKETTE
FORMAT
1. We strongly prefer manuscripts typed on IBM-compatible computers, with
operating system MS DOS (versions 3.2 or higher), and wordprocessing package
WordPerfect (4.2 or higher).

2. We also accept files in most other wordprocessing packages, that run under
MS DOS, and Apple Macintosh diskettes.

3. If this combination is not available to you, please contact us as soon as
possible.

4. If you work with the Graphical User Interface Windows or on a Macintosh
computer, use only regular fonts like Courier, Times, Helvetica or standard
Symbol.

DO's
1. File. Identify your file clearly with a sensible name. Make absolutely sure
that you send us your final version, and that the printout is identical to

what you have saved on the diskette.

2. Consistency. Be absolutely consistent and check the use of punctuation, abbreviations, capitals and lower case in headings, spelling, etc. If possible, use the spelling checker on your computer.

3. Special characters. If the ASCII character set or the character set(s) of your wordprocessing package does not contain the special characters you need, key in a code between angle brackets, < >, and use this each and every time you want the character to appear. You could, for example, use <gamma> for a lower case Greek gamma and <Gamma> for an upper case Greek gamma. Make the code self-explanatory. Note: Always supply us with a list of the codes that you have used!

4. Headings. Start headings etc. flush left, with two space lines above (i.e. three Hard Returns) and one space line below (two Hard Returns). Distinguish different levels of headings and be consistent.

5. Paragraphs. Indent all paragraphs with a [TAB] code, and separate them from one another with one Hard Return.

6. Block quotations should be indented with an [Indent] code and should have one space line (i.e. two Hard Returns) above and below.

7. Figures should be submitted in camera-ready form. The position of the figure in the text should be indicated in the margins of the hard copy. Figure legends should be placed at the end of your file.

8. Tables. We prefer tables to be submitted in camera-ready form. If you also put your tables on diskette, please separate columns with [TAB] codes (not with spaces) and, consequently, adjust the tabular stops to position the columns.

9. Equations. One-line equations without fractions can be typeset from the diskette when they are keyed in as plain text. Other equations can not be used from the diskette: they will be typeset manually from the hard copy.

10. References and Notes. Strictly follow the Instructions for Authors of the journal in which the article will be published for the style of referencing and the use of notes.

DON'Ts

1. Hyphenation. Do not hyphenate words at the end of a line. Use only one hyphen for words such as "well-being", and "re-do" and use two hyphens for sequences of dates and years such as "conference dates are 12--15 September, 1992", "age groups between 20--30 years are welcome", and page number indications in References, e.g. "pp. 240--243".

2. Hard Returns. Do not use Hard Returns except when absolutely necessary, such as at the end of paragraphs, headings, etc. Otherwise, let the word wrap feature of your wordprocessor do this work for you.

3. TAB feature and Spacebar. If you need more than one space between two items, e.g. when you write in columns, always use the [TAB] feature of your wordprocessing package. Use the spacebar only for separating words from one another. Do not use the spacebar to format tables, for centering or laying out

texts, or for any other form of line or page formatting.

DELIVERING YOUR ARTICLE

1. Always supply us with both the hard-copy (printout) version of your final text and the diskette.

2. Label your diskette properly, giving exact details on operating system and software used.

3. Always retain a backup copy of your diskette.

Copyright

COPYRIGHT

1. An author, when quoting from someone else's work or when considering reproducing an illustration or table from a book or journal article, should make sure that he is not infringing a copyright.

2. Although in general an author may quote from other published works, he should obtain permission from the holder of the copyright if he wishes to make substantial extracts or to reproduce tables, plates or other illustrations. If the copyright-holder is not the author of the quoted or reproduced material, it is recommended that the permission of the author should also be sought.

3. Material in unpublished letters and manuscripts is also protected and must not be published unless permission has been obtained.

4. Submission of a paper will be interpreted as a statement that the author has obtained all necessary permissions.

5. A suitable acknowledgement of any borrowed material must always be made.

6. Upon acceptance of an article by the journal, the author(s) will be asked to transfer the copyright of the article to the publisher. This transfer will ensure the widest possible dissemination of information.

PROOFS

1. Copy editing of manuscripts is performed by the staff of Kluwer. The author is asked to check the galley proofs for typographical errors and to answer queries from the copy editor.

2. Kluwer, at its discretion, is entitled to recover from the author of any paper or report published in the journal, any cost occasioned by the alterations made by the author in the printer's proof other than correction of typesetting errors and essential additions which update information in the paper; the latter preferably as sentences at the end of existing paragraphs or as new paragraphs.

REPRINTS

1. 25 reprints will be supplied free of charge.

2. Additional reprints can be ordered on a reprint order form which is included with the proofs.

3. UNESCO coupons are acceptable as payment for extra reprints.

SUBMISSION OF MANUSCRIPTS
Submission of an article is understood to imply that the article is original
and unpublished and is not being considered for publication elsewhere.

If the address to which proofs should be sent is different from the
correspondence address, authors are kindly requested to indicate this.

Papers should be submitted to Editorial Office

Editorial Office
    Ms Hella Courgeau (assistant editor)
    INED
    27, rue du Commandeur
    75675 Paris Cedex 14 - FRANCE
    Tel.: 33(1)42 18 20 00 Fax: 33(1)42 18 21 99

Editorial Committee
    Daniel Courgeau (editor)
    INED
    David Coleman (editor)
    University of Oxford
    Dpt of Applied Social Studies and Social Research
    Barnett House, Wellington square
    Oxford OX1 2ER- UNITED KINGDOM
    Tel.: 44(0)1865 270 345 Fax: 44(0)1865 270 324

Book review Editor
    Clara Mulder
    University of Uhecht
    P.O. Box 80115
    3508 TC Utrecht
    Tel.: 31 30 2532243 Fax: 31 30 2540604

EUROPEAN JOURNAL OF POPULATION is published by Kluwer Academic Press, P.O. Box
17, 3300 AH Dordrecht, The Netherlands. Phone (31) 78 524400, Fax (31) 78
524474.

EXPLORATIONS IN ECONOMIC HISTORY

ADDRESS FOR SUBMISSION :

PROFESSOR LARRY NEAL, EDITOR
EXPLORATIONS IN ECONOMIC HISTORY
UNIVERSITY OF ILLINOIS
328 DAVID KINLEY HALL
1407 WEST GREGORY DRIVE
URBANA, IL 61801
USA
217-333-8153
217-333-1398 (Fax)
E-Mail : l-neal@uiuc.edu

CIRCULATION DATA :

Reader : Academic

Frequency of Issue : Quarterly

Copies Per Issue : Less than 1000

Subscription Price : 126.00 US$
    Foreign : 140.00 US$

Sponsorship : Profit Oriented Corp.

PUBLICATION GUIDELINES :

Manuscript Length : 50 Maximum

Copies Required : Three

Computer Submission : Yes

Format : IBM Compatible + hard copy

Fees to Review : 0.00 US$

REVIEW INFORMATION :

Type of Review : Blind Review

No. of External Reviewers : Two

No. of In House Reviewers : One

Acceptance Rate : 11-20%

Time To Review : 4-6 months

Reviewer's Comments : Yes

Fees to Publish : 0.00 US$

Invited Articles : 5% or less

MANUSCRIPT TOPICS : ACCOUNTING INFORMATION SYSTEMS;
    ECONOMIC HISTORY

PUBLICATION GUIDELINES :

MANUSCRIPT GUIDELINES/COMMENTS :

1. EXPLORATIONS IN ECONOMIC HISTORY publishes research papers of scholarly merit on a wide range of topics in economic history. The focus is wide, encompassing all aspects of economic change, all historical times, and all geographical places. Topics of interest include economic development, income distribution, urbanization, poverty, human resource development, as well as the more traditional topics of business enterprise, finance, agriculture, manufacturing, and transportation improvements. Preference is given to the use of quantitative methods and explicit theoretical analysis, but all approaches to historical inquiry are welcome.

2. Original papers only will be considered. Manuscripts are accepted for review with the understanding that the same work has not been and will not be published nor is presently submitted elsewhere, and that its submission for publication has been approved by all of the authors and by the institution where the work was carried out; further, that any person cited as a source of personal communications has approved such citation. Written authorization may be required at the Editor's discretion. Articles and any other material published in EXPLORATIONS IN ECONOMIC HISTORY represent the opinions of the author(s) and should not be construed to reflect the opinions of the Editor(s)

and the Publisher.

3. Authors submitting a manuscript do so on the understanding that if it is accepted for publication, copyright in the article, including the right to reproduce the article in all forms and media, shall be assigned exclusively to the Publisher. The Publisher will not refuse any reasonable request by the author for permission to reproduce any of his or her contributions to the Journal.

4. FORM OF MANUSCRIPT. Manuscripts should be submitted in triplicate (1 original and 2 photocopies), typed double-spaced on one side of 8.5 x 11 inch white bond paper with 1 inch margins on all sides. Page 1 should contain the article title, author(s) name(s) and affiliation(s), a short running head (abbreviated form of title) not exceeding 40 characters including letters and spaces, and the name and complete mailing address of the person to whom correspondence should be sent. At the bottom of Page 1 any footnotes to the title (indicated by ╆, *, ₭). Page 2 should contain a 100-word abstract, double-spaced. Each page of the manuscript should be numbered.

5. FIGURES. All artwork should be numbered in order of appearance with Arabic numerals. Short descriptive captions for each figure, legends, and sources should be typed in order, doublespaced on a separate page.

6. Line drawings must be originals in black India ink on white paper. Lettering should be uniform and large enough to be legible after a reduction of 50 - 60%. Halftone artwork should be glossy prints ready for reproduction. The author should consider the proportions of the printed page in planning artwork (a maximum size of 5 x 7 inches is desirable). Illustrations in color can be accepted only if the authors defray the cost.

7. TABLES. All tabular material should be numbered in order of appearance in text (with Arabic numerals). They should be typed double-spaced on a separate page. Each table should have a short descriptive title typed above it. Footnotes to the table (indicated by superscript lowercase letters) should be typed at the bottom of the table.

8. FOOTNOTES to the text should be indicated by superscript Arabic numerals cited in order throughout the article. They should be typed double-spaced on a separate page.

9. REFERENCES should be cited in text by the author and publication date in parentheses, e.g., Smith (1988). If more than one paper was published in a given year, the correct style is Smith (1987a) and Smith (1987b). References should be listed alphabetically at the end of the article typed double-spaced on separate page. Note the following examples:

Boyer, G.R. (1985), "An Economic Model of the English Poor Law Circa 1780-1834". Explorations in Economic History 22, 129-167.

Gottlieb, M. (1983), A Theory of Economic Systems. New York: Academic Press. Chaps. 2, 3.

Rainwater, L., and Rein M. (1983). "The Growing Complexity of Economic Claims in Welfare Societies". In S.E. Spiro and E. Yuchtman-Yaar (Ed.), Evaluating the Welfare State: Social and Political Perspectives. NewYork: Academic Press. pp.111-129.

10. PROOFS. Proofs will be sent to the author with a reprint order form. Authors will be charged for alterations in excess of 10% of the cost of composition.

11. REPRINTS. Twenty-five (25) reprints of each article (without covers) will be supplied free of charge. Additional reprints may be ordered. A reprint form will accompany the proofs.

FACILITIES

ADDRESS FOR SUBMISSION :

EDWARD FINCH, EDITOR
FACILITIES
THE UNIVERSITY OF READING
DEPARTMENT OF CONSTRUCTION MANAGEMENT
  AND ENGINEERING
WHITEKNIGHTS, P.O. BOX 219
READING, RG6 2AW
UK

E-Mail : e.f.finch@reading.ac.uk

CIRCULATION DATA :

Reader : Business Persons &
         Academic

Frequency of Issue : 13 Times/Year

Copies Per Issue :

Subscription Price : 1139.00 US$

Sponsorship : Profit Oriented Corp.

PUBLICATION GUIDELINES :

Manuscript Length : 2,000-4,000 words

Copies Required : Three

Computer Submission : No

Format : N/A

Fees to Review : 0.00 US$

REVIEW INFORMATION :

Type of Review : Blind Review

No. of External Reviewers : Two

No. of In House Reviewers : One

Acceptance Rate :

Time To Review : 2-3 months

Reviewer's Comments :

Fees to Publish : 0.00 US$

Invited Articles :

MANUSCRIPT TOPICS : COST ACCOUNTING; REAL ESTATE;
  PEOPLE, PROPERTY AND PROCESS MANAGEMENT

PUBLICATION GUIDELINES :

MANUSCRIPT GUIDELINES/COMMENTS :

ABOUT THE JOURNAL
Articles submitted to the journal should be original contributions and should
not be under consideration for any other publication at the same time.
Submissions should be sent to:

THE EDITORS
Dr Edward Finch, Department of Construction Management and Engineering, The
University of Reading, Whiteknights, PO Box 219, Reading RG6 2AW, UK. E-mail:
<e.f.finch@reading.ac.uk> and Fari Akhlaghi, Unit for Facilitied Management
Reaearch, Sheffield Hallam University, UK. E-mail: <FAKHLAGHI@SHU.AC.UK.

EDITORIAL OBJECTIVES
The term "facilities" is used to describe the physical environment that is
occupied and utilized by an organization in order to carry out its various
functions. "Facilities management" (FM) is a hybrid management discipline that
combines people, property and process management expertise to provide vital
services in support of the organization.

FACILITIES

FACILITIES is interested in all areas relating to briefing, design, construction and use of facilities and in the emerging technologies that support organizational functions at the workplace. FACILITIES is also interested in innovations in theory, tools, legislation, analysis techniques and applications of new ideas in the wide spectrum of the facilities management discipline. The journal aims to maintain a crucial balance between "academic" -and "practitioner" -based contributios, both to satisfy the needs of its readership and also to meet the development requirements of this important and expanding field. Outstanding case studies which give detailed exposition of how different organizations have realized significant achievements in any aspect of facilities design, planning and management are particularly encouraged.

FACILITIES is the first journal in the field of facilities management with an "academic refereed" content combined with other contributions in the form of new ideas, news, research findings, case examples, book reviews and editorials. In addition to being the natural place for publication by FM scholars, the journal aims to be a key publication vehicle among eminent researchers in all the relevant traditional academic fields who recognize facilities management as a fertile ground for furthr development of their work. In all this, the journal always aims to remain relevant and useful to the forward-thinking senior professional practitioner looking for information on management and operational innovations.

FACILITIES will, therefore, publish original and authoritative papers that contribute to the advancement of research and practice in facilities management and its related fields. FACILITIES has an international outlook and draws from contributions worldwide. The journal only prints contributions that have not been published elsewhere in English. The Editor, however, may consider an article which has previously been published in another language. In such cases the author must make this clear. Valuable conference papers will also be considered from time to time if the Editor considers the further dissemination of the work through FACILITIES to be particularly supportive of the journal's editorial objectives.

THE REVIEWING PROCESS
Each paper submitted is subject to the following review procedures:

(1) It is reviewed by the editor for general suitability for this publication.
(2) If it is judged suitable two reviewers are selected and a double blind review process takes place.
(3) Based on the recommendations of the reviewers, the editors then decide whether the particular article should be accepted as it is, revised or rejected.

ARTICLE FEATURES AND FORMATS REQUIRED OF AUTHORS
There are a number of specific requirements with regard to article features and formats which authors should note carefully:

1. Word length
Articles should be between 2,000 and 4,000 words in length.

2. Title
A title of not more than eight words in length should be provided.

3. Autobiographical note
A brief autobiographical note should be supplied including full name, appointment, name of organization and e-mail address.

4. Word processing
Please submit to the Editor three copies of the manuscript in double line spacing with wide margins.

5. Headings and sub-headings
These should be short and to-the-point, appearing approximately every 750 words. Headings should be typed in capitals and underlined; sub-headings should be typed in upper and lower case and underlined. Headings should not be numbered.

6. References
References to other publications should be in Harvard style. They should contain full bibliographical details and journal titles should not be abbreviated. For multiple citations in the same year use a, b, c immediately following the year of publication. References should be shown as follows:

* Within the text - author's last name followed by a comma and year of publication all in round brackets, e g. (Fox, 1994).

* At the end of the article a reference list in alphabetical order as follows:
  (a) For books:
      surname, initials, year of publication, title, publisher, place of publication, e.g. Casson, M. (1979), Alternatives to the Multinational Enterprise, Macmillan, London.
  (b) For chapter in edited in book:
      surname, initials, year, title, editor's surname, initials, title, publisher, place, pages, e.g.
      Bessley, M. and Wilson, P. (1984), "Public policy and small firms in Britain", in Levicki, C. (Ed.), Small Business Theory and Policy, Croom Helm, London, pp. 111-26.
  (c) For articles:
      surname, initials, year, title, journal, volume, number, pages, e.g.
      Fox, S. (1994), "Empowerment as a catalyst for change: an example from the food industry", Supply Chain Management, Vol. 2 No. 3, pp. 29-33.

If there is more than one author list surnames followed by initials. All authors should be shown.
Electronic sources should include the URL of the electronic site at which they may be found.

Notes/Endnotes should be used only if absolutely necessary. They should be identified in the text by consecutive numbers enclosed in square brackets and listed at the end of the article.

7. Figures, charts, diagrams
Use of figures, charts and diagrams should be kept to a minimum and information conveyed in such a manner should instead be described in text form. Essential figures, charts and diagrams should be referred to as figures and numbered consecutively using arabic numerals. Each figure should have a brief title and labelled axes. Diagrams should be kept as simple as possible

FACILITIES

and avoid unnecessary capitalization and shading In the text, the position of the figure should be shown by typing on a separate line the words "take in Figure 1".

8. Tables
Use of tables should be kept to a minimum. Where essential, these should be typed on a separate sheet of paper and numbered consecutively and independently of any figures included in the article. Each table should have a number in roman numerals, a brief title, and vertical and horizontal headings. In the text, the position of the table should be shown by typing on a separate line the words "take in Table 1". Tables should not repeat data available elsewhere in the paper.

9. Photos, illustrations
Half-tone illustrations should be restricted in number to the minimum necessary. Good glossy bromide prints should accompany the manuscripts but not be attached to manuscript pages. Illustrations unsuitable for reproduction, e.g. computer-screen capture, will not be used. Any computer programs should be supplied as clear and sharp print outs on plain paper. They will be reproduced photographically to avoid errors.

10. Emphasis
Words to be emphasized should be limited in number and italicized. Capital letters should be used only at the start of sentences or in the case of proper names.

11. Abstracts
Authors must supply an abstract of 100-150 words when submitting an article. It should be an abbreviated, accurate representation of the content of the article. Major results, conclusions and/or recommendations should be given, followed by supporting details of method, scope or purpose. It should contain sufficient information to enable readers to decide whether they should obtain and read the entire article.

12. Keywords
Up to six keywords should be included which encapsulate the principal subjects covered by the article. Minor facets of an article should not be keyworded. These keywords will be used by readers to select the material they wish to read and should therefore be truly representative of the article's main content.

PREPARATION FOR PUBLICATION
13. Final submission of the article
Once accepted by the Editor for publication, the final version of the article should be submitted in manuscript accompanied by a 3.5" disk of the same version of the article marked with: disk format; author name(s); title of article; journal title; file name. This will be considered to be the definitive version of the article and the author should ensure that it is complete, grammatically correct and without spelling or typographical errors.

In preparing the disk, please use one of the following formats:
- for text prepared on a PC - AMI Pro, FrameMaker, Office Writer, Professional write, RTF, Word or WordPerfect;
- for text prepared on a Macintosh system - FrameMaker, MacWrite, MS Works, Nisus 3, RTF, Word, WordPerfect WriteNow or ASCII

FACILITIES

- for graphics, figures, charts and diagrams, please use one of the following formats:

File type	Programs	File extension
Windows Metafile	Most Windows programs	.wmf
WordPerfect Graphic	All WordPerfect software	.wpg
Adobe Illustrator	Adobe Illustrator	.ai
	Corel Draw	
	Macromedia Freehand	
Harvard Graphics	Harvard Graphics	.cgm
PIC	Lotus graphics	.pic
Computer/Graphics Metafile	Lotus Freelance	.cgm
DXF	Autocad	.dxf
	Many CAD programs	
GEM	Ventura Publisher	.gem
Macintosh PICT	Most Macintosh Drawing	

Only vector type drawings are acceptable, as bitmap files (extension .bmp, .pcx or .gif) print poorly. If graphical representations are not available on disk, black ink line drawings suitable for photographic reproduction and of dimensions appropriate for reproduction on a journal page should be supplied with the article.

If you require technical assistance in respect of submitting an article please consult the relevant section of MCB's World Wide Web Literati Club on http://www.mcb.co.uk/literati/nethome.htm or contact Mike Massey at MCB, e-mail: mmassey@mcb.co.uk

14. Journal Article Record Form
Each article should be accompanied by a completed and signed Journal Article Record Form. This form is available from the Editor or can be downloaded from MCB's World Wide Web Literati Club on http://www.mcb.co.uk/literati/nethome.htm

15. Author proofs
Where author proofs are supplied, they will be sent to corresponding authors who will be expected to correct and return them within five days of receipt or the article will be published without author corrections. The publisher is not responsible for any error not marked by the author on the proof Corrections on the proof are limited to typesetting errors; no substantial author changes are allowed at this stage.

COPYRIGHT
Authors submitting articles for publication warrant that the work is not an infringement of any existing copyright and will indemnify the publisher against any breach of such warranty. For ease of dissemination and to ensure proper policing of use, papers and contributions become the legal copyright of the publisher unless otherwise agreed.

FACILITIES is published by MCB University Press, 60/62 Toller Lane, Bradford, West Yorkshire BD8 9BY, UK. Tel: +44 1274 777700, Fax: +44 1274 785201. Internet URL: http://www.mcb.co.uk Modem Link: +44 1274 481703

FINANCE AND DEVELOPMENT

ADDRESS FOR SUBMISSION :

CLAIRE LIUKSILA, EDITOR
FINANCE AND DEVELOPMENT
INTERNATIONAL MONETARY FUND
700 19TH STREET,N.W.
WASHINGTON, DC 20431
USA
202-623-8768
202-623-4738 (Fax)

CIRCULATION DATA :

Reader : Business Persons &
        Academic

Frequency of Issue : Quarterly

Copies Per Issue : Over 25,000

Subscription Price :
  Airmail per year : 20.00 US$

Sponsorship : Professional Assoc.

PUBLICATION GUIDELINES :

Manuscript Length :

Copies Required :

Computer Submission : No

Format : N/A

Fees to Review : 0.00 US$

REVIEW INFORMATION :

Type of Review : Blind Review

No. of External Reviewers :

No. of In House Reviewers : Over 3

Acceptance Rate :   50 %

Time To Review : One month or less

Reviewer's Comments : Yes

Fees to Publish : 0.00 US$

Invited Articles : Over 50%

MANUSCRIPT TOPICS : ECONOMETRICS;
  GOVERNMENT & NON-PROFIT ACCOUNTING; INTERNATIONAL FINANCE;
  PORTFOLIO & SECURITY ANALYSIS; PUBLIC POLICY ECONOMICS; ECONOMICS;
  FINANCE & INVESTMENTS; INTERNATIONAL BUSINESS

PUBLICATION GUIDELINES : Chicago Manual of Style

MANUSCRIPT GUIDELINES/COMMENTS :

INVITED ARTICLES: 100%
This is an "in-house" journal, that is a journal that publishes material
prepared by the staff of the IMF and the World Bank. The only exception to
this is the series of "Guest Articles" by outside authors at the express
invitation of the Editor.

Accepts Advertising.

FINANCE INDIA

ADDRESS FOR SUBMISSION :

DR. JAIDEV AGARWAL, EDITOR
FINANCE INDIA
INDIAN INSTITUTE OF FINANCE
P.O. BOX 8486
ASHOK VIHAR II
DELHI, 110052
INDIA
011-91-11-7136257
011-91-11-7454128 (Fax)

CIRCULATION DATA :

Reader : Business Persons &
          Academic

Frequency of Issue : Quarterly

Copies Per Issue : 1001-2000

Subscription Price : 60.00 US$
    Institution : 80.00 US$

Sponsorship : Non Profit Corp.

PUBLICATION GUIDELINES :

Manuscript Length : No Limit

Copies Required : Three

Computer Submission : No

Format : N/A

Fees to Review : 20.00 US$

REVIEW INFORMATION :

Type of Review : Blind Review

No. of External Reviewers : Two

No. of In House Reviewers : One

Acceptance Rate : 11-20%

Time To Review : 2-3 months

Reviewer's Comments : Yes

Fees to Publish : 0.00 US$

Invited Articles : 5% or less

MANUSCRIPT TOPICS : ACCOUNTING THEORY & PRACTICE; AUDITING;
   CAPITAL BUDGETING; COST ACCOUNTING; ECONOMETRICS; ECONOMIC HISTORY;
   GOVERNMENT & NON-PROFIT ACCOUNTING; INSURANCE;
   INTERNATIONAL & ECONOMIC DEVELOPMENT; INTERNATIONAL FINANCE;
   PORTFOLIO & SECURITY ANALYSIS; PUBLIC POLICY ECONOMICS; REAL ESTATE

PUBLICATION GUIDELINES :

MANUSCRIPT GUIDELINES/COMMENTS :

OBJECTIVE
FINANCE INDIA is the official publication of Indian Institute of Finance. The
primary aim of the Journal is to promote research by disseminating the results
of such research in Finance, Accounting and related areas. The Journal is
intended to provide scholars a major forum for interdisciplinary and
intradisciplanary study of various aspects of Finance.

The Journal publishes articles, research papers, abstracts of doctoral
dissertations, contents of articles published in different journals, book
reviews, abstracts of books recently published, an extensive bibliography on
one of the areas related to Finance, and relevant statistics on Indian
economy, money and banking, international trade and finance, public sector
enterprises and industry.

The Journal is published four times a year in March, June, September and
December.

EDITORIAL CORRESPONDENCE
All correspondence relating to articles, research papers, etc. for FlNANCE INDIA should be submitted to the Chief Editor, Prof. J. D. Agarwal, or to Managing Editor, Dr. Manju Agarwal, Indian Institute of Finance, P.O. Box 8486, Ashok Vihar II, Delhi-110052, India. All articles, research papers, book reviews, etc. should be original and must not be published elsewhere. As far as possible the articles and research papers should make positive contribution towards theoretical knowledge in the area of Finance and Accounting or alternatively should have practical bias. All papers submitted are screened by Managing Editor or a member of the editorial board and sent for blind review to two experts.

IIF assumes no responsibility for the views expressed by the authors. All rights reserved, reproduction in any manner, in whole or in part, in English or in any other language, is not permitted without prior permission.

INSTRUCTIONS FOR AUTHORS/FORMAT AND STYLE

a. Authors should submit three copies of their manuscript, clearly typed with double spacing; Verbatim inset quotations should be single spaced.

b. The cover page shall contain the title of the manuscript, the author's name, affiliation including acknowledgment if any. This page will be removed before the manuscript is sent to referees. The first page of text should show the title but NOT the author's name.

c. Each manuscript should include an abstract of about 100 words.

d. The introductory section must have no heading or number. Subsequent headings should be given Roman numerals. Subsection headings should be lettered A, B, C, etc.

e. The article should end with a non-technical summary statement of the main conclusions. Lengthy mathematical proofs and very extensive detailed tables should be placed in the appendix. The author should make every effort to explain the meaning of mathematical proofs.

f. FOOTNOTES. Footnotes in the text must be numbered consecutively and typed on a separate page, double spaced, following the reference section. Footnotes to the tables must also be double spaced and typed on the bottom of the page with the table.

g. TABLES. Tables must be numbered consecutively with Roman numerals. Please check that your text contains a reference to each table. Type each table on a separate page. Authors must check tables to be sure that amounts add up to the totals shown and that the title, column headings, captions, etc. are clear and put to point.

h. FIGURES. Figures must be titled and numbered consecutively with Arabic numerals.

i. EQUATIONS. All but very short mathematical expressions should be displayed on a separate line and centered. Equations must be numbered consecutively on the right margin, using Arabic numerals in parentheses.

j. REFERENCES. References must be typed on a separate page, double spaced, at the end of the paper.

k. Please check your manuscript for clarity, grammar, spelling, punctuation, and consistency of references to minimize editorial changes.

FINANCIAL ANALYSTS JOURNAL

ADDRESS FOR SUBMISSION :

W. VAN HARLOWE III, EDITOR
FINANCIAL ANALYSTS JOURNAL
P.O. BOX 3668
5 BOAR'S HEAD LANE
CHARLOTTESVILLE, VA 22903
804-980-9775
804-963-6826 (Fax)
E-Mail : faj@aimr.org

CIRCULATION DATA :

Reader : Investment Professionals
Frequency of Issue : 6 Times/Year
Copies Per Issue : Over 25,000
Subscription Price : 150.00 US$
Sponsorship : Professional Assoc.

PUBLICATION GUIDELINES :

Manuscript Length : Up to 20
Copies Required : Five
Computer Submission : No
Format : N/A
Fees to Review : 100.00 US$

REVIEW INFORMATION :

Type of Review : Blind Review
No. of External Reviewers : Two
No. of In House Reviewers : One
Acceptance Rate : 11-20%
Time To Review : 2-3 months
Reviewer's Comments : Yes
Fees to Publish : 0.00 US$
Invited Articles : 5% or less

MANUSCRIPT TOPICS : PORTFOLIO & SECURITY ANALYSIS

PUBLICATION GUIDELINES :

MANUSCRIPT GUIDELINES/COMMENTS :

PHILOSOPHY
The FINANCIAL ANALYSTS JOURNAL publishes original research in investment
analysis, investment management and related subjects for a highly
sophisticated readership dominated by the 23,000 investment practitioners who
are members of the Association for Investment Management and Research (AIMR).
We seek articles that are practitioner-oriented, forward-looking, and
rigorous. Articles should enhance an analyst's human capital by providing
insights and wisdom unavailable from other sources.

Articles must be fresh, original, well-documented and carefully reasoned,
clearly stating the implicatins for praticing analysts. They must be written
in plain language that is both direct and conversational. Articles must be
educationally meritorious or topically interesting. All aspects of the
professional investor's environment are suitable topics.

FORM. Submit manuscripts double-spaced on single sides of standard paper.
Include a one-paragraph abstract of no more than 100 words on a separate
sheet. Place mathematics and statistical notions not essential to the
intuitive substance of the article in an appendix. Footnotes, tables, and
charts must follow the text; place only one table or chart per page. Provide a

FINANCIAL ANALYSTS JOURNAL

title page containing your name, affiliation, address, and telephone number along with the same information about any coauthors. Names and affiliations should not appear on any other pages of the manuscript.

MECHANICS: Submit five copies of the manuscript to the address below. Include a nonrefundable $100 submission fee payable to AIMR.

FINANCIAL COUNSELING AND PLANNING

ADDRESS FOR SUBMISSION :

SHERMAN HANNA, EDITOR
FINANCIAL COUNSELING AND PLANNING
OHIO STATE UNIVERSITY
DEPT. OF FAMILY RESOURCE MANAGEMENT
174 CAMPBELL HALL
1787 NEIL AVENUE
COLUMBUS, OH 43210-1295
USA
614-292-4584
614-292-7536 (Fax)
E-Mail : hanna.1@osu.edu

Change in Editor's Address
  May Occur in : 12/31/94

CIRCULATION DATA :

Reader : Academic

Frequency of Issue : 1 Times/Year

Copies Per Issue : Less than 1000

Subscription Price : 60.00 US$
  Membership/Inst. : 120.00 US$
  Membership/Student : 30.00 US$

Sponsorship : Professional Assoc.

PUBLICATION GUIDELINES :

Manuscript Length : 16-20

Copies Required : Four

Computer Submission : No

Format : N/A

Fees to Review : 0.00 US$

REVIEW INFORMATION :

Type of Review : Blind Review

No. of External Reviewers : Three

No. of In House Reviewers : Zero

Acceptance Rate : 45 %

Time To Review : 2-3 months

Reviewer's Comments : Yes

Fees to Publish : 0.00 US$

Invited Articles : 5% or less

MANUSCRIPT TOPICS : INSURANCE; PORTFOLIO & SECURITY ANALYSIS;
  FINANCIAL COUNSELING THEORY

PUBLICATION GUIDELINES : American Psychological Association

MANUSCRIPT GUIDELINES/COMMENTS :

WEBSITE: http://www.hec.ohio-state.edu/hanna

Individuals and institutions other than libraries may receive FINANCIAL
COUNSELING AND PLANNING by becoming members of the Association for Financial
Counseling and Planning Education. Members receive a quarterly newsletter in
addition to the journal. The 1991 membership dues are $60 for regular members,
$30 for student members, and $120 for institutional memberships. A library of
a nonprofit institution may subscribe to the journal for $60 per year. All
inquiries about dues and subscriptions should be directed to:
    Association for Counseling and Planning Education
    Tahira Hira, Executive Director
    1096 Le Barron Hall
    Iona State University
    Ames, IA 50011

FINANCIAL COUNSELING AND PLANNING

FINANCIAL COUNSELING AND PLANNING is intended to be a journal for educators and practicing financial planners and counselors. The journal includes research reports as well as descriptions of innovative approaches to education and practice. The conclusions of your manuscript should outline implications for practitioners and educators in detail.

MANUSCRIPT PREPARATION
1. Mail four paper copies of the double-spaced manuscript, including one original, to the editor. Include a cover letter with the current address and telephone number of the contact author.

2. The separate title page should include footnote giving affiliation and contact person's address and telephone number. Anonymity during the review process is ensured.

3. The title of article should be centered at the top of the abstract page. Abstract should not be more than 150 words. Up to three key words, separated by commas, should be arranged in alphabetical order at the bottom of the abstract.

4. Double space all text and triple space between paragraphs. Triple space before headings of sections within the paper and double space after headings before starting the text for that section. Be sure to avoid hard carriage returns except between paragraphs.

5. References in the text should be arranged in chronological order and WITH a comma between the author(s)' last name and date. Example: (Hanna, 1989). Be sure that references in the text agree with those in the reference list. Use correct dates and spelling of names.

6. All statistical and mathematical copy should follow APA guidelines. Be sure to INCLUDE degrees of freedom, etc. in the appropriate way. Use "N" and "n" and other statistical symbols correctly.

7. References should follow APA (Third edition) style. This includes the author(s)' last name, first and middle initials and year of publication in parentheses followed by a period. Then, write the title of the article with only the first letter of the first word capitalized (journals and proceedings are all capitalized) and follow the title with a period. List the journal title, follow it with a comma, the volume underlined and followed by a comma, and the page numbers. Single-space each reference, with double spaces between references. The second and subsequent lines of a reference should be indented five spaces. Arrange references in alphabetical order with one exception: articles by the same author are arranged chronologically. Include issue number of journals ONLY if each issue begins with page one. BE SURE to include page numbers of chapters in edited books. Be sure to include all information.

8. Integrate tables into the text. Separate the table from text with two thick horizonal lines: one above and the other below the table. Use DECIMAL (numeric) tabs for table data. Pay particular attention to NOTES for tables. NOTE: PLEASE PUT TABLES THAT ARE NOT ESSENTIAL TO THE MAIN NARRATIVE OF THE MANUSCRIPT IN AN APPENDIX. AUTHORS SHOULD TRY TO REDUCE THE NUMBER OF TABLES IN ARTICLES. ALL IMPORTANT RESULTS SHOULD BE REFERRED TO IN THE TEXT. IT IS NOT SUFFICIENT TO REFER THE READER TO A TABLE!

FINANCIAL COUNSELING AND PLANNING

9. Integrate figures into the text. Photocopied figures will not be acceptable for final submission of accepted manuscripts. If possible draw figures using appropriate graphics programs or a program which allows it to be read into WordPerfect.

10. Mail to Sherman Hanna, Department of Family Resource Management, 174 Campbell Hall, 1787 Neil Ave., Columbus, Ohio 43210-1295. For questions, call (614) 292-4584 or send INTERNET message to hanna.1@OSU.edu. (FINAL submissions of ACCEPTED manuscripts should be on PC disks, preferably in WordPerfect 6.0 or 5.1. For instructions on preparation, contact the editors.)

FINANCIAL ENGINEERING AND THE JAPANESE MARKETS

ADDRESS FOR SUBMISSION :

TAKEAKI KARIYA, EDITOR
FINANCIAL ENGINEERING AND THE
 JAPANESE MARKETS
HITOTSUBASHI UNIVERSITY
THE INSTITUTE OF ECONOMIC RESEARCH
KUNITACHI, TOKYO, 186,
JAPAN
81 425 721101 EXT 4830
81 425 754856 (Fax)
E-Mail : cr00055@s4v.cc.hit-u.ac.jp

Change in Editor's Address
 May Occur in : 06/30/03

CIRCULATION DATA :

Reader : Academic

Frequency of Issue : 3 Times/Year

Copies Per Issue : Less than 1000

Subscription Price : 217.50 US$

Sponsorship : Professional Assoc.

PUBLICATION GUIDELINES :

Manuscript Length : 21-25

Copies Required : Four

Computer Submission : No

Format : N/A

Fees to Review : 0.00 US$

REVIEW INFORMATION :

Type of Review : Editorial Review

No. of External Reviewers : One

No. of In House Reviewers : One

Acceptance Rate : 40 %

Time To Review :

Reviewer's Comments : Yes

Fees to Publish : 0.00 US$

Invited Articles : 5% or less

MANUSCRIPT TOPICS : COST ACCOUNTING; ECONOMETRICS;
 PORTFOLIO & SECURITY ANALYSIS; FINANCIAL ENGINEERING, DERIVATIVE SECURITIES

PUBLICATION GUIDELINES :

MANUSCRIPT GUIDELINES/COMMENTS :

FINANCIAL ENGINEERING AND THE JAPANESE MARKETS publishes empirical and/or
theoretical research articles on financial time series, pricing models for
various financial assets including derivatives, global asset allocation,
trading strategies for investment, optimization methods etc. Papers with
empirical analysis using the Asian market data are preferred.

FINANCIAL ENGINEERING AND THE JAPANESE MARKETS is published by Kluwer Academic
Press, P.O. Box 17, 3300 AH Dordrecht, The Netherlands. Phone (31) 78 524400,
Fax (31) 78 524474.

FINANCIAL MANAGEMENT

ADDRESS FOR SUBMISSION :

DOUGLAS R. EMERY, EDITOR
FINANCIAL MANAGEMENT
BINGHAMTON UNIVERSITY
SCHOOL OF MANAGEMENT
BINGHAMTON, NY 13902-6015
USA
607-777-2316
607-777-4487 (Fax)

Change in Editor's Address
  May Occur in : 10/15/99

CIRCULATION DATA :

Reader : Academic

Frequency of Issue : Quarterly

Copies Per Issue : 10,001-25,000

Subscription Price : 50.00 US$

Sponsorship : Professional Assoc.

PUBLICATION GUIDELINES :

Manuscript Length : 16-20

Copies Required : Five

Computer Submission : N/A

Format : N/A

Fees to Review : 100.00 US$
  Members 20.00 US$
  Nonmem. Doctoral Stu 50.00 US$

REVIEW INFORMATION :

Type of Review : Blind Review

No. of External Reviewers : Two

No. of In House Reviewers : Zero

Acceptance Rate : 11-20%

Time To Review : 2-3 months

Reviewer's Comments : Yes

Fees to Publish : 0.00 US$

Invited Articles : 5% or less

MANUSCRIPT TOPICS : CAPITAL BUDGETING;
  PORTFOLIO & SECURITY ANALYSIS; CORPORATE FINANCE

PUBLICATION GUIDELINES : Chicago Manual of Style

MANUSCRIPT GUIDELINES/COMMENTS :

FINANCIAL MANAGEMENT serves both academicians and practitioners who are
concerned with the financial management of nonfinancial businesses, financial
institutions, and public and private not-for-profit organizations. FINANCIAL
MANAGEMENT's editorial policy is designed to promote interest and knowledge of
issues in management and decision-making at the level of the firm. The
principal criteria of publishability are originality, rigor, currency,
practical relevance, instructiveness, and clarity. Papers previously published
elsewhere are not eligible for publication as regular articles in FINANCIAL
MANAGEMENT.

Submit five copies of manuscripts to the Editor.

Each paper must be accompanied by a submission fee for manuscript evaluation:
$20 for FMA members, $100 for nonFMA members, and $50 for doctoral students
who are not FMA members. The $100 and $50 non-member submission fees include a
one-year membership in FMA for the submitting author Make checks payable to
FINANCIAL MANAGEMENT. This journal includes information about joining FMA.

FINANCIAL MANAGEMENT

Manuscripts are evaluated anonymously Names of authors should not appear on the article itself. Attach a separate cover page that includes the title, authors, and title and affiliation of each author to one copy of the article. Double space the text with ample margins.

To each copy of the manuscript, attach an executive summary of not more than 800 words in length and a short, one-paragraph (approximately 100 word) abstract of the article. Both should be on separate pages, headed by the title of the paper. Practitioners are the target audience of the executive summaries. The executive summary should convey to the readers the practical importance of the paper-what need the research addresses or how the research impacts current financial management practices and strategies. Authors should devote at least one paragraph to implementation issues and to recommended corporate actions in the executive summary. The abstract should provide a brief overview of the paper.

Avoid tedious mathematical expressions. When algebraic terms do appear in the text, accompany them with a clear explanation. Each equation should be numbered consecutively, with the number in parentheses and flush with the right margin. Place derivations and proofs in an appendix. When submitting a paper for review, please provide supplemental sheets showing all steps in algebraic derivations so that the reviewers do not have to re-create them.

Tables and figures should appear on separate pages labeled in numerical order and grouped at the end of the text Label tables at the top and follow the heading with a description of the table in sufficient detail so that it is capable of standing alone. Label figures at the bottom. Include marginal notation in the article for the approximate placement of all tables and figures.

Minimize extensive content footnotes.

Place references in an unnumbered, alphabetical list at the end of the manuscript. Provide all relevant publication information available (i.e., season/month, year, city and state, author(s), etc.) Examples of references are provided below:

REFERENCES

Baldwin, C., 1991, "The Impact of Asset Stripping on the Cost of Deposit Insurance," Harvard Business School Working Paper 92-053 (December).

Commerce Clearing House, 1993,1994 U.S. Master Tax Guide, Chicago, IL.

Brick, I.E. and O. Palmon, 1993, "The Tax Advantages of Refunding Debt by Calling, Repurchasing, and Putting," Financial Management (Winter), 96-105

Myers, S.C., 1993, "Finance Theory and Financial Strategy," in D.H. Chew, Jr., Ed., The New Corporate Finance, New York, NY, McGraw-Hill, 90-97.

Smith, C.W., Jr. and C.W. Smithson, 1990, The Handbook of Financial Engineering, New York, NY, Harper Business.

Cite references in the text by citing the author(s) name(s) and then the year of publication in parentheses.

FINANCIAL MANAGEMENT

Authors of accepted articles must supply camera-ready artwork for all charts and/or graphs. Camera-ready means a professional drawing on white paper in India ink or a clean, laser-printed copy of computer-generated charts and/or graphs.

Authors of accepted papers must supply a word-processed copy of their article on an IBM-formatted disk. (Macintosh disks may cause significant delay in publications.) Any questions about disk preparation should be directed to the Managing Editor, Financial Management Association, University of South Florida, College of Business Administration, Tampa, FL 33620-5500, TEL 813-974-2084, FAX 813-974-3318, e-mail fma@bsn01.bsn.usf.edu

FINANCIAL MANAGER (THE)

ADDRESS FOR SUBMISSION :

MARIE KUECHELL, EDITOR
FINANCIAL MANAGER (THE)
C/O BCFM/BCCA
701 LEE STREET, #640
DES PLAINES, IL 60016
USA
847-296-0200
847-296-7510 (Fax)

CIRCULATION DATA :

Reader : Business Persons,
   Academic, &
   Broadcast/Cable/Financial

Frequency of Issue : Bi-Monthly

Copies Per Issue : 2001-3000

Subscription Price : 49.00 US$

Sponsorship : Professional Assoc.

PUBLICATION GUIDELINES :

Manuscript Length : 1-10

Copies Required : One

Computer Submission : Yes

Format : See Guidelines

Fees to Review : 0.00 US$

REVIEW INFORMATION :

Type of Review : N/A

No. of External Reviewers : One

No. of In House Reviewers : Two

Acceptance Rate : 80 %

Time To Review :

Reviewer's Comments :

Fees to Publish : 0.00 US$

Invited Articles : 6-10%

MANUSCRIPT TOPICS : ACCOUNTING INFORMATION SYSTEMS;
 ACCOUNTING THEORY & PRACTICE; AUDITING; CAPITAL BUDGETING; COST ACCOUNTING;
 INSURANCE; INTERNATIONAL FINANCE; PORTFOLIO & SECURITY ANALYSIS;
 PUBLIC POLICY ECONOMICS; TAX ACCOUNTING; FINANCE & INVESTMENTS;
 TAXES; LEGAL ISSUES; HUMAN RESOURCES; MUSIC LICENSING

PUBLICATION GUIDELINES :

MANUSCRIPT GUIDELINES/COMMENTS :

THE FINANCIAL MANAGER is the official publication of the Broadcast Cable
Financial Management Association (BCFM) and CREDIT TOPICS is the official
publication of the Broadcast Cable Credit Association (BCCA), published six
times per year.

Articles of interest to the BCFM and BCCA membership and our readers are
accepted at the discretion of the BCFM, BCCA and the Editors of THE FINANCIAL
MANAGER and CREDIT TOPICS. Topics of interest include, but are not limited to:

* financial and accounting,
* management information,
* human resources, and
* regulatory and legal subjects related to broadcast, cable and radio.

The following guidelines are applicable to all articles submitted.

FINANCIAL MANAGER (THE)

FORMAT
Academic and scientific manuscripts are not appropriate. Articles should be in a magazine style with appropriate attribution. First and second person should be avoided, and as a rule, the Associated Press guidelines for punctuation, grammar and style apply.

CONTENT
Editorial perspectives are accepted only with prior approval from the Editor. Advertorials and promotional pieces will not be accepted for publication. Display space may be purchased for publication of these items, with approval from the Editor.

LENGTH
No minimum article length, nor limit of space is imposed. Authors are encouraged to concisely provide information and adequate detail.

GRAPHICS
Photographs, charts and illustrations relevant to the content of the article are accepted and encouraged. Please see mechanical requirements for further detail.

REVIEW
All articles submitted should be absolutely final. In the event that an article is significantly edited by the editorial staff, the author will be given the opportunity to review such edits. Only one set of corrections to these edits will be permitted.

SUBMISSION DATES
Submission dates for publication are as follows:

EDITION	SUBMISSION DUE
December/January	October 15
February/March	December 15
April/May	February 15
June/July	April 15
August/September	June 15
October/November	August 15

MECHANICAL REQUIREMENTS
Articles must be submitted as final with hard copy, and text and graphics on a 3.5" computer diskette. Appropriate formats include:

TEXT*	GRAPHICS, 1 & 2 COLOR
Microsoft Word	Microsoft Excel
WordPerfect 5.1 or earlier	Quark Express
Rich Text Format	EPS or Tiff files
Text Only	Black & white photos
ASCII	Color photos
*Windows, Mac and DOS.	

Articles may be sent to: THE FINANCIAL MANAGER
                            c/o BCFM/BCCA
                            701 Lee Street, Suite 640
                            Des Plaines, IL 60016

Inquiries to the editor may be directed to: Marie Kuechel, Editor
                                                847.359.7371
                                                847.359.7388 Fax

FINANCIAL REVIEW

ADDRESS FOR SUBMISSION :

G.C. PHILIPPATOS & H.A. BLACK, EDITORS
FINANCIAL REVIEW
UNIVERSITY OF TENNESSEE
COLLEGE OF BUSINESS ADMINISTRATION
426 STOKELY MANAGEMENT CENTER
KNOXVILLE, TN 37996-0540
USA
423-974-1713
423-974-3100 (Fax)
E-Mail : finrev@utkux.utcc.utk.edu

CIRCULATION DATA :

Reader : Academic

Frequency of Issue : Quarterly

Copies Per Issue : 2001-3000

Subscription Price : 15.00 US$
    Institution : 50.00 US$

Sponsorship : Professional Assoc.

PUBLICATION GUIDELINES :

Manuscript Length : 20-25

Copies Required : Four

Computer Submission : No

Format : N/A

Fees to Review : 30.00 US$

REVIEW INFORMATION :

Type of Review : Blind Review

No. of External Reviewers : Two

No. of In House Reviewers : Two

Acceptance Rate : 6-10%

Time To Review : 1-2 months

Reviewer's Comments : Yes

Fees to Publish : 0.00 US$

Invited Articles : 5% or less

MANUSCRIPT TOPICS : CAPITAL BUDGETING; COST ACCOUNTING; INSURANCE;
    INTERNATIONAL FINANCE; PORTFOLIO & SECURITY ANALYSIS;
    FINANCIAL MARKETS, DOMESTIC AND INTERNATIONAL;
    FINANCIAL DERIVATIVES; BANKING & FIN. INSTITUTIONS

PUBLICATION GUIDELINES :

MANUSCRIPT GUIDELINES/COMMENTS :

INVITED ARTICLES: 1% or less
COMPUTER SUBMISSIONS are not accepted up front. We request a disk (3 1/2" or 5
1/4") and hard copy upon acceptance of the paper.

1. SUBMISSIONS: Send four copies of the manuscript to the editors with the
appropriate fee ($30 for Eastern Finance Association members and $45 for
nonmembers).

2. AUTHOR INFORMATION: Include the following information on the first page of
the manuscript:
    a. title
    B. author(s)
    c. institutional affiliation
    d. address
    e. telephone number
Reviewers will not receive this page. On the next page of the manuscript,
include the title and the abstract.

FINANCIAL REVIEW

3. ABSTRACT: Include a one-paragraph abstract of no more than 100 words. Do not include references, footnotes, or abbreviations in the abstract.

4. TYPING FORMAT: Double-space the text, the footnotes, and the references. Leave wide margins for ease of editing and of typesetting.

5. HEADINGS AND SUBHEADINGS: Use no more than three levels of headings. Center first-level headings and capitalize all letters. Begin second-level headings at the left margin and capitalize the first letter of the first word and of major words. Indent third-level headings five spaces from the left margin and capitalize the first letter. Underline third-level headings and end these with a period. Do not use letters or numbers before headings (e.g., I, ll or A, B, etc.).

6. FOOTNOTES: Mark with an asterisk the initial footnote identifying the author's(s') affiliation. Keep footnotes to a minimum. Number footnotes consecutively throughout the text with superscript Arabic numerals.

7. EQUATIONS. Number consecutively only those equations that are referenced in the text. Indent equations and place numbers in parentheses at the right margin. Type equations clearly with one space before and after mathematical function signs except in subscripts and superscripts. Type the main components, the equal sign, and the fraction baron the main line of typing. Spell out in the right margin any handwritten Greek letters used in equations. Write on one line mathematical expressions used within a paragraph.

8. NUMBER OF SIGNIFICANT DIGITS: In results of calculations, keep numbers of significant digits constant, not exceeding four.

9. TABLES: Type tables on separate pages after the text of the paper. Center the word "TABLE" followed by an Arabic numeral above the body of the table. Separate headings in a table from the title of the table and from the body of the table with solid lines. Use a solid line to end the table or to separate the body of the table from table footnotes. Mark table footnotes with asterisks. When referring to a specific table in the text of the paper, capitalize only the first letter of the word "Table" (e.g., Table 1).

10. FIGURES: Provide figures in camera-ready form of a professional quality. (Initially, photocopies are acceptable.) When referring to specific figures in the text, capitalize only the first letter (e.g., Figure 1). When labeling figures, capitalize the first letter in the word and number with Arabic numerals (e.g., Figure 1). In figure titles, capitalize the first letter of the first word and of major words.

11. REFERENCES: List references alphabetically by author's last name at the end of the paper, numbered with bracketed Arabic numerals. Include only those references cited in the text. Cite references in the text by enclosing the number of the reference in brackets.

12. STYLES OF REFERENCES: Include the following facts in references.

Books:
1. name of author(s), editor(s), or institution/business responsible for writing the book;
2. full title;

3. series (if any);
4. volume number;
5. edition;
6. city of publication;
7. publisher's name; and;
8. date of publication.

For example:
[1] Smith, John D., Paul Doe, and David Rose, Jr. References: A Guide to Format. New York: Publishers, Inc., 1982.

Articles:
1. name of author(s);
2. title;
3. name of periodical;
4. volume number and date;
5. pages occupied by article.

Use full name rather than initials whenever possible. For example:
[2] Smith, John D., "A Complex Model". Journal of Irreproducible Results 15 (September 1985): 115-348.

13. PROFESSIONAL PRESENTATION: To minimize editorial changes, check the manuscript for clarity, grammar, spelling, punctuation, and consistency of references.

FINANCIAL SERVICES REVIEW: JOURNAL OF INDIVIDUAL FINANCIAL MANAGEMENT

ADDRESS FOR SUBMISSION :

KAREN EILERS LAHEY, EDITOR
FINANCIAL SERVICES REVIEW: JOURNAL OF
  INDIVIDUAL FINANCIAL MANAGEMENT
UNIVERSITY OF AKRON
COLLEGE OF BUSINESS ADMINISTRATION
DEPARTMENT OF FINANCE
AKRON, OH 44325-4803
330-972-6330
330-972-5970 (Fax)
E-Mail : KLAHEY@UAKRON.EDU

Change in Editor's Address
  May Occur in : 06/30/98

CIRCULATION DATA :

Reader : Academic

Frequency of Issue : Quarterly

Copies Per Issue : Less than 1000

Subscription Price : 70.00 US$
  Member of AFS : 30.00 US$
  Library : 155.00 US$

Sponsorship : Professional Assoc.

PUBLICATION GUIDELINES :

Manuscript Length : 26-30
Copies Required : Four
Computer Submission : No
Format : N/A
Fees to Review : 0.00 US$

REVIEW INFORMATION :

Type of Review : Blind Review
No. of External Reviewers : Two
No. of In House Reviewers : Zero
Acceptance Rate : 11-20%
Time To Review : 1-2 months
Reviewer's Comments : Yes
Fees to Publish : 0.00 US$
Invited Articles : 5% or less

MANUSCRIPT TOPICS : ACCOUNTING INFORMATION SYSTEMS; INSURANCE;
  INTERNATIONAL FINANCE; PORTFOLIO & SECURITY ANALYSIS; REAL ESTATE;
  FINANCIAL SERVICES

PUBLICATION GUIDELINES : American Psychological Association

MANUSCRIPT GUIDELINES/COMMENTS :

FINANCIAL SERVICES REVIEW (FSR) is the official publication of the Academy of
Financial Services. The purpose of this refereed academic journal is to
encourage rigorous empirical research that examines individual behavior in
terms of financial planning and services. In contrast to the many corporate or
institutional journals that are available in finance, the focus of this
journal is on individual financial issues.

The FSR journal provides a forum for those who are interested in the
individual prospective on issues in the areas of Banking/Banking Services,
Education in Financial Services, Employee Benefits, Estate and Tax Planning,
Financial Counseling, Financial Planning, Insurance, Investments, Mutual
Funds, Nonbank Financial Institutions, Pension and Retirement Planning, and
Real Estate. While the annual meeting in October provides an opportunity to
discuss and present these topics to colleagues, the journal allows a much
wider audience of those interested in this subject matter.

FINANCIAL SERVICES REVIEW: JOURNAL OF INDIVIDUAL FINANCIAL MANAGEMENT

To encourage the development of curricula in financial services at the university level, appropriate pedagogical papers are accepted for publication. This represents a new area for the FSR journal. Manuscripts are encouraged that present ideas about appropriate content, methods of teaching, and materials. Authors of new and revised textbooks and materials (including computer programs) are also encouraged to submit their work for review by members of the Academy. The reviews will be published in a new section that provides for rigorous analysis of published materials that are available to those teaching at universities and colleges who wish to consider them for use in their classes.

Contributions from practitioners who are actively involved in financial planning, financial services, and professional associations are welcome. While the primary purpose of this journal is the publication of traditional academic empirical research, the Academy believes that it is important to encourage the cross fertilization of ideas and an exchange of information of interest to both academicians and practitioners. Thus, the new editor seeks manuscripts from practitioners that present innovative ideas and new information in financial planning and services or suggest new avenues of research for academics.

The journal will also start an AFS Notes Section. It will feature brief notes, responses to recent papers, comments, and letters to the editors. This is your opportunity as a member of the Academy of Financial Services to give us the benefit of your thoughts in a format much briefer than a journal article.

In 1997, the journal will become a quarterly publication. The addition of two more issues a year will allow publication of additional academic empirical research as well as the new features that are described above. If you have ideas for manuscripts or are interested in accepting the significant responsibility of producing a special issue of the journal, contact the new editor with your thoughts.

REVIEWER GUIDELINES

The FINANCIAL SERVICES REVIEW (FSR) is the official publication of the Academy of Financial Services (AFS). Its focus is to investigate and expand the frontiers of knowledge on individual behavior in terms of financial planning and financial services. To encourage the development of curricula in financial services at the university level, appropriate pedagogical papers are accepted.

The market niche for the journal is individual investment issues as opposed to corporate or institutional issues. FSR is interested in manuscripts that provide an individual viewpoint in one of the following 12 categories: (1) Banking/Banking Services, (2) Education in Financial Services, (3) Employee Benefits, (4) Estate/Tax Planning, (5) Financial Counselling, (6) Financial Planning, (7) Insurance, (8) Investments, (9) Mutual Funds, (10) Nonbank Financial Institutions, (11) Pension/Retirement Planning, (12) Real Estate.

It is the Goal of FSR to publish manuscripts that:
1. Contribute to the literature of the individual investor.
2. Would be of interest to academics or practitioners, or both.
3. Use appropriate research methodology and statistical analysis.
4. Are well written.

FINANCIAL SERVICES REVIEW: JOURNAL OF
INDIVIDUAL FINANCIAL MANAGEMENT

Please keep in mind the following in preparing your report on the manuscript you have accepted for review:

1. In addition to publishing worthy manuscripts, FSR has a responsibility to help prospective authors improve the quality of their research and its presentation. Consequently, the job of the reviewer is both to help the editor make the accept/reject decisions and to provide the authors with suggestions for improvement of their research.

2. Fill out the Reviewer Evaluation Form and explain your overall publication recommendation. If you feel the manuscript is not acceptable for the Financial Services Review, but might be more appropriate for another journal, please indicate this in your comments. In addition, be sure to provide detailed comments that would help the authors improve their manuscript. These comments will remain anonymous unless you request otherwise.

FINANCIER (THE)

ADDRESS FOR SUBMISSION :

ANNE ZISSU, ED. & CHARLES STONE, CO-ED.
FINANCIER (THE)
602 WASHINGTON SQUARE, SUITE 1806
PHILADELPHIA, PA 19106
215-829-1354
215-829-1376 (Fax)
E-Mail : http://www.the-financier.com

PUBLICATION GUIDELINES :

Manuscript Length : 16-20
Copies Required : Two
Computer Submission : No
Format : N/A
Fees to Review : 0.00 US$

CIRCULATION DATA :

Reader : Business Persons
Frequency of Issue : 5 Times/Year
Copies Per Issue : 2001-3000
Subscription Price : 125.00 US$
Sponsorship :

REVIEW INFORMATION :

Type of Review : Blind Review
No. of External Reviewers : One
No. of In House Reviewers : Two
Acceptance Rate : 5% or less
Time To Review : 1-2 months
Reviewer's Comments : Yes
Fees to Publish : 0.00 US$
Invited Articles : Over 50%

MANUSCRIPT TOPICS : ACCOUNTING THEORY & PRACTICE; CAPITAL BUDGETING;
COST ACCOUNTING; INSURANCE; INTERNATIONAL FINANCE;
PORTFOLIO & SECURITY ANALYSIS; TAX ACCOUNTING; FINANCIAL ENGINEERING

PUBLICATION GUIDELINES : Chicago Manual of Style

MANUSCRIPT GUIDELINES/COMMENTS :

THE FINANCIER: ANALYSES OF CAPITAL AND MONEY MARKET TRANSACTIONS is an applied
periodical composed of analyses that examine how public authorities and
private enterprises raise capital. Each issue of THE FINANCIER will explore
multiple dimensions of a single theme. Legal experts, financial economists,
accountants, treasurers, financial engineers, chief financial officers and
bankers will contribute the papers which compose THE FINANCIER. THE FINANCIER
will be published five times per year.

THE FINANCIER is designed to be a three way conduit between the supply,
demand, and academic sides of the capital and money markets. The two main
criteria against which all papers will be judged are 1) the extent to which
they clarify one or multiple facets of capital and/or money market
transactions 2) the clarity and logic of the analysis. The editors encourage
the submission of case studies. Space in THE FINANCIER will be allocated to
book and literature reviews.

Papers written for THE FINANCIER should address at least one of the following
dimensions of a capital or money market transaction: the architecture of a

transaction, the evaluation of specific structural elements, legal issues, accounting issues, political environment, regulatory constraints, historical precedents, logistics of issuing securities, analysis of marketing strategies, relative value of a specific security design, analysis of innovations associated with a transaction, analysis of weaknesses and flaws in specific financial transactions, evaluation of the role of a specific financial institution or class of institutions in raising capital, commentary on financing trends in specific markets, or the analysis of strategies and tactics employed to raise capital. An appropriate length for a paper is between 4,000 and 18,000 words. Quality rather than quantity is the binding constraint.

Invited papers will be reviewed by a member of the Advisory Board or an Editor. Unsolicited papers will be reviewed by an anonymous referee. The time necessary for the review process dictates that unsolicited papers must be submitted to THE FINANCIER four months prior to the publication month of the targeted issue. The choice of papers that compose each issue of THE FINANCIER is the sole responsibility of the Editors.

FORUM FOR SOCIAL ECONOMICS

ADDRESS FOR SUBMISSION :

PATRICK J. WELCH, EDITOR
FORUM FOR SOCIAL ECONOMICS
SAINT LOUIS UNIVERSITY
DEPARTMENT OF ECONOMICS
3674 LINDELL BLVD.
ST. LOUIS, MO 63108
USA
314-977-3814
314-977-3897 (Fax)

CIRCULATION DATA :

Reader : Academic

Frequency of Issue : 2 Times/Year

Copies Per Issue : Less than 1000

Subscription Price : 5.00 US$
   Institution : 7.00 US$
   Outside U.S.A. : 13.00 US$

Sponsorship : Professional Assoc.

PUBLICATION GUIDELINES :

Manuscript Length : Less Than 25

Copies Required : Two

Computer Submission : Yes

Format : WordPerfect Preferred

Fees to Review : 0.00 US$

REVIEW INFORMATION :

Type of Review : Blind Review

No. of External Reviewers :

No. of In House Reviewers : One

Acceptance Rate : 11-20%

Time To Review : 2-3 months

Reviewer's Comments : Yes

Fees to Publish : 0.00 US$

Invited Articles : Over 50%

MANUSCRIPT TOPICS : ACCOUNTING INFORMATION SYSTEMS;
   PUBLIC POLICY ECONOMICS

PUBLICATION GUIDELINES :

MANUSCRIPT GUIDELINES/COMMENTS :

THE FORUM FOR SOCIAL ECONOMICS is published twice a year by the Association
for Social Economics at Saint Louis University.

THE FORUM FOR SOCIAL ECONOMICS aims to facilitate communication and discussion
in the field of social economics. Its mission is to examine the normative
dimensions of economics and of economic life and to provide a forum for the
timely dissemination of the results of scholarly work in the field. In
addition to the traditional fields of inquiry in social economics broadly
considered, the editors welcome scholarly contributions examining the
relationship between social economics and philosophy, theology, linguistics,
and other disciplines.

Like the REVIEW OF SOCIAL ECONOMICS (RSE), the FORUM is a scholarly, peer-
reviewed journal. The editors of the FORUM from time to time invite scholars
to contribute papers on special topics and publish symposia as well as
selected papers from meetings sponsored by the Association. The editors are
also willing to consider critical essays, and other contributions that depart
from the traditional research journal format. The relationship and difference

FORUM FOR SOCIAL ECONOMICS

between the FORUM and the RSE (both published by the ASE) can be compared to the relationship between the JOURNAL OF ECONOMIC PERSPECTIVES and the AMERICAN ECONOMIC REVIEW (both published by the American Economic Association.)

The Association for Social Economics (ASE) is one of the seven original member organizations of the Allied Social Sciences Associations (ASSA). Every year the ASE organizes a number of sessions for the annual ASSA meetings, as well as sessions for several regional meetings.

Contributions published, or to be published, in Volume 25 of the FORUM include: "Shifting the Paradigm: Value and Feminist Critiques of Economics" by Diana Strassman and Livia Polanyi, "Truth, Self, and Feminism" by Kenneth Lux and Mark A. Lutz, "Personalism and the Problem of Scarcity" by Peter L. Danner (with Comment by M. Douglass Meeks), "Putting in Politics: A Review of Economic Models with Endogenous Determination of Policy" by Douglas Marcouiller.

Also to be published is a symposium: "Economics and Religion: Views From Within the Profession." Included in this collection are "Theological Visions in Economics and Religion" by Paul Heyne, "In what Sense, if any, is 'Economics' distinct from 'Religion,' and why does it Matter?" by A.M.C. Waterman, "Christian Roots of Capitalist Civilization" by Salim Rashid, and "The God of the Poor: Economics and Religion in Latin America" by Douglas Marcouiller.

Published, or to be published, book reviews are Tyranny of Kindness: Dismantling the Welfare System to End Poverty in America by Theresa Funiciello, and Ideas, Interests, and American Trade Policy by Judith Goldstein (both reviewed by Robert Prasch), Political Economy of Fairness by Edward E Zajac (reviewed by Thomas Ross), and The Misunderstood Economy: what counts and how to count it by Robert Eisner (reviewed by Timothy Yeager).

INSTRUCTIONS TO AUTHORS
(1) Manuncripts should be sent to the editor.

(2) Authors' names, affiliations, and addresses should be clearly identified on the manuscript.

(3) Two copies of the manuscript along with a file of the manuscript on diskette should be sent The author's software package should be identified on the diskette.

(4) The manuscript should include an abstract of no more than 150 words.

(5) Authors should use endnotes and cite references alphabetically at the end of the manuscript.

FREEMAN

ADDRESS FOR SUBMISSION :

BETH HOFFMAN, MANAGING EDITOR
FREEMAN
THE FOUNDATION FOR ECONOMIC EDUCATION
30 S. BROADWAY
IRVINGTON-ON-HUDSON, NY 10533
914-591-7230
914-591-8910 (Fax)
E-Mail : freeman@westnet.com

CIRCULATION DATA :

Reader : Business Persons &
        Academic
Frequency of Issue : Monthly
Copies Per Issue : 10,001-25,000
Subscription Price : 30.00 US$
Sponsorship : Non Profit Corp.

PUBLICATION GUIDELINES :

Manuscript Length : 25
Copies Required : One
Computer Submission : Yes
Format : WordPerfect
Fees to Review : 0.00 US$

REVIEW INFORMATION :

Type of Review : Editorial Review
No. of External Reviewers :
No. of In House Reviewers : Zero
Acceptance Rate : 11-20%
Time To Review : One month or less
Reviewer's Comments : Yes
Fees to Publish : 0.00 US$
Invited Articles : 5% or less

MANUSCRIPT TOPICS : ECONOMETRICS; ECONOMIC HISTORY

PUBLICATION GUIDELINES : Chicago Manual of Style

MANUSCRIPT GUIDELINES/COMMENTS :

We welcome the opportunity to consider thoughtful articles exploring the principles underlying a free-market economy--private property, voluntary exchange, limited government. We publish scholarly articles as well as ones written in a more popular style. Nonfiction is preferred.

Though a necessary part of the literature of freedom is the exposure of collectivistic cliches and fallacies, our aim is to emphasize and explain the positive case for individual responsibility and choice. Especially important is the methodology of freedom: Self-improvement, in contrast to compulsory reform of others. We try to avoid name-calling and personality clashes, and find satire of little use as educational device. Nor do we advocate or sponsor political action as a cure for problems cause by government intervention.

MANUSCRIPT PREPARATION
Manuscripts should be typed, double-spaced, accompanied by a letter including the author's name, address, telephone number and a brief biographical sketch.

Manuscript length may vary, but should not exceed 5000 words. Shorter articles and book reviews are welcomed. If you wish your manuscript returned, please enclose a stamped, addressed envelope.

FREEMAN

Facts and quotations cited should be fully documented, with any footnotes at the end of the manuscript. Charts, drawings, and photographs can be accomodated.

We prefer to purchase full rights to an article, but will withhold further rights at the author's request. While original manuscripts are preferred, we occasionally reprint articles.

Payment of 10 cents a word is made at the time of publication.

We encourage a preliminary inquiry, outline or short precis and will respond promptly.

Send manuscripts to the Editor.

FUTURES

ADDRESS FOR SUBMISSION :

JANE STIUGNELL, EDITOR
FUTURES
ELSEVIER SCIENCE
STOVER COURT
BANPFLYDE STREET
EXERTER DEVON, EX1 2AH
ENGLAND
44 0 1392 251558
44 0 1392 425370 (Fax)

CIRCULATION DATA :

Reader : Business Persons &
          Academic

Frequency of Issue : 10 Times/Year

Copies Per Issue : 1001-2000

Subscription Price : 235.00 U.K.$
   Overseas : 250.00 U.K.$

Sponsorship :

PUBLICATION GUIDELINES :

Manuscript Length : 6-more than 20

Copies Required : Three

Computer Submission : No

Format : N/A

Fees to Review : 0.00 US$

REVIEW INFORMATION :

Type of Review : Blind Review

No. of External Reviewers : Two

No. of In House Reviewers : One

Acceptance Rate : 21-30%

Time To Review : 2-3 months

Reviewer's Comments : Yes

Fees to Publish : 0.00 US$

Invited Articles : 31-50%

MANUSCRIPT TOPICS : INTERNATIONAL & ECONOMIC DEVELOPMENT;
   PUBLIC POLICY ECONOMICS; STRATEGIC MANAGEMENT POLICY;
   FORECASTING/ SOCIETY,ECONOMY,TECHNOLOGY,POLITICS

PUBLICATION GUIDELINES :

MANUSCRIPT GUIDELINES/COMMENTS :

FUTURES is an international journal published 10 times a year, every month
except January and July. It covers the developing methods and practice of
long-term forecasting for decision and policy making on the future of man,
society, economy, technology, and politics. It provides opportunities for the
publication of material which may represent divergent ideas and opinions. The
editors do not necessarily agree with the views expressed in the pages of
FUTURES.

Contributions should relate to the development and application of forecasting
techniques, or to subjects appropriate to long-term policy making. The editors
of FUTURES also welcome news and reports, covering industrial, governmental or
educational activities in this field, and information on forthcoming events
and publications. Entries for the "Meetings" page should be received at least
two months before the date of publication of the respective issue. Letters to
the editors intended for publication should be so marked.

The recommended length for the main articles is 4000-6000 words, plus
illustrations; for contributions to the sections "Viewpoint", "Essay", etc.

the ideal length is 2500 words. Reports, news items, etc. should not exceed 100 words in length. Contributions should be sent direct to the editorial offices. Three copies of the manuscript should be submitted, typed on one side of the paper, double spaced.

Contributions are normally received with the understanding that their content is unpublished material and is not being submitted for publication elsewhere; otherwise the authors should consult the editors when submitting the manuscript. Translated material which has not previously been published in English will also be considered. If any figure, table or a part of the text from previously published material is included in a manuscript, the author should obtain written permission to reproduce from the copyright holder.

The editors reserve the right to edit all contributions, including letters, but authors will receive proofs for approval before publication.

POINTS OF STYLE
The title of a contribution should not exceed 50 characters including spaces between the words. The title page should include full names of authors, professional affiliations and the address the authors wish to appear in the journal.

Each contribution submitted for publication as a main article should be accompanied by an abstract not exceeding 150 words.

The text should be organized under appropriate cross-headings.

References should be numbered consecutively in the text and listed at the end of an article. It is also desirable to incorporate into this list footnotes, if any. (Extensive use of footnotes is discouraged.) References should conform to the following style:

JOURNALS	S. Dedijer, 'The 1984 global system: intelligent systems, development stability and international security', Futures, February 1984, 16 (1), pages 18-37.
BOOKS	J.S. Gould, The Mismeasure of Man (Boston, MA, USA, Harvard University Press, 1982) pages 324-325.

Line drawings should be clear, but unless they are very complicated (e.g. a map) they will be redrawn to FUTURE'S style.

PROOFS
Authors of articles are sent page proofs for checking before publication. Only corrections can be accepted at this stage.

REPRINTS
Authors of articles will receive 50 free reprints shortly after publication. Further reprints (in minimum quantities of 100) can be ordered at prices which can be obtained from the publishers.

COPYRIGHT
Before publication, authors are requested to sign a copyright transfer form. This allows the publisher to sanction reprints and photocopies and to reprint complete issues or volumes.

FUTURES RESEARCH QUARTERLY

ADDRESS FOR SUBMISSION :

TIMOTHY MACK, EDITOR-IN-CHIEF
FUTURES RESEARCH QUARTERLY
WORLD FUTURE SOCIETY
7910 WOODMONT AVENUE #450
BETHESDA, MD 20814
USA
301-656-8274
301-951-0394 (Fax)
E-Mail : echard@tmn.com

CIRCULATION DATA :

Reader : Academic

Frequency of Issue : Quarterly

Copies Per Issue : 1001-2000

Subscription Price : 60.00 US$
  Library : 75.00 US$

Sponsorship : Professional Assoc.

PUBLICATION GUIDELINES :

Manuscript Length : 16-20

Copies Required : Three

Computer Submission : Yes

Format : N/A

Fees to Review : 0.00 US$

REVIEW INFORMATION :

Type of Review : Blind Review

No. of External Reviewers : Three

No. of In House Reviewers : Two

Acceptance Rate : 38 %

Time To Review : 4-6 months

Reviewer's Comments : No

Fees to Publish : 0.00 US$

Invited Articles :

MANUSCRIPT TOPICS : ECONOMETRICS;
  INTERNATIONAL & ECONOMIC DEVELOPMENT; PUBLIC POLICY ECONOMICS;
  FUTURES RESEARCH AND METHODOLOGY

PUBLICATION GUIDELINES : Chicago Manual of Style

MANUSCRIPT GUIDELINES/COMMENTS :

1. The Editors of FUTURES RESEARCH QUARTERLY invite manuscripts from
professionals worldwide whose contributions fall within the broad spectrum
defined in our Editorial Policy statement. We are especially seeking the
following types of material:
  a. Methodological and conceptual;
  b. Papers based on research, analysis and modeling (the substantive
     outcomes of futures research);
  c. Papers aimed at government and corporate planners and other
     practicing/professional futurists;
  d. Articles about futures research practitioners (individuals,
     institutional or at a national level) and their contributions to the
     art/discipline.

2. Our prime objective is high quality. Bear in mind, however, that we seek
dialog between communities of theoreticians, practitioners and
users/beneficiaries, all with different backgrounds. The need, therefore, is
for clarity and simplicity of expression rather than academic obfuscation.
This is a journal by and for professionals; however, assumptions as to the

FUTURES RESEARCH QUARTERLY

technological sophistication of the reader should be avoided to the extent possible.

3. Manuscripts are evaluated anaonymously by at least 3 members of the Editorial Board. Accepted manuscripts will be subject to minor editing to conform to journal format and standards. Substantive revisions, if any, will be returned to the author for approval.

4. Manuscripts should be addressed to: Futures Research Quarterly c/o World Future Society, with the name, address and phone number of the author serving as principal contact. To facilitate anonymous review, all identifying information about the author(s) should be on a separate sheet. Material should be typed, single-sided clean copy, double-spaced with ample margins. Manuscripts should not normally exceed 6000 words. Citations and other references should be limited to essential entries, numbered in sequence, and should be typed (double-spaced) on a separate page and placed following the last page of text. Authors should follow any commonly accepted authority as to style. Tables and graphics should be camera ready, or professional quality, and placed at the end of the manuscripts with a clearly visible notation in the text to indicate approximate placement. Photographs and halftones cannot be included.

5. The author should retain the original manuscript, since submissions will not normally be returned. Authors within the US should submit manuscripts in quadruplicate; single copies will be accepted from overseas contributors. Ten copies of the issue containing the article, once published, will be provided free of charge to each author. Larger quantities can be made available at moderate cost.

GENEVA PAPERS ON RISK AND INSURANCE THEORY

ADDRESS FOR SUBMISSION :

PROFESSOR HARRIS SCHLESINGER, EDITOR
GENEVA PAPERS ON RISK AND
  INSURANCE THEORY
UNIVERSITY OF ALABAMA
DEPARTMENT OF FINANCE
BOX 870224
TUSCALOOSA, AL 35487
USA
205-348-7858
205-348-0590 (Fax)
E-Mail : hschlesi@cba.ua.edu

CIRCULATION DATA :

Reader : Academic

Frequency of Issue : 2 Times/Year

Copies Per Issue : Less than 1000

Subscription Price : 144.00 US$

Sponsorship : Non Profit Corp.

PUBLICATION GUIDELINES :

Manuscript Length : Any

Copies Required : Four

Computer Submission : No

Format : N/A

Fees to Review : 0.00 US$

REVIEW INFORMATION :

Type of Review : Editorial Review

No. of External Reviewers : Two

No. of In House Reviewers : Zero

Acceptance Rate : 21-30%

Time To Review : 2-3 months

Reviewer's Comments : Yes

Fees to Publish : 0.00 US$

Invited Articles : 6-10%

MANUSCRIPT TOPICS : COST ACCOUNTING; INSURANCE;
  ECONOMICS OF UNCERTAINTY

PUBLICATION GUIDELINES :

MANUSCRIPT GUIDELINES/COMMENTS :

GEORGIA BUSINESS AND ECONOMIC CONDITIONS

ADDRESS FOR SUBMISSION :

LORENA M. AKIOKA, EDITOR
GEORGIA BUSINESS AND ECONOMIC
   CONDITIONS
UNIVERSITY OF GEORGIA
TERRY COLLEGE OF BUSINESS
SELIG CENTER FOR ECONOMIC GROWTH
ATHENS, GA 30602
USA
706-542-4085
706-542-3835 (Fax)

CIRCULATION DATA :

Reader : Business Persons &
         Academic

Frequency of Issue : Bi-Monthly

Copies Per Issue : 3001-4000

Subscription Price :
  Free on request : 0.00 US$

Sponsorship : University

PUBLICATION GUIDELINES :

Manuscript Length : 10-20

Copies Required : Two

Computer Submission : Yes

Format : Word 5.0 or Later

Fees to Review : 0.00 US$

REVIEW INFORMATION :

Type of Review : Blind Review

No. of External Reviewers : Zero

No. of In House Reviewers : Over 3

Acceptance Rate : 50 %

Time To Review : 2-3 months

Reviewer's Comments : No

Fees to Publish : 0.00 US$

Invited Articles : Over 50%

MANUSCRIPT TOPICS : COST ACCOUNTING; ECONOMIC HISTORY;
   GOVERNMENT & NON-PROFIT ACCOUNTING; PUBLIC POLICY ECONOMICS; REAL ESTATE;
   ECONOMICS; FINANCE

PUBLICATION GUIDELINES : Chicago Manual of Style

MANUSCRIPT GUIDELINES/COMMENTS :

Manuscripts must be Georgia-specific and not highly technical.

GLOBAL BUSINESS AND FINANCIAL REVIEW

ADDRESS FOR SUBMISSION :

DAVID J. KIM, EDITOR
GLOBAL BUSINESS AND FINANCIAL REVIEW
INDIANA STATE UNIVERSITY
SCHOOL OF BUSINESS
CENTER FOR RESEARCH AND MANAGEMENT
  SERVICES
TERRE HAUTE, IN 47809
USA
812-237-2117
812-237-7675 (Fax)
E-Mail : mfdjk@befac.indstate.edu

CIRCULATION DATA :

Reader : Business Persons &
         Academic

Frequency of Issue : 2 Times/Year

Copies Per Issue : Less than 1000

Subscription Price : 30.00 US$
  Institution : 80.00 US$
  Student : 15.00 US$

Sponsorship : Profit Oriented Corp. &
              University

PUBLICATION GUIDELINES :

Manuscript Length : 16-20

Copies Required : Three

Computer Submission : No

Format : N/A

Fees to Review : 30.00 US$
  For GBFR Subscribers 20.00 US$

REVIEW INFORMATION :

Type of Review : Blind Review

No. of External Reviewers : Two

No. of In House Reviewers : One

Acceptance Rate :

Time To Review : 2-3 months

Reviewer's Comments : Yes

Fees to Publish : 0.00 US$

Invited Articles : 11-20%

MANUSCRIPT TOPICS : AUDITING; CAPITAL BUDGETING;
  INTERNATIONAL FINANCE; PORTFOLIO & SECURITY ANALYSIS; FINANCE & INVESTMENTS;
  INTERNATIONAL BUSINESS; STRATEGIC MANAGEMENT POLICY;
  ORGANIZATIONAL BEHAVIOR AND THEORY; APPLIED RESEARCH IN ALL BUSINESS FIELDS

PUBLICATION GUIDELINES : Chicago Manual of Style

MANUSCRIPT GUIDELINES/COMMENTS :

The Style Guide forr JOURNAL OF INTERNATIONAL BUSINESS STUDIES is also
acceptable for GBFR.

The GLOBAL BUSINESS & FINANCE REVIEW (GBFR) is a refereed journal published
twice annually in the spring and fall by the Center for Research and
Management Services, School of Business, Indiana State University.

SUBMISSION:
The GBFR invites articles dealing with domestic and international aspects of
accounting, finance, management, and marketing. Authors are requested to
submit four copies of the manuscript and follow THE CHICAGO MANUAL OF STYLE.
An abridged style guide including the most common requirements is provided
herein for your convenience.

GLOBAL BUSINESS AND FINANCIAL REVIEW

Each submission should be accompanied by a fee of $20 for GBFR subscribers. Nonsubscribers should include $30 with submission, to be applied toward a one-year subscription. Authors will receive confirmation when their manuscripts are received.

FORMAT:
* The length of the manuscript should not exceed 20 pages, double spaced, using 1 inch margins. Tables and figures should be provided on separate sheets with insert notation within manuscript.

* The cover page should include the manuscript title, author's name and full title, as well as complete address, zip code, phone number, fax number, and email address.

* The first page should include the title of the manuscript and an abstract of 100 words or less. Please do not include name(s) of author(s) on first page.

* Number pages in sequence. Include pages in the following order:
  1- cover page
  2- title page and abstract (no author names)
  3- article
  4- end notes (if applicable)
  5- appendices (if applicable)
  6- references (required)
  7- tables and/or figures in order of insertion

ACCEPTANCE:
Editorial decisions regarding acceptance of articles will be sent to authors within 90 days of submission.

Upon acceptance, author must provide the following:
* Copy of the manuscript on 3 1/2" disk. Word Perfect or Microsoft Word is preferred. Other acceptable wordprocessing programs include Works WP, MacWrite, WordStar, Professional Write, Ami Pro, Framemaker, XYWrite, Word PC, WriteNow, and OfficeWriter. DOS or Macintosh formats are equally acceptable. PLEASE NOTE REGARDING WORD PROCESSING: Use hard returns at end of paragraphs and headings only. Use tab spaces sparingly- one tab at beginning of each paragraph and ONE tab between columns on tables.

* Author biography of 50-75 words including education, professional affiliation and accomplishments, and other publications of note.

* Two hard copies printed from disk, including all pages. Tables, figures, and illustrations must be provided camera-ready on separate pages.

STYLE GUIDE
Refer to THE CHICAGO MANUAL OF STYLE for complete style guidelines. Attached is an easy reference to style issues most commonly encountered.

The following style requirements are based on THE CHICAGO MANUAL OF STYLE. Please refer to this publication for additional guidelines regarding style usage.

PROFESSIONAL PRESENTATION:
To minimize editorial changes, please check manuscript for clarity, grammar,

GLOBAL BUSINESS AND FINANCIAL REVIEW

spelling, punctuation, and consistency of references before submission. Avoid inconsistency in the use of abbreviations, terminology, and in citation of references.

HEADINGS:
Use headings to denote various sections of article. Do not underline headings. A main heading should be centered and capitalized. A secondary heading should be centered with only the major words capitalized.

NUMBERS:
General rule in using figures or words:

* Spell out whole numbers from one through ninety-nine in ordinary text.

* Spell out any whole number followed by hundred, thousand, million, etc.

* If a number between one thousand and ten thousand can be expressed in terms of hundreds, that style is preferred to figures: (i.e. fifteen hundred words).

* Spell out numbers that represent approximations (i.e. some forty thousand people).

* Spell out round numbers that are even thousands: i.e. two hundred thousand.

* Very large numbers may be expressed in figures (i.e. 2.3 million).

* The general rule applies to ordinal as well as cardinal numbers: i.e. ninth, 125th.

* The preferred figure form of the ordinals second and third is with d alone, not nd and rd: i.e. 122d, 123d.

* Numbers applicable to the same category should be treated alike within the same context: i.e. There are 25 graduate students in the philosophy department, 56 in the classics department, and 117 in the hundred romance languages department.

Physical quantities:
* Scientific usage: physical quantities such as distances, lengths, areas, volumes, pressures, etc., are expressed in figures, whether whole numbers or fractions: i.e. 45 miles, 3 cubic feet, 10° C, 10.5° F

* Nonscientific text: such quantities should be treated according to the rules governing the spelling out of numbers: i.e. The temperature dropped twenty degrees in less than an hour. The entries were typed on three-by-five-inch index cards.

* Quantities consisting of both whole numbers and fractions should be expressed in figures: i.e. 8 1/2-by-11-inch paper.

* If an abbreviation or symbol is used the quantity should always be expressed by a figure: i.e. 55 MPH, 35-mm film, 3 1/2", 36°.

Percentages and decimal fractions:
* Percentages and decimal fractions are set in figures in all copy.

GLOBAL BUSINESS AND FINANCIAL REVIEW

* In scientific and statistical copy use the symbol "%" for a percentage, in humanistic copy use the word percent.

* In scientific contexts decimal fractions of less than 1.00 are set with an initial zero is the quantity expressed is capable of equaling or exceeding 1.00: i.e. a mean of 0.73, the ratio 0.85.

* If the quantity never equals 1.00, as in probabilities, levels of significance, correlation coefficients, factor loadings, etc., no zero is used: i.e. p<.05, R=.10.

Money:
* Isolated references to amounts of money are spelled out or expressed in figures in accord with the general rules. If the number is spelled out, so is the unit of currency, and if figures are used, the symbol "$" precedes them.

Dates:
* Exact dates should be written in the sequence day-month-year, without internal punctuation: i.e. 27 April 1981. After an exact date has been used, an elliptical reference to another date in the same month is spelled out i.e. On 5 November the national elections took place. By the morning of the sixth, returns for all but a few precincts were in.

Time of day:
* Times of day in even, half, and quarter hours are usually spelled out in text matter: i.e. half past three, midnight, quarter of four, seven o'clock. But figures are used when the exact moment of time is to be emphasized: i.e. The program is televised at 2:30 in the afternoon. We can catch the 6:20 P.M. train.

CITING SOURCES IN TEXT:
* Use the author-date system when citing references within text: last name of an author and the year of publication of the work, with no punctuation between them.

* For works with two or three authors: (Meredith and Lewis 1979) (Wynken, Blynkin, and Nodd 1988). Note that "and" is preferred, not "&"

* For more than three authors use the name of the first followed by "et al." (Zipursky et al. 1959).

* When citing within text, follow the author's name with date enclosed in parentheses: i.e. Wynken, Blynkin, and Nodd (1988) believe that...

* When citing for a direct quote, include the page number with reference: i.e. (Smith 1978, 74) - note that p. or pp. is omitted with page numbers.

REFERENCES:
A list of references cited in text (alphabetical, by author's last name, and including first initials) should follow the notes at the end of the manuscript. Authors should make certain that there is a complete reference for every citation in the text and that the cited dates and spelling of author names in both text and references be in agreement.

GLOBAL BUSINESS AND FINANCIAL REVIEW

Following are examples of common reference citations. Please note style used for author name, date, capitalization of titles, publisher, journal, etc.

Author(s): last name followed by initials on author listed first, subsequent authors list initials followed by last name. Use "and" instead of "&" and end author listing with a period.

Follow list of authors with date of publication, no parentheses, period. List book titles in italics, capitalize first word only; subtitles after title separated by colon, capitalize first word only.

Book reference: follow title with period then city of publication: (colon) name of publisher.

Journals and periodicals: name of article with no quotation marks, no italics, first word only capitalized, follow article title with period. Next list name of journal in italics. Volume, issue, page numbers should immediately follow name of journal, no italics.

The title of an unpublished paper is treated like the title of a journal article. Follow title with "Unpublished dissertation" and the location or sponsoring body.

REFERENCE LISTING EXAMPLES:
Book with one author:
Lynton, E.A. 1984. The missing connection between business and the
   universities. New York: Collier McMillan.

Book with more than one author:
Porter, L.W. and L.E. McKibbin. 1988. Management education and development.
   New York: McGraw-Hill.

Journal (note if multiple issues place in parentheses after volume number):
Dunning, J.H. 1988. The eclectic paradigm of international production: A
   restatement and some possible extensions. Journal of International Business
   Studies, 19(4):1-31.

Chapter/article excerpt from edited book:
Hill, H. 1992. Manufacturing industry. In A. Booth, ed., The boom and after:
   Indonesian economic policy and performance in the Soeharto era, 204-57.
   Singapore: Oxford University Press.

Unpublished paper or dissertation:
Christie, A. 1995. Equity risk, the opportunity set, production costs and
   debt. Unpublished manuscript, University of Rochester.

Proceedings of meetings and symposia:
Briggs, R.O. and N.C. Romano, Jr. 1992. Learning to think/thinking to learn.
   Proceedings of the 10th Annual National Anniversary Conference of the
   Association of Management, Las Vegas.

Citation from document, no author:
International Directory of Corporate Affiliations. 1991. (Vol. I, September).
   Wilmette, IL: National Register Publishing.

Computer program:
Fernandes, F.D. 1972. Theoretical prediction of interference loading on
  aircraft stores, [Computer program]. Pomona, CA: General Dynamics, Electrc
  Dynamics Division.

TABLES, FIGURES, AND ILLUSTRATIONS:
Provide each table, figure, or illustration camera-ready, on separate sheets
in order of insertion. Label each and indicate placement within article.

****
Table 1 here
****

PERMISSION TO QUOTE:
Blanket permission is granted to any individual wanting to use articles
appearing in the GLOBAL BUSINESS & FINANCE REVIEW for education purposes.
Written permission from the Center for Research and Management Services or the
Editors is not required. All other requests to quote or republish should be
submitted in writing to the Center for Research and Management Services,
School of Business, Indiana State University, Terre Haute, IN 47809-5402.

COPYRIGHT:
Articles submitted for consideration are reviewed with the understanding that
they are substantially new, have not been previously published in whole
(including book chapters) or in part (including exhibits), have not been
previously accepted for publication, are not under consideration by any other
publisher, and will not be submitted elsewhere until a decision is reached
regarding their publication in GBFR. The only exception is papers in
conference proceedings; the author should indicate the conference in which a
version of the submission originally appeared.

In the publication agreement provided to authors upon acceptance of articles,
authors are asked to assign the copyright to the Center for Research and
Management Services (sponsor), thus granting all rights for the contribution
so that author and sponsor may be protected from the consequences of
unauthorized use. Authors will have the right, however, after publication to
reprint the contribution without charge in any book of which he or she is
author or editor.

GLOBAL FINANCIAL JOURNAL

ADDRESS FOR SUBMISSION :

MANUCHEHR SHAHROKHI, EDITOR-IN-CHIEF
GLOBAL FINANCIAL JOURNAL
CALIFORNIA STATE UNIVERSITY
CRAIG SCHOOL OF BUSINESS
FRESNO, CA 93740
USA
209-278-4058
209-278-4911 (Fax)
E-Mail : mshahrok@csufresno.edu

Change in Editor's Address
  May Occur in : 12/01/99

CIRCULATION DATA :

Reader : Business Persons &
        Academic

Frequency of Issue : 2 Times/Year

Copies Per Issue : 1001-2000

Subscription Price : 60.00 US$
  Institution : 125.00 US$

Sponsorship : Profit Oriented Corp. &
              University

PUBLICATION GUIDELINES :

Manuscript Length : 16-20

Copies Required : Four

Computer Submission : Yes

Format : WP 5.1 & ASCII required

Fees to Review : 25.00 US$
  GFI Members 15.00 US$

REVIEW INFORMATION :

Type of Review : Blind Review

No. of External Reviewers : One

No. of In House Reviewers : Two

Acceptance Rate : 11-20%

Time To Review : 2-3 months

Reviewer's Comments : Yes

Fees to Publish : 0.00 US$

Invited Articles : 5% or less

MANUSCRIPT TOPICS : ACCOUNTING THEORY & PRACTICE; CAPITAL BUDGETING;
  INTERNATIONAL FINANCE; PORTFOLIO & SECURITY ANALYSIS; TAX ACCOUNTING

PUBLICATION GUIDELINES :

MANUSCRIPT GUIDELINES/COMMENTS :

The mission of GFJ is to advance applied research by providing a forum for the
exchange of ideas and techniques for academicians and practitioners in global
finance. The primary criteria for publication are originality, quality,
practicality, instruction, clarity and contribution to the field of global
finance.

Manuscripts and editorial communications should be addressed to the Editor.

MANUSCRIPT PREPARATION
1. SUBMISSION. Submit three copies of your manuscript, retaining the original
for your files. Manuscripts will not be returned. A fee of $25 ($15 for GFJ
subscribers) must accompany each submission. Make checks payable to GLOBAL
FINANCE JOURNAL.

2. IDENTIFICATION. To maintain anonymity in the review process, only the title
should appear on the manuscript. Attach a cover page with the title of the

manuscript, the author(s), affiliations(s) and any acknowledgements or credits.

3. ABSTRACT. Include an abstract of 150 words or less on a separate page.

4. TYPING. Type all copy double-spaced, allowing one-inch margins on all sides.

5. EQUATIONS. Equations within the text should be centered on a separate line and numbered consecutively on the right margin in parentheses.

6. TABLES AND FIGURES. Each table must be typed on a separate page and placed at the end of the article. Tables should have brief descriptive titles and be numbered consecutively. Figures should have explanatory captions and be numbered consecutively. Indicate the approximate locations of tables/figures in the text with a phrase such as [INSERT TABLE 1 HERE].

Upon acceptance of an article, author(s) must furnish camera-ready artwork for all figures in a professional drawing on white paper.

7. FOOTNOTES. Footnotes should be sequentially numbered using superscript numbers and typed on a separate page in an appendix titled "NOTES".

8. REFERENCES. Cite references in the text by placing the appropriate reference number(s) in brackets, e.g., [3,8]. List all references in numbered, alphabetical order by author in an appendix titled "REFERENCES".

Periodicals: cite the title of the work in quotations followed by the title of the periodical (underlined), volume number, month and year of publication, and page numbers.

Books: underline title, followed by publisher, city of publication, date and page numbers. Unpublished works: cite the title of the work in quotations, followed by meeting where presented for organization for which it was prepared, city and date.

The GLOBAL FINANCE JOURNAL follows a blind review process. Authors will be sent letters indicating decisions by the editor following review of the submissions. Copies of reviewers' comments will be mailed to authors of reviewed submissions.

GOVERNMENT ACCOUNTANTS JOURNAL

ADDRESS FOR SUBMISSION :

MARIE FORCE, EDITOR
GOVERNMENT ACCOUNTANTS JOURNAL
2200 MOUNT VERNON AVENUE
ALEXANDRIA, VA 22301
USA
703-684-6931 EXT 104
703-684-6345 (Fax)
E-Mail : AGAPUBS@aol.com

CIRCULATION DATA :

Reader : Gov't Accountants, Auditors
Frequency of Issue : Quarterly
Copies Per Issue : 10,001-25,000
Subscription Price : 55.00 US$
Sponsorship : Professional Assoc.

PUBLICATION GUIDELINES :

Manuscript Length : 15-18
Copies Required : Three
Computer Submission : Yes
Format : WordPerfect 5.1
Fees to Review : 0.00 US$

REVIEW INFORMATION :

Type of Review : Blind Review
No. of External Reviewers : Two
No. of In House Reviewers :
Acceptance Rate : 40 %
Time To Review : 2-3 months
Reviewer's Comments : Yes
Fees to Publish : 0.00 US$
Invited Articles : 5% or less

MANUSCRIPT TOPICS : ACCOUNTING INFORMATION SYSTEMS; AUDITING;
  COST ACCOUNTING; GOVERNMENT & NON-PROFIT ACCOUNTING

PUBLICATION GUIDELINES :

MANUSCRIPT GUIDELINES/COMMENTS :

As published in the quarterly JOURNAL.

Type of Reader: Government Accountants, Auditors, Budget Analysts

GROWTH AND CHANGE: A JOURNAL OF URBAN AND REGIONAL POLICY

ADDRESS FOR SUBMISSION :

SCOTTIE KENKEL, EDITOR
GROWTH AND CHANGE: A JOURNAL OF
  URBAN AND REGIONAL POLICY
UNIVERSITY OF KENTUCKY
349 B&E BUILDING
LEXINGTON, KY 40506-0034
USA
606-257-1588
606-257-7671 (Fax)
E-Mail : grc003@ukcc.uky.edu

CIRCULATION DATA :

Reader : Academic &
        Public and Private

Frequency of Issue : Quarterly

Copies Per Issue : 1001-2000

Subscription Price : 36.00 US$
  Institution : 77.00 US$

Sponsorship : University

PUBLICATION GUIDELINES :

Manuscript Length : Up to 20 or so

Copies Required : Five

Computer Submission : Yes

Format : For publication/WdPerf. or

Fees to Review : 0.00 US$

REVIEW INFORMATION :

Type of Review : Blind Review

No. of External Reviewers : Three

No. of In House Reviewers : Two

Acceptance Rate : 21-30%

Time To Review : 2-3 months

Reviewer's Comments : Yes

Fees to Publish : 0.00 US$

Invited Articles : 5% or less

MANUSCRIPT TOPICS : COST ACCOUNTING;
  INTERNATIONAL & ECONOMIC DEVELOPMENT; PUBLIC POLICY ECONOMICS;
  ECO.GEOGRAPHY;PUBLIC POL.;REGIONAL ECO.;DEMOGRAPHY

PUBLICATION GUIDELINES : Chicago Manual of Style

MANUSCRIPT GUIDELINES/COMMENTS :

1. GROWTH AND CHANGE: A JOURNAL OF URBAN AND REGIONAL POLICY is an interdisciplinary, refereed research quarterly focusing primarily on regional science, regional economic development, and related policy issues. Established in 1970 and sold internationally, it serves as a useful forum for scholars and practitioners in economics, geography, finance, regional and urban planning, agricultural economics, and other fields. Each issue contains articles, notes, perspectives, and book reviews. For more information as to our range of interests, see recent copies of the journal.

2. Papers are accepted for consideration with the understanding that they are not being considered for publication elsewhere, and that the material infringes upon no other material protected by a copyright. All articles appearing in the GROWTH AND CHANGE are copyrighted by the journal. We try to give as speedy an initial internal review as is consistent with careful judgment.

3. Article length should be approximately 3,500 words or less. Submit fivecopies of manuscripts, typed double-spaced on one side of 8-1/2 by 11 inch

white paper. Leave at least a one-inch margin all around.
4. Please give your name, position title, and institutional affiliation on a separate cover page, along with the title of the article. Avoid referring to yourself in the article in such a way as to jeopardize your anonymity to reviewers.

5. Use the author-date system with alphabetical reference as described in the most recent edition of the CHICAGO MANUAL OF STYLE.

6. Follow the CHICAGO MANUAL OF STYLE. Number tables and figures with Arabic numerals and type the title, all in capital letters, at the top, with source notes and footnotes at the bottom. Use a separate sheet for each table or figure. Tables should be at least double-spaced, with more rows than columns if possible.

7. There are two considerations here: clarity for the reader and cost of typesetting. In general, follow the suggestions in the CHICAGO MANUAL OF STYLE. Please number mathematical expressions and formulas with Arabic numerals in parentheses and place them flush left of the page. Immediately below, define terms in paragraph form.

DO NOT submit manuscript for review on disk. Send 3 1/2" disk (formatted in WordPerfect or Word) for publication.

HARVARD BUSINESS REVIEW

ADDRESS FOR SUBMISSION :

EDITOR
HARVARD BUSINESS REVIEW
SOLDIERS FIELD
BOSTON, MA 02163
USA
617-495-6800
617-495-9933 (Fax)
E-Mail : hbr_editorial@hbsp.harvard.edu

CIRCULATION DATA :

Reader : Business Persons

Frequency of Issue : Bi-Monthly

Copies Per Issue : Over 25,000

Subscription Price : 75.00 US$

Sponsorship : University

PUBLICATION GUIDELINES :

Manuscript Length : 2-30

Copies Required : Three

Computer Submission : Yes

Format : Macintosh

Fees to Review : 0.00 US$

REVIEW INFORMATION :

Type of Review : Editorial Review

No. of External Reviewers : Zero

No. of In House Reviewers : Over 3

Acceptance Rate : 5% or less

Time To Review : 1-2 months

Reviewer's Comments : No

Fees to Publish : 0.00 US$

Invited Articles : 31-50%

MANUSCRIPT TOPICS : ACCOUNTING INFORMATION SYSTEMS;
   ACCOUNTING THEORY & PRACTICE; AUDITING; CAPITAL BUDGETING; COST ACCOUNTING;
   ECONOMETRICS; ECONOMIC HISTORY; GOVERNMENT & NON-PROFIT ACCOUNTING;
   INSURANCE; INTERNATIONAL & ECONOMIC DEVELOPMENT; INTERNATIONAL FINANCE;
   PORTFOLIO & SECURITY ANALYSIS; PUBLIC POLICY ECONOMICS; REAL ESTATE;
   TAX ACCOUNTING

PUBLICATION GUIDELINES : Chicago Manual of Style

MANUSCRIPT GUIDELINES/COMMENTS :

1. CHICAGO MANUAL OF STYLE

2. EDITORIAL AIMS:
The aims of HBR are to develop a keener, more responsible sense of leadership
among policymaking businessmen, both in the United States and abroad; to
increase businessmen's understanding of concepts and methods of professional
management, and approaches to the art of management. Thus, HBR seeks to
educate business leaders; it is an educational arm of the Harvard Business
School.

3. AUDIENCE
The audience to which HBR is addressed sets the tone for articles and
features. Traditionally, HBR's primary audience has been top management in
U.S. industry. Today the audience is broader and includes top management in
Western Europe and Japan as well. Secondary audiences include:

HARVARD BUSINESS REVIEW

    A. Younger managers who aspire to top management responsibilities,
    B. Policy-making executives in government,
    C. Policy makers in non-commercial organizations, such as health and
       welfare, and
    E. Professional people (e.g., lawyers, engineers) interested in the
       viewpoint of the business management.

During the past decade, the secondary audiences have assumed a steadily larger proportion of the total readership, although the primary audience has grown in absolute numbers.

4. CONTENT AND APPROACH:

HBR seeks to inform executives about what is taking place in management, but it also wants to challenge them and stretch their thinking about the policies they make, how they make them, and how they administer them. It does this by presenting articles that provide:
    A. In-depth analyses of issues and problems in management, and
    B. Wherever possible, guidelines for thinking out and working toward
       resolutions of these issues and problems.

To attain this goal, we publish regular articles on a broad range of management topics from accounting to world business. These articles account for about 80% of the editorials material in an issue.

Feature articles take up the remaining space.

5. CRITERIA FOR JUDGING MANUSCRIPTS:

A variety of criteria are used to judge manuscripts submitted. An article must:
    1. Discuss, in depth, a new or developing aspect or problem of business, an
       issue that affects management significantly, or conditions that affect
       the merger in his or her role as an executive.

    2. Probe analytically into the causes of and possible solutions to problems
       confronting business administrators and policy makers, so that they will
       find it helpful.

    3. Stimulate and broaden the manager's thinking.

    4. Reflect the values of corporate experience, wherever possible (short
       examples from actual experience are useful to this end).

    5. Stand as a carefully reasoned presentation, a connected argument in
       favor of the author's viewpoint, even where his or her purpose is to
       debate both sides of an issue.

    6. Analyze new concepts, developing trends, and matters in the news. Relate
       new facts and experiences that put previous research in a different
       light.

6. PROCEDURE:

As a first step in submission, it is generally advisable to submit an outline of your proposed article. We can then give you our reactions as to:
    A. Whether the topic and approach are suitable, and
    B. What kind of emphasis should be given to the material.

If there is a problem of overlap with another published or recently accepted article for future publication, we can alert you to that fact. An outline has some special advantages. You can:

1. Spell out what ground you intend to cover in each section.

2. Indicate the thread of the article -- the transitions by which you plan to move from section to section.

3. In an introductory paragraph or two, explain your exact purpose in addressing the HBR audience.

4. Indicate the conclusions at which you will arrive at the end of the article.

An outline of this kind need not be long -- two to four typewritten pages usually do the trick. It should be a full-sentence outline. In addition, it is helpful to draft the first couple of pages of the proposed article attaching these to the outline or other prospectus. (Because of the brevity of items in IDEAS FOR ACTION -- a maximum of five double-spaced typewritten pages -- you need not go through the preliminary outline stage with contributions intended for that feature.)

7. MANUSCRIPT PREPARATION:

All manuscripts should be typewritten and double-spaced. Headings should be inserted in such a manner that main sections and subsections can be distinguished.

Footnotes should be kept to a minimum.

Charts, if submitted with a manuscript, should be sketched in sumcient detail that their point is clear.

Charts need not be submitted in finished form, however, as our Art Director prepares all charts for the printer after discussion with the Editors working on the manuscript.

We have no rigid requirements as to length. Features and regular articles generally range from 5 to 25 double-spaced typewritten pages.

Unless you know or have been working with one editor in particular, address your manuscript to: The Editors, HARVARD BUSINESS REVIEW, Soldiers Field, Boston, MA 02163. You will receive an acknowledgement of receipt. Please allow several weeks for a reply from one of the staff.

If your article is accepted for publication, one of the editors will write you. After he or she has finished editing it, you will be sent a copy of the edited version for your approval and any necessary corrections before it is sent to the printer. If we feel your article is not right in its present form but might be usable with revision, we will write you with suggestions for changing it. If the article is not suitable for HBR, in our opinion, we will return it to you with a letter describing our reactions.

HARVARD BUSINESS REVIEW

Most articles are published two and one-half to five months after acceptance. The scheduling obviously depends on a variety of factors, such as timeliness of subject matter, the number of articles already on hand for publication, the balance of editorial material, etc.

We pay a modest honorarium for articles accepted. In addition, we supply an author with 100 complimentary reprints of his or her article. Additional reprints can be obtained at published prices for years after publication.

We have no objection to co-authorship of an article, provided one author serves as our contact if revisions are needed and when we send out the edited manuscript for approval.

8. WHO ARE OUR AUTHORS?:

Many prospective authors ask us who writes for HBR, and whether we accept submission of unsolicited manuscripts. Here are the facts.

In recent years we have been receiving nearly 1000 manuscripts a year for consideration, and the number of submissions continues to increase. We print 13 to 14 articles per issue, averaging about 80 per year, so it is clear that we use somewhat less than 10% of the articles submitted to us. In addition, we receive almost as many outlines or proposed manuscripts and speeches saying, "We hope you can adapt for publication". In short, we are not without articles and manuscript ideas from which to choose.

The bulk of these submissions come in unsolicited or "over the transom" as we say in the editorial world -- but many of the articles that HBR publishes are the results of direct solicitation by our editors. The editors spend a good amount of their time on article solicitation in subject areas in which they consider the unsolicited flow to be of insufficient quality or quantity. Unlike many other management-directed publications, HBR publishes few articles written by professional writers or by its own staff.

9. THE ARTICLE DEVELOPMENT PROCESS:

The creation of a good article resembles, on a small scale, any new product development project. It can usefully be broken down into these steps: Idea generation, market testing, design and writing.

IDEA GENERATION:
For most of us, the first staff is the most difficult of all. Where do good article ideas come from? Except for spontaneous inspiration -- the rare light bulb suddenly aglow over the cranium -- there probably are only three important sources of insights that can yield good articles for a magazine like HBR.

1. PERSONAL EXPERIENCE
Sometimes you will come away from an engagement or a series of engagements, with a sense of real excitement, convinced that you have got hold of a concept, an approach, or a set of observations that could advance the state of management art. Occasionally you will be right.

Another person may find it necessary to prime the pump a bit. One way of doing this is to take half an hour, after finishing an important engagement, to put down on paper the most significant professional insight you gained from the experience. Try to generalize it. Ask yourself whether it has valid and useful management implications. Consider whether you have, or can get, the evidence to support it. This approach won't work every time, but if you go through the exercise each time you finish an engagement, your chances of coming one day upon a valid article idea should be very good indeed.

2. IDEA FILES

Be on the lookout for ideas and facts and quotes, related and unrelated -- from other studies, from your professional reading, from books or magazines or newspapers. Slip them into your idea file and forget about them for the time being. When a dozen or so items have accumulated, review them someday in a spare hour. Synergy among disparate but related ideas can produce an innovative and important article theme. Or, if an article idea comes along from some other source, items from your idea file are almost certain to be useful in supporting your argument or giving an interesting new twist to your approach.

3. RESEARCH, NOTABLY SURVEYS

Surveys reliably produce new because their output is facts, not opinion. Typically, the facts they produce -- properly analyzed and interpreted -- give the business reader some sort of yardstick by which to measure his or her own or the company's performance against others. Businessmen are eager for such yardsticks, and business magazines in general are hungry for articles that provide the. Moreover, surveys need not be large, elaborate, or statistically sophisticated to be a productive source of articles. Even a very modest research effort can pay off handsomely if it explores an area of real current concern to a large number of businessmen.

Given an apparently promising article from on one of these sources, what tests can be applied to determine whether it will be worth pursuing? The foremost useful criteria seem to be freshness or originality, usefulness, breadth of appeal, and simplicity. Let us take each in turn:

FRESHNESS:

Any good article adds something to present knowledge, pushed back horizons, cuts through complexity to give a new insight, or at the very least, presents familiar phenomena in a new and revealing light. The first step in checking out an article idea, therefore, is to make sure you are not reinventing the wheel. Explore what has been published in the same general subject area, for the same general audience. If you find that the ground has already been covered in whole or in part, you had better abandon your idea or modHy it to minimize overlap.

Quite frequently, prospective authors are tempted to dismiss as academic the questions of whether someone else has said the same thing before. when you repeatedly see supposedly sophisticated executives committing a particularly egregious blunder, it is easy to convince yourself that an article pointing out how to avoid the pitfall in questions is exactly what the world needs. This, of course, is a fallacy. If the path to salvation has already been clearly pointed out in print, it's obvious that something other than the written words will be required to make those blundering managers change their ways. If they read articles at all, they probably know better already and if they don't, they probably won't read yours.

Originality (or novelty, if you prefer) is often just a matter of seeing familiar phenomena in a new light. It may present a fresh synthesis of existing elements. Or it may consist of a familiar concept or technique in a fresh but relevant setting. (It ought not to consist of untested ideas for setting the world, or some corner of the world, straight. If you are not a recognized authority, no one is likely to be much interested in your proposals for reform unless they are supported by empirical evidence.)

Another sort of novelty arises from discerning, analyzing, and interpreting change in the real world -- external trends and developments that can be detected through research, observation, or reflection. Bear in mind, though, that the discovery of an unrecognized problem unless the objective evidence for it is exceedingly strong, seldom makes for a successful article. It's difficult enough to convince a reader that you have a remedy to a problem that already worries him. If you have to persuade him of the existence of the problem as well, you have set yourself a needlessly difficult task.

USEFULNESS:
Assuming your article idea has passed the test of freshness, the next question is its value to the reader. Will it help him or her act more wisely, effectively, confidently, or profitably.

BREADTH OF APPEAL:
A good article idea is relevant to the interests of executives in a variety of industries. Perhaps your real concern is with a few thousand businessmen in particular, or with one or two industries, but that does not mean the article can be aimed only at those people. If, because of its tone, the choice of its examples, or the selection of data, it sounds specialized or exclusive, it is likely to be rejected by the HBR staff. While we know we can't make every article interesting to every subscriber, we do our best to see that every article can interest at least several broad, major groups of businessmen.

SIMPLICITY:
This final test is a most important one, for the sharper your focus, the more deeply you can penetrate your topic -- and the more lasting the impression you will make. Try to distill your idea into 100 words that will command a businessman's attention and interest. If you can't do it, you almost certainly need to do some more hard thinking.

Assuming that your idea has passed all four tests, you may wish to try it out on a colleague or two, a friend you have found helpful, or possibly an editorial consultant with whom you've worked closely and whose judgment you can respect. Do so by all means, but wait until you have got the concept well defined. Underdeveloped ideas are vulnerable things, so it is wise to be quite clear about your idea, convinced of its value, and prepared to back it up before inviting criticism.

10. MARKET TESTING:

It seldom makes sense to embark on the hard work of writing without reasonable assurance that someone will want to publish your article. In most cases, this is readily determined. Write a short description of the article idea -- topic, scope, practical reader appeal and the gist of your message - for submission to an HBR editor. Keep it brief, unpretentious, and to the point. If the editor encourages you -- particularly if he or she offers specific suggestions regarding content or approach -- you will be able to proceed with some confidence.

Should you be turned down by our editor, don't abandon hope. Try other magazines. Editors may reject article ideas for many reasons, not all related to their intrinsic merits. Two or three unexplained rejections, of course, would suggest a return to the drawing board. But if your idea has passed all the test above, this is unlikely to happen.

11. DESIGNING PRESENTATION:

Assuming an HBR editor has expressed positive interest in your idea, the next step is normally to decide on the key structural elements of your article - the title, the lead, the body of the text, and the conclusion.

1. TITLING YOUR ARTICLE

A brilliant title can enhance the impact of your article, but is seldom critical to getting it accepted and published. Some magazines, in fact, are very free about retitling articles to suit their own notions of reader appeal. Searching for a title is important for another reason, however. It can greatly help you to focus your ideas and clarify your concepts further. Inability to think of a decent title, in fact, may be grounds for suspecting that you still haven't got your idea into proper focus.

A good title should serve a three-fold function: Engaging the reader's interest, telling him or her what the article is about and giving him or her a reason to read it -- a benefit, expressed or implied. Ideally, it will have brevity, freshness, and some sort of come-on. Though the editors may change it later on (for reasons of length, compatibility with other titles in the issue, etc.), it will help start their imaginations going -- and perhaps help to "sell" the article to them.

A simple test of brevity is whether your title will fit in one line of title-size type in the magazine; in general, the shorter the better. Freshness, unfortunately, comes a little harder. About all you can do is experiment. Forget (if you can) the wom-out word combinations like "challenge to management" and "keys to success", and give your own powers of invention free rein. As for come-on, it may be an implied promise of benefit, a whiff of controversy, or a striking metaphor. If it's sufficiently intriguing, the other criteria needn't be taken so seriously. "Marketing Myopia", the title of one of the most widely read articles ever published in HBR, was hardly explicit, but it was provocative. Usually, though, the come-on is less cryptic. For example:

Challenge -- "The Coming Scramble for Executive Talent"
Promise -- "Use Your Hidden Cash Resources"
Topic Interest -- "Can Management be Multinationalized?"

2. WRITING THE LEAD

If the title is the bait that engages the reader's interest, the lead -- that is, the first page or so of the article -- is the barb that hooks him. A good title and lead together can double your readership; a bad lead alone can halve it. And "bad" in this context means boring or misleading.

HARVARD BUSINESS REVIEW

A common pitfall in writing leads is to take too long establishing the place of the subject in the scheme of things. Try to come to the point as quickly as possible with a fact, a quote, or a questions that crystallizes the problem or the topic with which you're concerned and relate it strongly to the reader's own interests.

Another good way to start an article is with a concrete example. If you can think of a real-life incident that strikingly characterizes the problem, you will be off to a strong start. Follow it up by briefly defining your topic, emphasizing its importance (if that isn't already obvious), and giving the reader a quick preview of your argument -- i.e., the organization of the article.

3. SELECTING A STRUCTURE

How your article should be organized depends very much on the nature of the message. If it's an exposition of survey findings, you might take up your findings industry by industry, or function by function, or if it's that sort of survey, explore the common denominators of success and contrast them with the common denominators of failure. If the article is essentially an interpretation of trends, you might consider first the factual evidence, then the future course of events as you see them, and finally the implications for management in certain key areas. If the article is a problem and solution, or "how-to~ piece, you might choose to discuss the manifestations of the problem, its causes, and steps to its solution, in that order. And if your message is an argument in the narrower sense -- an attempt to prove a proposition -- you would naturally do so by identifying the issues and exploring the evidence for each.

In working up your outline -- try to avoid the pitfall of over-organization. As a rough rule of thumb, if there are more than four major sections to your outline, exclusive or lead and conclusion, you probably need to simplify. Another bad sign is more than three levels of structure, as indicated by major and minor side heads and the like. Still another pitfall to avoid is excessive reviewing and previewing -- telling the reader what you're about to tell him, then telling him, and finally telling him what you've told him. This is appropriate in some reports where the reader needs a guide through the labyrinth. But it shouldn't be necessary in a well organized article.

4. DEVELOPING THE CONCLUSIONS

A natural tendency when you come to the last page of the article is simply to summarize -- to give the reader a concise resume of the journey he's just completed. The temptation should usually be resisted. A good conclusion will add something new, but relevant, to the article -- a clinching bit of evidence, or ideally, something to do on Monday morning.

12. WRITING OUT THE IDEAS:

Hundreds of books have been written on the craft of writing, and many of them are loaded with valuable insights. But no one ever learned to write from a book. In writing, as in goH or guitar playing, you learn by doing. How you should go about writing is a very personal thing. Some people are able to dictate coherent prose; others, who can't and know it, prefer to write in longhand. Whatever your approach, you owe it to yourself to edit your own copy. Never be satisfied with your first draft, and look critically on your second. If you're hard on your own work in the beginning, it may not require major surgery later on with someone else's hands. Moreover, your writing skills will develop more rapidly as a result.

Writing for business magazines requires no special literary talent; al it takes is intelligence and a little basic technique. The technique can be summed up in these guidelines:

First and most important, KEEP YOUR READERS IN FOCUS. Consider their motives. They want ideas or information. They want, perhaps, practical help. Or they want to satisfy their curiosity. In any case, they certainly do not want to be bored or baffled. Try to say what you have to say as clearly and as crisply as you can. Don't confuse the reader by talking around the subject. Don't make statements whose implications are unclear, or arouse expectations you can't fulfill. Try to anticipate the reader's questions and give him or her reasonable, intelligible, and useful answers.

Second, KEEP IT SIMPLE. As Theodore Roosevelt once remarked, "Writings are useless unless they are read, and they cannot be read unless they are readable". This doesn't mean confining yourself to words of one syllable. But remember the demands on your readers' time and the limits of their patience. In all probability they are reading fast. If you express yourself in needlessly complicated fashion, you'll either confuse them or annoy them, and in either case you're likely to lose them.

Third, BE SPECIFIC. Use concrete details. Be definite in your statements. Don't say, "The manufacturing facility represented a major capital investment". Say, if you can, "The company invested $20 million in its new polystyrene plant". That tells the reader more and what it has lost in stateliness it has gained in vigor. Don't say, "The plant manager's disappointing performance eventually precipitated disciplinary action on the part of senior management". Say, "Six months later the plant manager found himself out of a job".

While examples are almost always needed in the body of an article to support general assertions, one or two for each major point should be enough, unless the point is so circumstantial, in fact, they can sometimes be no more than a sentence or two. They should always be specific enough, however, to have the ring of realty. Of course, disguises of names and places may be needed to avoid embarrassment.

Fourth, OMIT NEEDLESS WORDS. Strunk and White put the point nearly in THE ELEMENTS OF STYLE:

"Vigorous writing is concise. A sentence should contain no unnecessary words, a paragraph no unnecessary lines and a machine no unnecessary parts. This requires not that the writer make all his sentences short, or that he avoid all detail and treat his subject only in outline, but that every word tell."[1]

By the same token, it is helpful in writing for the HBR audience to avoid subtle qualifications -distinctions so delicate, or simply so trivial, that they obscure your main points instead of clarifying them. Most of your readers probably lack the time and patience to appreciate shades of grey. If you hedge your message about with too many qualifiers and modifiers. It may not register at all.

Fifth and last, TRY NOT TO PREACH. Don't, for example, try to tell readers how the MUST manage a business. Instead, tell them how others have benefited from the use of the approach and let them draw their own conclusions. More than advice, they will welcome information on how other organizations have dealt with a particular problem -- information they can put to work to help them manage work more effectively. There is hardly anything you might wish to say in an article that cannot be said without lecturing or preaching to the reader.

September, 1976

1. William S. Strunk, Jr., and E.B. White, THE ELEMENTS OF STYLE (New York, The Macmillan Co., 1959), p. ix.

HEALTHCARE FINANCIAL MANAGEMENT

ADDRESS FOR SUBMISSION :

CHERYL STACHURA, EDITOR
HEALTHCARE FINANCIAL MANAGEMENT
HEALTHCARE FINANCIAL MANAGEMENT ASSN.
TWO WESTBROOK CORP. CENTER, SUITE 700
WESTCHESTER, IL 60154
USA
708-531-9600, EXT. 385
708-531-0032 (Fax)

CIRCULATION DATA :

Reader : Healthcare Financial Managers

Frequency of Issue : Monthly

Copies Per Issue : Over 25,000

Subscription Price : 75.00 US$

Sponsorship : Professional Assoc.

PUBLICATION GUIDELINES :

Manuscript Length : 8-10

Copies Required : Five

Computer Submission : Yes

Format : WordPerfect 5.1/Windows 95

Fees to Review : 0.00 US$

REVIEW INFORMATION :

Type of Review : Blind Review

No. of External Reviewers : Three

No. of In House Reviewers : One

Acceptance Rate : 40 %

Time To Review : 2-3 months

Reviewer's Comments : Yes

Fees to Publish : 0.00 US$

Invited Articles : 21-30%

MANUSCRIPT TOPICS : ACCOUNTING INFORMATION SYSTEMS;
 ACCOUNTING THEORY & PRACTICE; AUDITING; CAPITAL BUDGETING; COST ACCOUNTING;
 GOVERNMENT & NON-PROFIT ACCOUNTING; INSURANCE;
 PORTFOLIO & SECURITY ANALYSIS; PUBLIC POLICY ECONOMICS; TAX ACCOUNTING;
 ACCOUNTING; ECONOMICS; FINANCE & INVESTMENTS; STRATEGIC MANAGEMENT POLICY;
 HEALTHCARE REFORMS; REIMBURSEMENT; MANAGEMENT INFORMATION SYSTEMS (MIS);
 HOSPITAL ADMINISTRATION; MANAGED & LONG TERM CARE;
 PHYSICIAN GROUP PRACTICE; INTEGRATED DELIVERY SYST

PUBLICATION GUIDELINES :

MANUSCRIPT GUIDELINES/COMMENTS :

ADDITIONAL MANUSCRIPT TOPICS: ELECTRONIC DATA INTERCHANGE, AMBULATORY CARE

1. HEALTHCARE FINANCIAL MANAGEMENT is a professional journal published monthly
by the Healthcare Financial Management Association as a service to its
members. The Journal's readers are financial managers of hospitals, managed
care plans, physician group practices, integrated delivery systems, long-term
care facilities, and other healthcare organizations. Articles address a wide
variety of subjects, including capital finance, accounting, financial
management, financial reporting, audit and control, productivity, strategic
planning and marketing, benefits and compensation, cost management,
information systems, alternative delivery systems, and long-term care, managed
care, ambulatory care, reimbursement, electronic data interchange, integrated
healthcare reform, health systems, and physician relations.

HEALTHCARE FINANCIAL MANAGEMENT

2. Articles in HFM are directed to three audiences. The principal audience is healthcare administrators, chief financial officers, vice presidents of finance, controllers, business managers, office managers, and other individuals responsible for implementing administrative and financial procedures in healthcare management. The second audience contains lawyers, accountants, investment bankers, commercial bankers, leasing executives, and financial consultants with an interest or specialty in health care. The tertiary audience includes those concerned with capital financing in the healthcare field, including public policy makers.

3. When submitting manuscripts for publication, the author should provide a full name, academic or professional title, complete address, and telephone number.

4. Manuscripts should be submitted on plain typing paper (8 1/2" x 11"), typed double space with 1" margins. The manuscript should be no longer than 12 pages, including graphs, charts, and tables, and should include a three-paragraph summary of the article. If footnotes are used, they are to be designated in superscript, alphabetically in the text (for example, not-for-profit hospitals) and follow this form on the footnote page:
Books:
  a. Grimaldi, Paul L. and Micheletti, Julie A. Diagnosis Related Groups. Chicago, Ill.: Pluribus Press. 1983. pp. 2-4.
Articles:
  b. Zelman, William; McLeod, Katherine; Dieter, Frank A.; and Sulver, James D. "Approaching cost reduction through responsibility centers". Healthcare Financial Management. Vol. 38 No. 9. September 1984. pp. 20-24.
These footnotes should be placed on a separate page at the end of the manuscript.

5. Include NO bibliography.

6. The author should also suggest a title for the submitted manuscript. It should be short, concise, and include an active verb (for example, "Ten hospitals forge new directions and strategies"). The author must realize, however, that the title may need to be reworded by the editors because of space constraints.

7. When submitting a manuscript, include five doublespaced copies for editing and review. Delete or omit author names or affiliations on the first page of text of four of the copies, as reviewers are not given author names when reviewing manuscripts for HFM.

8. Tables, charts, and graphs help emphasize and clarify points in the article and should be used when possible. They should be reproduced or drawn neatly but need not be camera ready. When citing tables, charts, or graphs in the text, the author should refer to them as "exhibits" and number them consecutively (for example, Exhibit 1). The actual chart, graph, or table should include an exhibit designation and title (for example, Exhibit 1: The age distribution of hospital charges).

9. HFM stresses clear, straightforward, expository style. Avoid humor, sarcasm, slang, or jargon. Be concise, communicating your ideas in as few words as possible. Also, use subheads whenever appropriate. Subheads divide the article into smaller, more understandable parts.

10. Because HFM's primary audience includes practitioners in the healthcare field, articles should be practical rather than theoretical. Whenever appropriate, illustrate points with examples from personal experience.

11. Manuscripts accepted for publication are edited by the staff for content (organization, accurate information, and so on), style (grammar, punctuation,and spelling), and length. Standards for style are set by the staff to follow professional publishing practices. Although the editors try to preserve the author's personal writing style, decisions on style and content are at the discretion of the editors.

12. Manuscripts submitted to HFM will be reviewed by a panel of healthcare financial management experts, before being accepted for publication. Reviewers consider each manuscript on the basis of timeliness, usefulness to Journal readers, contribution to the professional literature, and technical accuracy. If the reviewers believe that the manuscript is not appropriate for publication, the author is notified by letter. If the reviewers believe additional clarification or information is needed, the author is asked to make corrections before a decision can be made. If the manuscript is accepted, the author is notified by letter and asked to sign a manuscript release form and provide a biography and a black and white photograph. The biography should include full names, degrees, credentials, academic or professional titles, affiliations, publications, and complete addresses. Six to eight weeks should be allowed for completion of the review process.

13. The editors of HFM do not wish to promote any commercial service, product, or organization. Therefore, submitted manuscripts should be generic in nature. Specific commercial products, services or organizations should not be mentioned.

14. HFM follows a policy of exclusive publication. Articles published elsewhere are not accepted. Furthermore, HFM assumes sole copyright of any article published in HFM. Permission is required of the Editor before an article can be copied or reproduced. Requests for reprinting an article must be directed in writing to the Editor.

15. The editors will discuss potential topics and react to outlines of possible articles. Written queries should be sent to the Editor.

16. HFM operates on a three month lead schedule. That is, the staff begins working on an issue at least three months before the publication date. When combined with the time taken for editing and review, it is not unusual for at least six months to elapse from the time a manuscript is received until it is published. Other factors affecting the publication date are the existing backlog of manuscripts already accepted, the subject matter of the manuscripts (an article on a similar topic may have appeared recently), or the theme of the issue.

17. HFM does not pay authors for publishing manuscripts. We send three complimentary copies of the issue to the author when an article appears.

18. When an article appears in HFM, the author will be provided with information on how to purchase various quantities of reprints of the article.

HISTORY OF POLITICAL ECONOMY

ADDRESS FOR SUBMISSION :

C.D.W. GOODWIN, EDITOR
HISTORY OF POLITICAL ECONOMY
DUKE UNIVERSITY
DEPARTMENT OF ECONOMICS
BOX 90097
DURHAM, NC 27708-0097
USA
919-684-3936
919-681-7869 (Fax)
E-Mail : goodwin@econ.duke.edu

CIRCULATION DATA :

Reader : Academic

Frequency of Issue : Quarterly

Copies Per Issue : 1001-2000

Subscription Price : 60.00 US$

Sponsorship : University

PUBLICATION GUIDELINES :

Manuscript Length : 16-20

Copies Required : Three

Computer Submission : No

Format : N/A

Fees to Review : 0.00 US$

REVIEW INFORMATION :

Type of Review : Editorial Review

No. of External Reviewers : Two

No. of In House Reviewers : One

Acceptance Rate : 21-30%

Time To Review : 2-3 months

Reviewer's Comments : Yes

Fees to Publish : 0.00 US$

Invited Articles : 5% or less

MANUSCRIPT TOPICS : ACCOUNTING INFORMATION SYSTEMS;
  ECONOMIC HISTORY; HISTORY OF ECONOMIC THOUGHT

PUBLICATION GUIDELINES : Chicago Manual of Style

MANUSCRIPT GUIDELINES/COMMENTS :

1. "HISTORY OF POLITICAL ECONOMY is devoted to the development of economic analysis and exploration of the relations of theory and analysis to policy, to other disciplines, and to social history in general."

2. Only original unpublished material can be considered; author's signature on "Agreement to Publish" form is a precondition of publication. For speedier consideration, submit three copies of the typescript. It should be emphasized that all material (text, excerpts, lists, tables, footnotes, references) MUST be typed double-spaced; no single-spaced material can be accepted. Authors are expected to furnish any drawings for their articles in reproducible form upon acceptance of articles for publication.

3. Books for review should be sent to the Book Review Editor, Professor S. Todd Lowry, Department of Economics, Washington and Lee University, Lexington, VA 24450, USA.

HUMANOMICS

ADDRESS FOR SUBMISSION :

MASUDUL A. CHOUDHURY, EDITOR
HUMANOMICS
UNIVERSITY COLLEGE OF CAPE BRETON
SCHOOL OF BUSINESS
SYDNEY, NS BIP 6L2
CANADA
902-539-5300
902-562-0119 (Fax)
E-Mail : mchoudhu@sparo.uccb.ns.ca

CIRCULATION DATA :

Reader : Academic

Frequency of Issue : Quarterly

Copies Per Issue : Less than 1000

Subscription Price : 359.00 US$

Sponsorship : Professional Assoc.

PUBLICATION GUIDELINES :

Manuscript Length : 26-30

Copies Required : Two

Computer Submission : Yes

Format : WordPerfect 5.1

Fees to Review : 0.00 US$

REVIEW INFORMATION :

Type of Review : Blind Review

No. of External Reviewers : One

No. of In House Reviewers : One

Acceptance Rate : 90 %

Time To Review : 1-2 months

Reviewer's Comments : Yes

Fees to Publish : 0.00 US$

Invited Articles :

MANUSCRIPT TOPICS : ECONOMETRICS; PUBLIC POLICY ECONOMICS;
  PHILOSOPHY; COMPARATIVE STUDIES; INTERDISCIPLINARY

PUBLICATION GUIDELINES : Chicago Manual of Style

MANUSCRIPT GUIDELINES/COMMENTS :

Journal of HUMANOMICS on a continuing basis; presently publishing Vol. 13, No.
1997. Articles may be interdisciplinary in nature focusing on the systemic
interrelationship between ethics/morality/public policy and socioeconomic,
institutional, scientific, developmental issues. Scientific papers including
mathematical ones must note this condition. Clearly constructed diagrams,
tables, mathematical equations are to be submitted where applicable.

Send two copies of paper to Professor M.A. Choudhury, Editor and Director of
the Centre of Humanomics.

The Centre of Humanomics is a formally established intellectual association of
university professors from around the world at the University College of Cape
Breton, Sydney, Nova Scotia. It is devoted to the ethico-economic study of
major socio-economic issues in world perspective. The main objective of the
Centre is to disseminate scholarly views and writings of social thinkers and
personalities on ethico-economic issues for the awareness, education and
interest of informed readership. The programmes of the Centre of Humanomics
are: editorship of the international academic journal HUMANOMICS; publication
of occasional refereed monographs on ethico-economic issues, organisation of

HUMANOMICS

occasional learned seminars and conferences in the area of ethico-economics, socio-scientific epistemology and globally interactive systems. For all of this the Centre seeks active participation in ethico-economic research and deliberations from the world intellectual community.

Humanomics is catalogued in the Journal of Economic Literature and is entered in the CD-ROM of JEL.

INDIAN ECONOMIC REVIEW

ADDRESS FOR SUBMISSION :

V. PANDIT, EDITOR
INDIAN ECONOMIC REVIEW
UNIVERSITY OF DELHI
DELHI SCHOOL OF ECONOMICS
DELHI 110007,
INDIA
91 11 725 7005
91 11 725 7159 (Fax)
E-Mail : ier@cdedse.ernet.in

CIRCULATION DATA :

Reader : Academic

Frequency of Issue : 2 Times/Year

Copies Per Issue : Less than 1000

Subscription Price : 30.00 US$
  Institution : 50.00 US$

Sponsorship : University

PUBLICATION GUIDELINES :

Manuscript Length : 21-25

Copies Required : Three

Computer Submission : Yes

Format : Word Perfect 6.0

Fees to Review : 0.00 US$

REVIEW INFORMATION :

Type of Review : Blind Review

No. of External Reviewers : One

No. of In House Reviewers : One

Acceptance Rate : 40 %

Time To Review : 2-3 months

Reviewer's Comments : Yes

Fees to Publish : 0.00 US$

Invited Articles : 5% or less

MANUSCRIPT TOPICS : ECONOMETRICS;
  INTERNATIONAL & ECONOMIC DEVELOPMENT; INTERNATIONAL FINANCE;
  PORTFOLIO & SECURITY ANALYSIS; PUBLIC POLICY ECONOMICS; DEVELOPMENT POLICY;
  MACROECONOMIC POLICY; HOUSEHOLD BEHAVIOUR; THEORY OF THE FIRM

PUBLICATION GUIDELINES :

MANUSCRIPT GUIDELINES/COMMENTS :

INDIANA BUSINESS REVIEW

ADDRESS FOR SUBMISSION :

CAROL O. ROGERS, MANAGING EDITOR
INDIANA BUSINESS REVIEW
INDIANA UNIVERSITY
GRADUATE SCHOOL OF BUSINESS
INDIANA BUSINESS RESEARCH CENTER
10TH AND FEE LANE
BLOOMINGTON, IN 47405
USA
812-855-5507
317-274-3312 (Fax)
E-Mail : Rogersc@indiana.edu

CIRCULATION DATA :

Reader : Business Persons

Frequency of Issue : Monthly

Copies Per Issue : 3001-4000

Subscription Price :
  Free to Indiana Res. : 0.00 US$

Sponsorship : University

PUBLICATION GUIDELINES :

Manuscript Length : 11-15

Copies Required : Two

Computer Submission : Yes

Format : Mac or PC

Fees to Review : 0.00 US$

REVIEW INFORMATION :

Type of Review : Editorial Review

No. of External Reviewers : Zero

No. of In House Reviewers : Two

Acceptance Rate : 50 %

Time To Review : 1-2 months

Reviewer's Comments : No

Fees to Publish : 0.00 US$

Invited Articles : 31-50%

MANUSCRIPT TOPICS : COST ACCOUNTING; ECONOMETRICS; ECONOMIC HISTORY;
  INTERNATIONAL & ECONOMIC DEVELOPMENT; PUBLIC POLICY ECONOMICS; DEMOGRAPHICS

PUBLICATION GUIDELINES : Chicago Manual of Style

MANUSCRIPT GUIDELINES/COMMENTS :

INVITED ARTICLES: 75%

The IBR is a journal relating to the state of Indiana. It publishes articles
discussing the state's economy and demographics and trends in those areas.
Once a year we publish issues devoted to national, state, and local forecasts.

Morton Marcus, our editor, reviews all manuscripts and makes the final
decision on what is published.

INSTITUTIONAL INVESTOR

ADDRESS FOR SUBMISSION :

DAVID CUDBACK, EDITOR
INSTITUTIONAL INVESTOR
488 MADISON AVENUE
NEW YORK, NY 10022
USA
212-224-3105

CIRCULATION DATA :

Reader :

Frequency of Issue :

Copies Per Issue :

Subscription Price :

Sponsorship :

PUBLICATION GUIDELINES :

Manuscript Length :

Copies Required :

Computer Submission : No

Format : N/A

Fees to Review : 0.00 US$

REVIEW INFORMATION :

Type of Review : N/A

No. of External Reviewers :

No. of In House Reviewers :

Acceptance Rate :

Time To Review :

Reviewer's Comments : No

Fees to Publish : 0.00 US$

Invited Articles :

MANUSCRIPT TOPICS : PORTFOLIO & SECURITY ANALYSIS

PUBLICATION GUIDELINES :

MANUSCRIPT GUIDELINES/COMMENTS :

The articles in this magazine are prepared primarily by the reporting staff.

INSURANCE: MATHEMATICS & ECONOMICS

ADDRESS FOR SUBMISSION :

S. KLUGMAN, EDITOR
INSURANCE: MATHEMATICS & ECONOMICS
DRAKE UNIVERSITY
COLLEGE OF BUSINESS ADMINISTRATION
DES MOINES, IA 50311
USA
515-271-4097
515-271-2001 (Fax)
E-Mail : SKLUGMAN@ACAD.DRAKE.EDU

CIRCULATION DATA :

Reader : Academic

Frequency of Issue : Quarterly

Copies Per Issue :

Subscription Price :
  Dutch Florins : 822.00

Sponsorship : Profit Oriented Corp.

PUBLICATION GUIDELINES :

Manuscript Length : 16-20

Copies Required : Three

Computer Submission : No

Format : N/A

Fees to Review : 0.00 US$

REVIEW INFORMATION :

Type of Review : Editorial Review

No. of External Reviewers : Two

No. of In House Reviewers : One

Acceptance Rate : 21-30%

Time To Review : 4-6 months

Reviewer's Comments : Yes

Fees to Publish : 0.00 US$

Invited Articles : 5% or less

MANUSCRIPT TOPICS : ACCOUNTING INFORMATION SYSTEMS; ECONOMETRICS;
  INSURANCE; PUBLIC POLICY ECONOMICS; ACTUARIAL SCIENCE

PUBLICATION GUIDELINES :

MANUSCRIPT GUIDELINES/COMMENTS :

AIMS AND SCOPE
INSURANCE: MATHEMATICS AND ECONOMICS is an international journal which intends
to strengthen communication between individuals and groups who produce and
apply research results in insurance mathematics, thus helping to correct the
current fragmentation of research in the field. The journal feels a particular
obligation to facilitate closer cooperation between those who carry out
research in insurance mathematics and insurance economics (whether actuaries
or non-actuaries) and practicing actuaries who are interested in the
implementation of the results. To this purpose, INSURANCE: MATHEMATICS AND
ECONOMICS will publish high quality papers of international interest,
concerned with either the theory of insurance mathematics or the inventive
application of it, including empirical or experimental results. Papers which
combine several of these aspects are particularly welcome, as are survey
papers of a pedagogical nature.

The subject matter of the journal includes the theory, models and
computational methods of life insurance (including pension systems, social
insurance, and health insurance), of non-life insurance, and of reinsurance
and other risk-sharing arrangements. It also includes, under the heading

INSURANCE: MATHEMATICS & ECONOMICS

insurance economics, innovative insurance applications of results from other fields, such as probability and statistics, computer science and numerical analysis, economics, operations research and management science, and risk management.

INSTRUCTIONS TO AUTHORS
Manuscripts should preferably be written in English. Manuscripts written in German and French can also be considered for publication.

Manuscripts can be submitted (in triplicate) to any of the three following addresses:

    R. Kaas, Universiteit van Amsterdam, Instituut voor Actuariaat en Econometrie, Roetersstraat 11, 1018 WB Amsterdam, The Netherlands.

    S. Klugman, College of Business Administration, Drake University, Des Moines, IA 50311, USA.

    G.C. Taylor, Coopers & Lybrand, Coopers & Lybrand Tower, Level 32, 580 George Street, Sydney, N.S.W. 2000, Australia.

Submission of a manuscript will be held to imply that it contains original unpublished work and is not being submitted for publication elsewhere and that, if the work received official sponsorship, it has been duly released for open publication.

Upon acceptance of an article, the author(s) will be asked to transfer copyright of the article to the publisher. This transfer will ensure the widest possible dissemination of information.

Manuscripts should be typewritten on one side of the paper only, double spaced with wide margins. All pages should be numbered consecutively. References, tables and legends for figures should be typed on separate pages. The legends and titles on tables and figures must be sufficiently descriptive such that they are understandable without reference to the text.

The first page of the manuscript should contain the following information: (i) the title; (ii) the name(s) and institutional affiliation(s) of the author(s); (iii) an abstract of no more than thirty lines; (iv) a list of keywords, and (v) an abbreviated title. A footnote on the same sheet should give the name and the present address of the author to whom proofs and reprint ordor form should be addressed.

All mathematical symbols which are not typewritten should be specified and listed separately. Unusual symbols or notations should be identified in the margins. Awkward mathematical notations which require special typesetting procedures must be avoided. The numbers identifying displayed mathematical expressions should be placed in parentheses at the right margin. Parts of text should not be subject to this numbering.

Illustrations should be provided in triplicate (1 original drawn in black ink on white paper + 2 photocopies). Care should be taken that lettering and symbols are of a comparable size. The drawings should not be inserted in the text and should be marked on the back with figure numbers, title of paper, and name of author. All graphs and diagrams should be referred to as figures and should be numbered consecutively in the text in arabic numerals. Illustrations of insufficient quality which have to be drawn by the publisher will be charged to the author.

Footnotes should be numbered consecutively and typed, double spaced, in a separate list at the end of the paper. In the text, footnotes, which should be kept to a minimum, are indicated by superscript numbers alone.

References should be ordered alphabetically, in a separate list like the following examples:

Arrow, K.J. (1970). Essays in the Theory of Risk-Bearing. North-Holland, Amsterdam.
Beckman, J.A. (1974). A new collective risk model. Transactions of the Society of Actuaries 25, 789-806.
Jewell, WS. (1975). Model variations in credibility theory. In: Credibility: Theory and Applications, 133-244. Academic Press, New York.

Note that journal titles should not be abbreviated. In the text, references to publications should appear as follows: Smith (1969) reported that..." or "This problem has been a subject in literature before [e.g., Smith (1969, p. 102)]". The author should make sure that there is a strict one-to-one correspondence between the names (years) in the text and those on the list.

Tables should be numbered consecutively in the text in arabic numerals.

Any manuscript which does not conform to the above instructions may be returned for the necessary revision before publication.

Page proofs will be sent to the authors. Corrections other than printer's errors may be charged to the author. Twenty five reprints of each paper are supplied free; additional reprints are available at cost it they are ordered when the proof is returned.

INTERNAL AUDITING

ADDRESS FOR SUBMISSION :

STEPHEN H. COLLINS, MANAGING EDITOR
INTERNAL AUDITING
RIA GROUP
395 HUDSON STREET
NEW YORK, NY 10014
212-367-6398
212-367-6718 (Fax)

PUBLICATION GUIDELINES :

Manuscript Length : 11-20

Copies Required : Two

Computer Submission : Yes

Format : WordPerfect 5.1

Fees to Review : 0.00 US$

CIRCULATION DATA :

Reader : Business Persons,
        Academic, &
        Internal Auditors

Frequency of Issue : Quarterly

Copies Per Issue : 4001-5000

Subscription Price : 115.00 US$

Sponsorship : Profit Oriented Corp.

REVIEW INFORMATION :

Type of Review : Editorial Review

No. of External Reviewers : Two

No. of In House Reviewers : Two

Acceptance Rate : 45 %

Time To Review : 1-2 months

Reviewer's Comments : No

Fees to Publish : 0.00 US$

Invited Articles : 31-50%

MANUSCRIPT TOPICS : AUDITING; ECONOMETRICS; INTERNAL AUDITING

PUBLICATION GUIDELINES : Chicago Manual of Style

MANUSCRIPT GUIDELINES/COMMENTS :

SPONSORSHIP: Warren Gorham & Lamont (RIA Group)
SUBSCRIPTION PRICE: Academic discounts are given.

INTERNAL AUDITING seeks articles that are primarily practice oriented and that
will be of interest to directors of internal auditing and their staff. The
intent of Internal Auditing is to provide operational and implementational
guidance to internal auditors.

The major areas for articles are:
*   Operations auditing
*   Financial auditing
*   EDP auditing
*   Audit department administration
*   Relationships with external auditors, management and the Board
*   Risk assessment
*   Oral and written reporting

It is expected that most articles will fall in the 3000 to 5000 word range.
The subject matter should be the final determinant of length, and this range
may be broken in either direction in individual cases.

INTERNAL AUDITING

Authors should bear in mind that articles published are intended to be read by busy people. The article should get to the point and not digress into extraneous areas.

While a how-to approach is preferred, we are interested in receiving articles that are controversial or unusual in their viewpoint so long as the topic should be of interest to our audience.

Articles are initially screened by the Editor-in-Chief and the editors. Promising manuscripts are sent to two external reviewers for their comments and review. Final decisions of acceptance are made by the editors.

MANUSCRIPT STYLE

Every publication seeks a certain degree of uniformity of style in the papers written by its several authors. We, too, seek a certain level of writing that, though not so heavy handed as the NEW YORKER or the HARVARD BUSINESS REVIEW, which make all articles seem to have been written by the same person, will create an impression of unity in a reader's mind.

Technical writers use too much punctuation, too much emphasis, and too many stops and starts in their writing. Some, though not all, of our authors have been infested with the disease. Some examples follow:

PARENTHESES. Parentheses should be used to insert data that is not part of the discussion. Parentheses are not designed to permit an author to carry on two unrelated discussions simultaneously.

Correct:
    The American Institute of CPA's (AICPA) has decreed...

Incorrect:
    Some of the characteristics of the standard accountants report (e.g., the uncertainty qualification) are under review.

    Can an accountant apply poolings of interest accounting (as defined in APB Opinion 15) without first...?

QUOTATION MARKS. Quotation marks are used to identify words used by others, not to cast doubt or to emphasize and to identify words being used as words instead of ideas. When quotation marks are used to identify a term being defined, this should be done only the first time and not throughout the discussion.

Correct:
    The term "window period" means the period after issuance of a report during which...

Incorrect:
    An event during the "window period" may require dual dating.

UNDERLINING. A fair quota of words to be underlined would be two words per article. Emphasis is a matter of phraseology and writing, not typography.

FOOTNOTES. Identify sources of material in References. As to footnotes with additional information, a fair quota is five footnotes for contra discussions. If a thing is worth saying, put it in the text.

TITLES OF PUBLISHED WORKS. Some publications call for underlined titles indicating to the printer that italics should be used. We use this form in the reference notes but in the text the correct title surrounded by quotation marks is used the first time a publication is identified, thus:

> In 1984 the SEC issued Financial Reporting Release 17. (FRR 17) "Oil and Gas Producers - Full Cost Accounting Practices." Thereafter refer simply to FRR 17.

As to other publications:

> FULL TITLE
> ABBREVIATION
>
> Statement of Financial Accounting
> Standards No. 80 SFAS 80
>
> Statement of Auditing
> Standards 49   SAS 49
>
> Statement of Internal Auditing Standards
> No. 3   SIAS 3

PREPARATION OF MANUSCRIPTS:

1. Use only 8-1/2 x 11" white bond paper. Do not use "erasable" paper.

2. ALL MANUSCRIPT COPY -- text, footnotes, charts, quotations and everything else -- MUST BE TYPED DOUBLE-SPACED, on one side of the paper only.

3. All footnotes are to be double-spaced and typed on a separate page at the end of the manuscript. They should be numbered consecutively throughout the article starting from 1.

4. Footnotes should be limited to identification of sources referred to in the text. We believe that anything worth saying should be said in the text of the paper although occasionally small exceptions will be made. We do not ordinarily publish bibliographies.

5. Minor changes should be made between the lines of the typescript, not in the margins. That is, typographical errors and slight corrections of the text or footnotes may be written (please print) on the manuscript in pen. If corrections are lengthy or complex, retype the entire manuscript page.

6. Illustrations accompanying manuscripts should be numbered, provided with suitable legends (again, typed double-spaced on 8-1/2 x 11" sheets), and marked lightly in pencil on the back with the name of the author and the title of the article. Illustrations such as original drawings or graphs are to be drawn in black India ink. Typewritten or freehand lettering is not acceptable. All lettering must be done professionally. Do not staple or paper clip illustrations between sheets of cardboard before mailing.

7. Tables and exhibits should be numbered consecutively.

8. Use headings and subheadings extensively. Center main headings within the article, type secondary headings flush left with the left-hand margin.

9. Keep the punctuation simple. Most authors overuse parentheses, italics and quotations marks which are simply edited out in the publication process.

10. If an article includes any previously copyrighted material (other than short quotations), the publisher must have letters of permission to reprint from the copyright holder and from the author if he or she is not the copyright holder. These letters must be submitted at the same time as the manuscript.

11. Internal Auditing normally publishes articles only if they have not yet appeared or since been accepted for publication elsewhere. There is generally no objection, however, to having articles that appear in Internal Auditing reprinted in other publications at a later date, if appropriate permission is requested from the publisher.

12. Three copies of each manuscript should be submitted for review.

INTERNAL AUDITOR

ADDRESS FOR SUBMISSION :

MS. ANNE GRAHAM, EDITOR
INTERNAL AUDITOR
THE INSTITUTE OF INTERNAL AUDITORS
249 MAITLAND AVENUE
ALTAMONTE SPRINGS, FL 32701-4201
USA
407-830-7600
407-831-5171 (Fax)

CIRCULATION DATA :

Reader : Business Persons

Frequency of Issue : Bi-Monthly

Copies Per Issue : Over 25,000

Subscription Price : 60.00 US$
  2 Years : 108.00 US$
  3 Years : 156.00 US$

Sponsorship : Professional Assoc.

PUBLICATION GUIDELINES :

Manuscript Length : 11-15

Copies Required : Four

Computer Submission : No

Format : N/A

Fees to Review : 0.00 US$

REVIEW INFORMATION :

Type of Review : Blind Review

No. of External Reviewers : Three

No. of In House Reviewers : Two

Acceptance Rate : 21-30%

Time To Review : 2-3 months

Reviewer's Comments :

Fees to Publish : 0.00 US$

Invited Articles : 5% or less

MANUSCRIPT TOPICS : AUDITING; CAPITAL BUDGETING; BUSINESS EDUCATION;
  INTERNAL AUDITING; ETHICS; ISO 9000; BENCHMARKING;
  MANAGEMENT INFORMATION SYSTEMS (MIS); ORGANIZATIONAL BEHAVIOR AND THEORY;
  FRAUD; DISASTER RECOVERY

PUBLICATION GUIDELINES : Chicago Manual of Style

MANUSCRIPT GUIDELINES/COMMENTS :

More Manuscript Topics: TQM, Global Technology
Copies per Issue: 40,000

1. CHICAGO MANUAL OF STYLE

2. Our primary audience is the internal auditing professional in practice all over the globe. Our readers hold top management positions in the multicorporate world and the public sector; they are found in private industry, nonprofit organizations, and local and national governments. From vice presidents to entry-level staff auditors, the majority are members of the Institute and actively support the development of their profession.

3. The Journal has secondary audiences of professionals in such fields as public accounting, education, information systems, and security. The steady growth of these audiences plus a broadening membership base has increased the total readership each year. A respected reference, the Journal's articles are reprinted and translated in books and periodicals around the world.

4. Each issue of the Journal carries special interest material much of which comes from our readers. If you wish to send an item, look for the address published in that department or send it directly to the Journal and we will forward it to the department editor.

5. The Round Table. One of our most popular departments, it includes "short stories" from auditors who tell how they discovered and solved problems in their companies. Submit one or two typewritten, double-spaced pages describing the problem, how it was discovered, what was done to fix it, and include the benefit to the company such as a monetary saving. Individual anonymity is voluntary and assured; the sources are usually listed as an IIA Chapter or an anonymous offering.

6. Fraud Findings. Only discovery and resolution of fraud are presented here. Events must be based on actual facts, but names of individuals or companies involved will not be mentioned. Submissions are usually a few pages long and include a brief narrative of the case, the key clue uncovering the fraud, steps taken to facilitate the audit, motivation of the perpetrator, control weaknesses, and action taken to prevent recurrence.

7. Letters. We encourage readers to write letters on timely, professional issues or to comment on published articles. Letters must be signed and should be no longer than 700 words because space is limited. All letters will be edited for purposes of clarity or space.

8. THE IA also has two departments that are "semi-contributory".

9. Professional standards bulletins are prepared for information only by the Standards Information Service Subcommittee of the Institute's Professional Standards and Responsibilities Committee. If you have a question concerning the STANDARDS FOR PROFESSIONAL PRACTICE OF INTERNAL AUDITING, please send it to us and our experts will try to answer it.

10. Readings include reviews of books (periodicals are not reviewed) we believe to be of interest to internal auditors. If you know of a book that we have not yet reviewed, but that you would like to read an opinion on before purchasing, please send us the name of the book and its publisher's name and address.

11. "Computers & Auditing" provides audit professionals with information about how other audit organizations have integrated the personal computer into their operations. The column features software product reviews, tips from end-user auditors, and examples of auditor-developed applications.

12. In addition to our Outstanding Contributor Certificates, which are given for the finest articles we publish, each year we honor the article judged best by our review board by awarding the author the coveted John B. Thurston Award for literary excellence. The author also travels to IIA's international conference -- all expenses paid.

13. Write clearly and concisely. Get directly to the point, make your point in as few words as possible, and use simple language.

14. Define terms that may not be well known. Avoid jargon and cliches that may confuse the reader or send them running for the dictionary. On first

mention, spell out abbreviations or initials such as IIA, GAO, USPS.
Remember: While some computer terms are "universal" not all computer systems
use the same term to mean the same thing. If in doubt, define!

15. For crisp writing, use the active voice. Too often a passive voice
statement such as "it was decided" leaves the reader questioning "who
decided?" Anticipate your readers' questions and give them reasonable and
useful answers.

16. Subheads give the reader a break between main sections of a manuscript and
provide points of quick reference for a reader searching for a particular
thought or concept.

17. Be sure all direct quotes are accurate and contribute to your topic. Be
aware of what constitutes libel. Indicate your source. If you cannot
attribute a quote to a publication, we may have to rephrase the idea or delete
the quote and any reference to it altogether. When quoting a speech, identify
the speaker, the date of delivery and the event.

18. Our footnote style is the standard reference style, for example: Alan S.
Glazer and Henry R. Jaenicke, A FRAMEWORK FOR EVALUATING AN INTERNAL AUDIT
FUNCTION (Altamonte Springs, Florida: Foundation for Auditability Research
and Education, Inc., 1980), pp. 35-37.

19. The average published article is five or six pages, so limit the length of
your manuscript to 18-25 pages including exhibits. The manuscript should be
typed and double-spaced with margins no less than 1-1/4 inches wide. Letter
quality computer printouts are acceptable.

20. Exhibits should be concise, separated from the body of the manuscript, and
detailed enough to make their message clear. Our staff will prepare them to
fit the publications' specifications, so original art is necessary only for
unique items.

21. Keep footnotes to a minimum. They are necessary to indicate the source of
an assertion or a fact that is not widely known, or to guide the reader to
more detailed information. Please put the footnote and group all footnotes at
the end of the manuscript.

22. Submit the original and three copies of the manuscript. We need the name,
address, and telephone number of the author, even when the manuscript is
submitted through the local IIA chapter.

23. Mail your material to INTERNAL AUDITOR, 249 Maitland Avenue, P.O. Box
1119, Altamonte Springs, FL 32715-1119.

24. The review process for the INTERNAL AUDITOR generally takes about six
weeks. Three members of our editorial advisory board, selected for their
compatibility to your topic, will receive a "blind" copy of your manuscript
and evaluate it for its interest to auditors, quality of writing, technical
soundness, timeliness, and originality.

25. Although every manuscript we receive is judged on its own merits, we
follow these general criteria:

Does the manuscript deal with a problem, issue, or condition that is the concern of people in the auditing profession?

Is this a new concern or a new approach to a continuing concern?

Does the author discuss it in enough depth to help the reader (who is, more often that not, an internal auditor)?

Does the author support the discussion with examples drawn from actual experience?

Does the manuscript offer any solutions to the problem discussed?

Does the manuscript stand as a carefully reasoned presentation?

Does the manuscript add significantly to what has already been published about the subject in the IA about elsewhere?

26. Not every manuscript must cover all of these criteria, but inclusion of them increases the chances for acceptance of a manuscript.

INTERNATIONAL ADVANCES IN ECONOMIC RESEARCH

ADDRESS FOR SUBMISSION :

JOHN M. VIRGO, EDITOR-IN-CHIEF
INTERNATIONAL ADVANCES IN ECONOMIC
  RESEARCH
SOUTHERN ILLINOIS UNIVERSITY
ATLANTIC ECONOMIC SOCIETY
CAMPUS BOX 1101
EDWARDSVILLE, IL 62026-1101
618-692-2291
628-692-3400 (Fax)
E-Mail : jvirgo@eniac.ac.siue.edu

CIRCULATION DATA :

Reader : Academic

Frequency of Issue : Quarterly

Copies Per Issue : Less than 1000

Subscription Price : 30.00 US$
  Institution : 90.00 US$

Sponsorship : Professional Assoc.

PUBLICATION GUIDELINES :

Manuscript Length : 26-30

Copies Required : Two

Computer Submission : Yes

Format : ASCII or WordPerfect 6.1

Fees to Review : 115.00 US$
  Members/At.Econ.Soc. 65.00 US$

REVIEW INFORMATION :

Type of Review : Blind Review

No. of External Reviewers : Two

No. of In House Reviewers : One

Acceptance Rate : 11-20%

Time To Review : 1-2 months

Reviewer's Comments : Yes

Fees to Publish : 28.00 US$
  Members/At.Econ.Soc. 18.00 US$

Invited Articles : 5% or less

MANUSCRIPT TOPICS : ACCOUNTING THEORY & PRACTICE; AUDITING;
  ECONOMETRICS; ECONOMIC HISTORY; INTERNATIONAL & ECONOMIC DEVELOPMENT;
  INTERNATIONAL FINANCE; PUBLIC POLICY ECONOMICS

PUBLICATION GUIDELINES :

MANUSCRIPT GUIDELINES/COMMENTS :

FORMAT AND MARGINS

Limit the paper to no more than 15 single-spaced, typewritten pages, including
references and footnotes. Use white, 8 1/2 x 11 or 8 1/2 x 14 inch paper.

Cover Page
1. Limit the title of the manuscript to no more than 10 words.

2. The title should include the name of the author and coauthors and their
affiliations. The cover page is the only page of the manuscript in which the
authors and coauthors names and affiliations should be listed.

3. List the JEL category and name under which the paper primarily belongs.

4. State any disclaimers to the paper.

5. The cover page should indicate the name, address, phone, and fax number of the correspondence person.

Manuscript Pages
1. Place the title of the paper at least one inch from the top of the page.

2. Triple space. Place the heading "ABSTRACT" flush left and in all capital letters, followed by an abstract of no longer than 125 words. The JEL category under which the paper primarily belongs should appear at the end of the abstract.

3. Triple space before starting the body of the manuscript.

4. Double space between all paragraphs, headings, and subheadings.

Type Style
Papers should be typed using CG Times or Times Roman type style in 10 point elite.

Headings
All headings are to be typed flush with the left margin. Main headings should be in all capital letters. Subheadings should be italicized or underlined (when italics are not available) and in capital and lower case.

REFERENCES AND FOOTNOTES
1. Be certain to separate references from footnotes. References are works cited within the text. Footnotes are explanatory remarks about a specific point in the text.

2. Footnotes should appear at the end of the text of the manuscript, followed by the references. Indent the first line of each footnote. Number footnotes consecutively throughout the paper, not page by page.

3. Double space between the last line of text and the first footnote. Double space between the last footnote and the start of references.

4. The headings "FOOTNOTES" and "REFERENCES" should be in all capital letters, typed flush with the left margin.

5. Alphabetize all references by author's last name (with last name first for the primary and secondary authors).

6. Indent the second and subsequent lines of each reference. Include the full title of journal, volume number, issue number, month, year, and page numbers. Example:
    Musgrave, Richard A. "The Three Branches Revisited," Atlantic Economic Journal, 17, 1, March 1989, pp. 1-7.

References Within the Text of the Manuscript
1. When you reference a publication in the text, insert the author's last name and the year of publication in brackets, including specific page numbers where necessary. Place it at the end of the sentence or before quoted matter.

2. If reference is made to two or more works by the same author in the same year, designate them as follows: 1986a, 1986b. Example:

INTERNATIONAL ADVANCES IN ECONOMIC RESEARCH

This form of analysis has received attention in the literature [Pfouts, 1994b, pp. 20-7].

TABLES AND FIGURES

1. Tables and figures should be placed in the body of the paper. Limit tables and figures to those that are absolutely necessary for the presentation.

2. The words "TABLE" and "FIGURE" should be in all capital letters and centered.

3. Number all tables and figures in Arabic numerals. The title of the table or figure appears on a separate line and is centered and typed in capital and lower case. Examples:

TABLE I
Rank Order of OECD Countries

FIGURE 3
Efficiency of Supply and Demand

4. Double space before all tables and figures and triple space after. The information in the table or figure should be typed within the width and length margins noted above.

5. Upon notification of paper acceptance, authors are required to have all figures and graphs professionally drawn. If graphic facilities are not available, the AES can have the work done by an outside company with the author billed at our cost (about $75.00 per graph).

MATHEMATICAL NOTATION

Mathematical notation should be eliminated or minimized whenever possible. Notation that is of general knowledge (e.g., Cobb-Douglas production function LaGrangian multiplier, Euler's theorem) should not be included. Only include mathematical techniques or equations that make new contributions to the literature.

Avoid repeated listing of the arguments of functions where these can be omitted without causing confusion. Do not make repeated use of time or sectoral subscripts and superscripts if they can be suppressed without ambiguity.

All mathematical notation must be typed. Hand written notation and symbols will not be accepted. If created on computer, an equation box with automatic height, 400 point width, and centered content is preferred.

DISKETTE SUBMISSION

Submit 2 hard copies of the manuscript along with a copy of your paper on either 5 1/4 or 3 1/2 inch diskette using WordPerfect 6.1 or earlier versions. Authors who do not have the facilities to provide IAER with diskettes using WordPerfect 6.1 or earlier versions have two options. First, if there are no equations and mathematical notations, the paper can be submitted in ASCII format using IBM compatible software. Second, an author of a manuscript with equations and mathematical notation has the option of having the full manuscript typeset by the AES. The charge for this service is $100.

INTERNATIONAL ADVANCES IN ECONOMIC RESEARCH

SUBMISSION FEE AND DEADLINE

IAER will consider manuscripts directly submitted. However, special attention will be given to authors who have presented papers at the AES conferences and have incorporated comments received at the meetings into a final version of their manuscript for submission to the reviewers of IAER. Submission fees are waived for papers resulting from conference presentations if submitted within one month after completion of the conference. Submissions after that date, and all non-conference manuscripts, will be charged a $65.00 submission fee for members and $115.00 for nonmembers.

Mail two copies and the diskette containing your paper using WordPerfect 6.1 or an earlier version or ASCII to John M. Virgo, Editor-in-Chief.

PUBLICATION FEE

Upon acceptance, there is a publication fee of $18 per manuscript page for AES members and $28 per manuscript page for nonmembers. One complimentary copy of the issue in which your article appears will be provided.

INTERNATIONAL ECONOMIC REVIEW

ADDRESS FOR SUBMISSION :

EDITOR
INTERNATIONAL ECONOMIC REVIEW
UNIVERSITY OF PENNSYLVANIA
3718 LOCUST WALK
PHILADELPHIA, PA 19104-6297
USA
215-898-5841
215-573-2072 (Fax)

PUBLICATION GUIDELINES :

Manuscript Length : Less than 50

Copies Required : Four

Computer Submission : No

Format : N/A

Fees to Review : 40.00 US$
    Subscriber 15.00 US$

CIRCULATION DATA :

Reader : Academic

Frequency of Issue : Quarterly

Copies Per Issue :

Subscription Price : 50.00 US$
    Institution : 165.00 US$
    Student : 20.00 US$

Sponsorship : University

REVIEW INFORMATION :

Type of Review : Editorial Review

No. of External Reviewers : Two

No. of In House Reviewers : Two

Acceptance Rate : 11-20%

Time To Review : 4-6 months

Reviewer's Comments : Yes

Fees to Publish : 0.00 US$

Invited Articles : 5% or less

MANUSCRIPT TOPICS : AUDITING; ECONOMETRICS;
    INTERNATIONAL & ECONOMIC DEVELOPMENT; INTERNATIONAL FINANCE;
    PUBLIC POLICY ECONOMICS; QUANTITATIVE ECONOMICS

PUBLICATION GUIDELINES : Chicago Manual of Style

MANUSCRIPT GUIDELINES/COMMENTS :

Submit 4 copies of manuscript on 8 1/2 by 11 inch white paper. The manuscript
length may not exceed 50 pages. There is a $40 submission fee for
nonsubscribers and a $15 submission fee for subscribers. Authors may subscribe
to the REVIEW when submitting a paper by sending $65. Please make your check
payable to the University of Pennsylvania.

Please use these guidelines in preparing your paper for the Review. All parts
of your paper must be entirely double-spaced (a blank line between each line
of type) including text, footnotes and references. Your paper must be single
sided (do not use both sides of the page).

1. The first page should include the title, the author(s) name, and an
abstract of not more than 100 words.

2. Affiliation appears on the last page of the text, before the Appendix (if
any), or references.

3. Textual Subdivisions: Sections are numbered consecutively in Arabic numerals, beginning with the introduction. Subsections, if numbered at all, are consecutive, as, e.g., 1.1,1.2.

4. The Appendix should appear after the end of the paper, before the references. The need for more than one appendix should be handled as subsections of the single appendix.

5. Theorems, Lemmas, Corollaries, Remarks, Definitions, etc., are numbered consecutively in Arabic numerals.

6. Equations may be set in the text or centered as display equations. Some or all of the display equations may be numbered, and if so, Arabic numbers should be used either consecutively throughout the paper (1,2,3) or within sections (2.1,2.2,3.1). Please place the equation number in parentheses at the far left, the equation in the center, and the running variable on the right side, as shown:

$$(1) \qquad\qquad P = T + q \qquad\qquad q = 2,..,r$$

7. All unusual symbols should be identified. A clear distinction should be made between:
   A. Capital and lower case letters
   B. Subscripts, superscripts and ordinary letters or numbers
   C. Zero and the letter "o" or "O"
   D. K and kappa, u and mu, v and nu, n and eta, letter "el" and numeral "1" and prime sign.

8. Figures are numbered consecutively in arabic numbers. Rough drawings may be submitted initially and professional drawings prepared after acceptance by the Editor.

9. Tables should be numbered consecutively in Arabic numeral. Rows and columns must be clearly separated with column heads marked.

10. Footnotes should be numbered consecutively and double-spaced. They may appear at the bottom of each page or at the end of the text. Acknowledgement, if any, should be made in footnote 1, with superscript to the author's name.

11. References

A. When citing references in the text, include the author's (and co-author's, if any) lastname, the date of publication, and page numbers, if applicable. "et al." may be used with three or more authors. If the citation is given in parentheses, do not enclose the date in an additional set of parentheses or brackets.
   A similar procedure is explored by Arrow (1963, pp. 10-12).
   This argument is discussed in Krantz, et al. (1971).
   This argument is discussed in Krantz, Luce, Suppes and Tversky (1971).
   (See Hellwig 1977 for a detailed discussion.)

B. References should be listed alphabetically (by author--within author chronologically--and title) and must be double-spaced on a separate sheet at the end of the paper.

INTERNATIONAL ECONOMIC REVIEW

PUBLISHED SOURCES

Book: Author(s), Title (city of Publication: Publisher, Year).

Arrow, K. J., Social Choice and Individual Values, 2nd edition (New York: Wiley, 1963).

Krantz, H. D., R. D. Luce, P. Suppes and A. Tversky, Foundations of Measurement (New York: Academic Press, 1971).

Samuelson, P. A., "Pure Theory of Public Expenditure and Taxation," in J. Margolis and H. Guitton, eds., Public Economics (New York: Macmillan, 1969), 98-123.

Article: Author(s), "Title," Journal vol.# (Year), page #s.

Kramer, G. H., "On a Class of Equilibrium Conditions for Majority Rule," Econometrica 41 (March 1973), 285-297.

UNPUBLISHED SOURCES

Author(s), "Title," type of paper, University or Foundation, Year.

Chiang, S. C., "Imperfect Information and Quality Upgrading," Ph.D. Dissertation, Cornell University, 1983.

Halvorsen, R. and T. Smith, "A Test of the Theory of Exhaustible Resources," mimeo, University of Washington, 1986.

Schworm, W. E., "User Cost of Capital," Discussion Paper No. 77-22, Department of Economics, University of British Columbia, July 1977.

For cases not covered above, please include all information (i.e., series title, volume number, translator, reprint information).

INTERNATIONAL JOURNAL

ADDRESS FOR SUBMISSION :

JAVED KHOKHAR, ESQUIRE, EDITOR
INTERNATIONAL JOURNAL
SILVERSTEIN & MULLENS
1776 K STREET, N.W.
WASHINGTON, DC 20006
USA
202-452-7963
202-452-7989 (Fax)

CIRCULATION DATA :

Reader : International Tax Practitioner
Frequency of Issue : Monthly
Copies Per Issue : 2001-3000
Subscription Price : 371.00 US$
Sponsorship : Profit Oriented Corp.

PUBLICATION GUIDELINES :

Manuscript Length : Any
Copies Required : One
Computer Submission : Yes
Format : WordPerfect
Fees to Review : 0.00 US$

REVIEW INFORMATION :

Type of Review : Editorial Review
No. of External Reviewers : Zero
No. of In House Reviewers : One
Acceptance Rate : 21-30%
Time To Review : 1-2 months
Reviewer's Comments : Yes
Fees to Publish : 0.00 US$
Invited Articles : Over 50%

MANUSCRIPT TOPICS : ACCOUNTING THEORY & PRACTICE;
  PUBLIC POLICY ECONOMICS; ACCOUNTING; CURRENT INTERNATIONAL TAX ISSUES

PUBLICATION GUIDELINES : Blue Book

MANUSCRIPT GUIDELINES/COMMENTS :

INTERNATIONAL JOURNAL OF ACCOUNTING, EDUCATION AND RESEARCH

ADDRESS FOR SUBMISSION :

ANDREW D. BAILEY, EDITOR
INTERNATIONAL JOURNAL OF ACCOUNTING,
  EDUCATION AND RESEARCH
UNIVERSITY OF ILLINOIS
320 COMMERCE WEST BUILDING, BOX 109
1206 SOUTH STREET
CHAMPAIGN, IL 61820
USA
217-333-4545
217-244-6565 (Fax)
E-Mail : barbs2@commerce.cba.uiuc.edu

CIRCULATION DATA :

Reader : Academic

Frequency of Issue : Quarterly

Copies Per Issue : 1001-2000

Subscription Price : 25.00 US$

Sponsorship : University

PUBLICATION GUIDELINES :

Manuscript Length : 20

Copies Required : Two

Computer Submission : Yes

Format : WordPerfect 5.1

Fees to Review : 0.00 US$

REVIEW INFORMATION :

Type of Review : Blind Review

No. of External Reviewers : Three

No. of In House Reviewers :

Acceptance Rate : 37 %

Time To Review : 4-6 months

Reviewer's Comments : Yes

Fees to Publish : 0.00 US$

Invited Articles :

MANUSCRIPT TOPICS : ACCOUNTING INFORMATION SYSTEMS;
  ACCOUNTING THEORY & PRACTICE; AUDITING; CAPITAL BUDGETING; COST ACCOUNTING;
  ECONOMETRICS; ECONOMIC HISTORY; GOVERNMENT & NON-PROFIT ACCOUNTING;
  INSURANCE; INTERNATIONAL & ECONOMIC DEVELOPMENT; INTERNATIONAL FINANCE;
  PORTFOLIO & SECURITY ANALYSIS; PUBLIC POLICY ECONOMICS; REAL ESTATE;
  TAX ACCOUNTING; BUSINESS EDUCATION; INTERNATIONAL BUSINESS

PUBLICATION GUIDELINES : Chicago Manual of Style

MANUSCRIPT GUIDELINES/COMMENTS :

All manuscripts submitted for consideration should be typed on 8-1/2 X 11"
paper and should be double-spaced throughout, including synopsis, footnotes,
and bibliography. At least two copies should be submitted for review. Margins
should be appropriately wide to facilitate editing. The title of the paper,
the author's name, rank, and affiliation, and any acknowledgments should
appear on the first page of the body of the manuscript. All pages, as well as
bibliography, exhibits, and appendices, should be serially numbered. The
beginning of each paragraph should be indented. Footnotes may be placed either
at the bottom of the appropriate page, or on a separate page. Each manuscript
should be accompanied by a brief synopsis of the article explaining its
international significance.

HEADINGS
All major headings with the manuscript should be in capital letters. They
should not be numbered. Subheadings should be in capital and lower case

letters on a separate line beginning at the left margin. If third-level headings are used, they should begin at the left margin and should end with a period. The text will follow on the same line immediately.

EXHIBITS
Each exhibit should be titled and numbered. A textual reference should be made to each exhibit. It would be helpful if the author would indicate by marginal notation where each exhibit should be placed. These instructions will be followed as printing practices allow.

FOOTNOTES
Footnotes should be numbered consecutively throughout the manuscript with superscript Arabic numerals. Citations should not be made in brackets in the text. Mathematical symbols should not have footnote numbers attached. Entries for books should include author's name, title of the work underlined, and, in parentheses, place of publication, name of publisher, and date of publication. For journals, author's name, title of article within quotation marks, title of journal underlined, date of issue in parentheses, and page numbers should be included. Please see the following examples:

1William A. Dymsza, Multinational Business Strategy (New York: McGraw-Hill, 1972), 49-53.
2Geoffrey Holmes, "Replacement Value Accounting", Accountancy)March 1972), 4-8.

BIBLIOGRAPHY
Manuscript may include a bibliography at the end of the paper. If so, such references are not to be limited to those references cited in the text. Each entry should contain all data necessary for identification. Citations should be arranged in alphabetical order. Multiple works by the same author should be listed according to chronological order of publication. Examples are listed below.

Robert L. Aliber and Clyde P. Stickney. "Accounting Measures of Foreign Exchange Exposure -- The Long and Short of It". Accounting Review, January 1975, 44-57.

American Institute of Certified Public Accountants. Accounting Research Bulletin No. 43. New York: AICPA, 1953.

_____. "Financial Statements Restated for General Price Level Changes". Statement of the Accounting Principles Board No. 3. New York: AICPA, 1969.

Leonard Lorensen and Paul Rosenfield. "Management Information and Foreign Inflation". Journal of Accountancy, December 1974, 98-102.

Lawrence Revsine. Replacement Cost Accounting. Englewood Cliffs, N.J.: Prentice-Hall, 1973.

MATHEMATICAL NOTATION
Mathematical notation should be stated as simply as possible so as to simplify typesetting. Alignment should clearly indicate superscript and subscripts. Equations which are numbered should have the numbers in parentheses flush with the right-hand margin.

INTERNATIONAL JOURNAL OF APPLIED QUALITY MANAGEMENT

ADDRESS FOR SUBMISSION :

PHILIP H. SIEGEL, EDITOR
INTERNATIONAL JOURNAL OF APPLIED
  QUALITY MANAGEMENT
MONMOUTH UNIVERSITY
SCHOOL OF BUSINESS
DEPARTMENT OF ACCOUNTING & BUSINESS LAW
WEST LONG BEACH, NJ 07740-1895
908-571-7523
908-263-5290 (Fax)
E-Mail : psiegel@mondec.monnouth.edu

CIRCULATION DATA :

Reader : Business Persons &
         Academic

Frequency of Issue : 2 Times/Year

Copies Per Issue : 1001-2000

Subscription Price : 75.00 US$
  Library : 175.00 US$

Sponsorship : Profit Oriented Corp. &
              Professional Assoc.

PUBLICATION GUIDELINES :

Manuscript Length : 21-25

Copies Required : Four

Computer Submission : No

Format : N/A

Fees to Review : 45.00 US$

REVIEW INFORMATION :

Type of Review : Blind Review

No. of External Reviewers : Two

No. of In House Reviewers : One

Acceptance Rate : 21-30%

Time To Review : 4-6 months

Reviewer's Comments : Yes

Fees to Publish : 0.00 US$

Invited Articles : 5% or less

MANUSCRIPT TOPICS : ACCOUNTING INFORMATION SYSTEMS; COST ACCOUNTING;
  QUALITY MANAGEMENT

PUBLICATION GUIDELINES : American Psychological Association

MANUSCRIPT GUIDELINES/COMMENTS :

Follow JAI PRESS procedures. Editor will supply further detail.

INTERNATIONAL JOURNAL OF FINANCE

ADDRESS FOR SUBMISSION :

PROFESSOR DILIP K. GHOSH, EDITOR
INTERNATIONAL JOURNAL OF FINANCE
206 RABBIT RUN DRIVE
CHERRY HILL, NJ 08003
USA
609-424-2262
609-424-6007 (Fax)
E-Mail : duwt62a@prodigy.com

CIRCULATION DATA :

Reader : Academic

Frequency of Issue : Quarterly

Copies Per Issue : 1001-2000

Subscription Price : 40.00 US$
    Institution : 125.00 US$

Sponsorship : Profit Oriented Corp.

PUBLICATION GUIDELINES :

Manuscript Length :

Copies Required : Four

Computer Submission : Yes

Format : WordPerfect 5.1

Fees to Review : 50.00 US$
    Subscribers 45.00 US$

REVIEW INFORMATION :

Type of Review : Blind Review

No. of External Reviewers : Two

No. of In House Reviewers : One

Acceptance Rate : 11-20%

Time To Review : 2-3 months

Reviewer's Comments : Yes

Fees to Publish : 0.00 US$

Invited Articles : 5% or less

MANUSCRIPT TOPICS : ACCOUNTING INFORMATION SYSTEMS;
    CAPITAL BUDGETING; INTERNATIONAL FINANCE; PORTFOLIO & SECURITY ANALYSIS;
    MARKETS AND INSTITUTIONS

PUBLICATION GUIDELINES :

MANUSCRIPT GUIDELINES/COMMENTS :

PUBLICATION GUIDELINES are given only after the paper is accepted for
publication.

EDITORIAL POLICY
It is the editorial policy of THE INTERNATIONAL JOURNAL OF FINANCE that this
journal is not for works in "international finance" alone. It is committed to
publishing new theoretical as well as empirical results representing a
measurable contribution to the existing body of knowledge in the fields of
financial management, investments, capital market theory, portfolio theory,
financial institutions and markets, and foreign exchange and international
finance.

Submit four copies of the manuscript with appropriate submission fee ($35or
subscribers and $45 for non-subscribers) to

Professor Dilip K. Ghosh
The International Journal of Finance   206 Rabbit Run Drive

INTERNATIONAL JOURNAL OF FINANCE

Cherry Hill, NJ 08003
MANUSCRIPTS should conform to the following guidelines:

In general, manuscripts should follow THE CHICAGO MANUAL OF STYLE.

Double-space all text, including verbatim quotations, which should be inset.

Center primary headings, using Roman numerals, and begin subsection headings at the left-hand margin.

FOOTNOTES: Keep footnotes to a minimum. Footnotes should appear on a separate page at the end of the main text.

Manuscripts accepted for publication must be submitted in hard copy form and on a 5-1/4 floppy disk. THE INTERNATIONAL JOURNAL OF FINANCE uses WORDPERFECT. However, other word processing programs such as WORD, WORDSTAR, MULTIMATE can be used.

On the title page, include the TITLE, AUTHOR'S NAME, AFFILIATION, AND COMPLETE ADDRESS FOR CORRESPONDENCE INCLUDING THE TELEPHONE NUMBER.

CAMERA READY copy of each diagram must be provided with the accepted manuscript.

INTERNATIONAL JOURNAL OF FORECASTING

ADDRESS FOR SUBMISSION :

ROBERT FILDES, EDITOR
INTERNATIONAL JOURNAL OF FORECASTING
LANCASTER UNIVERSITY
DEPARTMENT OF MANAGEMENT SCIENCE
LANCASTER, LA1 4YX
ENGLAND
44-1524-593879
44-1524-844885 (Fax)
E-Mail : r.fildes@lancaster.ac.uk

CIRCULATION DATA :

Reader : Academic

Frequency of Issue : Quarterly

Copies Per Issue : 1001-2000

Subscription Price : 389.00 US$

Sponsorship : Professional Assoc.

PUBLICATION GUIDELINES :

Manuscript Length : 16-20

Copies Required : Four

Computer Submission : Yes

Format : MS-DOS

Fees to Review : 0.00 US$

REVIEW INFORMATION :

Type of Review : Blind Review

No. of External Reviewers : Two

No. of In House Reviewers : One

Acceptance Rate : 21-30%

Time To Review : 4-6 months

Reviewer's Comments : Yes

Fees to Publish : 0.00 US$

Invited Articles : 6-10%

MANUSCRIPT TOPICS : ECONOMETRICS;
   INTERNATIONAL & ECONOMIC DEVELOPMENT; PUBLIC POLICY ECONOMICS

PUBLICATION GUIDELINES :

MANUSCRIPT GUIDELINES/COMMENTS :

See AIMS, SCOPE AND STANDARDS; OBJECTIVITY; and REPLICABILITY at the end of
these guidelines.

(1) Papers must be in English or French. Referees will be asked to consider
the value of the paper relative to its length.

(2) Submission of a paper implies that it contains original work that has not
previously been published and that is not being submitted for publication
elsewhere. Publication in a limited distribution "Proceedings" does not
disqualify a paper. If the author has published similar findings elsewhere,
please cite and explain how the current paper differs.

(3) Submit four copies of the paper to any of the four editors (not to
associate editors). See addresses on the inside front cover of each issue. The
editors do not accept responsibility for damage or loss of papers submitted.

(4) Submision of accepted papers as electronic manuscripts, i.e., on disk with
accompanying manuscript, is encouraged. Electronic manuscripts have the

advantage that there is no need for rekeying of text, thereby avoiding the possibility of introducing errors and resulting in reliable and fast delivery of proofs. The preferred storage medium is a 5.25 or 3.5 inch disk in MS-DOS format, although other systems are welcome, e.g., Macintosh (in this case, save your file in the usual manner; do not use the option "save in MS-DOS format"). Do not submit your original paper as electronic manuscript but hold on to the disk until asked for this by the Editor (in case your paper is accepted with out revisions). Do submit the accepted version of your paper as electronic manuscript. Make absolutely sure that the file on the disk and the printout are identical. Please use a new and correctly formatted disk and label this with your name; also specify the software and hardware used as well as the title of the file to be processed. Do not convert the file to plain ASCII. Ensure that the letter "l" and the digit "1", and also the letter "O" and digit "O" are used properly, and format your article (tabs, indents, etc.) consistently. Characters not available on your word processor (Greek letters, mathematical symbols, etc.) should not be left open but indicated by a unique code (e.g., gralpha, <alpha>, @, etc., for the Greek letter a). Such codes should be used consistently throughout the entire text; a list of codes used should accompany the electronic manuscript. Do not allow your word processor to introduce word breaks and do not use a justified layout. Please adhere strictly to the general instructions below on style, arrangement and, in particular, the reference style of the journal.

(5) Double space everything. Type on one side only. Use wide margins.

(6) The first page should contain the title of the paper and each author's name, affiliation, address, and telephone and fax numbers. Correspondence will be with the first author unless requested otherwise.hor unless requested otherwise.

(7) The second page should give only a brief descriptive title.

(8) The third page should contain an abstract of not more than 150 words. Summarize the principal findings and how they were obtained. Explain why the findings are important for researchers and for practitioners. Be specific.

(9) Keywords should also appear on the third page.

(10) Provide a biographical sketch of not more than 100 words for each author.

(11) Start the paper on the fourth page; do not relist the title or authors.

(12) Use major and minor headings to aid readability. Headings should be short. Side headings should be underlined. Paragraph headings should be underlined, followed by a colon.

(13 Footnotes should be kept to a minimum. If used, they should be numbered consecutively and placed after the references.

(14) References should include only relevant sources, presumably those with evidence or methodology. In the text, references should appear for papers as "Klein (1984)", or for books as Box and Jenkins (1970, p. 245)". At the end of the manuscript, the references should be listed alphabetically by surname of the first author. Use the following format:

INTERNATIONAL JOURNAL OF FORECASTING

For articles: Gardner, E.S., Jr. and E. McKenzie, 1985, "Forecasting trends in time series", Management Science, 31, 1237-1246.
For books: Cook, T.D. and D.T. Campbell, 1979, Quasi-Experimentation (Houghton Mifflin, Boston).
For collective works: Kahneman, D. and A. Tversky, 1982, "Intuitive prediction: Biases and corrective procedures", in: D. Kahneman, P. Slovic and A. Tversky, eds., Judgment Under Uncertainty: Heuristics and Biases (Cambridge Univertsity Press, Cambridge, UK), 414-421.
Authors should ensure that there is a strict one-to-one correspondence between the authors' names (years) in the text and those in the reference list.

(15) In general, only published papers should be cited. If published, indicate how copies may be obtained.

(16) Use simple notation. Our readership crosses many disciplines. Avoid unusual symbols and Greek letters if possible.

(17) If mathematical derivations are needed, put them in an Appendix. (18) Quotations should be kept to a minimum. Authors must obtain written permission from the publisher to use a quotation that exceeds 250 words.

(19) Tables and Figures should be placed on separate pages. Figures should be photoready with descriptive headings. Provide explanatory labels for the rows and columns of a table. Place tables and figures at the end of the paper, and mark the number, title of paper, and name of author on the back. Illustrations that have to be redrawn by the publisher will be charged to the author.

(20) Simplify the presentation of data! Round data to no more than three digits. Organize tables and charts to aid understanding.

(21) Readability is important, especially in that the readers come from different countries, disciplines, and types of institutions. One way to assess readability is the Gunning Fog Index, G. It provides the educational grade level needed to understand the material. The formula is:
$$G = 0.4(S+W),$$
where S is the average sentence length (words per sentence) and W is the percentage of words with 3 or more syllables (not counting common prefixes and suffixes). Try to keep the index for your paper below 16. Guidelines for effective and simple writing can be found in W. Strunk, Jr. and E.B. White, 1979, THE ELEMENTS OF STYLE (Macmillan, New York).

(22) Authors should fully disclose their methods and data. Due to space limitations, it is often advisable to provide the data to the editors separately to put on file. Tell readers how to obtain additional details. The disclosure of data will be considered in the decision of whether to publish the paper.

(23) Evidence of prior peer review is helpful, such as a listing of the occasions on which this paper has been presented, and a list of colleagues who have reviewed the paper.

(24) Authors are invited to provide names, addresses, and fields of interest of 4 to 6 persons outside their own institution who are qualified to act as referees. We will try to use at least one of these as a referee.

(25) After acceptance of the paper, all correspondence should be addressed to the Editor-in-Chief.

(26) Page proofs will be sent to the (first) author. Please proofread carefully. Corrections other than printer's errors may be charged to the author. 25 reprints of each paper are supplied free of charge; additional reprints are available at cost if they are ordered when the proof is returned.

AIMS, SCOPE AND STANDARDS

The INTERNATIONAL JOURNAL OF FORECASTING is the official publication of the International Institute of Forecasters (IIF) and shares its aims and scope. The INTERNATIONAL JOURNAL OF FORECASTING publishes high quality refereed papers covering all aspects of forecasting. Its objective (and that of the IIF) is to unify the field and to bridge the gap between theory and practice. The intention is to make forecasting useful and relevant for decision and policy makers who need forecasts. The journal places strong emphasis on empirical studies, evaluation activities, implementation research and ways of improving the practice of forecasting. For empirical studies, the journal gives preference to papers that compare "multiple hypotheses" (two or more reasonable hypotheses).

Papers published in the INTERNATIONAL JOURNAL OF FORECASTING encompass the following areas:
1. Evaluation of forecasting methods and approaches
2. Forecasting application in business government and the military
3. Implementation research
4. Judgemental / psychological aspects of forecasting
5. Impact of uncertainty on decision making
6. Seasonal adjustments
7. Marketing forecasting
8. Time series forecasting
9. Organizational aspects of forecasting
10. Economic and econometric forecasting
11. New products forecasting
12. Financial forecasting
13. Time series analysis
14. Economic analysis
15. Production forecasting
16. Technological forecasting
17. Legal and political aspects

OBJECTIVITY

To ensure fairness and objectivity, blind reviewing will be used. Furthermore, authors of controversial papers are invited to attach a "Note to Referees". This note would describe the model (hypotheses) and possible outcomes, but not the results. The referees would be asked to evaluate the methodology and to predict the outcomes prior to reading the paper. They would then review the entire paper and complete the regular Referee's Rating Sheet.

REPLICABILITY

For empirical studies, the description of the method and the data should be sufficient to allow for replication. Where this is not possible because of space restrictions the authors should submit to the editors a complete description of the method and a copy of all data used. If this is not feasible due to costs, include summaries and samples of the data If the data are confidential submit disguised data. Authors should also be prepared to make information available to interested readers. The IJF encourages replication studies.

PUBLICATION INFORMATION
INTERNATIONAL JOURNAL OF FORECASTING (ISSN 0169-2070). Members of the IIF will receive the International Journal of Forecasting as part of their membership. Please address all your requests regarding orders and subscription queries to: Elsevier Science B.V., PO. Box 211, 1000 AE Amsterdam, The Netherlands. Tel. 31-20-5803642 Fax 31-20-5803598.

US MAILING NOTICE: INTERNATIONAL JOURNAL OF FORECASTING is published quarterly by Elsevier Science B.V. (Molenwerf 1 Postbus 211 1000 AE Amsterdam). Annual subscription price in the USA is US$389.00 (valid in North Central and South America only) including air speed delivery.
USA POSTMASTERS: send address changes to International Journal of Forecasting, Publications Expediting Inc, 200 Meacham Avenue, Elmont NY 11003. Airfreight and mailing in the USA by Publication Expediting.

INTERNATIONAL JOURNAL OF GAME THEORY

ADDRESS FOR SUBMISSION :

DOV SAMET, EDITOR
INTERNATIONAL JOURNAL OF GAME THEORY
TEL AVIV UNIVERSITY
THE LEON RECANATI GRADUATE SCHOOL OF
  BUSINESS ADMINISTRATION
FACULTY OF MANAGEMENT
TEL AVIV, 69978
ISRAEL

E-Mail : dsamet@post.tau.ac.il

CIRCULATION DATA :

Reader : Academic

Frequency of Issue : Quarterly

Copies Per Issue : Less than 1000

Subscription Price :
  North America : 377.00 US$
  Other Countries : 520.00 D.M.$

Sponsorship : Profit Oriented Corp.

PUBLICATION GUIDELINES :

Manuscript Length :

Copies Required : Four

Computer Submission : No

Format : N/A

Fees to Review : 0.00 US$

REVIEW INFORMATION :

Type of Review : Editorial Review

No. of External Reviewers : Two

No. of In House Reviewers : Zero

Acceptance Rate :

Time To Review :

Reviewer's Comments : Yes

Fees to Publish : 0.00 US$

Invited Articles :

MANUSCRIPT TOPICS : COST ACCOUNTING; ECONOMETRICS; GAME THEORY

PUBLICATION GUIDELINES :

MANUSCRIPT GUIDELINES/COMMENTS :

AREA EDITOR "GAMES AND EXPERIMENTS"
    RONALD M. HARSTAD, RUTCOR, Rutgers University, New Brunswick, NJ 08903-
    5062, USA. E-mail: RonIJGT@rutcor.rutgers.edu

The journal publishes original research, surveys, and state-of-the-art
articles with rigorous mathematical contents in the field of game theory and
its applications in mathematical economics, management science, political
science, biology, and other fields. The journal investigates a broad range of
notions relating to competition, strategic optimization, equilibrium,
information, bargaining, coalition behavior and equitable allocation.

A section on "Games and Experiments" includes experimental research on
behavior in game situations. In addition, the INTERNATIONAL JOURNAL OF GAME
THEORY offers a "Listing Service" concerning research memoranda, discussion
papers etc., indicating the names and addresses of the authors. For inclusion
in this service send the paper with name(s) and address(es) of the authors to
Fioravante Patrone, Department of Mathematics, University of Genova, Via
Dodecaneso 35, 16146 Genova, Italy. E-mail: patrone@dima.unige.it

INTERNATIONAL JOURNAL OF GAME THEORY

The INTERNATIONAL JOURNAL OF GAME THEORY contains original articles on the theory of games and its applications. The Journal was founded by Oskar Morgenstern in 1971. The Editorial Board of the journal is composed of prestigious scientists who represent a broad international base.

GAME THEORY is a collection of theoretical methods and mathematical models for the study of conflict and cooperation. It is concerned with the observation, understanding, resolution and management of conflict situations involving two or more decision makers with different objectives. Its articles investigate a broad range of notions relating to competition, strategic optimization, equilibrium, information, bargaining, coalitional behavior and equitable allocation.

This journal is the primary international periodical devoted exclusively to game theoretical developments. It contains fundamental research contributions in English written by distinguished experts from around the world on all aspects of game theory. These papers are of basic interest to both quantitatively oriented scientists in many fields and to a broad range of specialists throughout the mathematical and decision science communities.

INSTRUCTIONS TO AUTHORS
Manuscripts are accepted for review with the understanding that the same work has not been published, and is not under consideration for publication elsewhere.
Four copies of every manuscript should be submitted to the Editor.

When preparing manuscripts for the journal, please note the following items.

1. Form and content of the manuscript should be carefully checked to exclude the need for later corrections, as papers will be made up to pages immediately after typesetting. Any subsequent changes in the text will be charged to the authors.

The desired positions of figures and tables must be marked in the margin of the manuscript. Manuscripts must be typed on one side of the paper only and with wide margins. References and legend should be typed on separate sheets.

The author receives page proofs (2 sets) of his paper with provisional page numbers. These provisional numbers may be referred to during correction. The final page numbers are inserted by the publisher when an issue is ready for press.

2. The first manuscript page should provide the title, names of all authors, names of institutes or firms, any footnotes to the title, address to which proofs are to be sent, and running title.

3. Each paper is to be preceded by a short summary in English, which should not exceed 12 typewritten lines.

4. Words to be set in italics for emphasis should be underlined.

5. Footnotes to the text should be avoided.

6. Figures are to be numbered consecutively. For direct reproduction, lettered ink drawings are required.

INTERNATIONAL JOURNAL OF GAME THEORY

Computer printouts are accepted, provided they are black enough.

Do not paste the illustrations in the manuscript; enclose them on separate sheets.

7. Tables are to be numbered separately from the illustrations and each table should have a title.

8. Formulas are to be typewritten whenever possible. Special signs are to be marked in colour. Formulas should be numbered consecutively on the right-hand side of the page.

9. The list of references should include only publications cited in the text. The references should be listed in alphabetical order under the first author's name.
Citations in the text should be by author and year.

Examples for references
Bennett E, Wooders M (1979) Income Distribution and Firm Formation. J of Comparative Economics 3:304-317

Basar T (1986) A Tutorial on Dynamic and Differential Games. In Basar T (ed) Dynamic Games and Applications in Economics, Springer-Verlag, Berlin Heidelberg New York Tokyo pp 1-25

A total of 30 offprints of each paper will be supplied free of charge. Additional reprints can be ordered at cost price.

INTERNATIONAL JOURNAL OF GOVERNMENT AUDITING

ADDRESS FOR SUBMISSION :

DON R. DRACH, EDITOR
INTERNATIONAL JOURNAL OF GOVERNMENT
 AUDITING
INT'L. ORGANIZ. OF SUPREME AUDIT INSTIT.
U.S. GENERAL ACCOUNTING OFFICE
441 G STREET, N.W., ROOM 7806
WASHINGTON, DC 20548
USA
202-512-4707
202-512-4021 (Fax)
E-Mail : drachd@gao.gov

CIRCULATION DATA :

Reader : Business Persons &
          Auditors/Financial Managers

Frequency of Issue : Quarterly

Copies Per Issue : 1001-2000

Subscription Price : 5.00 US$

Sponsorship : Professional Assoc.

PUBLICATION GUIDELINES :

Manuscript Length : 6-10

Copies Required : Two

Computer Submission : Yes

Format : WP 5.1

Fees to Review : 0.00 US$

REVIEW INFORMATION :

Type of Review : Editorial Review

No. of External Reviewers : Two

No. of In House Reviewers : One

Acceptance Rate : 11-20%

Time To Review : 2-3 months

Reviewer's Comments : No

Fees to Publish : 0.00 US$

Invited Articles : 11-20%

MANUSCRIPT TOPICS : ACCOUNTING INFORMATION SYSTEMS; AUDITING;
   COST ACCOUNTING; GOVERNMENT & NON-PROFIT ACCOUNTING;
   STRATEGIC MANAGEMENT POLICY; OPERATIONS RESEARCH/STATISTICS;
   PUBLIC ADMINSTRATION

PUBLICATION GUIDELINES :

MANUSCRIPT GUIDELINES/COMMENTS :

INTERNATIONAL JOURNAL OF INTELLIGENT SYSTEMS IN ACCOUNTING, FINANCE, & MGT.

ADDRESS FOR SUBMISSION :

DANIEL E. O'LEARY, EDITOR
INTERNATIONAL JOURNAL OF INTELLIGENT
  SYSTEMS IN ACCOUNTING, FINANCE, & MGT.
UNIVERSITY OF SOUTHERN CALIFORNIA
GRADUATE SCHOOL OF BUSINESS
LOS ANGELES, CA 90089-1421
USA
213-740-4856
213-747-2815 (Fax)
E-Mail : OLEARY@RCF.USC.EDU

CIRCULATION DATA :

Reader : Business Persons &
          Academic

Frequency of Issue : Quarterly

Copies Per Issue : 1001-2000

Subscription Price : 75.00 US$
  Institution : 150.00 US$

Sponsorship : Profit Oriented Corp. &
              University

PUBLICATION GUIDELINES :

Manuscript Length : 20+

Copies Required : Four

Computer Submission : Yes

Format : N/A

Fees to Review : 0.00 US$

REVIEW INFORMATION :

Type of Review : Blind Review

No. of External Reviewers : Three

No. of In House Reviewers : Zero

Acceptance Rate : 11-20%

Time To Review : 2-3 months

Reviewer's Comments : Yes

Fees to Publish : 0.00 US$

Invited Articles :

MANUSCRIPT TOPICS : ACCOUNTING INFORMATION SYSTEMS; AUDITING;
  CAPITAL BUDGETING; COST ACCOUNTING; ECONOMETRICS; INSURANCE;
  INTERNATIONAL FINANCE; PORTFOLIO & SECURITY ANALYSIS; TAX ACCOUNTING;
  APPLICATIONS OF THE ABOVE & BANKING APPLICATIONS

PUBLICATION GUIDELINES : Chicago Manual of Style

MANUSCRIPT GUIDELINES/COMMENTS :

TYPE OF READER:
Academics and Practitioners in Finance, Accounting and Taxation, Management
Information Systems, Information Science, Artificial Intelligence, Cognitive
Science, Computer Science.

MANUSCRIPT TOPICS:
The Journal publishes original material concerned with all aspects of
intelligent systems in business-based applications. It is devoted to the
improvement and further development of the theory and practice of intelligent
systems design, development and implementation. The Journal provides a
communication forum for advancing theory and practice of the application of
intelligent systems in business settings.

Published papers take and investigate a number of different issues, including
"research perspectives," emerging technologies, existing technologies,
verification and validation, cognitive models, cognitive science, the impact

of intelligent systems on organizations, the integration of different
technologies such as databases and intelligent systems.

MANUSCRIPT GUIDELINES:
1. Authors should send FOUR COPIES of their manuscript to Daniel E. O'Leary,
Editor. Authors should keep a copy of their paper. No manuscripts or
illustrations will be returned unless specifically requested.

2. Only original papers (not published or simultaneously submitted elsewhere),
in the English language, will be considered for the journal. LENGTH of typical
papers is between 20 and 40 typescript pages, but submissions outside these
limits may be discussed with the Editor.

3. Copyright of accepted papers will be vested in the publisher, and authors
must include with their paper a completed copy of the standard journal
publishing agreement which may be copied from the first issue in each volume
or obtained from the Editor.

4. Submissions should be typed DOUBLE-SPACED with wide margins on one side
only of each sheet, and the first page must show ONLY the full TITLE OF THE
PAPER, the NAME OF THE AUTHOR (or coauthors), the affiliations of the author
(or coauthors) as they are to be printed, and the FULL POSTAL ADDRESS OF THE
FIRST NAMED AUTHOR, to whom all correspondence and proofs will be sent unless
otherwise requested. Please include phone and fax numbers.

5. AN ABSTRACT of about 150 words, which should summarize the whole paper not
just the conclusions, must be on a separate sheet at the beginning of the
paper, with the full title repeated.

6. TABLES AND FIGURES should be on separate sheets, consecutively numbered,
and their desired position indicated in the text, with a separate sheet of
clearly numbered CAPTIONS. FOOTNOTES should be avoided, but if absolutely
necessary they should be placed at the end of the paper, after the references,
numbered consecutively. TABLES should have explanatory headings, and should
not repeat data in the text.

7. Figures should be supplied CAMERA READY about twice final size. Line
drawings should be in black on white paper with clear lettering and
photographs must be original prints or negatives, not photocopies. COMPUTER
PRINTOUT must be clear and sharp.

8. Written COPYRIGHT PERMISSION is required, for tables, text extracts or
illustrations from other copyright sources, and it is the author's
responsibility to obtain this for submission with the manuscript.

9. REFERENCES in the text should be NAME (DATE), e.g. Jones (1987), and listed
in full at the end of the paper in alphabetical order by author. E.g.,

Jones, Il, Great Title of Paper, International Journal of Intelligent
Systems in Accounting, Finance and Management, Vol. 3, Number 3, 1991,
pp. 121-134. (Journal reference)

Jones, Il, Great Book Title, John Wiley and Sons, England, 1991. (Book
reference)

INTERNATIONAL JOURNAL OF INTELLIGENT
SYSTEMS IN ACCOUNTING, FINANCE, & MGT.

Jones, Il, Great Title of Chapter, In Editor: Title of Volume. John Wiley and Sons, England, 1991. (Chapter reference)

10. Mathematical symbols can be typewritten or handwritten. Symbols or Greek letters should be identified separately in the margin. Distinguish clearly between CAPITAL or lowercase letters, between letter O and zero, between letter l and number 1, and other instances when confusion might occur.

11. The publishers will supply reprints of each paper and more copies can be ordered on the form supplied to the first named author with the proofs of the paper.

12. Authors will be requested to submit an electronic version of the paper, if it is accepted.

INTERNATIONAL JOURNAL OF SOCIAL ECONOMICS

ADDRESS FOR SUBMISSION :

JOHN C. O'BRIEN, EDITOR
INTERNATIONAL JOURNAL OF SOCIAL
  ECONOMICS
CALIFORNIA STATE UNIVERSITY - FRESNO
5241 NORTH MAPLE AVENUE
FRESONRD, WEST YORKSHIRE, CA 93740-0054
USA
209-278-2842
209-278-7987 (Fax)
E-Mail : <john_obrien@csufresno.edu>

CIRCULATION DATA :

Reader : Academic

Frequency of Issue : Monthly

Copies Per Issue :

Subscription Price : 3699.00 US$

Sponsorship : Profit Oriented Corp.

PUBLICATION GUIDELINES :

Manuscript Length : 26-30

Copies Required : Three

Computer Submission : No

Format : N/A

Fees to Review : 0.00 US$

REVIEW INFORMATION :

Type of Review : N/A

No. of External Reviewers : Two

No. of In House Reviewers : Two

Acceptance Rate : 21-30%

Time To Review : One month or less

Reviewer's Comments : Yes

Fees to Publish : 0.00 US$

Invited Articles : 21-30%

MANUSCRIPT TOPICS : ACCOUNTING INFORMATION SYSTEMS; COST ACCOUNTING;
  SOCIAL ECONOMICS; SOCIOLOGY; SOCIO ECONOMICS

PUBLICATION GUIDELINES :

MANUSCRIPT GUIDELINES/COMMENTS :

ABOUT THE JOURNAL
Articles submitted to the journal should be original contributions and should
not be under consideration for any other publication at the same time.
Submissions should be sent to:

THE EDITOR
Professor John Conway O'Brien, California State University - Fresno, 5241
North Maple Avenue, Fresno, CA 93740-0054, USA.
E-mail: <john_obrien@csufresno.edu>

EDITORIAL OBJECTIVES
To provide social economists with philosophical discussions of research
findings and commentary on international developments in social economics.

THE REVIEWING PROCESS
Each paper submitted is reviewed by the editor for general suitability for
publication and the decision whether or not to publish is made in consultation
with members of the editorial board or other subject matter experts.

INTERNATIONAL JOURNAL OF SOCIAL ECONOMICS

ARTICLE FEATURES AND FORMATS REQUIRED OF AUTHORS
There are a number of specific requirements with regard to article features
and formats which authors should note carefully:
1. Word length
Articles should be between 3,000 and 6,000 words in length.

2. Title
A title of not more than eight words in length should be provided.

3. Autobiographical note
A brief autobiographical note should be supplied including full name,
appointment, name of organization and e-mail address.

4. Word processing
Please submit to the Editor three copies of the manuscript in double line
spacing with wide margins.

5. Headings and sub-headings
These should be short and to-the-point, appearing approximately every 750
words. Headings should be typed in capitals and underlined; sub-headings
should be typed in upper and lower case and underlined. Headings should not be
numbered.

6. References
References to other publications should be in Harvard style. They should
contain full bibliographical details and journal titles should not be
abbreviated. For multiple citations in the same year use a, b, c immediately
following the year of publication. References should be shown as follows:

* Within the text - author's last name followed by a comma and year of
  publication all in round brackets, e g. (Fox, 1994).

* At the end of the article a reference list in alphabetical order as
  follows:
  (a) For books:
      surname, initials, year of publication, title, publisher, place of
      publication, e.g. Casson, M. (1979), Alternatives to the Multinational
      Enterprise, Macmillan, London.
  (b) For chapter in edited in book:
      surname, initials, year, title, editor's surname, initials, title,
      publisher, place, pages, e.g.
      Bessley, M. and Wilson, P. (1984), "Public policy and small firms in
      Britain", in Levicki, C. (Ed.), Small Business Theory and Policy, Croom
      Helm, London, pp. 111-26.
  (c) For articles:
      surname, initials, year, title, journal, volume, number, pages, e.g.
      Fox, S. (1994), "Empowerment as a catalyst for change: an example from
      the food industry", Supply Chain Management, Vol. 2 No. 3, pp. 29-33.

If there is more than one author list surnames followed by initials. All
authors should be shown.

Electronic sources should include the URL of the electronic site at which they
may be found.

INTERNATIONAL JOURNAL OF SOCIAL ECONOMICS

Notes/Endnotes should be used only if absolutely necessary. They should be identified in the text by consecutive numbers enclosed in square brackets and listed at the end of the article.

7. Figures, charts, diagrams

Use of figures, charts and diagrams should be kept to a minimum and information conveyed in such a manner should instead be described in text form. Essential figures, charts and diagrams should be referred to as figures and numbered consecutively using arabic numerals. Each figure should have a brief title and labelled axes. Diagrams should be kept as simple as possible and avoid unnecessary capitalization and shading In the text, the position of the figure should be shown by typing on a separate line the words "take in Figure 1".

8. Tables

Use of tables should be kept to a minimum. Where essential, these should be typed on a separate sheet of paper and numbered consecutively and independently of any figures included in the article. Each table should have a number in roman numerals, a brief title, and vertical and horizontal headings. In the text, the position of the table should be shown by typing on a separate line the words "take in Table 1". Tables should not repeat data available elsewhere in the paper.

9. Photos, illustrations

Half-tone illustrations should be restricted in number to the minimum necessary. Good glossy bromide prints should accompany the manuscripts but not be attached to manuscript pages. Illustrations unsuitable for reproduction, e.g. computer-screen capture, will not be used. Any computer programs should be supplied as clear and sharp print outs on plain paper. They will be reproduced photographically to avoid errors.

10. Emphasis

Words to be emphasized should be limited in number and italicized. Capital letters should be used only at the start of sentences or in the case of proper names.

11. Abstracts

Authors must supply an abstract of 100-150 words when submitting an article. It should be an abbreviated, accurate representation of the content of the article. Major results, conclusions and/or recommendations should be given, followed by supporting details of method, scope or purpose. It should contain sufficient information to enable readers to decide whether they should obtain and read the entire article.

12. Keywords

Up to six keywords should be included which encapsulate the principal subjects covered by the article. Minor facets of an article should not be keyworded. These keywords will be used by readers to select the material they wish to read and should therefore be truly representative of the article's main content.

PREPARATION FOR PUBLICATION

13. Final submission of the article

Once accepted by the Editor for publication, the final version of the article

INTERNATIONAL JOURNAL OF SOCIAL ECONOMICS

should be submitted in manuscript accompanied by a 3.5" disk of the same version of the article marked with: disk format; author name(s); title of article; journal title; file name. This will be considered to be the definitive version of the article and the author should ensure that it is complete, grammatically correct and without spelling or typographical errors.

In preparing the disk, please use one of the following formats:
- for text prepared on a PC - AMI Pro, FrameMaker, Office Writer, Professional write, RTF, Word or WordPerfect;
- for text prepared on a Macintosh system - FrameMaker, MacWrite, MS Works, Nisus 3, RTF, Word, WordPerfect WriteNow or ASCII
- for graphics, figures, charts and diagrams, please use one of the following formats:

File type	Programs	File extension
Windows Metafile	Most Windows programs	.wmf
WordPerfect Graphic	All WordPerfect software	.wpg
Adobe Illustrator	Adobe Illustrator	.ai
	Corel Draw	
	Macromedia Freehand	
Harvard Graphics	Harvard Graphics	.cgm
PIC	Lotus graphics	.pic
Computer/Graphics		
Metafile	Lotus Freelance	.cgm
DXF	Autocad	.dxf
	Many CAD programs	
GEM	Ventura Publisher	.gem
Macintosh PICT	Most Macintosh Drawing	

Only vector type drawings are acceptable, as bitmap files (extension .bmp, .pcx or .gif) print poorly. If graphical representations are not available on disk, black ink line drawings suitable for photographic reproduction and of dimensions appropriate for reproduction on a journal page should be supplied with the article.

If you require technical assistance in respect of submitting an article please consult the relevant section of MCB's World Wide Web Literati Club on http://www.mcb.co.uk/literati/nethome.htm or contact Mike Massey at MCB, e-mail: mmassey@mcb.co.uk

14. Journal Article Record Form
Each article should be accompanied by a completed and signed Journal Article Record Form. This form is available from the Editor or can be downloaded from MCB's World Wide Web Literati Club on http://www.mcb.co.uk/literati/nethome.htm

15. Author proofs
Where author proofs are supplied, they will be sent to corresponding authors who will be expected to correct and return them within five days of receipt or the article will be published without author corrections. The publisher is not responsible for any error not marked by the author on the proof Corrections on the proof are limited to typesetting errors; no substantial author changes are allowed at this stage.

COPYRIGHT
Authors submitting articles for publication warrant that the work is not an

INTERNATIONAL JOURNAL OF SOCIAL ECONOMICS

INTERNATIONAL JOURNAL OF SOCIAL ECONOMICS is published by MCB University Press, 60/62/ Toller Lane, Bradford, West Yorkshire BD8 9BY, UK. Tel: +44 1274 777700, Fax: +44 1274 785200 or 785201.

INTERNATIONAL JOURNAL OF THE ECONOMICS OF BUSINESS

ADDRESS FOR SUBMISSION :

H.E. FRECH III, EDITOR
INTERNATIONAL JOURNAL OF THE ECONOMICS
  OF BUSINESS
UNIVERSITY OF CALIFORNIA
ECONOMICS DEPARTMENT
SANTA BARBARA, CA 93106
805-893-2124
805-893-2124 (Fax)
E-Mail : frech@econ.ucsb.edu

CIRCULATION DATA :

Reader : Academic

Frequency of Issue : 3 Times/Year

Copies Per Issue : Less than 1000

Subscription Price : 58.00 US$
  Library : 218.00 US$

Sponsorship : Profit Oriented Corp.

PUBLICATION GUIDELINES :

Manuscript Length : 26-30

Copies Required : Four

Computer Submission : No

Format : N/A

Fees to Review : 0.00 US$

REVIEW INFORMATION :

Type of Review : Editorial Review

No. of External Reviewers : Two

No. of In House Reviewers : Zero

Acceptance Rate : 11-20%

Time To Review : 2-3 months

Reviewer's Comments : Yes

Fees to Publish : 0.00 US$

Invited Articles : 6-10%

MANUSCRIPT TOPICS : COST ACCOUNTING; INSURANCE;
  INTERNATIONAL FINANCE; PORTFOLIO & SECURITY ANALYSIS;
  PUBLIC POLICY ECONOMICS; INDUSTRIAL ORGANIZATION

PUBLICATION GUIDELINES :

MANUSCRIPT GUIDELINES/COMMENTS :

INTERNATIONAL JOURNAL OF THE ECONOMICS OF BUSINESS is an international
refereed journal published three times a year. It presents original research
in economics that is clearly applicable to business or related public policy
problems or issues. The term 'business' is used in its widest sense to
encompass both public and private sector--governmental, private non-profit and
cooperative organizations, as well as profit-seeking enterprises. Services and
distribution will be included along with manufacturing and extractive
industries. Coverage will include the less developed and former Eastern Bloc
countries, as well as industrialized countries. INTERNATIONAL JOURNAL OF THE
ECONOMICS OF BUSINESS will carry papers relating to three main spheres: THE
ORGANIZATION--to analyse and aid decision-making and the internal organization
of the business; THE INDUSTRY--to analyse how businesses interact and evolve
within and across industries; THE EXTERNAL ENVIRONMENT--to show how public
policy, technological developments and other outside forces affect business
behaviour.

EDITORIAL CORRESPONDENCE from all authors outside North America should be
addressed to either Eleanor Morgan, School of Management, University of Bath,

INTERNATIONAL JOURNAL OF THE ECONOMICS OF BUSINESS

Claverton Down, Bath BA2 7AY, UK or Mick Silver, Cardiff Business School, University of Wales, Colum Drive, Cardiff CF1 3EU, UK. Correspondence from North American authors should be addressed to H.E. Frech III, Economics Department, University of California, Santa Barbara, CA 93106, USA. Details concerning the preparation and submission of articles can be found on the inside back cover.

The journal is sponsored by Carfax Publishing Company, P.O. Box 25, Abingdon, Oxfordshire OX14 3UE, UK. The Journal is published three times a year in February, July and November. These three issues constitute one volume. An annual index and title page is bound in the November issue.

INTERNATIONAL JOURNAL OF TRANSPORT ECONOMICS

ADDRESS FOR SUBMISSION :

PROFESSOR GIANROCCO TUDDI, EDITOR
INTERNATIONAL JOURNAL OF TRANSPORT
  ECONOMICS
VIA G.A. GUATTANI, 8
00161 ROME, ITALY
06-8555950

CIRCULATION DATA :

Reader : Academic

Frequency of Issue : 3 Times/Year

Copies Per Issue : Less than 1000

Subscription Price : 90.00 US$

Sponsorship : University

PUBLICATION GUIDELINES :

Manuscript Length : 16-20

Copies Required : Two

Computer Submission : Yes

Format : ASCII

Fees to Review : 0.00 US$

REVIEW INFORMATION :

Type of Review : Blind Review

No. of External Reviewers : One

No. of In House Reviewers : One

Acceptance Rate : 11-20%

Time To Review : 2-3 months

Reviewer's Comments : Yes

Fees to Publish : 0.00 US$

Invited Articles : 31-50%

MANUSCRIPT TOPICS : ACCOUNTING INFORMATION SYSTEMS; COST ACCOUNTING

PUBLICATION GUIDELINES :

MANUSCRIPT GUIDELINES/COMMENTS :

AIMS OF THE REVIEW
The main aim of the review is to bring together the research work being done in the field of Transport Economics and arrange it organically in the form of a synthesis between theory and fact.

The situation facing transport economics is one in which old problems remain to be solved and new ones have been created by a wider range of information and improved methods of analysis.

In addition, foreseeable development in the internal logic of theories and the formulation of fresh hypotheses to interpret complex phenomena, both economic and non-economic, are becoming the object of further research for which the review is intended to be a medium of expression and comparison. It is important in this respect to stress the fact that transport economics is prepared to take advantage of contributions from allied sciences and combine with them in providing a more convincing interpretation of realities together with solutions to concrete problems. Within this framework the contributions to the review from inside and outside Italy, though differing in standpoint and cultural background, will all be expected to maintain a rigorous standard of scientific scholarship.

INTERNATIONAL JOURNAL OF TRANSPORT ECONOMICS

INFORMATION FOR CONTRIBUTORS

Manuscripts should be submitted to the editor in two typed copies with double-spacing and with a wide left-hand margin. They will be examined on the understanding that their content has not been already published and is not being submitted for publication elsewhere. Each paper should be summarized in an abstract of about 400 words so as to enable the reader to know whether the paper is pertinent to his needs.

The language of the Journal is English.

Communications and research notes as a rule should not exceed 15 printed pages including diagrams and tables.

The author is requested to provide the editor with any information that might be worthwhile including in the section: "Contributors to this issue".

Names of journals and titles of books should be underlined (Italics).

Figures must be submitted in a form suitable for good reproduction, have a brief descriptive title and be professionally drawn so that they will be clear and legible when reduced to final size. If halftone reproductions are included, the author is requested to submit glossy prints.

Tables should have a brief descriptive title and should be clearly headed in order to be fully understandable even without reference to the text.

The author will be asked to incorporate least cost mathematical notation, avoid circumflexes, bars, dots, and tildes, so far as possible, because these must be set by hand; superscripts or subscripts are to be preferred. Fractions should, whenever possible, be written in the form $(a + bQ)/(2Pj)$. Roots should be written as fractional powers.

Reprints. A total of 25 reprints of each paper will be supplied free of charge. Additional copies may be ordered.

INTERNATIONAL LABOUR REVIEW

ADDRESS FOR SUBMISSION :

MARTHA F. LOUTFI, EDITOR-IN-CHIEF
INTERNATIONAL LABOUR REVIEW
INTERNATIONAL LABOUR OFFICE
4, ROUTE DES MORILLONS
CH-1211 GENEVE 22,
SWITZERLAND
(41-22) 799 6510/799 6111
(41-22) 798 8685 (Fax)
E-Mail (use Telex: 415647 ilo ch)

CIRCULATION DATA :

Reader : Academic

Frequency of Issue : Bi-Monthly

Copies Per Issue : 5001-10,000

Subscription Price : 70.00 US$

Sponsorship :

PUBLICATION GUIDELINES :

Manuscript Length : 20-30

Copies Required : Two

Computer Submission : Yes

Format : WIN WP OR Word

Fees to Review : 0.00 US$

REVIEW INFORMATION :

Type of Review : Editorial Review

No. of External Reviewers : One

No. of In House Reviewers : Two

Acceptance Rate : 11-20%

Time To Review : 2-3 months

Reviewer's Comments : Yes

Fees to Publish : 0.00 US$

Invited Articles : 31-50%

MANUSCRIPT TOPICS : ECONOMETRICS; PUBLIC POLICY ECONOMICS;
   LABOR RELATIONS & HUMAN RESOURCE MGT (HRM);
   LABOUR LAW; SOCIAL SECURITY; LABOUR MGT RELATIONS;
   LABOUR MARKET POLICY; TRAINING POLICY

PUBLICATION GUIDELINES :

MANUSCRIPT GUIDELINES/COMMENTS :

THE INTERNATIONAL LABOUR ORGANIZATION
The International Labour Organization was founded in 1919 to advance the cause
of social justice and, by so doing, to contribute to ensuring universal and
lasting peace. A Unique feature of its structure is that representatives of
workers and employers take part with government representatives in the
International Labour Conference, in the Governing Body of the ILO and in many
of its regional and other meetings.

Over the years, the ILO has built up a code of international labour standards
in the form of Conventions and Recommendations relating to freedom of
association, employment and training policy, conditions of work, social
security, industrial relations and other labour and social matters.

A major part of the ILO's work consists in the provision of expert advice and
technical assistance to member States. Much of this operational activity lies
in such fields as labour legislation, employment promotion, enterprise
development, social security, occupational safety and health, labour

statistics, workers' education and industrial relations. The International Centre for Advanced Technical and Vocational Training, in Turin, provides courses for instructors, supervisors and managers.

INTERNATIONAL LABOUR OFFICE
    Telegrams INTERLAB GENEVE
    Telex 415647 ilo ch
    Facsimile (41-22) 798 86 85
    Telephone (41-22) 799 6111
    http://www.unic.org/ilo

The INTERNATIONAL LABOUR REVIEW is published by the International Labour Office (ILO) in Geneva, Switzerland. It seeks to contribute to a wider understanding of labour and employment issues by publishing: the results of original research and analysis on questions of international interest as signed articles; perspectives on current and emerging issues; and reviews of recent publications.

SUBMISSION OF MANUSCRIPTS

1. Articles may be prepared by invitation of the Editor-in-Chief on -the basis of an agreed outline describing the subject, the hypothesis examined and sources used. Unsolicited manuscripts are considered on their merits and in relation to the overall programme of the Review. All manuscripts are subject to assessment by experts in the relevant technical departments of the ILO and by independent advisers.

2. Manuscripts may be submitted in English, French or Spanish; if translated from another language, the original should also be provided.

3. Contributions should be accompanied by a statement that they have not already been published, and that they will not be submitted for publication elsewhere without the agreement of the Editor-in-Chief

4. It is understood that manuscripts accepted for publication are subject to editorial revision and that the right of publication in any form or language is reserved by the ILO.

5. Manuscripts-preferably no longer than 6500 words-should be typed with double spacing throughout. A clean original, a copy and a 100-word abstract should be provided, together with a diskette in WordPerfect, Word for Windows and/or ASCII.

6. The preferred form of citation is the inclusion in the text, within parentheses, of the author's last name, the year of publication and, for direct citations, the page number, with the corresponding reference provided in an alphabetical list of references placed at the end of the manuscript. All notes should be numbered consecutively throughout the article, except those in tables and figures.

7. Bibliographical references should indicate: for books, author's full name, title of book (in italics), place of publication, publisher and year of publication (within parentheses) and page(s) cited; for articles, author's full name, title of article in inverted commas (quotes), title of periodical (in italics), place of publication (within parentheses), date, volume and

issue numbers, and pages. Titles of articles, books and periodicals should be given in the original language.

8. Tables should be numbered consecutively and presented separately, one to a page, at the end of the text. The data on which diagrams and figures are based should be provided. No text should be included within diagrams. Tables and diagrams should bear a descriptive title and any notes should be numbered.

9. Authors must observe the usual rules and practices regarding the reproduction of copyright material in their articles, assuming responsibility for obtaining permission where appropriate.

10. No material shall be published which is in conflict with the aims and purposes of the Organization.

11. The designations employed in ILO publications, which are in conformity with United Nations practice, and the presentation of material therein do not imply the expression of any opinion whatsoever on the part of the ILO concerning the legal status of any country, area or territory or of its authorities, or concerning the delimitation of its frontiers. Reference to names of firms and commercial products and processes does not imply their endorsement by the ILO, and any failure to mention a particular firm, commercial product or process is not a sign of disapproval.

12. Authors are strongly advised to consult one or more recent issues of the International LABOUR Review before submitting manuscripts for publication.

INTERNATIONAL ORGANIZATION

ADDRESS FOR SUBMISSION :

PETER GOUREZITCH, DAVID LAKE, EDITORS
INTERNATIONAL ORGANIZATION
UCSD
GRADUATE SCHOOL OF INTERNATIONAL
 RELATIONS AND PACIFIC STUDIES
9500 GILMAN DRIVE
LA HOYA, CA 92093-0519
USA
619-534-4034
619-822-1556 (Fax)
E-Mail : io@ucsd.edu

Change in Editor's Address
 May Occur in : 12/31/01

CIRCULATION DATA :

Reader : Academic

Frequency of Issue : Quarterly

Copies Per Issue : 2001-3000

Subscription Price : 35.00 US$
 Institution : 80.00 US$

Sponsorship :

PUBLICATION GUIDELINES :

Manuscript Length : Any

Copies Required : Three

Computer Submission : Yes

Format : WordPerfect 5.1

Fees to Review : 0.00 US$

REVIEW INFORMATION :

Type of Review : Blind Review

No. of External Reviewers : Two

No. of In House Reviewers : One

Acceptance Rate : 6-10%

Time To Review : 2-3 months

Reviewer's Comments : Yes

Fees to Publish : 0.00 US$

Invited Articles :

MANUSCRIPT TOPICS : ECONOMETRICS;
 INTERNATIONAL & ECONOMIC DEVELOPMENT; INTERNATIONAL FINANCE;
 PUBLIC POLICY ECONOMICS

PUBLICATION GUIDELINES : Chicago Manual of Style

MANUSCRIPT GUIDELINES/COMMENTS :

Our prime focus is original research on international relations and
international political economy. Manuscript topics include: Trade,
Environment, International Institutions and Law, Securtity and Alliances,
Conflict, Negotiation, European Integration, Foreign Policy. Papers should
make some contribution to economic or political theory.

INTERNATIONAL ORGANIZATION invites the submission of manuscripts on all
aspects of world politics and international political economy. Manuscripts
should be addressed to the editor.
Manuscripts should be double-spaced and submitted in triplicate, along with an
abstract and author's note.
Footnotes should be numbered consecutively, typed double-spaced, and placed at
the end of the manuscript. Authors may expect a decision within two months of
the Editor's receipt of a manuscript.
Statements of fact and opinion appearing in INTERNATIONAL ORGANIZATION are

INTERNATIONAL ORGANIZATION

INTERNATIONAL REGIONAL SCIENCE REVIEW

ADDRESS FOR SUBMISSION :

ANDREW M. ISSERMAN, EDITOR
INTERNATIONAL REGIONAL SCIENCE
  REVIEW
WEST VIRGINIA UNIVERSITY
REGIONAL RESEARCH INSTITUTE
MORGANTOWN, WV 26506-6825
USA
619-534-4034
619-740-4298 (Fax)
E-Mail : irer@wvnvm.wvnet.edu

CIRCULATION DATA :

Reader : Academic

Frequency of Issue :   3 Times/Year

Copies Per Issue : 2001-3000

Subscription Price : 18.00 US$
  Library : 35.00 US$
  Member : 6.00 US$

Sponsorship : University

PUBLICATION GUIDELINES :

Manuscript Length : 16-40

Copies Required : Four

Computer Submission : Yes

Format : DOS or Windows(Wd,WP,ASCII)

Fees to Review : 0.00 US$

REVIEW INFORMATION :

Type of Review : Blind Review

No. of External Reviewers : Three

No. of In House Reviewers : Zero

Acceptance Rate : 11-20%

Time To Review : 2-3 months

Reviewer's Comments : Yes

Fees to Publish : 0.00 US$

Invited Articles :

MANUSCRIPT TOPICS : INTERNATIONAL & ECONOMIC DEVELOPMENT;
  PUBLIC POLICY ECONOMICS; REAL ESTATE;
  REGIONAL ECONOMICS; INDUSTRIAL LOCATION

PUBLICATION GUIDELINES :

MANUSCRIPT GUIDELINES/COMMENTS :

Manuscript Topics: Regional Economics, Industrial Location, Economic
Development, Methods of Economic Analysis

The INTERNATIONAL REGIONAL SCIENCE REVIEW is a refereed journal published
three times a year by the Regional Research Institute of West Virginia
University. Regional Science began in the 1950's as a multidisciplinary effort
to strengthen the regional and spatial aspects of theoretical and quantitative
research in the social sciences--particularly economics, geography, and
demography--and to improve the analytical foundations of urban and regional
planning. Since then regional scientists have developed methods and
theoretical frameworks specifically designed for spatial analysis and have
extended and adapted concepts and techniques from several disciplines through
the innovative incorporation of the spatial dimension.

The INTERNATIONAL REGIONAL SCIENCE REVIEW seeks important papers that...
...review the literature on key topics in regional science or describe recent
trends in regional phenomena, thereby identifying new research directions and
significant policy questions.

INTERNATIONAL REGIONAL SCIENCE
REVIEW

...analyze planning and policy issues in which the spatial dimension plays a central role, such as regional economic development, industrial location, population distribution, and natural resource utilization and protection.

...present improvements in analytical methods for regional and spatial analysis, describe new methods, or demonstrate creative applications of existing methods.

... advance regional science and its component fields, whether theoretically, conceptually, empirically, or otherwise.

MANUSCRIPT SUBMISSION

In a cover letter, the authors should verify that the manuscript has not been published and is not being considered for publication elsewhere. Four copies of the manuscript, typed double-spaced, should be submitted. It is not necessary to send the original of either the manuscript, figures, graphs, or maps. Authors with access to Bitnet who would like immediate confirmation that their manuscripts have been received should include their Bitnet or Internet address in their cover letters.

Submitted manuscripts need not follow the REVIEW'S format for references, notes, and section headings; however, manuscripts accepted for publication must be typed according to the REVIEW'S specifications and must be accompanied by a computer disk containing the text. An abstract of no more than 100 words should accompany the manuscript.

Manuscripts and inquiries regarding editorial matters should be sent to the Editor.

INTERNATIONAL REVIEW OF APPLIED ECONOMICS

ADDRESS FOR SUBMISSION :

MALCOLM SAWYER, EDITOR
INTERNATIONAL REVIEW OF APPLIED
  ECONOMICS
UNIVERSITY OF LEEDS
SCHOOL OF BUSINESS & ECONOMIC STUDIES
EES BUILDING
LEEDS, LS2 9JT
ENGLAND
44 0 153 233 4484
44 0 113 233 4465 (Fax)
E-Mail : mcs@bes.leeds.ac.uk

CIRCULATION DATA :

Reader : Academic

Frequency of Issue : 3 Times/Year

Copies Per Issue : Less than 1000

Subscription Price :

Sponsorship :

PUBLICATION GUIDELINES :

Manuscript Length : 20+

Copies Required : Three

Computer Submission : No

Format : N/A

Fees to Review : 0.00 US$

REVIEW INFORMATION :

Type of Review : Editorial Review

No. of External Reviewers : Two

No. of In House Reviewers : One

Acceptance Rate : 21-30%

Time To Review : 2-3 months

Reviewer's Comments : Yes

Fees to Publish : 0.00 US$

Invited Articles : 5% or less

MANUSCRIPT TOPICS : INTERNATIONAL & ECONOMIC DEVELOPMENT;
  PUBLIC POLICY ECONOMICS

PUBLICATION GUIDELINES :

MANUSCRIPT GUIDELINES/COMMENTS :

This journal is devoted to the application of economic ideas to the real
world. Applied economics will be interpreted to include both the publication
of empirical work and the application of economics to the evaluation and
development of economic policies. The interaction between empirical work and
economic policy is an important feature of the INTERNATIONAL REVIEW.

The INTERNATIONAL REVIEW publishes papers by authors from many countries, and
has appointed an international advisory board. It publishes papers which draw
lessons from the experience of one country for other countries and those
making multinational comparisons of economic experience.
The review publishes articles and book reviews in the area of applied,
policy-oriented economics. It adopts a broadly left-of-centre perspective on
economic policy, both within that perspective it will not be identified with
any specific theoretical or political position. It strives to publish
articles dealing with policy issues and adopting theoretical positions on
current issues which are neglected in mainstream journals. The house style of
the review will be rigorous analysis written in a relatively non-technical way
to give the review a wide appeal extending outside the usual academic audience
for economics journals.

INTERNATIONAL REVIEW OF APPLIED ECONOMICS

NOTES TO AUTHORS ON THE PREPARATION OF TYPESCRIPTS

1. THE TYPESCRIPT should be prepared on good quality A4 or quarto paper, double-spaced and with generous margins at head, foot and left and right-hand margins. The top copy should be submitted together with a photocopy or corrected carbon.

2. STYLE. Please follow (or ask your typist to follow) these notes:

i.   Use 'z' not 's' where there is an alternative, and in general follow the first variant given by the SHORTER OXFORD ENGLISH DICTIONARY, e.g. realize, idealize, analyse, advertise.

ii. DATES: '16 January 1980' not 'January 16, 1980'.

iii. NUMBERS: Adopt a rule that all numbers under 10 should be spelt out in letters except where attached to a unit of quantity (e.g. 1mm or 3kg) or where the context makes this awkward (e.g. use spelt-out forms at the beginning of a sentence).

iv. Avoid excessive capitalization. For titles of books and articles, capitals should be used for the initial letter of the first word only. For the titles of journals and series, the initial letter of all principal words should be capitalized.

v.   Use italics for emphasis very sparingly.

vi. ABBREVIATIONS: Initial letter of abbreviations should be typed with no full point (e.g. UK, UNESCO, BBC). Abbreviations in which the last letter of the word should also have no full point (e.g. Mr, St, - but no., str., etc.).

3. HEADINGS. In dividing articles under headings, please weight your headings by writing A, B, C etc. in the margin of the page:

A:	subheading	numbered	1,	2,	3	etc
B.	subsubheading	"	1.1,	1.2,	1.3	etc.
C.	subsubsubheading	"	a,	b,	c	etc.

Please avoid using more than three weights of subheading.

4. All illustrations should be separate from the manuscript with a list of captions, but their place in the text should be marked in the margin.

5. Tables should be typed on separate sheets. Indicate in the margin of the text where the tables should be placed.

6. Use endnotes for discursive comments, and not for documentation. Superscripts for location of notes should be inserted in the text and all notes collected at the end of the paper under NOTES. In the case of an acknowledgement or brief author's statement, this should go as an unnumbered note before the main textual notes.

7. In general, the use of mathematics should be kept to a low level as the journal is intended for a non-technical audience. Where mathematics is

INTERNATIONAL REVIEW OF APPLIED
ECONOMICS

considered essential, avoid unusual symbols where common ones will do, and place distinguishing marks after symbols rather than above.

8. REFERENCES should follow the Harvard system. In the typescript references should be indicated by giving the author's name and year of publication (with page references where necessary). For example:

> ... a quality which Liebenstein (1967, 153) calls 'x-efficiency'.

> Piaget points out that 'between two structures of different levels there can be no one-way reduction, but rather there is reciprocal assimilation... ' (1972a, 93).

> The references should be listed in full AT THE END OF THE ARTICLE in alphabetical order and in the following form:

a. Journal article
Liebenstein, H. 1966: Allocative efficiency versus x-efficiency. American Economic Review 61, 392-415.

(i.e. no quote marks around the title of the article and minimum capitalization.)

b. Book
Olson, M. 1965: The logic of collective action. Cambridge, Massachusetts: Harvard University Press.

c. Article in a book
Wiesbrod, B.A. 1965: Geographic spillover effects and the allocation of resources to education. In Margolis, J., editor, The public economy of urban communities, Washington, D.C.: Government Printing Office, 33-50.

d. Book in a series
Bunge, W. 1966: Theoretical geography, second edition. Lund Studies in Geography, Series C, General and Mathematical Geography 1, Lund: Gleerup.

NOTES

i.   Please indicate in brackets at the end of reference the number of pages in mimeographed articles and publications.

ii. If several papers by the same author and from the same year are cited, a, b, c, etc. should be added to the year of publication (1972a, 1972b, etc.).

iii. The use of the phrase et al. (=et alia) to indicate multiple authorship is permissible in the text, but not in the list of references, where all names should be given.

iv. No journal titles should be abbreviated. If in exceptional circumstances any abbreviations are used then they should be listed at the beginning of the references.

INTERNATIONAL REVIEW OF APPLIED ECONOMICS

9. COPYRIGHT. Please provide the publishers with a list of all matter in the following categories, including full information of work cited, author, date, publisher and page references:

i.   All maps, diagrams, figures and photographs (forms are available from the publishers).

ii. Single passages of prose exceeding 250 words, or scattered passages totalling more than 400 words from any one work.

     UK copyright extends to fifty years after the death of the author or fifty years after publication of a scholarly edition.

10. Proofs will be supplied only once in the form of page proofs. Please remember that:

i.   proof corrections are disproportionately expensive. For example, the insertion of three commas on a page will frequently cost as much as, or more than, the original setting cost of the entire page.

ii. if you return proofs even a few days after the date stipulated, it may be too late to include corrections in the final version of the journal.

INTERNATIONAL REVIEW OF ECONOMICS & FINANCE

ADDRESS FOR SUBMISSION :

H. BELADI (ECONOMICS), C. CHEN (FINANCE)
INTERNATIONAL REVIEW OF ECONOMICS
  & FINANCE
EDITORS
UNIVERSITY OF DAYTON
SCHOOL OF BUSINESS ADMINISTRATION
300 COLLEGE PARK
DAYTON, OH 45469-2241
USA
513-229-3073
513-229-2477 (Fax)
E-Mail : IREF@UDAYTON.EDU

CIRCULATION DATA :

Reader : Academic

Frequency of Issue : Quarterly

Copies Per Issue :

Subscription Price : 60.00 US$
  Institution : 150.00 US$

Sponsorship : University

PUBLICATION GUIDELINES :

Manuscript Length : 16-25

Copies Required : Three

Computer Submission : No

Format : N/A

Fees to Review : 30.00 US$

REVIEW INFORMATION :

Type of Review : Blind Review

No. of External Reviewers : Two

No. of In House Reviewers : One

Acceptance Rate : 11-20%

Time To Review : 2-3 months

Reviewer's Comments : Yes

Fees to Publish : 0.00 US$

Invited Articles : 5% or less

MANUSCRIPT TOPICS : CAPITAL BUDGETING; COST ACCOUNTING;
  ECONOMETRICS; ECONOMIC HISTORY; INTERNATIONAL & ECONOMIC DEVELOPMENT;
  INTERNATIONAL FINANCE; PORTFOLIO & SECURITY ANALYSIS;
  PUBLIC POLICY ECONOMICS; CORPORATE FINANCE; GENERAL ECONOMIC THEORY

PUBLICATION GUIDELINES : JAI Press

MANUSCRIPT GUIDELINES/COMMENTS :

EDITORS: HAMID BELADI (ECONOMICS) AND CARL R. CHEN (FINANCE)

OBJECTIVES AND SCOPE
With the globalization of all aspects of economics and finance, there is an
increasing interdependence between these two disciplines. The objective of the
INTERNATIONAL REVIEW OF ECONOMICS AND FINANCE is to publish original
theoretical/empirical articles on ALL ASPECTS of economics and finance. This
journal publishes papers of high quality that significantly contribute to the
knowledge of economics and finance and/or research that facilitates the
communication between the real and the financial sectors of the economy. The
editors are particularly interested in articles which contain a new
theoretical result and/or empirical findings which are likely to be of use or
interest to other researchers. IREF is a blind refereed publication which also
contains a book review section.

INTERNATIONAL REVIEW OF ECONOMICS & FINANCE

MANUSCRIPT PREPARATION

1. Papers submitted must be in English, clearly typed with double-spacing.

2. Papers should be sent in triplicate to the Editor(s). Submission of a paper will be held to imply that it is original unpublished work, that a significant part of it has not already been published, and that it is not being submitted for publication elsewhere. There is a $30 U.S. submission fee. Make check payable to INTERNATIONAL REVIEW OF ECONOMICS AND FINANCE.

3. Manuscripts may be typed, xeroxed, or mimeographed, but must be 8.5 x 11 paper with wide margins. All pages should be numbered consecutively, with titles and subtitles being kept short. Diagrams, tables, and references should be typed on separate pages with corresponding titles and legends being sufficiently descriptive as to be understandable without reference to the text. The dimensions of figure axes and body of tables must be clearly labeled in English. Tables should be numbered consecutively in the text in arabic numerals and typed on separate sheets. All unessential tables should be eliminated from the manuscript. Indicate the approximate location of tables/figures in the text with a phrase such as [INSERT TABLE 1 HERE].

4. The cover page of the manuscript should contain the following information (in order): (i) the title, (ii) the names(s) of the author(s), (iii) the affiliation(s) of the author(s), and (iv) any acknowledgements or credits. At the bottom of the same page, provide the name, current address and telephone number of the author to whom proofs and reprint order forms should be addressed. Include an abstract of 150 words or less on a separate page. The first page of text should show the title but not the author's name.

5. Lengthy mathematical proofs should be placed in an appendix. Where all of the steps involved in a formula have not been shown, it is very beneficial to present the full derivation of the formula on a separate sheet of paper. This will be used to assist referees but will not be published. Significant formulas should be numbered consecutively on the right-hand side of the page, as (1), (2), etc.

6. All graphs and diagrams should be labeled as figures and numbered consecutively in the text in arabic numerals. Upon acceptance of an article, author(s) must furnish camera-ready artwork in triplicate for all figures in a professional drawing on white paper (one original in black ink and two photocopies accepted). Any illustrations provided which must be redrawn by the publisher will be charged to the author(s).

7. Footnotes should be numbered consecutively with superscript arabic numerals and the number of footnotes should be kept to a minimum. Footnotes should be typed on a separate page, double-spaced, following the reference section.

8. References cited in the text must appear in the reference list; conversely, each entry in the reference list must be cited in the text. References must be typed on a separate page, double-spaced, at the end of the paper.

For Periodicals:
Black, F., and Scholes, M. "The Valuation of Option Contracts and a Test of Market Efficiency." Journal of Finance, 27 (May 1972): 399-418.

INTERNATIONAL REVIEW OF ECONOMICS & FINANCE

Jones, R.W. "The Structure of Simple Ceneral Equilibrium Models." Journal of Political Ecomomv, LXXII (Dec 1965): 557-72.

For Books:
Santomero, A.M. Current Views on the Bank Capital Issue. Washington: Association of Reserve City Banks, January 1983.

Any manuscript not conforming to the above guidelines may be returned to the authors for revision before publication. Page proofs will be sent to the author(s). Corrections required other than printer's errors may be charged to the author(s).

INTERNATIONAL REVIEW OF FINANCIAL ANALYSIS

ADDRESS FOR SUBMISSION :

GEORGE M. FRANKFURTER, EDITOR
INTERNATIONAL REVIEW OF FINANCIAL
  ANALYSIS
LOUISIANA STATE UNIVERSITY
COLLEGE OF BUSINESS ADMINISTRATION
DEPARTMENT OF FINANCE
2163 CEBA
BATON ROUGE, LA 70803
504-388-6369
504-388-6366 (Fax)
E-Mail : fifran@lsuvm.sncc.lsu.edu

CIRCULATION DATA :

Reader : Academic

Frequency of Issue : 3 Times/Year

Copies Per Issue : Less than 1000

Subscription Price :

Sponsorship : Profit Oriented Corp.

PUBLICATION GUIDELINES :

Manuscript Length :

Copies Required : Three

Computer Submission : No

Format : N/A

Fees to Review : 35.00 US$

REVIEW INFORMATION :

Type of Review : Blind Review

No. of External Reviewers : Two

No. of In House Reviewers : One

Acceptance Rate : 11-20%

Time To Review : 2-3 months

Reviewer's Comments : Yes

Fees to Publish : 0.00 US$

Invited Articles : 5% or less

MANUSCRIPT TOPICS : ACCOUNTING INFORMATION SYSTEMS;
  INTERNATIONAL FINANCE

PUBLICATION GUIDELINES :

MANUSCRIPT GUIDELINES/COMMENTS :

SUBMISSION OF MANUSCRIPTS
1. An original manuscript is accepted for review with the understanding that it was not published elsewhere and its submission for publication has been approved by all the authors and their respective institutions.

2. Authors submitting a manuscript for publication understand that if it is accepted for publication, copyright in the article shall be assigned to the Publisher of the INTERNATIONAL REVIEW OF FINANCIAL ANALYSIS.

3. Only manuscripts submitted in English will be considered for publicaiton. The author(s) is(are) responsible for correct spelling and punctuation, accurate quotations with page numbers, complete and accurate references, relevant content, coherent organization and legible appearance.

4. The review process cannot begin until the $35.00 submission fee, paid by check drawn to the INTERNATIONAL REVIEW OF FINANCIAL ANALYSIS in U.S. currency, is received.

5. Three copies of the manuscript must be submitted to the editor of IRFA.

INTERNATIONAL REVIEW OF FINANCIAL ANALYSIS

These must be typed double-spaced on white paper, using only one side.
6. The upper limit on the length of a manuscript is 75,000 ASCII characters
(without tables). Still, concise writing is advised as brevity is a major
factor in a favorable publication decision.

7. The mailing addresses, as well as telephone and fax numbers (if any) of
each author should be included. This information should appear only on the
title page and no where else in the manuscript. Correspondence is generally
sent to the first author unless he/she is unavailable.

8. Authors must resubmit accepted manuscripts on a double-density
IBM-PC-readable diskette, in both WordPerfect 5.1 and ASCII format. All tables
must be saved separately in ASCII format.

9. Once a resubmitted manuscript is received at our editorial offices, IRFA
reserves the right to edit it in the interest of style and proper English. A
copy of the final version as it will be submitted to the printer is sent to
the first author, along with a Publication Agreement.

THE REVIEW PROCEDURE
1. After an initial screening, papers are sent to an associate editor familiar
with the main tenor of the work. The associate editor reads the paper and
requests the evaluation of two referees, one of whom might be himself. Upon
receiving the referees' evaluation, the associate editor makes reccomendation
for disposition. The final decision, based on this material, is then made by
the editor of IRFA.

2. Every effort will be made to have a constructive and timely reviewing
process. Even in the instance of completely negative decision, the review is
designed to provide feedback to the author. Our goal is to reach a decision
and provide feedback to the authors within two to three months.

3. If a manuscript is accepted, the first author is required to mail back to
IRFA, within 14 days of the postmark of the letter of acceptance, a signed and
binding copyright agreement. The author(s) of an accepted manuscript is (are)
also responsible for obtaining pemission to quote from copyrighted work cited
in the manuscript.

4. If a manuscript is rejected, or when modifications and changes in the paper
are recommended against the better judgment of the author(s), a letter of
appeal may be filed with the editor. This letter should include detailed,
point-by-point rebuttal of the review in a polite and professional manner.

4. Upon examination of the letter of appeal, the editor will decide whether to
send the paper, the original review material and the letter of appeal to
another associate editor. In such instance, the recommendation of the second
associate editor will be final.

PREPARING A MANUSCRIPT ONCE IT HAS BEEN ACCEPTED

ASSEMBLY OF THE MANUSCRIPT
Number pages of the manuscript consecutively at the top right, and arrange
them as follows:
    1. Title Page   (first page)
    2. Abstract   (second page)

INTERNATIONAL REVIEW OF FINANCIAL ANALYSIS

3. Text   (third page and on--number first text page as page 1)
4. Appendices   (Start each on a separate page)
5. Acknowledgments (start on a new page)
6. Notes   (start on a new page)
7. References   (start on a new page)
8. Tables   (start each on a separate page)
9. Figures   (start each on a separate page)

TITLE PAGE
The title page inclludes four elements:
1. The title in uppercase letters, boldfaced and centered.
2. The authors in uppercase and lowercase letters, centered. Use full names (e.g., John J. Jones or John Jacob Jones, not J. Jones or JJ. jones).
3. An abbreviated title to be used as a running head, if the title exceeds 70 characters. Keep the running head under 70 characters and type it in uppercase letters, centered and identified (e.g., "Running Head: BRITISH OPTIONS MARKET BEHAVIOR").
4. Affiliation and mailing address of each author, centered at the bottom of the page in uppercase and lowercase letters.

ABSTRACT
The manuscript's second page is an abstract of 150 words or less. Type the word "ABSTRACT" in boldfaced, uppercase letters, centered at the top of the page. Do not use equations or mathematical symbols in the abstract.

TEXT
Begin the manuscript on the third page (numbered page 1). The sections of the text follow without a break. The purpose of the paper should be revealed by the second or third paragraph.

HEADINGS. The three levels should appear as follows:
1. flush left all uppercase heading, boldfaced, with Roman numerals.
2. Uppercase and lowercase heading, boldfaced, indented five spaces from the left margin.
3. Uppercase and lowercase heading, underlined or italicized, indented five spaces from the left margin.

PERSONS, VOICES AND TENSES. Only the third person should be used, never first or second (e.g., "it" or "they," never "I" or "we"). Use the passive voice in describing the paper (e.g., "...in Section II a review of the literature is offered."). Use the present tense in describing prior research and results (e.g., "Brown (1985) finds that..."). Use the past tense in describing the accumulation of data and running of texts (e.g., "...three months of positive returns were observed...").

PARAGRAPHS AND MARGINS. Indent the first line of each paragraph five spaces. Use flush left, ragged right margin setups.

QUOTATIONS. Direct quotations must be accurate. Incorporate quotations of 40 words or less into the text and enclose them with double quotation marks ("). display quotations of more than 40 words as a double-spaced block with no quotation marks, indented five spaces from both the left and right margins. Accompany any direct quotation by a reference citation in the text including the author, year of publication, and page number(s). If copyrighted works are quoted at length, it is the author's responsibility to obtain written

INTERNATIONAL REVIEW OF FINANCIAL ANALYSIS

permission; a copy of such permission must accompany the manuscript.
EQUATIONS. Set equations off from the text by double-spacing twice above and twice above and twice below the equation. Equations referenced in the text should be numbered with Arabic numerals enclosed in parentheses (e.g., "(1)"). Equations not actually referenced in the text must not be numbered.

STATISTICAL AND MATHEMATICAL SYMBOLS. Make every effort to type all signs and symbols; otherwise, draw them accurately by hand. Type subscripts half a line below the symbol and superscripts half a line above the symbol. Identify symbols that may be hard to read or ambiguous, and do not use the same symbol or letter to designate two different things. For example, if k is used as a subscript, if must not be used again as a variable. Since variables appear italicized in printed text, they must be underlined or italicized in typed copy, as well.

APPENDICES

Double-space the appendices and begin each on a separate page. Center the word "APPENDIX" at the top of the page in boldfaced, all uppercase letters with an identifying capital letter based on the order in which the appendix is mentioned in the text (e.g., "APPENDIX A"). iF THERE IS ONLY ONE APPENDIX, DO NOT USE AN IDENTIFYING LETTER.

ACKNOWLEDGMENTS

Acknowledgments must appear only on one page, separate from the rest of the text. Type the word "ACKNOWLEDGMENTS(S)" in boldfaced, all uppercase letters, flush left at the top of the page. Type the acknowledgement itself as a double-spaced single paragraph.

NOTES

Notes mentioned in the text are numbered consecutively with superscripted numbers, and appear as endnotes after the "acknowledgments" page. At the top of the page, type the word "Notes" in boldfaced, uppercase and lowercase letters, flush left. Indent the first line of each note five spaces, type the note number and a period (not using superscripted type, e.g., "1."), then indent five more spaces and begin the text of the note. Use the same margins on the note page as are used in the text. Single-space within the notes and double-space between each note.

Do not use either op. cit. or loc. cit. Ibid. is acceptable. Notes that merely refer the reader to one of the references should be included in the text rather than as an endnote. For example, "...prior research in Smith (1980)..." or "...dominant portfolios (see Jones 1989)."

REFERENCES

Follow THE CHICAGO MANUAL OF STYLE (13th edition, page 422). References cited in the text must appear in the reference list and each entry in the reference list must be cited in the text, either by a note or parenthetically. It is the author's responsibility to make certain that each source refeenced appears in both places and that the text citation and reference list are identical. If at all practical, translate foteign language volumes, parts and editions into their English equivalents. List single-author entries before multiauthor entries beginning with the same name, and list all entries with the same authorship chronologically.

INTERNATIONAL REVIEW OF FINANCIAL ANALYSIS

Book references include:
1. Author's full name (initials acceptable but not preferred)
2. Date of publication
3. Complete title of the book
4. Editor, compiler, or translator (if any)
5. Series and/or volume number (if any)
6. Edition number (if not the original)
7. Facts of publication: city where published, publisher

Periodical article references include:
1. Author's full name (initials acceptable but not preferred)
2. Date of the volume or issue
3. Complete of title of the article
4. Name of the periodical
5. Volume number of periodical
6. Page numbers of the article

Unpublished material references include:
1. Author's full name (initials acceptable but not preferred)
2. Date of last revision
3. Complete title of the document
4. Folio number or other identifying material
5. Name of collection or university
6. Depository, if applicable
7. City where collection is located

TABLES
Tables are numbered consecutively in the order in which they are first mentioned in the text, and are identified by the boldfaced word "Table" and an Arabic numeral, as well as an appropriate title (e g., "Table 6: Portfolio Size"). When referring table in the text, identify it by its numbered label rather than its location in the text (e.g, "Table 6" not "the table on p. 32"). Double-space each table, regardless of length. When setting up tables, do not abbreviate table headings. Limit the use of rules to horizontal rules only. Notes to the tables should appear at the bottom of each table, marked with asterisks.
Begin each table on a separate page. Type the manuscript title (or running head) in the upper right hand corner of every page containing a table. Indicate the table's placement in the text by inserting a legend such as "TABLE 6 ABOUT HERE," set off double-spaced above and below.

FIGURES
Figures are also numbered consecutively in the order in which they are first mentioned in the text and are identified by the word "Figure" and an Arabic numeral, as well as an appropriate caption (e.g., "Figure 4: A mean-parameterized path subject to general linear constraints."). When referring to a figure in the text, identify it by its numbered label rather than its location in the text (e.g., "Figure 4" not "the figure on p. 48"). Charts and illustrations are considered to be figures and must be submitted in a form suitable for reproduction without redrawing or retouching.

Begin each figure on a separate page. Type the manuscript title (or running head) in the upper right-hand corner of every page containing figure. Indicate the figure's placement in the text by inserting a legend such as "FIGURE 4 ABOUT HERE", set off double-spaced above and below.

INTERNATIONAL TAX JOURNAL

ADDRESS FOR SUBMISSION :

WALTER F. O'CONNOR, EDITOR
INTERNATIONAL TAX JOURNAL
FORDHAM UNIVERSITY
GRAD. SCHOOL OF BUSINESS ADMININSTRATION
113 WEST 60TH STREET
NEW YORK, NY 10023
USA
212-636-6122
212-765-5573 (Fax)
E-Mail : oconnor@mary.fordham.edu

CIRCULATION DATA :

Reader : Business Persons

Frequency of Issue : Quarterly

Copies Per Issue : 1001-2000

Subscription Price : 136.00 US$

Sponsorship : Profit Oriented Corp.

PUBLICATION GUIDELINES :

Manuscript Length : 16-20+

Copies Required : One

Computer Submission : Yes

Format : WordPerfect 5.1 or ASCII

Fees to Review : 0.00 US$

REVIEW INFORMATION :

Type of Review : Blind Review

No. of External Reviewers : Two

No. of In House Reviewers : One

Acceptance Rate : 50 %

Time To Review : One month or less

Reviewer's Comments : No

Fees to Publish : 0.00 US$

Invited Articles : 5% or less

MANUSCRIPT TOPICS : ACCOUNTING INFORMATION SYSTEMS;
  ACCOUNTING THEORY & PRACTICE; AUDITING; CAPITAL BUDGETING;
  INTERNATIONAL FINANCE; PORTFOLIO & SECURITY ANALYSIS; TAX ACCOUNTING

PUBLICATION GUIDELINES :

MANUSCRIPT GUIDELINES/COMMENTS :

1. Articles should provide practical information and ideas about
international tax practice. Articles should cover matters of importance to
practitioners, and cover tax, legal, and business planning aspects affecting
clients with international tax situations.

2. Be sure to include both your address and telephone number where you may be
reached during business hours. While the utmost care will be given to all
manuscripts, we cannot accept responsibility for unsolicited manuscripts.
Article accepted for publication are subject to editorial revision. There is
no payment for articles; authors will receive 10 copies (to be shared by
multiple authors) of their published articles.

3. Type manuscript on one side of the paper only, on 8-1/2" x 11"
good-quality white bond. Please do not use "erasable" paper. Use one-inch
margins and double spacing. Generally, article manuscript should be
approximately 15 to 35 typed pages. On acceptance, submit a computer disk of
the article in WordPerfect 5.1 or ASCII.

INTERNATIONAL TAX JOURNAL

4. Within your article, use headings and subheadings to break up and emphasize your points. Type headings and subheadings flush left.

5. Type footnotes separately, double spaced, at the end of the main manuscript. Footnote and reference citations should generally follow the "Harvard Blue Book".

6. With your article, please include a brief biographical note.

7. Any artwork, e.g., flow charts, original drawings, or graphs, must be provided in camera-ready form. Typewritten or free-hand lettering is not acceptable; all lettering must be done professionally. Do not staple or paper clip illustrations and put all illustrations between sheets of cardboard before mailing, to prevent folds. Note: We will typeset tubular material, which you may provide in typewritten form as part of your manuscript.

8. Except in rare cases, INTERNATIONAL TAX JOURNAL publishes articles only if they have not yet appeared or been accepted for publication elsewhere. If you are considering submission of previously published material, please correspond with the Editor first to determine if such submission is suitable. We will generally be pleased to consider articles for prior publication adapted from book-length works in progress but, again, request advance notice so that we may work out necessary copyright arrangements.

9. If you are reprinting any previously copyrighted material in your article, other than short quotations, you must submit with your manuscript letters of permission from the copyright holder and from the author (if he or she is not the copyright holder).

10. We will own and retain the copyright to all of the articles we publish, together with the right to reprint them in any republication of the Journal in any form or media. You may reprint your article for personal use, provided you do not do so for resale and provided the Journal, and Panel Publishers, a division of Aspen Publishers, Inc. as the Journal's publisher, are given appropriate credit if and when you reprint the article. We will be happy to provide you with appropriate credit-line language. (Should you wish to have your own article reprinted or reissued in a book or periodical to be sold or distributed by another publisher or organization, you must obtain prior written permission from us.)

INTERNATIONAL TRADE JOURNAL

ADDRESS FOR SUBMISSION :

KHOSROW FATEMI, EDITOR
INTERNATIONAL TRADE JOURNAL
TEXAS A&M INTERNATIONAL UNIVERSITY
5201 UNIVERSITY BOULEVARD
LAREDO, TX 78041-1999
USA
210-326-2480
210-326-2479 (Fax)
E-Mail : fatemi@tamiu.edu

CIRCULATION DATA :

Reader : Academic

Frequency of Issue : Quarterly

Copies Per Issue : Less than 1000

Subscription Price : 70.00 US$
  Member of ITFA : 45.00 US$

Sponsorship : University

PUBLICATION GUIDELINES :

Manuscript Length : 16-20

Copies Required : Four

Computer Submission : Yes

Format : WordPerfect

Fees to Review : 0.00 US$

REVIEW INFORMATION :

Type of Review : Blind Review

No. of External Reviewers : Two

No. of In House Reviewers : One

Acceptance Rate : 11-20%

Time To Review : 4-6 months

Reviewer's Comments : Yes

Fees to Publish : 0.00 US$

Invited Articles : 6-10%

MANUSCRIPT TOPICS : ACCOUNTING THEORY & PRACTICE; COST ACCOUNTING;
   ECONOMETRICS; INTERNATIONAL & ECONOMIC DEVELOPMENT; INTERNATIONAL FINANCE;
   PUBLIC POLICY ECONOMICS; INTERNATIONAL ECONOMICS; COMMERCIAL POLICY

PUBLICATION GUIDELINES :

MANUSCRIPT GUIDELINES/COMMENTS :

EDITIORIAL POLICY
The INTERNATIONAL TRADE JOURNAL is a refereed journal published for the
enhancement of research in international trade. Its editorial objective is to
provide a forum for the scholarly exchange of research findings in, and
significant conceptual or theoretical contributions to, the field.

The INTERNATIONAL TRACE JOURNAL welcomes contributions not only from
researchers in academia but also from practitioners of international trade
with significant research findings in the field.

The Journal's scope includes, but is not limited to, the following:
*   International Trade Theory
*   International Trade Relations
*   Commercial Policy
*   Trade and Development
*   International Trade Organizations and Agreements
*   National Studies
*   Regional Studies

INTERNATIONAL TRADE JOURNAL

The INTERNATIONAL TRADE JOURNAL is published quarterly by the Institute for International Trade, Texas A&M International University. The responsibility for such views expressed, and accuracy of facts given, are those of the authors. Such opinions do not necessarily reflect the position of Texas A&M International University or the Institute for International Trade; nor that of the Editor or the Editorial Advisory Board of the Journal.

PREPARATION AND SUBMISSION OF ARTICLES

Articles are invited from all researchers with significant conceptual or theoretical findings or with major contributions to any aspect of international trade.

Prospective authors should also keep in mind the following:

* The International Trade Journal accepts manuscripts on the understanding that their contents are original and that the manuscript has not been submitted elsewhere. The International Trade Journal has the copyright to all its published articles.

* Manuscripts accepted for review are refereed by two or more scholars, at least one of whom is a member of the Editorial Advisory Board of the Journal.

* Four copies of the manuscript should be submitted.

* Manuscripts should be between 4000 and 8000 words. They should be double-spaced and typed on standard letter-size (11 x 8.5) paper.

* The cover page should include the author's name, his institutional affiliation, and the title of the paper.

* All manuscripts should include an abstract of not more than 150 words on a separate page.

* All manuscripts should also include a biographical sketch, not to exceed 100 words, of the author on a separate page.

* The first page of the text should include the title of the article but not the author's name.

* Each table, chart and graph should be put on a separate page. The authors are responsible for providing camera-ready copies of their charts, graphs, and tables.

* No footnotes should be used.

* A complete bibliography should be at the end of the manuscript. References cited in text must be in the bibliography.

* Submit manuscripts to: The International Trade Journal
                          Texas A&M International University
                          5201 University Boulevard
                          Laredo, Texas 784041-1999

IS AUDIT & CONTROL JOURNAL

ADDRESS FOR SUBMISSION :

PATRICIA K. DAHLBERG, ASSOC. PUBLISHER
IS AUDIT & CONTROL JOURNAL
INFORMATION SYSTEMS AUDIT AND CONTROL
  ASSOCIATION
3701 ALGONQUIN ROAD, SUITE 1010
ROLLING MEADOWS, IL 60008
USA
708-253-1545 EXT 453
708-253-1443 (Fax)
E-Mail : publication@isaca.org

CIRCULATION DATA :

Reader : Business Persons

Frequency of Issue : Bi-Monthly

Copies Per Issue : 10,001-25,000

Subscription Price : 40.00 US$
  Outside U.S. : 50.00 US$

Sponsorship : Professional Assoc.

PUBLICATION GUIDELINES :

Manuscript Length : 11-15

Copies Required : Three

Computer Submission : Yes

Format : ASCII,MS Word,WP:PC or MAC

Fees to Review : 0.00 US$

REVIEW INFORMATION :

Type of Review : Editorial Review

No. of External Reviewers : Over 3

No. of In House Reviewers : Two

Acceptance Rate : 50 %

Time To Review : 2-3 months

Reviewer's Comments : No

Fees to Publish : 0.00 US$

Invited Articles : Over 50%

MANUSCRIPT TOPICS : ACCOUNTING INFORMATION SYSTEMS;
  COMPUTER SECURITY, AUDITING & CONTROL PRACTICES

PUBLICATION GUIDELINES :

MANUSCRIPT GUIDELINES/COMMENTS :

Thank you for your interest in the IS AUDIT & CONTROL JOURNAL, the official
journal of the Information Systems Audit and Control Association (formerly the
EDP Auditors Association).

The Journal provides important information on industry advancements and
professional development to those involved in the IS audit, control and
security community. Each issue focuses on a new technical topic relevant to
our readers.
The Journal is published bi-monthly and combines short columns with longer
feature articles.

1996 EDITORIAL CALENDAR
Topics for 1996 include the following
* Internet control and security,
* Information integrity;
* Risk assessment;
* IS Auditor's Buyer's Guide;
* Electronic data interchange; and
* Control self-assessment.

IS AUDIT & CONTROL JOURNAL

Other topics for which we're accepting manuscripts include application development controls, audit automation, benchmarking client/server issues, contingency planning, e-mail security, encryption, LANs, VANs, WANs, security standards and architecture, electronic commerce, and privacy and information protection.

WHY INVEST IN BECOMING PUBLISHED?
Publishing an article in the IS AUDIT & CONTROL JOURNAL offers you several benefits. It places your name in front of your peers, establishes you as an expert in a technical area of IS audit and control, and enables you to exchange ideas with your colleagues.

WHO MAY WRITE??
Authors should cover either new developments in the field or in-depth technically oriented subjects. Major feature should have broad appeal and focus on practical matters; purely theoretical material is not solicited. Authors are not required to be Association members.

Original submissions should be offered exclusively to the IS AUDIT & CONTROL JOURNAL. However, finished manuscripts are also considered. Advertising and public relations agency submissions generally are not accepted for feature articles, but are for the "Product Overview" or "Case Study" columns.

OUR READER PROFILE
The ISA AUDIT & CONTROL JOURNAL's 25,000 readers are a combination of Association members and paid subscribers in 92 countries around the world. The paid subscribers include university libraries worldwide, and copies are circulated within organizations in a wide range of industries and government. According to a recent reader survey, more than 98 percent of those responding report reading each bimonthly issue of the Journal. The majority of our readers refer to back issues and can recall specific information found in past issues within the last several years.

TYPES OF ARTICLES ACCEPTED
All manuscripts on subjects relevant to the Journal's readers will be considered for publication.

We accept and consider articles for the following sections: Guest Editorial, Perspectives, and Case Study. Articles submitted for these departments should be from two to four double-spaced pages in length, and must adhere to the Journal's style conventions. Articles may be edited for length.

A strong article will co-mingle the pertinent facts with references to personal experience, and use anecdotes to illustrate the author's key points. Quotations from other experts involved also add to the article's depth.

An article should not simply repeat information gleaned from existing literature. Instead, it should draw lessons from such material and include the author's conclusions about the impact of this information on the practice of IS auditing.

Articles based on surveys or questionnaires must include a brief analysis of the results, with evaluations as to the significance of the responses and tabulations. Include the number of respondents and indicate when and where the study was done.

IS AUDIT & CONTROL JOURNAL

We strongly encourage you to include exhibits, graphics and artwork for an article. These will assist the reader in comprehending and retaining the information in your article, and will make the layout of the Journal more appealing. Such items are treated as text manuscripts requiring the same warranties and assignments.

The New Products/Book Review sections provide an impartial evaluation to our readers. While we generally assign reviews, we do accept review submissions from an independent source. Articles submitted for this section should be from one to two double-spaced pages. Product illustrations or photographs are helpful.

SUBMISSION REQUIREMENTS
The following guidelines must be followed when formatting your document for submission to the Journal:

TYPEWRITTEN (matrix printer output is acceptable if it is letter or near-letter quality); double-spaced between paragraphs; one side to a page; and on pages that measure 8 1/2 x 11 inches or are A4 sized.

SUBMIT TWO HARD COPIES of the article and one disk formatted in Word Perfect (IBM compatible), Microsoft Word (IBM or Macintosh), or ASCII on a 3 1/2-inch diskette. Diskettes should be dearly labeled with the author's name, article title, date, software and version used.

Also, when saving the document, choose the SAVE AS option in the File Menu. Select SAVE AS "Mac 5.1 format." Or, SAVE AS "Text Only."

THESE DOCUMENTS PARAMETERS must be followed when formatting your file:
* Hyphenation OFF;
* Double spacing,
* Margins - 1 and 80;
* Page numbering - Upper Right;
* Right justify - OFF;
* No automation headers/footers (type them manually);
* Standard Printer Spec; and
* AVOID special characters or keys (e.g., indents - instead use TAB for the indent key).

GRAPHICS AND ARTWORK should be submitted both in hard copy and on disk.

ARTICLE LENGTH should be from 2,500 to 3,000 words. Even major articles are seldom more than 4,000 words. (Articles may be edited for length.)

ARTICLE STYLE should be structured as explained in the box on p. 3, as well as follow the CHICAGO MANUAL OF STYLE.

USE ENDNOTES at the end of your article, rather than footnotes, to credit your sources.

AUTHORS should include a brief biography including current position, background, professional affiliations, and books or articles published.

MATERIAL should be written in English. Other languages will be accepted only after discussion with the editor.

IS AUDIT & CONTROL JOURNAL

REVIEW PROCESS
Manuscripts submitted to the Journal are acknowledged by the staff upon receipt. Manuscripts are subject to review by one or more members of the Editorial Board of the Information Systems Audit and Control Association.

The review process generally takes eight weeks, depending on the length of the article and its complexity. When the review process is complete, the author will be informed whether the manuscript has been accepted for publication (with or without revisions).

Each article published in the Journal becomes part of our overall copyright. We request authors ask for perrmission to reprint their articles and include a statement "Reprinted with permission of the IS AUDIT & CONTROL JOURNAL, Vol. X, year, pages xx-xx."

Accepted articles are placed in the inventory of unpublished articles until scheduled for publication. In general articles are published within three to nine months of their acceptance.

The Association sends authors five copies of the issue in which the article appears. There is no honorarium for Journal authors.

Manuscripts for publication in the IS AUDIT & CONTROL JOURNAL are edited according to THE CHICAGO MANUAL OF STYLE. Revisions are made by the author.

The IS AUDIT & CONTROL JOURNAL is published by the Information Systems Audit and Control Association. For more information, call the associate publisher at + 1.708.253.1545.

COPYRIGHT AND REPRINTS
The Information Systems Audit and Control Association obtains first International serial rights to any published manuscript in the IS AUDIT & CONTROL JOURNAL. While every effort is made to preserve the author's (or authors') style, the Journal Editorial Board and staff reserves the right to edit articles.

Article reprints are available after publication. For more information, contact the Journal's associate publisher.

SEND YOUR ARTICLE TO...
Please send your manuscripts or direct your questions regarding editorial policy to:
Patricia K. Dahlberg, Associate Publisher
IS AUDIT & CONTROL JOURNAL
Information Systems Audit and Control Association
3701 Algonquin Road, Suite 1010
Rolling Meadows, IL 60008, USA
+ 1.708.253.1545, ext.453.

STYLE CONVENTIONS - IS AUDIT & CONTROL JOURNAL

I. HEADINGS
A. Major headings should be flush left and capitalized.
Example: SECURITY AUDITS OF IMS

IS AUDIT & CONTROL JOURNAL

B. Subheadings should also begin at the left margin (flush left), but at the should have an initial capital letter, rather than be all caps.
Example: Importance of Program Control Procedures

C. Sub subheads under subheads should be indented five spaces. In this case, only the first word needs to be capitalized.

II. ENDNOTES
A. Endnotes in text should be numbered sequentially and listed on a separate page(s) at the end of the article. Each endnote should include the full name of the reference, e.g., author, book, date, and page number(s).
Example:
In the United States, forgers started with a counterfeit check drawn on a Los Angeles business account, and proceeded with an elaborate scheme that defrauded a Midwestern bank out of $700,000.

 Bradford, Michael. "Thieves Sting Banks with High-Tech Forgeries." Business Insurance. March 2, 1992. p.14.

III. TABLES, EXHIBITS, FIGURES AND ILLUSTRATIONS
These should be on separate pages, properly labeled. In the text of the article, please indicate where each table, exhibit, or figure should be placed, e.g., "Place Exhibit I here." Exhibits and Tables should have Roman numerals (I, II, III); figures should take Arabic numerals (1,2,3).

A Checklist for Success
HELPFUL HINTS FOR GETTING PUBLISHED IN THE JOURNAL

Drafting a manuscript takes time and practice. Crafting your article to fit each publication's style requires an eye for editorial detail. Here are some tips regarding the IS Audit & CONTROL JOURNAL that will help you in becoming published:

__ Keep your colleagues in mind. Remember that while you are writing for a sophisticated audience, both in technical training and in education, they also are busy. So be concise when expressing your ideas. Use subheadings to break up the text and make skimming easier.

__ Follow a journalistic style. Keep your writing concise, provide details that illustrate your position and follow a logical progression of ideas. Vary your sentence lengths to make reading easier and to help engage the reader.

__ Write in the active voice using active verbs.

__ Use specific examples and case histories to illustrate points. (But be careful not to promote an individual, company, product or service.)

__ Address your readers in a friendly, conversational tone. Avoid unnecessarily complex vocabulary, cliches and excessive jargon.

__ Add subheads to signal topic changes and use bullets to make points easier to read.

__ Provide a summary of the major points of your article at the end.

IS AUDIT & CONTROL JOURNAL

__ If your article becomes too long, consider separating some of the copy to form a sidebar. Sidebars should include supporting facts or data and should be no longer than 300-350 words.

__ Provide supporting tables, figures, charts or artwork along with your manuscript. Tables and charts should be sent on separate pages. Captions should be included that explain the relevance and significance of these supporting items.

__ Give your article a final edit to eliminate unnecessary words. Make sure paragraphs flow smoothly and logically.

__ And be sure to double-check facts and figures.

Thankyou for your interest! And goodluck!!

ISSUES IN ACCOUNTING EDUCATION

ADDRESS FOR SUBMISSION :

WANDA A. WALLACE, EDITOR
ISSUES IN ACCOUNTING EDUCATION
EVE BORNHAUSER, EDITORIAL ASSISTANT
COLLEGE OF WILLIAM AND MARY
SCHOOL OF BUSINESS ADMINISTRATION
WILLIAMSBURG, VA 23185
USA
757-221-2936
757-221-2937 (Fax)
E-Mail : emborn@dogwood.tyler.wm.edu

CIRCULATION DATA :

Reader : Academic

Frequency of Issue : Quarterly

Copies Per Issue : 5001-10,000

Subscription Price : 45.00 US$

Sponsorship : Professional Assoc.

PUBLICATION GUIDELINES :

Manuscript Length : 20

Copies Required : Four

Computer Submission : No

Format : N/A

Fees to Review : 50.00 US$

REVIEW INFORMATION :

Type of Review : Blind Review

No. of External Reviewers : Three

No. of In House Reviewers : One

Acceptance Rate : 11-20%

Time To Review : 2-3 months

Reviewer's Comments : Yes

Fees to Publish : 0.00 US$

Invited Articles : 5% or less

MANUSCRIPT TOPICS : ACCOUNTING INFORMATION SYSTEMS;
    ACCOUNTING THEORY & PRACTICE; AUDITING; CAPITAL BUDGETING; COST ACCOUNTING;
    GOVERNMENT & NON-PROFIT ACCOUNTING; INTERNATIONAL & ECONOMIC DEVELOPMENT;
    INTERNATIONAL FINANCE; PORTFOLIO & SECURITY ANALYSIS; TAX ACCOUNTING

PUBLICATION GUIDELINES : American Review Style

MANUSCRIPT GUIDELINES/COMMENTS :

1. The purpose of ISSUES IN ACCOUNTING EDUCATION is to provide useful
information to accounting faculty to assist in the teaching of accounting
courses and to assist in the understanding of student and faculty performance
and behavior. Papers that present research related to this purpose, that
provide insights into the teaching function, or that describe methods or
materials that can be used in the classroom will be considered for
publication. Authors should communicate in a direct and easily understood
manner. Examples and illustrations are frequently helpful. Papers should
contain descriptions of the methods used to support and validate the
conclusions reached by the authors.

2. Authors should submit four copies of their papers along with the $50
submission fee to the editor. Checks should be made payable to ISSUES IN
ACCOUNTING EDUCATION. A submission provides a representation by the author
that the paper is not currently under review by any other journal.

ISSUES IN ACCOUNTING EDUCATION

3. Papers submitted to the journal are screened by the editors. Those that are considered inappropriate or for which there appears to be a low probability of acceptance will be returned to the author promptly. The submission fee will not be returned.

4. Those papers that pass the initial screening will be sent to two to three reviewers for evaluation. A double blind review procedure is used. The reviewers are asked to provide a recommendation to accept or reject the paper, or to return it for revision. This review process takes approximately four to eight weeks. Approximately 15 to 20 percent of the papers submitted to the journal are eventually accepted for publication. Most of these papers are revised one or more times before acceptance. The lag between submission of a paper and publication generally is between eight and twelve months.

5. Authors are requested to use the following guidelines in preparing manuscripts for submission:

6. An abstract of no more than 150 words should accompany the manuscript. The abstract should contain a concise statement of the purpose of the paper, the primary methods or approaches used, and the main results or conclusions.

7. The paper should be double spaced throughout, including abstract, footnotes, and references.

8. Footnotes, references, tables, and figures should appear on separate pages.

9. Tables and figures should be numbered serially using Arabic numerals. The table number (TABLE 1) and a title should appear at the top of the page in caps. The tables and figures should stand along. Abbreviations should be avoided, and when used, should be explained in footnotes. Headings should be clear. Vertical lines normally should not be used. Horizontal lines should separate the title from the headings and the headings from the body. Figures should be prepared in a form suitable for printing.

10. Headings and subheadings should be used throughout the paper. The title and major headings should be in caps and centered. Subheadings should be flush with the left margin, underlined, and not in caps. Headings and subheadings should not be numbered.

11. Footnotes should be used sparingly. References should be noted in the text using the date of publication in brackets. For example: Wright [1986, p. 27]. The reference list should use the following format:

Wright, A., "On the Use of an Available Prior Examination Policy", Issues in Accounting Education (Spring 1986), pp. 24-36.

12. The title page should list the authors names, titles, affiliations, telephone numbers, and any acknowledgements. The authors and their affiliations should not be identified anywhere else in the paper.

13. Permission is granted to reproduce any of the contents of ISSUES for use in courses of instruction, so long as the source and American Accounting Association copyright are indicated in any such reproductions.

ISSUES IN ACCOUNTING EDUCATION

14. Written application must be made to the Editor for permission to reproduce any of the contents of ISSUES for use in other than courses of instruction -- e.g., books of readings. The applicant must notify the author(s) in writing of the intended use of each reproduction.

15. Except as otherwise noted, the copyright has been transferred to the American Accounting Association for articles appearing in this journal. For those articles for which the copyright has not been transferred, permission to reproduce must be obtained directly from the author.

JOURNAL OF ACCOUNTANCY

ADDRESS FOR SUBMISSION :

EDITOR
JOURNAL OF ACCOUNTANCY
AMERICAN INSTITUTE OF CPAS
1211 AVENUE OF THE AMERICAS
NEW YORK, NY 10036
USA
201-938-3456
201-938-3329 (Fax)
E-Mail : ckatz@aicpa.org

CIRCULATION DATA :

Reader : Accountants (CPAs)

Frequency of Issue : Monthly

Copies Per Issue : Over 25,000

Subscription Price : 40.00 US$

Sponsorship : Professional Assoc.

PUBLICATION GUIDELINES :

Manuscript Length : 10

Copies Required : Five

Computer Submission : Yes

Format : None Special

Fees to Review : 0.00 US$

REVIEW INFORMATION :

Type of Review : Editorial Review

No. of External Reviewers : Three

No. of In House Reviewers : One

Acceptance Rate : 6-10%

Time To Review : 2-3 months

Reviewer's Comments : No

Fees to Publish : 0.00 US$

Invited Articles : 31-50%

MANUSCRIPT TOPICS : ACCOUNTING INFORMATION SYSTEMS;
ACCOUNTING THEORY & PRACTICE; AUDITING; CAPITAL BUDGETING; COST ACCOUNTING;
ECONOMETRICS; ECONOMIC HISTORY; GOVERNMENT & NON-PROFIT ACCOUNTING;
INSURANCE; INTERNATIONAL & ECONOMIC DEVELOPMENT; INTERNATIONAL FINANCE;
PORTFOLIO & SECURITY ANALYSIS; PUBLIC POLICY ECONOMICS; REAL ESTATE;
TAX ACCOUNTING; INTERNATIONAL BUSINESS; SMALL BUSINESS ENTREPRENEURSHIP

PUBLICATION GUIDELINES : Chicago Manual of Style

MANUSCRIPT GUIDELINES/COMMENTS :

The JOURNAL OF ACCOUNTANCY is a national monthly magazine for the accounting
profession. It is the one publication in the United States that covers the
whole field of accounting. The Journal keeps its readers abreast of technical
and professional developments of significance to accountants and to anyone
with an interest in accounting.

READERS
Over 40% of Journal readers are in public practice and another 40% are in
business and industry. The remainder are government personnel, educators or
students. Most of those in public practice work in small or midsized firms or
sole practitioners.

Articles should be addressed to generalists, not specialists. Most readers are
well-versed in general accounting or business topics but not necessarily in
highly technical specialized areas. It is expected that specialists will look

to other publications and commercial services for more detailed information on technical subjects. But they must all look to the Journal to keep informed of general developments outside their own fields.

OBJECTIVES
Journal readers have a variety of interests that require diversity of editorial content. The magazine covers the full range of issues in accounting, auditing, taxation, professional developments, management advisory services, practice management and education, among other areas.

Articles should have broad appeal and should focus on practical situations and applications. Those that are entirely theoretical or are derived wholly from secondary sources are rarely accepted. Those based on studies or surveys should draw conclusions from the research, analyze their impact on the profession and offer insights or advice that will be useful to readers.

SUBJECT MATTER
Feature articles in the Journal generally fall into one of three categories:

*   Practical. These discuss problems encountered by most or many accountants and offer ideas or guidelines for resolving them. (See "Recovering Fees in Bankruptcy" by Gregg D. Johnson, September 88, page 66.)

*   Professional issues. These address issues facing the profession in general and the impact they could or should have. (See "Our Profession in the Year 2000: A Blueprint of the Future" by Robert Mednik, Aug. 88, page 54.)

*   Technical. These usually cover new standards or practices that will affect accountants or accounting. They are meant to explain developments and detail what effect they will have. (See "The Auditor's New Guide to Errors, Irregularities and Illegal Acts" by D.R. Carmichael, Sept. 88, page 40.

The Journal also accepts articles for its regular departments. These should be short, service-oriented pieces that offer practical, hands-on information. They are particularly useful when based on the author's own experience.

STYLE
Articles should be concise and clear. Keep sentences short and simple. If technical jargon or complicated terms must be used, follow them with brief explanations for those unfamiliar with the subject.

Introductory paragraphs should indicate what the article is about and why the reader should be interested in it. When essential, background information on the topic should be included here. The rest of the article should relate to subjects mentioned in the introduction.

Feature articles should be a maximum of 2,500 words (10 double-spaced, typed pages): department pieces, a maximum of 1,000 words (4 double-spaced, typed pages).

Authors should include manuscripts a separate brief description of one or two most important points they would like readers to take away from the article.

Feature articles should be accompanied by an executive summary. These are short pieces (150-200 words) that will be run in boxes with features. They are meant to give readers a glimpse of what the article is about and to highlight its main points.

Essential references should be woven into the narrative; do not use footnotes.

MANUSCRIPT REQUIREMENTS
Manuscripts should be typewritten, double spaced and on one side of the paper. If possible, five copies should be submitted to facilitate the reviewing process.

The Journal has computer hardware and software that enable us to process accepted manuscripts electronically. We have a Wang VS/Wang PC system. A manuscript prepared on a Wang 5-1/4 inch double-sided, double-density diskette either in OIS Wang Word Processing or in Wang PC Word Processing is the easiest for us to process. We also can read and convert manuscripts written on Multimate, Wordstar, WordPerfect or Displaywrite programs into ASCII text on a 5-1/4 inch double-sided, double-density diskette also are acceptable.

We encourage authors to submit manuscript on diskette. If a manuscript is rejected, the diskette will be returned.

THE EDITORIAL AND REVIEW PROCESS
The Journal uses editorial advisers and a board of consultants to assist the editors in selecting high quality material for publication. The group of advisers consists of about 45 professionals with broad experience. This group includes public accounting practitioners from firms of varying sizes, accountants in industry and education, and those with particular expertise in various accounting specialties.

Manuscripts submitted to the Journal are acknowledged by the editors and forwarded to reviewers. They read manuscripts and return them to the editors with their evaluations and recommendations. The elements considered include readability, technical soundness, originality and interest to readers. The review process generally takes eight weeks. Reviewers are asked to make one of three recommendations.

Reviewers may favor publication, suggest that an article be revised before it is published, or recommend that an article not be published. All manuscripts receive a careful, judicious review and every effort is made to assist the author in revising and editing a manuscript if, in the opinion of the reviewers, it would contribute to accounting literature.

Once an article is accepted for publication, it is assigned to a Journal editor. That editor contacts the author to discuss the manuscript and any recommended changes. After all revisions have been made, the article is edited to conform to Journal style. The author is sent a final, edited manuscript for review and final approval. The article should not be rewritten at this time, but authors should make essential changes. The article then goes into Journal inventory until it is selected. Authors are informed by mail when a definite publication date has been set.

Regrettably, there is no provision in the Journal's budget for payment of honoraria for published articles. However, as a token of appreciation, authors of feature articles receive a specially bound copy of the issue containing their article as well as ten copies of the issue.

JOURNAL OF ACCOUNTING & ECONOMICS

ADDRESS FOR SUBMISSION :

R.BALL, R.L.WATTS, J.L. ZIMMERMAN, EDS.
JOURNAL OF ACCOUNTING & ECONOMICS
UNIVERSITY OF ROCHESTER
WILLIAM E. SIMON GRADUATE SCHOOL OF
  BUSINESS ADMINISTRATION
ROCHESTER, NY 14627
716-275-4063
716-442-6323 (Fax)
E-Mail : pratt@mail.ssb.rochester.edu

CIRCULATION DATA :

Reader : Academic

Frequency of Issue : Quarterly

Copies Per Issue : 1001-2000

Subscription Price : 70.00 US$

Sponsorship : Profit Oriented Corp.

PUBLICATION GUIDELINES :

Manuscript Length : 20+

Copies Required : Four

Computer Submission : Yes

Format : MS-DOS/PC-DOS OR Macintosh

Fees to Review : 180.00 US$
  Subscriber 150.00 US$

REVIEW INFORMATION :

Type of Review : Blind Review

No. of External Reviewers : One

No. of In House Reviewers : Zero

Acceptance Rate : 11-20%

Time To Review : 1-2 months

Reviewer's Comments : Yes

Fees to Publish : 0.00 US$

Invited Articles : 5% or less

MANUSCRIPT TOPICS : ACCOUNTING INFORMATION SYSTEMS;
  ACCOUNTING THEORY & PRACTICE; AUDITING; COST ACCOUNTING;
  GOVERNMENT & NON-PROFIT ACCOUNTING; TAX ACCOUNTING

PUBLICATION GUIDELINES :

MANUSCRIPT GUIDELINES/COMMENTS :

AIMS AND SCOPE:
The JOURNAL OF ACCOUNTING AND ECONOMICS encourages the application of economic
theory to the explanation of accounting phenomena. The theories of the firm,
public choice, government regulation, and agency theory, in addition to
financial economics, can contribute significantly to increasing our
understanding of accounting. The JAE provides a forum for the publication of
the highest quality manuscripts which employ economic analyses of accounting
problems. A wide range of methodologies are encouraged and covered: the
determination of accounting standards, government regulation of corporate
disclosure, the information content and role of accounting numbers in capital
markets, the role of accounting in financial contracts and in monitoring
agency relationships, the theory of the accounting firm, government regulation
of the accounting profession, statistical sampling and the loss function in
auditing, and the role of accounting within the firm (managerial accounting).

SUBMISSION FEE:
A submission fee is used to encourage quicker response from the referees who are paid a nominal fee if they return the manuscript within three weeks. The submission fee of $150 must accompany all manuscripts submitted by authors who currently subscribe to the JOURNAL OF ACCOUNTING AND ECONOMICS and $180 for non-subscribers. The submission fee will be refunded for all accepted manuscripts (unless it was previously waived). There are no page charges. Cheques should be made payable to the JOURNAL OF ACCOUNTING AND ECONOMICS and must be in U.S. currency.

INSTRUCTIONS TO AUTHORS
(1) Papers must be in English.

(2) Papers for publication should be sent in triplicate to:
       Professors Ray Ball, Ross L. Watts or Jerold L. Zimmerman
       William E. Simon Graduate School of Business Administration
       University of Rochester, Rochester, NY 14627, USA

Submission of paper will be held to imply that it contains original unpublished work and is not being submitted for publication elsewhere. The Editors do not accept responsibility for damage or loss of papers submitted. Upon acceptance of an article, author(s) will be asked to transfer copyright of the article to the publisher. This transfer will ensure the widest possible dissemination of information.

(3) Submission of accepted papers as ELECTRONIC MANUSCRIPTS, i.e., on disk with acccompanying manuscript, is encouraged. Electronic manuscripts have the advantage that there is no need for rekeying of text, thereby avoiding the possibility of introducing errors and resulting in reliable and fast delivery of proofs. The preferred storage medium is a 5.25 or 3.5 inch disk in MS-DOS format, although other systems are welcome, e.g., Macintosh (in this case, save your file in the usual manner; do not use the option "save in MS-DOS format"). Do not submit your original paper as electronic manuscript but hold on to the disk until asked for this by the Editor (in case your paper is accepted without revisions). So submit the accepted version of your paper as electronic manuscript. Make absolutely sure that the file on the disk and the printout are identical. Please use a new and correctly formatted disk and label this with your name; also specify the software and hardware used as well as the title of the file to be processed. Do not convert the file to plain ASCII. Ensure that the letter "l" and digit "1", and also the letter "O" and digit "0" are used properly, and format your article (tabs, indents, etc.) consistently. Characters not available on your word processor (Greek letters, mathematical symbols, etc.) should not be left open but indicated by a unique code (e.g., gralpha, <alpha>, @, etc., for the Greek letter a). Such codes should be used consistently throughout the entire text; a list of codes used should accompany the electronic manuscript. Do not allow your word processor to introduce word breaks and do not use a justified layout. Please adhere strictly to the general instructions below on style, arrangement, and, in particular, the reference style of the journal.

(4) Manuscripts should double-spaced with wide margins and printed on one side of the paper only. All pages should be numbered consecutively. Titles and subtitles should be short. References, tables and legends for figures should be printed on separate pages.

(5) The first page of the manuscript should contain the following information: i. the title; ii. the names(s) and institutional affiliation(s) of the author(s); iii. an abstract of not more than 100 words. A footnote on the same sheet should give the name, address, telephone and fax numbers of the corresponding author.

(6) The first page of the manuscript should also contain at least one classification code according to the Classification System for Journal Articles as used by the JOURNAL OF ECONOMIC LITERATURE; in addition, up to five key words should be supplied.

(7) Acknowledgements and information on grants received can be given in a first footnote, which should not be included in the consecutive numbering of footnotes.

(8) Footnotes should be kept to a minimum and numbered consecutively throughout the text with superscript Arabic numerals. They should be double spaced and not include displayed formulae or tables.

(9) Displayed formulae should be numbered consecutively throughout the manuscript as (1), (2), etc. on the right-hand margin of the page. In cases where the derivation of formulae has been abbreviated it is of great help to referees if the full derivation can be presented on a separate sheet (not to be published).

(10) References to publications should be as follows: "Smith (1992) reported that..." or "This problem has been studied previously (e.g., Smith et al., 1969)". The author should make sure that there is a strict one-to-one correspondence between the names and years in the text and those on the list. The list of references should appear at the end of the main test (after any appendices, but before tables and legends for figures). It should be double spaced and listed in alphabetical order by author's name. References should appear as follows:

For monographs
Hawawini, G. and I. Swary, 1990, Mergers and acquisitions in the U.S. banking industry: Evidence from the capital markets (North-Holland, Amsterdam).

For contributions to collective works
Brunner, K. and A.H. Meltzer, 1990, Money supply, in: B.M. Friedman and F.H. Hahn, eds., handbook of monetary economics, Vol. 1 (North-Holland, Amsterdam) 357-396.

For periodicals
Griffiths, W. and G. Judge, 1992, Testing and estimating location vectors when the error covariance matrix is unknown, Journal of Econometrics 54, 121-138.

Note that journal titles should not be abbreviated.

(11) Illustrations will be reproduced photographically from originals supplied by the author; they will not be redrawn by the publisher. Please provide all illustrations in QUADRUPLICATE (one high-contrast original and three photocopies). Care should be taken that lettering and symbols are of a comparable size. The illustrations should not be inserted in the text, and should be marked on the back with figure number, title of paper, and author's

name. All graphs and diagrams should be referred to as figures and should be numbered consecutively in the text in Arabic numerals. Illustrations for papers submitted as electronic manuscripts should be in traditional form.

(12) Tables should be numbered consecutively in the text in Arabic numerals and printed on separate sheets.

Any manuscript which does not conform to the above instructions may be returned for the necessary revision before publication.

Page proofs will be sent to the corresponding author. Proofs should be corrected carefully; the responsibility for detecting errors lies with the author. Corrections should be restricted to instances in which the proof is at variance with the manuscript. Extensive alterations will be charged. Twenty-five reprints of each paper are supplied free of charge to the corresponding author; additional reprints are available at cost if they are ordered when the proof is returned.

NOTES FOR ELECTRONIC TEXT PREPARATION

1. GENERAL
The word-processed text should be in single column format. Keep the layout of the text as simple as possible; in particular, do not use the word-processor's options to justify the text or to hypenate the words.

2. TEXT PREPARATION
The electronic text should be prepared in a way very similar to that of coventional manuscripts (see also Guide for Authors). The list of references, tables and figure legends should be compiled separately from the main text. Do NOT reserve space for the figures and tables in the text; instead, indicate their approximate locations, either directly in the electronic text or on the manuscript.

3. SUBMISSION
The final text should be submitted both in manuscript form and on diskette. Use standard 3.5" or 5.25" diskettes for this purpose. Both double density (DD) and high density (HD) diskettes are acceptable. Make sure, however, that the diskettes are formatted according to their capacity (HD or DD) before copying the files onto them.

It is recommended to store the main text, list of references, tables and figure legends in separate text files with clearly identifiable file names (for example, with extensions .TXT, .REF, .TBL, .FIG).

The format of the files depends on the wordprocessor used. Texts made with DEC WPS PLUS, DisplayWrite, First Choice, IBM Writing Assistant, Microsoft Word, Multimate, PFS:Write, Professional Writer, Samna Word, Sprint, TEX, Total Word, Volkswriter, Wang PC, Word-MARC, WordPerfect, Wordstar, or files supplied in DCA/RFT format can be readily processed. In all other cases the preferred text format is ASCII.

Essential is that name and version of the wordprocessing program and the type of computer on which the text was prepared is clearly indicated on the diskette label or the accompanying checklist.

JOURNAL OF ACCOUNTING & ECONOMICS

The manuscript may contain parts (e.g. formulas or complex tables) or
last-minute corrections which are not included in the text on diskette;
however, if this is the case then the differences with the diskette version
should be clearly marked on the manuscript.

Illustrative material (original figures or high-quality glossy prints, or
photographs showing a sharp contrast) should be included separately.

ELECTRONIC TEXT CHECKLIST

Please complete this list where appropriate and include it with the diskette.

Journal: _____
Title: _____
Author(s): _____

COMPUTER   WORDPROCESSOR

_ IBM compatible   _ DEC WPS PLUS (2)   version:_____
_ Macintosh (1)   _ DisplayWrite (3)   version:_____
                                      _ First Choice   version:_____
DISKETTE   _ IBM Writing Assistant version:_____
                                      _ Microsoft Word   version:_____
_ formatted with MS-DOS/PC-DOS   _ Multimate   version:_____
_ formatted with Macintosh OS   _ PFS:Write   version:_____
                                      _ Professional Writer   version:_____
                                      _ Samna Word   version:_____
                                      _ Sprint   version:_____
                                      _ TEX   version:_____
                                      _ Total Word   version:_____
                                      _ Volkswriter   version:_____
FILE FORMAT (if different from   _ Wang PC   version:_____
 wordprocessor's original format)   _ WordMARC   version:_____
                                      _ WordPerfect   version:_____
_ ASCII   _ Wordstar   version:_____
_ DCA/RFT
_ DEC/DX   _ Other (specify) (4)_____

Diskette contents: _____
                   _____
Remarks: _____
         _____

(1) In view of the further text processing on a MS-DOS compatible system
submission of text files on MS-DOS formatted diskettes is recommended.

(2) Files should be submitted in DX format (option "CV" from the DEC-WPS
Document Processing Menu).

(3) Files created with DisplayWrite 4 should be submitted in DCA/RFT format by
means of the Display Write "Convert Documents" utility.

(4) Submission of the text files in ASCII format is strongly recommended.

JOURNAL OF ACCOUNTING AND COMPUTERS

ADDRESS FOR SUBMISSION :

WILLILAM J. READ, PROFESSOR, MG.ED.
JOURNAL OF ACCOUNTING AND COMPUTERS
BENTLEY COLLEGE
DEPARTMENT OF ACCOUNTANCY
WALTHAM, MA 02154-4705
USA
617-891-2525
617-891-2896 (Fax)
E-Mail : wread@bentley.edu

CIRCULATION DATA :

Reader : Academic

Frequency of Issue : 1 Times/Year

Copies Per Issue : 4001-5000

Subscription Price :

Sponsorship : Profit Oriented Corp.

PUBLICATION GUIDELINES :

Manuscript Length : 11-15

Copies Required : Four

Computer Submission : No

Format : N/A

Fees to Review : 0.00 US$

REVIEW INFORMATION :

Type of Review : Blind Review

No. of External Reviewers : Two

No. of In House Reviewers : One

Acceptance Rate : 40 %

Time To Review : 2-3 months

Reviewer's Comments : Yes

Fees to Publish : 0.00 US$

Invited Articles : 5% or less

MANUSCRIPT TOPICS : ACCOUNTING INFORMATION SYSTEMS;
   ACCOUNTING THEORY & PRACTICE; AUDITING; COST ACCOUNTING; TAX ACCOUNTING

PUBLICATION GUIDELINES : Accounting Review

MANUSCRIPT GUIDELINES/COMMENTS :

FORMAT

All manuscripts should be typed and double-spaaced on a 8-1/2 x 11" paper.
Allow a margin of at least 1 inch on all sides of a page. Number all pages,
including exhibits, consecutively. Authors should include a cover sheet
showing the title of the article and name(s) and affiliation(s) of the
author(s). In order for our blind review process to be effective, the article
title, but not the author's name, should be repeated on the page following the
cover sheet. All exhibits hsould be placed at the end of an article and
referenced for insertion at the appropraite point in the article.

An ABSTRACT of a paragraph or two should precede each article briefly
summarizing the article's contents and/or its focus or purpose.

LITERATURE REFERENCES

References to works of other authors or studies should be noted in square
brackets in the text of the article and should contain the author's name, year
of publication of the work cited, and page numbers where appropriate. For

example, [Kick and Wells, 1989] or [Benke, 1989, p. 60]. References in the text should provide sufficient information to refer the reader to the References list.

A References list should accompany the article, including all literature cited in the text as well as other relevant material. This list should appear at the end of the article and list all references in alphabetical order by the last name of the first author. Only the first initial of each author's first name is necessary.

Examples:

Nikolai, L., and j. Bazley, Intermediate Accounting, 4th ed. (Kent Publishing Co., 1988).
Boles, M., and T.J. Mock, "Attitudes Toward a Consulting or MAS Tract in an Accounting Curriculum", Kent/Bentley Journal, Vol. IV (Fall 1988), pp. 1-13.

FOOTNOTES should be used for notes to the textual material that are not necessary to the discussion in the text itself. Number footnotes consecutively.

SUBMISSION PROCEDURE

Submit one original and four copies of papers to the managing editor of the Journal.

Complimentary copies will be made available at conventions. Individuals can write directly to:

Marketing Department
South-Western Publishing Company
501 Madison
Cincinnati, OH 45227-1490

JOURNAL OF ACCOUNTING AND FINANCE RESEARCH

ADDRESS FOR SUBMISSION :

ROGER CALCOTE, EDITOR
JOURNAL OF ACCOUNTING AND FINANCE
  RESEARCH
AMERICAN ACADEMY OF ACCOUNTING & FINANCE
220 OLIVER DRIVE
BROOKHAVEN, MS 39601
601-833-9741
E-Mail :pfuller@ccaix.jsums.edu

Change in Editor's Address
  May Occur in : 01/27/01

CIRCULATION DATA :

Reader : Academic

Frequency of Issue : Quarterly

Copies Per Issue : Less than 1000

Subscription Price : 135.00 US$

Sponsorship : Professional Assoc.

PUBLICATION GUIDELINES :

Manuscript Length : 11-15

Copies Required : Three

Computer Submission : No

Format : N/A

Fees to Review : 180.00 US$
  If Attend AAAFR Meet 90.00 US$

REVIEW INFORMATION :

Type of Review : Blind Review

No. of External Reviewers : Two

No. of In House Reviewers : Two

Acceptance Rate : 21-30%

Time To Review : 2-3 months

Reviewer's Comments : Yes

Fees to Publish : 0.00 US$

Invited Articles : 5% or less

MANUSCRIPT TOPICS : ACCOUNTING INFORMATION SYSTEMS;
  ACCOUNTING INFORMATION SYSTEMS; ACCOUNTING THEORY & PRACTICE; AUDITING;
  CAPITAL BUDGETING; COST ACCOUNTING; GOVERNMENT & NON-PROFIT ACCOUNTING;
  INSURANCE; INTERNATIONAL FINANCE; PORTFOLIO & SECURITY ANALYSIS;
  REAL ESTATE; TAX ACCOUNTING; PERSONAL FINANCE

PUBLICATION GUIDELINES :

MANUSCRIPT GUIDELINES/COMMENTS :

Associate Editor: Philip Fuller, DBA

The JOURNAL OF ACCOUNTING AND FINANCE RESEARCH is the official publication of
the American Academy of Accounting and Finance. The Journal is published
semiannually and will begin quarterly publication with Volume 2 in the Spring
of 1996.

Papers published in The Journal were presented at a previous annual meeting of
the Academy and went through a review process. Only papers presented at the
Academy's annual meeting and published in the proceedings of the annual
meeting are considered for The Journal. Unsolicited manuscripts are not
accepted.

The Academy's annual meeting is held in New Orleans, Louisiana during the
first or second week of December.

JOURNAL OF ACCOUNTING AND FINANCE RESEARCH

Requests for information about the Academy, The Journal or the annual meeting should be sent to American Academy of Accounting and Finance, 220 Oliver Dr., Brookhaven, MS 39601, USA.

FORMAT INSTRUCTIONS
All instructions that follow are mandatory for the final copy of your paper that you will submit by March 1, 1997. These instructions are laidout in the format you should use. We are following the style of Accounting Horizons, generally.

TITLE
The title should be in CG Times (Scalable) size 16 font, all capital letters, centered at the top of the first page, and beginning on or near the 1.50" line. Titles of more than one line should be single spaced.

AUTHORS
The author(s), name(s) and affiliation(s) should be centered and single spaced, beginning on the second line below the title. Do not use titles such as Dr. or Assistant Professor, etc. Use CG Times (Scalable) size 14 font. The rest of the paper should be in CG Times (Scalable) size 12 font.

HEADINGS
All headings should be in bold type. First-level headings should be centered and set in all caps. Second-level headings should be set flush left with initial caps. Do not use headings other than these two. Separate headings from preceding and succeeding text by one line space.

ABSTRACT
Introduce the paper with an abstract of approximately 150-200 words. Begin in the left column with the first-level heading, "ABSTRACT."

BODY
The body of the paper should be single spaced and should follow the abstract. Use a first-level heading of some type after the abstract and before the first paragraph of the body of the paper to separate the two.

Figures and Tables
Figures and tables should be placed either "in-column" or at the top of the page as close as possible to where they are cited. First-level headings state the table or figure number and may be followed by second-level subheadings. A sample of a full page table is shown at the top of the next page and a sample of an "in-column" table follows.

TABLE I		
Margins		
Column	Left	Right
1	1.00	7.50
Space Between Columns .5		

Scalable fonts smaller than CG 12 may used be to fit a table "in-column" provided, in the authors opinion, the data is still legible.

JOURNAL OF ACCOUNTING AND FINANCE RESEARCH

TABLE 2
Checklist for Papers

___ Prepare using WordPerfect (any version)
___ Submit disk copy on 3.5" disk (final version only)
___ Submit four (4) hard copies printed on 300 dot per inch (minimum) laser printer
___ Use CG Times (Scalable), size 12 font (or the nearest thing to it available on your laser printer) for the body of the paper
___ Title of paper: All caps, bold type, single-spaced, centered across both columns. Use CG Times (Scalable), size 16 font
___ Authors: include affiliations. Use CG Times (Scalable), size 14 font
___ Headings: Only two allowed; 1st level, all caps, centered, bold; 2nd level, initial caps, flush left, bold
___ Scale tables and figures to avoid use of paste, glue, or tape
___ Lay-out: two columns, except for title, authors, and tables and figures

___ Margins:	Top	Bottom	Column	Left	Right
	0.875"	0.75"	1	1.00"	4.00"
			2	4.50	7.50

___ Headers: Include a blank two-line header on each page
___ Page numbers: Do not type in; lightly pencil on back of pages
___ Number of pages: Limited to 15
___ Submit the final version of your paper by March 1, 1997.

CALLING REFERENCES
Use Accounting Horizons style for calling references.

FOOTNOTES
The use of footnotes is strongly discouraged.

EQUATIONS
All equations should be place on a separate line and numbered consecutively, with the equation numbers placed within parentheses and aligned against the right margin.

$$R_i = f(X_i) \qquad\qquad\qquad (1)$$

REFERENCES (BIBLIOGRAPHY)
Since the bibliography should only include those references cited in the paper, it should be referred to as "REFERENCES", a first-level heading. References should be listed at the end of the paper and follow ACCOUNTING HORIZON style.

APPENDICES
Appendices should immediately follow the body of the paper, precede the references, and should be referred to as "APPENDIX", a first-level heading. If you have more than one appendix, number each consecutively with a second-level heading.

TYPING AND PRINTING INSTRUCTIONS

WORD PROCESSING SOFTWARE AND TYPE SIZE
Papers are to be prepared using WordPerfect (any version through 6.1) and submitted on a 3.5" disk as well as four (4) in laser-printed, hard-copy. The

JOURNAL OF ACCOUNTING AND FINANCE
RESEARCH

preferred type is "CG Times (Scalable) size 12. This document is prepared in that type. If not available on your laser printer, please use the type font that most closely matches this.

LAYOUT AND MARGINS
Except for the title and author(s) information, papers are to be laid out using WordPerfect's Balanced Newspaper Column feature. Set the column margins as follows:

Column	Left	Right
1	1.00	4.00
2	4.50	7.50

All paragraphs should be indented 0.3". Set the top and bottom margins of the paper at 0.875" and 0.75" respectively. Use 'Full Justification' and be sure to turn WordPerfect's hyphenation feature on to obtain reasonable appearing spacing. Do not skip a line between paragraphs

SPACING
Single space the body of the paper. Double space before and after all headings. Triple space after the last authors' name preceding the abstract heading.

PAGE NUMBERS
Don't type in page numbers. Keep pages in sequence and lightly pencil in the page number on the back of each page.

HEADERS
Include a blank two-line header in CG Scale 12 on each page after the title page. Failure to include the blank header will affect pagination and can result in the return of your paper for correction.

JOURNAL OF ACCOUNTING AND PUBLIC POLICY

ADDRESS FOR SUBMISSION :

LAWRENCE GORDON & STEPHEN LOEB, EDITORS
JOURNAL OF ACCOUNTING AND PUBLIC
  POLICY
UNIVERSITY OF MARYLAND
COLLEGE OF BUSINESS & MANAGEMENT
COLLEGE PARK, MD 20742
USA
301-405-2255 OR 2207
301-314-9157 (Fax)
E-Mail : SLOEB@BMGTMAIL.UMD.EDU

CIRCULATION DATA :

Reader : Academic

Frequency of Issue : Quarterly

Copies Per Issue :

Subscription Price :

Sponsorship : Profit Oriented Corp.

PUBLICATION GUIDELINES :

Manuscript Length : No Limit

Copies Required : Three

Computer Submission : No

Format : N/A

Fees to Review : 0.00 US$

REVIEW INFORMATION :

Type of Review : N/A

No. of External Reviewers : Two

No. of In House Reviewers :

Acceptance Rate : 11-20%

Time To Review : 2-3 months

Reviewer's Comments : Yes

Fees to Publish : 0.00 US$

Invited Articles :

MANUSCRIPT TOPICS : ACCOUNTING INFORMATION SYSTEMS;
  ACCOUNTING THEORY & PRACTICE; AUDITING; CAPITAL BUDGETING; COST ACCOUNTING;
  GOVERNMENT & NON-PROFIT ACCOUNTING; TAX ACCOUNTING

PUBLICATION GUIDELINES : Chicago Manual of Style

MANUSCRIPT GUIDELINES/COMMENTS :

All manuscripts should be submitted to the Editors. Manuscripts are submitted with the understanding that they are original, unpublished works and are not being submitted elsewhere.

MANUSCRIPT. Submit the original and three photocopies of the manuscript, typed double-spaced on 8-1/2 X 11 in. bond paper. On the title page include names and addresses of authors, academic or professional affiliations, and the complete address of the author to whom proofs and reprint requests should be sent. Also provide a running title of less than 45 characters and spaces, which will appear on alternate pages in the journal. Include an Abstract and a list of Key Words that best code the contents of the article for indexing purposes. The text proper begins on the following page and ends with a citation of acknowledgments, whenever appropriate. References, tabular material, figure captions, and footnotes follow. Tables and figures are numbered in order of their appearance with Arabic numerals, and each should have a brief descriptive title. Footnotes to the text are numbered consecutively with superior Arabic numerals.

JOURNAL OF ACCOUNTING AND PUBLIC POLICY

MATHEMATICAL NOTATION. Use typewritten letters, numbers, and symbols whenever possible. Identify boldface, script letters, etc. at their first occurrence. Distinguish between one and the letter "l" and between zero and the letter "o" whenever confusion might result.

REFERENCES. Citation in the text is by name(s) of author(s), followed by year of publication in parentheses. For references authored by more than two contributors use first author's name and et al. For multiple citations in the same year use a, b, c after year of publication.

ILLUSTRATIONS. Unmounted, glossy, black and white photographs or India ink drawings on white paper should accompany the original copy of the manuscript. Photocopies are suitable for the other three copies of the manuscript. To facilitate identification and processing, on the back of each figure write the number, first author's name, and indicate which side is the top. Captions appear on a separate page.

PROOFS AND REPRINTS. The corresponding author will receive proofs, which should be corrected and returned within ten days of receipt. The author is responsible for proofreading the manuscript; the publisher is not responsible for any error not marked by the author on proof. Corrections on proof are limited to printer's errors; no substantial author changes are allowed at this stage. Reprints may be ordered prior to publication; consult the price list accompanying proofs.

COPYRIGHT. Upon acceptance of an article by the journal, the author(s) will be asked to transfer copyright of the article to the publisher. Elsevier Science Publishing Co., Inc. This transfer will insure the widest possible dissemination of information under the U.S. Copyright Law.

JOURNAL OF ACCOUNTING AUDITING AND FINANCE

ADDRESS FOR SUBMISSION :

JEFFREY CALLEN, EDITOR
JOURNAL OF ACCOUNTING AUDITING
   AND FINANCE
NEW YORK UNIVERSITY
STERN SCHOOL OF BUSINESS
40 WEST 4TH STREET, SUITE 312
NEW YORK, NY 10012-1118
USA
212-998-0059
212-998-4001 (Fax)
E-Mail : jcallen@stern.nyu.edu

CIRCULATION DATA :

Reader : Academic

Frequency of Issue : Quarterly

Copies Per Issue : Less than 1000

Subscription Price : 85.00 US$
   2 Years : 160.00 US$

Sponsorship : University

PUBLICATION GUIDELINES :

Manuscript Length : 20+

Copies Required : Three

Computer Submission : No

Format : N/A

Fees to Review : 50.00 US$

REVIEW INFORMATION :

Type of Review : Blind Review

No. of External Reviewers : One

No. of In House Reviewers : One

Acceptance Rate : 5% or less

Time To Review : 2-3 months

Reviewer's Comments : Yes

Fees to Publish : 0.00 US$

Invited Articles : 5% or less

MANUSCRIPT TOPICS : ACCOUNTING INFORMATION SYSTEMS;
   ACCOUNTING THEORY & PRACTICE; AUDITING; CAPITAL BUDGETING; COST ACCOUNTING;
   ECONOMETRICS; ECONOMIC HISTORY; GOVERNMENT & NON-PROFIT ACCOUNTING;
   INSURANCE; INTERNATIONAL & ECONOMIC DEVELOPMENT; INTERNATIONAL FINANCE;
   PORTFOLIO & SECURITY ANALYSIS; PUBLIC POLICY ECONOMICS; REAL ESTATE;
   TAX ACCOUNTING

PUBLICATION GUIDELINES :

MANUSCRIPT GUIDELINES/COMMENTS :

1. Under new editorship, the JOURNAL OF ACCOUNTING, AUDITING, AND
FINANCE(JAAF) has a new orientation. High quality, academic refereed articles
will be accompanied by non-academic renderings of accepted manuscripts, and
published simultaneously. These will be written in less technical language
and directed to the practitioner.

2. The Journal will consider papers covering a broad spectrum of topics in
finance. These may include, but not necessarily be restricted to, analytical
or empirical contributions in areas such as theories of market equilibrium,
concepts of "efficient markets", normative or descriptive theories of
financial management, and investment decisions under uncertainty.

3. A serious attempt will be made to process manuscripts promptly. Upon
acceptance of a paper, the author will be asked to provide a concise,

non-academic version, describing the research problem, design, methodology, results and implications for practitioners. A professional editor will be available to assist the author in editing and styling the abbreviated version. As a result, the work will be read by both academic peers and a wide audience of practitioners, the latter typically not having been exposed to research written in technical, academic language. Thus, the condensed version will provide the critical bridge between the academic and professional communities.

4. Three copies of each manuscript should be submitted to: Joshua Ronen, Editor, Journal of Accounting, Auditing, and Finance, Vincent C. Ross Institute of Accounting Research, New York University - Schools of Business, 300 Tisch Hall, 40 West Fourth Street, New York, NY 10012.

5. Use only 8-1/2" x 11" white bond paper. Do not use "erasable" paper. All manuscript copy, including text, footnotes, charts, quotations, etc., must be typed double-spaced, on one side of the paper only.

6. Sources of material should be numbered in brackets consecutively in the text throughout the article, starting with (1). These references are to be typed on a separate page entitled "References" at the end of the manuscript. Minor changes should be made between the lines of the typescript, not in the margins. That is, typographical errors and slight corrections of the text or footnotes may be written (please print) on the manuscript in pen. If corrections are lengthy or complex, retype the entire manuscript page.

7. Illustrations accompanying manuscripts should be numbered, provided with suitable legends (again, typed double-spaced on 8-1/2 x 11" sheets), and market lightly in pencil on the back, with the name of the author and the title of the article. Illustrations such as original drawings or graphs are to be drawn in black India ink. Typewritten or freehand lettering is not acceptable. All lettering must be done professionally. Do not staple or paper clip illustrations. Put all illustrations between sheets of cardboard before mailing, to prevent folds. Tables and exhibits should be numbered consecutively. Center main headings within the article, type secondary headings flush with the left-hand margin.

8. A strong effort should be made to keep the punctuation simple. Most authors overuse parentheses, italics and quotation marks which are simply edited out in the publication process.

9. If an article includes any previously copyrighted material (other than short quotation), the publisher must have letters of permission to reprint from the copyright holder and from the author if he or she is not the copyright holder. These letters must be submitted at the same time as the manuscript.

10. The Journal normally publishes articles only if they have not yet appeared or been accepted for publication elsewhere. There is generally no objection, however, to having articles that appear in the Journal reprinted in other publications at a later date, if appropriate permission is requested from the publisher at that time.

11. Authors of accepted papers will be furnished with copies of the issue in which their paper appears.

JOURNAL OF ACCOUNTING CASE RESEARCH

ADDRESS FOR SUBMISSION :

ELDON GARDNER, EDITOR
JOURNAL OF ACCOUNTING CASE RESEARCH
UNIVERSITY OF LETHBRIDGE
ACCOUNTING EDUCATION RESOURCE CENTRE
4401 UNIVERSITY DRIVE
LETHBRIDGE, ALBERTA, T1K 3M4
CANADA
403-329-2726
403-329-2038 (Fax)
E-Mail : gardej@cetus.Mngt.Uleth.Ca

CIRCULATION DATA :

Reader : Academic

Frequency of Issue : 2 Times/Year

Copies Per Issue : Less than 1000

Subscription Price : 60.00 US$

Sponsorship : Professional Assoc.

PUBLICATION GUIDELINES :

Manuscript Length : Any

Copies Required : Five

Computer Submission : No

Format : N/A

Fees to Review : 0.00 US$

REVIEW INFORMATION :

Type of Review : Blind Review

No. of External Reviewers : Two

No. of In House Reviewers : Zero

Acceptance Rate : 21-30%

Time To Review : 2-3 months

Reviewer's Comments : Yes

Fees to Publish : 60.00 US$
    Subscriber   0.00 US$

Invited Articles : 5% or less

MANUSCRIPT TOPICS : ACCOUNTING INFORMATION SYSTEMS;
   ACCOUNTING THEORY & PRACTICE; CAPITAL BUDGETING; COST ACCOUNTING;
   ECONOMETRICS; GOVERNMENT & NON-PROFIT ACCOUNTING; TAX ACCOUNTING

PUBLICATION GUIDELINES :

MANUSCRIPT GUIDELINES/COMMENTS :

EDITORIAL POLICY
The JOURNAL OF ACCOUNTING CASE RESEARCH publishes cases on accounting and
related topics, and educational manuscripts related to the use of case
materials in accounting. Cases and Teaching Notes should be separated, and
notes and references should appear at the end of the manuscript double-spaced
manuscripts, on one side of the paper only, submitted with a diskette in
WordPerfect (5.1, 5.2 or 6.0) containing all of the case material and teaching
notes, are requested.

Cases submitted for review should have a separate title page with names and
affiliations of all authors thereon. No names or references to the individuals
involved in writing the case should be contained in the manuscript itself.

Cases should have a clear set of issues on which decisions are required, and
they should be well written in the English or French language. Any exhibits,
tables, graphs or charts should be prepared in camera-ready form on separate
pages, preferably in WordPerfect 5.1 or 6.0 compatible form. A detailed

teaching note is required, including some indication of courses in accounting for which the case is suitable; classroom format; other possible areas of use for the case; issues for discussion; directions for analysis, and any background material that would be relevant or appropriate for the case.

All cases submitted for review should be available for publication without restriction, unless a sponsoring agency (such as a research funding agency or post-secondary educational institution) also holds a copyright. Under such circumstances, the agency should be willing to allow publication in the JOURNAL OF ACCOUNTING CASE RESEARCH, subject to minimal restrictions on use by subscribers.

Cases submitted for review should be accompanied by a forwarding letter that contains either or both of the following, as applicable:

1. The source of the material and the authorization of the provider of the material for publication of the case in the JOURNAL OF ACCOUNTING CASE RESEARCH by the Accounting Education Resource Centre.
2. A statement that any other material not provided by a specific source, as in (1), has been obtained from fictional or public domain sources, and that no copyrighted material has been used without permission.

It is the policy of the journal to have a minimum of two blind reviews, by qualified academic and/or professional reviewers, of all materials considered for publication. Reviewers are provided with guidelines by the Centre, and their recommendations are given a careful and thorough consideration in publication decisions. The ultimate decision on publication, however, rests with the Editor and the Management Board of the Centre.

The copyright on all published cases will be held by the Accounting Education Resource Centre jointly with the author unless otherwise stated. Publication in other venues will be allowed by the journal if permission is requested in writing and a suitable royalty arrangement (if applicable) is made.

The following note is placed at the bottom of the first page of any case accepted for publication:

> This case was prepared by John Doe of the University of Big City, Big City, State, County as the basis for class discussion rather than to illustrate either effective or ineffective handling of a managerial situation. Distributed by the Accounting Education Resource Centre, The University of Lethbridge, ⓐ 199x. All rights reserved to the author and to the Accounting Education Resource Centre. Permission to use the case in classes of instruction, without restriction is provided to subscribers of the journal unless otherwise stated.

SUBMISSION OF CASES
Five copies of cases and articles should be submitted (with teaching notes where applicable) to the Editor. Facsimile copies are not acceptable for publication, but authors may submit a copy in this manner for preliminary consideration by the editor.

Previously published material, or materials under review for publication elsewhere are not acceptable. Materials presented to workshops or in Proceedings are not construed to be previously published.

JOURNAL OF ACCOUNTING CASE RESEARCH

THERE IS NO SUBMISSION FEE FOR SUBSCRIBERS TO THE JOURNAL OF ACCOUNTING CASE RESEARCH. NON-SUBSCRIBERS ARE REQUIRED TO PAY THE ANNUAL SUBSCRIPTION FEE, OR DEMONSTRATE THAT IT HAS BEEN PAID, PRIOR TO REVIEW OF MATERIALS SUBMITTED.

It is the intention of the Centre to continue the bi-annual Accounting Case Writing Competitions. Deadlines for submission in even numbered years will be announced in the journal and in other appropriate venues. Prizes ($2000-first, $1,000-second, $500-third) for the next competition will be announced in 1996 through the journal and through advertisements sent to interested parties. Cases submitted after April 30, 1996 and before the next deadline will be considered by the Centre as entrants for the next competition at the discretion of the authors.

All manuscripts will be reviewed regardless of intents to enter the competition. Entrants to the competition and all other authors will be advised of the reviewers' comments as soon as possible, but these comments and any other amendments will not be considered by the judges. Normal turn-around time will be about three months.

For manuscript submissions and case copyright information, contact the Editor.

JOURNAL OF ACCOUNTING EDUCATION

ADDRESS FOR SUBMISSION :

KENT ST. PIERRE, EDITOR
JOURNAL OF ACCOUNTING EDUCATION
UNIVERSITY OF DELAWARE
COLLEGE OF BUSINESS ECONOMICS
DEPARTMENT OF ACCOUNTING
NEWARK, DE 19716-2715
USA
302-831-1793
302-831-6750 (Fax)
E-Mail : KENT.STPIERRE@MVS.UDEL.EDU

CIRCULATION DATA :

Reader : Academic

Frequency of Issue : Quarterly

Copies Per Issue : 1001-2000

Subscription Price : 72.00 US$

Sponsorship : Profit Oriented Corp.

PUBLICATION GUIDELINES :

Manuscript Length : None Required

Copies Required : Four

Computer Submission : No

Format : N/A

Fees to Review : 0.00 US$

REVIEW INFORMATION :

Type of Review : Blind Review

No. of External Reviewers : Three

No. of In House Reviewers : Zero

Acceptance Rate : 11-20%

Time To Review : 4-6 months

Reviewer's Comments : Yes

Fees to Publish : 0.00 US$

Invited Articles : 5% or less

MANUSCRIPT TOPICS : ACCOUNTING INFORMATION SYSTEMS;
   ACCOUNTING THEORY & PRACTICE; AUDITING; COST ACCOUNTING;
   GOVERNMENT & NON-PROFIT ACCOUNTING; TAX ACCOUNTING;
   THE ABOVE TOPICS WITH EDUCATION FOCUS

PUBLICATION GUIDELINES :

MANUSCRIPT GUIDELINES/COMMENTS :

1. The JOURNAL OF ACCOUNTING EDUCATION (JAEd) is a refereed journal dedicated
to promoting excellence in teaching and stimulating research in accounting
education. The Journal provides a forum for exchanging ideas, opinions, and
research results among accounting educators in community colleges, four-year
colleges and universities and graduate institutions.

2. The JAEd has three sections: A Main Section, a Teaching and Educational
Notes Section and a Case Section. Articles in the Main Section presents
in-depth analyses of the topics discussed. The Teaching and Educational Notes
section is designed to further the goal of providing a forum. This section
contains short papers with information of interest to readers of the JAEd.
The Case Section contains cases for classroom use.

3. All manuscripts are sent to an associate editor who selects two reviewers
for a blind review. The reviewers use three criteria for evaluating papers:
    1. readability;   2. relevance; and   3. reliability.

JOURNAL OF ACCOUNTING EDUCATION

The evaluation for readability is two-fold. First, it is necessary to ensure that the paper can be readily understood by accounting educators involved in the area discussed in the paper. References should not impede the flow of the paper, and unnecessary or obscure jargon should not be used. The details of the statistical methodology should be in the body of the paper. The statistical methodology is necessary for the review, but may not be published with the paper.

4. Worthy papers are reviewed twice for grammar; once before the reviewers receive it and a second time prior to publication. It is preferred that a paper be examined closely by a grammarian before it is submitted for review. Poor readability can impede the ability of a reviewer to evaluate the contribution of a paper, and may lead to rejection. All papers accepted for publication in the JAEd must have a high level of readability.

The second criterion is relevance. A paper is relevant if it has the potential to influence the process of educating accounting students. A paper that appeals to a broad spectrum of JAEd readers or is unique or innovative has a better probability of influencing the process of educating accounting students, and is more relevant than a paper without these features.

The third criterion is reliability. A paper is reliable if the conclusions of the paper can be reasonably inferred from the arguments. Reliability is not hard to assess when a paper is statistical or involves empirical research with which the reviewer is familiar. Authors can improve the probability of acceptance of a paper by including a section on the limitations of the research techniques.

5. When a paper relies on verbal analysis, reliability is harder to assess. Reviewers have to depend on their own knowledge of the subject to ensure the arguments are relevant to the question addressed and that the paper is internally consistent.

6. The heart of a quality journal is the presentation of meaningful content in readable and usable form. The staff of the JAEd is committed to ensuring these high standards.

7. Authors should send four copies of their manuscript for review. There is no review fee for subscribers. Nonsubscribers should send a check for U.S. $58.00 with their manuscript. The fee will be applied to a one-year subscription.

8. A letter to the Editor must be enclosed requesting review and possible publication; the letter must also state that the manuscript has not been previously published and is not under review for another journal. The corresponding author's address and telephone number (as well as any upcoming address change) should be included. This individual will receive all editorial correspondence.

9. Manuscripts for ALL SECTIONS should be submitted to the the Editor, Professor Kent St. Pierre, at the University of Delaware. Upon acceptance for any publication, the author(s) must complete a Transfer of Copyright Agreement form.

10. All manuscripts should be typed double-spaced on 8-1/2" x 11" bond paper.

11. The title page should list
    1. the article;
    2. the authors' names and affiliations at the time the work was conducted;
    3. corresponding authors' address and telephone number;
    4. a concise running title;
    5. an unnumbered footnote giving a complete mailing address for reprint requests; and
    6. any acknowledgements

12. An abstract should be submitted that does not exceed 150 words in length. This should be typed on a separate page following the title page.

13. Manuscripts should be carefully prepared using the PUBLICATION MANUAL OF THE AMERICAN PSYCHOLOGICAL ASSOCIATION, 3rd ed., 1983, for style. The reference section must be double-spaced and works cited must be listed. Avoid abbreviations of journal titles and incomplete information.

Sample Journal Reference:
Raymond, M.J. (1964). The treatment of addiction by aversion conditioning with apomorphine. Behaviour Research and Therapy, 3, 287-290.

Sample Book Reference:
Barlow, D.H., Hayes, S.C., & Nelson, R.O. (1984). The scientist practitioner: Research and accountability in clinical and educational settings. New York: Pergamon Press.

14. For tables and figures, do not send glossy prints, photographs or original artwork until acceptance. Copies of all tables and figures should be included with each copy of the manuscript. Upon acceptance of a manuscript for publication, original, camera-ready figures and any photographs must be submitted, unmounted and on glossy paper. Photocopies, blue ink or pencil are not acceptable. Use black India ink, and type figure legends on a separate sheet. Write the article title and figure number lightly in pencil on the back of each.

15. Authors with access to an Apple IIc, IIe, IBM-PC or compatible personal computer are encouraged to use Manuscript Manager/APA Style, a software program available from Pergamon Journals that automatically formats manuscripts according to APA requirements.

16. Page proofs of the article will be sent to the corresponding author. These should be carefully proofread. Except for typographical errors, corrections should be minimal, and rewriting the text is not permitted. Corrected page proofs must be returned within 48 hours of receipt. Along with the page proofs, the corresponding author will receive a form for ordering reprints and full copies of the issue in which the article appears. Twenty-five (25) free reprints are provided; orders for additional reprints must be received before printing in order to qualify for lower publication rates. All coauthor reprint requirements should be included on the reprint order form.

JOURNAL OF ACCOUNTING LITERATURE

ADDRESS FOR SUBMISSION :

BIPIN AJINKYA & WILLIAM MESSIER,JR., EDS
JOURNAL OF ACCOUNTING LITERATURE
UNIVERSITY OF FLORIDA
ACCOUNTING RESEARCH CENTER
GAINSEVILLE, FL 32611
USA
352-392-0155
352-392-8882 (Fax)
E-Mail : MESSIER@DALE.CBA.UFL.EDU

CIRCULATION DATA :

Reader : Business Persons &
         Academic

Frequency of Issue : 1 Times/Year

Copies Per Issue : Less than 1000

Subscription Price : 22.00 US$
  Library : 32.00 US$

Sponsorship : University

PUBLICATION GUIDELINES :

Manuscript Length : No Limit

Copies Required : Three

Computer Submission : No

Format : N/A

Fees to Review : 25.00 US$

REVIEW INFORMATION :

Type of Review : Editorial Review

No. of External Reviewers : Two

No. of In House Reviewers :

Acceptance Rate : 21-30%

Time To Review : 2-3 months

Reviewer's Comments : Yes

Fees to Publish : 0.00 US$

Invited Articles :

MANUSCRIPT TOPICS : ACCOUNTING THEORY & PRACTICE; ECONOMIC HISTORY

PUBLICATION GUIDELINES :

MANUSCRIPT GUIDELINES/COMMENTS :

JOURNAL OF ACCOUNTING RESEARCH

ADDRESS FOR SUBMISSION :

EDITOR
JOURNAL OF ACCOUNTING RESEARCH
UNIVERSITY OF CHICAGO
GRADUATE SCHOOL OF BUSINESS
CHICAGO, IL 60637
USA
312-702-7460
312-702-0458 (Fax)
E-Mail : JAR@gsb.uchicago.edu

CIRCULATION DATA :

Reader : Academic

Frequency of Issue : 3 Times/Year

Copies Per Issue : 2001-3000

Subscription Price :
  Academician/Student : 70.00 US$
  Library/Practitioner : 86.00 US$

Sponsorship :

PUBLICATION GUIDELINES :

Manuscript Length : Varies w/Topic

Copies Required : Two

Computer Submission : No

Format : N/A

Fees to Review : 50.00 US$

REVIEW INFORMATION :

Type of Review : Editorial Review

No. of External Reviewers :

No. of In House Reviewers :

Acceptance Rate :

Time To Review :

Reviewer's Comments : Yes

Fees to Publish : 0.00 US$

Invited Articles : 5% or less

MANUSCRIPT TOPICS : ACCOUNTING THEORY & PRACTICE; AUDITING;
  COST ACCOUNTING; GOVERNMENT & NON-PROFIT ACCOUNTING; TAX ACCOUNTING

PUBLICATION GUIDELINES : Chicago Manual of Style

MANUSCRIPT GUIDELINES/COMMENTS :

No. of External and In House Reviewers, and Acceptance Rate: Varies

1. The JAR accepts for review unpublished, original research in the fields of empirical, analytic and experimental accounting.

2. All material should be typed DOUBLE SPACED including text, footnotes references and appendices. Leave at least 1 1/2 inch margins at top, bottom, and sides of each page. If possible, send the typed original of all material, not a xerox copy. If you must submit a xerox, please be sure all pages are clean and clear. All xerox copies should be one-sided. Footnotes are to be typed DOUBLE SPACED and placed together at the end of the manuscript. They should not appear at the bottom of pages within the text.

3. REFERENCES: If references are given in the text or notes, the following form should be used: White [1970, p. 104] states, "...." or (see Green and Black [1975], White [1970; 1974]). Place dates of publication in square brackets, not in parentheses. References are to be typed DOUBLE SPACED and placed at the end of the manuscript. Place references in alphabetical order and do not number them. Give place of publication as well as publisher and

date of publication for books cited. Do not put the author's name in all capitals. Include in your references only those works which are cited in the text. And please double check that all references cited in the text appear in the References. (See a recent copy of the Journal for other questions of style in the references.)

4. MATHEMATICAL EXPRESSIONS: Mathematical expressions should be indented or centered on the page. If they are numbered, the number should appear in parentheses at the right hand margin of the page.

The same format should be used consistently throughout the paper. Long equations may begin at the left margin and extend into the right margin. Vectors should be underlined to distinguish them from other expressions. Vectors will be set in boldface type. If an underbar is not a vector, please make a note on a separate sheet of paper for the copy editor.

5. ENUMERATIONS: Enumerations or lists should be displayed in paragraph form. Numbers and letters used to enumerate items should be set in parentheses. An example is given below:

    Sample firms met the following criteria:
    1. listed on the Compustat data base for the years 1970 to 1980,
    2. market value of common equity greater than $200 million, and
    3. earnings forecast data available in VALUE LINE.

6. TABLES AND FIGURES: Each table is to be typed on a separate sheet of paper. The information contained in the body of the table may be single spaced; textual material in the table (such as footnotes) should be double spaced. Tables are to be numbered with Arabic (not Roman) numerals. Example: TABLE 1, TABLE 2, etc. (note that TABLE is in capitals). The title of a table is to be typed in capitals and lowercase, not in all capitals. Example: Summary of Data from Period 1. Tables should avoid vertical rules and should have a double rule at the top and a single rule at the bottom, before the notes (if any). Also, DO NOT send table which have been reduced through xerographic process. Instead, send the LARGE ORIGINALS(S).

7. Figures are photographed and reproduced in the Journal from original copy (i.e., they are not typeset). Therefore, it is imperative that camera ready figures be professionally drawn in black ink on high contrast copy paper. The figures must be of sufficiently high quality to be photographed. Also, the figure axes and any symbols that are part of the figure must be drawn by the artist. The legend should be typed on a separate sheet of paper since it will be typeset. If a figure is drawn on graph paper, please be sure the paper is lined in blue (which will not reproduce in the photograph) NOT in green, red, or black.

8. The legends, labels and footnotes for all figures and tables should be sufficiently complete to make the table or figure self-contained. In other words, the reader should be able to understand the table or figure without reading the text. The following items should appear somewhere in the legend, column labels, row labels, axis labels, or footnotes:

    1. Description of the content of the numbers or symbols in the body of the table or the content of the figure. This description should include the dimensions of all numbers, e.g., daily returns.

JOURNAL OF ACCOUNTING RESEARCH

2. Sample description, including size, period and, if relevant, a subsample description.
3. Definition, in words, of the symbols, equations and terms used in the figure or table.

9. Notes to the copy editor should be submitted on a separate sheet of paper.

JOURNAL OF ACCOUNTING RESEARCH ISSN: 021-8456
SUBSCRIPTION RATES (U.S. & OTHER COUNTRIES) Volumes 34-35 (1996-97)
From January 1, 1996 to December 31, 1997

	Academician or Student	Other (Library, Practitioners, etc.)
Each volume includes Spring, Autumn and Supplement issues.		
1996 (vol. 34)	$ 70	$ 86
1997 (vol. 35)	70	86
1996 and 1996 (vol. 34 and 35)	125	160
Single issue	34	44

Volumes 1-33 (1963-95)
From 1963 to 1995 inclusive
Each volume includes Spring, Autumn and Supplement issues.
(Volumes 1-3 do not have Supplements)

1 year	$ 63	$ 78
Single issue	30	40

IF AIR MAIL IS DESIRED, AN ADDITIONAL PAYMENT OF $50.00 IS REQUIRED PER VOLUME ($15.00 PER ISSUE).

Checks should be made payable to the JOURNAL OF ACCOUNTING RESEARCH in U.S. dollars. Foreign subscribers should send checks drawn on an American bank or an international money order.

We cannot accept credit cards or postal money orders.

Please address all correspondence to : JOURNAL OF ACCOUNTING RESEARCH
Graduate School of Business
University of Chicago
1101 E. 58th Street
Chicago, IL 60637 USA

JOURNAL OF ACCOUNTING, ETHICS & PUBLIC POLICY

ADDRESS FOR SUBMISSION :

ROBERT W. MC GEE, EDITOR
JOURNAL OF ACCOUNTING, ETHICS &
  PUBLIC POLICY
DUMONT INSTITUTE FOR PUBLIC POLICY
  RESEARCH
236 JOHNSON AVENUE
DUMONT, NJ 07628
201-501-8574
201-387-0744 (Fax)
E-Mail : Dumontinst@aol.com

CIRCULATION DATA :

Reader : Business Persons &
         Academic

Frequency of Issue : Quarterly

Copies Per Issue :

Subscription Price : 60.00 US$

Sponsorship :

PUBLICATION GUIDELINES :

Manuscript Length : 16-25

Copies Required : Three

Computer Submission : No

Format : N/A

Fees to Review : 0.00 US$

REVIEW INFORMATION :

Type of Review : Blind Review

No. of External Reviewers : Two

No. of In House Reviewers : One

Acceptance Rate :

Time To Review : 1-2 months

Reviewer's Comments : Yes

Fees to Publish : 0.00 US$

Invited Articles :

MANUSCRIPT TOPICS : ACCOUNTING INFORMATION SYSTEMS;
  ACCOUNTING THEORY & PRACTICE; PUBLIC POLICY ECONOMICS; ETHICS

PUBLICATION GUIDELINES :

MANUSCRIPT GUIDELINES/COMMENTS :

JOURNAL OF ACCOUNTING, ETHICS & PUBLIC POLICY is a new journal; therefore, there are no percentages given on acceptance rates nor circulation data.

READERSHIP: Practicing accountants, academics, anyone interested in accounting ethics and/or public policy.

DESIRED LENGTH: The preferred length is 15-25 pages, double-spaced. However, we are more interested in quality than quantity, so a shorter or longer length will also be considered.

NUMBER OF COPIES: 3

SUBJECT MATTER: Any topic that overlaps the areas of accounting and ethics, accounting and public policy or ethics and public policy.

SUBMISSION OR PUBLICATION CHARGES: None

BLIND REVIEW: Yes, after the editor has determined that the paper is suitable for refereeing.

JOURNAL OF ACCOUNTING, ETHICS & PUBLIC POLICY

SELECTION CRITERIA: The paper must be well-written and on a topic included under preferred subject matter.

APPROXIMATE REVIEW PERIOD: One to two months.

APPROXIMATE LEAD TIME TO PUBLICATION AFTER ACCEPTANCE: An abstract will be posted on our website and perhaps other places within 30 days after final acceptance. The article will appear in paper form within 1-3 months thereafter.

STYLE REQUIREMENTS: The cover page should include only the title of the paper and the names, addresses, institutional affiliations and telephone numbers of all authors. Acknowledgments, if any, should also be included here. The first page of the article should include the title and a 100 to 150 word abstract (indented). All references are to be by footnote. There is no reference section at the end of the article. The first time an article is cited, full particulars should be given. For example: Murray N. Sabrin, "Issues in Tax Reform," Northwestern Journal of Taxation, Vol. 14:2 (Fall, 1995), 422-437, at 425. Pages 422-437 represent the place where the article may be found. Page 425 refers to the page where the thought or quote may be found. Shorter citations may be given for subsequent references. For example, Sabrin at 436. Books should be cited as follows: Tibor R. Machan, Accounting Ethics (New York: Basic Books, 1996), 162. To cite items other than articles or books, use your best judgment.

COPYRIGHT: The JOURNAL OF ACCOUNTING, ETHICS & PUBLIC POLICY retains the right to publish articles in any format without compensation to the authors. Authors retain the right to reprint without permission of this journal. Anyone may distribute copies of any article for classroom use without permission, provided the source is clearly indicated, unless the article indicates that the author retains the copyright, in which case the author's permission must first be obtained. Reprints for inclusion in a book or other publication require permission of the Journal.

SEND SUBMISSIONS TO: The Editor.

SPONSOR OF PUBLICATION: The Dumont Institute for Public Policy Research.

JOURNAL OF AGRICULTURAL AND APPLIED ECONOMICS

ADDRESS FOR SUBMISSION :

CHUNG HUANG, MICHAEL WETZSTEIN, EDITORS
JOURNAL OF AGRICULTURAL AND APPLIED
  ECONOMICS
UNIVERSITY OF GEORGIA
CONNOR HALL
ATHENS, GA 30602-7509
706-542-0758
706-542-0739 (Fax)
E-Mail : JABE@agecon.uga.edu

Change in Editor's Address
  May Occur in : 06/01/98

CIRCULATION DATA :

Reader : Academic

Frequency of Issue : 2 Times/Year

Copies Per Issue : 1001-2000

Subscription Price : 15.00 US$

Sponsorship : Professional Assoc.

PUBLICATION GUIDELINES :

Manuscript Length : 21-25

Copies Required : Four

Computer Submission : No

Format : N/A

Fees to Review : 0.00 US$

REVIEW INFORMATION :

Type of Review : Blind Review

No. of External Reviewers : Two

No. of In House Reviewers : Zero

Acceptance Rate : 50 %

Time To Review : 2-3 months

Reviewer's Comments : Yes

Fees to Publish : 65.00 US$

Invited Articles : 21-30%

MANUSCRIPT TOPICS : ACCOUNTING INFORMATION SYSTEMS; ECONOMETRICS;
  PUBLIC POLICY ECONOMICS; AGRICULTURAL, ENVIRONMENTAL, NATURAL RESOURCES

PUBLICATION GUIDELINES : Chicago Manual of Style

MANUSCRIPT GUIDELINES/COMMENTS :

Contributors of manuscripts which closely adhere to the following guidelines
will receive prompt and efficient consideration.

1. COVER LETTER. Indicate (a) why the manuscript would interest JAAE readers;
(b) whether material in the manuscript, in whole or in part, has been
submitted for publication elsewhere; and (c) that the material in the
manuscript does not infringe upon other published material protected by
copyright.

2. COVER PAGE. The JAAE uses a system of blind reviews. Thus, all copies of
the manuscript should have a removable cover page that provides the authors'
names and institutional affiliations. Materials for review should not identify
the authors.

3. FORMAT. Manuscripts should be typed on good quality 8 1/2" by 11" paper
with 1.25" margins. Use 12-point Times Roman or a similar type style and size.
Double space all material throughout the manuscript, including the abstract,
acknowledgments, footnotes, references, and tables. Type only on one side of
the paper and do not use right-margin justification.

JOURNAL OF AGRICULTURAL AND APPLIED ECONOMICS

4. ABSTRACT. On a separate page, include an abstract not to exceed 100 words, followed by no more than eight key words, listed in alphabetical order.

5. FOOTNOTES. Number footnotes consecutively throughout the manuscript. Type the content of the footnotes on separate pages placed immediately after the main text. Footnotes should not be used for citations or directives to other literature. Reference citations should be incorporated into the text.

6. TABLES. Place each table on a separate page at the end of the text, immediately following the last footnote page.

7. REFERENCES. Place all references, cited in the text, alphabetized by author's last name on separate pages after the text, immediately following the last table page. Citations may appear parenthetically or as part of the text. Within the text, use parentheses rather than brackets for citations. Spell out up to three author last names; for works with four or more authors, include only the first author followed by "et al." When citing a direct quote, include page number(s). Do not specify the publication year unless there is more than one reference by the same author.

8. FIGURES. Place each figure, chart, or graph on a separate page immediately following the last reference page.

9. MATHEMATICAL FORMULATION. Use Arabic numbers enclosed in parentheses placed flush left on the first line of the equation. Number equations consecutively throughout the manuscript. Indent the equation after the equation number. Punctuate all mathematical material.

10. PUBLICATION COSTS. Authors submitting manuscripts are expected to assume obligation for payment of page charges. Page charges currently are $65 per printed page.

11. COPYRIGHT. The JAAE is copyrighted. Authors are required to sign a release form which will prohibit publication of material contained in the article elsewhere unless specific permission is granted by the editors.

12. COPIES. Send four clean copies to the Editors.

JOURNAL OF AGRICULTURAL AND APPLIED ECONOMICS is sponsored by Southern Agricultural Economics Association.

JOURNAL OF APPLIED CORPORATE FINANCE

ADDRESS FOR SUBMISSION :

DON CHEW, EDITOR
JOURNAL OF APPLIED CORPORATE FINANCE
STERN STEWART AND CO.
40 WEST 57TH STREET, 20TH FLOOR
NEW YORK, NY 10019
USA
212-261-0714
212-581-6420 (Fax)

CIRCULATION DATA :

Reader : Business Persons

Frequency of Issue : Quarterly

Copies Per Issue : 10,001-25,000

Subscription Price : 95.00 US$
  Aademic/Library : 50.00 US$

Sponsorship : Profit Oriented Corp.

PUBLICATION GUIDELINES :

Manuscript Length : 11-20

Copies Required : One

Computer Submission : Yes

Format : N/A

Fees to Review : 0.00 US$

REVIEW INFORMATION :

Type of Review : N/A

No. of External Reviewers :

No. of In House Reviewers :

Acceptance Rate :

Time To Review :

Reviewer's Comments :

Fees to Publish : 0.00 US$

Invited Articles : Over 50%

MANUSCRIPT TOPICS : COST ACCOUNTING; INTERNATIONAL FINANCE;
  PORTFOLIO & SECURITY ANALYSIS;
  CAPITAL STRUCTURE, RISK MANAGEMENT (DERIVATIVES);
  CORPORATE PERFORMANCE MEASUREMENT; INCENTIVE COMPENSATION

PUBLICATION GUIDELINES :

MANUSCRIPT GUIDELINES/COMMENTS :

JOURNAL OF APPLIED ECONOMETRICS

ADDRESS FOR SUBMISSION :

M. HASHEM PESARAN, EDITOR
JOURNAL OF APPLIED ECONOMETRICS
UNIVERSITY OF CAMBRIDGE
FACULTY OF ECONOMICS AND POLITICS
SIDGWICK AVENUE
CAMBRIDGE, CB3 9DE
UK
44-1223-335291
44-1223-335471 (Fax)
E-Mail : gs111@econ.cam.ac.uk

CIRCULATION DATA :

Reader : Academic

Frequency of Issue : Bi-Monthly

Copies Per Issue : Less than 1000

Subscription Price : 75.00 U.K.$
  Elsewhere : 115.00 US$

Sponsorship : Profit Oriented Corp.

PUBLICATION GUIDELINES :

Manuscript Length : 16-20

Copies Required : Four

Computer Submission : No

Format : N/A

Fees to Review : 0.00 US$

REVIEW INFORMATION :

Type of Review : Editorial Review

No. of External Reviewers : Three

No. of In House Reviewers : Zero

Acceptance Rate : 11-20%

Time To Review : 4-6 months

Reviewer's Comments : Yes

Fees to Publish : 0.00 US$

Invited Articles : 5% or less

MANUSCRIPT TOPICS : COST ACCOUNTING; ECONOMETRICS;
  INTERNATIONAL FINANCE

PUBLICATION GUIDELINES :

MANUSCRIPT GUIDELINES/COMMENTS :

CO-EDITORS
STEVEN DURLAUF, Department of Economics, University of Wisconsin, 1180
Observatory Drive, Madison, WI 53706, USA. Email: durlauf@macc.wisc.edu

JOHN GEWEKE, Department of Economics, University of Minnesota, 271 19th Avenue
South, Minneapolis, MN 55455, USA. Email: geweke@atlas.socsci.umn.edu

ARIE KAPTEYN, Center for Economic Research, Tilburg University, PO Box 90153,
5000 LE Tilburg, The Netherlands. Email: kapteyn@kub.nl

JOHN RUST, Department of Economics, University of Wisconsin, 1180 Observatory
Drive, Madison, WI 53706, USA. Email: jrust@thor.econ.wisc.edu

BOOK REVIEW EDITOR
MICHAEL MCALEER, Department of Economics, University of Western Australia,
Nedlands, Perth WA 6009, Australia. Email: mmcaleer@ecel.uwa.edu.au

SOFTWARE REVIEW EDITOR AND COORDINATOR OF THE DATA ARCHIVE
JAMES MACKINNON, Department of Economics, Queen's University, Kingston,

JOURNAL OF APPLIED ECONOMETRICS

Ontario, K7l 3N6, Canada. Email: jgm@qed.econ.queensu.ca

AIMS AND SCOPE

The JOURNAL OF APPLIED ECONOMETRICS is a bi-monthly international journal which aims to publish articles of high quality dealing with the application of existing as well as new econometric techniques to a wide variety of problems in economics and related subjects, covering topics in measurement, estimation, testing, forecasting and policy analysis. The emphasis is on the careful and rigorous application of econometric techniques and the appropriate interpretation of the results.

The intention of the JOURNAL OF APPLIED ECONOMETRICS is to provide an outlet for innovative, quantitative research in economics which cuts across areas of specialisation, involves transferable techniques, and is easily replicable by other researchers.

NOTES FOR CONTRIBUTORS

1. Four copies of each manuscript should be submitted to the Editor.

2. Only original papers will be accepted, and copyright in published papers will be vested in the publisher. Papers are accepted for review only on the condition that they are not under review by another journal. Papers of special interest delivered at conferences may be accepted if copyright has not been previously surrendered. Copyright laws require that the transfer of copyright from authors to publisher must be explicit to enable the publisher to ensure maximum dissemination of the author's work. A copy of the Copyright Transfer Agreement to be used for the JOURNAL OF APPLIED ECONOMETRICS is reproduced in each volume. Additional copies are available from the Journal editors or from the publishers, or contributors may photocopy the agreement from this journal. A copy of this agreement signed by the author, must accompany every article submitted for publication.

3. The language of the Journal is English.

4. Fifty offprints of each paper and one copy of the Journal issue in which it appear will be provided free of charge. Additional copies may be purchased on a offprint order form which will accompany the proofs.

5. Proofs will be sent to authors so they can correct printers errors only.

6. Manuscripts should be typed double-spaced with wide margins, on one side of the paper only and submitted in quadruplicate. Illustrations should be submitted with the manuscript on separate sheets. There is no maximum length for contributions, but authors should write concisely.

7. The title should be brief, typed on a separate sheet and the author's name should be typed on the line below the title; the affiliation and address should follow on the next line. In the case of co-authors, respective addresses and affiliations should be clearly indicated. Authors should also give telephone, fax and electronic mail contact details. Correspondence, proofs and reprints will be sent to the first-named author, unless otherwise indicated.

8. The body of the manuscript should be preceded by a Summary (maximum length 100 words) which should be a summary of the entire paper, not of the conclusions alone. The summary will appear at the head of the article when

published.

9. The paper should be reasonably subdivided into sections and, if necessary, subsections.

10. Mathematical symbols should be typewritten. Greek letters and unusual symbols should be identified separately in the margin. Distinction should be made between capital and lower case letters; between the letter O and zero; between the letter l, the number one and prime; between k and kappa. Superscripts and subscripts should be displayed clearly above and below the line respectively. All equations should be numbered consecutively, and the numbers should be placed in parentheses in the right hand margin.

11. Half-tone illustrations are to be restricted in number to the minimum necessary. Good, glossy bromide prints should accompany the manuscripts and should not be attached to manuscript pages. Photographs should be enlarged sufficiently to permit clear reproduction in half-tone after reduction. If words or numbers are to appear on a photograph two prints should be sent, the lettering being clearly indicated on the print only. All should be clearly identified on the back with the figure number and author's name.

Colour illustrations will be accepted if the Editor considers them necessary and if the costs are borne by the author(s).

12. Line drawings should be supplied on a separate sheet at the same size as the intended printed version (so no enlargement or reduction is required), maximum width 140 mm. Lettering on the artwork should be set in 8pt type. Computer-generated artwork must be submitted as laser printed output at a resolutin of 600 dots per inch on high quality paper. Dot matrix printer output is unacceptable. Tints are to be avoided; hatching should be used instead. Drawn artwork should be carefully lettered and drawn in balck ink. Provide copies as well as the originals, all of which should be clearly identified on the back with the figure number and the author's name.

Artwork on disk is preferred on 3.5 inch PC or Macintosh format disk in a dedicated drawing package, such as Adobe Illustrator/Corel Draw/Macromedia Freehand not presentation, spreadsheet or database packages. Each graphic should be in a separate file, should conform to the information above and be supplied as a source (original) file as well as .EPS file, if different. Provide a hard copy print out of each figure, clearly identified.

13. Figure legends should be typed on a separate sheet and placed at the end of the manuscript. The amount of lettering on a drawing should be reduced as far as possible by transferring it to the legend.

14. It is the author's responsibility to obtain written permission to quote material which has appeared in another publication.

15. Tables should be numbered consecutively and titled. All table columns should have an explanatory heading. Tables should not repeat data which are available elsewhere in the paper, e.g. in a line diagram.

16. References to published literature should be quoted in the text by giving the author's name, year of publication, and, where needed for a quote, the page number, e.g. Stone (1954, p. 511). References should be listed alphabetically in a section labelled 'References' at the end of the paper.

JOURNAL OF APPLIED ECONOMETRICS

[Underline titles of journal and books.]
Journal references should be arranged thus, giving journal titles in full:
   Mellander, E., A. Vredin and A. Warne (1992), 'Stochastic trends and economic fluctuations in a small open economy', Journal of Applied Econometrics, 7, 369-394.

Book references should be given as follows:
   Amemiya, T. (1985), Advanced Econometrics, Blackwell, Oxford.
   Hansen, B. E. (1993), 'The likelihood ratio test under nonstandard conditions: testing the Markov switching model of GNP', in M. H. Pesaran and S.M. Potter (eds.), Nonlinear Dynamics, Dhaos and Econometrics, Wiley, Chichester.

17. No manuscript or figures will be returned following publication unless a request for return is made when the manuscript is originally submitted.

18. The publisher will do everything possible to ensure prompt publication. It will therefore be appreciated if manuscripts and illustrations conform from the outset to the style of the journal. Corrected proofs must be returned to the publishers within ten days to minimize the risk of the author's contribution having to be held over to a later issue.

19. Authors will be expected to make available a complete set of data used as well as any specialized computer programs employed, preferably in a machine-readable form. In cases where there are restrictions on the dissemination of the data the responsibility of obtaining the required permission to use the data rests with the interested investigator and not with the author. The condition of making available the specialized computer programs can be met either by providing a program listing or by allowing other investigators to use the program on an installation to which public access is possible. Authors of accepted papers are expected to deposit their data in electronic form onto the journal's data archive. Copies of the Guidelines for Users of the JOURNAL OF APPLIED ECONOMETRICS Data Archive can be obtained from the journal editors or the publishers. The Guidelines will also be published in the journal from time to time.

JOURNAL OF BANK COST & MANAGEMENT ACCOUNTING

ADDRESS FOR SUBMISSION :

AL SCHNEIDER, EDITOR
JOURNAL OF BANK COST & MANAGEMENT
  ACCOUNTING
NABCA
P.O. BOX 458
NORTHBROOK, IL 60065-0458
847-272-4233
847-272-6445 (Fax)
E-Mail : NABCA@MCS.NET

CIRCULATION DATA :

Reader : Business Persons

Frequency of Issue : 3 Times/Year

Copies Per Issue : Less than 1000

Subscription Price : 90.00 US$
  International : 100.00 US$

Sponsorship : Professional Assoc.

PUBLICATION GUIDELINES :

Manuscript Length : 16-20

Copies Required : Two

Computer Submission : Yes

Format : Almost any WP

Fees to Review : 0.00 US$

REVIEW INFORMATION :

Type of Review : Editorial Review

No. of External Reviewers : One

No. of In House Reviewers : One

Acceptance Rate : 70 %

Time To Review : 1-2 months

Reviewer's Comments : No

Fees to Publish : 0.00 US$

Invited Articles : 5% or less

MANUSCRIPT TOPICS : ACCOUNTING INFORMATION SYSTEMS;
  ACCOUNTING THEORY & PRACTICE; AUDITING; CAPITAL BUDGETING; COST ACCOUNTING

PUBLICATION GUIDELINES :

MANUSCRIPT GUIDELINES/COMMENTS :

CALL FOR PAPERS

The JOURNAL OF BANK COST & MANAGEMENT ACCOUNTING, published by the National
Association for Bank Cost & Management Accounting, seeks articles on issues
relevant to management accounting in financial institutions. Articles should
be on a subject of interest to practitioners in the field of bank cost and
management accounting and should reflect the views of the author. Authors
should not hesitate to submit articles that present a minority or unusual view
as long as that view is effectively presented. A sample copy of the Journal
will be provided to prospective authors upon request.

The Journal is published three times a year and distributed to 500 subscribers
worldwide. The Journal generally publishes articles that have not appeared or
been accepted for publication elsewhere. Exceptions to this policy may be
approved if the author obtains a release from the copyright holder.

Authors of accepted papers will be furnished with six (6) copies of the issue
in which their paper appears. Where multiple authors are involved, each author
will be given four (4) copies. Complete address and telephone information for

each author should be included with each article submitted. The publisher will pay $100 for each published article.

GUIDELINES FOR PREPARATION OF MANUSCRIPTS

FORMAT - The entire manuscript, including text, footnotes, charts, and quotations, must be typed, double-spaced on plain 8 1/2" x 11" paper, leaving one-inch margins on all sides. The title of the article and author's name and title should appear on page one of the manuscript. Headings should be used to give structure to the article and to order the text in a logical format. The premise of the article and the conclusion(s) should be clearly stated.

LENGTH - Manuscripts may be of any length in the above format, generally over ten pages. The final determinant of an acceptable length is the subject matter of the article. The Editor reserves the right to edit manuscripts for length.

STYLE - Punctuation should be kept simple, adding to the readability of the article. Tables and exhibits should be numbered and printed on separate sheets of paper whenever possible; they should be clearly referenced in the body of the manuscript. Footnotes should include the author's name, title of reference, publisher, and date. Unless a direct quote is used, no page or volume numbers are required in the footnotes. References or bibliographies should be typed on a separate page, entitled "References", at the end of the manuscript.

REVIEW AND EDITING

SUBMISSION - Authors are strongly encouraged to submit their manuscripts on computer disk in any major software program format; one clear paper copy of the manuscript must be included with each disk. (Call NABCA with any questions about disk format.) Alternatively, two copies (one original, one photocopy) of each manuscript may be submitted to the Editor at the address shown above. If an article includes copyrighted material (other than short quotations), submissions must be accompanied by a letter of permission to reprint from the copyright holder.

REVIEW/EDITING - Articles are screened by the Editor and may be sent out to reviewers for comment in certain cases. Manuscripts are evaluated based on coverage of the subject and whether it will be of interest to readers. Each manuscript is edited for grammar, punctuation, and structure, and may be returned to the author with suggestions for rewriting.

If a manuscript is accepted for publication, a release form will be sent to the author. The signed release form must be returned within 15 days. Published articles become the property of the National Association for Bank Cost & Management Accounting and may not be reprinted without the written permission of the publisher.

JOURNAL OF BANKING AND FINANCE

ADDRESS FOR SUBMISSION :

GIORGIO P. SZEGO, EDITOR
JOURNAL OF BANKING AND FINANCE
C/O ASSOCIAZIONE BANCARIA ITALIANA
PIAZZA DEL GESU 49
00186 ROMA,
ITALY
39-6-8387631
39-6-86214805/86207513 (Fax)
E-Mail : E.CARULLI@AGORA.STM.IT

CIRCULATION DATA :

Reader : Business Persons,
        Academic, &
        Banks & Financial Institutions

Frequency of Issue : 8 Times/Year

Copies Per Issue : 1001-2000

Subscription Price : 751.00 DFL.

Sponsorship : Profit Oriented Corp. &
              Professional Assoc.

PUBLICATION GUIDELINES :

Manuscript Length : 2-35

Copies Required : Four

Computer Submission : No

Format : N/A

Fees to Review : 130.00 US$
  Subscribers 65.00 US$
  By submission/author 130.00 US$

REVIEW INFORMATION :

Type of Review : Blind Review

No. of External Reviewers : Two

No. of In House Reviewers : Zero

Acceptance Rate : 11-20%

Time To Review : 4-6 months

Reviewer's Comments : Yes

Fees to Publish : 0.00 US$

Invited Articles : 5% or less

MANUSCRIPT TOPICS : COST ACCOUNTING; INSURANCE;
   INTERNATIONAL & ECONOMIC DEVELOPMENT; INTERNATIONAL FINANCE;
   PORTFOLIO & SECURITY ANALYSIS; BANKING

PUBLICATION GUIDELINES :

MANUSCRIPT GUIDELINES/COMMENTS :

ACCEPTANCE RATE: 9-12%, TIME TO REVIEW: 2-6 months

SPONSORSHIP: Italian Bankers Associations and Banks

The aim of the JOURNAL OF BANKING AND FINANCE is to provide an outlet for the
increasing flow of scholarly research concerning financial institutions and
the money and capital markets within which they function. The emphasis will
primarily be on applied and policy-oriented research. The Journal is thus
intended to improve communications between, and within, the academic and other
research communities and those members of financial institutions, both private
and public, national and international, who are responsible for operational
and policy decisions.

JOURNAL OF BUSINESS

ADDRESS FOR SUBMISSION :

DOUGLAS W. DIAMOND, EDITOR
JOURNAL OF BUSINESS
UNIVERSITY OF CHICAGO
GRADUATE SCHOOL OF BUSINESS
1101 EAST 58TH STREET
CHICAGO, IL 60637
USA
773-702-7140
773-702-0458 (Fax)
E-Mail : job@uchicago.gsb.edu

CIRCULATION DATA :

Reader : Academic

Frequency of Issue : Quarterly

Copies Per Issue : 2001-3000

Subscription Price : 22.00 US$

Sponsorship : University

PUBLICATION GUIDELINES :

Manuscript Length :

Copies Required : Three

Computer Submission : No

Format : N/A

Fees to Review : 0.00 US$

REVIEW INFORMATION :

Type of Review : Blind Review

No. of External Reviewers : One

No. of In House Reviewers : One

Acceptance Rate : 11-20%

Time To Review : 2-3 months

Reviewer's Comments : Yes

Fees to Publish : 0.00 US$

Invited Articles : 5% or less

MANUSCRIPT TOPICS : ACCOUNTING INFORMATION SYSTEMS;
ACCOUNTING THEORY & PRACTICE; AUDITING; CAPITAL BUDGETING; COST ACCOUNTING;
ECONOMETRICS; ECONOMIC HISTORY; GOVERNMENT & NON-PROFIT ACCOUNTING;
INSURANCE; INTERNATIONAL & ECONOMIC DEVELOPMENT; INTERNATIONAL FINANCE;
PORTFOLIO & SECURITY ANALYSIS; PUBLIC POLICY ECONOMICS; REAL ESTATE;
TAX ACCOUNTING

PUBLICATION GUIDELINES :

MANUSCRIPT GUIDELINES/COMMENTS :

1. ALL MANUSCRIPTS MUST BE DOUBLE-SPACED (text, references footnotes, etc.).
Allow right and left-hand margins of at least 1-1/2 inches each.

2. FIRST PAGE OF MANUSCRIPT
    A. Title should be at least 2 inches from the topic edge of the page.
    B. Allow 1-inch space, and on a separate line type the name(s) of the
        author(s).
    C. One inch below this, on a separate line, type author(s) affiliation.
    D. On a separate sheet, an abstract of not more than 100 words.

3. REFERENCES FOLLOW THE TEXT. They should be typed on a separate page or
pages in alphabetical order by authors' last names. Each line after the first
line of each reference should be indented 1/2 inch. All references must be
referred to in the text by author's name and year of publication. Note that
journal titles should not be abbreviated. Reference style is as follows:

JOURNAL OF BUSINESS

A. For periodicals
>Jones, R.Y., and Brown, E.B. 1985. Transactions costs and the stock market. Journal of Business 23 (April): 178-85.
>Smith, J.D. 1960. Economic theory. Journal of Political Economy 67 (May): 126-42.

B. For a book title
>Donahue, C.L. The Economics of Western Europe. 2 vols. New York: Oxford University Press.

C. For contributions to collective works
>Smith, J.D. 1942. Predictions in economic theory. In C.E. Lang (ed.), Sociology as a Force. 2d ed. New York: Farrar & Rinehart.

In the text, references should appear as follows: "Smith (1942) showed that..." For multiple references by the same author in the same year, alphabetize by article title, adding a after the first reference date, b after the second, etc. For example:

>Jones, C.D. 1971a. Social Trends. Boston: Beacon Press.
>Jones, C.D. 1971b. Tax deductions. Finance 7 (December): 218-35.
>In the text they are referred to as Jones (1971a), or (Jones 1971a).

4. FOOTNOTES (typed paragraph style) should be placed together on typed sheets following the references. They should be numbered in order and correspond with the numbers in the text. In both places, footnote numbers should be shown as superscripts (i.e., slightly above the line). For example:

>(Text)...in that study3 (footnote)
>3 Numerous studies have shown that

Footnotes are not necessary if only used to refer to a work cited. In this case, the information should be placed in the text in parenthesis. Example: (see Jones 1956, pp. 8-15). Footnotes are only necessary for further explanation of something within the text. An acknowledgement footnote should be unnumbered and should precede any numbered footnotes.

5. TABULAR MATERIAL
Each table should be on a separate sheet of paper following the footnotes. Each table should be numbered and should be referred to in order in the text.

6. ILLUSTRATIONS
Each illustration (figure) should be on a separate sheet of paper and should follow the tabular material. Legends for the illustrations should be typed in order on a sheet of paper which should accompany the illustrations. All illustrations should be referred to in order in the text as figure 1, figure 2, etc.

7. MISCELLANEOUS
Any unusual symbols or abbreviations in the text should be identified in the margin (in pencil). PLEASE PREPARE ONE ORIGINAL TYPESCRIPT (NOT A CARBON) AND ONE CLEAR XEROX COPY OF THE MANUSCRIPT.

8. INSTRUCTIONS FOR PREPARATION OF FIGURES
Illustrations are expensive; be certain that yours are essential and do not repeat material presented in the text.

9. Make black-and-white drawings with India ink on pure white stock or tracing paper. Fuzzy lines and shades of gray will not reproduce clearly. Printed transparent overlays with patterns of lines, dots, strippling, or cross-hatching are available commercially for different degrees of reduction. If these are needed, mount them so that the pattern does not obscure printing or other critical material underneath. Be sure that the overlay is attached securely everywhere, with no air bubbles beneath. Draw graphics on coordinate paper printed in pale blue so that the grid will not reproduce. Orange, yellow, green, and red grids reproduce as black.

10. All lettering should be made in India ink also. Mechanical aids are available for drawing the lettering. For the readers' convenience, arrange all lettering to be read from of position.

11. Cite all illustrations in the text (as Figure X), numbering them in one consecutive series. A circled note in the margin, enables the editor or printer to place the figure correctly in the text.

12. Art work submitted with the manuscript ordinarily should be 8-1/2 by 11 inches or smaller. Plan line drawings for reduction of 50% or more; this will minimize flows. Remember that not only the overall dimensions but also the thickness of individual lines, spaces, and letters will be reduced proportionally.

JOURNAL OF BUSINESS & FINANCE LIBRARIANSHIP

ADDRESS FOR SUBMISSION :

CHARLES POPOVICH, HEAD LIBRARIAN
JOURNAL OF BUSINESS & FINANCE
  LIBRARIANSHIP
THE OHIO STATE UNIVERSITY
BUSINESS LIBRARY/110 PAGE HALL
1810 COLLEGE ROAD
COLUMBUS, OH 43210-1395
614-292-2136
614-292-7859 (Fax)
E-Mail : POPOVICH.1@OSU.EDU

CIRCULATION DATA :

Reader : Academic

Frequency of Issue : Quarterly

Copies Per Issue : 1001-2000

Subscription Price : 36.00 US$
  Institution : 75.00 US$

Sponsorship :

PUBLICATION GUIDELINES :

Manuscript Length : 10-50

Copies Required : Four

Computer Submission : Yes

Format : 3.5" WordPerfect 6.0

Fees to Review : 0.00 US$

REVIEW INFORMATION :

Type of Review : Blind Review

No. of External Reviewers : Two

No. of In House Reviewers : One

Acceptance Rate : 50 %

Time To Review : 2-3 months

Reviewer's Comments : Yes

Fees to Publish : 0.00 US$

Invited Articles : 21-30%

MANUSCRIPT TOPICS : ACCOUNTING INFORMATION SYSTEMS;
  ACCOUNTING THEORY & PRACTICE; AUDITING; CAPITAL BUDGETING; COST ACCOUNTING;
  ECONOMETRICS; ECONOMIC HISTORY; GOVERNMENT & NON-PROFIT ACCOUNTING;
  INSURANCE; INTERNATIONAL & ECONOMIC DEVELOPMENT; INTERNATIONAL FINANCE;
  PORTFOLIO & SECURITY ANALYSIS; PUBLIC POLICY ECONOMICS; REAL ESTATE;
  TAX ACCOUNTING; ANY BUSINESS & FINANCE TOPIC;
  TOPICS MUST DISCUSS SOME RELATIONSHIP TO LIBRARIES

PUBLICATION GUIDELINES :

MANUSCRIPT GUIDELINES/COMMENTS :

NOTE: ALL MANUSCRIPT TOPICS *MUST* DISCUSS SOME RELATIONSHIP TO LIBRARIES.
JBFL is a "peer review" journal which is published quarterly by the Haworth
Press. It is devoted to publishing articles of importance to information
professionals who are involved with, or have an interest in, the creation,
organization, dissemination, retrieval, and use of business and finance
information. Articles generally pertain to the needs of information
professionals in business and finance libraries and information centers or
services outside of the traditional library setting. JBFL is not only an
outlet for practice-oriented articles, but also a forum for new empirical
studies on librarianship related to business and finance information. Also,
many of the articles reflect the multinational and international scope of
today's business community.

FOR AN INFORMATIONAL "INSTRUCTIONS FOR AUTHORS" BROCHURE, CONTACT THE EDITOR.

JOURNAL OF BUSINESS AND ECONOMIC PERSPECTIVES

ADDRESS FOR SUBMISSION :

DR. BOB FIGGINS, EDITOR
JOURNAL OF BUSINESS AND ECONOMIC
  PERSPECTIVES
UNIVERSITY OF TENNESSEE AT MARTIN
SCHOOL OF BUSINESS ADMINISTRATION
MARTIN, TN 38238
USA
901-587-7226
901-587-7241 (Fax)
E-Mail : bfiggings@utm.edu

CIRCULATION DATA :

Reader : Academic

Frequency of Issue : 2 Times/Year

Copies Per Issue : Less than 1000

Subscription Price : 10.00 US$
  Institution : 35.00 US$

Sponsorship : University

PUBLICATION GUIDELINES :

Manuscript Length : 16

Copies Required : Three

Computer Submission : Yes

Format : Request Style Sheet

Fees to Review : 15.00 US$

REVIEW INFORMATION :

Type of Review : Blind Review

No. of External Reviewers : Two

No. of In House Reviewers : One

Acceptance Rate : 21-30%

Time To Review : 4-6 months

Reviewer's Comments : No

Fees to Publish : 0.00 US$

Invited Articles : 5% or less

MANUSCRIPT TOPICS : ACCOUNTING INFORMATION SYSTEMS;
  ACCOUNTING THEORY & PRACTICE; AUDITING; CAPITAL BUDGETING; COST ACCOUNTING;
  ECONOMIC HISTORY; GOVERNMENT & NON-PROFIT ACCOUNTING; INSURANCE;
  INTERNATIONAL & ECONOMIC DEVELOPMENT; INTERNATIONAL FINANCE;
  PORTFOLIO & SECURITY ANALYSIS; PUBLIC POLICY ECONOMICS; REAL ESTATE;
  APPLIED ECONOMICS

PUBLICATION GUIDELINES : Chicago Manual of Style

MANUSCRIPT GUIDELINES/COMMENTS :

Manuscripts related to popular aspects of Business and Economics are
solicited. All articles of interest to both practitioners and academics in
business will be considered.

LENGTH OF ARTICLES. Ordinarily, articles should not exceed sixteen typewritten
pages, double-spaced.

MATHEMATICS. The use of mathematics and graphics should be kept at a minimum.
Avoid technical jargon. Number equations. In identifying variables in
formulas, capitalize only the initial letter of abbreviations except where
common usage indicates otherwise.

SUBMISSION OF ARTICLES. Send three copies of all articles to the address
above. We regret that we are unable to return or store manuscripts.

JOURNAL OF BUSINESS AND ECONOMIC PERSPECTIVES

REVIEW. Before publication, manuscripts are reviewed by the Editor and one or more readers to be sure the material is appropriate for the Journal. On occasion, revisions may be suggested to the author to make the material of the greatest possible use to Journal readers.

TYPING. The manuscript should be double-spaced throughout. This applies to text, footnotes, references, and figure legends. Use standard 8-1/2 X 11 white paper. Submit three copies and keep another for your own use.

Type on one side only. Leave a 1 inch margin on all four sides of the text. Mathematical symbols must be clearly represented--typed if at all possible. Make sure that final changes are made on all three copies.

TITLE PAGE AND SUMMARY. Use a cover page which shows the title of the paper, the name of the author(s) with their titles, institutional affiliations, and telephone numbers. Include on this page a summary of the article in 150 words or less. If appropriate,add as a footnote material about previous publications or other information which can be used to identify the author(s).

CORRECTIONS AND INSERTIONS. Keep corrections in the manuscript to a minimum. Retype any page on which more than a few changes are necessary. Do not write in the margins. Type lengthy insertions on a separate page and mark the place in the text where the insertion is to appear. This page should also indicate that the insertion follows. (For example, number the insertion follows. (For example, number the insertion 12a. Page 12 should be marked "Followed by p. 12a.")

FOOTNOTES. Use footnotes sparingly. Number sequentially. Type footnotes double-spaced on a separate page at the end of the article. In general, avoid lengthy explanatory footnotes. This material can usually be incorporated in the text.

SECTION HEADINGS. If sparingly used, section headings and subheadings enhance the readability of an article. Do not try to indicate typographical style, but show the relative weights by using all capital letters for the main headings (i.e. CONCLUSIONS) and initial capital letters (only) for words in the subheadings (i.e., Test Results).

TABLES AND CHARTS. Avoid excessively long tables. Type tables and charts on pages separate from the text. Captions of all figures should be consistent. Capitalize the first letter in all words in main headings (i.e. Test Results). For captions of lessor importance in the column headings or subs, capitalize only the first letter of the initial word (i.e., Goodness of fit.)

REFERENCES. Type double-spaced with each item beginning flush left. For entries requiring more than one line, run-over lines should be indented. Authors in the references should be listed alphabetically; do not number the entries. Citations for books should contain author's last name, first name and middle initials followed by full title of the book, place of publication, publisher, and publication (copyright) date. The following example illustrates the desired form and punctuation.

Smith, Arthur G., Economics, New York: Godwin, 1978.

JOURNAL OF BUSINESS AND ECONOMIC PERSPECTIVES

Journal articles should include (in addition to author and title, as above) the name of the journal, date, volume, and page. For example:

Smith, Arthur G., "Teaching Economics," Journal of Economic Education, Spring 1976, 7, 4-12.

Vibhakar, Ashvin P., and Kennedy, Robert E., "Alternate Estimates of the Cost of Equity Capital: Electric Utilities Revisited," Journal of Business and Economic Perspectives, Fall 1982, 8, 1-22.

In referring to references in the text of the article, use the author's name, publication date, and page number (if needed). For example: "... as the date indicates (Smith,1978, p. 456)" or "...as Smith (1978) has stated..."

JOURNAL OF BUSINESS FINANCE & ACCOUNTING (JBFA)

ADDRESS FOR SUBMISSION :

RICHARD J. BRISTON, MANAGING EDITOR
JOURNAL OF BUSINESS FINANCE &
  ACCOUNTING (JBFA)
UNIVERSITY OF HULL
DEPARTMENT OF ACCOUNTING & FINANCE
HULL, HU6 7RX
ENGLAND
0 1482-466221
0 1482-466377 (Fax)

CIRCULATION DATA :

Reader : Academic

Frequency of Issue : 8 Times/Year

Copies Per Issue : 1001-2000

Subscription Price : 126.00 US$
  Library : 321.00 US$

Sponsorship :

PUBLICATION GUIDELINES :

Manuscript Length : 11-20

Copies Required : Three

Computer Submission : No

Format : N/A

Fees to Review : 75.00 US$
  Personal Subscribers 37.50 US$

REVIEW INFORMATION :

Type of Review : Blind Review

No. of External Reviewers : Two

No. of In House Reviewers : One

Acceptance Rate : 11-20%

Time To Review :

Reviewer's Comments : Yes

Fees to Publish : 0.00 US$

Invited Articles : 5% or less

MANUSCRIPT TOPICS : ACCOUNTING THEORY & PRACTICE; CAPITAL BUDGETING;
  COST ACCOUNTING; ECONOMETRICS; INTERNATIONAL FINANCE;
  PORTFOLIO & SECURITY ANALYSIS; CAPITAL MARKET ANALYSIS

PUBLICATION GUIDELINES :

MANUSCRIPT GUIDELINES/COMMENTS :

TIME TO REVIEW: 3-4 months
LENGTH OF MANUSCRIPT: 11-20 pages, but occasionally both longer and shorter
are accepted - shorter papers as "Notes".

1. All manuscripts should be submitted to: The Editors, JOURNAL OF BUSINESS
FINANCE & ACCOUNTING. Manuscripts are considered on the understanding that
they are original, unpublished works not concurrently under consideration for
publication elsewhere. The receipt of manuscripts will be acknowledged, but
the editors and publishers can accept no responsibility for any loss or
non-return of manuscripts. Suitable manuscripts will be given anonymous
review, following which a copy of any review report will be supplied together
with the editors' decision. As regards papers accepted for publication, the
author(s) will be asked to transfer copyright to the publishers. Authors are
requested to follow JBFA's manuscript and style requirements closely, to
minimize later delay or redrafting: a fuller leaflet of "Information for
Contributors" is available from the editorial office on request. In

particular, authors should draft their papers and footnotes etc. to avoid identifying themselves directly or indirectly, to help ensure a fair review.

2. SUBMISSION FEE. A submission fee is required for each manuscript submitted to JBFA (other than Replies or Rejoinders), including rewritten and resubmitted manuscripts which had previously been rejected with advice that a rewritten paper could be reconsidered, subject to a further review assessment. However, in all cases the required submission fees are reduced by one-half if the designated author can confirm being a paid-up current subscriber to JBFA. The rates of submission fees may alter with inflation: the latest rates are printed on the inside front cover of the current issue of the journal. Submission fees should accompany the relevant manuscript, in the form of a cheque or draft made payable to the University of Hull or JBFA. If only the half-rate fee is sent, a cover note should give definite confirmation that the author is currently a paid-up subscriber.

3. MANUSCRIPT REQUIREMENTS. Submit three photocopies of the manuscript (together with any submission fee), typed double-spaced (preferably on international-size A4 paper). On the title page include the names, titles and institutional affiliations of all the author(s), and also the complete address of the designated author to whom decisions, proofs and reprint request should be sent. Also provide a running title of fewer than 50 characters and spaces, which will appear on alternate pages in the journal. If the paper is to include any acknowledgements these should be typed as a footnote on the title page. The second page should repeat the full title of the paper, (but not the author(s)' names) and contain the Abstract of the paper, not exceeding 100 words for full-length papers, or 60 words for shorter Notes, Comments, Replies or Rejoinders. The third page may repeat the full title of the paper (but not the author(s)' names) and here the text proper begins. The main text should be followed by any appendices, by any footnotes (which should be kept to the essential minimum, identified in the text by superscript numerals and listed together at the end, not separately at the bottom of each page), and by the list of source references (see below). Tables and figures should be numbered in order of their appearance with Arabic numerals, and each should have a concise descriptive title (and source, where relevant).

4. REFERENCES. Citation in the text is by name(s) of author(s), followed by year of publication (and page numbers where relevant) in parentheses. For references authored by more than two contributors use the first author's name and 'et al.'. For multiple citations in the same year use a, b, c, immediately following the year of publication. The source reference list should be typed in alphabetical order, and in accord with the following examples of style.

Amey, L.R. (1979a), Budget Planning and Control Systems (Pitman, 1979).

_____ (1979b), "Budget Planning: A Dynamic Reformulation", Accounting and Business Research (Winter 1979), pp. 17-24.

Lee, T.A. (1981), "Cash Flow Accounting and Corporate Financial Reporting" in Essays in British Accounting Research, M. Bronwich and A. Hopwood, eds. (Pitman, 1981), pp. 63-78.

Peasnell, K. V., L.C.L. Skerratt and P.A. Taylor (1979), "An Arbitrage Rationale for Tests of Mutual Fund Performance", Journal of Business Finance & Accounting (Autumn 1979), pp. 373-400.

JOURNAL OF BUSINESS FINANCE &
ACCOUNTING (JBFA)

5. MATHEMATICAL AND STATISTICAL MATERIAL. Mathematical notation should be used only when its rigour and precision are essential to comprehension, and authors should explain in narrative format the principal operations performed. Preferably detailed mathematical proofs and statistical support should be relegated to appendices. Any equations used should be numbered sequentially in parentheses positioned flush with the right-hand margin. Whilst the journal does not wish to publish unnecessary mathematical or statistical detail, or specimen questionnaires, supplementary information of these kinds may be of assistance to the editors and reviewers in assessing papers, and authors are invited to submit such supporting evidence as separate documents clearly marked as being for information rather than publication.

6. ILLUSTRATIONS. All graphs, charts, etc. submitted with papers must be referred to in the text, and be fully legible and clearly related to scales on the axes. If illustrations are numerous, a proportion may have to be deleted unless the author is able to supply artwork of camera-ready quality or to reimburse the journal for the cost of artwork.

7. PROOFS, OFFPRINTS AND PRIZES. The designated author will receive proofs, which should be corrected and returned within ten days of receipt. This author is responsible for proofreading the manuscript: the editors/publishers are not responsible for any error not marked by the author on the proofs. Corrections to proofs are limited to rectifying errors: no substantial author's changes can be allowed at this stage unless agreement to pay full costs if communicated with the return of proofs. Similarly, offprints in excess of the twenty-five free copies automatically supplied to the designated author (for sharing among any co-authors) must be ordered at the time of the return of proofs, in accord with the instructions and price list accompanying the proofs. Following publication, papers (other than papers authored by members of the Board) will be eligible for consideration of merit by the Board of Editors for the award of the Paish Prize in honour of Professor F.W. Paish (for papers in Business Finance) or the Baxter Prize in honour of Professor W.T. Baxter (for papers in Accounting and Control). The prizes may be awarded annually and are currently of the value of ú100 each.

8. COMMENTS AND REPLIES. The journal welcomes non-trivial Comments on papers previously published in JBFA. To avoid publishing Comments based on misunderstanding, and to obtain Replies quickly so that they can be published simultaneously with the Comments, it is required that draft Comments should be sent to the original authors for their reactions, prior to any formal submission to the editors for publication.

JOURNAL OF BUSINESS FORECASTING METHODS & SYSTEMS

ADDRESS FOR SUBMISSION :

C.L. JAIN, PH.D., PROFESSOR
JOURNAL OF BUSINESS FORECASTING
  METHODS & SYSTEMS
ST. JOHN'S UNIVERSITY
COLLEGE OF BUSINESS ADMINISTRATION
DEPARTMENT OF ECONOMICS AND FINANCE
JAMAICA, NY 11432
USA
718-990-7314
718-544-9086 (Fax)
E-Mail : FORECAST@NYIO.NET

CIRCULATION DATA :

Reader : Business Persons &
          Academic

Frequency of Issue : Quarterly

Copies Per Issue : 3001-4000

Subscription Price : 60.00 US$
  Foreign : 90.00 US$

Sponsorship : Profit Oriented Corp.

PUBLICATION GUIDELINES :

Manuscript Length : 6-10

Copies Required : Three

Computer Submission : Yes

Format : WordPerfect

Fees to Review : 0.00 US$

REVIEW INFORMATION :

Type of Review : Blind Review

No. of External Reviewers : Two

No. of In House Reviewers : One

Acceptance Rate : 21-30%

Time To Review : 2-3 months

Reviewer's Comments : Yes

Fees to Publish : 0.00 US$

Invited Articles : 5% or less

MANUSCRIPT TOPICS : ACCOUNTING INFORMATION SYSTEMS;
  ACCOUNTING THEORY & PRACTICE; AUDITING; CAPITAL BUDGETING; COST ACCOUNTING;
  ECONOMETRICS; GOVERNMENT & NON-PROFIT ACCOUNTING; INSURANCE;
  PORTFOLIO & SECURITY ANALYSIS

PUBLICATION GUIDELINES : Chicago Manual of Style

MANUSCRIPT GUIDELINES/COMMENTS :

The JOURNAL OF BUSINESS FORECASTING METHODS & SYSTEMS is published by Graceway Publishing Company, P.O. Box 159, Station C, Flushing, NY 11367. The editor is C.L. Jain, Ph.D., Professor, College of Business Administration, St. John's University, Jamaica, NY 11432, to whom articles should be submitted.

The Journal is designed to keep business managers abreast of developments in forecasting methods and systems and to help them gain a better understanding of, and appreciation for, the forecasting function. Articles dealing with forecasting methods applicable to manufacturing, processing, wholesaling, retailing, and service industries and financial institutions are invited.

Both descriptive and prescriptive methods may be discussed in such areas as finance, sales, marketing, production, inventory management, labor force levelling, new product introduction, technology, etc.

JOURNAL OF BUSINESS FORECASTING
METHODS & SYSTEMS

There is no restriction on the professional disciplines of those whose
articles may be published; articles receive equal consideration.
The criteria are that:
1. the author demonstrate professional competence in the subject
2. the contents of the paper indicate that the author has taken existing
    knowledge into account
3. the methods described can be replicated by others in the same or
    different industry
4. the subject is handled in such a manner that it is understandable to
    business managers whose backgrounds may not include an advanced degree
    in mathematics

The last-mentioned criterion places the onus upon the those in the forecasting
profession for communicating their concepts to users who constitute the
largest segment of the Journal's readership. While the editors do not
underestimate the need for, or importance of, mathematical modes, or wish to
discourage their use, contributors should recognize that unless the business
manager understands the material he/she cannot put it to use.

We suggest, therefore that, wherever possible, authors divide articles into
two parts: the first should describe the method of system in common business
language to capture the interest of the non-technical business manager; the
second part should present the mathematical formulations required by the
technician, whose help may be solicited by the business manager in adopting
the system.

In those instances where the material does not lend itself to the structure
described above, authors may incorporate the models within the body of the
text. However, when this method is adopted the models should be explained in
common business language in a brief paragraph within brackets; examples of
business oriented situations represented by the symbolic language of the model
are effective in achieving the objective.

Whether either of the above suggestions is adopted (or some other of the
author's choosing), the author should strive for reader comprehension, keeping
in mind that the reader of the Journal, as pointed out earlier, is not an
academician. He/she is, nevertheless, willing and able to learn what the
technician has to offer.

Articles dealing with any subject on a purely theoretical level should not be
submitted; pragmatism is the guide by which papers are judged.

Articles are subject to a blind review by an Editorial Advisory Board composed
of technicians and business users. The latter determine the value of the
material to a business enterprise and judge the method of presentation on the
basis of the ease of comprehension by business users; the technicians judge
the technical adequacy of the method or system presented, with emphasis on the
extent to which the author has used existing knowledge.

There is no limitation on length; however, authors should be mindful of:
1. the limited time available to an executive and
2. the executive propensity to devote time to those subjects that capture
    and hold his/her interest and promise to help him/her achieve personal
    and company goals.

JOURNAL OF BUSINESS FORECASTING
METHODS & SYSTEMS

The editors insist on clear and concise writing. The multi-disciplinary composition of the Journal's readership dictates that authors eschew professional jargon. Care should be exercised to avoid ambiguity, which arises from loose sentence construction, poor punctuation and careless choice of words. Clarity is enhanced by limiting the number of thoughts in one sentence to two; one is better. Contrary to warnings you may have received from instructors in creative writing courses, repetition of a word or phrase in the same paragraph contributes to clarity in technical literature. Avoid pompous language.

Articles should be typewritten double-spaced with no more than 40 characters and spaces per line. Submit papers in triplicate to the editor at the above address. Computer printouts of tables, graphs or other material are acceptable, provided they are legible. Line drawings should be clear and ready-for-camera. Do not submit photographs clipped from printed material; only original black/white glossy photos are acceptable. After article is accepted, it has to be furnished on a disk in WordPerfect format. Type tables and graphs on separate sheets.

Avoid footnotes; place explanatory material in the body of the text within brackets. Where footnotes cannot be avoided, type them on a separate sheet(s) of paper. References should always appear on a separate sheet(s).

Type the title and the name(s) of the author(s) on one sheet of paper, give the affiliation of each author, the address(es), telephone number(s), and fax number(s). Type the abstract on a second sheet; identify the abstract by repeating the first three or four words of the title. Start the manuscript on the third page; repeat the first three or four words of the title in the upper left corner of each page of the manuscript.

The author is responsible for obtaining permission to use copyrighted material. Permission to use data obtained while employed by an organization shall be obtained by the author from a responsible officer of the organization, if its identity is disclosed in the article. Such permission shall be in writing and a copy submitted to the editor. At his discretion, the editor may ask a responsible officer of an identified organization to reply to any critical comments of the organization appearing in an article.

JOURNAL OF BUSINESS IN DEVELOPING NATIONS

ADDRESS FOR SUBMISSION :

DR. JOHN A. PARNELL, EDITOR
JOURNAL OF BUSINESS IN DEVELOPING
  NATIONS
NORTH CAROLINA CENTRAL UNIVERSITY
SCHOOL OF BUSINESS
DURHAM, NC 27707
919-560-6277
919-560-6163 (Fax)
E-Mail : jparnell@nccu.campus.mci.net

CIRCULATION DATA :

Reader : Academic

Frequency of Issue : 3 Times/Year

Copies Per Issue :

Subscription Price :
  Free @ Web Site : 0.00 US$

Sponsorship : University

PUBLICATION GUIDELINES :

Manuscript Length : 16-20

Copies Required : Four

Computer Submission : No

Format : N/A

Fees to Review : 0.00 US$

REVIEW INFORMATION :

Type of Review : Blind Review

No. of External Reviewers : Three

No. of In House Reviewers : Zero

Acceptance Rate : 11-20%

Time To Review : 1-2 months

Reviewer's Comments : Yes

Fees to Publish : 0.00 US$

Invited Articles : 5% or less

MANUSCRIPT TOPICS : COST ACCOUNTING;
  INTERNATIONAL & ECONOMIC DEVELOPMENT; INTERNATIONAL FINANCE;
  DEVELOPING NATIONS

PUBLICATION GUIDELINES : American Psychological Association

MANUSCRIPT GUIDELINES/COMMENTS :

CALL FOR PAPERS
The JOURNAL OF BUSINESS IN DEVELOPING NATIONS, an international refereed
electronic journal, serves as an outlet for the publication of conceptual and
empirical business research, broadly defined, with specific applications to
developing nations . The journal will be published in electronic form with its
first issue in early 1997, available free of charge to researchers throughout
the world. Its home page can be accessed at
                http://www.nscu.edu/business/journal.htm.
Its editorship welcomes conceptual and empirical submissions from academic
researchers and business professionals in all functional areas of business
including such topics as:
* Successes and failures in businesses in developing nations
* Economic development strategies, including privatization, in developing
  nations
* Case studies of business organizations in developing nations
* Conceptual and empirical applications of existing models to developing
  nations
* Comparisons of organizational processes in all functional areas of business

JOURNAL OF BUSINESS IN DEVELOPING NATIONS

in developing nations to those in developed countries
The journal's editorship broadly defines the domain of developing nations.
However, studies addressing issues in less-researched regions of the
developing world such as Africa, South America, and the Middle East are
especially welcome.

The journal is supported by a competent and diverse editorial review board,
representing all functional areas of business in many parts of the world.

SUBMISSION GUIDELINES

Papers will be blind-refereed and judged on the following criteria:
1. Interest to a broad scholarly audience representing all functional areas of
   business.
2. Timeliness of subject matter and integration with recently published work
   in the field.
3. For conceptual papers, extent to which models are complete and free from
   logical flaws. For empirical papers, application of appropriate statistical
   tools.
4. Clarity and writing style.
5. The presentation of clear and supported practical implications and
   recommendations.

Please note that manuscripts should be prepared in APA format with several
notable exceptions:

1. Author(s) should be identified only on the title page. The title page
should include the names, addresses, telephone and fax numbers, and e-mail
addresses of all authors. The second page should include the title and a
50-100 word abstract which clearly argues why the general manager should read
the article. The body of the paper should begin on the third page, followed by
figures and tables. The body should contain about 12-18 pages of double-spaced
text. A disk containing a Microsoft Word 6.0 compatible file of the paper
should also be submitted.

2. Coverage of previous literature should be minimized in manuscripts that
report on empirical studies. Implications for practitioners should be
maximized and highlighted.

3. The number of tables and figures should be kept to a minimum and placed on
separate pages with the corresponding number and title.

4. To facilitate international mailing, manuscripts should be printed on both
sides of the paper. Insert one blank line between headings and typed material
and between paragraphs. Single space references. The body of the paper should
contain approximately 10-15 double-spaced pages, utilizing a 12-point font and
one-inch margins throughout.
5. Accepted manuscripts must be prepared precisely accordingly to format and
submitted on IBM computer disk in Microsoft Word 6.0 or compatible form.

Submit four clear copies of the manuscript to the current editor. Every effort
will be made to complete the review and provide detailed reviewer comments
within 45 days. Inquiries about research in progress are welcome. All
correspondence should be addressed to the Editor.

JOURNAL OF BUSINESS ISSUES

ADDRESS FOR SUBMISSION :

J.K. BURCH, EDITOR
JOURNAL OF BUSINESS ISSUES
P.O. BOX 15228
TALLAHASSEE, FL 32317
904-894-1333
904-894-1333 (Fax)

CIRCULATION DATA :

Reader : Academic

Frequency of Issue : 2 Times/Year

Copies Per Issue : Less than 1000

Subscription Price : 40.00 US$

Sponsorship :

PUBLICATION GUIDELINES :

Manuscript Length : 21-25

Copies Required : Three

Computer Submission : No

Format : N/A

Fees to Review : 50.00 US$

REVIEW INFORMATION :

Type of Review : Blind Review

No. of External Reviewers : One

No. of In House Reviewers : One

Acceptance Rate : 40 %

Time To Review : 2-3 months

Reviewer's Comments : Yes

Fees to Publish : 15.00 US$

Invited Articles : 5% or less

MANUSCRIPT TOPICS : ACCOUNTING INFORMATION SYSTEMS;
 ACCOUNTING THEORY & PRACTICE; AUDITING; CAPITAL BUDGETING; COST ACCOUNTING;
 ECONOMETRICS; ECONOMIC HISTORY; GOVERNMENT & NON-PROFIT ACCOUNTING;
 INSURANCE; INTERNATIONAL & ECONOMIC DEVELOPMENT; INTERNATIONAL FINANCE;
 PORTFOLIO & SECURITY ANALYSIS; PUBLIC POLICY ECONOMICS; REAL ESTATE;
 TAX ACCOUNTING; ALL BUSINESS AREAS

PUBLICATION GUIDELINES : American Psychological Association

MANUSCRIPT GUIDELINES/COMMENTS :

The Journal solicits unpublished manuscripts not currently under consideration
by another pubilcation. Papers submitted in connection with a formal program
may be submitted provided the manuscript does not appear in whole or in part
(other than a brief abstract) in the proceedings of the event. Each author
must provide the Editor wlth a statement that the manuscript or a similar one
has not been published and is not, nor will be, under consideration for
publication elsewhere while being reviewed by the JOURNAL OF BUSINESS ISSUES.
Manuscripts with more than four authors are discouraged.

Manuscripts should be typed on 8 1/2" by 11" good quality white paper and be
double spaced, except for indented quotations. Only one side of the page
should be used. Margins of at least one inch from the top, bottom, and sides
should facilitate editing and duplication.

JOURNAL OF BUSINESS ISSUES

Manuscripts should include a cover page which indicates the author's name, address, affiliation, and any acknowledgements. The author should not be identified anywhere else in the manuscript.

Manuscripts should Include a separate abstract page not exceeding 250 words. The title but not the author's name and affiliation should appear on the abstract. The abstract should contain a concise statement of the purpose of the manuscript, the primary methods or approaches used, and the significance of the findings and contribution.

In order to be assured of an anonymous review, authors should not identify themselves directly or indirectly in the text of the paper. Reference to unpublished working papers and dissertations should be avoided. If necessary, authors may indicate the reference is being withheld because of self-citation.

Tables, figures, and exhibits should appear on separate pages. Each should be numbered and have a title.

Indent all new paragraphs with a tab. Place two spaces between each sentence. Use tabs to align columns in charts and exhibits rather than spacing over with the space bar.

Footnotes and references should appear at the end of the manuscript. However, every effort should be made to incorporate material into the body of the paper.

Three copies of each manuscript and a diskettes containing the manuscript using WordPerfect 5.1 should be submitted along with a submission fee of $50, payable to JOURNAL OF BUSINESS ISSUES.

THE JOURNAL IMPOSES PAGE FEES ON ALL ACCEPTED MANUSCRIPTS. The fees are necessary to offset the very substantial cost of publishing the Journal. The page fee is $15 per Journal page and is due only after the manuscript is accepted for pubilcation. Manuscript copyright will be transferred to the JOURNAL OF BUSINESS ISSUES.

THE JOURNAL OF BUSINESS ISSUES is a double-blind refereed Journal publishing articles of interest to Business faculty members. The Journal is an independent academic Journal dedicated to excellence in Business.

JOURNAL OF COMMON MARKET STUDIES

ADDRESS FOR SUBMISSION :

SIMON BULMER & ANDREW SCOTT, EDITORS
JOURNAL OF COMMON MARKET STUDIES
UACES SECRETARIAT
KING'S COLLEGE LONDON
STRAND
LONDON, WC2R 2LS
UK
0171 240 0206
0171 836 2350 (Fax)

Change in Editor's Address
  May Occur in : 01/09/98

CIRCULATION DATA :

Reader : Academic

Frequency of Issue : Quarterly

Copies Per Issue : 1001-2000

Subscription Price : 136.00 US$
  Institution : 280.00 US$

Sponsorship : Profit Oriented Corp.

PUBLICATION GUIDELINES :

Manuscript Length : Up to 8,000 wds.

Copies Required : Three

Computer Submission : No

Format : N/A

Fees to Review : 0.00 US$

REVIEW INFORMATION :

Type of Review : Blind Review

No. of External Reviewers : Two

No. of In House Reviewers : One

Acceptance Rate : 11-20%

Time To Review : 2-3 months

Reviewer's Comments : Yes

Fees to Publish : 0.00 US$

Invited Articles : 6-10%

MANUSCRIPT TOPICS : ECONOMETRICS;
  INTERNATIONAL & ECONOMIC DEVELOPMENT; EUROPEAN AFFAIRS

PUBLICATION GUIDELINES :

MANUSCRIPT GUIDELINES/COMMENTS :

AIMS AND SCOPE
JOURNAL OF COMMON MARKET STUDIES is a leading journal in the field, publishing
high quality, accessible articles on the latest EU issues. For more than 30
years JOURNAL OF COMMON MARKET STUDIES has been the forum for the development
and evaluation of theoretical and empirical issues in the politics and
economics of integration, focusing principally on developments within the
European Union.

JOURNAL OF COMMON MARKET STUDIES aims to achieve a disciplinary balance
between political science and economics, including the various sub-disciplines
such as monetary economics, fiscal policy, political economy, public policy
studies, public administration and international relations. In addition to
mainstream theoretical and empirical articles, JOURNAL OF COMMON MARKET
STUDIES publishes shorter pieces which focus on specific policy areas or which
report the results of specialised research projects. Each year a special issue
is devoted to a comprehensive review of the activities of the European Union
in the previous year.

JOURNAL OF COMMON MARKET STUDIES

JOURNAL OF COMMON MARKET STUDIES is committed to deepening the theoretical understanding of European integration. It will continue to develop as the primary forum for the analysis of all aspects relating to the process of European integration.

COVERAGE

* a forum for theoretical debate
* interdisciplinary in scope
* comprehensive analysis of the European Union
* a key resource for academics and policy-makers
* occasional thematic special issues
* book reviews covering all relevant publications
* comparative studies of international integration
* covers political forces, institutions and public policy of the EU
* examines economic dynamics of integration
* regular analysis of policy areas

MANUSCRIPTS

1. Manuscripts of mainstream articles, shorter manuscripts for EUROPEAN AGENDA and correspondence relating to the Journal should be sent to the Editors of the JOURNAL OF COMMON MARKET STUDIES.

2. Manuscripts are welcome on all areas covered by the Journal as set out in the policy statement on the inside front cover.

3. Three copies of any manuscript should be submitted. Each copy must be typed on one side of the paper only, using double spacing throughout (including any footnotes and references). Authors should indicate the length of the article and the inclusion of any diagrams. Articles should be accompanied by a note of the author's name and affiliation and by an abstract not exceeding 100 words. The abstract should summarize the main argument of the article.

4. Mainstream articles should not exceed 8000 words.

5. Shorter research notes, short notes raising matters for scientific debate, and occasional reviews of important policy developments are published in EUROPEAN AGENDA. These should not exceed 4000 words.

6. Bibliographical references should be incorporated into the text using the author-date system, with page numbers where necessary. All references should be listed alphabetically at the end of the article. For journal articles, the volume and issue number, month and year of publication and inclusive page numbers should be provided. Bibliographical references should follow the style used in this issue.

7. Footnotes should be numbered consecutively, and should not solely comprise references.

8. Manuscripts which do not conform to this format, if accepted, may be subject to delay, since it is not possible to have them typeset until suitable copy has been supplied.

9. The Journal is indexed in the Journal of Economic Literature and in ABC POLSCI: A Bibliography of Contents: Political Science and Government.

10. Each article contributor receives 20 free offprints of his or her article, together with a copy of the issue in which it appears. Each review contributor receives 4 free offprints of the review section together with a copy of the issue in which his or her review appears.

THE EUROPEAN UNION: THE ANNUAL REVIEW OF ACTIVITIES, published each Autumn, is included in the annual subscription to JOURNAL OF COMMON MARKET STUDIES.

The purpose of THE EUROPEAN UNION: THE ANNUAL REVIEW OF ACTIVITIES is to provide an information resource which can be used as a reference tool for teaching and research by all who are interested in European Union Affairs.

Each edition of THE EUROPEAN UNION: THE ANNUAL REVIEW OF ACTIVITIES includes a useful chronology of key events during the preceding year and an evaluation of key issues and developments which provide a succinct yet comprehensive guide to the progress of EU policy and plans.
Regular features include:
    Governance and Institutional Developments
    Internal Policy Developments   External Policy Developments
    Developments in the Economies of the European Union
    Developments in European Law
    Developments in the Member States
    A Guide to the Documentation of the European Community/Union
    Chronology of Key Events
    Books on European Integration.

The Journal is published by Blackwell Publishers, 238 Main Street, Cambridge, MA, 02142, USA. Tel 617-547-7110, Fax 617-547-0789.

JOURNAL OF COMPARATIVE ECONOMICS

ADDRESS FOR SUBMISSION :

JOSEF C. BRADA, EDITOR
JOURNAL OF COMPARATIVE ECONOMICS
ARIZONA STATE UNIVERSITY
DEPARTMENT OF ECONOMICS
TEMPE, AZ 85287-3806
USA
602-965-6524
602-965-0748 (Fax)
E-Mail : ATJCB@ASUVM.INRE.EDU.ASU

CIRCULATION DATA :

Reader : Academic

Frequency of Issue : Bi-Monthly

Copies Per Issue : 1001-2000

Subscription Price : 129.00 US$
  Member of Assn. : 58.00 US$

Sponsorship : Professional Assoc.

PUBLICATION GUIDELINES :

Manuscript Length : 26-30

Copies Required : Three

Computer Submission : Yes

Format : After accepted/WP 5.1

Fees to Review : 0.00 US$

REVIEW INFORMATION :

Type of Review : Blind Review

No. of External Reviewers : Two

No. of In House Reviewers : Zero

Acceptance Rate : 11-20%

Time To Review : 2-3 months

Reviewer's Comments : Yes

Fees to Publish : 0.00 US$

Invited Articles : 5% or less

MANUSCRIPT TOPICS : COST ACCOUNTING; ECONOMETRICS; ECONOMIC HISTORY;
  INTERNATIONAL & ECONOMIC DEVELOPMENT; COMPARATIVE ECONOMIC SYSTEMS

PUBLICATION GUIDELINES :

MANUSCRIPT GUIDELINES/COMMENTS :

The JOURNAL OF COMPARATIVE ECONOMICS is devoted to the analysis and study of
contempporary, historical, and hypothetical economic systems. Such analyses
may involve comparisons of the pcrformance of different economic systems or
subsystems, studies linking outcomes to system characteristics in one economy
or investigations of the origin and evolution of one or more economic systems.
Empirical, theoretical, and institutional approaches are equally welcome.
Empirical analyses should display appropriate sensitivity to the problems of
comparing data generated by different economic systems and seek to employ
methodologies that permit the researcher to distinguish between the effects of
the system and of other causal variables on observed outcomes. Theoretical
work that develops new ways of viewing economic systems and their operation or
explains the behavior of systems or of agents within a system will also be
considered for publication. Authors of technical papers are requested to
provide a verbal explanation of their results as part of their conclusions.
Although papers limited to the description of institutions will generally not
be published by the Journal, such descriptions accompanied by the analysis of
the interaction of the institution with the system are also weleome. The
Journal is open to all viewpoints and ideologies. Nevertheless, authors should
recognize that the Editor will not publish material that, in his opinion,

cannot be expected to command the assent of the readership due to deficient or inadequate methodology.

It is the policy of the Journal to provide authors with an editorial decision within three months of the receipt of submissions.

Manuscripts should be submitted in triplicate to the Editor.

Manuscripts are accepted for review with the understanding that the same work will not be nor is presently submitted elsewhere; that its submission for publication has been approved by all of the authors; and that any person cited as a source of personal communications has approved such citation.

Authors submitting a manuscript do so on the understanding that if it is accepted for publication, copyright in the article, including the right to reproduce the article in all forms and media, shall be assigned exclusively to the Publisher. The Publisher will not refuse any reasonable request by the author for permission to reproduce any of his or her contributions to the journal.

Any statements in the article once it is accepted by the Editor remain the sole responsibility of the author(s), including personal communications from other scholars. They represent only the opinions of the author(s) and should not be construed to reflect the opinions of the Editors, the Association, or the Publisher.

MANUSCRIPTS SHOULD BE PREPARED ACCORDING TO THE STYLE RULES OUTLINED BELOW. DEVIATION FROM THESE RULES MAY CAUSE PUBLICATION DELAYS.

FORM OF MANUSCRIPT. Submit manuscripts in English in triplicate, typed double-spaced on one side of 8 1/2 x 11-inch white paper. All pages should be numbered. Page 1 should contain the article's title, author(s) name(s) and affiliation(s) (name of institution, city state and zip code); the complete mailing address of the author to whom proofs should be sent; and a suggested running head (abbreviated form of the title of less than 35 xharacters. Page 2 should contain a short abstract of approximately 100 words. The abstract will appear at the beginning of the article in the journal; use the abstract format and classification numbers which are required by the JOURNAL OF ECONOMIC LITERATURE.

LIST OF SYMBOLS. A complete list of symbols used in the manuscript must be included. All symbols should be identified typographically, not mathematically. This list will not appear in print, but it is essential to avoid costly author's corrections in proof. Distinguish between "oh" and "zero"; "ell" and "one"; "kappa" and "kay"; etc. All letters used as symbols will be set in italics unless a special type (e.g., Greek, boldface, script) is specified. Note that if the equations are handwritten in the text, then the list of symbols should also be handwritten.

EQUATIONS. All displayed equations should conform to the author's list of symbols and be typewritten, if possible, or neatly handwritten. All equations to which reference is made in the text should be numbered consecutively, with optional subdivision by sections; equation numbers should be placed in parentheses against the right margin.

FOOTNOTES. Number footnotes consecutively, with superscript Arabic numerals, beginning with the article title. They should be typed double-spaced on a separate page.

TABLES. Number all tables consecutively with Arabic numerals. Each table should be typed double-spaced on a separate page. All tables should have titles. If footnotes to the table are necessary they should be indicated by superscript italic letters, a, b, c, and should be typed immediately below the table. Indicate in the margins where you would prefer to have the table inserted.

FIGURES. All illustrations are to be considered as figures and should be provided as camera-ready copy. Number the figures consecutively; type their legends double-spaced on a separate page, not on the figures themselves. Plan figures to fit the proportions of the printed page (approximately 5 X 7- or 8 x 10-inch originals). Figures should be professionally drawn and lettering should be planned so that it will be legible after a reduction of 50 to 60%. Indicate in the margins where you would prefer to have the figures inserted. Illustrations in color can be accepted only if the authors defray the cost.

REFERENCES. All references should be cited in the text by the author's surname and date of publication, e.g., Smith and Jones (1984) or (Smith, 1984) and typed double-spaced. All references should be listed at the end of the article in alphabetical order by authors' surnames. All authors should be listed by last name first, first name last. Abbreviations of journal titles should conform to general usage in economics. The following reference styles should be used in the reference list.
References that are books:
  Desia, Padma, Ed., Marxism, Central Planning, and the Soviet Economy Cambridge, MA: MIT Press, 1983.

References that are government documents:
  Ericson, Paul G., and Miller, Ronald S., "Soviet Foreign Economic Behavior: A Balance of Payments Perspective." In Soviet Economy in a Time of Change, Vol. 2, pp. 208-244. Comp. of Papers, Joint Econ. Comm., U. S. Congress. Washington, D. C.: U. S. Govt. Printing Office, 1979.

References that are journal articles:
  Furuboln, Eirik G., and Pejovich, Svetozar, "Property Rights and Economic Theory: Survey of Recent Literature." J. Econ. Lit. 10, 4:1137-1162, Dec. 1972.

References that are chapters in edited volumes:
  Swain, Nigel, "The Evolution of Hungary's Agricultural System since 1967." In Paul Hare, H. Radice, and N. Swain. Eds., Hungary: A Decade of Economic Reform, pp. 225-251. London: Allen & Unwin, 1981.

PROOFS. Proofs will be sent to the Author. Authors are responsible for correcting the proofs of their article. Authors will be charged for changes (other than corrections of printing errors) in excess of 10% of the cost of composition.

REPRINTS. Reprint order forms will accompany the proofs. Fifty reprints without covers will be provided free of charge. Additional reprints may be purchased from the Publisher.

JOURNAL OF CONSTRUCTION ACCOUNTING & TAXATION

ADDRESS FOR SUBMISSION :

STEPHEN COLLINS, EDITOR
JOURNAL OF CONSTRUCTION ACCOUNTING
  & TAXATION
RIA GROUP
395 HUDSON STREET
NEW YORK, NY 10014
212-367-6398
212-367-6718 (Fax)

CIRCULATION DATA :

Reader : Business Persons &
        Academic

Frequency of Issue : Quarterly

Copies Per Issue : 4001-5000

Subscription Price : 137.00 US$

Sponsorship :

PUBLICATION GUIDELINES :

Manuscript Length : 11+

Copies Required : Two

Computer Submission : Yes

Format : WordPerfect 5.1

Fees to Review : 0.00 US$

REVIEW INFORMATION :

Type of Review : Blind Review

No. of External Reviewers : Two

No. of In House Reviewers : One

Acceptance Rate : 50 %

Time To Review : 1-2 months

Reviewer's Comments : No

Fees to Publish : 0.00 US$

Invited Articles : Over 50%

MANUSCRIPT TOPICS : ACCOUNTING INFORMATION SYSTEMS;
  ACCOUNTING THEORY & PRACTICE; CONSTRUCTION ACCOUNTING & TAXATION

PUBLICATION GUIDELINES : Chicago Manual of Style

MANUSCRIPT GUIDELINES/COMMENTS :

JOURNAL OF CORPORATE ACCOUNTING
AND FINANCE

ADDRESS FOR SUBMISSION :

EDWARD J. STONE, EDITOR
JOURNAL OF CORPORATE ACCOUNTING
  AND FINANCE
JOHN WILEY & SONS, INC.
605 THIRD AVENUE
NEW YORK, NY 10158-0012
718-931-7235

PUBLICATION GUIDELINES :

Manuscript Length : 16-20

Copies Required : Two

Computer Submission : Yes

Format : Wd. 6.0/ WdPer./Others

Fees to Review : 0.00 US$

CIRCULATION DATA :

Reader : Business Persons

Frequency of Issue : Quarterly

Copies Per Issue :

Subscription Price : 208.00 US$
  Outside North Amer. : 232.00 US$

Sponsorship : Profit Oriented Corp.

REVIEW INFORMATION :

Type of Review : Blind Review

No. of External Reviewers : One

No. of In House Reviewers : One

Acceptance Rate : 40 %

Time To Review : One month or less

Reviewer's Comments : No

Fees to Publish : 0.00 US$

Invited Articles : 11-20%

MANUSCRIPT TOPICS : ACCOUNTING THEORY & PRACTICE; COST ACCOUNTING

PUBLICATION GUIDELINES :

MANUSCRIPT GUIDELINES/COMMENTS :

The JOURNAL OF CORPORATE ACCOUNTING AND FINANCE is directed to corporate
accounting and financial executives and outside auditors and accountants
working with corporations.

Articles should address this readership and be informative, analytical, and
practical, but not highly technical. We seek material that will offer our
readership new insights into, and new approaches to, corporate finance and
accounting issues.

Manuscripts are considered for publicatin with the understanding that they
represent original material, and are offered exclusively and without fee to
The JOURNAL OF CORPORATE ACCOUNTING AND FINANCE.

ARTICLES MUST NOT HAVE BEEN PUBLISHED PREVIOUSLY AND MAY NOT SIMULTANEOUSLY BE
SUBMITTED ELSEWHERE.

An ORIGINAL and TWO COPIES of the manuscript must be submitted. Any
accompanying artwork or exhibits must be submitted as black and white
originals suitable for reproduction.

JOURNAL OF CORPORATE ACCOUNTING AND FINANCE

Articles should range from 3,700-7,500 WORDS (15-30 pages), double-spaced on one side only of 8 1/2" x 11" heavy-duty white bond paper.

MARGINS should be set to allow for 55 CHARACTERS PER LINE. A 1 1/2" margin should be left at the top and bottom of each manuscript page.

Try to use as FEW FOOTNOTES as possible. If they are indispensable to the subject, they should appear DOUBLE-SPACED ON A SEPARATE PAGE at the end of the article.

Send PHOTOCOPIES OF THE ORIGINAL SOURCE OF LENGTHY QUOTATIONS. This enables us to confirm the absolute accuracy of the quotation.

Please seek CLARITY, BREVITY, AND PERTINENCE. Titles of articles should be short and clear. All accepted manuscripts are subject to editing.

A BRIEF -50 words or less- BIOGRAPHICAL SKETCH of the author should accompany the article. The sketch should name the author's position, company or other professional organization, and field of expertise.

A 100-to-125 word SUMMARY OF THE ARTICLE should also be provided.

All unsolicited manuscripts must be accompanied by a self-addressed, stamped envelope. Otherwise, they cannot be returned to the author.

Address articles to the Editor at John Wiley & Sons, Inc.

JOURNAL OF CORPORATE FINANCE

ADDRESS FOR SUBMISSION :

KENNETH LEHN, EDITOR
JOURNAL OF CORPORATE FINANCE
UNIVERSITY OF PITTSBURGH
GRADUATE SCHOOL OF BUSINESS
MERVIS HALL
PITTSBURGH, PA 15260
USA
412-648-2034
412-648-2875 (Fax)
E-Mail : lehn@katz.business.pitt.edu

CIRCULATION DATA :

Reader : Academic

Frequency of Issue : Quarterly

Copies Per Issue : Less than 1000

Subscription Price :

Sponsorship : Profit Oriented Corp.

PUBLICATION GUIDELINES :

Manuscript Length :

Copies Required :

Computer Submission : N/A

Format : N/A

Fees to Review : 85.00 US$
    Subscriber 50.00 US$

REVIEW INFORMATION :

Type of Review : Blind Review

No. of External Reviewers : Two

No. of In House Reviewers : One

Acceptance Rate : 21-30%

Time To Review : 4-6 months

Reviewer's Comments : Yes

Fees to Publish : 0.00 US$

Invited Articles : 5% or less

MANUSCRIPT TOPICS : CAPITAL BUDGETING; COST ACCOUNTING;
  CORPORATE CONTROL; CORPORATE GOVERNANCE

PUBLICATION GUIDELINES :

MANUSCRIPT GUIDELINES/COMMENTS :

JOURNAL OF CORPORATE TAXATION

ADDRESS FOR SUBMISSION :

EUGENE M. KRADER, MANAGING EDITOR
JOURNAL OF CORPORATE TAXATION
WARREN, GORHAM AND LAMONT, INC.
90 FIFTH AVENUE
NEW YORK, NY 10011
USA
212-971-5194
212-971-5025 (Fax)

CIRCULATION DATA :

Reader : Lawyers & Accountants
Frequency of Issue : Quarterly
Copies Per Issue : 4001-5000
Subscription Price : 130.00 US$
Sponsorship : Profit Oriented Corp.

PUBLICATION GUIDELINES :

Manuscript Length : 20+
Copies Required : Two
Computer Submission : Yes
Format : N/A
Fees to Review : 0.00 US$

REVIEW INFORMATION :

Type of Review : Editorial Review
No. of External Reviewers : One
No. of In House Reviewers : One
Acceptance Rate : 21-30%
Time To Review : 2-3 months
Reviewer's Comments : Yes
Fees to Publish : 0.00 US$
Invited Articles : 21-30%

MANUSCRIPT TOPICS : COST ACCOUNTING; TAX ACCOUNTING;
  CORPORATE TAXATION

PUBLICATION GUIDELINES : Chicago Manual of Style

MANUSCRIPT GUIDELINES/COMMENTS :

JOURNAL OF COST ANALYSIS

ADDRESS FOR SUBMISSION :

DR. ROLAND D. KANKEY, EDITOR
JOURNAL OF COST ANALYSIS
AFIT/LSQ
2950 P. STREET, BUILDING 641
WRIGHT-PATTERSON AFB, OH 45433
USA
513-255-6280
513-476-7988 (Fax)
E-Mail : RKANKEY@AFIT.AF.MIL

CIRCULATION DATA :

Reader : Military(related)Cost Analysis

Frequency of Issue : 2 Times/Year

Copies Per Issue : 2001-3000

Subscription Price :

Sponsorship : Professional Assoc.

PUBLICATION GUIDELINES :

Manuscript Length : 16-20

Copies Required : Five

Computer Submission : No

Format : N/A

Fees to Review : 0.00 US$

REVIEW INFORMATION :

Type of Review : Blind Review

No. of External Reviewers : Two

No. of In House Reviewers : One

Acceptance Rate : 21-30%

Time To Review : 2-3 months

Reviewer's Comments : Yes

Fees to Publish : 0.00 US$

Invited Articles : 5% or less

MANUSCRIPT TOPICS : CAPITAL BUDGETING; COST ACCOUNTING;
  ECONOMETRICS; COST ESTIMATE; COST ANALYSIS

PUBLICATION GUIDELINES :

MANUSCRIPT GUIDELINES/COMMENTS :

STYLE
The Society of Cost Estimating and Analysis is a multidisciplinary
organization, with interest in a variety of subjects that deal with estimation
and analysis of costs in a variety of contexts, and with systems and concepts
that affect costs and their estimation/analysis. This clearly encompasses
subsets of accounting, statistics, forecasting, economics, and
production/operations management. Due to this multi-disciplinary character, we
are interested in papers from a variety of fields, and are reasonably liberal
regarding style.

Please avoid extensive footnoting. Generally these can be either included in
the text or attached. If the paper uses survey data, please include a copy of
the survey when you submit the paper. If the paper reports results from a data
set, please include the data set as an attachment. (Extensive data sets will
not be published, but may be needed by the referees.) Please place lengthy
derivations in an appendix, with adequate detail to allow the reader to
replicate the computations. Since the referees will need to check all steps of
derivations and proofs, a supplement (not for publication) which details these
steps is recommended.

JOURNAL OF COST ANALYSIS

The title (first) page should contain the title, with the author(s) name(s), affiliation(s) and address(es). The next page should be the first page of the paper, with the title at the top. The paper should not identify the author(s) except on the title page.

Please double space the paper, with at least one inch margins. Figures and tables may be included in the text, or attached for the initial submission. Final copies will require separate, camera ready, figures and tables.

PROCEDURE
Submit five copies of the paper to the Editor.
One copy will be maintained as a file copy, while the other four are sent to an appropriate Associate Editor who will manage the referee process. The first author (or designee) will be notified of receipt, and of the results of the referee process after each iteration. The paper may be accepted without changes, accepted pending minor changes, judged tentatively acceptable pending major revisions, or rejected. Most papers will require at least minor changes before publication. The editors will attempt to keep the referee cycle at a reasonable length.

JOURNAL OF COST MANAGEMENT

ADDRESS FOR SUBMISSION :

BARRY J. BRINKER, EDITOR
JOURNAL OF COST MANAGEMENT
THE RIA GROUP
395 HUDSON STREET
NEW YORK, NY 10014
USA
212-367-6376
212-367-6305 (Fax)
E-Mail : Barry_Brinker_@_WGLRIAI

CIRCULATION DATA :

Reader : Business Persons

Frequency of Issue : Bi-Monthly

Copies Per Issue : 5001-10,000

Subscription Price : 135.00 US$

Sponsorship :

PUBLICATION GUIDELINES :

Manuscript Length : 16-20

Copies Required : Three

Computer Submission : Yes

Format : WordPerfect 5.1

Fees to Review : 0.00 US$

REVIEW INFORMATION :

Type of Review : Blind Review

No. of External Reviewers : One

No. of In House Reviewers : One

Acceptance Rate : 21-30%

Time To Review : 2-3 months

Reviewer's Comments : Yes

Fees to Publish : 0.00 US$

Invited Articles : 6-10%

MANUSCRIPT TOPICS : ACCOUNTING INFORMATION SYSTEMS; COST ACCOUNTING

PUBLICATION GUIDELINES :

MANUSCRIPT GUIDELINES/COMMENTS :

HARDCOPIES AND WORD PROCESSING FILES
* Please provide two copies double-spaced of each article.

* File Format: Please save files in a WordPerfect 5.1 format (preferably on a 3 1/2" disk). Note that even if you use some other word processing package, you can usually save your file in WordPerfect format or at least in ASCII format. (If not, we can probably translate your file to a format we can use; just let us know what format the file is in.)

* Submit hardcopies and files to:
        Barry J. Brinker, Editor
        The RIA Group
        395 Hudson Street
        New York, New York 10014
        (212) 367-6376 fax (212) 367-6305

AUHOR BIOGRAPHIES
* Provide brief author biographies, including names, titles, affiliations, and cities. We avoid printing other information (e.g., professional certifications or other books or articles you have written).

JOURNAL OF COST MANAGEMENT

* We send articles out for a blind review by our board of advisors, so put authors' names and bios on a separate page.

* Put acknowledgments, thanks, etc. at the end of the authors' biographies rather than in a note (example: "John Doe is cost manager at Hewlett-Packard in Palo Alto, California. The author would like to thank George Lincoln, manager of Hewlett-Packard's plant in Atlanta, Georgia, for his help with this article.")

ABSTRACTS AND EXECUTIVE SUMMARIES
* Please prepare a one-paragraph summary of the article.
* Also prepare an executive summary--i.e., about four or five key points made in the article. The key points can be sentences adapted from the one-paragraph summary.

HEADINGS
* Use headings and subheadings liberally to organize the text, break up gray text, and help readers find what important topics. The headings and subheadings of an article should correspond to an outline of the material (i.e., they should reflect an organizing plan).

* Only the first words of headings are capitalized in the JOURNAL OF COST MANAGEMENT.

* In titles and headings, most two- and three-letter articles (e.g., a, an, the) are not capitalized.

* Only two headings are used: #1 heads and #2 heads. The style for #1 heads is boldface, while #2 heads are italicized.

* Don't have a subheading follow a heading directly. Text must intervene, even if it just says something like this: "the following paragraphs explain this in more detail."

LISTS
* Lists: Please break up the text to increase its readability by using numbered or bulleted lists. Generally, put a semicolon after each item, followed by "and" for the next-to-last item (very short items may need no punctuation; very long items may end better with a period).

* Use bulleted lists when you have not mentioned the number of items or when the number of items is not important:
    Example:
    Here are some things to consider:
        *   Now is the time;
        *   For every good man; and
        *   To come to the aid of his country.

* Numbered lists: Indicate the beginning of a numbered list with the code "@NL:", then use numbering and a tab for each item.
    Example:
    Here are three important things to consider:
        1.   Now is the time;
        2.   For every good man; and
        3.   To come to the aid of his country.

JOURNAL OF COST MANAGEMENT

EXHIBITS
* Call everything--e.g., graphs, tables, charts, etc.--an "exhibit."

* Exception: occasionally we run sidebars, which can be labeled and referred to as sidebars rather than exhibits.

* Number exhibits sequentially throughout each article; i.e., the first exhibit in each article is "Exhibit 1, " the second is "Exhibit 2," etc.

* Please place each exhibit on a separate page at the end of the hardcopy and of the corresponding word processing file.

* Each exhibit must have a title and must be referred to in the text (e.g., "As Exhibit 3 shows...").

* After the first reference to each exhibit, please add a parenthetical annotation in the text like this: "[Exhibit X goes about here]" so that we know where to place each exhibit.

* If an exhibit is taken from a previously published source (e.g., a book), get written permission and add a source line to the bottom of the exhibit. The source line should provide all information usually given in an endnote.

* We can do any artwork needed (e.g., arrows, graphs, flowcharts), but please type any words or text shown in exhibits.

CITATIONS
* We print endnotes, not footnotes. Use as few as possible, and only for cites to published works, not for further explanations or elaborations (which should be included in the text--perhaps parenthetically--or simply deleted).

* Please use our (old-fashioned) note style, not the commonly used academic style (i.e., a parenthetical note in the text such as "(Cooper 1992)" that refers to a bibliography included at the end of the article).

* Latin: we avoid Latin words, phrases, and abbreviations in notes.

* For citations of periodicals, please provide author names, article title in quotation marks, title of periodical underlined, issue number or date, and page numbers.
     Example:
     "1.   Neal Clausing, "But What's My Cost," Journal of Cost Management
            (Fall 1990): 52-56."

* For citations of books, please provide author names, title (underlined), publisher, city of publisher, year of publication, and page numbers (if specific page numbers are referred to).
     Example:
     "1.   E.M. Goldratt and R.E. Fox, The Race (Croton-on-Hudson, NY: North
            River Press, Inc., 1986): 102-104."

PUNCTUATION AND STYLISTIC CONVENTIONS
* Serial commas: use commas before each item in a list of three or more (i.e., include a comma before the "and" that precedes the final item: "x, y, and z" rather than "x, y and z")

JOURNAL OF COST MANAGEMENT

* "Paper": In referring to an article, use "article" (or column) rather than "paper."
* Acronyms: Certain acronyms recur repeatedly (e.g., ABC, ABM, TQM). Nevertheless, the first time a term is used, spell it out and show the acronym in parentheses. For the rest of the article, show only the acronym.
* "%" vs. "percent": We write out "percent" in text (e.g., 12 percent) but use the symbol "%" in formulas or in tables. We use numerals in front of "percent" (e.g., "6 percent" rather than "six percent").
* Periods (spaces after): Use only one space after periods.
* Dashes: To indicate a dash, type two hyphens with no spaces before or after ("...**...").
* Punctuation with quotation marks: Periods and commas generally precede an and quote (i.e., "end of sentence.").
* Hyphens: We generally avoid hyphens, though we do hyphenate compound adjectives (e.g., "activity-based" costing, "forward-thinking" managers).

USAGE, GRAMMAR
* Use a spell checker and--if you have one--a grammar checker.
* First person: Avoid using the first person (e.g., I, we, our) and the second person (you, yours).
* Avoid passive constructions (not "Passive constructions are avoided...").
* Firm/company: Usually use "company" rather than "firm" (though law and accounting partnerships can be called firms).
* Prior to/before: Use "before"
* "With respect to" or "as to": Just say "about" or "on"
* During or within/in: "in" is usually sufficient
* "Different than"/"different from": latter preferred
* Towards/toward: Use toward
* "and/or": Use just "and" or "or," not both.
* Upon/on: Usually just say "on"
* That/which: Use "that" for relative clauses (i.e., "which" clauses usually must be preceded by a comma)
* In order to: Delete "in order" and just say "to"
* Service/serve: Use serve as in "to serve customers"
* Utilize/use: usually avoid "utilize" in favor of "use"
* All of/all; usually all is enough ("all the people there..." instead of "all of the people there")
* Whether or not/whether: "whether" suffices
* He/she vs. he; avoid "he/she" or "he or she." Note that this problem can usually be finessed (e.g., by rephrasing, using the plural form, or repeating the antecedent).
* It's/its; use "its" correctly
* Proactive/active: don't use "proactive"
* Data base/database. Make it one word.
* "Such": the word "such" can often be avoided
* "As well as": usually "and" or "also" is adequate
* "Not only xxx, but..." is an overworked construction
* "As" or "since": Avoid using these words as substitutes for "because"
* Between/among: "Among" is not obligatory when more than two persons or objects are being discussed; indeed, "between" is preferable when each item is regarded individually (e.g., "a treaty between France, Spain, and Italy" is perfectly correct)

JOURNAL OF CULTURAL ECONOMICS

ADDRESS FOR SUBMISSION :

MARK CRAIN, EDITOR
JOURNAL OF CULTURAL ECONOMICS
KLUWER ACADEMIC PUBLISHERS
EDITORIAL JOURNALS OFFICE
P.O. BOX 17
3300 AA DORDRECHT,
THE NETHERLANDS
703-993-2325
703-993-2325 (Fax)
E-Mail : MCRAIN@GMU.edu

CIRCULATION DATA :

Reader : Academic

Frequency of Issue : Quarterly

Copies Per Issue : Less than 1000

Subscription Price : 256.00 US$
  SCE Members : 45.00 US$

Sponsorship : Professional Assoc.

PUBLICATION GUIDELINES :

Manuscript Length : 16-20

Copies Required : Three

Computer Submission : No

Format : N/A

Fees to Review : 0.00 US$

REVIEW INFORMATION :

Type of Review : Editorial Review

No. of External Reviewers : Two

No. of In House Reviewers : One

Acceptance Rate : 11-20%

Time To Review : 4-6 months

Reviewer's Comments : Yes

Fees to Publish : 0.00 US$

Invited Articles : 6-10%

MANUSCRIPT TOPICS : ACCOUNTING INFORMATION SYSTEMS;
  GOVERNMENT & NON-PROFIT ACCOUNTING; PUBLIC POLICY ECONOMICS;
  PERFORMING & VISUAL ARTS

PUBLICATION GUIDELINES : Chicago Manual of Style

MANUSCRIPT GUIDELINES/COMMENTS :

The Journal is sponsored by the Association of Cultural Economics
International.

AIMS AND SCOPE. Cultural Economics is the application of economic analysis to
the area of all the creative and performing arts, the heritage and cultural
industries, whether publicly or privately owned. It is concerned with the
economic organization of the cultural sector and with the behavior of
producers, comsumers and policymakers in that sector. Scientific inquiry in
public economics, the theory of the firm, the theory of organizations and
public choice, all apply in the cultural field.

The perspective of the cultural economic field is open to a range of
approaches, mainstream and radical, neoclassical, welfare economics, public
policy and institutional. It has attracted contributions from some of the most
eminent economists of our time, and it is steadily growing as an area of
economic inquiry; it is increasingly accepted by policy-makers as an important
aspect of cultural decision-making.

JOURNAL OF CULTURAL ECONOMICS

The editors and editorial board of the JOURNAL OF CULTURAL ECONOMICS seek to attract the attention of the whole economics profession to this branch of economics, as well as those in related disciplines and practitioners with an interest in economic issues. The Journal publishes original papers that deal with the theoretical development of cultural economics as a subject, the application of econonmic analysis to the field of culture, and the dissemination of economic ideas in the area of cultural policy.

SUBMISSION OF MANUSCRIPTS. Articles should be submitted in quadruplicate to: The Journal of Cultural Economics, Editorial Journals Office, Kluwer Academic Publishers, P.O. Box 17, 3300 AA Dordrecht, The Netherlands.

MANUSCRIPT PREPARATION. Final versions of accepted papers should be all double-spaced with 1-inch margins. Include:

1. A TITLE PAGE, with the article's title, the author's name(s) and permanenet affiliation(s), and the author's current address, telephone and fax numbers, for sending proofs and offprints.

2. A SECOND PAGE containing an abstract of not more than 100 words, plus two to six key words.

3. The TEXT OF THE ARTICLE. The location of tables and figures should be indicated in the text. Equation numbers should be placed flush right. References to sources should be in the form: Smith (1989, pp. 14-17) or (Smith, 1989, pp. 14-17) as appropriate.

4. NOTES. Notes are to be typed double-spaced in a separate section beginning on a new page following the text. An acknowledgement note should be keyed with an asterisk at the author's name on the title page. Other notes should be keyed to superscript arabic numbers at the end of sentences in the text.

5. REFERENCES are to be typed double-spaced in a separate section. Underline or italicize book and journal titles. Examples:
For monographs
Throsby, C.D. and Withers, G.A. (1979) The Economics of the Performing Arts. Edward Arnold, London.

For contributions to collective works
Peacock, Alan (1992) "Economics, Cultural Values and Cultural Policies", in Ruth Towse and Abdul Khakee, eds. Cultural Economics. Springer, Heidelberg.

For periodicals
Pommerchoe, Werner W. and Frey, Bruno S. (1990) "Public Promotion of the Arts; A Survey of Means". Journal of Cultural Economics 14: 73-95.

Note that the journal titles should not be abbreviated.

6. TABLES come after the References. They should be numbered consecutively in the text in roman numerals. Each should be titled and typed double-spaced, beginning on a separate page. Tables should be typed on separate pages. The legends and titles on tables must be sufficiently descriptive such that they are understandable without reference to the text. The body of tables must be clearly labelled in English. Explain all abbreviations. Notes to tables are

designated by superscript letters a, b, c,...

7. FIGURES for accepted manuscripts are to be in professional-quality, camera-ready form; i.e. drawn in India ink on drafting paper on high-quality white paper. Lettering should be legible after reduction to size. Provide the original plus two copies. The drawings should not be inserted in the text and should be legible after reduction to size. Provide the original plus two copies. The drawings should not be inserted in the text and should be marked on the back with figure numbers, title of paper, and name of author. All graphs and diagrams should be referred to as figures and should be numbered consecutively in the text in Arabic numerals. Legends for figures should be typed on separate pages. The legends and titles of figures must be sufficiently descriptive such that they are understandable without reference to the text. The dimensions of figure axes must be clearly labelled in English.

8. UNITS. Any numerical results in dimensional form should be presented in SI units.

9. Important formulae (displayed) should be numbered consecutively throughout the manuscript as (1), (2) etc., on the right-hand side of the page.

Any manuscript which does not conform to the above instructions may be returned for the neccessary revisions before publication. Compliance with JOURNAL OF CULTURAL ECONOMICS Information for Authors will be required before a manuscript is accepted.

PROOFS AND OFFPRINTS. Authors will be sent page proofs and should return the corrected proofs within three days of receipt. Alterations other than typesetting errors may be charged to the author. The first-mentioned author will receive 25 free copies. Further copies can be ordered when returning page proofs.

THE KLUWER ACADEMIC PUBLISHERS INFORMATION SERVICE KAPIS. This free Internet service is available at the following URL: http://www.wkap.nl

JOURNAL OF DEFERRED COMPENSATION: NON QUALIFIED PLANS & EXEC. COMPENSATION

ADDRESS FOR SUBMISSION :

BRUCE J. MC NEIL, EDITOR-IN-CHIEF
JOURNAL OF DEFERRED COMPENSATION: NON
  QUALIFIED PLANS & EXEC. COMPENSATION
DOHERTY, RUMBLE & BUTLER
3500 FIFTH STREET TOWERS
150 SOUTH FIFTH STREET
MINNEAPOLIS, MN 55402-4235
USA
612-340-5589
612-340-5584 (Fax)

CIRCULATION DATA :

Reader : Business Persons

Frequency of Issue : Quarterly

Copies Per Issue : Less than 1000

Subscription Price : 156.00 US$

Sponsorship : Profit Oriented Corp.

PUBLICATION GUIDELINES :

Manuscript Length : 21-25

Copies Required : Two

Computer Submission : N/A

Format : N/A

Fees to Review : 0.00 US$

REVIEW INFORMATION :

Type of Review : Editorial Review

No. of External Reviewers : One

No. of In House Reviewers : One

Acceptance Rate :

Time To Review : One month or less

Reviewer's Comments : No

Fees to Publish : 0.00 US$

Invited Articles : 31-50%

MANUSCRIPT TOPICS : ACCOUNTING THEORY & PRACTICE; INSURANCE;
  PUBLIC POLICY ECONOMICS; TAX ACCOUNTING; EMPLOYEE BENEFITS

PUBLICATION GUIDELINES :

MANUSCRIPT GUIDELINES/COMMENTS :

JOURNAL OF DEFERRED COMPENSATION: NON QUALIFIED PLANS & EXEC. COMPENSATION is
devoted to providing practical information and ideas on matters of importance
to professionals who deal with tax, legal, and business planning aspects of
pensions and related benefits in their practices. The Journal encourages
contributions from lawyers, accountants, benefits administrators, the academic
community, and others interested in the field of pension planning and
compliance.

JOURNAL OF DEFERRED COMPENSATION: NON QUALIFIED PLANS & EXEC. COMPENSATION
emphasizes quality and clarity of exposition. Reviewers consider the following
criteria in assessing submissions: value of the information to the Journal's
audience, substantive contribution to the broadly defined field of
nonqualified deferred compensation and executive benefits, and overall quality
of manuscript. The decision to publish a given manuscript is made by the
Editor-in-Chief, relying on the recommendations of the reviewers.

Submission of a manuscript clearly implies commitment to publish in the
journal. Papers previously published or under review by other journals and

articles adapted from book-length works-in-progress will be considered under acceptable copyright arrangements.

MANUSCRIPT SPECIFICATIONS: Manuscripts submitted for publication should not exceed 40 typewritten pages; the publisher encourages submission of shorter papers. All textual material -- including notes and references -- must be double spaced in a full-size nonproportional typeface (e.g., 12 pt. Courier), on one side only of 8-1/2" x 11" good quality paper, with 1-1/2" margins all around. All pages must be numbered. Notes and references must be placed separately, double-spaced, as endnotes; footnote format is unacceptable. Improperly prepared manuscripts will be returned for repreparation.

Within the article, use short subheadings for organization and emphasis. Include a cover sheet with title, author's address and affiliations, mailing address, and phone and fax numbers. To ensure anonymity in the review process, the first page of the text should show only the title of the submission.

Artwork, including tables, charts, and graphs, must be of camera-ready quality. Each should be on a separate page placed at the end of the text, with proper placement indicated within text (e.g., "Insert Table 2 here").

Three high-quality copies of the manuscript should be submitted to the Editor-in-Chief. Include an abstract of 125 to 150 words and a biographical statement of 50 words or less.

ACCEPTANCE. Once an article has been formally accepted, the author must submit the article to the publisher in two formats: two high-quality manuscript copies and a WordPerfect or ASCII computer file on 3-1/2" floppy diskette labeled with file type and name, software version, article title, and author's name.

Copyright is retained by the publisher, and articles are subject to editorial revision. There is no payment for articles; authors receive ten copies of the issue in which the article is published. Manuscripts not accepted for publication are not returned. Authors should keep a copy of any submission for their files.

Manuscript submissions and inquiries should be directed to: Editor-in-Chief

For business and production matters, contact:

> Journal of Deffered Compensation
> Panel Publishers
> 36 West 44th Street
> New York, NY 10036

JOURNAL OF DERIVATIVES (THE)

ADDRESS FOR SUBMISSION :

STEPHEN FIGLEWSKI, EDITOR
JOURNAL OF DERIVATIVES (THE)
NEW YORK UNIVERSITY
STERN SCHOOL OF BUSINESS
44 WEST 4TH STREET, SUITE 9-160
NEW YORK, NY 10012-1126
USA
212-998-0712
212-995-4220 (Fax)

CIRCULATION DATA :

Reader : Business Persons

Frequency of Issue : Quarterly

Copies Per Issue : 2001-3000

Subscription Price : 300.00 US$
  Academics : 75.00 US$

Sponsorship : Profit Oriented Corp.

PUBLICATION GUIDELINES :

Manuscript Length : 16-20

Copies Required : Three

Computer Submission : Yes

Format : WordPerfect

Fees to Review : 0.00 US$

REVIEW INFORMATION :

Type of Review : Editorial Review

No. of External Reviewers : Two

No. of In House Reviewers : Zero

Acceptance Rate :

Time To Review : 2-3 months

Reviewer's Comments : No

Fees to Publish : 0.00 US$

Invited Articles : Over 50%

MANUSCRIPT TOPICS : ECONOMETRICS; PORTFOLIO & SECURITY ANALYSIS

PUBLICATION GUIDELINES :

MANUSCRIPT GUIDELINES/COMMENTS :

CONTENT GUIDELINES
THE JOURNAL OF DERIVATIVES is devoted exclusively to contigent claims. The
goal of JOD is to be the interface between practitioners and academics, and
between theory and practice, in the area of derivative securities and markets.
Articles should be on topics of interest to a broad audience of sophisticated
practitioners and academics, and written in a clear and accessible style.

Strict academic standards for the consistency and correctness of theoretical
reasoning and empirical results do apply. A relatively high level of
mathematical analysis is acceptable where appropriate -- derivatives are
inherently mathematical -- but only what is necessary and appropriate to the
material. the math should be expressed in as clear and simple a form as
possible, and separable to the maximum extent possible from the logical flow
of the discussion, so that articles can be understood by the more casual
reader who does not wish to follow the math step by step.

Submissions are encouraged in the areas of:

* Theory and practice of trading in any exchange-traded or OTC derivative
  product.

JOURNAL OF DERIVATIVES (THE)

* Valuation and risk assessment models for derivative instruments and securities with derivative features.
* Risk management applications of derivatives.
* Empirical studies of behavior of derivatives prices and markets.
* Regulatory issues (from an economic as opposed to a legal perspective).
* Application of derivatives concepts to other areas, such as incurance, corporate finance, and banking.

SUBMISSION GUIDELINES

Please refer to the following guidelines when submitting a manuscript for publication. We may return any paper to the author for revisions that does not follow these instructions. The editors reserve the right to make changes for clarity and consistency.

1. Submit four copies of the manuscript double-spaced with wide margins and pages numbered. The front page should include the authors' full names, titles, addresses, zip codes, and phone and fax numbers.

2. References, endnotes, tables, and figures should appear on separate pages at the end of the text.

3. Limit references principally to works cited in the text and list them alphabetically. Citations in the text should appear as "Smith [1990] suggests that..." Use page numbers for quotes.

4. Minimize the number of endnotes. use periods instead of commas between authors' names and titles of references. Use superscript Arabic numbers in the text and on the endnote page.

5. Number and title all exhibits, with one to a page. Write out the column heads and legends; they should be understandable without reference to the text. Submit graphs in camera-ready form; we cannot draw graphs for you.

6. Center each equation on a separate line, numbered consecutively with Arabic numbers, in parentheses in the right margin. Identify Greek letters in the margin for the typesetter. Please make clear markings, in a color other than black, when inserting Greek letters or equations into the text.

7. Immediately upon acceptance of the article, THE JOURNAL OF DERIVATIVES' copyright agreement form must be signed, and a diskette of the article must be sent to the Editorial Production Director (address below).

8. After acceptance of the article, further changes can only be made at the galley stage, except with the permission of the editor.

SEND 3 COPIES TO:
Stephen Figlewski, Editor
The Journal of Derivatives
New York University
Stern School of Business
44 West 4th Street, Suite 9-160
New York, NY 10012-1126

SEND 1 COPY TO:
Noelle Schultz
Editorial Production Director
The Journal of Derivatives
488 Madison Avenue
New York, NY 10022
Tel: (212)224-3193/Fax: (212)224-3527

THE JOURNAL OF DERIVATIVES is published by Institutional Investor, Inc., 488 Madison Avenue, New York, NY 10022. Tel: 212-224-3545 Fax: 212-224-3527.

JOURNAL OF DEVELOPING AREAS

ADDRESS FOR SUBMISSION :

NICHOLAS C. PANO, GENERAL EDITOR
JOURNAL OF DEVELOPING AREAS
WESTERN ILLINOIS UNIVERSITY
MACOMB, IL 61455
USA
309-298-1108
309-298-2865 (Fax)
E-Mail : SE-Schisler@WIU.EDU

CIRCULATION DATA :

Reader : Academic

Frequency of Issue : Quarterly

Copies Per Issue : 1001-2000

Subscription Price : 29.00 US$
    Institution : 39.00 US$

Sponsorship : University

PUBLICATION GUIDELINES :

Manuscript Length : 20-35

Copies Required : Three

Computer Submission : Yes

Format : N/A

Fees to Review : 0.00 US$

REVIEW INFORMATION :

Type of Review : Blind Review

No. of External Reviewers : Three

No. of In House Reviewers : One

Acceptance Rate : 11-20%

Time To Review : 4-6 months

Reviewer's Comments : Yes

Fees to Publish : 0.00 US$

Invited Articles : 5% or less

MANUSCRIPT TOPICS : COST ACCOUNTING; ECONOMETRICS;
    INTERNATIONAL & ECONOMIC DEVELOPMENT; INTERNATIONAL FINANCE;
    PUBLIC POLICY ECONOMICS; MARKETING THEORY & APPLICATIONS;
    BUSINESS LAW & PUBLIC RESPONSIBILITY; INTERNATIONAL BUSINESS;
    SMALL BUSINESS ENTREPRENEURSHIP; STRATEGIC MANAGEMENT POLICY;
    GENERAL BUSINESS; INTERNATIONAL TRADE; BANKING;;
    ORGANIZATIONAL BEHAVIOR,THEORY, DEVELOPMENT;
    COMMUNICATION; ECONOMICS; FINANCE & INVESTMENTS;
    OPERATIONS RESEARCH/STATISTICS

PUBLICATION GUIDELINES : Chicago Manual of Style

MANUSCRIPT GUIDELINES/COMMENTS :

1. Manuscripts should have Third World focus.

2. Scholars of any discipline and country may submit manuscripts that
    1. present the conclusions of original research pertinent to
       understanding development or
    2. provide comprehensive and analytical summaries of the current state of
       knowledge on development within specific regions and time periods.

3. Individuals other than scholars who by reason of profession, experience, or
residency feel qualified to evaluate specific aspects of development, may also
submit manuscripts which embody their personal views. These will be considered
as potential editorial comments.

4. Manuscripts should be in English and should follow the University of Chicago A MANUAL OF STYLE, 14th ed. rev. (1993).

5. All manuscripts must be either typed or xeroxed and double-spaced throughout. Three copies should be submitted. If accepted, a manuscript must be submitted on computer disk.

6. The author's identify should not be evident in either text or footnotes; anonymity of author and referees is a basic principle of the JDA evaluation process.

7. Notes should be double-spaced at the end of the paper. The JDA uses the short title form to refer to works previously cited; op. cit, and loc, cit. are not acceptable.

8. All manuscripts should be final, clean copy in article form; chapters of dissertations, preliminary drafts, and scripts for speeches should not be submitted for evaluation.

9. Manuscripts previously published in another language, or for which later publication plans exist, will not be considered - nor will manuscripts which embody the essence of previously published work.

10. Publication costs require that tabular material be kept to essential levels.

11. Return postage should be included if the author wishes one copy of the manuscript returned when the evaluation is completed.

12. All submitted manuscripts will be acknowledged. Those deemed suitable for evaluation will be read by at least three independent referees. The required evaluation time is generally from three to six months, but longer periods are sometimes required.

13. The author will be notified of the Editorial Staff's decision upon publication in one of the following ways:
    1. rejected;
    2. rejected with major revision and complete reevaluation required if resubmitted;
    3. accepted with specific revision required before final acceptance; or
    4. accepted with no revision or only minor revision suggested.

14. All accepted manuscripts are subject to normal editing. The edited copy is sent for the author's approval before the copy is sent to press.

15. Authors of published articles will receive five copies of the issue. If desired, offprints must be ordered when the proofed edited manuscript is returned to the JDA.

16. Manuscripts should be sent to: General Editor, Journal of Developing Areas, Western Illinois University, Macomb, Illinois 61455, U.S.A.

JOURNAL OF DEVELOPMENT ECONOMICS

ADDRESS FOR SUBMISSION :

PROFESSOR PRANAB BARDHAN, EDITOR
JOURNAL OF DEVELOPMENT ECONOMICS
UNIVERSITY OF CALIFORNIA AT BERKELEY
DEPARTMENT OF ECONOMICS
BERKELEY, CA 94720
USA
510-642-0823
510-642-0563 (Fax)
E-Mail : jde@econ.berkeley.edu

CIRCULATION DATA :

Reader : Academic

Frequency of Issue : Bi-Monthly

Copies Per Issue :

Subscription Price : 135.00 US$

Sponsorship : Profit Oriented Corp.

PUBLICATION GUIDELINES :

Manuscript Length : 26-30

Copies Required : Three

Computer Submission : Yes

Format : MS DOS

Fees to Review : 60.00 US$

REVIEW INFORMATION :

Type of Review : Editorial Review

No. of External Reviewers : Two

No. of In House Reviewers :

Acceptance Rate : 21-30%

Time To Review : 4-6 months

Reviewer's Comments : Yes

Fees to Publish : 0.00 US$

Invited Articles : 5% or less

MANUSCRIPT TOPICS : ECONOMETRICS;
  INTERNATIONAL & ECONOMIC DEVELOPMENT; PUBLIC POLICY ECONOMICS;
  SPACE DEVEL. IN POLITICAL, ECONOMIC, LEGAL, SOCIAL

PUBLICATION GUIDELINES :

MANUSCRIPT GUIDELINES/COMMENTS :

AIMS AND SCOPE:
The JOURNAL OF DEVELOPMENT ECONOMICS publishes papers relating to all aspects
of economic development - from immediate policy concerns to structural
problems of underdevelopment. The emphasis is on quantitative or analytical
work, which is relevant as well as intellectually stimulating.

BOOK REVIEWS:
The JOURNAL OF DEVELOPMENT ECONOMICS will include book reviews which will be
in greater depth and longer than usual. Books for review should be addressed
to Clive Bell, Department of Economics, Vanderbilt University, Nashville, TN
37235, U.S.A.

(1) Papers must be in English.

(2) Papers for publication should be sent in triplicate to the Editor.

Submission of a paper will be held to imply that it contains original
unpublished work and is not being submitted for publication elsewhere. The

Editor does not accept responsibility for damage or loss of papers submitted. Upon acceptance of an article, author(s) will be asked to transfer copyright of the article to the publisher. This transfer will ensure the widest possible dissemination of information.

(3) Submission of accepted papers as ELECTRONIC MANUSCRIPTS, i.e., on disk with accompanying manuscript, is encouraged. Electronic manuscripts have the advantage that there is no need for rekeying of text, thereby avoiding the possibility of introducing errors and resulting in reliable and fast delivery of proofs. The preferred storage medium is a 5.25 or 3.5 inch disk in MS-DOS format, although other systems are welcome, e.g., Macintosh (in this case, save your file in the usual manner; do not use the option 'save in MS-DOS format').

Do not submit your original paper as electronic manuscript but hold on to disk until asked for this by the Editor (in case your paper is accepted without revisions).

Do submit the accepted version of your paper as electronic manuscript. Make absolutely sure that the file on the disk anf the printout are identical. Please use a new and correctly formatted disk and label this with your name; also specify the software and hardware used as well as the title of the file to be processed. Do not convert the file to plain ASCII. Ensure that the letter 'I' and digit '1', and also the letter 'O' and digit '0'are used properly, and format your article (tabs, indents, etc.) consistently. Characters not available on your word processor (Greek letters, mathematical symbols, etc.) should not be left open but indicated by a unique code (e.g. gralpha, [alpha], @, etc., for the Greek letter a. Such codes should be used consistently throughout the entire text; a list of codes used should accompany the electronic manuscript. Do not allow your word processor to introduce word breaks and do not use a justified layout. Please adhere strictly to the general instructions below on style, arrangement and, in particular, the reference style of the journal.

(4) Manuscripts should be double spaced, with wide margins, and printed on one side of the paper only. All pages should be numbered consecutively. Titles and subtitles should be short. References, tables, and legends for figures should be printed on separate pages.

(5) The first page of the manuscript should contain the following information: (i) the title; (ii) the name(s) and institutional affiliation(s) of the author(s); (iii) an abstract of not more than 100 words. A footnote on the same sheet should give the name, address, and telephone and fax numbers of the corresponding author [as well as an e-mail address].

(6) The first page of the manuscript should also contain at least one classification code according to the Classificaiton System for Journal Articles as used by the JOURNAL OF ECONOMIC LITERATURE; in addition, up to five key words should be supplied.

(7) Acknowledgements and information on grants received can be given in a first footnote, which should not be included in the consecutive numbering of footnotes.

(8) Footnotes should be kept to a minimum and numbered consecutively

throughout the text with superscript Arabic numerals.

(9) Displayed formulae should be numbered consecutively throughout the manuscript as (1), (2), etc. against the right-hand margin of the page. IN CASES WHERE THE DERIVATION OF A FORMULAE HAS BEEN ABBREVIATED, IT IS OF GREAT HELP TO THE REFEREES IF THE FULL DERIVATION CAN BE PRESENTED ON A SEPARATE SHEET (NOT TO BE PUBLISHED).

(10) References to publications should be as follows: 'Smith (1992) reported that...' or 'This problem has been studied previously (e.g., Smith et al., 1979)'. The author should make sure that there is a strict one-to-one correspondence between the names and years in the text and those on the list. The list of references should appear at the end of the main text (after any appendices, but before tables and legends for figures). It should be double spaced and listed in alphabetical order by author's name. References should appear as follows:

For monographs
Hawawini, G. and I. Swary, 1990, Mergers and acquisitions in the U. S. banking industry: Evidence from the capital markets (North-Holland, Amsterdam).

For contributions to collective works
Brunner, K. and A.H. Meltzer, 1990, Money supply, in : B.M. Friedman and F.H. Hahn, eds., Handbook of monetary economics, Vol. 1 (North-Holland, Amsterdam) 357-396.

For periodicals
Griffiths, W. and G. Judge, 1992, Testing and estimating location vectors when the error covariance matrix is unknown, Journal of Econometrics 54, 121-138. Note that journal titles should not be abbreviated.

(11) Illustrations will be reproduced photographically from originals supplied by the author; they will not be redrawn by the publisher. Please provide all illustrations in QUADRUPLICATE (ONE high-contrast original and THREE photocopies). Care should be taken that lettering and symbols are of a comparable size. The illustrations should not be inserted in the text, and should be marked on the back with figure number, title of paper, and author's name. All graphs and diagrams should be referred to as figures, and should be numbered consecutively in the text in Arabic numerals. Illustrations for papers submitted as electronic manuscripts should be in traditional form.

(12) Tables should be numbered consecutively in the text in Arabic numerals and printed on separate sheets.

Any manuscript which does not conform to the above instructions may be returned for the necessary revision before publication.

Page proofs will be sent to the corresponding author. Proofs should be corrected carefully; the reponsibility for detecting errors lies with the author. Correctins should be restricted to instances in which the proof is at variance with the manuscript. Extensive alterations will be charged. Twenty-fine reprints of each paper are supplied free of charge to the corresponding author; additional reprints are available at cost if they are ordered when the proof is returned.

JOURNAL OF DEVELOPMENT STUDIES

ADDRESS FOR SUBMISSION :

ADMINISTRATIVE EDITOR
JOURNAL OF DEVELOPMENT STUDIES
FRANK CASS & CO., LTD.
900 EASTERN AVENUE
LONDON, 1G2 7HH
UK
+44 0181 599 8866
+44 0181 599 0884 (Fax)
E-Mail : 100067.1576@compuserve.com

CIRCULATION DATA :

Reader : Academic

Frequency of Issue : Bi-Monthly

Copies Per Issue : 1001-2000

Subscription Price : 65.00 US$
  Institution : 195.00 US$

Sponsorship :

PUBLICATION GUIDELINES :

Manuscript Length : 16-20

Copies Required : Three

Computer Submission : Yes

Format : Any

Fees to Review : 0.00 US$

REVIEW INFORMATION :

Type of Review : Editorial Review

No. of External Reviewers : Two

No. of In House Reviewers : Two

Acceptance Rate : 6-10%

Time To Review : 1-2 months

Reviewer's Comments : Yes

Fees to Publish : 0.00 US$

Invited Articles : 5% or less

MANUSCRIPT TOPICS : ECONOMETRICS;
  INTERNATIONAL & ECONOMIC DEVELOPMENT; PUBLIC POLICY ECONOMICS

PUBLICATION GUIDELINES :

MANUSCRIPT GUIDELINES/COMMENTS :

MANAGING EDITORS: David Booth, Department of Sociology and Anthropology,
University of Hull; Christopher Colclough, Institute of Development Studies at
University of Sussex; Colin Kirkpatrick, Development and Project Planning
Centre, University of Bradford. BOOK REVIEW EDITOR: Pramit Chaudhuri,
University of Sussex.

Articles submitted to the Journal should be original contributions and should
not be under consideration for any other publication at the same time; if an
article is under consideration by another publication, authors should clearly
indicate this at the time of submission.

Each typescript should be submitted in duplicate, typewritten on one side only
and double-spaced throughout, with ample margins. It should conform to the
Journal style outlined below. Pages, including those containing illustrations,
diagrams or tables, should be numbered consecutively.

If the article is typed on a word-processor, the disk should accompany the
typescript. Disks should be labelled with the title of the article, the
author's name and the software used.

JOURNAL OF DEVELOPMENT STUDIES

Any figures and tables must be clearly produced ready for photographic reproduction, type area 114 mm x 185 mm. No vertical or horizontal rules are necessary in tables. The source should be given below the table.

There is no standard length for articles, but 5-6,000 words is a useful target.

Authors are entitled to 25 free offprints and a copy of the issue in which their article appears. Copyright in articles published in the Journal rests with the publisher.

STYLE
Current Journal style should be followed closely. The author's institutional affiliation should appear as a footnote on the first page, together with any acknowledgments. The article should begin with an indented, underlined summary of less than 100 words of the contents and conclusions of the article.

NOTES
(a) Simple references without accompanying comments: to be inserted at appropriate place in text, underlined and in squared brackets stating author's surname, publication date of work referred to, and relevant pages.
e.g. [Brown, 1979: 33-71].

(b) References with comments: to appear as Notes, indicated consecutively throughout the article by raised numerals corresponding to the list of notes placed at the end.

(c) Book titles and names of journals should be underlined; titles of articles should be in inverted commas.

A REFERENCE LIST should appear after the list of notes. It should contain all the works referred to, listed alphabetically by author's surname (or name of sponsoring body where there is no identifiable author). Style should follow: author's surname, forename and/or initials, date of publication, title of publication, place of publication, and publisher. [Underline title of journal or book.] Thus:

Brown, A.E., 1968a, Development Economics, London: MacRoutledge.
Brown, A.E., 1968b, 'Agricultural Policy in India'. Journal of Development
          Studies, Vol.2, No.3.

House style: British spelling throughout, NB: -ise endings NOT -ize, Dates: 28 January 1968. Single quotes; double within single.

AUTHORS should retain at least one complete copy of their articles; unsolicited manuscripts will be returned only on specific request. While every effort will be made for the safe keeping of manuscripts, the Editors cannot accept responsibility for any damage or loss which may occur.

SUBSCRIPTION ORDERS AND ENQUIRIES should be sent to the Journals Subscription Department, Frank Cass & Co. Ltd. (address, phone, fax, email are same as editorial address given above.)

JOURNAL OF DEVELOPMENTAL ENTREPRENEURSHIP

ADDRESS FOR SUBMISSION :

WILLIAM LEWIS RANDOLPH, MANAGING EDITOR
JOURNAL OF DEVELOPMENTAL
  ENTREPRENEURSHIP
NORFOLK STATE UNIVERSITY
SCHOOL OF BUSINESS AND ENTREPRENEURSHIP
2401 CORPREW AVENUE
NORFOLK, VA 23504
757-683-2563
757-683-2506 (Fax)
E-Mail : WRANDOLPH@VGER.NSU.EDU

CIRCULATION DATA :

Reader : Academic &
        Micro Enterprise Fund Mgrs.

Frequency of Issue : 2 Times/Year

Copies Per Issue : 1001-2000

Subscription Price : 50.00 US$
  Institution : 125.00 US$

Sponsorship : Non Profit Corp.

PUBLICATION GUIDELINES :

Manuscript Length : 16-20

Copies Required : Four

Computer Submission : No

Format : N/A

Fees to Review : 0.00 US$

REVIEW INFORMATION :

Type of Review : Blind Review

No. of External Reviewers : Two

No. of In House Reviewers : One

Acceptance Rate : 21-30%

Time To Review : 2-3 months

Reviewer's Comments : Yes

Fees to Publish : 0.00 US$

Invited Articles : 6-10%

MANUSCRIPT TOPICS : COST ACCOUNTING; PUBLIC POLICY ECONOMICS;
  DEVELOPMENTAL ENTRENEURSHIP

PUBLICATION GUIDELINES : American Psychological Association

MANUSCRIPT GUIDELINES/COMMENTS :

The JOURNAL OF DEVELOPMENTAL ENTREPRENEURSHIP is soliciting the submission of
high quality, original manuscripts in the area of developmental
entrepreneurship. Send all submissions to William Lewis Randolph.

PURPOSE
The JOURNAL OF DEVELOPMENTAL ENTREPRENEURSHIP (JDE) provides a forum for the
dissemination of descriptive, empirical, and theoretical research that focuses
on issues concerning microenterprise development among economically
disadvantaged groups. In the developed nations, the economically disadvantaged
are usually minorities and women, while in less developed nations the
economically disadvantaged can be the majority of the population.
Microenterprise development entails training prospective entrepreneurs in
business skills and providing access to start-up capital.

The intended audience for the journal are scholars who study issues of
developmental entrepreneurship and professionals involved in governmental and
non-governmental efforts to facilitate entrepreneurship among the economically
disadvantaged. Articles will cover a broad range of topics, including:

JOURNAL OF DEVELOPMENTAL
ENTREPRENEURSHIP

* Challenges and opportunities unique to minority and female entrepreneurs
* Microenterprise funds
* Legislation that encourages entrepreneurship and community development
* Governmental and corporate set-aside programs for minorities and women
* International programs in developmental entrepreneurship
* Private sector small business lending practices
* Education and training for aspiring entrepreneurs

EDITORIAL POLICY
The JDE is a double-blind refereed journal that publishes quality articles on issues and topics concerning developmental entrepreneurship. We especially welcome articles that critically address specific programs and efforts to increase entrepreneurship among women and minorities. Program successes as well as failures provide valuable lessons for researchers and program managers. Given the broad range of readership, we value readability and practicality.

Only unpublished, non-copyrighted manuscripts should be submitted. Revised versions of papers previously published in Proceedings are acceptable if the author has retained the copyright. Submission of a paper will imply that it contains original unpublished work and is not submitted for publication elsewhere.

The editors will rigorously pursue a policy of timely and meaningful reviews. One goal is to provide an editorial decision within two months of receipt of a submission. The editor will notify the author concerning any delay if we cannot meet this goal. After initial screening, the editor will send papers to reviewers who are familiar with the main topic of the work. Upon receiving the reviewers' evaluations, the editor makes the final decision based on this material.

After a manuscript is accepted, we require the corresponding author to return a signed and binding copyright agreement to JDE. The author of an accepted manuscript is also responsible for obtaining permission to quote from copyrighted work cited in the manuscript. The author must also provide the manuscript's final version in an electronic file on a diskette.

We will publish the Journal in the spring and fall each year, commencing with the Spring 1996 issue. Address subscription inquiries and orders to the Managing Editor. Annual subscription rates:

     Institutions: North America $125   Individuals: North America $50
                   Elsewhere $140   Elsewhere $65
(Please remit by check or money order in US$ made out to the Norfolk State University Foundation.)

MANUSCRIPT GUIDELINES
Authors must submit four copies of their manuscript, clearly typed with double spacing. Use only one side of the paper and one inch margins to facilitate editing. Manuscript text should be no longer than twenty double-spaced pages.

Arrange the pages of the manuscript as follows:
* The title page with title, author's name, institutional affiliation, running head for publication and name, mailing address, phone and fax numbers of the corresponding author

JOURNAL OF DEVELOPMENTAL
ENTREPRENEURSHIP

* Second page; repeat title then the abstract of 100 to 200 words, followed by
  a list of 4-5 keys used for indexing purposes
* Third page and following; text
* References (start on a separate page)
* Author note (start on a separate page)
* Footnotes (start on a separate page)
* Tables (start on a separate page)
* Figures (place each on a separate page)

The article should end with a non-technical summary statement of the main
conclusions. Place lengthy mathematical proofs and very extensive detailed
tables in an appendix or omit entirely. Attempt to eliminate all content
footnotes. The Journal follows the PUBLICATION MANUAL of the American
Psychological Association.

Sponsors of the Journal are Norfolk State University Foundation and the
Coleman Foundation.

YOUR NAME _____

PHONE NUMBER _____

JOURNAL'S NAME_____

EDITOR'S ADDRESS _____

_____

_____

_____

_____

YOUR NAME _____

PHONE NUMBER _____

JOURNAL'S NAME_____

EDITOR'S ADDRESS _____

_____

_____

_____

_____

BUSINESS REPLY MAIL

FIRST CLASS   PERMIT NO. 52   BEAUMONT, TEXAS

POSTAGE WILL BE PAID BY ADDRESSEE

CABELL PUBLISHING COMPANY - A,E & F
Box 5428, Tobe Hahn Station
Beaumont, Texas 77726-9904

BUSINESS REPLY MAIL

FIRST CLASS   PERMIT NO. 52   BEAUMONT, TEXAS

POSTAGE WILL BE PAID BY ADDRESSEE

CABELL PUBLISHING COMPANY - A,E & F
Box 5428, Tobe Hahn Station
Beaumont, Texas 77726-9904